Hungarian Yearbook 2022

eleven

Hungarian Yearbook of International Law and European Law
Volume 10 HYIEL 2022

Aim and scope

Hungarian Yearbook of International Law and European Law is a collection of articles written mostly by Hungarian authors covering developments in the field of international law and European law, and progress in domestic implementation and application of these fields of law. The online archives consist of all the articles published in the book series since 2013. The Yearbook articles analyse well-known Hungary-related cases and their assessment from the perspective of Hungarian legal experts. Moreover, the articles offer a comprehensive picture of the state of application and implementation of EU law and international law in Hungary.

Submission of articles

Manuscripts should be submitted by email to the editorial team at editors@hungarianyearbook.com. The instructions for authors are available from www.hungarianyearbook.com.

Publisher
Eleven International Publishing, Hofweg 9D, P.O. Box 85576, 2508 CG The Hague, info@elevenpub.com, www.elevenpub.com.

Subscriptions
The Hungarian Yearbook of International Law and European Law is published once a year. Individual annual subscription rates for 2022 are € 128 (online) and € 179,50 (access via IP). Prices exclude VAT. For more information or to request a quote, please contact info@elevenpub.com.

ISSN 2666-2701

Hungarian Yearbook of International Law and European Law
2022 (10) 1

Table of Contents

EDITORIAL

Editorial Comments: Symbol of Symbols. The Significance of the *Gabčíkovo-Nagymaros* Case from a Personal Perspective

Foreword to Vol. 10 (2022) of the Hungarian Yearbook of International Law and European Law*

*Péter Kovács***

Together with the release of Vol. 10 (2022) of the Hungarian Yearbook of International Law and European Law, Pázmány Péter Catholic University hosts an international conference dedicated to the 25th anniversary of the ICJ's *Gabčíkovo-Nagymaros* judgment. One of the authors of this year's thematic chapter, Boldizsár Nagy, was part of the Hungarian team preparing the submissions, others participated at the oral interventions under the direction of James Crawford, György Szénási, Alexandre Charles Kiss, who all passed away since then. The Editor-in-Chief of the Hungarian Yearbook, Marcel Szabó, took part in the post-judgment negotiations on the execution of the judgment and the transposition of the abstract legal principles into operative bilateral commitments.

My humble personal contributions are of a different nature: during my diplomatic service in Paris between 1990-1994, I prepared certain background press-materials about the roots of the litigation, the impact of the newly emerging environmental ideas on the Antall-government and the Hungarian parliament, elected in the first free elections organized after the return to the parliamentary liberal democracy in 1989/1990.

While for Hungary, the Gabčíkovo-Nagymaros project and abandoning it became the symbol of the change of the regime, it was also clear that the accomplishment of the project with all its officially emphasized alleged 'advantages' was the symbol of political and economic independence, sovereignty and national pride for Slovakia.

At the same time, Hungary, Czechoslovakia (and after the secession Czechia and Slovakia), Poland, Romania, *etc.* sought to integrate into the different European and Euro Atlantic organizations (Council of Europe, EU, NATO, *etc.*), knowing that the most important members of these organizations expect the

* This contribution was written in my personal capacity, the thoughts expressed therein cannot be attributed to the ICC.

** Péter Kovács: chairman of the Editorial Board, Hungarian Yearbook of International Law and European Law; professor of international law, Pázmány Péter Catholic University, Budapest; judge, International Criminal Court, the Hague (2015-2024).

doi: 10.5553/HYIEL/266627012022010001001

prior settlement of real or potential conflicts between these countries (see the Balladur-plan, the European Pact on Stability, *etc.*). This had an impact on the legal and diplomatic thinking, which emphasized that while problems surrounding the Gabčíkovo-Nagymaros project are truly serious, nevertheless, the most important thing is that Hungary and Slovakia are ready to litigate their dispute before the ICJ. This was also a symbol because as we all know, during the communist period, the refusal of the jurisdictional competence of the ICJ was a *sine qua non* of the international legal doctrine of the member states of the Warsaw Pact and the Comecon.[1]

For a while, I also served as a contact-person between the French international legal counsels, Pierre-Marie Dupuy and Alain Pellet, ready to support the Hungarian case and the Hungarian foreign ministry. (As it is well known – yet for different reasons that I was not officially informed of, and consequently I am not aware of – the Hungarian government took the decision to only engage professor Dupuy. Not surprisingly, Professor Pellet, was at once asked to join the Slovak team.[2]) I am particularly honored that despite this regrettable decision of Hungary, Alain Pellet became a friend and supported subsequently, and without any hesitation my career as an international lawyer. In this context, the *Gabčíkovo-Nagymaros* dispute is for me also a personal symbol of professional fortune, professional cooperation and friendship.

Another example for the nature of my small contributions is the organization of the infrastructural background of a meeting of the Hungarian team which was held for different reasons at our Paris embassy. When the official submissions were in the stage of finalization, I had to bring the 5 volumes, arriving in a diplomatic bag to a law firm specialized in ICJ litigation (or, just the other way round – I cannot recall with certainty: I had to collect the 5 volumes at the law firm and take them to the embassy to forward them to our foreign ministry.)

After the judgment was delivered in 1997, I also analyzed the 'positive' and 'negative' elements in a manuscript which appeared in French in the German Yearbook of International Law.[3]

When the foreign ministry organized in the autumn of 1997 (or at the beginning of 1998) a meeting between members of parliament and international lawyers from academia on the interpretation of the judgment, I gave voice to a critical remark concerning the submitted Hungarian translation of the judgment, which seemed to be misleading at a crucial point, *i.e.* what is to be done with the

1 Péter Kovács, 'The Effect of the Change of Political Regime on the Hungarian Doctrine of International Law', *in* András Jakab *et al.* (eds.), *The transformation of the Hungarian legal order 1985-2005: transition to the rule of law and accession to the European Union*, Alphen aan den Rijn, Kluwer Law International, 2007, pp. 453-463.

2 Alain Pellet, 'The Gabčíkovo-Nagymaros Case: a Personal Recollection', *in* Serena Forlati *et al.* (eds.), *The Gabčíkovo-Nagymaros Judgment and Its Contribution to the Development of International Law*, Brill, Nijhoff, Leiden, Boston, 2020, pp. 3-11.

3 Péter Kovács, 'Quelques considérations sur l'appréciation et l'interprétation de l'arrêt de la Cour Internationale de Justice, rendu dans l'affaire Gabčíkovo-Nagymaros', *German Yearbook of International Law*, Vol. 41, 1998, pp. 252-266.

doi: 10.5553/HYIEL/266627012022010001001

Nagymaros part of the project and what to do with the Čunovo complexum. My remark was about the use of small letters and capital letters, which may seem to be a petty problem, however, in this case, it had a tremendous impact on the interpretation of the text. The English text of the judgment used a capital letter to write Treaty only when it referred to the 1977 Treaty concerning the construction and operation of the Gabčíkovo-Nagymaros System of Locks.[4] Generally, the ICJ wrote about it in this way: the 1977 Treaty. In para. 144, it is however only Treaty. Even if the year is missing, the content is evident. In para. 146 the ICJ tried to show a reasonable way forward for the Parties to get out of the deadlock created by the mutual violations of international legal commitments. In this paragraph the word treaty is featured twice, first in with a capital letter and somewhat later, in small letters:

> "146. The Court also concludes that Variant C, which it considers operates in a manner incompatible with the *Treaty*, should be made to conform to it. By associating Hungary, on an equal footing, in its operation, management and benefits, Variant C will be transformed from a de facto status into *a treaty-based* régime." [emphasis added]

4 "144. The 1977 *Treaty* not only contains a joint investment programme, it also establishes a régime. According to the Treaty, the main structures of the System of Locks are the joint property of the Parties; their operation will take the form of a co-ordinated single unit; and the benefits of the project shall be equally shared. Since the Court has found that the *Treaty* is still in force and that, under its terms, the joint régime is a basic element, it considers that, unless the Parties agree otherwise, such a régime should be restored.

145. Article 10, paragraph 1, of the *Treaty* states that works of the System of Locks constituting the joint property of the contracting parties shall be operated, as a co-ordinated single unit and in accordance with jointly agreed operating and operational procedures, by the authorized operating agency of the contracting party in whose territory the works are built. Paragraph 2 of that Article states that works on the System of Locks owned by one of the contracting parties shall be independently operated or maintained by the agencies of that contracting party in the jointly prescribed manner. The Court is of the opinion that the works at Čunovo should become a jointly operated unit within the meaning of Article 10, paragraph 1, in view of their pivotal role in the operation of what remains of the Project and for the water-management régime. The dam at Čunovo has taken over the role which was originally destined for the works at Dunakiliti, and therefore should have a similar status Čunovo has taken over the role which was originally destined for the works at Dunakiliti, and therefore should have a similar status.

146. The Court also concludes that Variant C, which it considers operates in a manner incompatible with the *Treaty*, should be made to conform to it. By associating Hungary, on an equal footing, in its operation, management and benefits, Variant C will be transformed from a de facto status into a *treaty-based* régime. It appears from various parts of the record that, given the current state of information before the Court, Variant C could be made to function in such a way as to accommodate both the economic operation of the system of electricity generation and the satisfaction of essential environmental concerns. Regularization of Variant C by making it part of a single and indivisible operational system of works also appears necessary to ensure that Article 9 of the Treaty, which provides that the contracting parties shall participate in the use and in the benefits of the System of Locks in equal measure, will again become effective." [emphasis added]. ICJ, *Case concerning the Gabčíkovo-Nagymaros Project (Hungary v Slovakia)*, judgment, ICJ Reports 1997, pp. 79-80.

The message is that a new international convention should be concluded in order to regulate the works as they stand, but bilateralizing its operation, economic management and achieving environmentally friendly (or at least neutral) operation. Because the Hungarian translation of the ministry used capital letters in both instances, it suggested the *quasi* identity of the future convention with the content of the 1977 Treaty.[5] This was amplified by the use of the definite article in the Hungarian text in contrast with the indefinite article in the English text.[6]

5 *See* the still accessible text produced by the foreign ministry (in Hungarian): A Nemzetközi Bíróság 1997. szeptember 25-ei ítélete, Bős-Nagymaros vízlépcsőrendszer (Magyarország/Szlovákia), a magyar Külügyminisztérium által készített fordítás:

"144. Az 1977-es Szerződés nem egyszerűen egy közös beruházási program, de egy rendszert is létrehozott. A Szerződés szerint a zsiliprendszer fő létesítményei a Felek közös tulajdonát képezik; működtetésük egy összehangolt, egységes egészként történik, és a beruházás előnyeiből egyenlő arányban részesednek a Felek. Mivel a Bíróság arra a megállapításra jutott, hogy a *Szerződés* hatályban van, és feltételei alapján ez a közös rendszer kulcsfontosságú, ez azt jelenti, hogy hacsak a Felek másként nem állapodnak meg, ezt a rendszert helyre kell állítani.

145. A *Szerződés* 10. cikk (1) bekezdése kimondja, hogy a vízlépcsőrendszert, amely a Felek közös tulajdonát képező, összehangolt egységes egészként közösen elfogadott üzemszabályzat szerint azon szerződő fél által felhatalmazott üzemeltető szerv üzemelteti, amely fél területén a létesítmény épült. Ugyanezen cikk 2. bekezdése leírja, hogy csak az egyik fél tulajdonában lévő vízlépcső létesítmények, ugyanezen szerződő fél nevén, önálló üzemeltetés és fenntartás alá esnek, a közösen előírt módon. A Bíróság azon a véleményen van, hogy a dunacsúnyi létesítményeknek a 10. cikk (1) bekezdése alapján egy közösen üzemeltetett egységnek kell lennie, a beruházás fennmaradó részének működésében játszott sarkalatos szerepe és a vízgazdálkodási rendszer miatt. A dunacsúnyi gát vette át azt a szerepet, amelyet eredetileg a dunakiliti létesítménynek szántak, ezért ugyanolyan státusszal kell rendelkeznie.

146. A Bíróság továbbá arra a következtetésre jutott, hogy a C Variáns jelenlegi üzemeltetése összeegyeztethetetlen a *Szerződéssel*, azt ennek megfelelővé kell tenni. Magyarország bevonásával, egyenlő mércével mérve az üzemeltetésben, irányításban és a hasznokban, a C-Variánst a de facto helyzetből *a Szerződésen alapuló renddé* kell átalakítani. A Bíróság a beterjesztett anyagok alapján arra a következtetésre jutott, hogy a C-variáns üzemeltethető úgy is, hogy megfeleljen az elektromos energiatermelőrendszer gazdaságos működtetésének és kielégítse a lényeges környezeti aggályokat. A Szerződés 9. cikkének újbóli érvényesítése érdekében – amely meghatározza, hogy a Feleknek a vízlépcsőrendszer használatában és hasznában egyenlően kell részesedniük – szükségesnek látszik a C-variáns olyan szabályozása, mely azt egy egységes és oszthatatlan üzemeltetési rendszer részévé teszi." [emphasis added]. *See* at http://realzoldek.hu/dok/Kerenyi/hagai_itelet.pdf.

6 Compare the formula "*into a treaty-based régime*" with "*a Szerződésen alapuló renddé*" which is, in English, *a regime based on the Treaty (instead of "based on a treaty")*.

doi: 10.5553/HYIEL/266627012022010001001

This was thus far removed from the meaning of the English and the French texts. Even if the French text uses only small letters writing *traité ou le traité de 1977*, but in para. 146 it refers to a *"régime conventionnel"*.[7]

I note that there is at least one equally accessible translation, and its author seems to be also the foreign ministry.[8] When translating the message of para. 146, it arrives at an acceptable result,[9] but it is to be emphasized that contrary to the English text, it always uses – as the French text of the judgment

7 "146. La Cour conclut également que la variante C, qu'elle a estimé fonctionner d'une manière incompatible avec le *traité*, devrait être mise en conformité avec ce dernier. L'association de la Hongrie, sur un pied d'égalité, à l'exploitation, à la gestion et aux bénéfices de la variante C, aura pour effet que le statut de fait qui s'applique à cette dernière fera place a *un régime conventionnel.* Il ressort des différents éléments du dossier qu'en l'état actuel des informations soumises a la Cour la variante C semble pouvoir fonctionner d'une façon qui permette à la fois l'exploitation économique du système de production d'électricité et la satisfaction des préoccupations écologiques essentielles. Régulariser la variante C en en faisant une partie intégrante d'un système d'ouvrages opérationnel unique et indivisible apparaît également nécessaire pour donner de nouveau effet à l'article 9 du traité, qui prévoit que les parties contractantes participeront, à parts égales, à l'utilisation et aux avantages du système d'écluses." C.I.J. Recueil 1997, pp. 79-80.

8 Translation made by the Ministry of Foreign Affairs of Hungary (in Hungarian), at www.bos-nagymaros.hu/jog/haga/pagehaga.htm.

9 "144. Az 1977. évi szerződés nemcsak egy beruházás közös kivitelezését írja elő, hanem egy rendszert is létrehoz. A *szerződés* szerint a vízlépcsőrendszer fő létesítményei a felek közös tulajdonát képezik; működtetésük összehangolt, egységes egészként történik, és a beruházás előnyeiből egyformán részesednek. Mivel a bíróság arra a megállapításra jutott, hogy a szerződés még mindig érvényben van és a *szerződés* értelmében a közös rendszer alapvető elem, a bíróság úgy ítéli meg, hogy ezt a közös rendszert vissza kell állítani, hacsak a felek nem egyeznek meg másképpen.

145. A szerződés 10. cikkének 1. bekezdése szerint a szerződő felek közös tulajdonát képező vízlépcsőrendszert összehangolt egységes egészként közösen elfogadott üzemszabályzat szerint azon szerződő fél által felhatalmazott üzemeltető szerv üzemelteti, amelyik fél területén a létesítmény épült. Ugyanennek a cikknek a 2. bekezdése arról rendelkezik, hogy a vízlépcsőnek csak az egyik fél tulajdonában lévő létesítményeit a tulajdonos szerződő fél üzemeltető szerve függetlenül üzemelteti és tartja karban a közösen előírt módon. A bíróság azon a véleményen van, hogy a dunacsúni létesítménynek közös üzemeltetésűnek kell lennie a 10. cikk 1. bekezdésének értelmében, mivel rendkívül fontos szerepet játszik a beruházás megmaradt részének működtetésében és a vízszabályozási rendszer szempontjából is. A dunacsúni duzzasztógát azt a szerepet vette át, amelyet eredetileg a dunakilitinek szántak, ennélfogva hasonló státusba kell kerülnie.

146. A bíróság azt is megállapította, hogy a C-variánst, amelynek üzemeltetési módját a *szerződésben* foglaltakkal összeegyeztethetetlennek ítéli, úgy kell üzemeltetni, hogy az megfeleljen a szerződés előírásainak. Ha Magyarország egyenlő félként bekapcsolódik működtetésébe, irányításába, és előnyeiből is részesül, a C-variáns a jelenlegi de facto státusból *szerződéses alapú* üzemeltetési rendszerbe kerül át. A dokumentumok különböző részleteiből úgy tűnik, a bíróság rendelkezésére álló információ jelenlegi állása szerint, hogy a C-variáns működtethető úgy, hogy mind az áramtermelő rendszer gazdaságos működtetésének, mind az alapvető környezetvédelmi követelményeknek eleget tegyen. A C-variáns szabályossá tétele oly módon, hogy egy egységes és oszthatatlan rendszer részévé teszik, azért is szükséges, hogy a szerződés 9. cikkének eleget lehessen tenni, amely kimondja, hogy a szerződő feleknek együttesen kell részt venniük a rendszer használatában, és azonos mértékben kell részesedniük a vízlépcsőrendszer hasznából." [emphasis added]. *See* at www.bos-nagymaros.hu/jog/haga/hagaiitelet.htm.

doi: 10.5553/HYIEL/266627012022010001001

does – small letters when referring to the 1977 Treaty. (This implies that this translation, which is stylistically very different from the one submitted to the MPs, might have been made by another person on the basis of the French text, even though the authentic version of the judgment was in English.)

The criticized – and at that time only – *quasi* official translation submitted to the MPs is also the symbol of how a well-balanced legal text can have diametrically opposite consequences according to the lobbying of the heavy industry and construction business on the one hand, and the hard-line green activists on the other.[10]

It is also a symbol for politics: when it became public that secret negotiations had been launched under Gyula Horn's government (1994-1998), resulting in an agreement being parafied containing a commitment to build the Nagymaros-part of the project, the governmental coalition split and subsequently failed in the parliamentary elections. Since then, the four conservative Orbán-governments, and the two socialist-liberal governments (the Medgyessy/Gyurcsány government between 2002-2006 and then Gyurcsány/Bajnai government between 2006-2010) treated the issue as a hot potato. Negotiations were launched and managed without any transparency and apparently without any hurry. And, as a matter of fact, without any real result.

The *Gabčíkovo-Nagymaros* judgment is a symbol of a divide in Hungarian society: while during the change of political regime it was the symbol of unity and freedom, today, it seems that it is very difficult to find a shared concept of what to do. *"Pride and prejudice"*, attachment to positions, *inertia*, business, economy and regional lobbying are all wound up in it.

The *Gabčíkovo-Nagymaros* judgment however, is also a symbol for all those who specialize in international environmental law. Its most important principles on environment, precaution or state responsibility were reiterated in several other ICJ judgments.[11]

Those who know me, will probably know that I like biking. When I was riding alongside the Austrian part of the famous *Donauradweg*, I came across several dams and dikes: this is certainly not the *natura intacta*, but they are far from being atrocious and have become part of the scenery. On the other hand, when I bike at Nagymaros (or if I am uphill in the Visegrád fortress) I am very happy that the panorama seen from this historically symbolic medieval castle is not disrupted by huge concrete constructions.

10 Needless to say that my article published in the German Yearbook of International Law is very far from the position of the industrial lobby – although it certainly doesn't coincide with that of green intransigence.

11 *See e.g.* ICJ, *Case concerning armed activities on the territory of the Congo (Democratic Republic of Congo v Uganda)*, judgment, ICJ Reports 2005, para. 259, p. 257; ICJ, *Case concerning application of the Convention on the prevention and punishment of Genocide (Bosnia and Herzegovina v Serbia and Montenegro)*, judgment, ICJ Reports 2007, para. 460, p. 233; ICJ, *Case concerning pulp-mills on the river Uruguay (Argentina v Uruguay)*, judgment, ICJ Reports 2010, paras. 76, 185, 194, and 273 on pp. 48-49, 76-79 and 103-104. Not surprisingly in cases related with natural environment, pleadings and dissents returned often also to the 1997 *Gabčíkovo-Nagymaros* judgment.

doi: 10.5553/HYIEL/266627012022010001001

I know and regret that the current conditions in the 'old-Danube' area are sorely problematic from an environmental point of view. It is also clear, however, that the so-called "environmental catastrophe" or "ecological catastrophe" forecasted by so many influential experts, did not occur. It is also a question whether 25 years were enough to understand and model the future.

When preparing this short introduction, I tried to go through my Hungarian colleagues' academic writings on the judgment[12] and the efforts surrounding its hitherto unsuccessful implementation.[13] I have the impression that the presence of symbols is so important on both the Hungarian and Slovak sides in face of the lack of execution of the ICJ judgment and the sea snake-like bilateral negotiations. That is perhaps the reason why it not easy to reach an agreement based solely, or (let us admit) mostly on international law.

***

This year's thematic chapter centers around the topic of the ICJ's judgment in *Gabčíkovo-Nagymaros*, which was rendered exactly a quarter of a century ago. Confusion still persists as to how the judgment should be implemented by the

12 In alphabetical order and only in an exemplificative manner: László Bodnár, 'A nemzetközi szerződések megszűnésének kérdései a nemzetközi bíróságnak a bős-nagymarosi beruházás ügyében hozott ítéletében', *Acta Universitatis Szegediensis: Acta juridica et politica*, Vol. 58, 2000, pp. 81-90; János Bruhács, 'The International River Law in the Early 2000's', *in* Péter Kovács (ed.), *International law: a Quiet Strength. Miscellanea in memoriam Géza Herczegh,* Pázmány Press, Budapest, 2011, 231-249; Géza Herczegh, 'Bős-Nagymaros', *Valóság*, Vol. 47, Issue 2, 2004, pp. 1-20; Gábor Kecskés, 'A Nemzetközi Bíróság ítélkezési gyakorlata a környezeti tárgyú ügyekben', *Állam- és Jogtudomány*, Vol. 56, Issue 3, 2015, pp. 55-79; Boldizsár Nagy, 'A felek és a Nemzetközi Bíróság jogi álláspontja a Gabčíkovo (Bős)-Nagymarosi perben', *in* János Vargha (ed.), *A hágai döntés*, Enciklopédia, Budapest, 1997, pp. 141-178; Anikó Raisz, 'A környezetvédelem helye a nemzetközi jog rendszerében', *Miskolci Jogi Szemle*, Vol. 6, Issue 1, 2011, pp. 90-108.

13 Gábor Baranyai & Gábor Bartus, 'Anatomy of a deadlock: A systemic analysis of why the Gabčíkovo-Nagymaros dam dispute is still unresolved', *Water Policy*, Vol. 18, 2016, pp. 39-49; Lívia Mátis (ed.), *A Duna védelmében – a hágai döntés után*, Batthyány Lajos Alapítvány, Budapest, 1998; Boldizsár Nagy, 'The ICJ Judgment in the Gabčíkovo-Nagymaros Project Case and its Aftermath: Success or Failure?', *in* Marco BeNatar, & Tamar Meshel (eds.), *A Bridge over Troubled Waters: Dispute Resolution in the Law of International Watercourses and the Law of the Sea*, Brill, Nijhoff, Leiden, 2020, pp. 21-60; Boldizsár Nagy, 'Az elmaradt rendszerváltás: Bős-Nagymaros harminc éve', *Ellensúly*, 2019/3, pp. 102-113; Zsófia Nagy, 'Egy konfliktus konstrukciói. Térértelmezések Bős kapcsán', *Tér és Társadalom*, Vol. 28, Issue 1, 2014, pp. 62-83; Marcel Szabó, 'The Legal Position of Hungary and Slovakia after the Judgment of the ICJ in the Gabčíkovo-Nagymaros Case', *in* Péter Kovács (ed.), *International Law at the Turn of the Millennium – the Hungarian Approach,* Szent István Társulat, Budapest, 2000, pp. 59-76; Marcel Szabó, 'Gabčíkovo-Nagymaros Dispute – Implementation of the ICJ Judgement', *Environmental Policy and Law*, Vol. 39, Issue 2, 2009, 97-102; Marcel Szabó, 'The Implementation of the Judgment of the ICJ in the Gabčíkovo-Nagymaros Dispute', *Iustum Aequum Salutare,* Vol. 5, Issue 1, 2009, pp. 15-25; Marcel Szabó, 'Implementation of the 25th September, 1997 Judgement of the International Court of Justice – Comparing Theoretical Perspectives and Practice', *in* Kovács (ed.) 2011, pp. 271-283; Marcel Szabó, 'A bős-nagymarosi vízlépcsőper és utóélete – két évtized távlatából', *in* Gábor Kajtár & Pál Sonnevend (eds.), *A nemzetközi jog, az uniós jog és a nemzetközi kapcsolatok szerepe a 21. században: tanulmányok Valki László tiszteletére,* ELTE Eötvös, Budapest, 2021, pp. 483-198; János Ede Szilágyi, *Vízjog. Aktuális kihívások a vizek jogi szabályozásában*, Miskolc, 2013.

doi: 10.5553/HYIEL/266627012022010001001

states. In their contributions, our authors undertook to elaborate on circumstances of the judgment and the role and effect of the decision 25 years on. *Boldizsár Nagy* describes the arguments presented by Hungary and Slovakia in the proceedings, while *Malgosia Fitzmaurice* points out that the *Gabčíkovo-Nagymaros* judgment was a milestone in the development of modern water law. *Christina Binder* draws attention to the fact that the traditional law of the treaties toolbox is insufficient when dealing with environmental disputes and in his paper, *Ottavio Quirico* seeks to substantiate the *erga omnes* nature of the right and duty to a sustainable climate. *Alexandra R. Harrington* analyzes the *Gabčíkovo-Nagymaros* judgment, making the claim that it is the bedrock of international environmental law, transcending the confines of water law and impacting on the development of environmental law as a whole. Finally, *Katalin Sulyok* discusses the shift in the reliance on scientific knowledge in international environmental disputes before the ICJ.

***

On behalf of the entire Editorial Team, I wish you a good read and hope you enjoy the current Volume of our Yearbook. I also hope to welcome you among the authors of Vol. 11 (2023) of the Hungarian Yearbook of International Law and European Law. The thematic chapter of Vol. 11 (2023) is open for submissions dealing with the war between Ukraine and Russia and its impact on the development of international and European law. Please feel free to submit your contribution (to be published in any of our chapters) with us no later than 15 April 2023, in accordance with our Style Guide and Call for papers (available at our website, www.hungarianyearbook.com).

doi: 10.5553/HYIEL/266627012022010001001

The Gabčíkovo-Nagymaros Project Case Judgment: 25 Years On

Buds to Blossom Later

The Precautionary Principle, Environmental Impact Assessment and Intergenerational Equity in the Gabčíkovo-Nagymaros Project Case and Thereafter

Boldizsár Nagy[*]

Abstract

Why did the ICJ fail to apply the precautionary principle, the duty to conduct environmental impact assessment and the respect for intergenerational equity in the Gabčíkovo-Nagymaros Project Case in 1997? Why and how has it circumvented these concepts/principles then, most of which later emerged in its subsequent jurisprudence – that is the central question of this article. It reviews the international legal status of these concepts before the judgment was adopted in 1997, the arguments of the parties in the written and oral pleadings referring (or not) to these concepts and the "afterlife" of the three concepts/principles, showing that in the 25 years after the judgment environmental impact assessment became a firmly established international legal obligation, the precautionary principle exerts stronger influence but is still somewhat debated as to its precise content, especially outside the EU and intergenerational equity (fairness to future generations) has remained a guiding principle upon which no direct claim may be based, but that may change soon in light of the climate litigation reviewed. The hardly visible undercurrent of the text suggests that had these concepts/principles been adopted by the international community by 1997, the ICJ could have reached a different conclusion. But time was not ripe for that in 1997.

Keywords: ICJ, Gabčíkovo-Nagymaros judgment, intergenerational equity, international environmental law, precautionary principle.

"When technical questions are discussed, in particular concerning cases related to environmental protection, it seems to me that the files constituted by the parties are abusively technical and abstruse – or in any case, incomprehensible for

* Boldizsár Nagy: associate professor of law, Central European University, Vienna; counsel of Hungary at the ICJ during the Gabčíkovo-Nagymaros litigation.

doi: 10.5553/HYIEL/266627012022010001002

normally constituted jurists who have only limited training in chemistry, geology or hydrographics." (Alain Pellet, 2008)[1]

1. Mapping the Subject

This article represents a dialogue[2] with the judgment of the ICJ in the *Gabčíkovo-Nagymaros Project Case*[3] and its impact (or lack of it) on the use of three inter-related concepts: the environmental impact assessment (EIA), the precautionary principle and intergenerational equity, that is the position of future generations. As such, it does not aim at an overall analysis of the judgment or its impact. That

1 Alain Pellet, 'The Anatomy of Courts and Tribunals', *The Law and Practice of International Courts and Tribunals*, Vol. 7, Issue 3, 2008, p. 282.

2 The author was involved in the dispute on the Hungarian side between 1989 and 2010, including as counsel for Hungary in the ICJ case. Therefore, the interpretation of the judgment proposed in this article is not of the impartial observer but of someone who fully identifies with the standpoint the Hungarian party represented before the ICJ, and whose preferences coincided with those of the Hungarian Government as expressed before the litigation, during it and – with a year break in 1997-1998 – during the negotiations on the implementation of the judgment until 2010. Naturally, every effort is made to remain faithful to the facts and only to offer possible interpretations within the established.

3 ICJ, *Case concerning the Gabčíkovo-Nagymaros Project (Hungary v Slovakia)*, judgment, ICJ Reports 1997, p. 7.

doi: 10.5553/HYIEL/266627012022010001002

has been accomplished by many scholars elsewhere,[4] including the present author.[5]

4 From the early literature the five articles ('Symposium: The Case Concerning the Gabčíkovo-Nagymaros Project') published in Vol. 8, Issue 1, 1998 of the *Yearbook of International Environmental Law* should be mentioned. The *Leiden Journal of International Law* produced a "thematic issue" (Vol. 11, Issue 2, 1998). Case notes appeared in several journals, including the *American Journal of International Law* (by Peter H. F. Bekker, Vol. 92, Issue 2, 1998, pp. 273-278), the *International and Comparative Law Quarterly* (by Phoebe N. Okowa, Vol. 47, Issue 3, 1998, pp. 688-697). From the ensuing literature a narrow selection would include: Daniel Reichert-Facilides, 'Down the Danube: the Vienna Convention on the Law of Treaties and the Case concerning the Gabčíkovo-Nagymaros Project', *in* Scott Davidson (ed.), *The Law of Treaties*, Ashgate, Darthmouth, 2004, pp. 474-494; Philippe Sands, 'Watercourses, Environment and the International Court of Justice: The Gabčíkovo-Nagymaros Case', *in* Salman M.A. Salman & Laurence Boisson de Chazournes, *International watercourses: enhancing cooperation and managing conflict*, World Bank, 1998, 103-125; Stephen Stec, 'Do Two Wrongs Make a Right? Adjudicating Sustainable Development in the Danube Dam Case', *Golden Gate University Law Review*, Vol. 29, Issue 3, 1999, pp. 317-397; John Fitzmaurice, 'The ruling of the International Court of Justice in the Gabčíkovo-Nagymaros Case: A Critical Analysis', *European Environmental Law Review*, Vol. 9, Issue 2, 2000, pp. 80-87; Cesare P. Romano, *The Peaceful Settlement of International Environmental Disputes A Pragmatic Approach*, Kluwer, 2000; Ellen Hey, 'International water law placed in a contemporary environmental context: the Gabčíkovo-Nagymaros case', *Physics and Chemistry of the Earth, Part B: Hydrology, Oceans and Atmosphere*, Volume 25, Issue 3, 2000, pp. 303-308; Marcel Szabó, 'The Legal Position of Hungary and Slovakia after the Judgment of the ICJ in the Gabčíkovo-Nagymaros Case', *in* Péter Kovács (ed.), *International Law at the Turn of the Millennium – the Hungarian Approach*, Szent István Társulat, Budapest, 2000, pp. 59-76; Steven M. Schwebel, 'The Judgment of the International Court of Justice in the case concerning the Gabčíkovo-Nagymaros project (Hungary/Slovakia)', *in* Steven M. Schwebel, *Justice in International Law. Further selected writings*, Cambridge University Press, Cambridge, 2011, pp. 113-123; Stephen Deets, 'Constituting interests and identities in a two-level game: understanding the Gabčíkovo-Nagymaros Dam conflict', *Foreign Policy Analysis*, Vol. 5, Issue, 1, 2009, pp. 37-56; Marcel Szabó, 'The Implementation of the Judgment of the ICJ in the Gabčíkovo-Nagymaros Dispute', *Iustum Aequum Salutare*, Vol. 5, Issue 1, 2009, pp. 15-25; Marcel Szabó, 'Gabčíkovo-Nagymaros Dispute – Implementation of the ICJ Judgment', *Environmental Policy and Law*, Vol. 39, Issue 2, 2009, pp. 97-102; Marcel Szabó, 'Implementation of the 25th September, 1997 Judgement of the International Court of Justice – Comparing Theoretical Perspectives and Practice', *in* Péter Kovács (ed.), *International law: a Quiet Strength. Miscellanea in memoriam Géza Herczegh*, Pázmány Press, Budapest, 2011, pp. 271-283; Gábor Baranyai & Gábor Bartus,'Anatomy of a deadlock: a systemic analysis of why the Gabčíkovo-Nagymaros dam dispute is still unresolved', *Water Policy*, Vol. 18, 2016, pp. 39-49; Serena Forlati *et al.* (eds.), *The Gabčíkovo-Nagymaros judgment and its contribution to the development of international law*, Brill, 2020, with 15 chapters taking up different aspects of the case. Marcel Szabó, 'A bős-nagymarosi vízlépcsőper és utóélete – két évtized távlatából', *in* Gábor Kajtár & Pál Sonnevend (eds.), *A nemzetközi jog, az uniós jog és a nemzetközi kapcsolatok szerepe a XXI. században*, ELTE Eötvös, Budapest, 2021, pp. 483-498.

5 This author has published several pieces on the dispute, of which Boldizsár Nagy, 'The Danube Dispute: Conflicting Paradigms', *The New Hungarian Quarterly*, 1992/128, pp. 56-65; Boldizsár Nagy, The ICJ Judgment in the Gabčíkovo-Nagymaros Project case and its aftermath: success or failure?, *in* Marco Benatar & Tamar Meshel (eds.), *A Bridge over Troubled Waters: Dispute Resolution in the Law of International Watercourses and the Law of the Sea*, Brill/Nijhoff, 2021, pp. 21-60, are primarily relevant.

doi: 10.5553/HYIEL/266627012022010001002

1.1. *The Aim*

The goal here is to show, how the duty to pursue EIA, the precautionary principle, and the care for the interests of future generations were inchoate in both the dispute and the judgment, without being able play a decisive role. The proposal is that the judgment was an opportunity to transform their potential into actuality in the Aristotelian sense. These ideas could have had the power to deeply influence or right away determine the content of the judgment. They had the potential, but under the historic circumstances and the ICJ's disposition they could not exert it, the actuality did not come forward, the potential was not brought to fruition. It took time until later judgments led to the blossoming of flowers that earlier were only buds bursting the bark of the *Gabčíkovo-Nagymaros Project Case*.

Before we delve into the details of the text and of subsequent developments, let us very briefly recall the salient elements of the case.

1.2. *The Barrage System*

After earlier tentative plans to utilize the hydropotential of the Danube and under pressure from CMEA[6] and the Soviet Union in the sixties, Czechoslovakia and Hungary developed the 'Joint Investment Programme', that contained all the important elements of the later system by 1964.[7] A two element barrage system was to be built where the lower hydropower unit would enable the upper hydropower unit to operate in a 'peak mode', holding back the waterflow of the Danube for 10-18 hours. After the elaboration of the detailed plans, the intergovernmental treaty setting forth the main elements and the mutual obligations of the parties was adopted on 16 September 1977 (1977 Treaty).[8] This stipulated the location of the upper barrage at Gabčíkovo, then in Czechoslovakia, and the lower barrage about 120 kilometers downstream at Nagymaros. The planned system entailed a 60 km2 reservoir between Bratislava and Dunakiliti, wherefrom a 17 km long artificial headrace canal was to deliver the waterflow to the combined 720 MW capacity turbines of the hydropower station built at the end of the headrace canal at Gabčíkovo, roughly 3 km from the Danube river border on the Czechoslovak side.[9] Another artificial canal, the tailrace canal, also dug into fertile land far away from the riverbed, was to bring back the waterflow to the main riverbed, leaving a 41 rkm stretch of the main riverbed to be fed with a meagre average of 2-3% of the waterflow.

The continuous (run-of-the-river) hydropower station at the Nagymaros barrage would have had 158 MW built-in capacity, so its main aim was not electricity generation but keeping the Danube navigable when the Gabčíkovo

6 Council of Mutual Economic Assistance, the intergovernmental organization tasked with the management of the economic co-operation of the Socialist states.

7 Hungarian Memorial, para. 2.34.

8 Treaty concerning the Construction and Operation of the Gabčíkovo-Nagymaros System of Locks (Hungary and Czechoslovakia), 16 September 1977, 1109 UNTS 236; also published in *International Legal Materials*, Vol. 32, Issue 5, 1992, pp. 1247-1290. (1977 Treaty).

9 *See* the detailed description relying on the 1977 Treaty at paras. 28-29 of the judgment and the sketch-maps in para. 18.

doi: 10.5553/HYIEL/266627012022010001002

weirs were closed and no water was to be discharged from the reservoir in order to collect the water for peak (hour) operation.[10] In terms of costs, control and reaping the benefits, the 1977 treaty envisaged a "single and indivisible operational system"[11] in which both parties would have equal share.

In bilateral relations Hungary raised environmental concerns first in 1981 and then again, in a more resolute way in 1989. It first suspended and after fruitless negotiations with Czechoslovakia abandoned the construction of the second barrage at Nagymaros and did not complete the weir at Dunakiliti that was to divert the Danube into the artificial headrace canal. In response and during further similarly unsuccessful negotiations in 1989-1991, Czechoslovakia proceeded to the construction of installations at Čunovo 10 kilometers upstream from Dunakiliti where it controlled both embankments with a view to unilateral diversion of the Danube.[12]

The presently operating set of installations is called Variant 'C' (as it was one of the several options considered by Czechoslovakia)[13] and it entails full control by Slovakia over water management and navigation in the bypass canal (headrace + tailrace canal) since the diversion of the Danube on 24-27 October 1992. Hungary's significant investments into the Gabčíkovo power plant and the right bank dyke of the reservoir, as well as its investment in digging the tailrace canal appear as sunken costs. Its hydropotential used at Gabčíkovo for electric energy production is not compensated in any manner, nor does Hungary have access to its equitable and reasonable share of the Danube waterflow between rkms 1851 (the Čunovo diversion) and rkm 1810 (the confluence of the bypass canal and the old riverbed at Szap.)

1.3. The Environmental and Ecological Concerns that Justify the Paramount Role of the Three Principles

The essence of the dispute has been identified in many ways,[14] some stressing the treaty law elements,[15] others the law of responsibility, and still others the international water-law components or the environmental aspects.[16] Obviously, from a broader perspective, the case was a political dispute and a competition

10 For a comparison: it is roughly equal to one photovoltaic power plant planned in Serbia near Zaječar (CWP to install 150 MW Solarina solar power plant near Zaječar, at https://bbj.hu/economy/energy/green-energy/cwp-europe-unit-to-build-150-mw-pv%C2%A0plant-in-zajecar-serbia); or roughly 75 wind turbines (The Anholt Offshore Wind Farm in Denmark has 400 MW capacity, at https://ramboll.com/projects/re/anholt-offshore-wind-farm).

11 Article 1 of the 1977 Treaty.

12 *See* paras. 23, and 66 of the judgment.

13 Slovak Memorial, paras. 5.15-5.23

14 *See e.g.* the thematic issue of the *Leiden Journal of International Law*, or the *Yearbook of International Environmental Law*, cited above. The publication commemorating the 20th anniversary of the ICJ judgment, Forlati *et al.* (eds.) 2020 discusses the case under three main headings, that of Treaties, international responsibility and sustainable development.

15 "I think we were right in considering that it was first of all a treaty law case." Alain Pellet, 'The Gabčíkovo-Nagymaros Case: A Personal Recollection', *in* Forlati *et al.* (eds.) 2020, p. 7

16 "[...] environmental issues [...] could in fact be described as the very essence of the case." Okawa 1998, p. 694.

doi: 10.5553/HYIEL/266627012022010001002

between an industrial, modern approach and a post-industrial, ecological approach.[17]

Here it is appropriate to concentrate on the environmental and in a narrower sense the ecological concerns that invite the three notions/principles at the center of this article.

The Hungarian Memorial and all later submissions, including the oral pleadings devoted considerable space to these concerns and the damages and risks associated with the Original Project,[18] as well as with Variant 'C'.[19] The surface and subsurface waters were of prime concern. The decreased water flow in the main riverbed, reduced to a fragment of the actual discharge (that was to be diverted to the bypass channel) threatened with the drying up of the last inland delta in Europe, comprising several hundred square kilometers in the form of two large islands (Szigetköz and Zitny Ostrov) with an unusually dense branch system in the flood plain area supporting unique wetlands. Substantive deterioration of water quality including the danger of eutrophication also belonged to expected surface water changes.

The aquifer below these two large islands was (and still is) threatened. The aquifer under the Hungarian side has the sustainable capacity to yield 750 million liters of potable water per day. Similar resources on the Slovak side resources are even larger. The fear was that the deteriorating quality of the infiltrating water containing heavy metals and other pollutants would in an irreversible manner pollute this aquifer rendering the water not potable or necessitate complicated and financially prohibitively expensive treatment.

At the lower section, upstream and downstream of the Nagymaros Barrage, the expected river morphological changes would have significantly reduced the quantity and impaired the quality of the water produced by the bank filtered wells operating in the affected area. These wells supply the drinking water of the 1.9 million inhabitants living in the Hungarian capital. The water gained from the wells in the area that would have been affected by the Nagymaros Barrage is of such quality that it needs no treatment at all, thanks to the natural process of bank filtering.

The two islands below Bratislava, Zitny Ostrov and Szigetköz and the branches criss-crossing them form the last inland delta in Europe. They contain unique flora and fauna and are vital sites of aquatic life. The loss of connection

17 Nagy 1992; John Fitzmaurice, *Damming the Danube: Gabčíkovo and post-communist politics in Europe*, Routledge, 1998; János Vargha, 'Vízerő és politika', *in* János Vargha (ed.), *A hágai döntés*, Enciklopédia, Budapest, 1997, pp. 221-287.

18 "Original Project" refers to the set of installations and mode of operation in the original plans supporting the 1977 Treaty, including the "Joint Contractual Plan" containing all the details, adopted in 1976.

19 Hungarian Memorial, pp. 147-179, paras. 5.30-5.140; Hungarian Counter-Memorial, pp. 34-81, paras. 1.50-1.177, and pp. 153-171, paras. 3.15-3.81. Two tomes were devoted to these issues as Vol. 5, Part I and II to the Hungarian Memorial, one as Volume 2 of the Annexes to the Hungarian Counter-Memorial. The Hungarian Reply summarized the concerns and addressed the Slovak arguments proposed in the Slovak Counter-Memorial in response to the Hungarian position in the Hungarian Memorial at pp. 48-65, paras. 1.100-1.144, accompanied by one more volume containing the "scientific rebuttal" of the Slovak position (Vol. 2 of the Annexes).

doi: 10.5553/HYIEL/266627012022010001002

between the side arms and the main riverbed of the Danube, the decreased water discharge and ground water levels and the lack of floods would have had devastating impact on the flood plain ecosystems of the affected area, including disappearance of species and reduced biodiversity. Disappearance of certain aquatic habitats and a significant impairment of fisheries was also expected.

Other risks related to navigation (which is totally blocked for ships larger than small boats in the main riverbed between Čunovo and Sap), landscape and recreational values, 45 archaeological sites including remnants of Roman watch-towers and geological and geophysical risks were also associated with the Original Project.[20]

The unilateral diversion of the Danube in 1992 and the continuous operation ever since of Variant 'C' has re-arranged the set of risks and damages: most of those related to the Nagymaros barrage (that had not been built) and the 123 km long reservoir between it and the upstream confluence of the bypass canal and the main riverbed did not materialize. As Gabčíkovo is more-or-less continuously operating, the sedimentation pattern in the Čunovo reservoir is very different from the original plan to which one may add that the water quality of the river has dramatically improved due to the collapse of Socialist heavy industry and owing to EU requirements, so the threat of the pollution of the aquifer has decreased. On the other hand, the length of the river without normally fluctuating discharge was extended by 10 kilometers, the abrupt diversion wreaked havoc in the ecosystems, and the present artificial water supply system cannot maintain the conditions that prevailed in the area before construction had started.[21]

2. The Three Buds: Environmental Impact Assessment, Precaution and Intergenerational Equity

Let us not start with trying to determine whether these were or now are rules, principles, concepts or approaches. Here, in the introduction to their detailed discussion the aim is to clarify why other similarly relevant concepts, like the idea of sustainable development, principles of the use of international watercourses, the duty to prevent transboundary harm and many more are excluded from this study. The reasons for that omission are threefold: either these other concepts do not belong to the dense normative space the three suggested topics create (like the principle of reasonable and equitable use of shared resources) or they have been extensively discussed in academia and had a fairly fixed meaning by the time

20 For a concise listing of these and further risks *see* the Hungarian Reply, para. 1.102.

21 "We can conclude that construction of the Gabčíkovo Waterworks, similar to other river regulations [references to studies], leads to the slow degradation of rare and endangered habitats of the softwood floodplain forests in the Danube inland delta. Analysis of changes in the species composition and ecological factors revealed that all three studied sites have undergone negative changes over the last 23 years." Mária Petrášová-Šibíková *et al.*, 'Effect of the Gabčíkovo Waterworks (Slovakia) on riparian floodplain forest ecosystems in the Danube inland delta: vegetation dynamics and trends', *Biologia*, Vol. 72, Issue 7, 2017, p. 732.

doi: 10.5553/HYIEL/266627012022010001002

the judgment was rendered (principle of prevention) or, lastly, they are so complex and elusive that their discussion would deserve and require disproportional space and effort within the frame of this paper (sustainable development).

Consequently, I chose environmental impact assessment, precaution and the interests (or rights?) of future generations as the central themes of this paper. I did so because of their inherent linkages and the dense normative space they create.[22] Precaution is applied in order to save present and future generations from irreversible and/or devastating harm under circumstances of uncertainty, when no full scientific evidence can be produced.[23] Environmental impact assessment is the measure to be applied to assess the risk of that harm together with identifying the concrete, clearly foreseeable consequences of the planned activity.

The essence of the Gabčíkovo-Nagymaros Project dispute was located in the center of this normative space. Hungary believed that the project's possible impacts have not been assessed in a holistic way, which could only be done in the form of a methodically flawless, comprehensive environmental impact assessment that would investigate not only the planned barrage system but also its alternatives, be it energy production or solution to the navigational problems or flood protection. The country suspended the construction at Nagymaros, and a few months later at the upper section in 1989, precisely to accomplished this. Why? Because there were good reasons to believe that the operation of the Original Project would lead to serious and irreversible damage in many ways, among others threatening the drinking water supply of several millions of people. Harm would not necessarily immediately manifest itself. The yet untapped resources under Szigetköz and Zitny Ostrov served as reservoirs to supply the drinking water needs of future generations not only in the two affected countries, but more widely, the future generations who may live in areas with water pressure and scarcity. The degradation of the habitats and ecologically valuable areas may in fact take decades, depriving future generations from biodiversity, agricultural, aquacultural and forestry resources and recreational values on the long run.

That was the core of the dispute: could it be established with scientific certainty that no such harm was threatening, that the interests and choices of future generations to come were not jeopardized? In order to answer that question the parties ought to have engaged in an environmental impact assessment that could have dispelled any reasonable doubt as to the viability of the project. Hungary was of the view that the risk was real and present, its nature and probability ought to be specified in a comprehensive environmental impact assessment in order to protect the interests of present and future generations even against threats that may not be proven with full scientific certainty.

22 For the link between precaution and environmental impact assessment, *see* Antônio Augusto Cançado Trindade, 'Principle 15 Precaution', *in* Jorge E. Vinuales (ed.), *The Rio Declaration on Environment and Development: A Commentary,* Oxford University Press, Oxford, 2015.

23 A more precise definition will be offered later.

doi: 10.5553/HYIEL/266627012022010001002

Czechoslovakia and – after 31 December 1992 – the successor state to the project, Slovakia did not share this approach. It believed that appropriate investigations had been completed to exclude serious and or irreversible damage and so one could assume that intergenerational equity was not jeopardized. Slovakia was of the view that negative impacts on the environment or the malfunctioning of the system can be rectified by engineering and similar measures and denied that precaution was a justiciable rule/principle of international law. One may say the first was a postmodern, sustainability-oriented approach, the second an industrial, modern, growth-oriented approach.

It all depended on the Court: was it ready to adopt an environmentally progressive, activist approach, reinforcing nascent norms or did it want to play safe by applying norms that it could have applied fifty years earlier as well. For the sake of this study the research question to be answered is: what was the substance and the international law status of the three concepts at the time of the procedure (1993-1997); how did the Court relate to them then; and has its approach – and the overall international legal perception – changed in the subsequent quarter of a century?

3. Environmental Impact Assessment

This, and the following section and will be divided into three subsections: *(i)* the first will briefly review the status of the legal concept up to the adoption of the judgment on 25 September 1997, that is their history before and during the ICJ procedure. *(ii)* The second subsection in each section will review how the parties and the ICJ dealt with the concept in the case. *(iii)* Finally, a third subsection will explore their 'life' after the judgment.

3.1. The Status of EIA before the Judgment

It was not until 2010 that the full Court admitted that undertaking an environmental impact assessment (EIA) was "a requirement under general international law".[24] In 1995 *ad hoc* judge Palmer nominated by New Zealand in the second *New Zealand versus France* case[25] ventured into saying that "customary international law *may* have developed a norm of requiring environmental impact assessment where activities may have a significant effect on the environment"[26] (emphasis added).

Clearly, the duty to conduct an EIA (when certain risks were entailed) was not a rule that the ICJ would apply as part of the foundation of its judgment in

24 ICJ, *Pulp Mills on the River Uruguay (Argentina v Uruguay)*, judgment, ICJ Reports 2010, p. 14, para. 204.

25 ICJ, *Request for an Examination of the Situation in Accordance with Paragraph 63 of the Court's Judgment of 20 December 1974 in the Nuclear Tests (New Zealand v France) Case*, ICJ Reports 1995, p. 288.

26 Id. Dissenting Opinion of Judge Geoffrey Palmer, para. 91.

doi: 10.5553/HYIEL/266627012022010001002

the 1990s, no matter how strongly some parties were pushing for it.[27] But what was its status at the time?

The history of EIA is well rehearsed.[28] At national level the starting point was the US National Environmental Policy Act of 1969.[29] It early on combined the EIA with the goal to "fulfil the responsibilities of each generation as trustee of the environment for succeeding generations".[30] By 1992 both Hungary and Czechoslovakia had dedicated rules on environmental impact assessment.[31]

Globally, the adoption of Principle 17 of the 1992 Rio Declaration[32] prescribing it as a duty of states was the most important step. In Europe the turning point was the 1991 (Espoo) Convention on Environmental Impact Assessment in a Transboundary Context[33] concluded under the aegis of the UN Economic Committee for Europe, whereas the EU (then: European Economic Community) adopted its first directive on EIA in 1985.[34]

One can assume that the core ideas of the EIA had crystallized by the early nineties. In a more recent publication, Neil Craik summarizes them as follows:

> "1 An EIA shall be required prior to the commencement of a planned activity that is likely to have a significance environmental impact on the territory of another state or in areas beyond national jurisdictions.
> 2 EIA primarily applies to physical undertakings and much less to policies, plans, and programs.
> 3 The contents of an EIA shall be determined by domestic law, but ought to be sufficient to allow states to evaluate the environmental impacts, both direct and indirect, of the activity, as well as potential mitigation measures, in accordance with due diligence.
> 4 In case significant environment impact is likely, the obligation to notify the potentially affected states, inform them about the results of the EIA, and to consult with a view to resolving any outstanding concerns emerges.

27 *See* the next subsection.

28 Neil Craik, 'Environmental Impact Assessment', *in* Vinuales (ed.) 2015, p. 451; Philippe Sands *et al.*, *Principles of international environmental law, 4th edition*, Cambridge University Press, Cambridge, 2018, pp. 657-681.

29 Pub. L. 91-190 as amended USC 42§ 4321-47. In force since 1 January 1970.

30 Id. Section 101.

31 Czechoslovakia: Czech National Council Act on Environmental Impact Assessment (No. 244/1992); Hungary: Governmental Decree No. 86/1993. (VI. 4.) on the temporary regulations of EIA of certain activities.

32 UN Conference on Environment and Development, *Rio Declaration on Environment and Development*, 14 June 1992, UN Doc. A/Conf.151/5/Rev.1, Principle 17. Two important predecessors were the UNEP Goals and Principles of Environmental Impact Assessment UNEP Res. GC14/25, 14th Sess. (1987), endorsed by GA Res. 42/184, UN GAOR, 42nd Session, UN Doc. A/Res/42/184 (1987) ('UNEP EIA Goals and Principles'), and the World Bank's Operational Policy on environmental Assessment OP 4.01 first introduced in 1989.

33 Convention on Environmental Impact Assessment in a Transboundary Context, 25 February 1991.

34 Council Directive 85/337/EEC on the Assessment of the Effects of Certain Public and Private Projects on the Environment.

doi: 10.5553/HYIEL/266627012022010001002

5 EIA processes shall provide opportunities for public participation.
6 States who undertake activities are under a continuous obligation to monitor environment impacts, where monitoring is found to be reasonably necessary."[35]

3.2. Environmental Impact Assessment in the Gabčíkovo-Nagymaros Project Case – Position of the Parties and the ICJ

The Slovak Memorial only mentions the term 'environmental impact assessment' once, when referring to a professional group, that conducted a large study commissioned by Hungary.[36] It writes extensively about all the disparate scientific studies conducted in the past and dealing with the expected impact of the Original Project, but nowhere does it make an effort to place them into the legal and epistemological frame of the EIA. None of the documents referred to in the previous subsection, not even the Rio Declaration appears in the text. Remarkably, when arguing for the legality of Variant 'C', the point dealing with the (alleged) conformity of the unilateral diversion of the Danube and the operation of the Gabčíkovo power plant with "rules and principles of international law that regulate shared watercourses",[37] Slovakia limits itself to the principle of reasonable and equitable share and ignores duties related to EIA as providing information, notification and negotiation, not to mention the involvement of the affected public.

The Slovak perception was that the Hungarian environmental arguments throughout the different phases of the dispute were merely pretexts camouflaging first economic, and later political purposes. It claimed that the motivation of the social movements attacking the project was political as was that of the government which after 1990 identified with the goals of the environmental movements, but at no time was opposition to the completion of the project supported by solid scientific evidence.[38]

The mentality of Slovakia is best reflected by the bold statement ending the description of the Original Project:

> "It had been found that the environment would benefit to a high degree from the Project and that any negative impacts could be mitigated at the same time as the parties' development goals were realized."

35 Neil Craik, 'Environmental Impact Assessment" *in* Yann Aguila & Jorge E. Vinuales (eds.), *A Global Pact for the Environment: Legal Foundations,* C-EENRG, Cambridge, 2019, pp. 69-70.
36 Slovak Memorial, para. 2.27.
37 Id. Chapter VII, Section 3 E, paras. 7.772-7.86.
38 Id. para. 3.56. To taste the unique style of the Slovak Memorial, read this concluding sentence of para. 3.56, summarizing why the first democratically elected government of Hungary opposed the project: "After the political changes in Hungary, opposition to the G/N Project became an *idée fixe* in the political program of the party that assumed power, because such opposition had played an important role in the struggle for power in 1989 and 1990 and in its outcome."

doi: 10.5553/HYIEL/266627012022010001002

This is the quintessentially modern, industrial approach: everything is fine, the goal is "development", *i.e.* growth, there are no risks to consider and if nevertheless something goes wrong, we will fix it.

The Hungarian Memorial dealt more extensively with the duty to conduct an EIA. It noted the domestic criticism (coming, among others, from the Hungarian Academy of Sciences) against the studies conducted in the mid-eighties, according to which the studies were not complex, failed a rigorous methodology and did not adequately investigate alternatives to the project.[39] The more extensive treatment of EIA appears in the context of Variant 'C' in which both the Espoo Convention and the Rio Declaration are invoked, primarily as sources of an obligation to inform and consult.[40] The Hungarian Memorial also mentions EIA as an obligation that has developed after the conclusion of the 1977 Treaty and therefore can be an element contributing to the evidence supporting the claim that a fundamental change of circumstances has occurred since the conclusion of the Treaty.[41]

The counter-memorials predictably brought a more intensive engagement with EIA. *Slovakia* essentially continued to ignore EIA as a legal norm, and opted for a bifurcated strategy: on the one hand it challenged the evidence about the future threats presented by the Hungarian side by purporting to refute certain details.[42] On the other hand, it continuously moved the dispute to the field of water management, equitable and reasonable share and economic benefits,[43] not refraining from occasionally simply distorting the Hungarian evidence.[44] The general tenor of the Counter-Memorial is reflected by the following quote:

> "The general principles of contemporary international environmental law do not operate in isolation from other norms of international law including the principle of *pacta sunt servanda*, or from other values of the international community. In particular, those principles, properly understood, inform but do not thwart the efforts of countries to develop for the benefit of present and future generations. Yet if Hungary's view of the general international law of the environment were followed to its logical conclusion it would mean that no dams or other development projects could be constructed on international watercourses because they would alter the natural environment."

39 Hungarian Memorial, paras. 3.52-3.

40 Id. Chapter 7, Section C 2.

41 Id. para. 10.76.

42 Slovak Counter-Memorial, para. 8.16 "Unfortunately, the WWF publications in relation to the GNBS Project are characterized by a lack of in depth in scientific study and a prejudice against the Project."

43 Chapter IX, Section 3, paras. 9.45-9.79.

44 Para. 4.29 claims that the quotes taken from the Hungarian Academy of Sciences study presented in that paragraph showed they were a clear "statement by the Hungarian Academy of Sciences (HAS) of the priority of economic interests over environmental concerns." In reality, the HAS study called for further research into the expected impacts and suggested to temporarily or definitely avoid the construction of the second barrage in order to eliminate the "adverse side effects" of the project. *Cf.* Hungarian Memorial Annexes, Vol. 5, Part I, p. 11.

doi: 10.5553/HYIEL/266627012022010001002

Hopefully there is no need to stress that Hungary never objected to the utilization of the international watercourse, it simply aspired to what the ICJ was to declare later: that the Project may only operate if it is environmentally sound.[45]

The *Hungarian Counter-Memorial* devoted considerable space to EIA. The Counter-Memorial's main text addressed it in two sections[46] and a whole annexed volume was devoted to the scientific evaluation of the GNBS and Variant 'C', chapter 7 of which dealt exclusively with the EIA.[47] The essence of the Hungarian position may be summarized in the following way. *(i)* Environmental impact assessment is a project evaluation technique that includes a process which aims at the complex and interrelated ascertainment of the expected environmental, social, and economic impacts of the planned intervention and its alternatives, including no action at all and consists of the procedural steps and of an environmental impact statement, the criteria of which have changed since the 1970s and are still not fixed. The process also includes subsequent monitoring and evaluation.[48] *(ii)* Isolated studies related to a project do not add up to an EIA, no matter how many of these are available. What is critical is

> "the scope of the issues addressed, the quality of each study, and the extent to which the different studies have been integrated so as to provide a coherent overview of the environmental problems posed."[49]

In the context of the failure to carry out an environmental impact assessment of Variant 'C' the Hungarian Counter-Memorial notes that the items named, but not reproduced in an Annex of the Slovak Memorial[50] constitute a "motley collection of studies" that neither individually, nor collectively constitute an EIA. It further stresses that not "one of these studies purports to address the overall environmental impacts of Variant 'C', or its effects on such matters as biodiversity or water quality on the Hungarian side."

By the Reply phase, EIA became an important issue for both parties. The Slovak Reply engages the Hungarian argument early on, according to which no proper EIA was ever executed. It once again proposes that the much criticized studies (on both sides) in effect provided appropriate information, making mitigation of the harmful impact possible. What the Slovak Republic does not do is to reflect on what an EIA should look like, what the criteria ought to be, and

45 According to the ICJ, the 1977 Treaty requires "the Parties, in carrying out their obligations to ensure that the quality of the water in the Danube is not impaired and that nature is protected, [and] to take new environmental norms into consideration when agreeing upon the means to be specified in the Joint Contractual Plan." ICJ judgment, para. 112.

46 Hungarian Counter-Memorial, Chapter I , Section C, paras. 1.20-1.41. and Chapter 3, Section B, paras. 3.11-3.14.

47 Id. Annexes, Volume 2.

48 Id. para. 1.20, and Chapter 7 in Volume 2.

49 Id. para. 124.

50 Slovak Memorial, Annex 36.

doi: 10.5553/HYIEL/266627012022010001002

how the set of studies available at different time periods correspond (or don't correspond) to these criteria.

Instead, it claims that general international law could only regulate matters that were not regulated by the 1977 Treaty and asserts that "nature protection" was in fact regulated by the Treaty. It further asserts that in any event, the 1977 Treaty was *lex specialis*, even in relation to later developed general principles of international environmental law.[51]

The Hungarian Reply devotes twenty paragraphs to showing that no proper EIA was made before or subsequent to the 1977 Treaty, and highlights how the "Bioproject" studies that were claimed to have assessed the impacts of the Original Project were never handed over to Hungary.[52] It also stresses that Slovakia applied for EU funds (PHARE) to create a "proper impact assessment model" and pointed out that the Slovak experts had indicated that an adequate study was lacking.[53]

The oral pleadings essentially repeated the parties' well-rehearsed positions. Professor Wordsworth on behalf of Slovakia stressed that

> "there was no duty under international law in the pre-Treaty period to carry out a proper environmental impact assessment, whatever that may be, and Hungary's contention is anyway contradicted by the evidence annexed to its own Memorial."[54]

There were three statements in this sentence: *(i)* first, that EIA was not compulsory before 1977 (true, but Hungary never claimed the opposite); *(ii)* second, that nobody knows what a proper EIA may be (in 1997 there were quite many, including the Hungarian delegation who knew what it ought to be); and *(iii)*, finally that in fact there was an Environmental Impact Statement annexed to the Hungarian Memorial (that would be the 1985 statement by the Hungarian company involved in the construction of the barrage system, which was a far cry from a decent environmental impact statement as substantiated by Hungary in the oral phase.)[55]

Hungary yet again stressed the lack of a comprehensive EIA that would identify the impact of changing one environmental factor (*e.g.* water level) on others (*e.g.* flora, fauna, land use, *etc.*)[56] It also showed, that major items such as seismological threats had not been addressed adequately and reassuringly.[57]

The words of Professor McCaffrey speaking on behalf of Slovakia lead to the question the ICJ had to answer concerning EIA:

51 Slovak Reply, para. 3.56.
52 Hungarian Reply, para. 1.68.
53 Id. para. 1.83.
54 Slovak Oral Pleadings, CR 97/7, 24 March 1997, p. 42.
55 Hungarian Oral Pleadings, CR 97/12, 10 April 1997, pp 34-36.
56 Id. p. 53, CR 97/7, 7 March 1997.
57 Id. pp. 56-57.

doi: 10.5553/HYIEL/266627012022010001002

> "Hungary is thus saying that the Parties' assessment of the Project's environmental impact was not *"adequate"* – in the sense that it did not measure up to today's standards. But surely this can have no legal relevance."[58]

Therefore, the ICJ had to decide if EIA was indeed legally irrelevant, and also, what adequacy would mean if it actually was relevant. The ICJ did not say that conducting an EIA in the above-described meaning was obligatory in 1997 or earlier. In other words, it did not acknowledge its customary law character as of September 1997. It should have done so, at least according to Hungary and Judge Weeramantry, who in his much-quoted separate opinion noted that

> "Environmental Impact Assessment (EIA) has assumed an important role in this case. In a previous opinion [*New Zealand v France*, 1995 – BN] I have had occasion to observe that this principle was gathering strength and international acceptance, and had reached the level of general recognition at which this Court should take notice of it [Footnotes omitted]."[59]

In 1997 the judge went further and stated that in his view environmental law would "read into treaties which may reasonably be considered to have a significant impact upon the environment, a duty of environmental impact assessment" and a duty of monitoring during the operation of the scheme.[60]

If the ICJ's treatment of sustainable development was "cryptic",[61] its approach to the EIA was no less obscure. It invented its own language to circumscribe what ought to be done, without subjecting the states to well-established and more-or-less well defined international environmental law. It established that "the concerns expressed by Hungary for its natural environment in the region affected by the Gabčíkovo-Nagymaros Project related to an 'essential interest' of that State."[62] The ICJ noted that

> "the Project's impact upon, and its implications for, the environment are of necessity a key issue. The numerous scientific reports which have been presented to the Court by the Parties – even if their conclusions are often contradictory – provide abundant evidence that this impact and these implications are considerable."[63]

Further, it stressed that

58 Slovak Oral Pleadings, CR 97/9, 25 March 1997, p. 40.

59 ICJ, *Gabčíkovo-Nagymaros*, Separate Opinion of Judge Weeramantry, p. 111.

60 Id. p. 112.

61 Boyle 1997, p. 18.

62 ICJ, *Gabčíkovo-Nagymaros*, judgment, para. 53.

63 Id. para. 140.

doi: 10.5553/HYIEL/266627012022010001002

> "awareness of the vulnerability of the environment and the recognition that environmental risks have to be assessed on a continuous basis have become much stronger in the years since the Treaty's conclusion."[64]

Did this "stronger recognition" of the fact that "environmental risks have to be assessed on a continuous basis" lead to the conclusion that EIA is mandatory, as it includes the preliminary assessment of future risks and the continuous lookout for later possible risks? No. Neither did the Court acknowledge retroactively that in 1989 the construction should have been submitted to an EIA (if that was not yet a legal requirement in 1977). Nor did it believe that in 1997 the duty to complete an EIA when determining the future form of the project was compulsory and part of "rules of general international law" that determine the relationship between the Parties next to the 1977 Treaty, which is *lex specialis*, but "open to adapt to emerging norms of international law".[65]

The language the ICJ used in the much-quoted para. 140 to determine the course of environmental action is this:

> "In order to evaluate the environmental risks, current standards must be taken into consideration. This is not only allowed by the wording of Articles 15 and 19, but even prescribed, to the extent that these articles impose a continuing – and thus necessarily evolving – obligation on the parties to maintain the quality of the water of the Danube and to protect nature.
>
> The Court is mindful that, in the field of environmental protection, vigilance and prevention are required on account of the often irreversible character of damage to the environment and of the limitations inherent in the very mechanism of reparation of this type of damage. [...]
>
> [...] the Parties together should look afresh at the effects on the environment of the operation of the Gabčíkovo power plant. In particular they must find a satisfactory solution for the volume of water to be released into the old bed of the Danube and into the side-arms on both sides of the river."

Vigilance, prevention, fresh look.[66] We are almost there, even if "vigilance" is not an international environmental law term,[67] and much less is fresh look. The international community was to wait another 13 years until the pieces of the puzzle fell together in *Pulp Mills*,[68] and we learnt that due diligence is the mother of prevention, and vigilance and due diligence is only exercised if an EIA had been conducted. But that is a story for the next subchapter.

64 Id. para. 112.
65 Id. paras. 132, and 112.
66 For a careful analysis, *see* Makane Moïse Mbengue, 'On Sustainable Development: a Conversation with Judge Weeramantry' and Leslie-Anne Duvic-Paoli, 'Vigilance and Prevention. The Contribution of the Gabčíkovo-Nagymaros Judgment', both *in* Forlati *et al.* (eds.) 2020.
67 Duvic-Paoli 2020, p. 202.
68 ICJ, *Pulp Mills on the River Uruguay (Argentina v Uruguay)*, judgment, ICJ Reports 2010, p. 14.

doi: 10.5553/HYIEL/266627012022010001002

3.3. *EIA after the 1997 Judgment*

This section cannot give a comprehensive overview of the development of the concept/principle over the last 25 years.[69] Instead, it is limited to presenting a few milestones to show how the bud broke to become a flower. The Draft Articles on Prevention of Transboundary Harm from Hazardous Activities adopted by the International law Commission in 2001[70] deals "with activities [...] which involve a risk of causing significant transboundary harm through their physical consequences",[71] and prescribes that the authorization of such an activity "shall, in particular, be based on an assessment of the possible transboundary harm caused by that activity, including any environmental impact assessment."[72]

The ILC did not specify who should conduct the assessment, what the content of the risk assessment should be and which type of activities should be subjected to EIA, but in respect of the third question, it has always been clear that the probability, the magnitude and the irreversibility of the potential (transboundary) impact/harm is decisive.[73]

The *Pulp Mills* case between Uruguay and Argentina related to the pulp mill (Orion, later Botnia) established on the bank of the Uruguay river. The river was the subject of a bilateral treaty (Statute) between Uruguay and Argentina which, among others, prescribed that the parties shall co-ordinate, to avoid any change in the ecological balance[74] and to protect and preserve the aquatic environment and, in particular, to prevent its pollution, by prescribing appropriate rules and adopting appropriate measures.[75]

In paras. 185 and 194 the ICJ recalled its words from the *Gabčíkovo-Nagymaros* judgment about the need for prevention and vigilance and to look afresh at the environmental effects of the operation of the project. Then it uttered the words already expected in the *Gabčíkovo-Nagymaros Project Case*:

> "[T]he obligation to protect and preserve, [...] has to be interpreted in accordance with a practice, which in recent years has gained so much acceptance among States that it may now be considered a requirement under general international law to undertake an environmental impact assessment where there is a risk that the proposed industrial activity may have a significant adverse impact in a transboundary context, in particular, on a shared resource. Moreover, due diligence, and the duty of vigilance and prevention which it implies, would not be considered to have been exercised, if a party planning works liable to affect the régime of the river or the quality

69 *See e.g.* Philippe Sands *et al.* 2018, pp. 657-681.

70 *Yearbook of the International Law Commission*, 2001, Vol. II, Part Two.

71 Article 1 of the Draft Articles.

72 Article 7 of the Draft Articles.

73 For the relation of the ILC Draft, the Espoo Convention and the *Pulp Mills* judgment *see* Alan Boyle, 'Developments in the International Law of Environmental Impact Assessments and their Relation to the Espoo Convention', *Review of European Community & International Environmental Law*, Vol. 20, Issue 3, 2011, p. 227.

74 Article 36 of the Statute.

75 Article 41 of the Statute.

> of its waters did not undertake an environmental impact assessment on the potential effects of such works."

So here is the new construct: the customary law requirement of due diligence (also confirmed by the ILC draft articles) incorporates two norms: *(i)* the duty to prevent significant transboundary harm, and *(ii)* the duty to be vigilant. These twin norms require (presume) the conduct of an EIA. Could the same reasoning have been presented in 1997? Yes, it could. But the Court shields itself from criticism by assuming that this was the result of the developments of "recent years."

Two more recent cases of the ICJ involved EIA. *(i)* The first, itself a double (united) case[76] related to building a road next to the San Juan river on the side of Costa Rica in response to certain military activities carried out by Nicaragua on Costa Rican territory. Both parties accused each-other with failing to conduct an appropriate EIA and causing transboundary environmental harm. According to Costa Rica, Nicaragua breached the procedural obligations to carry out an appropriate transboundary environmental impact assessment of its dredging works, and to notify and consult with Costa Rica regarding those works. The situation resembled the *Gabčíkovo-Nagymaros* dispute to the extent that there was an environmental impact study conducted by Nicaragua which, together with other studies, it considered as fulfilling the obligation of carrying out EIA. Costa Rica claimed that these indeed existed, but were not an adequate EIA. The ICJ repeated that EIA is obligatory if there is a risk of significant transboundary harm, but going beyond *Pulp Mills* it dropped the "industrial activity" condition and extended the obligation to any activity threatening with significant transboundary harm.[77] It again refrained from determining what an adequate EIA should contain.[78] This time the ICJ very clearly formulated the obligation to notify and consult.[79]

In the twin case, in which Nicaragua was the applicant, it claimed that Costa Rica breached its obligation under general international law to assess the environmental impact of the construction of the road before commencing it, particularly in view of the road's length and location. It also pointed out that the environmental impact studies produced by Costa Rica after the bulk of the construction work had been completed did not constitute an adequate environmental impact assessment.[80] Costa Rica's defense was that no risk of

76 ICJ, *Certain Activities carried out by Nicaragua in the Border Area (Costa Rica v Nicaragua) and Construction of a Road in Costa Rica along the San Juan River (Nicaragua v Costa Rica),* judgment, ICJ Reports 2015, p. 665.

77 Id. para. 104.

78 Id. Critically on that fact, *see* Katalin Sulyok, *Science and judicial reasoning: The legitimacy of international environmental adjudication,* Cambridge University Press, Cambridge, 2021, p. 79.

79 "If the environmental impact assessment confirms that there is a risk of significant transboundary harm, the State planning to undertake the activity is required, in conformity with its due diligence obligation, to notify and consult in good faith with the potentially affected State, where that is necessary to determine the appropriate measures to prevent or mitigate that risk." ICJ, *Certain Activities,* para. 104.

80 Id. para. 151.

doi: 10.5553/HYIEL/266627012022010001002

transboundary harm emerged with the construction, and in any case, it was acting in an emergency situation due to Nicaragua's military activities.[81] As a defense, it also referred to studies done during and after the construction.[82]

The case could have developed the doctrine if the ICJ had decided whether a state of emergency exempts the state from the duty to conduct an EIA. However, the ICJ denied the fact that an emergency was at hand, therefore, it refrained from answering the hypothetical question. Nevertheless, it went as far as to state that even if the emergency was a good ground to waive the EIA obligation, that ought to be regulated by international law, not simply by domestic law provisions.[83]

(ii) The second case is *Silala*,[84] in which the parties in the beginning invoked the duty to conduct an EIA. However, this was linked to Article 12 of the Convention on the Law of Non-Navigational Uses of International Watercourses[85] which requires that a notification on planned measures which may have a significant adverse effect upon other watercourse states be accompanied by available technical data and information, including the results of any environmental impact assessment.[86] Bolivia agreed with the idea that Article 12 of the Watercourses Convention reflects customary law.[87] By the time the dispute reached the hearings phase in 2022 the nature of the dispute had fundamentally changed, and it seems that EIA will not play a central role in the judgment.

To summarize this section: the record of the ICJ in the field of EIA is not a story of shining success. The ICJ, after long hesitation, arrived at the point of recognizing EIA as an international law obligation rooted in customary law if no concrete treaty obligation was at hand. However, it refrained from identifying customary rules on how the risk requiring an EIA should be established,[88] what the content of the EIA ought to be, especially whether alternatives, including inaction ought to be evaluated, what the role of public participation should be and how the adequacy or inadequacy of an environmental impact statement can be controlled by a tribunal. In essence, the question of how to merge scientific

81 Id. para. 146, and 148.

82 Id. para. 149.

83 Id. paras. 157-158.

84 ICJ, *Dispute over the Status and Use of the Waters of the Silala (Chile v Bolivia)*, filed with the Registry of the ICJ on 6 June 2016. Oral hearings between 1 and 14 April 2022, judgment pending at the time of submitting this manuscript.

85 Convention on the Law of Non-Navigational Uses of International Watercourses, signed at New York on 21 May 1997, UN Doc. A/RES/51/229 (1997). Memorial of the Republic of Chile, pp. 8-9, para. 1.17.

86 Id. p. 107, submission c).

87 Counter-Memorial of the Plurinational State of Bolivia, para. 156.

88 A pathetic illustration is the ICJ's handling of assessing whether there was a risk calling for an EIA in case of the Costa Rican road at the bank of San Juan. ICJ, *Certain Activities*, judgment, para. 155: "The possibility of natural disasters in the area caused by adverse events such as hurricanes, tropical storms and earthquakes, which would increase the risk of sediment erosion, must equally be taken into consideration." One could ask about the likelihood of other Acts of God and how they should be factored in when establishing the threshold level of risk calling for an EIA.

doi: 10.5553/HYIEL/266627012022010001002

risk assessment with legal procedural rules remained unanswered, and the norms enabling a tribunal to choose between competing scientific and engineering claims were not clarified by the ICJ.[89]

4. Precaution

Precaution is not prevention.[90] Prevention relates to an identified future impact/harm, that has to be prevented or at least mitigated if it reaches a certain threshold, such as being significant, serious or appreciable. The logical sequence starts with the age-old idea of responsibility/liability for harm/damage/injury being caused,[91] *sic utere tuo.*[92] The insight that compensation and restitution may be more difficult to achieve than avoiding the harm engendered the principle of prevention. This however, is not the subject of study here.

The focus of precaution is elsewhere than that of *sic utere tuo* and prevention: precaution is a method of dealing with (scientific) uncertainty.[93] The need for precaution does not stem from a future event that is certain. It is a technique of resource allocation, close to the logic of insurance. Invest now a modest resource or abstain from an action in order to be protected against an enormous and/or irreversible loss[94] that you may incur.

4.1. The Status of Precaution before the Judgment

The demand to act in a precautionary way is relatively new, it is linked to the late eighties-early nineties.[95] The 1987 Montreal Protocol on Substances that Deplete the Ozone Layer,[96] may have been the first multilateral treaty referring in its preamble to the "determination" of the parties to "take precautionary measures" to protect an environmental resource. The Declaration on Sustainable Development of the UNECE environment ministers in May 1990 may have been a further push in the right direction, for it declared that policies were to be based

89 Sulyok offers an incisive critique of the ICJ's treatment of EIA. Sulyok 2021, pp. 80-81.

90 Meinhard Schröder, 'Precautionary Approach/Principle', *Max Planck Encyclopedia of Public International Law*, 2014, online version, para. 4; Caroline E. Foster, *Science and the precautionary principle in international courts and tribunals: Expert evidence, burden of proof and finality,* Cambridge University Press, New York, 2011, p. 18.

91 The sentence intentionally combines consequences of international wrongful acts (responsibility) and those which arise as a consequence of accidents, hazardous activities or simply normal operation, which the young ILC used to refer to as "injurious consequences arising out of acts not prohibited by international law" (liability). Let us not replay the dispute whether this differentiation makes sense.

92 The usual references (*Trail Smelter, Corfu Channel, Lac Lanoux, etc.*) are to be found in the Hungarian Memorial, paras. 7.45-7.56.

93 A very competent and recent exposition of the principle is to be found in Nicolas de Sadeleer, *Environmental law principles: From political slogans to legal rules, 2nd edition,* Oxford University Press, Oxford, 2020, pp. 135-364.

94 This is intentionally a loose use of terms.

95 Schröder 2014, paras. 6-7, and 14; Foster 2011, p. 18.

96 16 September 1987, *International Legal Materials,* Vol. 26, 1987, p. 1550, *see* the Preamble and Article 6(2).

doi: 10.5553/HYIEL/266627012022010001002

on the precautionary principle. This meant that where "there are threats of serious or irreversible damage, lack of full scientific certainty should not be used as a reason for postponing measures to prevent environmental degradation".[97] The global assent came in Rio, 1992: the Declaration,[98] the Biodiversity Convention[99] as well as the Climate Change Convention[100] adopted in New York in the same year incorporated what they call the "precautionary principle" even though the formulations slightly differ, as the Declaration and the Climate Convention speak of "cost-effective measures", whereas the Biodiversity Convention does not incorporate that restriction (in its preamble). The formulation in the Rio Declaration, principle 15 reads:

> "In order to protect the environment, the precautionary approach shall be widely applied by States according to their capabilities. Where there are threats of serious or irreversible damage, lack of full scientific certainty shall not be used as a reason for postponing cost-effective measures to prevent environmental degradation."

The issue whether it is a principle, an approach or a set of measures had not been decided before the 1997 judgment, nor since.[101] Since the Amsterdam treaty was signed in 1997 and came into force in 1999 the TFEU refers to it as a principle upon which the Union's environmental policy must be based.[102] However, in 2013 in the final award in the *Indus Waters Kishenganga* arbitration the arbitral tribunal spoke of the precautionary approach (which it did not apply).[103] De Sadeleer comments:

> "US policy-makers prefer to use the term precautionary *approach* (PA) rather than precautionary *principle*; the latter term is preferred by the EU institutions. For our part, as we consider this an irrelevant debate, a semantic squabble between decision-makers, we will use the terms PP and PA interchangeably."[104]

Not only was its nature in question, but also its substance. Jonathan B. Wiener at the beginning of the millennium collected seven issue areas where uncertainty

97 Principle 7. *See Environmental Policy and Law*, Vol. 20, Issue 3, 1990, p. 100.
98 14 June 1992, UN Doc. A/CONF 151/26.
99 Convention on Biological Diversity, Rio de Janeiro, 5 June 1992, *International Legal Materials*, Vol. 31, Issue 4, 1992, p. 818.
100 Framework Convention on Climate Change, *International Legal Materials*, Vol. 31, Issue 4, 1992, pp. 849-873.
101 Makane Mbengue, 'Precaution', *in* Aguila & Vinuales (eds.) 2019, p. 77; Trindade 2015, "2.3.1. Principle or approach?"
102 Article 191(2) TFEU.
103 PCA, *Indus Waters Kishenganga Arbitration* (*Pakistan v India*), Final Award, 20 December 2013, para. 112.
104 De Sadeleer 2020, p. 136.

doi: 10.5553/HYIEL/266627012022010001002

prevailed.[105] It was unclear at that time whether the application of the precautionary principle was part of the risk assessment and risk management, or an alternative to it. Was it only applicable to the environment (as the Rio Declaration suggested) or more broadly to health, food and consumer safety? What degree of perceived risk triggered the principle/approach? What follows from precaution, a total stop of action or a need to reduce uncertainty related to the action? Should the cost of staying on the precautionary side matter (as the Rio Declaration suggests) or should they not (as in the case of introducing pharmaceuticals)? Does the principle require zero risk? Does it indeed lead to a shift of the burden of proof?

Interestingly many of these questions would not have played a significant role in applying the principle in the *Gabčíkovo-Nagymaros Project Case.* This is because the threat was clearly environmental, the risk enormous, the act suggested was not abandoning the project but reducing uncertainty, the costs were to be borne by both parties and would have been commensurate to the expected loss and the burden of proof was to be shared.

In order to understand what the task of the ICJ would have been, it is worth looking at the foundation of precaution. It entails a risk assessment phase and a risk management phase. The first is (largely) scientific, the second (largely) political.[106] The risk assessment can be divided into four segments: the identification of the hazard feared, its characterization, description of the expected exposure to the hazard and the characterization of the risk which is the hazard exerting its impact. Here is an example:[107] the Nagymaros dam may threaten the drinking water supply of Budapest – *identification of the hazard.* It may do so due to the changed morphological circumstances below the dam as the filtering function of the riverbed will deteriorate and infiltration conditions will change – *characterization of the hazard.* A large proportion of the population of Budapest, a city of 2 million would be exposed to drinking water shortages or a prohibitively expensive treatment of the bank-filtered water would be required – *exposure.* Quantifying this change in water yield and quality and the costs of remedial measures – *characterization of the risk.*

A lot of scientific uncertainties were entailed in the prognoses of the impact of the dam, since no mathematical model could precisely predict the behavior of the riverbed and its filtering capacity, yet there was enough certainty to fear large-scale negative impacts.

That is when the second phase starts: risk management. Faced with the risk that is established with inherent uncertainty, how to act? Take the risk hoping

105 Jonathan B. Wiener, 'Precaution', *in* Daniel Bodansky *et al.*, *The Oxford Handbook of International Environmental Law,* Oxford University Press, Oxford, 2007, pp. 602-603. The list I give does not exactly coincide with his.

106 De Sadeleer 2020, p. 213; and European Commission, *Communication from the Commission on the precautionary principle,* COM (2000) 1, 2 February 2000, pp. 13-14; and Annex III.

107 Another example probably closer to any reader on this Globe could have been COVID-19 vaccines and their experienced side effects and feared, unidentified long-term effects. Governments differed greatly in restricting some of them to certain groups of the population or banning them altogether from the country.

Hungarian Yearbook of International Law and European Law 2022 (10) 1
doi: 10.5553/HYIEL/266627012022010001002

that a technical fix will be invented if the hazard materializes or suspend action (construction) until the risk assessment leads to more detailed scientific and technical results that eliminate uncertainties to such a level, that either the unacceptable magnitude is revealed, or, on the contrary, the manageable size of the risk is established. The Commission's Communication highlights the political element in the risk management phase:

> "Decision-makers need to be aware of the degree of uncertainty attached to the results of the evaluation of the available scientific information. Judging what is an 'acceptable' level of risk for society is an eminently *political* responsibility. Decision-makers faced with an unacceptable risk, scientific uncertainty and public concerns have a duty to find answers. Therefore, all these factors have to be taken into consideration. [Emphasis in the original]"[108]

So what did representatives of decision-makers plead in the case?

4.2. *Precaution in the Gabčíkovo-Nagymaros Project Case – Position of the Parties and the ICJ*

Hungary, less than two years after its incorporation into the Rio Declaration pleaded the precautionary principle,[109] noting that "[a]lmost no new international instrument, whether regional or universal, drafted since 1989, ignores the precautionary principle" and stressed the importance of its inclusion into Article 2 of the Helsinki Convention on the Protection and Use of Transboundary Watercourses and International Lakes of 17 March 1992, drafted in the framework of the UN Economic Commission for Europe.[110] The argument openly appeared in the context of the claim that Czechoslovakia "failed to investigate the environmental problems caused by the implementation of the Barrage System".[111] In the context of the suspension of works at Nagymaros, the need to stop construction that threatens an essential interest with irreversible harm under circumstances of scientific uncertainty was extensively discussed, but the focus was kept on the legal foundation of necessity as a term of the law of responsibility.[112]

Slovakia first addressed the principle in the Counter-Memorial.[113] It developed a host of statements against the application of the precautionary principle in the

108 European Commission, *Communication from the Commission on the precautionary principle*, COM (2000) 1, 2 February 2000, para. 5 at p. 3.

109 Hungarian Memorial, p. 6.68. "One of the implications of the precautionary principle is that the causal link may be assumed in certain situations even in the absence of scientific certainty. Combined with the general obligation not to cause damage to another country's environment, this means that the State whose activities are likely to damage the environment of another State must show that the proposed action will not have such effects. If this cannot be done, the proposed activity must be modified or even abandoned."

110 Id. para. 6.66.

111 Id. para. 6.69.

112 Id. paras. 9.15-7; 9.19; 9.21; 9.29; and 10.76.

113 Slovak Counter-Memorial, paras. 9.23.4; and 9.80-9.94.

case, submitting that according to leading academics it was not a rule of general international law, that it was not an "absolute" principle, that in essence, it was due diligence which Slovakia had performed and that no serious or irreversible threatening damage was shown. The treatment of the burden of proof gave an opportunity to show the stylistic extravaganza of the Counter-Memorial's author(s):

> "Hungary seems to believe that its mere incantation of a 'likelihood of environmental harm' will bring such a likelihood into being or will at least force Slovakia to show that such a likelihood does not exist. Such a doctrine not only makes a mockery of the precautionary principle; it would have the dangerous consequence of thwarting, on the basis of absolutely no evidence, the legitimate efforts of States to develop."

One must wonder whether the incantation of "absolutely no evidence" can make the pile of evidence disappear, as if it had never existed. All in all, the apparent animosity towards the principle did not lead to the denial of its existence by Slovakia, just to the negation of its applicability to the case.

The *Hungarian Counter-Memorial* notes that the freshly concluded Sofia Convention on co-operation for the protection of the Danube river[114] in its Article 2(4) "proclaims that the precautionary principle constitutes a basis for all measures aiming at the protection of the Danube river and of the waters within its catchment area."[115] The very last section of the Hungarian Counter-Memorial dealing with remedies made it strikingly clear what Hungary was seeking:

> "The function of a court is to do justice between parties, not to require future generations to run unacceptable risks. [...] The primary Slovak contention in this case amounts to a request to the Court to return to this *ancien régime* in violation of the law, both as it was and as it has further evolved. Faced with such a demand, the Court, the principal judicial organ of the United Nations, is bound itself to apply a precautionary approach."[116]

In the Reply Slovakia once again asserted that both the Original Project and Variant 'C' were "consistent with the precautionary approach."[117] Its overall attitude towards general principles of environmental law, including the precautionary principle was that they were not applicable at all, but even if they were, only for the interpretation of the 1977 Treaty, and in fact, Czechoslovakia and Slovakia had always acted in accordance with these principles.[118]

114 Hungarian Counter-Memorial, Annexes, Vol. 3, Annex 71. or at www.icpdr.org/main/icpdr/danube-river-protection-convention.

115 Id. para. 4.30.

116 Id. paras. 7.25, and 7.38.

117 Slovak Reply, para. 3.54.

118 All these ideas are compressed into the Slovak Reply, para. 3.56.

doi: 10.5553/HYIEL/266627012022010001002

Hungary's Reply took a cautious stand on the legal status of the principle referring to the "strong evidence of [its] emerging acceptance".[119] In connection with the Original Project it stressed that it had "invoked the precautionary principle to seek a scientific re-examination of the likely consequences of the Original Project."[120] It also identified the increasing evidence showing a real risk of significant irreversible harm as a factor leading to the invocation of necessity.[121]

At the oral hearings Professor McCaffrey finally engaged with the principle in a serious way.[122] On the one hand, he repeated that facts – according to Slovakia – did not support the existence of the risk Hungary stated, on the other hand he claimed that "the conduct of the Parties in relation to the Project was fully compatible with the precautionary approach".[123] He denied that a genuine and substantial scientific debate existed, reaching the level of uncertainty that would have justified the application of the precautionary approach, but *in abstracto* conceded that

> "if there is a credible threat that an activity will cause serious or irreversible damage to the environment, cost-effective measures should be taken to prevent such damage – even if there is not *full* scientific certainty that the damage will occur."[124]

Hungary noted the agreement on the formulation in the Rio Declaration and stressed that in 1989 the

> "most cost-effective measures to be taken were further studies on the impacts of the project, especially Nagymaros and peak-power and the avoidance of irreversible measures such as the damming at Dunakiliti. Build Now, Investigate Later was simply incompatible with the precautionary approach."[125]

Thus, by the time the judgment was due, the parties converged around the core meaning of the principle, accepted that it should apply, but differed as to its relationship with the 1977 Treaty. Hungary was willing to give priority to it as a later norm of the same hierarchical standing (not as *jus cogens*), Slovakia insisting that it was just a tool of interpreting the Treaty, which in turn, was *lex specialis*.

But the essential debate related to the application of the principle. *(i)* The first question was whether a hazard had really been identified. *(ii)* The second, if that was indeed the case, did the evidence at hand show that the level of

119 Occasionally using the milder "approach" terminology.
120 Hungarian Reply, para. 1.58.
121 Id. para. 3.17.
122 Slovak Oral Pleadings, CR 9, at pp 33-37.
123 Id. p. 34.
124 Id. p. 35.
125 Hungarian Oral Pleadings, CR 12, at p. 61.

doi: 10.5553/HYIEL/266627012022010001002

uncertainty concerning the future risk was so high as to justify pausing construction and pursuing a further assessment of that risk.

The answer would have required the ICJ to take a stance on the legal status of precaution and to weigh the scientific evidence in respect of the future risk and the level of uncertainty. The ICJ did none, it evaded the answers.[126] As James Crawford observed:

> "Perhaps unusually, the Parties had been in agreement as to the content of the precautionary principle as a question of general international law. It is all the more surprising that the Court chose to sidestep the application of the principle."[127]

It is remarkable, how the ICJ avoided the principle in order to interpret the state of necessity conditions. In para. 54 of the judgment we read:

> "The word 'peril' certainly evokes the idea of 'risk'; that is precisely what distinguishes 'peril' from material damage. But a state of necessity could not exist without a 'peril' duly established at the relevant point in time; the mere apprehension of a possible 'peril' could not suffice in that respect. It could moreover hardly be otherwise, when the 'peril' constituting the state of necessity has at the same time to be "grave" and "imminent". "Imminence" is synonymous with "immediacy" or "proximity" and goes far beyond the concept of "possibility" [...] That does not exclude, in the view of the Court, that a 'peril' appearing in the long term might be held to be "imminent" as soon as it is established, at the relevant point in time, that the realization of that peril, however far off it might be, is not thereby any less certain and inevitable."[128]

This long quote is crucial: material damage is not required – merely a peril. That peril may be far out in time and still be imminent. What is decisive is that this peril is certain and inevitable. But if what is certain in the future is not material damage, it can only be a risk of damage – subject to the principle of precaution.[129] The ICJ appears to limit itself to discussing certain future "peril" and ignores future peril that is uncertain, but possible. The ICJ ignores precaution when constructing necessity. We might read this as a recognition of the principle of prevention (foreseeable damage) serving to justify ecological necessity, but certainly not that of precaution. In James Crawford's view, "Indeed the Court's

126 De Sadeleer 2020, p. 465; Szabó 2021, p. 493.

127 James Crawford, 'In dubio pro natura: The Dissent of Judge Herczegh', *in* Kovács (ed.) 2011, p. 262.

128 ICJ, *Gabčíkovo-Nagymaros*, judgment, para. 54. For an excellent and much clearer explanation of the terms and the uncertainty/ignorance related to them, *see* de Sadeleer 2020, p. 272.

129 Leslie-Anne Duvic-Pavoli offers the same interpretation of paras. 55-56. *See* Duvic-Paoli 2020, p. 196.

Hungarian Yearbook of International Law and European Law 2022 (10) 1
doi: 10.5553/HYIEL/266627012022010001002

own formulation of the doctrine of necessity touches upon aspects of the precautionary principle without either approving or applying it."[130]

However, the Judgment takes interesting turns. The ICJ "notes" that the "dangers ascribed to the upstream reservoir" above Nagymaros were "mostly of a long term nature" and remained uncertain.[131] But that uncertainty was caused by the indecision of whether Gabčíkovo would operate in a peak mode or not[132] – meaning that if the Original Project operated in a peak mode, the danger would be certain.

> "It follows that, even if it could have been established – which, in the Court's appreciation of the evidence before it, was not the case – that the reservoir would ultimately have constituted a 'grave peril' for the environment in the area, one would be bound to conclude that the peril was not 'imminent.'"[133]

But if the long-term certain peril qualifies as imminent, then here the danger/ peril was imminent. Except that the ICJ appreciated the evidence differently. How that appreciation was conducted by the bench remains a secret.[134] This is all the more intriguing, since the ICJ confesses in a much commented statement that:

> "Both Parties have placed on record an impressive amount of scientific material aimed at reinforcing their respective arguments. The Court has given most careful attention to this material, in which the Parties have developed their opposing views as to the ecological consequences of the Project. It concludes, however, that, as will be shown below, it is not necessary in order to respond to the questions put to it in the Special Agreement for it to determine which of those points of view is scientifically better founded."[135]

One wonders, how the ICJ could declare – after careful appreciation of the evidence – that the reservoir above Nagymaros was not a grave peril, if according to the judges it was not necessary to determine which of the views concerning the dangers the reservoir would cause was better founded scientifically.

In the end the ICJ came close to recognizing the precautionary principle in the already quoted para. 140 in which it spoke of itself being "mindful that, in the field of environmental protection, vigilance and prevention are required on

130 Crawford 2011, p. 261.
131 ICJ, *Gabčíkovo-Nagymaros*, judgment, para. 55.
132 Id.
133 Id.
134 Id. para. 54. A scathing critique of the ICJ dealing with scientific issues, including the employment of shadow experts appears in Sulyok 2021, pp. 82-84, and 87-88.
135 "[...] solid and legitimate conclusions can hardly be drawn regarding matters of ecological risks without considering the weight of relevant scientific reports submitted by the parties." Sulyok 2021, p. 82.

doi: 10.5553/HYIEL/266627012022010001002

account of the often irreversible character of damage to the environment [...]". That is read as an allusion to the precautionary principle.[136]

4.3. Precaution after the 1997 Judgment

The ICJ has never referred to the principle/approach as part of its own findings. In its arguments, New Zealand put great emphasis on the principle in an effort to reopen the dispute with France over nuclear testing, but the ICJ dismissed the request in 1995.[137] There was a passing remark in *Pulp Mills* with the important element that the approach does not lead to the reversal of the burden of proof.[138] The principle fared better in other tribunals, but the breakthrough was to come gradually and its acceptance may not be unconditional outside the EU. It is true that in 1998 the WTO did not give way to a precaution-based argument which the Commission called for in the dispute over beef hormones between the EU on the one side, and the US and Canada on the other, but it refrained from assessing whether it was a general principle of customary law.[139] The ITLOS went further both in the *Southern Bluefin Tuna* case between Australia and New Zealand, on the one hand, and Japan on the other (1999)[140] as well as in the *MOX Plant* case between Ireland and the UK (2000).[141] It referred to the content of the principle approvingly, without formally endorsing it.[142] The ITLOS became fully supportive of the principle with its Seabed Disputes Chamber in 2011, when it adopted its advisory opinion on "Responsibilities and obligations of States with respect to activities in the Area".[143] The Tribunal responded to questions of the Council of the International Seabed Authority that related to legal obligations[144] of States

136 Brian McGarry, 'Norms, Standards, and the Elusive Nomenclature of the Gabčíkovo-Nagymaros Judgment', *in* Forlati *et al.* (eds.) 2020, p. 220.

137 ICJ, *Request for an Examination of the Situation in Accordance with Paragraph 63 of the Court's Judgment of 20 December 1974 in the Nuclear Tests (New Zealand v France) Case,* Order of 22 September, ICJ Reports 1995, p. 288, paras. 5, and 34-35. More details in Sands *et al.* 2018, pp. 234-235.

138 ICJ, *Pulp Mills on the River Uruguay (Argentina v Uruguay),* judgment, ICJ Reports 2010, para. 164.

139 *European Communities – Measures concerning Meat and Meat Products (Hormones),* Report of the Appellate Body, WT/DS/26/AB/R and WT/DS/48/AB/R, 16 January 1998. "Whether it has been accepted by Member [of the WTO] as a principle of *general* or *customary* international law is less clear" 123. But the Appellate Body found it "unnecessary and probably imprudent" to take a position on that "important but abstract question". Id.

140 ITLOS, *Southern Bluefin Tuna (New Zealand v Japan; Australia v Japan),* Provisional Measures, Order of 27 August 1999, ITLOS Reports 1999, p. 280, para. 77: "in the view of the Tribunal, the parties should in the circumstances act with prudence and caution to ensure that effective conservation measures are taken to prevent serious harm to the stock of southern bluefin tuna."

141 ITLOS, *MOX Plant (Ireland v United Kingdom),* Provisional Measures, ITLOS No. 10, 3 December 2000. About the importance of the case, *see e.g.* Marcel Szabó, 'The MOX Plant case: the way towards Euro-chauvinism?', *in* Gyula Bándi (ed.), *The impact of ECJ jurisprudence on environmental law,* Szent István Társulat, Budapest, 2009, pp. 143-166.

142 Sands *et al.* 2018, pp. 236-237.

143 ITLOS, *Responsibilities and obligations of States with respect to activities in the Area,* Advisory Opinion, 1 February 2011, ITLOS Reports 2011, p. 10.

144 By comparing the different language versions of UNCLOS the Seabed Chamber established that the term "responsibility" in the relevant articles means "obligations" (and not responsibility for a wrongful act). Id. paras. 64-69, and 71.

doi: 10.5553/HYIEL/266627012022010001002

Parties to the Law of the Sea Convention with respect to the sponsorship of mining activities in the deep seabed, which is the common heritage of mankind (the Area), including the measures to be taken in the exercise of that responsibility.[145] Under the heading "direct obligations of sponsoring states", the Tribunal states that there is an obligation to apply the precautionary principle that is seen as a factor of due diligence. Due diligence is the duty of the Sponsoring State to ensure within its legal system "that a contractor so sponsored shall carry out activities in the Area in conformity with the terms of its contract and its obligations under this Convention".[146] The Nodules Regulations and the Sulphides Regulations transform the principle of precaution as enshrined in the Rio Declaration into binding obligation.[147] But the scope of the precautionary approach extends beyond the mining regulations.

> "[T]he precautionary approach is also an integral part of the general obligation of due diligence of sponsoring States, which is applicable even outside the scope of the Regulations. The due diligence obligation of the sponsoring States requires them to take all appropriate measures to prevent damage that might result from the activities of contractors that they sponsor. This obligation applies in situations where scientific evidence concerning the scope and potential negative impact of the activity in question is insufficient but where there are plausible indications of potential risks. A sponsoring State would not meet its obligation of due diligence if it disregarded those risks. Such disregard would amount to a failure to comply with the precautionary approach."

The ECtHR has adopted decisions which refer to precaution in other contexts, such as giving birth at home,[148] but its practice concerning precaution and the environment is minimal. Mostly the 2009 *Tatar versus Romania* case[149] is mentioned in which the ECtHR confirmed the applicability of the principle in an industrial hazard context.[150] However, it has to be noted that by the time of the decision Romania was a member of the EU and the court intensively relied on EU related documents before venturing into the more general remark.

145 Id. para. 1.
146 UNCLOS, Annex III, Article 4(4).
147 ITLOS, *Responsibilities and obligations of States with respect to activities in the Area, Advisory Opinion*, para. 127.
148 ECtHR, *Dubská and Krejzová v the Czech Republic (GC)*, Nos. 28859/11 and 28473/12, 15 November 2016. The risk assessment element was important, *see* paras. 135, and 182.
149 ECtHR, *Tatar v Romania*, No. 67021/01, 27 January 2009.
150 Id. para. 120 (in French).

doi: 10.5553/HYIEL/266627012022010001002

Limits must be set to this precursory review.[151] In his *opus magnum*, De Sadeleer lists and analyses the legal fields of water resources, fisheries, nature protection, hazardous substances, nuclear energy, electromagnetic fields and climate change in respect of which the precautionary principle has been implemented.[152] He reports on international, EU and national law and the jurisprudence within each field[153] and concludes that formulations of the principle vary among jurisdictions and among regulatory settings, reflecting different types of risk and levels of uncertainty.[154] A "risk of severe damage – and not irreversible or catastrophic – to health or the environment appears sufficient to trigger precaution."[155] All in all, he takes a stand in favor of its customary law status, finding that

> "[a]lthough some international courts have not always been favorable to the direct and autonomous application of the PP, we take the view that there has been repeated and widespread state practice accompanied by an *opinio juris* in order to crystallize precaution into a customary norm, at least from a European perspective." [Footnote omitted][156]

Similarly, Philippe Sands and his co-authors consider it a principle of customary international law and within the EU, a rule of customary law.[157] Foster back in 2011 was more cautious, but she still recognized the existence of the principle. According to her, the principle had

> "some legal effect in the sense that it has attracted an international consensus, increasingly informs states' approaches to environmental issues, and may be relied upon in the reasoning of international tribunals on substantive points."[158]

To summarize the above: evidence points to a general consensus on the existence of the principle addressing uncertainty when a hazard has been identified that entails a large scale or serious or irreversible risk, the occurrence of which may not (or has not yet) been proven with scientific certainty. That is a long way from the ICJ's perception that required a certain future damage as a precondition for suspending action that threatened an essential interest of a nation.

151 For a good overview of recent CJEU jurisprudence with further references, *see* Sara De Vido,'Science, precautionary principle and the law in two recent judgments of the Court of Justice of the European Union on glyphosate and hunting management', *Saggi – DPCE [Diritto Pubblico Comparato ed Europeo] online*, 2020/2, or János Ede Szilágyi. 'The Precautionary Principle's 'Strong Concept' in the Case Law of the Constitutional Court of Hungary', *Lex et Scientia International*, Vol. 26, Issue 2, 2019, pp. 88-112.

152 De Sadeleer 2020, p. 154.

153 Id. pp. 155-267.

154 Id. pp. 267-268.

155 Id. p. 268.

156 Id. p. 469.

157 Sands *et al.* 2018, p. 239.

158 Foster 2011, p. 244.

doi: 10.5553/HYIEL/266627012022010001002

5. Intergenerational Equity – The Interests/Rights of Future Generations

This section will not follow the structure of the previous two, as intergenerational equity, that is, paying due regard to the interests/rights to future generations may have more blurred contours than EIA and precaution, even though the idea is increasingly gaining ground in courtrooms and moves beyond hortatory statements which abound.

The editor of this volume, Hungarian Constitutional Court justice Marcel Szabó was the drafter of the 2018 decision of the Hungarian Constitutional Court in a subsurface water usage case, in which the Constitutional Court clearly connected the precautionary principle with future generations.

> "The responsibility deriving from the Fundamental Law for future generations[159] requires the legislator to assess and calculate the expected impact of its actions on the basis of scientific knowledge, in accordance with the precautionary principle and the principle of prevention."[160]

The Constitutional Court decision rules that the present generation is under an obligation to preserve choices for the future generation, the quality of the environment and the possibility to access these resources.[161]

With this reference to the three principles, we are at the foundation of the international legal theory of intergenerational equity, as first presented in 1989 by the pathbreaking monograph of Professor Edith Brown Weiss. There, she identified the conservation of options, of quality and of access as the three pillars of the theory of intergenerational fairness.[162]

Starting the section with a judgment of the Hungarian Constitutional Court may be a tribute to the fact that this text appears in the Hungarian Yearbook of International Law and European Law, but it also moves the substance of this paper forward as it stresses the connection between the precautionary principle and future generations.

The core of the theory, frequently referred to as the planetary trust, may be summarized as the right of each generation to "receive the planet in no worse condition than did the previous generation, to inherit comparable diversity in the natural and cultural resource bases, and to have equitable access to the use and

159 The relevant provision of the Fundamental Law is Article P(1): "Natural resources, in particular arable land, forests and the reserves of water; biodiversity, in particular native plant and animal species; and cultural artefacts, shall form the common heritage of the nation, it shall be the obligation of the State and everyone to protect and maintain them, and to preserve them for future generations."

160 Constitutional Court of Hungary, Decision No. 13/2018. (IX. 4.) AB, Reasoning [13]. For a detailed analysis *see* Szilágyi 2019, pp. 106-109; Marcel Szabó, 'The Precautionary Principle in the Fundamental Law of Hungary: Judicial Activism or an Inherent Fundamental Principle? An Evaluation of Constitutional Court Decision No. 13/2018. (IX. 4.) AB on the Protection on Groundwater', *Hungarian Yearbook of International Law and European Law*, Vol. 7, 2020, pp. 67-83.

161 Constitutional Court of Hungary, Decision No. 13/2018. (IX. 4.) AB, Reasoning [13].

162 Edith Brown Weiss, *In fairness to future generations: International law, common patrimony, and intergenerational equity*, United Nations University; Dobbs Ferry, Tokyo, Japan, 1989, pp. 40-45.

doi: 10.5553/HYIEL/266627012022010001002

benefits of the legacy."[163] Writing about the connection between precaution and intergenerational equity in 1998, Cameron, Wade-Gery and Abouchar[164] warn that we may not identify the utility of a present resource for future generations, therefore, precaution should not only extend to specific resource extraction industries. Talking about ozone and climate change they stress that under the threat of the disruption of life supporting endowments precaution should guide. Precaution is also needed, as the "real value of [a] resource or ecosystem to future generations may never be known and may be less or more than the cost to present generations of its preservation", therefore the precautionary principle should guide decisions.[165]

There are two roots of future generations appearing on the horizon of international law as entities whose rights/interests must be taken into account.[166] *(i)* The first root is the common heritage of mankind,[167] and *(ii)* the second is the principle of sustainable development and the implied environmental concerns.[168] The report of the UN Secretary General published in 2013[169] notes the philosophical and moral foundations and states that "[c]oncern for the needs of future generations therefore falls into the category of intergenerational equity or intergenerational justice, which is essentially the allocation of burdens and benefits across generations". It confronts the identity problem (Parfitt paradox),[170] namely that our deeds may change the person of the future beneficiaries, by recalling the suggestion of seeing them as holders of group rights or assuming the intergenerational identity of the community (or mankind) as such.[171] The detailed review in the report of references to future generations in international documents and national legislation and institutions, such as ombudspersons for future generations nevertheless ends with the UN Secretary General declaring that: "[a]t the international level, there exists no

163 Edith Brown Weiss, 'Our Rights and Obligations to Future Generations for the Environment', *American Journal of International Law*, Vol. 84, Issue 1, 1990, p. 202.

164 James Cameron *et al.*, 'Precautionary Principle and Future Generations', *in* Emanuel Agius & Salvino Busuttil (eds.), *Future generations and international law: Proceedings of the International Experts' Meeting held by the Future Generations Programme at the Foundation for International Studies, University of Malta*, Earthscan, London 1998, pp. 110-113.

165 Id. p. 112.

166 This is not the place to decide if future generations have (legal) rights and the present generations corresponding obligations. For a succinct exposition, *see* Brown Weiss 2019, pp. 56-57.

167 Boldizsár Nagy, 'Common Heritage of Mankind: The Status of Future Generations', *in Proceedings of the Thirty-First Colloquium on the Law of Outer Space*, International Institute of Space Law, Washington D.C., 1988, pp. 319-325.

168 World Commission on Environment and Development, *Our Common Future,* (1987) [Brundtland report], at https://sustainabledevelopment.un.org/content/documents/5987our-common-future.pdf.

169 *Intergenerational solidarity and the needs of future generations* UN Secretary General, UN Doc. A/68/322, 2013.

170 Derek Parfit, *Reasons and Persons*, Oxford University Press, Oxford, 1984.

171 UN Secretary General, UN Doc. A/68/322, 2013, paras. 22-23.

doi: 10.5553/HYIEL/266627012022010001002

legally binding instrument that specifically commits States to the protection of future generations."[172]

As regards the role of future generations in the pleadings, no separate legal argument was based on their interests or rights. Hungary quoted the letter of Prime Minister Németh from October 1989, in which he reminds his counterpart, Adamec on the duty to find a balance between construction and the demands of environmental protection and expresses his conviction that both governments were "guided by responsibility to future generations."[173] In the context of the termination of the 1977 Treaty, Hungary anticipated the argument of the ITLOS, to come almost a decade later (mixed with the idea of prevention) when it pleaded that:

> "Considering the present state of international law for the protection of the environment, a 'well-governed state' has a duty of diligence to avoid immediate and major risks to the health and livelihood of its present and future generations."[174]

As mentioned before, Slovakia put strong emphasis on sustainable development in its Counter-Memorial, so future generations got a few unspecific mentions. Beyond that Slovakia, in response to the above quote, assured readers that it was a well-governed state too, which protects present and future generations.[175] It also noted that "Slovakia shares with Hungary the belief that the emerging human right to the environment requires each generation to preserve and pass on its environmental patrimony to the next generation."[176] Slovakia offered no detail what this would mean in terms of quality, options, minimal standards. The Hungarian reply nevertheless noted this acceptance[177] and stressed that the actual impact "on that patrimony" was crucial and one could not wait until the "damage was serious or irreversible".[178] The Slovak Reply did not touch upon the position of future generations, the term "generation" was only combined with "electricity" and "power". During the oral hearing only Hungary mentioned the future generations, of which let me recall the prophetic words of Pierre-Marie Dupuy, who, before the closing of Hungary's first round of arguments recalled the "particular physiognomy" of the case and described it as being

> "both archaic and prophetic and is thus articulated, or more exactly torn between what is to come and what has been; it confronts us with an anachronistic dam project while at the same time obliging us to consider the rights of future generations."[179]

172 Id. para. 36.
173 Hungarian Memorial, para. 3.93.
174 Id. para. 10.39.
175 Slovak Counter-Memorial, para. 10.115.
176 Id. para. 10.116.
177 Hungarian Reply, para. 3.109.
178 Id.
179 Hungarian Oral Pleadings, CR 97/6, p. 62.

doi: 10.5553/HYIEL/266627012022010001002

Looking at the present position of future generations in international law, it may be noted that many of the old dilemmas are still with us.[180] In the Oxford Commentary to the Rio Declaration, published in 2015, Claire Molinari reviews the legal nature of Principle 3 ("The right to development must be fulfilled so as to equitably meet developmental and environmental needs of present and future generations"). Following an evaluation scholarly views she comes to the conclusion that it is still a guiding principle, "one that guides interpretation and provides context for decisions in international environmental law".[181] At the same time, she reminds us that both Judges Weeramantry and Cançado Trindade in their different dissenting opinions came closer to accepting intergenerational equity as a legal principle, albeit not expressly saying so.[182]

The field in which manifest change has occurred is that of litigation in the interest of future generations, particularly in the context of the climate crisis. By 2020, more than a thousand cases have been brought in the US, and several hundred have been brought in the rest of the world.[183] Due to space constraints they cannot be reviewed or analyzed here, therefore, only two more recent and famous cases will be mentioned.[184]

The first was decided by the Colombian Supreme Court in 2018.[185] In that case a group of young people complained about the fast deforestation of the Amazon and claimed that their rights to life, health, water, and food, was endangered as they would suffer harm from climate change when getting old. They requested the court to consider the principle of intergenerational equity both in relation to their own generation and generations to come.

> "In its decision, the Supreme Court of Colombia applied the principle of intergenerational equity to 'future generations, including the children who brought this action,' and it ordered the government to formulate an

180 Brown Weiss 2019, pp. 56-58.

181 Claire Molinari, 'Principle 3 From a Right to Development to Intergenerational Equity', *in* Vinuales (ed.) 2015, "2. Precaution and the obligation to carry out an environmental impact assessment". Similarly in 2020: Lydia Slobodian, 'Defending the Future: Intergenerational Equity in Climate Litigation', *Georgetown Environmental Law Review*, Vol. 32, Issue 3, 2020, p. 573.

182 Id.

183 Id. with further references.

184 A tribute has to be paid to *Oposa et al. v Fulgencio Factoran, Jr et al.*, [1993] GR, No 101083, in which the Philippines Supreme Court recognized that several minors, acting on behalf of themselves and future generations, had standing to challenge a timber licensing agreement the government had concluded with a private company; remarkably, the Court stated: "[E]very generation has a responsibility to the next to preserve the rhythm and harmony [of nature] for the full enjoyment of a balanced and healthful ecology. Put a little differently, the minors' assertion of their right to a sound environment constitutes, at the same time, the performance of their obligation to ensure the protection of that right for the generations to come." Quoted from: Helmut Philipp Aust & Georg Nolte (eds.), *The Interpretation of International Law by Domestic Courts. Uniformity, Diversity, Convergence*, Oxford University Press, Oxford, 2016, p. 122.

185 STC 4360-2018, at www.cortesuprema.gov.co/corte/wp-content/uploads/2018/04/STC4360-2018-2018-00319-011.pdf.

doi: 10.5553/HYIEL/266627012022010001002

> intergenerational pact for the life of the Colombian Amazon with active participation of the youth plaintiffs."[186]

The judgments' spirit is holistic, it not only assumes that the succeeding generations owe the duty of solidarity to each other, but postulates a unity of the humans and other species as well.[187]

In the European context a landmark decision is that of the German Constitutional Court.[188] The complainants asserted that the German Climate Change Act of 2019, that only had reduction targets up to 2030 and not beyond, unduly limited freedoms in the future after 2030 as it would require measures to achieve carbon neutrality that are much more drastic, than the ones foreseen until 2030. This means that the freedoms of those living beyond 2030 (including the applicants) would be unconstitutionally curtailed due to the lack of protection by the state, who failed to adopt a schedule that would more fairly distribute the burdens before and after 2030. The Constitutional Court recognized that

> "The state's duty of protection arising from Art. 2(2) first sentence GG [Constitution of Germany] also encompasses the duty to protect life and health against the risks posed by climate change, including climate-related extreme weather events such as heat waves, forest fires, hurricanes, heavy rainfall, floods, avalanches and landslides. It can furthermore give rise to an objective duty to protect future generations."[189]

In my view, what is decisive is that the German Constitutional Court extended protection to subsequent generations:

> "It follows from the principle of proportionality that one generation must not be allowed to consume large portions of the CO2 budget while bearing a relatively minor share of the reduction effort, if this would involve leaving subsequent generations with a drastic reduction burden and expose their lives to serious losses of freedom [...]."[190]

Summing up this section, the interests/needs/rights of future generations, the precise requirements of intergenerational equity may not be fixed in binding international treaties or may not have become the basis of a customary law rule,

186 Slobodian 2020, p. 578.

187 Niehaus, Manuela, 'Protecting Whose Children?: The Rights of Future Generations in the Courts of Germany and Colombia', *Verfassungsblog*, 23 March 2022, at https://verfassungsblog.de/protecting-whose-children/.

188 Order of the First Senate of the Court *(Beschluss des Ersten Senats)*, 24 March 2021, 1 BvR 2656/18, paras. 1-270, published on 29 April 2021. The full English version is available at www.bundesverfassungsgericht.de/SharedDocs/Entscheidungen/EN/2021/03/rs20210324_1bvr265618en.html.

189 *Bundesfervassungsgericht*, 'Constitutional complaints against the Federal Climate Change Act partially successful', Press Release No. 31/2021 of 29 April 2021.

190 Order of the First Senate, para. 192.

doi: 10.5553/HYIEL/266627012022010001002

but through national constitutions, institutions and jurisprudence related to climate, biodiversity, nuclear power and hazardous activities, intergenerational equity creates a frame that will in an increasing fashion guide the interpretation and application of any norm with the potential of long term impact. The formation of a general principle of law recognized by the major legal systems of the world may actually be taking place right before our eyes, successfully overcoming theoretical hurdles of identifying choices of future generations or questions of standing and representation.

6. Weaving the Threads Together (Conclusion)

I promised a dialogue with the judgment which at this point requires weaving the threads together. It is time to offer a larger frame, in which an alternative to the past in the present appears as the blossoming of the buds mentioned above.

The aim of writing this chapter was to show that if the case were to go to a court today, the outcome could be different. What was incipient in 1997 has become full blown. The potential of the case to end in a judgment that contributes to long term thinking, genuine sustainability and precautionary aversion of unduly large risks could materialize. The interests of succeeding generations could be respected and protected, subsurface and surface water resources and biodiversity would suffer much less damage.

Thirty years ago I had proposed that the dispute can offer two readings: a modern and a postmodern one. The first was chosen by Czechoslovakia and then Slovakia, the second can be associated with the position of Hungary in the ICJ case.[191]

Below is a table summarizing the dichotomies (Table 1).[192]

Environmental impact assessment, precaution and respect for intergenerational equity all belong to the postmodern mentality that does not make a fetish of growth, increased consumption based on an ever larger provision of energy and industrial goods produced with its help. Hungary was ready to suffer losses, including compensating Czechoslovakia for not building the Nagymaros barrage in order to relate to the environment and the ecological processes in a more respectful, sustainable way.[193]

In his book's second edition in 2020 De Sadeleer stresses that in his view "post-modernity is less a complete rupture with modernity than the rediscovery of the values underlying modernity within an evolving context".[194] In 1997 the ICJ was not yet ready to accomplish that rediscovery of underlying values of modernity. It remained a prisoner of the black and white letters of the law and a doctrine of treaty law that could have been applied exactly the same way a

191 I can't simply say "with the position of Hungary" as that position is volatile and frequently obscure. More on the recent decades in Nagy 2021. *See also* Nagy 1992.

192 First published in Nagy 1992, p. 57, slightly updated.

193 Hungarian Memorial, para. 9.24.

194 De Sadeleer 2020, p. 405.

Hungarian Yearbook of International Law and European Law 2022 (10) 1
doi: 10.5553/HYIEL/266627012022010001002

Table 1.

	Hungary	Czechoslovakia/Slovakia
Perspective	Long term perspective	Short term perspective
Value assessment	Discount rate low: high present value of future drinking water, near natural conditions	Discount rate high: hardly any value in the present of assets, resources to be consumed in remote future. Does not want to invest *now* for a return in fifty years
Care for posterity	Care for future generations, their life supporting systems and basic natural resources	Does not contemplate the situation of generations to come. "They should care for themselves, as we do for ourselves" – mentality.
Risk-management	Adoption of the precautionary principle regulating prudent behaviour in circumstances of uncertainty: according to this principle the lack of full and final scientific proof of future damage does not entitle going ahead; projects should be stopped even if there is "only" a high probability but not a certainty of the damage.	Belief in the technical fix: man is master of the universe, whatever he destroys, he can correct nothing is irreversible. A mere likelihood of immense future loss is not a reason to endure a qualitatively smaller, but certain present loss.
Market economy or else	Goods with no market value (the beauty of a landscape, the presence of irreplaceable archaeological sites, the richness of biodiversity) are nevertheless valuable, they deserve sacrifices including financial efforts.	Market economy dictates "reasonable market behaviour". Tradeable goods such as energy, navigational improvement have priority over symbolic values.
Survival vs growth	The goal is: balance with nature, sustainable existence (not necessarily development in terms of growth).	The goal is modernization in industrial terms, growth, expansion, domination over nature.

century earlier, all the calls for vigilance and references to the value of the environment notwithstanding. In 1997 the buds of postmodern, evolutive, future generations- and sustainability-oriented elements of environmental law that respect long term values no less than reward immediate state preferences could not yet burst the bark of traditional international law. But they were there, and 25 years on we can enjoy their late bloom.

doi: 10.5553/HYIEL/266627012022010001002

The Gabčíkovo-Nagymaros Case and Water Law

Malgosia Fitzmaurice[*]

Abstract

The Gabčíkovo-Nagymaros case is one of leading cases in international law, which has crystallized and evolved knowledge in many areas of international law. This case is also immensely important and instrumental for the development of water law. The ICJ observed the importance of a common right and cooperation in the shared resource and has laid down the foundation of the further development of modern water law. The ideas, which have originated in this case were later fully developed and unpacked in other cases of the ICJ dealing with water law, such as the Pulp Mills and Costa Rica/Nicaragua cases. The Court has emphasized the importance of the management of shared water resources and linked it to general environmental law. It has also supported and relied on the principle of equitable utilization. The ICJ confirmed the right of Hungary to an equitable and reasonable share of the resources of an international watercourse and supported the concept of common utilization of shared water resources. The ICJ adopted a very forward-looking approach to water law. It has taken into consideration the provisions of the 1997 Convention which was in force at the time, as codifying the principles of water law and shared water resources, such as equitable utilization principle and the no-significant harm rule. It may be said that the Gabčíkovo-Nagymaros case is a direct continuation and development of the River Oder case, which has laid down the foundations of contemporary international water law.

Keywords: water law, equitable utilization, no-significant harm rule, shared resource, Gabčíkovo-Nagymaros case.

1. Introduction

In *Gabčíkovo-Nagymaros*[1] the ICJ faced most challenging questions of international law, including the classical issues of the law of treaties; the law of state responsibility (including the interface between the two) while also dealing with and analyzing emerging and still evolving areas of international law, *i.e.* international environmental law and the law of international watercourses.

All these issues were closely related and, it may be said, have constituted a Gordian Knot of international law that was resolved by the ICJ. Not surprising, this case has generated an enormous body of literature, addressing all

* Malgosia Fitzmaurice: professor of international law, Queen Mary University of London.

1 ICJ, *Case concerning the Gabčíkovo-Nagymaros Project (Hungary v Slovakia)*, judgment, ICJ Reports 1997, p. 7.

doi: 10.5553/HYIEL/266627012022010001003

international law dilemmas raised by this case.[2] All aspects of this case were carefully analyzed, with a focus on classical international law themes.[3] The general view that has been expressed is that the ICJ has clarified many outstanding questions of international law, but equally has left many of them open and even missed the opportunity to provide definitive answers, in such matters as the uneasy relationship between the law of treaties and the law of state responsibility.[4] The ICJ has also dealt with international environmental law and water law, issues of which have formed the substantive fabric of the case.[5] The parts of the judgment which focused on the questions of the international environmental law and the law of international watercourses are particularly innovative, for at that time, many rules of both of these areas were evolving and in *statu nascendi*. Therefore, the ICJ was faced with a complex task of delving into issues in which there was very little judicial practice at the time, and whose fundamental principles were not fully formed and undisputed in substance, but

2 *See* in particular: Serena Forlati *et al.* (eds.), *The Gabčíkovo-Nagymaros Judgment and its Contribution to the Development of International Law*, Brill/Nijhoff, 2020.

3 *See e.g.* René Lefeber, 'The Gabčíkovo-Nagymaros Project and the Law of State Responsibility', *Leiden Journal of International Law*, Vol. 11, Issue 3, 1998, pp. 609-623; Phillippe Weckel, 'Convergence du droit des traités et du droit de la responsabilité internationale à la lumiére de l'Arret du 25 septembre 1997 de la Cour internationale de Justice relatif au projet Gabčíkovo-Nagymaros (Hongrie/Slovaquie)', *Revue Générale de droit International Public*, Vol. 102, 1998, pp. 647-684; Daniel Reichert-Facilides, 'Down the Danube: The Vienna Convention on the Law of Treaties and the Case Concerning the Gabčíkovo-Nagymaros Project', *International & Comparative Law Quarterly*, Vol. 47, Issue 4, 1998, pp. 837-854; Malgosia Fitzmaurice, 'The Gabčíkovo-Nagymaros Case: The Law of Treaties', *Leiden Journal of International Law*, Vol. 11, Issue 2, 1998, pp. 321-344; Jean D'Aspremont, 'Canonical Cross-Referencing in the Making of the law of International Responsibility', *in* Forlati *et al.* (eds.) 2020, pp. 22-40; Christina Binder & Jane Hofbauer, 'The Pacta Sunt Servanda Principle or the limits of Interpretation in the Gabčíkovo-Nagymaros Case Revisited', *in* Forlati *et al.* (eds.) 2020, pp. 58-77; Panos Merkouris, 'Termination of Treaties: Contribution of the Gabčíkovo-Nagymaros Judgment', *in* Forlati *et al.* (eds.) 2020, pp. 78-97; Serena Forlati, 'The Relationship between the Law of Treaties and the Law of State Responsibility', *in* Forlati *et al.* (eds.) 2020, pp. 109-130; Pierre Bodeau Livinec 'Circumstances Precluding Wrongfulness', *in* Forlati *et al.* (eds.) 2020, pp. 131-144; Loris Marotti & Paolo Palchetti, 'Of Restoring Compliance, *Lex Specialis* and Intersecting Wrongs: The Question of "Remedies" on Gabčíkovo-Nagymaros', *in* Forlati *et al.* (eds.) 2020, pp. 145-159.

4 Karel C. Wellens, 'The Court's Judgment in the Case Concerning Gabčíkovo-Nagymaros (Hungary/Slovakia): Some Preliminary Reflections', *in* Karel C. Wellens (ed.), *International Law: Theory and Practice. Essays in Honour of Eric Suy*, Martinus Nijhoff Publishers, 1998, pp. 765-799.

5 On the question of international environmental law *see e.g.* Johann G. Lammers, 'The Gabčíkovo-Nagymaros Case Seen in Particular from the Perspective of the Law of International Watercourse and the Protection of the Environment', *Leiden Journal of International Law*, Vol. 11, Issue 2, 1998, pp. 287-320; Leslie-Anne Duvic-Paoli, 'Vigilance and Prevention: The Contribution of the Gabčíkovo-Nagymaros Judgment', *in* Forlati *et al.* (eds.) 2020, pp. 193-206. On the water law, *see* Owen McIntyre, 'Environmental Protection of International Rivers', *Journal of Environmental Law*, Vol. 10, Issue 1, 1998, pp. 79-91; Charles B. Bourne, 'The Case Concerning the Gabčíkovo-Nagymaros Project: An Important Milestone in International Water Law', *Yearbook of International Law*, Vol. 8, Issue 1, 1997, pp. 6-12; Stephen Stec & Gabriel Eckstein, 'Of Solemn Oaths and Obligations: The Environmental Impact of the ICJ's Decision in the Case Concerning the Gabčíkovo-Nagymaros Project', *Yearbook of International Environmental Law*, Vol. 8, Issue 1, 1997, pp. 50.

doi: 10.5553/HYIEL/266627012022010001003

were merely the contours of emerging norms (or principles) with incipient content and uncertain legal force.

As noted above, all core issues in this case were entangled and it is not an easy task to separate them, focusing only on the one theme. However, since all aspects of the judgment were extensively analyzed elsewhere, I will confine myself to primarily dealing with the law of international watercourses in this case. This analysis will be further linked to other case-law of the ICJ dealing with the question of shared water resources. It must be mentioned that this aspect of the case (*i.e.* international watercourse law) is the least explored and analyzed in the vast literature devoted to this case.

2. The Background

The Danube River basin is the Europe's second largest river basin, with a total area of 801,463 km2. The Upper basin extends from the source of the Danube in Germany to Bratislava in Slovakia. The Middle basin is the largest of the three sub-regions, extending from Bratislava to the dams of the Iron Gate Gorge on the border between Serbia and Romania. The lowlands, plateaus and mountains of Romania and Bulgaria make up the Lower Basin of the River Danube. Finally, the river divides into three branches, forming the Danube Delta, which covers an area of about 6,750 km2. It has a unique biodiversity with about 2000 vascular plants and more than 5,000 animal species, including over 40 mammals, about 180 breeding birds, around 100 fish species, a dozen reptiles as well as amphibians. Changes to the river geography following such as the construction of dams, dikes, weirs and canals, disturb the aquatic environment, especially when it comes to migratory species, which cannot reach their spawning grounds.[6]

The River Danube was a subject of many international treaties, concluded before and after World War I and during the communist regime.[7] These, however, had very limited or no environmental provisions at all. The Gabčíkovo-Nagymaros project originated in 1951 and reflects another monumental construction of the Stalinist era. After many negotiations, the treaty's main objective emerged as energy production, with the secondary objectives of flood control and navigability. The first round of negotiations started in 1964 and resulted in the signing of the Rajka-Gonyu Agreement in 1968. By 1976, the Governments of Czechoslovakia and Hungary accepted a Joint Development Agreement for the project. These two states signed a treaty in 1977 in order to divert the course of the Danube through a series of dams and reservoirs. The Gabčíkovo-Nagymaros Project provided, *inter alia,* that "the Contracting Parties shall ensure [...] that the quality of the water in the Danube is not impaired as a result of the construction and operation of the System of Locks"[8] and to "take

6 Malgosia Fitzmaurice, 'The Gabčíkovo-Nagymaros Project: the Background of the Case', *in* Forlati *et al.* (eds.) 2020, p. 14.

7 On the history and the background of the dispute, *see* Id. pp. 14-15.

8 Article 15 of the 1977 Treaty.

doi: 10.5553/HYIEL/266627012022010001003

appropriate measures for the protection of fishing interests."[9] The treaty provided for completion in the period between 1986-1990.[10] According to the treaty provisions, the Danube was to have been diverted between river km 1842 and 1811 near Dunakiliti by a dam and a relief sluice from the original riverbed into an artificial canal on Czechoslovakian territory. Next to Gabčíkovo, a hydroelectric power plant with eight turbines and a capacity of 720 megawatts (MW) was to be erected. Beginning at the confluence of the canal into the original course of the Danube at river km 1811 until 1794, the riverbed was to have been deepened and its course regulated. Near Nagymaros at river km 1696, the treaty provided for a second, smaller power plant with an output of 158 MW, which was primarily to balance the fluctuation of the waterline. This would have been necessary, because the plant at Gabčíkovo was conceived as a peak-load electricity generation plant and would therefore have caused uneven water flow. The treaty foresaw a joint ownership of the main structure, comprising Dunakiliti Dam, the by-pass canal, the locks at Gabčíkovo-Nagymaros and provided for joint operation. The erection of the system was to be divided equally.[11] Hungary was supposed to perform all the construction in its own territory and 12 percent of the project value in Czechoslovakia.[12] The territorial scope of project was the area of 34 km of the Danube valley (Bratislava to Nagymaros),[13] with a reservoir positioned outside Bratislava. At Dunakiliti, a weir would divert water from the reservoir sending 90 percent of the flow through a diversion canal to the territory of Czechoslovakia and returning a small percentage of water to the original riverbed.[14] The diversion canal was an overground concrete construction, about 25 km long and over eighteen meters high, 274, to 70 meters wide. The canal would feed water through the 720 megawatt Gabčíkovo power plant before returning it to the Danube about 8.5 kms downstream.[15] The power plant in Gabčíkovo was supposed to operate in periodic surges, which would power the 160 megawatt power plant in Nagymaros.[16] The Nagymaros Dam was also designed to raise the water level in the 110 km area between Nagymaros and the diversion canal.[17]

3. The Judgment in the Gabčíkovo-Nagymaros Case and the Development of Water Law

As noted above, the questions of general international law (the law of treaties) concerning the continuing existence (or not) of the Treaty between the Slovak Republic and Hungary and the legality of the so-called Variant 'C' are closely

9 Article 20 of the 1977 Treaty.
10 Article 4(4) of the 1977 Treaty.
11 Article 1(1) of the 1977 Treaty.
12 Article 5(5) of the 1977 Treaty.
13 Articles 1(1) and 1(2) of the 1977 Treaty.
14 Article 1(2)(c) of the 1977 Treaty.
15 Article 1(2)(d) of the 1977 Treaty.
16 Article 1(3)(b) of the 1977 Treaty.
17 Fitzmaurice 2020, pp. 19-20.

doi: 10.5553/HYIEL/266627012022010001003

intertwined with substantive issues of international environmental law and international watercourse law (shared water resources). The separation of these questions is very difficult and in many relevant publications they were analyzed jointly.[18] However, from the ICJ's judgment I will try to distil the questions pertaining exclusively to the water law in this case, which will be followed by short presentation of the ICJ's more recent pronouncements in this area. The reason for such this approach is that the questions of water law in the *Gabčíkovo-Nagymaros* judgment as a separate subject-matter attracted the least attention by scholars, which in view of the ICJ's ongoing jurisprudence in this field, should be accorded more significance; meanwhile, the issues of general international law (the law of treaties and state responsibility) have been the main focus for international lawyers. It may be said that while the ICJ's views on international environmental law and sustainable development have been extensively analyzed, the law of international watercourses were mostly included as a part of environmental law analysis, not as an independent subject.

Suffice it to say that the ICJ has upheld the existence of the treaty and its binding force for Hungary and Slovakia (as the successor of Czechoslovakia). The pertinent treaty obligations binding on the parties derived from Articles 15, 19, and 20 which imposed respectively a duty of: ensuring non-impairment of the water quality of the Danube River; the protection of nature; and the protection of fishing interests. The ICJ has given guidance to the Parties to the dispute as to what are the objectives of the negotiations to be entered into on the basis of the Judgment. First, the parties were obliged to consider "in what way the multiple objectives of the Treaty can best be served, keeping in mind that all of them should be fulfilled".[19] These objectives were the production of hydroelectric energy and the improvement of the navigability of the Danube, flood control, the regulation of ice-discharge, and the protection of the natural environment. Importantly, all these objectives were of the equal value, thus, "none of these objectives has been given absolute priority over the other."[20] Bourne drew interesting and far reaching conclusions from the ICJ's lack of differentiated treatment of the objectives of the 1977 Treaty. He argued, correctly, that the parity among them meant that the environmental protection was not accorded preferential treatment, despite Hungary's argument that "the previously existing obligation not to cause substantive damage to the territory of another state had [...] evolved into an *erga omnes* obligation of prevention of damage pursuant to the 'precautionary principle'."[21] The analysis of the above statements of the ICJ, has evidenced in his view that the causing of significant harm in relation to the utilization of international watercourses was not treated by the ICJ as lawful and that the ICJ followed the provisions of the 1997 UN Convention on Non-Navigational Uses of International Watercourses (Watercourses Convention).[22]

18 *See e.g.* McIntyre 1998, Lammers 1998.
19 ICJ, *Gabčíkovo-Nagymaros,* judgment, para. 139.
20 Id. para. 135.
21 Id. para. 97; Bourne 1997, p. 7.
22 UNTS 2999; Bourne 1997, pp. 7-8.

doi: 10.5553/HYIEL/266627012022010001003

Bourne further argued that by not according priority to environmental protection, the ICJ has not at all referred to Articles 20 and 21 (the protection of the riparian environment) of the Watercourses Convention. He suggested that in these Articles

> "the words of Articles 20 and 21, which deal with ecology, the environment, and pollution, still echo the 'no significant harm' rule. It is doubtful, however, that these articles were intended to incorporate this rule, and the ICJ seems not to have interpreted them as doing so."[23]

The lack of supremacy accorded by the ICJ to international environmental law in its judgment does not mean, however, that the ICJ's judgment lack significance in this respect. As it was explained by Duvic-Paoli, in this judgment the ICJ consolidated its previous mention of international environmental law in the *Advisory Opinion in the Nuclear Weapons*[24] by the relying on the principle of prevention and situating international environmental law within the paradigm of sustainable development.[25] The ICJ has not elaborated on these aspects, nonetheless the judgment constituted a starting point for the ICJ's further elucidation of the principle of prevention and the due diligence obligation in relation to water law in *Pulp Mills*[26] and *Nicaragua/Costa Rica*.[27] Duvic-Paoli presented a nuanced analysis of the threshold of harm in the judgment. She observed that the ICJ failed to differentiate between two separate thresholds: the first one applicable to determine whether Hungary was facing the state of necessity, which is a circumstance precluding wrongfulness in the law of state responsibility; and the second one, applicable within the framework of international environmental law, to assess the applicability of the obligation of prevention. Therefore, the ICJ did not distinguish between the criteria applicable under state responsibility and international environmental law. The legal consequences of such an omission are quite significant. The threshold applicable in the realm of state responsibility is higher in defining the gravity and imminence of risk mandatory for the invoking of the state of (ecological) necessity than it is in relation to prevention. Therefore, even though the threshold was not met in relation to state responsibility, it might suffice regarding the avoidance of environmental harm, a scenario which, as Duvic-Paoli explained, the ICJ had "overlooked".[28]

In relation to the use of the Danube (the shared resource), the ICJ relied on the principle of equitable utilization. The ICJ confirmed Hungary's right "to an

23 Bourne 1997, p. 8.

24 ICJ, *Legality of the Threat or Use of Nuclear Weapons*, Advisory Opinion, ICJ Reports 1996, p. 226, para. 29.

25 Duvic-Paoli 2020, pp. 199-206.

26 ICJ, *Pulp Mills on the River Uruguay (Argentina v Uruguay)*, judgment, ICJ Reports 2010, p. 14.

27 ICJ, *Certain Activities carried out by Nicaragua in the Border Area (Costa Rica v Nicaragua) and Construction of a Road in Costa Rica along the San Juan River (Nicaragua v Costa Rica)*, judgment, ICJ Reports 2015, p. 665.

28 Duvic-Paoli 2020, p. 202, and pp. 201-202.

doi: 10.5553/HYIEL/266627012022010001003

equitable and reasonable sharing of the resources of an international watercourse", and "the concept of common utilization of shared water resources".[29] It stated that Slovakia, unilaterally assuming control of "a shared resource", had deprived Hungary of "its right to an equitable share of the natural resources of the Danube", and had thus "failed to respect the proportionality which is required by international law".[30] The purpose of the required negotiations was to find "an agreed solution that takes account of the objectives of the [1997] Treaty [...] as well as the norms of international environmental law and the principles of the law of international watercourses."[31] During the negotiations conducted in good faith, parties should discharge their obligations by implementing, *inter alia,* "the use, development and protection of the watercourse [...] in an equitable and reasonable manner".[32]

There is no doubt that it is in *Gabčíkovo-Nagymaros* that the ICJ made the most fundamental statement concerning the principle of sustainable development. The principle of equitable and reasonable utilization concerns the allocation of rights for the use and benefit of shared water resources based on the distributive concepts of equity, taking into account all relevant factors.[33] It should be noted that the principle of equitable utilization has been confirmed by the ICJ in the *Gabčíkovo-Nagymaros* and *Pulp Mills* cases as a fundamental principle of international watercourse cooperation.[34] In *Pulp Mills* this principle was linked directly to the concept of sustainable development, where the ICJ had stated that the "interconnectedness between equitable and reasonable utilization of a shared resource and the balance between economic development and environmental protection [...] is the essence of sustainable development."[35]

4. Some Reflections on the Fundamental Principles of the Watercourse Law and the Case Law of the ICJ

This section will be devoted to the analysis of the principle of equitable utlilization and the related principle of non (significant) harm. These principles are inexorably linked to due diligence, which will also be discussed. These principles will be illustrated by the ICJ's case law in relation to international watercourses, which developed these principles, first raised in its jurisprudence by *Gabčíkovo-Nagymaros*.

Without doubt the principle of equitable utilization of international watercourses is of fundamental nature. The Court derived it from the 1929 *River Oder* case where it stated as follows:

29 ICJ, *Gabčíkovo-Nagymaros,* judgment, para. 78.

30 Id. para. 85.

31 Id. para. 141.

32 Id. para. 150.

33 Owen McIntyre, 'Substantive Rules of International Law', *in* Alistair Rieu-Clarke *et al.* (eds.), *Routledge Handbook of Water Law and Policy,* Routledge, London, 2017, p. 238.

34 ICJ, *Gabčíkovo-Nagymaros,* judgment, para. 147; ICJ, *Pulp Mills,* judgment, para. 170.

35 ICJ, *Pulp Mills,* para. 177.

doi: 10.5553/HYIEL/266627012022010001003

> "[the] community of interest in a navigable river becomes the basis of a common legal right, the essential features of which are the perfect equality of al1 riparian States in the user of the whole course of the river and the exclusion of any preferential privilege of any one riparian State in relation to the others."[36]

The modern development of international law extended this principle to non-navigational uses of international watercourses as well, as evidenced by the adoption of the Convention of 21 May 1997 on the Law of the Non-Navigational Uses of International Watercourses.

The above statement of the ICJ emphasized several very important issues. It expressed the view that the principle of equitable utilization is derived from a community of interest in a river, which in turn is the basis of a common legal right, characterized by the equality of all riparian states. As McIntyre explains, "the existence of this community of interest requires an 'equitable and reasonable' balancing of State interests which accommodates the needs and uses of each State."[37] He also correctly states that the principle of equitable utilization has been widely recognized as a fundamental principle of watercourse cooperation both by scholars and in the practice of states.[38]

The Watercourse Convention further crystallized the principle of equitable utilization, stating, *inter alia*, in Article 5 that: "Watercourse states shall in their respective territories utilize an international watercourse in an equitable and reasonable manner. In particular, an international watercourse shall be used and developed by watercourse States with a view to attaining optimal and sustainable utilization thereof [...]." Article 6 provides a non-exhaustive list of factors relevant to equitable and reasonable utilization.[39] McIntyre observed that "to permit flexibility, the concept of 'equitable and reasonable' is necessarily vague and can only be determined in each case in the light of all relevant factors."[40]

The other fundamental principle of the use of international watercourses is the principle of no (significant) harm (see above), which is incorporated in Article 7 of the Watercourse Convention. The additional factor concerning water cooperation, which was not mentioned in the *Gabčíkovo-Nagymaros* judgment but analyzed in *Pulp Mills* and *Costa Rica v Nicaragua* cases, is due diligence, in

36 PCIJ, *Territorial Jurisdiction of the International Commission of the River Oder,* Judgment No. 16, 1929, PCIJ, Series A, No. 23, p. 27.

37 McIntyre 1998, p. 86.

38 Id.

39 "*(a)* Geographic, hydrographic, hydrological, climatic, ecological and other factors of a natural character; *(b)* The social and economic needs of the watercourse States concerned; *(c)* The population dependent on the watercourse in each watercourse State; *(d)* The effects of the use or uses of the watercourses in one watercourse State on other watercourse States; *(e)* Existing and potential uses of the watercourse; *(f)* Conservation, protection, development and economy of use of the water resources of the watercourse and the costs of measures taken to that effect; *(g)* The availability of alternatives, of comparable value, to a particular planned or existing use.'

40 McIntyre 1998, p. 86.

doi: 10.5553/HYIEL/266627012022010001003

connection with equitable utilization.[41] Due diligence in international watercourse law reflects the interplay amongst the two most fundamental principles: *(i)* the principle of equitable utilization; and *(ii)* the principle of no significant harm. They define the core of international watercourse law, that is, the relationship between upper and lower riparian states. The upper riparian states have supported the principle of equitable utilization, as adhering to this principle and acting diligently would release them from liability for environmental harm. Lower riparian states have been advocating for the principle of no significant harm, as it would allow them to seek remedies in cases of environmental harm, even if upper riparian states acted in observance of the principle of due diligence. Hence, the International Law Commission and the Sixth Legal Committee have decided to include Article 7(2) in the 1997 Watercourse Convention to grant lower riparian states some compensation in such situations. Where significant harm is nevertheless caused to another watercourse state, the states whose use caused such harm shall, in the absence of an agreement prior to such use, take all appropriate measures – having due regard for the provisions of Articles 5 and 6 and in consultation with the affected state – to eliminate or mitigate such harm and, where appropriate, to discuss the question of compensation.[42] In the *Costa Rica v Nicaragua* cases, the ICJ has made an important link between the due diligence obligation of conducting the environmental impact assessment (EIA) in general international environmental law and water law, which squarely falls under the category of all activities, which require such a procedure in the event of potentially causing significant adverse impact in a transboundary context. Due diligence in such a case also triggers a procedural obligation to carry out an EIA, notifying and consulting the potentially affected state if the EIA confirms there is a risk of significant harm.[43] Conversely, based on experts' opinion in Nicaragua, dredging activities did not carry such a risk, thus, there was no duty to conduct the EIA, notification or consultation *vis-à-vis* Costa Rica.[44] This case has not solved all issues which may rise in relation to shared water resources and the carrying out of the EIA (substantive and procedural obligations). The ICJ, it is argued, could have been more transparent in clarifying which activities require carrying out an EIA and what is the threshold of risk involved.[45] Further complexity is added with the application of the standard of due diligence to procedural obligations, which was expressly confirmed by the ICJ in *Pulp Mills*. In this case, the ICJ made certain statements that related to the substance of the duty of due diligence in relation to a shared watercourse. The ICJ stated that

41 Malgosia Fitzmaurice, 'Due Diligence in the Use of International Watercourses', *in* Heike Krieger *et al.* (eds.), *Due Diligence in the International Legal Order,* Oxford University Press, Oxford, 2020, p. 129.

42 Id. p. 130.

43 ICJ, *Costa Rica v Nicaragua cases*, judgment, para. 104. *See also* Rumiana Yotova, 'The Principle of Due Diligence and Prevention in International Environmental Law', *Cambridge Journal of International Law,* Vol. 75, Issue 3, 2016, p. 446.

44 Id. p. 446.

45 Id. p. 448.

doi: 10.5553/HYIEL/266627012022010001003

> "a State is thus obliged to use all of the means at its disposal in order to avoid activities which take place in its territory, or in any area under its jurisdiction, causing significant damage to the environment of another state",[46]

thus reaffirming the general obligation of prevention.[47] In *Pulp Mills* the ICJ confirmed the principle of prevention, which is based on due diligence and constitutes a core principle of international environmental law. This principle had initially been acknowledged in *Corfu Channel*,[48] then included in the *Nuclear Weapons Advisory Opinion*,[49] and relied upon in the ILC Articles on Prevention.[50] The ICJ specifically referred to the obligation of due diligence in protecting the shared river:

> "both Parties are therefore called upon, under Article 36, to exercise due diligence in acting through the Commission for the necessary measures to preserve the ecological balance of the river."[51]

The exercise of due diligence entails the adoption of appropriate rules and measures; a certain level of vigilance in their enforcement; the exercise of administrative control applicable to public and private operators; careful consideration of the technology to be used; the commission of an EIA; and notification informing and consulting potentially affected states.[52] Significant statements of the ICJ in this case concerned the legal character of due diligence, which was defined by it as an obligation of rather conduct than result (in accordance with general international law and the law of state responsibility).[53] The ICJ also observed that the obligation to carry out the EIA had become a requirement under international general law, in the case of activities which may have a significant adverse effect on the environment.[54] The ICJ, however, further stated that the scope and substance of the EIA are not specified by general international law. Each party must determine individually on a case-by-case basis what is required, while "having regard to the nature and magnitude of the proposed development and its likely adverse impact".[55]

According to the ICJ, two types of obligations – namely substantive and procedural – were laid down in the 1975 Statute of the River Uruguay and as the

46 ICJ, *Pulp Mills,* judgment, para. 101.

47 On the principle of prevention in general, *see* Leslie-Anne Duvic-Paoli, *The Prevention Principle in International Environmental Law*, Cambridge University Press, Cambridge, 2018; *see also* Alan Boyle, *Pulp Mills Case: A Commentary*, 2010, at www.biicl.org/files/5167_pulp_mills_case.pdf.

48 ICJ, *Corfu Channel Case (United Kingdom v Albania),* judgment, ICJ Reports 1949, p. 22.

49 ICJ, *Legality of the Threat or Use of Nuclear Weapons,* para. 29.

50 UN International Law Commission, *Draft Articles on Prevention of Transboundary Harm from Hazardous Activities*, at http://legal.un.org/ilc/texts/instruments/english/commentaries/9_7_2001.pdf.

51 ICJ, *Pulp Mills,* judgment, para. 187.

52 Id. para. 223.

53 Id. para. 182.

54 Id. para. 204.

55 Id. para. 205.

doi: 10.5553/HYIEL/266627012022010001003

Court stated they "complement one another perfectly, enabling the parties to achieve the object of the Statute which they set themselves in Article 1".[56] As it was noted above, the ICJ was of the view that these obligations were not contingent upon each other[57] and that the substantive aspect of the due diligence obligation does not impose an absolute duty to prevent harm. Instead, it is based on the due diligence principle, that is to say, states must meet the requirements of due diligence. The ICJ stated that a failure to meet the procedural obligation does not automatically amount to a violation of substantive obligations (such as the duty to prevent harm). The ICJ was of the view that

> "nowhere does the 1975 Statute indicate that a party may fulfil its substantive obligations by complying solely with its procedural obligations, nor that a breach of procedural obligations automatically entails the breach of substantive ones",[58]

and

> "the fact that the parties have complied with their substantive obligations does not mean that they are deemed to have complied *ipso facto* with their procedural obligations, or are excused from doing so."[59]

It may be observed that the ICJ's approach and reasoning regarding both substantive and procedural obligations in relation to shared watercourses and the EIA, appears to be opaque and not quite entirely convincing.[60] There is a host of questions relating to the relationship of these types of obligations, such as procedural obligations sequential to the substantive ones; does the duty of due diligence also pertain to substantive obligations; what are the type of activities which involve an obligation to carry out an EIA.[61] These uncertainties were not resolved by the *Costa Rica/Nicaragua* cases.

However, it may be argued that in light of the recent case law of the ICJ, procedural obligations pertaining to the management of the shared water resources have gained prominence. Cases decided by the ICJ also highlighted that many water agreements, concluded some time ago, contained such procedural obligations. An instructive example is *Pulp Mills* based on the interpretation of the 1975 Statute between Uruguay and Argentina. The Statute provided that, *inter alia*, through procedural obligations of information, consultation and negotiations, the state parties achieve the optimum and rational utilization of

56 Id. para. 77.
57 Id. paras. 77-78.
58 Id. para. 78.
59 Id.
60 *See e.g.* Jutta Brunnée, 'Procedure and Substance in International Environmental Law: Confused at Higher Level?', *European Society of International Law Reflections*, Vol. 5, Issue 6, 2016, p. 2, at http://esil-sedi.eu/?p=1344.
61 Id. p. 4.

doi: 10.5553/HYIEL/266627012022010001003

their shared watercourse.[62] The ICJ was clear in pointing out that Uruguay violated obligations of notification and consultation by not informing the joint administrative commission regarding the planned works. The ICJ also stated that in relation to the duty to negotiate, the unilateral authorization by Uruguay of pulp mills before the expiry of the negotiation period set out by the treaty, indicated a disregard for such a cooperative mechanism amounting to a breach of procedural obligations.[63]

The host of problems which the ICJ faced in the *Pulp Mills* and *Costa Rica/ Nicaragua* cases are very illustrative to problems encountered in the management of shared water recourses. Taken holistically, the approach to the joint management of such resources should have a due regard to the interdependence among recourses, habitats and ecosystems. Therefore, as it was stated in cases regarding shared mutual resources, "courts are expected to pay due regard to the shared interest in certain natural resources, and where necessary, the interests of the international community as a whole."[64] It is not at all surprising that an integrated approach to the management of the Danube River is an even more daunting task than in the bilateral context. The Danube flows through ten States: Germany, Austria, Slovakia, Hungary, Serbia, Romania, Bulgaria, Moldova, and Ukraine, and then discharges into the Black Sea. Therefore, the implementation of all the underlying water law principles (substantive and procedural) is a very complex matter, as according to the integrated approach, the interests of all riparian states should be considered, thus implying that a conflict resolution between the most directly concerned states should be conducted and resolved with a due regard to these other riparian states' interests and in a holistic manner. Pineschi emphasizes that there are a vast number of human activities conducted in the area of the entire Danube basin, potentially cumulatively affecting the entire region. Based on the data produced by the International Commission for the Protection of the River Danube, she states that a total of 59 dams were built along the Danube's first 1,000 km (from the sources to Gabčíkovo), which amounts to the Upper Danube being interrupted every 16 km on average. Therefore, it can hardly be characterized as fully free flowing.[65] Taking into consideration the common right of all riparian states, the principle of prevention must be applied to protect the environment across the whole river and for all riparian states. That was the premise on which Hungary based the application, invoking the principle of prevention, which was conceptualized as an *erga omnes* principle:

> "The main principle of international environmental law is that environmental degradation must be prevented. This principle of prevention which forms the

62 Laurence Boisson de Chazournes, *Fresh Water in International Law,* Oxford University Press, Oxford, 2nd edition, 2021, p. 270.

63 Id. ICJ, *Pulp Mills,* judgment, para. 149.

64 Laura Pineschi, 'Introduction to Part 2', *in* Forlati *et al.* (eds.) 2020, p. 51.

65 Id.

doi: 10.5553/HYIEL/266627012022010001003

> basis of all environmental law must be considered an *erga omnes* obligation."[66]

The view that ecological questions are of a multilateral character (operating *erga omnes*) rather than in a bilateral nature (operating *inter partes*) was shared by Judge Weeramantry.[67] The ICJ itself has not dwelt on the arguably special character of norms of international environmental law, noting that it was not necessary to pronounce on these issues as neither of the parties raised the question of the emergence of a new norm of international environmental law of a peremptory character since the conclusion of the 1977 Treaty.[68] As Pineschi observes, this very brief statement of the ICJ has been met with very mixed comments by scholars. Some of them have found the attitude of the ICJ very elusive; others agreed with its pragmatic approach, as there is only a remote possibility of any norm of international environmental law acquiring the status of a peremptory norm of international law.[69] However, it is undisputable that environmental prevention (also including water cooperation) involves a fine balancing of interests, in particular in the integrated approach. It was observed that in *Gabčíkovo-Nagymaros*, the ICJ has indeed moved from the no-harm principle of international environmental law towards the principle of prevention.[70] As Pineschi stated the same standards must be followed in the application of the principle of cooperation (which is based on procedural requirements) in cases of significant transboundary effect.[71]

5. The Judgment in the Gabčíkovo-Nagymaros Case and the Community of Interests

As it was referred to above, the ICJ relied on the notion of the community of interests of riparian states, which was introduced by the PCIJ in *River Oder*. The same case was mentioned by the Arbitral Tribunal in the *Rhine Chlorides Arbitration*. Therein, the Arbitral Tribunal added that "Solidarity between bordering states is undoubtedly a factor in their community of interests."[72]

It is often forgotten that community of interest and interests and solidarity in a common river was also expressed by the PCIJ's *Oscar Chin Case*, not only in

66 ICJ, *Memorial of the Republic of Hungary*, Vol. I, 2 May 1994, para. 6.63, pp. 200-201, cited in Pineschi 2020, p. 52.

67 ICJ, *Gabčíkovo-Nagymaros*, Separate Opinion of Judge (Vice-President) Weeramantry, paras. 88, and 118; Pineschi 2020, p. 52.

68 ICJ, *Gabčíkovo-Nagymaros*, judgment, para. 112.

69 Pineschi 2020, p. 53.

70 Laurence Boisson de Chazournes, 'Introduction to Part 4', *in* Forlati *et al.* (eds.) 2020, p. 264.

71 Pineschi 2020, p. 54.

72 The Rhine Chloride Arbitration Concerning the Auditing the Accounts (Netherlands-France), Award of 2004, para. 4, cited in Boisson de Chazournes 2021, p. 316.

doi: 10.5553/HYIEL/266627012022010001003

River Oder.[73] Judge van Eysinga commented on the legal character of the 1885 General Act of Berlin, which he describes as follows:

> "It will be seen from this survey that the Berlin Act presents a case in which a large number of states, which were territorially or otherwise interested in a vast region, endowed it with a highly internationalized statute, or rather a constitution established by treaty, by means of which the interests of peace, those of 'all nations' as well as those of the natives, appeared to be most satisfactorily guaranteed. [...] The General Act of Berlin does not create a number of contractual relations between a number of states, relations which may be replaced as regards some of these states by other contractual relations; it does not constitute a *jus dispositivum*, but it provides the Congo Basin with a régime, a statute, a constitution. This régime, which forms an indivisible whole, may be modified, but for this the agreement of all contracting Powers is required. An inextricable legal tangle would result if, for instance, it was held that the régime of neutralization provided for in Article II of the General Act of Berlin might be in force for some contracting Powers while it had ceased to operate for certain others."[74]

In the same case, Judge Schückling agreed fully with the aforementioned opinion of Judge van Eysinga. He added that

> "It is beyond doubt that the signatory states of the Congo Act desired to make it absolutely impossible, in the future, for some of their number only to amend the Congo Act, seeing that any modifications thus introduced would have been a danger to their vested rights in that vast region."[75]

Since then, international law has evolved towards the conceptualization of what has been defined as an international community by many scholars, such as Bruno Simma, progressing from bilateral relations towards a more 'socially conscious order', which is an amalgamate of the interests of the community and also of these states.[76] These developments have been reflected on a practical level by the 2001 Responsibility of States for Internationally Wrongful Acts (ARSIWA), *i.e.* Article 48, which allows the invocation of state responsibility by other than the directly affected state,[77] in protection of the collective interest, deriving from

73 PCIJ, *The Oscar Chin Case (United Kingdom v Belgium)* [1934] PCIJ Series A/B No. 63, 65. *See also* PCIJ, *Case of SS Wimbledon (Great Britain and Others v Germany)* [1923] PCIJ Series A No. 1, 15.

74 PCIJ, Individual Opinion of Judge van Eysinga, p. 133 and 134.

75 PCIJ, Separate Opinion of Judge Schücking, pp. 18-49.

76 Bruno Simma, 'From Bilateralism to Community Interest in International Law', *Collective Courses of the Hague Academy of International Law*, Vol. 250, 1994, p. 234.

77 *See also* James Crawford *et al.*, 'The ILC's Articles on State Responsibility Adopted For Internationally Wrongful Acts: Completion of the Second Reading', *European Journal of International Law*, Vol. 12, Issue 5, 2001, pp. 963-991; James Crawford, 'Responsibility for Breaches of Communitarian Norms: An Appraisal of Article 48 of the ILC Articles on State Responsibility of States for Internationally Wrongful Acts', *in* Ulrich Fastenrath *et al.*, *From Bilateralism to Community Interest*, Oxford University Press, Oxford, 2011, pp. 224-240.

doi: 10.5553/HYIEL/266627012022010001003

obligations *erga omnes* and *erga omnes partes.*[78] This Article is a departure from classical, international law, based on bilateral relations between states which allows standing to the state which is directly injured, as envisaged in Article 42 of ARSIWA to enforce to their vested rights in that vast region.

It was aptly observed that the ICJ has not explicitly applied the *erga omnes* (or *erga omnes partes*) dimension to environmental disputes. Such an example is the *Whaling in Antarctic* case, which has been brought by Australia (with New Zealand intervening), on, it may be said, the basis of the *erga omnes partes* principle, which was never mentioned in the judgment.[79] However, Australia in its pleadings claimed to be doing so, for which it was credited. According to Crawford, Australia invoked Japan's responsibility *erga omnes partes*.[80] During the proceedings, Australia claimed to act exclusively in the general interest. It argued that notwithstanding the fact that some of Japan's hunting activities have taking place in its territorial waters, it was not a directly injured state. It argued that every party has some interest in ensuring compliance by every other party with its obligations under the 1946 Whaling Convention. Accordingly, it claimed to be seeking to uphold the collective interest. Tams expressed the view that perhaps the *Whaling* case is a logical follow up to the 2011 judgment in *Belgium v Senegal* (see above). In that case, the ICJ surprised commentators by going out of its way to accept the applicant's standing to endorse a multilateral treaty protecting collective interests.[81] In this case, views were expressed that the current ecosystem approach and the notion of common heritage of humankind may be considered by states as matters that give rise to obligations *erga omnes* and *erga omnes partes* and, thus give rise to redress pursuant to Article 48 of the ARSIWA.[82]

We can see that was a little-known case before the PCIJ relating to the status of an international river, which also significantly contributed to the discourse on the community of interests.

6. Conclusions

There is no doubt that *Gabčíkovo-Nagymaros* is one of the leading cases in international law, which has crystallized and evolved knowledge in many areas of international law. The areas of international law, which are considered to be elucidated in the judgment are international environmental law; the law of

78 Crawford 2001, p. 976.

79 ICJ, *Whaling in the Antarctic (Australia v Japan: New Zealand intervening),* judgment, ICJ Reports 2014, p. 226; Pineschi 2020, p. 55.

80 Crawford 2011, p. 236.

81 Christian Tams, 'Roads not Taken, Opportunities Missed. Procedural and Jurisdictional Questions Sidestepped in the Whaling Judgment', *in* Malgosia Fitzmaurice & Dai Tamada (eds.), *Whaling in the Antarctic. Significance and Implications of the ICJ Judgment,* Brill/Nijhoff, Leiden, 2015, pp. 201-207.

82 Simone Borg, 'The Influence of International Case Law on Aspects of International Law Relating to Conservation of Living Marine Resources beyond National Jurisdiction', *Yearbook of International Environmental Law,* Vol. 23, Issue 1, 2017, pp. 57-71.

doi: 10.5553/HYIEL/266627012022010001003

treaties; and law of state responsibility. However, by writing this article, I have tried to demonstrated that this case is also immensely important from the perspective of the development of water law. The ICJ has noted the importance of a common right and cooperation in the shared resource laying, down the foundations for the further development of modern water law, which it continued in the above-mentioned and analyzed cases. The ICJ has also concluded that the 1977 Treaty has constituted a territorial regime within the meaning of Article 12 of the Vienna Convention on Succession in Respect of Treaties in line with the ILC's view that treaties concerning navigation rights on rivers are commonly regarded as candidates for inclusion in the category of territorial treaties which are unaffected by the succession of states.[83] The ICJ has demonstrated that principles such as prevention, sustainable development are of importance for water law. It may be stated that *Gabčíkovo-Nagymaros* has fomented further studies of water law and has had great practical significance. As such, it has proved to have an ever-lasting legacy in various areas of international law, including the water law.[84]

83 Lammers 1998, p. 319.

84 Attila Tanzi, 'Concluding Remarks. The Legacy of Landmark Case', *in* Forlati *et al.* (eds.) 2020, p. 229.

doi: 10.5553/HYIEL/266627012022010001003

The 25th Anniversary of the Gabčíkovo-Nagymaros Case

The Potential and Limits of International Law in Environmental Protection*

*Christina Binder***

Abstract

The article deals with the Gabčíkovo-Nagymaros case as one of the first true 'environmental cases' considered by the ICJ. On the basis of the ICJ's findings in the case, it examines the potential and limits of the traditional 'tool-box' of general international law when dealing with environmental concerns. Drawing on the ICJ's findings in the Gabčíkovo-Nagymaros case, the article more particularly argues that the circumstances precluding wrongfulness in the law of state responsibility (the necessity defence) and termination grounds of the law of treaties (supervening impossibility and fundamental change of circumstances) are most limited instruments to respond to the growing need for environmental protection. At the same time, a dynamic interpretation of treaty obligations offers certain opportunities to incorporate subsequent developments in environmental knowledge and to respond to environmental concerns. Finally, the article contextualizes these findings in a broader mise-en-perspective in light of the last 25 years, from three sides: a case-specific perspective, an institutional/ICJ perspective and through the lens of more recent jurisprudence of the ICJ in environmental matters.

Keywords: international environmental law, necessity defence, state responsibility, treaty termination, Gabčíkovo-Nagymaros judgment.

1. Introduction

The *Gabčíkovo-Nagymaros* case is one of the first true 'environmental cases' considered by the ICJ. It relates to a dam project on the Danube as agreed upon by Hungary and (then) Czechoslovakia in a bilateral treaty of 1977 and ecological concerns raised in particular by Hungary in relation to the project.[1] *Gabčíkovo-*

* The author wishes to thank Dr. Jane Hofbauer for helpful comments on an earlier draft of this paper.

** Christina Binder: professor of international law and international human rights law, Bundeswehr University Munich.

1 ICJ, *Case concerning the Gabčíkovo-Nagymaros Project (Hungary v Slovakia)*, judgment, ICJ Reports 1997, p. 7.

doi: 10.5553/HYIEL/266627012022010001004

Nagymaros's features of a 'typical' environmental case include developments in ecological knowledge and law relating to the environment subsequent to the conclusion of the 1977 Treaty, which led to a reconsideration of the project in Hungary.

The ICJ's findings of *Gabčíkovo-Nagymaros* evidence some of the challenges encountered when dealing with environmental protection within existing international legal frameworks. Indeed, international environmental law (IEL) is a comparatively new field of international law in rapid development and evolution. To account for these developments is demanding for general international law and its institutions, in this case, the ICJ. It is even trickier in view of the complexity of many environmental problems, which frequently require protection from future harm, despite a certain level of scientific uncertainty regarding the consequences of activities perceived as harmful to the environment. This is reflected in the partly disputed nature and scope of certain of IEL's key concepts such as the precautionary principle or sustainable development. The question indeed arises how to account for the specific challenges of environmental protection in the horizontally structured system of international law in lack of centralized institutions.

All this played a role in *Gabčíkovo-Nagymaros*, which explains the case's interest to examine the potential and limits of traditional public international law when dealing with environmental concerns. 25 years later, the *Gabčíkovo-Nagymaros* judgment merits an appraisal as to where we stand, especially in view of significant advancements in the field of IEL. Often, the question is posed on how the 'toolbox' of international law works when confronted with specific issues relating to the environment. Are the institutions and instruments of the general international law of treaties and state responsibility able and equipped to deal with ecological concerns? What can be learned from *Gabčíkovo-Nagymaros* in this respect? What is the legacy of the judgment 25 years on?

Such investigation seems particularly pertinent since the *Gabčíkovo-Nagymaros* case has been evaluated from opposite ends in literature as regards the ICJ's recognition of environmental concerns. While some commentators have positively assessed how the ICJ dealt with environmental protection in the case and welcomed the ICJ's clarification of relevant concepts,[2] others were more

2 *See e.g.* Makane Mbengue, 'On Sustainable Development: a Conversation with Judge Weeramantry', *in* Serena Forlati *et al.* (eds.), *The Gabčíkovo-Nagymaros Judgment and Its Contribution to the Development of International Law*, Brill Nijhoff, 2020, pp. 166 *et seq.* "pioneering in respect to the recognition of the environment". As stated by Laurence Boisson de Chazournes: "The ICJ has contributed to clarify concept or principle of sustainable development in international law and contributed to the progressive development of a *corpus* of norms and principles relating to environmental law." Laurence Boisson de Chazournes, 'Introduction to Part 4', *in* Forlati *et al.* (eds.) 2020, p. 163.

doi: 10.5553/HYIEL/266627012022010001004

critical, referring to a "missed opportunity"[3] or maintaining that the case has, if not slowed down, at least not advanced the development of IEL.[4]

Against this background, I start with a brief description of the key features of the case and the challenges encountered when it comes to environmental protection in international law (Section 2). Then I give an overview of the relevant instruments of international law in view of their potential to alleviate environmental concerns (Section 3). On that basis, I examine the ICJ's findings in *Gabčíkovo-Nagymaros* (Section 4). Finally, a broader *mise-en-perspective* contextualizes the case in light of the developments over the last 25 years (Section 5).

2. The Gabčíkovo-Nagymaros Case and the Environment

2.1. Background of the Gabčíkovo-Nagymaros Case[5]

As noted above, *Gabčíkovo-Nagymaros* concerns the use of the Danube by a joint dam project on which Czechoslovakia and Hungary had agreed in 1977 in a bilateral treaty, and the ensuing environmental degradation due to extensive use of water resources. The dam project provided for in the 1977 bilateral treaty envisaged a system of locks, in Gabčíkovo (then Czechoslovakia, today Slovakia) and Nagymaros (Hungary). The project stemmed from a time characterized by limited environmental considerations.[6] Still, in terms of the environment, the 1977 Treaty between (then) Czechoslovakia and Hungary already contained certain (broad) provisions envisaging the project's ecological consequences [commitment to uphold standards of water quality in the Danube (Article 15)]. The parties also committed themselves to "compliance with the obligation [imposed by international law] for the protection of nature arising in connection with the construction and operation of the System of Locks." (Article 19). More detailed measures to protect the ecology of the Danube were to be incorporated in a joint contractual plan. The Treaty did not contain a provision on termination.

With growing civic resistance to the project *inter alia* due to ecological concerns, Hungary suspended the works in 1989. In May 1992 it formally notified Czechoslovakia that the 1977 Treaty was terminated. More specifically,

3 *See* Mari Nakamichi's critical statement: "[The *Gabčíkovo-Nagymaros* case] was brought at a time of growing international concern for the environment. As such, the ICJ was presented with the opportunity to set a new standard for environmental protection in the next century, putting the spirit of countless international environmental agreements and conventions into effect. It explicitly declined to do so." Mari Nakamichi, 'The International Court of Justice Decision Regarding the Gabčíkovo-Nagymaros Project', *Fordham Environmental Law Journal*, Vol. 9, 1998, p. 363.

4 *Cf.* Brian McGarry: "[...] the terminologies of the Gabčíkovo-Nagymaros Judgment have – if not slowed – then at least failed to accelerate the clarification of general international environmental law." Brian McGarry, 'Norms, Standards, and the Elusive Nomenclature of the Gabčíkovo-Nagymaros Judgment', *in* Forlati *et al.* (eds.) 2020, p. 227; *see also* Laura Pineschi, 'Introduction to Part 2', *in* Forlati *et al.* (eds.) 2020, p. 43.

5 Tim Stephens, International Law and Environmental Protection, Cambridge University Press, Cambridge, 2009, pp. 177 *et seq.*; Nakamichi 1998.

6 *See* in general Stephens 2009, p. 175.

doi: 10.5553/HYIEL/266627012022010001004

Hungary relied on the one hand, on a "state of ecological necessity".[7] It also argued with impossibility of performance, declaring that it could not be "obliged to fulfil a practically impossible task, namely to construct a barrage system on its own territory that would cause irreparable environmental damage",[8] concluding that

> "by May 1992 the essential object of the Treaty – an economic joint investment which was consistent with environmental protection and which was operated by the two parties jointly – had permanently disappeared, and the Treaty had thus become impossible to perform."[9]

Hungary likewise argued a fundamental change of circumstances (Article 62 VCLT) *inter alia* due to a change of elements present at the conclusion of the 1977 Treaty which made that the Treaty had been transformed into a "prescription of environmental disaster".[10]

In a fourth argumentative strand, Hungary relied on the obligation of harm prevention and the principle of precaution.[11] At stake was thus the protection of the environment through the traditional means of international law, and related questions such as the scope and legal quality of key concepts of IEL.

2.2. The Gabčíkovo-Nagymaros Case and Environmental Protection in International Law

The protection of the environment in international law as emphasized in Hungary's arguments faces numerous, multidimensional challenges.

First, the environmental problems relied predominantly upon were in the future. There was thus a time gap between the argument and their materialization linked to the question of how to measure future damage, as such tainted with a level of uncertainty.[12] Expert knowledge and scientific studies were accordingly of fundamental relevance. More generally, the rapidly evolving knowledge on the environment and related legal developments posed challenges as regards their incorporation into the rather static/conservative field of general international (treaty) law.

This touched upon more fundamental questions of international (treaty) law: the focus on treaty stability which crystallizes in the pacta sunt servanda rule and 'freezes' law at the moment of a treaty's adoption which stands in an obvious

7 ICJ, *Gabčíkovo-Nagymaros,* judgment, para. 40.

8 Id. para. 94.

9 Id.

10 Id. para. 95.

11 Id. para. 97: "Finally, Hungary argued that subsequently imposed requirements of international law in relation to the protection of the environment precluded performance of the Treaty. The previously existing obligation not to cause substantive damage to the territory of another State had, Hungary claimed, evolved into an erga omnes obligation of prevention of damage pursuant to the "precautionary principle". On this basis, Hungary argued, its termination was "forced by the other party's refusal to suspend work on Variant C."

12 It was mainly prognosis-based, highly complex, relying on scientific evidence. *See e.g.* Counter Memorial of the Republic of Hungary, 5 December 1994.

doi: 10.5553/HYIEL/266627012022010001004

tension to the need to incorporate change/subsequent developments. In this respect, a balance between substance and procedure is at stake: substantive treaty rules and their possible (procedural) adaptation through interpretation or negotiations.

Moreover, while the conflict between Hungary and Slovakia is based on a classical bilateral treaty, from a broader perspective, Hungary's arguments transgress the bilateral/reciprocal dimensions of the dispute and relate to common concerns (environmental protection), *i.e.* community interests. Further questions concern therefore how best to account for these: how well equipped is the traditional toolbox of public international law to deal with environmental protection as a community interest?

3. The Toolbox of General International Law and Environmental Concerns

3.1. Termination and Non-Performance under the Laws of Treaties and State Responsibility as Substantive/Static Tools

The termination grounds of the law of treaties have inherent limitations when applied to environmental concerns. In light of the need to uphold the stability of treaty relations, conditions for successful invocation are very demanding. First, the substantive criteria for applying Articles 61 and 62 VCLT are restrictive and establish a high threshold of reliance.[13] Article 61 VCLT (supervening impossibility of performance) requires the permanent disappearance of an object indispensable for the performance of a treaty.[14] The latter must accordingly become impossible. Article 62 VCLT (fundamental change of circumstances)[15] is framed as a double negative – "may not be invoked [...] unless". It establishes the following demanding conditions: to successfully rely on Article 62, it is *inter alia* necessary that the circumstances which have changed have been unforeseen, an essential basis for the parties' consent to be bound by the treaty, and radically transform the extent of future obligations still to be performed under the treaty. It is worth noting that state practice and jurisprudence illustrate the most limited reliance on the grounds of treaty termination which have been so restrictively

13 Note that while Articles 61 and 62 VCLT are not directly applicable, they codify customary international law.

14 Article 61 VCLT: "1. A party may invoke the impossibility of performing a treaty as a ground for terminating or withdrawing from it if the impossibility results from the permanent disappearance or destruction of an object indispensable for the execution of the treaty. [...]"

15 Article 62 VCLT: "1. A fundamental change of circumstances which has occurred with regard to those existing at the time of the conclusion of a treaty, and which was not foreseen by the parties, may not be invoked as a ground for terminating or withdrawing from the treaty unless: *(a)* the existence of those circumstances constituted an essential basis of the consent of the parties to be bound by the treaty; and *(b)* the effect of the change is radically to transform the extent of obligations still to be performed under the treaty. [...]"

doi: 10.5553/HYIEL/266627012022010001004

formulated that they have – with one exception – never been accepted by an international tribunal.[16]

This high threshold of application will prevent reliance on these provisions for environmental protection considerations in the overwhelming majority of cases. Indeed, the general grounds of treaty termination appear of limited use to account for environmental concerns where dangers have often not sufficiently materialized to meet the demanding conditions required to successfully rely on the law of treaties' termination grounds.

Even in case of a successful reliance on Articles 61 and 62 VCLT, the legal consequences seem ill-suited for environmental protection since they only provide for termination (or suspension). Re-negotiation or an adaptation of the treaty to the new circumstances are not foreseen. This is based on an "all or nothing" approach and a static view, rather than a possible dynamic adaptation of a treaty in light of the changes. It does not sufficiently reflect the necessarily dynamic nature of environmental concerns in the context of inter-state cooperation.

Likewise, reliance on the necessity defense of the law of state responsibility (Article 25 of the ILC Articles on State Responsibility[17])[18] poses problems when it comes to ecological concerns. Also Article 25 is formulated as a double negative ("may not be invoked [...] unless"). It requires that an essential interest of a state be threatened by a grave and imminent peril; in this case, that the non-performance of the treaty be the only way to safeguard that interest, and that the state relying on necessity has not contributed to the situation (of ecological distress). Again, these demanding requirements are reflected in international

16 Christina Binder, 'The VCLT over the Last 50 Years: Developments in the Law of Treaties with a Special Focus on the VCLT's Rules on Treaty Termination', *Austrian Review of International and European Law*, Vol. 24, Issue 1, 2019, pp. 89-120. The exception is Judgment of 16 June 1998, *Case C-162/96, Racke,* ECLI:EU:C:1998:293, where the CJEU accepted the European Communities' reliance on Article 62 VCLT to justify the suspension of a cooperation agreement with the former Yugoslavia because of the ongoing war.

17 ILC, Responsibility of States for Internationally Wrongful Acts, General Assembly resolution 56/83 of 12 December 2001.

18 Article 25 of the ILC Articles on State Responsibility: "1. Necessity may not be invoked by a State as a ground for precluding the wrongfulness of an act not in conformity with an international obligation of that State unless the act: *(a)* is the only way for the State to safeguard an essential interest against a grave and imminent peril; and *(b)* does not seriously impair an essential interest of the State or States towards which the obligation exists, or of the international community as a whole. 2. In any case, necessity may not be invoked by a State as a ground for precluding wrongfulness if: *(a)* the international obligation in question excludes the possibility of invoking necessity; or *(b)* the State has contributed to the situation of necessity." To be precise, at stake in *Gabčíkovo-Nagymaros* was Article 25's "predecessor", Article 33 of the Draft Articles which contains the same elements. The state of necessity codifies customary international law.

doi: 10.5553/HYIEL/266627012022010001004

jurisprudence: reliance on necessity has only exceptionally been accepted by international tribunals.[19]

Moreover, the legal consequences in case of a successful reliance on necessity are problematic from the perspective of enduring environmental protection. On the one hand, successful reliance on necessity as a circumstance precluding wrongfulness only provides for temporary non-performance for the duration of the necessity. After the situation of necessity lapses, performance of the obligation must be resumed (Article 27 of the ILC Articles on State Responsibility).[20] This may pose problems in the context of ecological concerns, which are frequently characterized by indeterminate duration. A state of ecological necessity may thus put a treaty in a limbo. Another challenge is how to deal with compensation for the period of non-performance. The open formulation "without prejudice to [...] the question of compensation for any material loss [...]" of the pertinent Article 27 of the ILC Articles does not provide a clear answer.

In summary, the termination and non-performance grounds of general international law seem of limited use to respond to ecological concerns. They are, with their focus on treaty stability, highly restrictive in substantive terms and also end (or at best suspend) the treaty relationship. The options are thus binary, black and white, all or nothing, continuation in the established treaty framework or termination.

3.2. Evolutionary Interpretation as Procedural/Dynamic Tool

The toolbox of international law also disposes of more dynamic and procedural elements. Most importantly, treaty interpretation may be a means to incorporate subsequent changes in the treaty framework at hand. It may keep a treaty alive in light of rising ecological concerns.[21] Especially evolutionary interpretation [as read into Article 31(1) VCLT] and the principle of systemic integration [Article 31(3)(c) VCLT] are means to keep a treaty up-to-date in light of

19 *See* in particular the cases brought against Argentina before international investment tribunals, where Argentina consistently relied on the necessity defense to shield itself against claims brought by foreign investors in the context of the country's financial crisis 2001-2. For further reference *see* Christina Binder, 'Circumstances Precluding Wrongfulness', *in* Marc Bungenberg *et al.* (eds.), *International Investment Law – A Handbook,* Beck/Hart/Nomos, 2015, pp. 442-480.

20 Article 27 of the ILC Articles on State Responsibility: "Consequences of invoking a circumstance precluding wrongfulness: The invocation of a circumstance precluding wrongfulness in accordance with this chapter is without prejudice to: *(a)* compliance with the obligation in question, if and to the extent that the circumstance precluding wrongfulness no longer exists; *(b)* the question of compensation for any material loss caused by the act in question."

21 Article 31 VCLT (General rule of interpretation): "1. A treaty shall be interpreted in good faith in accordance with the ordinary meaning to be given to the terms of the treaty in their context and in the light of its object and purpose. [...] 3. There shall be taken into account, together with the context: *(a)* any subsequent agreement between the parties regarding the interpretation of the treaty or the application of its provisions; *(b)* any subsequent practice in the application of the treaty which establishes the agreement of the parties regarding its interpretation; *(c)* any relevant rules of international law applicable in the relations between the parties. [...]"

doi: 10.5553/HYIEL/266627012022010001004

subsequent developments, including those in environmental law.[22] I will discuss both in turn.

First, the evolutionary interpretation of a treaty serves to interpret a treaty in light of subsequent changes. More particularly, an evolutionary interpretation enables the parties or a judge to "redefine the meaning of a treaty without altering its nature".[23] While the concept of evolutionary interpretation is inherently vague, it has been frequently employed by international dispute settlement bodies to incorporate evolutionary elements in relation to the protection of the environment or human rights. This, even at the price of overshadowing the original intent of the parties.[24] The framework of the treaty may be broadened, from merely reciprocal obligations to the incorporation of common interests/environmental considerations. The principle of evolutionary interpretation has thus considerable potential for the incorporation of environmental concerns.

As regards developments in IEL, the principle of systemic integration [Article 31(3)(c) VCLT] may likewise prove to be helpful, insofar that it states that "any relevant rules of international law applicable in the relations between the parties" may be taken into account for interpretation. This gives room to refer to established rules of IEL (such as the no-harm rule). There is thus some potential to do justice to subsequent developments for the benefit of the environment.

At the same time, there are also limits to the incorporation of subsequent changes in environmental knowledge and law through treaty interpretation. First, the treaty text must allow for it.[25] The ultimate limit of evolutionary interpretation and systemic integration are always the provisions of the treaty. As stated in *Laguna del Desierto*, interpretation is "a judicial function, whose purpose is to determine the precise meaning of a provision, but which cannot change it."[26] Moreover, for the principle of systemic integration to apply, and to incorporate *e.g.* evolving rules of environmental law, the rules must be "applicable between the parties", *i.e.* they must be part of the established body of international law (as treaty law, customary law or general principles). This may pose limits to the incorporation of principles of IEL (such as the precautionary principle or the concept of sustainable development) which have not been codified in treaty law (or customary international law) yet,[27] and thus cannot be considered as "rules applicable between the parties" in accordance with Article 31(3)(c) VCLT by means of interpretation. At the same time, the clarification of the scope and

22 Another means might also be a reference to subsequent agreements or practice [Article 31(3)(a) and (b) VCLT].

23 *See* for further reference, Christina Binder & Jane Hofbauer, 'The *Pacta Sunt Servanda* Principle or the Limits of Interpretation: The *Gabčíkovo-Nagymaros* Case Revisited', *in* Forlati *et al.* (eds.) 2020, p. 70.

24 Id. p. 74.

25 This was, as likewise acknowledged by the ICJ, quite clearly the case for the 1977 Treaty. *See* below, Section 4.3.

26 *Dispute concerning the Course of the Frontier between BP 62 and Mount Fitzroy. 'Laguna del Desierto' (Argentina v Chile)*, 21 October 1994, 113 ILR p. 1, at 45 (para. 75).

27 Note that the principle of harm prevention, conversely, arguably codifies customary international law and could be relied upon in the context of Article 31(3)(c) VCLT.

doi: 10.5553/HYIEL/266627012022010001004

"hardening" of concepts and principles of IEL is an ongoing process. Ideally, the case law of the ICJ, shall contribute to this development.

3.3. Appreciation

The above demonstrates the difficulty to square the need for environmental protection with the classic framework of general international law and to apply the (restricted) toolbox of international law with the main options of termination/suspension and (limited) dynamic interpretation to address ecological concerns in an existing treaty framework (such as the 1977 Treaty). This evidences the tension between substance and procedure; the oscillation between the end of the treaty relationship (or cooperation in a project) and the latter's dynamic adaptation to subsequent changes.[28] In any case, to make international (treaty) law more responsive to the needs of environmental protection remains demanding. Certain answers are offered, at least initially, by the ICJ in *Gabčíkovo-Nagymaros*.

4. The Gabčíkovo-Nagymaros Judgment and the ICJ's Approach to Environmental Concerns

The *Gabčíkovo-Nagymaros* case is an excellent "show case" and "laboratory" as of how to live up to environmental needs, in particular in hindsight, 25 years after the judgment. There are various dimensions to this, including the recognition and further clarification of environmental concepts; the applicability of the toolbox of international law to ecological concerns; and the viability of further options.

4.1. Environmental Concepts and Values

In *Gabčíkovo-Nagymaros*, the ICJ recognized environmental concepts and ecological values to varying degrees and explicitness. First, positively, *the ICJ referred to the environment as value in itself:*

> "The Court recalls that it has recently had occasion to stress, in the following terms, the great significance that it attaches to the respect for the environment, not only for States but also for mankind: 'the environment is not an abstraction but represents the living space, the quality of life and the very health of human beings, including generations unborn. The existence of the general obligation of States to ensure that activities within their jurisdiction and control respect the environment of other States or of areas beyond national control is now part of the corpus of international law

28 An even further going turn to procedure might be positive – either by deferring to the treaty parties (negotiations, mediation) or, more long term, by means of institutionalization. *See* below Sections 4.3 and 5 for details.

doi: 10.5553/HYIEL/266627012022010001004

relating to the environment.' (Legality of the Threat or Use of Nuclear Weapons, Advisory Opinion, I.C.J. Reports 1996, pp. 241-242, para. 29.)"[29]

Also, though broadly, *the no-harm rule is arguably affirmed by the ICJ*.[30] More indirect is the ICJ's reference to the precautionary principle: the ICJ did not explicitly take up Hungary's reference to the principle but only implicitly recognized it through its reference to vigilance and due diligence.[31] Furthermore, the ICJ referenced the concept of sustainable development,[32] all while leaving open the concept's exact features, scope and legal quality, *i.e.* whether it codifies customary international law.[33] Finally, an obligation of cooperation to manage the risks of environmental damage derived from the principle of good faith may be read into the ICJ's findings in *Gabčíkovo-Nagymaros*.[34]

It becomes clear from the above that the ICJ acknowledged the value and need for environmental protection at least broadly. At the same time, the ICJ's findings remained rather in the abstract, did not define the legal quality and exact scope of concepts such as sustainable development[35] and omitted referencing other instruments for environmental protection, such as the obligation to conduct an environmental impact assessment.

4.2. Non-Performance and Treaty Termination

The *Gabčíkovo-Nagymaros* judgment moreover shed light on the limits of the application of the necessity defense in the law of state responsibility and the termination grounds of the law of treaties.

As far as state responsibility is concerned, the judgment confirmed the high threshold of ecological necessity. While recognizing the environment as an

29 ICJ, *Gabčíkovo-Nagymaros,* judgment, para. 53. At the same time, the ICJ adopted an anthropocentric approach and assessed the environment only in terms of the value the environment has for human beings: "[...] Their implementation thus requires a mutual willingness to discuss in good faith actual and potential environmental risks. It is all the more important to do this because as the Court recalled in its Advisory Opinion on the Legality of the Threat or Use of Nuclear Weapons, 'the environment is not an abstraction but represents the living space, the quality of life and the very health of human beings, including generations unborn' (ICJ Reports 1996, p. 241, para. 29; *see also* paragraph 53 above)." Id. para. 112.

30 *See* Anne Duvic-Paoli: "[...] the principle of prevention applies when two conditions are met relative to 1. The likelihood that harm will occur, and 2. Its magnitude. However, the Court did not engage in a full evaluation of the scientific evidence put to it regarding the quantitative and qualitative effects of the river diversion." Leslie-Anne Duvic-Paoli, 'Vigilance and Prevention: the Contribution of the Gabčíkovo-Nagymaros Judgment', *in* Forlati *et al.* (eds.) 2020, pp. 201, and 206. *See also* Boisson de Chazournes 2020, p. 164.

31 ICJ, *Gabčíkovo-Nagymaros,* judgment, para. 140: "[...] The Court is mindful that, in the field of environmental protection, vigilance and prevention are required on account of the often irreversible character of damage to the environment and of the limitations inherent in the very mechanism of reparation of this type of damage. [...]".

32 Id.; *see also* the reference to precautionary measures in para. 113,

33 Duvic-Paoli 2020, p. 197.

34 ICJ, *Gabčíkovo-Nagymaros,* judgment, paras. 17 and 140.

35 Note that it may be doubted whether such a complex/multidimensional concept such as sustainable development is at all suitable of further definition and sufficiently precise for codification.

doi: 10.5553/HYIEL/266627012022010001004

essential interest, the ICJ did not accept Hungary's ecological concerns as constituting a grave and imminent peril. It found that the ecological concerns were not sufficiently established in 1989, not imminent in the meaning of immediacy; and not the only way to deal with the danger, since Hungary could implement other mitigation measures without abandoning the work on the dam.[36]

In light of the ICJ's findings, the demanding threshold for a state of ecological necessity appears *de facto* impossible to meet. This largely precludes a due consideration of the precautionary principle. According to one commentator:

> "Several aspects of the Court's reasoning here are open to criticism. Although the Court stated that it was not necessary to reach a view as to which party's scientific evidence was better founded, the Court did in fact engage in a relatively detailed assessment of the gravity and imminence of the ecological risks asserted by Hungary. Moreover, in evaluating the evidence the Court effectively required Hungary to establish the alleged risks to a very high degree of scientific certainty, an approach which effectively precluded the operation of the precautionary principle. While this may well have been justified given the exceptional character of the necessity defense, the Court made no attempt to explain the relationship between the law of state responsibility and developing rules of international environmental law."[37]

Along similar lines, the ICJ's findings confirm the narrow framing of the VCLT's grounds of treaty termination (Articles 61 and 62 VCLT), which are ill-equipped to do justice to environmental concerns.[38] First, the ICJ left it open whether a legal regime (here: an economic joint investment which was consistent with environmental protection) was at all within the scope of Article 61 VCLT (impossibility of performance).[39] Moreover, the ICJ stated that as long as there was a means to "safeguard" the object (*i.e.* negotiations as foreseen in the 1977 Treaty), the application of Article 61 VCLT was precluded.[40] On that basis, the ICJ affirmed Article 61 VCLT's most restrictive (substantive) scope.

Similar conclusions may be drawn in relation to Article 62 VCLT. The findings of the ICJ in *Gabčíkovo-Nagymaros* illustrate the provision's most restrictive criteria of application.[41] The ICJ indeed rejected Hungary's reliance on Article 62 VCLT in view of the provision's high threshold (applicability only in

36 ICJ, *Gabčíkovo-Nagymaros*, judgment, paras. 55 and 57. *See* Stephens 2009, p. 178 for further reference.

37 Id.

38 For the sake of completeness, as regards a possible termination in view of the emergence of new requirements for the protection of the environment precluding the performance of the 1977 Treaty, the ICJ noted that neither of the parties had contended that new peremptory norms of environmental law had emerged subsequently to the adoption of the 1977 Treaty, and thus declined to consider it in the context of Article 64 VCLT. ICJ, *Gabčíkovo-Nagymaros*, judgment, para. 112; *see also* Nakamichi 1998, p. 362, for further reference.

39 ICJ, *Gabčíkovo-Nagymaros*, judgment, para. 103.

40 Id.

41 Id. para. 104.

doi: 10.5553/HYIEL/266627012022010001004

exceptional cases), that the change had not radically transformed the extent of the obligations still to be performed to accomplish the project and, also, by reason of the fact that the change was not entirely unforeseen.[42] What is more, once again, the ICJ drew the attention of the parties to procedural means to accommodate change in the framework of the 1977 Treaty (Articles 15, 19 and 20).[43]

In the judgment, the ICJ also hinted on the legal consequences of a successful reliance on Articles 61 and 62 VCLT: termination, which is diametrically opposed to the stability of treaty relations and the *pacta sunt servanda* rule, as a pillar of treaty law. The ICJ affirmed the importance of the *pacta sunt servanda* rule and rejected Hungary's reliance on the VCLT's termination provisions. It thus ultimately confirmed that treaty termination and non-performance grounds of general international law are of limited use to acknowledge environmental concerns.

4.3. *Treaty Interpretation and Negotiations*

As regards the potential of more procedurally focused techniques, *i.e.* treaty interpretation and negotiations, *Gabčíkovo-Nagymaros* offers light and shadow. On the one hand, the case highlights the techniques' potential to acknowledge ecological concerns. Concerning treaty interpretation, the ICJ indeed relied on dynamic considerations and referred to open elements as already provided in the framework of the 1977 Treaty.[44] For example, the ICJ observed that

> "newly developed norms of environmental law are relevant for the implementation of the Treaty and that the parties could, by agreement, incorporate them through the application of Articles 15, 19 and 20 of the Treaty. [...]".[45]

The ICJ likewise held that "[the Treaty was] not static but open to adapt to emerging norms of international law."[46] The broad terms of the 1977 Treaty contributed to achieving this result.[47] In particular, Separate Opinions to the judgment (see *e.g.* Vice-President Weeramantry's Opinion) highlighted the value of dynamic/evolutionary interpretation for incorporation of environmental concerns, with special reference to the long-term nature of the dam-project:

42 Id.

43 Id.

44 *See also* the Separate Opinion by Judge Bedjaoui: "Article 15, 19 and 20 of the 1977 Treaty are fortunately drafted in extremely vague terms (in them, reference is made to 'protection' – without any further qualification – of water, nature or fishing). In the absence of any other specification, respecting the autonomy of will implies precisely that provisions of this kind are interpreted in an evolutionary manner, in other words, taking account of the criteria adopted by the general law prevailing in each period considered." ICJ, *Gabčíkovo-Nagymaros,* judgment, Separate Opinion of Judge Bedjaoui, para. 7.

45 ICJ, *Gabčíkovo-Nagymaros,* judgment, para. 112.

46 Id.

47 Id. para. 140. *See* generally Laura Pineschi, 'Introduction to Part 2', *in* Forlati *et al.* (eds.) 2020, p. 45.

doi: 10.5553/HYIEL/266627012022010001004

> "If the Treaty was to operate for decades into the future, it could not operate on the basis of environmental norms as though they were frozen in time when the Treaty was entered into. This inter-temporal aspect of the present case is of importance to all treaties dealing with projects impacting on the environment [...] Environmental concerns are life and continuing concern whenever the project under which they arise may have been inaugurated."[48]

While broadly, *Gabčíkovo-Nagymaros* thus positively acknowledged the need to go with the dynamism in the development of IEL and knowledge.[49]

At the same time, the case also pointed to the limits of interpretation as means to read subsequent developments in IEL and knowledge into a treaty. By maintaining that there was no such thing as the approximate application of a treaty,[50] the ICJ affirmed that any interpretation had to remain within the treaty text.[51] Indeed, a further-reaching interpretation would constitute a revision and require the mutual consent of both parties.[52]

Moreover, the ICJ did not venture far in the interpretation of the 1977 Treaty's provisions.[53] Rather, the Court referred quite open-endedly to procedural obligations such as consultations and negotiations to incorporate evolving environmental norms. According to the ICJ,

> "[w]hat is required in the present case by the rule *pacta sunt servanda,* as reflected in Article 26 of the Vienna Convention of 1969 on the Law of Treaties, is that the Parties find an agreed solution within the co-operative context of the Treaty. [...]".[54]

48 Separate Opinion of Vice-President Weeramantry, p. 88 at .113-4

49 *See e.g.* Stephens 2009, pp. 186 *et seq.* "[...] Most important, however, were the Court's pronouncements on the impact of recent environmental norms upon an existing treaty regime. The judgment asserts the legitimacy of environmental concerns influencing the operation of a treaty concluded in the late 1970s, which did not have a strong focus on environmental protection. The Court effectively held that the parties could and should update this treaty framework in order to bring the joint dam project into conformity with contemporary international environmental standards."

50 The principle of approximate application, as put forward by Slovakia in the *Gabčíkovo-Nagymaros* case, relates back to the Separate Opinion of Sir Hersch Lauterpacht in *Admissibility of Hearings of Prisoners in South West Africa* who maintained: "It is a sound principle of law that whenever a legal instrument of continuing validity cannot be applied literally [...] it must [...] be applied in a way approximating most closely to its primary object. To do that is to give effect to the instrument - not to change it." ICJ, *Admissibility of Hearing of Prisoners in South West Africa*, Advisory Opinion of 1 June 1956, Separate Opinion of Sir Hersch Lauterpacht, ICJ Reports 1956, p. 46. *See* for details Binder & Hofbauer 2020, pp. 65 *et seq.*

51 In relation to Slovakia's variant 'C', the ICJ stated: "It is not necessary for the Court to determine whether there is a principle of international law or general principle of law of "approximate application" because, even if such a principle existed, it could by definition only be employed within the limits of the treaty in question. [...]" ICJ, *Gabčíkovo-Nagymaros,* judgment, para. 76.

52 Binder & Hofbauer 2020, p. 68.

53 Only once, the ICJ refers to third party involvement in view of the parties' disagreement. ICJ, *Gabčíkovo-Nagymaros,* judgment, para. 113.

54 Id. para. 142.

doi: 10.5553/HYIEL/266627012022010001004

This is reiterated in the operative part of the judgment, where the ICJ called on the parties to "negotiate in good faith" to "ensure the achievement of the objectives of the [1977 Treaty]" in light of the situation at hand.[55] The ICJ thus gave limited indications to the parties which are left "on their own" and fell short of exploring the full potential of evolutionary interpretation, as it could have done by drawing on the concept of sustainable development or Article 31(3)(c) VCLT, therewith guiding the parties in their application of the 1977 Treaty.

4.4. *Appreciation*

Overall, the *Gabčíkovo-Nagymaros* case is a realistic reflection of how environmental concerns were accounted for at the end of the last century, as concerns the 'classic' instruments of general international law (as discussed in Section 2). It points to insufficiencies; and shows, most importantly, the difficulties of applying the necessity defense and the grounds of treaty termination (Articles 61 and 62 VCLT). At the same time while the ICJ's push for negotiations between the parties rightly introduced a dynamic and procedural element, a somewhat further reaching guidance as to how negotiations should be conducted might have prevented the present stalemate in *Gabčíkovo-Nagymaros* which is still pending. Thus, the flexibility of a strong reliance on procedural means – in the absence of further guidance by the ICJ – proved to be a two-edged sword: promising to account for the inherent dynamism in (international) environmental law and knowledge, challenging when parties are unable to agree on how to proceed.

Also more generally, the *Gabčíkovo-Nagymaros* case throws light on the limitations of public international law in responding to ecological concerns. First, as a contentious case, it depended on party submissions. The need for environmental protection, common interests, were reflected upon only insofar as they coincided with the interests of a party to the dispute (here, Hungary's).[56] This points to the limits of environmental protection as "common interest" in these constellations. The protection of the environment in international law is even more demanding when it comes to "true" global concerns, such as climate change where the gap between reciprocal/*inter partes* and common interests increases.

Another challenge for the ICJ were its inherent institutional limitations, its lack of specialization/expertise in environmental matters and the necessary

55 Id. para. 155.

56 *See* for further reference Pineschi, 2020, pp. 54 *et seq.*; *see* generally Jutta Brunnée, 'International Environmental Law and Community Interests Procedural Aspects', *in* Eyal Benvenisti & Georg Nolte (eds.), *Community Interests Across International Law*, Oxford University Press, Oxford, 2018, p. 151; Jutta Brunnée, *Procedure and Substance in International Environmental Law*, The Hague Academy of International Law, Brill-Nijhoff 2020.

doi: 10.5553/HYIEL/266627012022010001004

reliance on outside independent scientific assessment.[57] A related issue is the difficulty of how to assess future environmental harm.[58]

In any case, *Gabčíkovo-Nagymaros*, as one of the first "true environmental cases" considered by the ICJ, was a stepping-stone for future developments in environmental matters. This calls for a broader perspective.

5. The Gabčíkovo-Nagymaros Case in Perspective

In retrospect, the *Gabčíkovo-Nagymaros* case may be considered from three perspectives on its 25th anniversary: a case-specific, an institutional/ICJ perspective and through the lens of subsequent case law/the development of environmental standards.

Firstly, *Gabčíkovo-Nagymaros* referred to broader questions of procedure versus substance, which is particularly relevant in IEL.[59] Procedures are tools to dynamically incorporate subsequent developments, increases in knowledge and environmental concerns. They are also important to flexibly respond to complex (future) situations and environmental problems where it may be difficult to be overly concrete in terms of substantive obligations. Still, too little guidance/substance and an exclusive reliance on procedures (negotiations) may also lead to a stalemate as has been the case in the *Gabčíkovo-Nagymaros* dispute so far. In view of the parties' stalemate, further proposals to join procedure and substance have been made. Concretely, a push to institutionalization has been argued for in academic literature in relation to the dispute.[60] It was held, that a Commission, such as the Danube Commission, could (have been) established to regulate and deal with contested environmental issues. Drawing on past experiences, factors for the success of such Commissions included the *(i)* independent agency of technical experts (not groups of government agents); *(ii)* a mandate of ongoing investigation, monitoring and dispute resolution; and *(iii)* a function as a central and ongoing coordinating institution.[61] In hindsight, such an institutionalized solution may have supported the parties (Hungary and Slovakia) in reaching an

57 *See* Pineschi 2020, pp. 55 *et seq.*; *see also* McGarry 2020, p. 227: "In Gabčíkovo-Nagymaros [...] preparations were made for a site visit by the Court between the first and second rounds of oral proceedings, in which setting the Court received 'technical explanations given by the representatives who had been designated for the purpose by the parties [...] Yet despite adding this site visit to what [the ICJ] viewed as an impressive amount of scientific evidence placed on record by the parties [...] the Court referenced this evidence only briefly in its judgment."

58 *See* generally UN, Gaps in international environmental law and environment-related instruments: towards a global pact for the environment, Report of the Secretary-General, A/73/419, 30 November 2018, p. 38: "In *Gabčíkovo-Nagymaros*, the International Court of Justice faced the difficult task of weighing the rights of parties under circumstances where the likelihood and extent of environmental harm remained unknown. This highlighted the paucity of rules or principles addressing unrealized harm, which is a problematic *status quo* in the light of the often-significant gap in time between acts and their effects on the environment." *See also* Nakamachi 1998, p. 364.

59 Brunnée 2018, p. 175.

60 Nakamachi 1998, pp. 366 *et seq.*

61 Id. pp. 370 *et seq.*

doi: 10.5553/HYIEL/266627012022010001004

agreement on the common dam project and the question of how to manage arising environmental concerns. More generally speaking, institutionalization through the establishment of joint Commissions may help address the usually technically and politically sensitive problems in projects with lasting environmental implications, such as the one at hand.

Secondly, from the *ICJ perspective* and in light of the ICJ's institutional limitations when dealing with complex environmental matters, several attempts to increase the ICJ's environmental expertise have been made. This seems even more important since an increasing number of cases brought before the Court concern environmental issues.[62] While the environmental chamber of the ICJ has never taken up its work and environmentally specialized judges were considered but dismissed as impractical,[63] especially subsequent case-law has shown the ICJ's progress in dealing with environmental expertise in complex scientific matters.[64] The ICJ has streamlined and professionalized its reliance on experts. This is a welcome development since well-chosen experts and considered reliance on expert opinion may counterbalance the ICJ's institutional deficits in environmental cases. Conversely, an issue which remains to be resolved and which the Court has considered only marginally so far, is the question of compensation/damage calculation in cases of environmental degradation/pollution.[65]

Thirdly, and more broadly speaking, the ICJ's approach to environmental problems has developed over the past 25 years. True, subsequent cases have not dealt as clearly with the traditional toolbox of international law and their application to environmental problems, as *Gabčíkovo-Nagymaros*. However, techniques (such as treaty interpretation) have been applied and the ICJ has further clarified concepts and principles of IEL. For example, the obligation to conduct an environmental impact assessment as a customary law obligation is affirmed in *Pulp Mills* (2010).[66] In *Whaling in the Antarctic* (2014),[67] an obligation

62 ICJ, *Pulp Mills on the River Uruguay (Argentina v Uruguay)*, judgment, ICJ Reports 2010; ICJ, *Certain Activities carried out by Nicaragua in the Border Area (Costa Rica v Nicaragua) and Construction of a Road in Costa Rica along the San Juan River (Nicaragua v Costa Rica)*, judgment, ICJ Reports 2015, p. 665; ICJ, *Whaling in the Antarctic (Australia v Japan, New Zealand intervening)*, judgment, ICJ Reports 2014, p. 226. *See also* the (albeit discontinued) *Pesticides* case which deals with transboundary environmental harm, including the impact on indigenous peoples. ICJ, *Case Concerning Aerial Herbicide Spraying (Ecuador v Colombia)*, Order of 13 September 2013, ICJ Reports 2013, p. 278.

63 *See* Cymie R. Payne, 'Judicial Development', *in* Lavanya Rajamani & Jacqueline Peel (eds.), *The Oxford Handbook of International Environmental Law*, 2nd edition, Oxford University Press, Oxford, 2020, p. 454; *see also* generally Brunnee 2018, p. 167.

64 *See e.g. Whaling in the Antarctic*, 2014; *see also Certain Activities and Construction of a Road*, 2015; *see* however also the shortcomings noted in the UN Report 2018, p. 38.

65 *See* in particular, ICJ, *Certain Activities carried out by Nicaragua in the Border Area (Costa Rica v Nicaragua)* on Compensation owed by Nicaragua to Costa Rica of 2 February 2018, ICJ General List No 150; *see also* ICJ, *Armed Activities on the Territory of the Congo (Democratic Republic of the Congo v. Uganda)*, judgment, ICJ Reports 2005, p. 168. *See* generally Jason Rudall, *Compensation for Environmental Damage under International Law*, Routledge, 2020, p. 5.

66 ICJ, *Pulp Mills*, judgment.

67 ICJ, *Whaling in the Antarctic*, judgment.

doi: 10.5553/HYIEL/266627012022010001004

to cooperate in good faith was confirmed[68] (although the preservation of the ecosystem as a general interest of the international community as a whole was not yet established).[69] The issue of compensation/damages calculation in case of environmental degradation, not at stake in *Gabčíkovo-Nagymaros*, has been an issue in *Armed Activities on the Territory of the Congo* (2005)[70] and in *Certain Activities carried out by Nicaragua in the Border Area* (2018).[71]

In summary, we can conclude that environmental matters are increasingly brought before the ICJ whose case law is in ongoing evolution. The ICJ is indeed uniquely placed to develop international law on the matter.[72] It thus seems safe to maintain that while *Gabčíkovo-Nagymaros* is a starting point, it is not the end of the story. Over the past 25 years, important developments have taken place, reflecting an incremental, albeit not revolutionary change in environmental protection.[73] Therein, *Gabčíkovo-Nagymaros* remains a landmark. This is also demonstrated by the references to this case made by other international tribunals. Especially the IACtHR has extensively referred to the ICJ's case law, including to *Gabčíkovo-Nagymaros*, in its Advisory Opinion on the Environment and Human Rights.[74] So, the toolbox of international law, while limited, is in ongoing development with more and more voices joining and adding to the chorus.

68 *See* generally Akiho Shibata, 'Good faith', *in* Lavanya Rajamani & Jacqueline Peel (eds.), *The Oxford Handbook of International Environmental Law*, 2nd edition, Oxford University Press, Oxford, 2020, pp. 376 *et seq.*

69 ICJ, *Whaling in the Antarctic*, judgment. Moreover, it was held that the *Whaling* case signalled an acceptance of standing in case of *erga omnes partes* obligations as environmental concerns. For further reference, *see* Christian J. Tams, 'Roads Not Taken, Opportunities Missed: Procedural and Jurisdictional Questions Sidestepped in the Whaling Judgment', *in* Malgosia Fitzmaurice & Dai Tamada (eds.), *Whaling in the Antarctic: Significance and Implications of the ICJ Judgment*, Brill, 2016, pp. 210-211; Brunnée 2020, pp. 139 *et seq.*

70 ICJ, *Armed Activities on the Territory of the Congo*, judgment.

71 ICJ, *Certain Activities and Construction of a Road*, compensation. *See* generally Payne 2020, pp. 457 *et seq.*; Rudall 2020, pp. 25 *et seq.*

72 The ICJ is indeed in a unique position to consider environmental protection with an authoritative voice. *See* Pineschi 2020. *See also* the criticism voiced in the Joint Dissenting Opinion of Judges Al-Khasawneh and Simma as regards the insufficient use of experts in *Pulp Mills*, ICJ Reports 2010, p. 108, para. 13: "[The use of scientific experts] would [...] have given the Court the opportunity of combining the rigour of the scientific community with the requirements of the courtroom – a blend which is indispensable for the application of the international rules for the protection of the environment and for other disputes concerning scientific evidence."

73 Payne 2020, p. 456.

74 IACtHR, *The Environment and Human Rights*, Advisory Opinion No 23/17 of 15 November 2017.

doi: 10.5553/HYIEL/266627012022010001004

The Gabčíkovo-Nagymaros Judgment after a Quarter Century

Transcending Jurisdictions to Advance Environmental Law

Alexandra R. Harrington[*]

Abstract

In 1997, the ICJ issued its judgment in the Gabčíkovo-Nagymaros case. Accompanied by the separate opinion issued by Judge Weeramantry, the Gabčíkovo-Nagymaros decision provided clarifications regarding treaty interpretation questions that are foundational to the ways in which international law is applied. Beyond this, however, the Gabčíkovo-Nagymaros decision has assumed a significant place in the development of environmental law at the international, regional and national levels. This article examines the Gabčíkovo-Nagymaros decision in light of the recent line of environmental rights cases, including those based in the emerging field of climate justice, in order to trace the ways in which the decision has transcended the limitations of time and geography to become a bedrock of environmental law. The article addresses the ways in which the Gabčíkovo-Nagymaros decision has transcended the context of a transboundary water rights claim between Hungary and Slovakia to become an element of emerging cases across the world. To this end, the article chronicles the ways in which the essential elements of the Gabčíkovo-Nagymaros decision are translated into and expanded by cases at the regional level and the national level. Ultimately, the article connects the nuanced fashion in which the Gabčíkovo-Nagymaros decision has grown to transcend the ICJ's jurisdiction in the case and become a truly internationalized base for the development of environmental laws and environmental rights. Finally, the conclusion of the article notes the potential for the Gabčíkovo-Nagymaros decision to continue transcending its initial application to a new generation of environmental concerns.

Keywords: sustainable development, transboundary consultation, environmental impact assessment, climate litigation, Gabčíkovo-Nagymaros judgment.

1. Introduction

In 1997, the ICJ issued its judgment in the *Gabčíkovo-Nagymaros* case. Accompanied by the separate opinion issued by Judge Weeramantry, the

* Alexandra R. Harrington: lecturer in law (environment), Lancaster University Law School.

doi: 10.5553/HYIEL/266627012022010001005

Gabčíkovo-Nagymaros decision provided clarifications regarding treaty interpretation questions that are foundational to the ways in which international law is applied. Beyond this, however, the *Gabčíkovo-Nagymaros* decision has assumed a significant place in the development of environmental law at the international, regional and national levels. Issued a mere five years after the international community came together to adopt the Rio Declaration alongside the UN Framework Convention on Climate Change, the UN Convention on Biological Diversity, and the UN Convention to Combat Desertification, the *Gabčíkovo-Nagymaros* decision was among the first in which the ICJ was asked to address environmental harms and impacts. In the quarter century that followed, international constructs of environmental law, environmental rights, and climate change related harms have grown exponentially and yet the *Gabčíkovo-Nagymaros* case continues to form the foundation upon which many of these concepts have been constructed.

This article examines the *Gabčíkovo-Nagymaros* decision in light of the recent line of environmental rights cases, including those based in the emerging field of climate justice, in order to trace the ways in which the decision has transcended the limitations of time and geography to become a bedrock of environmental law. The article begins by highlighting the critical elements of the *Gabčíkovo-Nagymaros* decision, including Judge Weeramantry's opinion, from the perspective of environmental law and rights. This discussion illuminates the ways in which the ICJ includes environmental impacts and harms as within the potential ambit of the doctrine of necessity in the state responsibility context.

Although there was ultimately a finding against Hungary's invocation of the doctrine based on the facts at issue, the explanation of environmental harms as sufficient in other circumstances was an important step for solidifying the place of environmental law as part of international law *per se*. The issue of transboundary harm and environmental damage as a continuous construct which requires ongoing consultation and information sharing between states is also discussed for its profound impact on how states are required to interact on environmental issues. Further, it describes the role of Judge Weeramantry's separate opinion as creating support for the evolution of environmental principles such as the principle of continuing environmental impact assessment, the principle of prevention, the principle of sustainable development, and the precautionary principle.

Building upon these discussions, the article then addresses the ways in which the *Gabčíkovo-Nagymaros* decision has transcended the context of a transboundary water rights claim between Hungary and Slovakia to become an element of emerging cases across the world. To do this, the article chronicles the ways in which the essential elements of the *Gabčíkovo-Nagymaros* decision are translated into and expanded by cases at the regional level and the national level. At the regional level, it focuses on the *Marangopoulos Foundation for Human Rights v Greece* decision from the European Committee of Social Rights, the *Advisory Opinion on the Right to a Healthy Environment* from the IACtHR, and the *Duarte Agostinho & Others v Portugal et al.* complaint currently before the ECtHR. These cases demonstrate the ways in which regional law has developed around many

doi: 10.5553/HYIEL/266627012022010001005

tenets from *Gabčíkovo-Nagymaros*, as well as the ways in which these tenets might be expanded in the future. At the national level, the article focuses on the *Urgenda Foundation v The Netherlands* case from the Dutch Supreme Court, the *Friends of the Irish Environment v Government of Ireland* case from the Irish Supreme Court, and the *Lamu et al. v Kenya* case from the Kenyan National Environmental Tribunal. These cases cut across issues and geography to demonstrate the evolution of *Gabčíkovo-Nagymaros* tenets through national court systems.

Following these discussions, the article connects the nuanced fashion in which the *Gabčíkovo-Nagymaros* decision has grown to transcend the ICJ's jurisdiction in the case and become a truly internationalized base for the development of environmental laws and environmental rights development. It notes the evolution of law regarding transboundary harm, the role of environmental law and rights, and the incorporation of the precautionary principle, the principle of prevention, the principle of sustainable development, and the principle of environmental impact assessment over the past quarter century. Finally, the conclusion of the article notes the potential for the *Gabčíkovo-Nagymaros* decision to continue transcending its initial application to a new generation of environmental concerns.

2. Critical Background from Gabčíkovo-Nagymaros

At a time when the world is faced with the increasingly urgent climate crisis, the short-term and long-term impacts of the COVID-19 pandemic, and the uncertainty caused by Russian actions in Ukraine, the *Gabčíkovo-Nagymaros* case serves a critical role for interpreting the future of international, regional and national law. Indeed, 25 years ago the ICJ gave the international community a decision – and separate opinion by Judge Weeramantry – which still serves as a vital guide for treaty interpretation and contractual agreements as well as state obligations to each other and the importance of environmental concerns. The articles throughout this volume of the Hungarian Yearbook of International Law and European Law pay *homage* to the many avenues in which the *Gabčíkovo-Nagymaros* case has provided key precedents. In this section, the focus will be largely on the elements of the case linked to environmental concerns, however the fulsome nature of the decision must be emphasized.

One of the essential arguments offered to justify the Hungarian actions was that of necessity.[1] In this context, the assertion was that the abrogation of the 1977 Treaty upon which the project was predicated was necessary in light of concerns regarding the impacts of the dam on the natural environment in the region.[2] From the outset, the ICJ reiterated the nature of the state of necessity as a customary international law principle that does not negate the wrongfulness of certain conduct at the state level but rather functions as an acceptable excuse for

1 ICJ, *Case concerning the Gabčíkovo-Nagymaros Project (Hungary v Slovakia)*, judgment, ICJ Reports 1997, p. 7.

2 Id. paras. 40-58.

doi: 10.5553/HYIEL/266627012022010001005

this conduct in light of exceptional circumstances.[3] In recognizing the customary elements of the necessity defense, the ICJ drew support from the work of the International Law Commission's (ILC) suggested requirements that govern the invocation of necessity as set out in Article 25 of the statement in Responsibility of States for Intentionally Wrongful Acts:

> "1 Necessity may not be invoked by a state as a ground for precluding the wrongfulness of an act not in conformity with an international obligation of that state unless the act: (*a*) is the only way for the state to safeguard an essential interest against a grave and imminent peril; and (*b*) does not seriously impair an essential interest of the state or states towards which the obligation exists, or of the international community as a whole.
>
> 2 In any case, necessity may not be invoked by a state as a ground for precluding wrongfulness if: (*a*) the international obligation in question excludes the possibility of invoking necessity; or (*b*) the state has contributed to the situation of necessity."[4]

While addressing these claims, the ICJ established that it had "no difficulty in acknowledging that the concerns expressed by Hungary for its natural environment in the region affected [...] related to an 'essential interest'" within the parameters of the necessity test elaborated by the ILC and adopted by ICJ jurisprudence.[5] Indeed, the ICJ highlighted and agreed with the ILC's articulation that "ecological preservation of all or some of [the] territory [of a state]" was an accepted aspect of necessity and that environmental concerns were increasing in legal spheres in the decades prior to *Gabčíkovo-Nagymaros*.[6] Further, the ICJ reiterated the statements of the advisory opinion on the *Legality of the Threat or Use of Nuclear Weapons* regarding "the great significance that it attaches to respect for the environment, not only for the states but also for the whole of mankind."[7] These considerations were not deemed to be sufficient in the abstract or with only partial information available to the state invoking necessity. However, the ICJ held that the ways in which Hungary asserted the potential negative impacts of the project as implemented were insufficiently asserted in terms of gravity and temporality at the time they were invoked in 1989.[8]

The ICJ's opinion next addressed the legality of various actions and remedial efforts undertaken by then-Czechoslovakia, including the contested Variant 'C' in the damming process, in relation to the Danube as an international waterway.[9] Set against this backdrop, the ICJ found that

3 Id. para. 51.
4 Id.
5 Id. para. 53.
6 Id.
7 Id.
8 Id. para. 54.
9 Id. para. 78.

doi: 10.5553/HYIEL/266627012022010001005

> "the suspension and withdrawal of that consent constituted a violation of Hungary's legal obligations, demonstrating, as it did, the refusal by Hungary of joint operation; but that cannot mean that Hungary forfeited its basic right to an equitable and reasonable sharing of the resources of an international watercourse."[10]

It went on to provide that the shared and equitable nature of watercourses is applicable to non-navigable waterways in the international context as well, thus further extending the transboundary concept of rights.[11] Using this understanding, the ICJ found that the then-state of Czechoslovakia had overreached the ability to claim proportionality in its responses to the Hungarian abrogation of the 1977 Treaty.[12]

Ultimately, the ICJ recognized the need for the States Parties to continue their negotiations regarding the implementation of the project and the parameters this should include as appropriate for establishing the environmental elements of project and potential negative impacts resulting from it.[13] As the ICJ explained:

> "Throughout the ages, mankind has, for economic and other reasons, constantly interfered with nature. In the past, this was often done without consideration of the effects upon the environment. Owing to new scientific insights and to a growing awareness of the risks for mankind – for present and future generations – of pursuit of such interventions at an unconsidered and unabated pace, new norms and standards have been developed, set forth in a great number of instruments during the last two decades. Such new norms have to be taken into consideration, and such new standards given proper weight, not only when States contemplate new activities but also when continuing with activities begun in the past. This need to reconcile economic development with protection of the environment is aptly expressed in the concept of sustainable development. For the purposes of the present case, this means that the Parties together should look afresh at the effects on the environment of the operation of the Gabčíkovo power plant. In particular they must find a satisfactory solution for the volume of water to be released into the old bed of the Danube and into the side-arms on both sides of the river."[14]

10 Id.

11 Id. para. 85; Mara Tignino & Christian Brethaut, 'The role of international case law in implementing the obligation not to cause significant harm', *International Environmental Agreements: Politics, Law and Economics*, Vol. 20, 2020, p. 639; Ibrahim Kaya, 'Implications of the Danube River Dispute on International Environmental Law', *Review of International Law and Politics*, Vol. 4, Issue 15, 2008, p. 97.

12 ICJ, *Gabčíkovo-Nagymaros*, judgment, para. 85.

13 Id. paras. 140-142; *see also* Nicolas Bremer, 'Post-environmental Impact Assessment Monitoring of Measures or Activities with Significant Transboundary Impact: An Assessment of Customary International Law', *Review of European, Comparative & International Environmental Law,* Vol. 26, Issue 1, 2017, p. 88.

14 ICJ, *Gabčíkovo-Nagymaros*, judgment, para. 140.

doi: 10.5553/HYIEL/266627012022010001005

In this way, the *Gabčíkovo-Nagymaros* can be seen as representing an endorsement of the need for meaningful consultations and discussions between states in which the current and future state of the environment and associated entities is at the heart of the determination. Thus, the case is a statement regarding the need to balance the interests of sovereignty with the interests of the environment as an entity that transcends boundaries and sovereignty.

Further to the majority opinion, then-Vice-President Weeramantry provided an impactful and stirring separate opinion that is centered on environmental and sustainability concerns raised in the case.[15] In this opinion, Judge Weeramantry discussed and provided the basis for entrenchment of the principle of sustainable development and, in his words, "the principle of continuing environmental impact assessment."[16] In articulating sustainable development as a legal principle, Judge Weeramantry envisioned a more robust legal ground for the incorporation of sustainable development in international law than the majority opinion, which considered it to be a "mere concept."[17] Indeed, Judge Weeramantry noted that this was the first case in which the ICJ was presented with assertions grounded in sustainable development tenets and highlighted the need for additional pronouncements because it would become an increasingly important legal and policy tool moving forward.[18] To emphasize this point, Judge Weeramantry detailed the origins of sustainable development in law and practice as well as the ways in which it increasingly developed into an accepted element of international treaty regimes and customary practice.[19]

As noted in the separate opinion, Judge Weeramantry had previously advocated for the idea of the principle of continuing environmental impact assessment in the nuclear testing and weapons cases.[20] In *Gabčíkovo-Nagymaros*, Judge Weeramantry broadened the scope of his articulated view of the principle to

> "clarify further the scope and extent of the environmental impact principle in the sense that environmental impact assessment means not merely an assessment prior to the commencement of the project, but a continuing assessment and evaluation as long as the project is in operation. This follows from the fact that EIA is a dynamic principle and is not confined to a pre-project evaluation of possible environmental consequences. As long as a project of some magnitude is in operation, EIA must continue, for every such project can have unexpected consequences; and considerations of prudence would point to the need for continuous monitoring. The greater the size and scope of the project, the greater is the need for a continuous monitoring of its effects, for EIA before the scheme can never be expected, in a matter so

15 Kaya 2008.
16 ICJ, *Gabčíkovo-Nagymaros*, judgment, para. 88.
17 Id. para. 85.
18 Id.
19 Id. paras. 85-95.
20 Id. para. 107.

Hungarian Yearbook of International Law and European Law 2022 (10) 1
doi: 10.5553/HYIEL/266627012022010001005

> complex as the environment, to anticipate every possible environmental danger."[21]

In tracing the evolution of the principle, Judge Weeramantry emphasized that the initial underpinnings began with the *Trail Smelter* case holdings regarding continuous monitoring and grew to include all phases of project development and implementation.[22] To achieve these goals and implement the *Gabčíkovo-Nagymaros* judgment, the separate opinion stresses the importance of national court systems to the implementation process.[23]

Thus, the ICJ's main decision in *Gabčíkovo-Nagymaros* and the separate opinion of Judge Weeramantry provide the platform for the protection of the environmental resources of both Hungary and Slovakia. At the same time, the precedent established by *Gabčíkovo-Nagymaros* was far deeper and broader than the dam, the river or the two states involved, as it provided international law with an understanding of how necessity can be successfully invoked with respect to environmental concerns and exigencies. Additionally, Judge Weeramantry's pronouncements in the separate opinions have established the groundwork for entrenching sustainable development, the precautionary principle, the principle of prevention and the use of environmental impact assessments as stable requirements of international law and practice.

3. Evolution of National and Regional Case Law

After 25 years, the lessons of the *Gabčíkovo-Nagymaros* case have truly become entrenched in the understanding of environmental issues and their evolution at the international, regional and national levels. Indeed, as the growth of environmentally based court challenges has accelerated across all levels of jurisprudence, the holdings and lessons of *Gabčíkovo-Nagymaros* continue to inform litigants and court systems as they seek to address complex claims which have bearing on current and future generations around the world.

The below discussion examines the ways in which various courts have applied the tenets of *Gabčíkovo-Nagymaros* in different jurisdictions, claims and allegations of harms. While not exhaustive of the entirety of case law which has been influenced by *Gabčíkovo-Nagymaros*, the cases discussed are typically prominent and have in many instances been used by other courts as sources of guidance and support in addressing similar claims. Perhaps the most obvious example of this is the *Urgenda Foundation v The Netherlands* case from the Dutch Supreme Court, which, while decided less than three years ago, has generated a spate of similar claims in countries around the globe. These cases demonstrate the diversity of venues in which *Gabčíkovo-Nagymaros* continues to serve as a tireless and persuasive source in name and in spirit. Not all of the cases below are as well known, yet the decision to include them was purposeful in that these are

21 Id.

22 Id. paras. 107-108.

23 Id. para. 113.

doi: 10.5553/HYIEL/266627012022010001005

typically cases from developing states that often do not attract as much global legal attention and yet are the site of significant environmental law claims.

3.1. *Regional Cases*

3.1.1. *Marangopoulos Foundation for Human Rights v Greece*

In 2007, the European Committee of Social Rights issued its decision on the merits in the *Marangopoulos Foundation for Human Rights v Greece* complaint.[24] The core questions raised by the complaint related to the Greek State's continued and expanded allowance of lignite mining within its territory as not properly regulated for potential environmental harms as well as public health threats.[25] The Committee applied international harm standards to address the issues raised in terms of environmental harms, particularly endorsing the findings of the ILC on the existence and gravity of state breeches of international obligations.[26]

Similar to the idea of continuing obligations in the fashioning of environmental standards and oversight from *Gabčíkovo-Nagymaros*, the Committee emphasized that

> "the Charter is a living instrument, whose purpose is to protect rights not merely theoretically but also in fact [...] [The Committee] therefore interprets the rights and freedoms set out in the Charter in the light of current conditions."[27]

Indeed, the Committee went further by seizing the opportunity to provide its opinion on the idea of interlinkages between human rights and environmental rights, especially the emerging concept of the right to a health environment.[28] This is an area of continued growth over the past 25 years, further allowing the *Gabčíkovo-Nagymaros* tenets to be expanded into cross-cutting realms featuring environmental issues.

The analysis necessary here merged considerations of health impacts from pollution and environmental damage associated with lignite mining in Greece and neighboring areas.[29] In this regard, the Committee stressed that

> "overcoming pollution is an objective that can only be achieved gradually. Nevertheless, States Party to the ECHR must strive to attain this objective within a reasonable time, by showing measurable progress and making best possible use of the resources at their disposal."[30]

24 ECSR, *Marangopoulos Foundation for Human Rights v Greece*, Complaint No. 30/2005 (7 June 2007).
25 Id. para. 1.
26 Id. para. 193.
27 Id. para. 194.
28 Id. paras. 195-196.
29 Id. paras. 197-204.
30 Id. para. 204.

Hungarian Yearbook of International Law and European Law 2022 (10) 1
doi: 10.5553/HYIEL/266627012022010001005

In conducting its analysis, the Committee noted that there were efforts to ensure some level of public participation, or at the very least information, regarding plans for lignite mining activities, however these measures were insufficient in terms of creating legally meaningful efforts at fulfilling national, EU and international law requirements.[31] As a result, the Committee determined that Greece was in violation of its obligations under the ECHR, as well as other nationally and internationally accepted legal norms.[32]

The *Marangopoulos Foundation* complaint created a legal space in which to expand the parameters of rights and obligations under the ECHR, particularly in terms of the expansion of environmental rights. Concomitantly, this extended the obligations of the state as well as the rights expectations of its citizens. In recognizing this, the Committee was then able to address questions of public participation in environmental impact and similar forms of assessment. That the process used in this instance was insufficient was not as impactful to the understanding of how far *Gabčíkovo-Nagymaros*'s effects can be seen, as was the fact that the Committee assumed the requirement of public participation based on appropriate information. Given the emerging nature of the nexus between health and environmental rights, this is a critical way in which *Gabčíkovo-Nagymaros* has transcended the context of water and associated biological diversity concerns.

3.1.2. *Advisory Opinion on the Environment and Human Rights*

The IACtHR had the occasion to express its findings on the parameters of the environment and human rights under various human rights treaties adopted under the auspices of the Organization of American States in 2017.[33] These findings were the result of a request for an advisory opinion on the topic by Colombia.[34] Given the IACtHR's jurisdictional parameters under the advisory opinion function, the IACtHR made the decision to expand the scope of the inquiry slightly in order to address "the interrelationship between human rights and the environment, and *(b)* the human rights affected by environmental degradation, including the right to a healthy environment" for context.[35] Thus, from the perspective of the ability to enjoy human rights enshrined at the international and regional levels, the IACtHR stressed that environmental rights and protections are critical.[36] In this way, the IACtHR stressed that it was part of a continuing spectrum of case law from the European and African human rights contexts in which similar connections were also recognized as a matter of law.[37] The IACtHR then went on to discuss the interrelationship between environmental concerns, human rights and sustainable development as

31 Id. paras. 197-216.
32 Id. para. 221.
33 IACtHR, *Advisory Opinion OC-23/17, The Environment and Human Rights* (15 November 2017).
34 Id.
35 Id. para. 46.
36 Id. Section VI(A).
37 Id. para. 50.

doi: 10.5553/HYIEL/266627012022010001005

established at the international level from the Stockholm Declaration onward to the Sustainable Development Goals.[38]

Through the Advisory Opinion, the IACtHR highlighted that the concept and application of the right to a healthy environment has shared and individual elements, and that the shared elements "constitutes a universal value that is owed both to present and future generations."[39] Overall, the IACtHR stressed that "[e]nvironmental degradation may cause irreparable harm to human beings; thus, a healthy environment is a fundamental right for the existence of humankind."[40] Critically, the IACtHR specifically extended the right to a healthy environment to include natural resources as rights holders, such as lakes, rivers and mountains,

> "not only because of the benefits they provide to humanity or the effects that their degradation may have on other human rights, such as health, life or personal integrity, but because of their importance to the other living organisms with which we share the planet that also merit protection in their own right."[41]

This, in practice, reflects what has been seen as a growing trend within global jurisprudence to officially recognize a variety of natural resources, such as rivers and mountains, as holding rights as a matter of law and designating certain Indigenous or other communities as representatives to speak for these resources in judicial and regulatory settings.

In establishing the parameters of the right to a healthy environment, the Advisory Opinion also emphasized the dichotomy between the substantive elements of the right, which cluster around individually held rights, and the procedural rights, which are inherently considered more systemic.[42] The latter rights include elements of public participation, transparency, and access to information.[43]

Critically, the Advisory Opinion directly addresses the role of obligations regarding transboundary and extraterritorial environmental damage.[44] Indeed, the extension of jurisdiction in this area to include extraterritoriality was noted as supported by existing case law in the Inter-American context.[45] The IACtHR stressed that the core obligation not to cause harm in the territory of another state is an accepted tenet of international law and that this was translatable to the environmental harms context.[46] The Advisory Opinion states that

38 Id. paras. 51-53.
39 Id. para. 59.
40 Id.
41 Id. para. 62.
42 Id. para. 63.
43 Id.
44 Id. Section VI(C).
45 Id. para. 95.
46 Id. paras. 96-98.

Hungarian Yearbook of International Law and European Law 2022 (10) 1
doi: 10.5553/HYIEL/266627012022010001005

> "The Court considers that states have the obligation to avoid transboundary environmental damage that can affect the human rights of individuals outside their territory. For the purposes of the American Convention, when transboundary damage occurs that effects treaty-based rights, it is understood that the persons whose rights have been violated are under the jurisdiction of the state of origin, if there is a causal link between the act that originated in its territory and the infringement of the human rights of persons outside its territory."[47]

In cases of transboundary damage, the exercise of jurisdiction by a state of origin is based on the understanding that it is the state in whose territory or under whose jurisdiction the activities were carried out that has the effective control over them and is in a position to prevent them from causing transboundary harm that impacts the enjoyment of human rights of persons outside its territory."[48]

As the IACtHR observed, these obligations apply irrespective of the legality or foreseeability of the damaging state's conduct at issue, provided the state had the opportunity to warn of the threat and/or prevent it where possible.[49] Thus, the Advisory Opinion can be seen as creating a variant on strict liability for transboundary environmental harms in that it applies regardless of fault or liability for the conduct as long as the threat of transboundary harm exists and there is a failure to advise the potentially impacted states.[50]

The Advisory Opinion then delved into issues of incorporating the precautionary principle, prevention and procedural aspects of enforcing environmental protection in general.[51] Regarding prevention, the IACtHR found that it should be the most influential and impactful driver of state practices as they relate to environmental concerns, noting the parameters of extraterritorial jurisdiction for harm responsibility and prevention requirements.[52] As the IACtHR explained,

> "any harm to the environment that may involve a violation of the rights to life and to personal integrity, in accordance with the meaning and scope of those rights as previously defined [...] must be considered significant harm. The existence of significant harm in these terms is something that must be determined in each specific case, based on the particular circumstances."[53]

It further amplified that circumstances are also important in assessing the level of protection involved, with the requirements increasing as the fragility of the environmental resources potentially impacted by state actions increases as well.[54]

47 Id. para. 101.
48 Id. para. 102.
49 Id. para. 103.
50 Id. paras. 102-103.
51 Id. para. 125.
52 Id. Section V(B)(B.1.a).
53 Id. para. 140.
54 Id. para. 142.

doi: 10.5553/HYIEL/266627012022010001005

To achieve the required elements of prevention at the state level, the IACtHR has recognized the existence of certain obligations, including the duty to regulate, encompassing environmental impact assessment procedure and conduct,[55] the duty to supervise and monitor, including environmental impact assessments initially as well as the oversight of their terms and implementation throughout the process,[56] the duty to require environmental impact assessments as a matter of law and policy,[57] the duty to develop a contingency plan,[58] and the duty to mitigate in the event of environmental damage.[59] These themes relate to the broadly articulated duty of states to cooperate in environmental issues that the IACtHR recognizes for the scope of state interactions overall.[60] Included in the ambit of this concept of duty is the state duty to notify when there are potential environmental issues that will have transboundary impacts,[61] the duty to negotiate with impacted states as well as consult directly with them[62] and to do so in good faith.[63]

Further, the Advisory Opinion stressed the fundamental nature of public participation in environmental decision-making processes.[64] As the Advisory Opinion explains,

> "this Court considers that the state obligation to ensure the participation of persons subject to their jurisdiction in decision-making and policies that could affect the environment, without discrimination and in a fair, significant and transparent manner, is derived from the right to participate in public affairs and, to this end, states must have previously ensured access to the necessary information."[65]

Thus, in the Advisory Opinion the IACtHR furthered the advancement of environmental rights and the duties of states to recognize them as part of their national and international obligations. This view is very much a furtherance of the *Gabčíkovo-Nagymaros* statements regarding the need to incorporate current and future impacts of activities on the environment. The Advisory Opinion also stresses the ways in which human rights and environmental rights have begun to coalesce in core judicial fora, allowing for an understanding of how environmental harms function *in toto* rather than as a compartmentalized viewpoint. It further underscores the role of *Gabčíkovo-Nagymaros* by including sustainable development in the connections between human rights and environmental law.

55 Id. paras. 146-151.
56 Id. paras. 152-155.
57 Id. paras. 156-161.
58 Id. para. 171.
59 Id. paras. 172-173.
60 Id. paras. 181-186.
61 Id. paras. 187-190.
62 Id. para. 197.
63 Id. paras. 201-205.
64 Id. paras. 226-228.
65 Id. para. 231.

doi: 10.5553/HYIEL/266627012022010001005

Additionally, the Advisory Opinion's pronouncements regarding transboundary and extraterritorial environmental damage assessment can be seen as reflecting the tenets of *Gabčíkovo-Nagymaros* and extending them to the broader extraterritorial concept. The inclusion of the precautionary principle and its intersection with the constructs of transboundary and extraterritorial environmental harms further advances and echoes in *Gabčíkovo-Nagymaros*. Similar connections exist with the enshrinement of the prevention principle and duties regarding the conduct and transparency of environmental impact assessments.

3.1.3. Duarte Agostinho & Others v Portugal et al.

In 2021, a group of youths from Portugal ended the drought of cases relating to climate issues at the ECtHR level by filing a claim against Portugal and 32 other State governments for damage to the environment due to climate change.[66] The claimants centered the focus of their claims on the continued, and indeed increasingly intense, forest fires occurring in Portugal each summer as a result of heatwaves that have registered historical levels from 2018 onward.[67] The claims are supported by scientific research projecting a dramatic increase in the number of heatwaves in Portugal between the date of filing and 2100, and attributing this increase to projections regarding global temperature rise.[68] The claimants also use scientific research to support assertions that global warming and increases in incidents of heat waves and forest fires have and will continue to have significant impacts on the health of current and future generations.[69] While the claimants are Portuguese and do allege wrong-doing by the Portuguese State, they also allege that each of the named respondent States are responsible for emissions contributing to global warming, climate change and, as a result, the environmental impacts experienced in Portugal.[70]

Much of the fundamental bases of the case are grounded in the Paris Agreement on Climate Change (Paris Agreement), as well as the overall UN Framework Convention on Climate Change (UNFCCC) system through which it was adopted.[71] Critical from the perspective of understanding how the core elements of the *Gabčíkovo-Nagymaros* case can be seen as transcending boundaries and influencing the growth of international law, the Paris Agreement contains requirements for a consistent cycle of reporting by State Parties on efforts taken to meet their obligations under the treaty regime on a 5-year basis, as well as a global stocktake requirement following each of these reporting cycles.[72] The purpose of the global stocktake is to ensure that there is a continually refreshed understanding of how the terms of the Paris Agreement are functioning, as well

66 *See* in general: Id.
67 ECtHR, *Duarte Agostinho & Others v Portugal et al.*, Application form, para. 16.
68 Id. para. 17.
69 Id. paras. 18-23.
70 Id. Annex para. 20.
71 *See* in general UN Framework Convention on Climate Change (1992); Paris Agreement on Climate Change (2015).
72 Article 4 Paris Agreement.

doi: 10.5553/HYIEL/266627012022010001005

as the gaps and challenges that exist for full implementation.[73] These lessons are intended to inform the development of future international law and policy, as well as the generation of responsive national laws and policies.[74] They are also transparent in the sense that they are open to the public for review.[75]

In framing their arguments before the ECtHR, the claimants stressed the ways in which the named states have been responsible for the overall global issues of emissions and associated climate change through their nations as sovereigns of the territories and actors under their jurisdiction.[76] Specifically, the claimants argued that

> "State contribute to climate change by *inter alia (a)* permitting release of emissions within national territory and offshore areas over which they have jurisdiction; *(b)* permitting export of fossil fuels extracted on their territory; *(c)* permitting import of goods the production of which involves release of emissions into the atmosphere; and *(d)* permitting entities within their jurisdictions to contribute to the release of emissions overseas, *e.g.* through their extraction of fossil fuels overseas or by financing such extraction."[77]

Although this case was filed within the last year and is not yet the subject of a full judicial opinion yet, it is mentioned here because it demonstrates a high-water mark in terms of where the environmental, sustainable development and transboundary elements of the *Gabčíkovo-Nagymaros* case have moved the discussion over the course of the past 25 years.

3.2. National Cases

3.2.1. Urgenda Foundation versus The Netherlands

As previously noted, one of the most influential decisions in the climate justice context was the 2019 decision of the Dutch Supreme Court in the *Urgenda Foundation versus The Netherlands* case.[78] In *Urgenda*, the Supreme Court was asked to decide whether the Netherlands was improperly carrying out its emissions reduction commitments under international and national laws by attempting to alter the reduction targets as had previously been established by the Dutch government.[79] These claims were brought under the terms of the ECHR as well as Dutch national law which, as the Supreme Court emphasized, is required in instances where environmental harms in one state threaten the broader welfare of other states.[80]

73 Id.
74 Id.
75 Id.
76 ECtHR, *Duarte Agostinho & Others v Portugal et al.*, Application form, paras. 9-10.
77 Id. para. 9.
78 *See* in general *Urgenda Foundation v The Netherlands*, No. 19/00135 (20 December 2019).
79 *See* in general Id.
80 Id. para. 5.5.3.

doi: 10.5553/HYIEL/266627012022010001005

In *Urgenda*, the Supreme Court recognized the importance of ensuring limitations on the global rate of temperature rise by 2050, stressing that all States have obligations in this regard and that the Netherlands, as a historically high-level source of emissions, has a high burden.[81] Further, the Supreme Court stressed that the climate obligations ascribed to the Netherlands and other States through their membership in the UNFCCC system – particularly the pronouncements of the various Conferences of the Parties – included the overall enshrinement of the 'no harm principle.'[82] The Supreme Court opinioned that this principle of international law could be extended to the climate context and that

> "this means that they can be called upon to make their contribution to reducing greenhouse gas emissions. This approach justifies partial responsibility: each country is responsible for its part and can therefore be called to account in that respect."[83]

By directly recognizing the connections between climate change, transboundary harm and State responsibility, echoes of the *Gabčíkovo-Nagymaros* tenets can be heard throughout the Dutch Supreme Court's ruling in *Urgenda*. These connections are further advanced in the component of the *Urgenda* decision addressing the incorporation of the no harm principle as a matter of state obligation in the environmental context.

3.2.2. *Friends of the Irish Environment versus Government of Ireland*

In July 2020, the Irish Supreme Court issued the *Friends of the Irish Environment versus Government of Ireland* decision.[84] The case originated in claims regarding the ways in which the Government of Ireland proposed and planned to implement requirements for periodic reporting regarding and updates to statutorily required plans for carrying out climate change related laws.[85] One of the fascinating aspects of the case, which embraces the understanding of environmental law as fundamental and evolving in international law, that was articulated by Judge Weeramantry in the *Gabčíkovo-Nagymaros* separate opinion, is that all sides of the issue and the Court agreed on the existence and importance of climate change.[86] Indeed, the Court devoted the opening section of its opinion to a discussion of the scientific basis for climate change and efforts to create laws and regulations to address it.[87]

This discussion is not, however, limited to climate change impacts in Ireland but rather extends to the global pressures faced as a result of climate degradation, and devoting a great deal of attention to the current and projected results in

81 Id. at paras. 4.5-4.7.
82 Id. para. 5.7.5.
83 Id.
84 *Friends of the Irish Environment v Government of Ireland*, Appeal No. 205/19 (31 July 2020).
85 *See* in general Id.
86 *See* in general Id.
87 Id. Section 3.

doi: 10.5553/HYIEL/266627012022010001005

developing states.[88] As the Court noted, "[w]hile it is widely acknowledged that urgent action is required in order to address climate change, urgency is assessed differently within the global community."[89] Further, the Court stressed that, in a somewhat novel situation,

> "[i]t can, however, safely be said that the consequences of failing to address climate change are accepted by both sides as being very severe with potential significant risk both to life and health throughout the world but also including Ireland. While the severity of that situation is not disputed, a number of commentaries on the likely impact of global warming were established in evidence before the High Court."[90]

In terms of content requirements and, vitally, fulfillment requirements for the Plan of implementation promulgated by the Government of Ireland, the Court was called upon to decide whether the intent was to create quantifiable benchmarks that necessitated accomplishment or to generate a set of aspirations.[91] While the Court noted that efforts to meet these obligations were partially achieved by adopting EU standards in the appropriate areas, it also stressed that this was not sufficient for full accomplishment without more in light of the needs and obligations of Ireland.[92]

When further examining the terms contained in the Plan, the Court noted that it was ostensibly intended to be implemented over the course of 33 years (from 2017 to 2050) and that there was a requirement for the Plan to be 5 years in duration at the outset but that, contrary to the Government's assertions, this was not the only period during which specific benchmarks had to be made.[93] Instead, the Court asserted that there was a continuing obligation over the full 33 year duration and that this required publication and public participation requirements for the Plan and continuing updates.[94] Specifically, the Court stated

> "it seems [...] that key objectives of the statutory regime are designed to provide both for public participation and for transparency around the statutory objective which is the achievement of the NTO by 2050."[95]

In establishing the compliance of the Plan with the Government's obligations under the Act creating it and statutory interpretation principles, the Court explained "

88 Id. Section 3.3.
89 Id. Section 3.4.
90 Id. Section 3.6.
91 Id. Section 4.
92 Id. Section 4.5-4.6.
93 Id. Section 6.20.
94 Id. Section 6.21.
95 Id. Section 6.22.

Hungarian Yearbook of International Law and European Law 2022 (10) 1
doi: 10.5553/HYIEL/266627012022010001005

> the Plan falls a long way short of the sort of specificity which the statute requires. I do not consider that the reasonable and interested observer would know, in any sufficient detail, how it really is intended, under current government policy, to achieve the NTO by 2050 on the basis of the information contained in the Plan. Too much is left to further study or investigation. In that context it must, of course, be recognized that matters such as the extent to which new technologies for carbon extraction may be able to play a role is undoubtedly itself uncertain on the basis of current knowledge. However, that is no reason not to give some estimate as to how it is currently intended that such measures will be deployed and what the effect of their deployment is hoped to be. Undoubtedly any such estimates can be highly qualified by the fact that, as the technology and knowledge develops, it may prove to be more or less able to achieve the initial aims attributable to it."[96]

Ultimately, the Court held that the Plan and the intention for Governmental updates to it fell short of the legal requirements in the Act and under existing Irish law.

In *Friends of the Irish Environment*, the recognition of environmental law's importance, as was articulated so clearly in the main *Gabčíkovo-Nagymaros* decision and in Judge Weeramantry's separate opinion, is notably accepted without hesitation as a matter of science and law. The case is also an important vehicle to understanding how the *Gabčíkovo-Nagymaros* tenets regarding responsibility of states for transboundary harms extend to the context of climate change responsibility and the contributions of states to global carbon emissions as well as reductions in emissions. Additionally, *Friends of the Irish Environment* demonstrates the ongoing requirement for the evaluation of the impacts of state actions, as enshrined in *Gabčíkovo-Nagymaros*, albeit in the context of a climate-related emissions reduction plan, rather than the implementation of damming proposals.

3.2.3. Lamu et al. versus Kenya

In the 2016 *Lamu et al. versus Kenya* case, the Kenyan National Environmental Tribunal addressed issues raised in connection with the national Kenya Vision 2030 initiative and its use of several coal fired power plants as part of methods to accomplish increased energy production.[97] Although an Environmental and Social Impact Assessment (ESIA) had been conducted as part of the requisite elements of national law, there was a challenge to the sufficiency of the ESIA.[98] The issues raised, and the Tribunal's certification of them on appeal, evinced a broad understanding of the procedural and substantive requirements for valid ESIA proceedings.[99] From the outset, the Tribunal established that

96 Id. Section 6.46.

97 *See* in general *Lamu et al. v Kenya*, Tribunal Appeal No. NET 196 of 2016 (2016).

98 *See* in general Id.

99 *See* in general Id.

doi: 10.5553/HYIEL/266627012022010001005

"the purpose of the Environment Impact Assessment (EIA) process is to assist a country in attaining sustainable development when commissioning projects. The United Nations has set Sustainable Development Goals (SDGs), which are an urgent call for action by all countries recognizing that ending poverty and other deprivations must go hand-in-hand with strategies that improve health and education, reduce inequality, and spur economic growth – all while tackling climate change and working to preserve our oceans and forests."[100]

In crafting the parameters of required public participation, the Tribunal began with the Rio Declaration and then moved outward from that point to international law and national legal and regulatory provisions.[101]

When applying these rules to the case at hand, the Tribunal explained the extent and purpose of the ESIA process as something that balances the interests of humanity with the interests of development and recognizes the inherent concerns of private individuals in this context.[102] Specifically, it provided that

"Human beings are justifiably concerned about the environmental impacts of projects to their location and especially where those projects are novel in nature. These environmental impacts are not restricted to the ecological effects alone but extend to other wider areas that affect their lives like the health impacts to them and their families, to their livelihood and economic opportunities, socio-cultural heritage and traditions. Being concerned about all these environmental effects of a project the people most affected by a project must therefore have a say on each and every aspect of the project and its impact. In carrying out a consultative process, it is not a must that every person must support the project nor can a proponent address every unreasonable demand and suggestion, but it is vital that even the most feeble of voices be heard and views considered."[103]

In light of this understanding and a noted lack of transparency or provision of information to the public sufficient for it to generate informed comments during the requisite portion of the ESIA procedure, the Tribunal found that the ESIA was indeed improperly executed.[104] The Tribunal clearly explained that

"it is important to point out that is imperative that those in administration be keen when faced with objections to projects, where objectors hold the view that the project may compromise the environment. This Tribunal cannot permit authorities to deal so nonchalantly with such objections. Such objections need to be taken seriously and need to be considered. Public

100 Id. para. 16.
101 Id. paras. 23-26.
102 Id. para. 50.
103 Id.
104 Id. paras. 69, and 75.

doi: 10.5553/HYIEL/266627012022010001005

> participation especially when it comes to EIAs are extremely critical and cannot be treated as a formality or inconvenience. It is at the very core of any EIA exercise. The EIA public participation process cannot be a mechanical exercise but a vibrant and dynamic activity where affected persons are engaged in a fair and reasonable manner."[105]

Further, the Tribunal addressed the adequacy of the mitigation efforts set out in the ESIA for the coal fired power plant operations and found them in part to be severely lacking.[106] It also found that efforts to apply the precautionary principle as part of the ESIA process were improperly implemented due to a lack of clarity.[107]

The *Lamu et al. versus Kenya* case demonstrates the power of a specialized court to incorporate the terms of the *Gabčíkovo-Nagymaros* decision in highly regulated contexts to ensure that the use of environmental impact assessments is enshrined in law and, at the practical level, is fully and meaningfully carried out.

4. Transcending Themes in Jurisprudence

The above review of the ways in which tenets from the *Gabčíkovo-Nagymaros* decision demonstrates the variety in geography and subject application of core elements such as recognition of the need to protect environmental concerns as a legitimate state interest and the requirement that states inform other states of potential transboundary impacts. These findings highlight the critical nature of the *Gabčíkovo-Nagymaros* decision across borders and within jurisdiction. Additionally, these cases highlight the ways in which principles of environmental impact assessment necessity, no harm, precaution, prevention and sustainable development have been developed from the *Gabčíkovo-Nagymaros* decision onward and are now foundational elements of international, European and national laws. Beyond this, however, these cases coalesce around several critical trends regarding the ways in which the fundamental legal principles of the *Gabčíkovo-Nagymaros* decision have been able to transcend time and place through judicial expansion and refinement.

Perhaps the most significant area of expansion is in the interrelationship between environmental rights, and concomitant requirements for environmental protections in law and practice, and other critical rights that have been recognized at the international, regional and national law levels. When the *Gabčíkovo-Nagymaros* decision was issued, the legal position of environmental rights and protections was still very much emerging, rendering the principles and tenets espoused all the more critical. After 25 years, the idea of environmental rights and the need for associated environmental protections being elements of state responsibility is enshrined in international treaty regimes as well as decisions of multiple courts at all levels. Further, these courts, as discussed above,

105 Id. para. 72.
106 Id. paras. 120-121.
107 Id. paras. 137-139.

doi: 10.5553/HYIEL/266627012022010001005

have recognized the interrelated – if not in fact interdependent – ties between environmental rights and human rights, as well as health-related rights. The decisions also make it clear that regional and national courts are increasingly recognizing environmental rights and the principle of sustainable development as inextricably linked as a matter of law.

The connections between environmental rights and human rights have also become clearly articulated in the evolutions of understanding transboundary impacts and state legal obligations. A vital aspect of the *Gabčíkovo-Nagymaros* decision, it will be recalled, was the obligation of a state regarding actual or potential transboundary harm generally, and transboundary harm in the environmental context in particular. What has emerged over the course of 25 years is the understanding that, as a matter of science and law, environmental harms and the threat of environmental damage extends beyond the transboundary context and is extraterritorial in reach. This is a critical distinction because it then allows the various courts to address broader questions of emissions reductions and impacts in the extraterritorial context, recognizing the global reach of pollution, rather than being limited to the transboundary context of environmental impacts in shared water or other resources. Such a shift in legal understandings of science as well as the contours of the law itself has formed the bedrock foundation upon which many climate justice cases have been, and continue to be brought in international, regional and national court systems. Regardless of the future success of these cases, this shift must be recognized as tied directly to the *Gabčíkovo-Nagymaros* decision and the legacy it has left.

Additionally, the extension of transboundary harms and impacts to extraterritorial harms and impacts has resulted in an increased willingness of courts to recognize that human rights issues are linked to environmental issues stemming from the extraterritoriality of environmental actions. As noted above, this shift can be seen in the changed understanding of fault and liability in instances of transboundary or extraterritorial harms. Indeed, as the scope of potential state obligations has expanded from transboundary to extraterritorial constructions, the elements necessary to establish liability can be argued to have decreased to nearly strict liability in some instances.

In terms of the no harm principle, the quarter century since the *Gabčíkovo-Nagymaros* decision has seen the entrenchment of this concept as a core element of international law obligations. Similarly, the principle of prevention has become a fundamental element in international law as well as regional and national laws across multiple jurisdictions. Overall, this correlates to the expansion of concepts of legal protections for natural resources and those who guard them as a matter of regional and national law.

Finally, a significant amount of growth has been seen over the past 25 years of jurisprudence regarding the role of environmental impact assessments and related concepts of public participation, public access to information and transparency in the governmental decision-making process. Whereas the principle of environmental impact assessment was identified in Judge Weeramantry's separate opinion as a guiding element of state decision-making, this was not included by the main opinion and remained very much persuasive

doi: 10.5553/HYIEL/266627012022010001005

authority. Courts at all levels have taken up this mantle, however, and some, such as the IACtHR, recognize this as a critical element of procedural law. While procedural law classification might lack some of the fundamental import of substantive rights, the designation of environmental impact assessments and associated elements as procedural elements vests them with an indelible place in the conduct of state decision-making. It also provides current and future generations a legal avenue through which to challenge decisions of the state in a concrete and measurable fashion. When used in cases that seek to expand the construct of environmental rights and state responsibility, the availability of a solid claim based on these types of procedural rights can be essential to chances of affecting change as a matter of law.

5. Conclusion

After a quarter century, the *Gabčíkovo-Nagymaros* decision has proven to be one of the most durable of ICJ decisions, transcending the parameters of its binding application as a matter of law to form the bedrock upon which the expansion of environmental rights and environmental law has occurred. While the issues at the heart of the case might still be the source of contention between Hungary and Slovakia after more than two decades, the precedent from *Gabčíkovo-Nagymaros* is far more deeply entrenched in the evolution of the way law views environmental protection, transboundary harms, and multiple principles.

While it is impossible to predict the future, the rapid increase in climate justice cases filed in jurisdictions across the world combined with the significant willingness of many courts and tribunals to hear and rule on these cases, indicates that environmental rights are becoming entrenched through case law even when the legislature fails to act. Indeed, the *Urgenda* case has seemingly served as a catalyst for many similar cases and has been cited by courts rendering decisions. Although *Urgenda* and the cases discussed in this article represent significant steps in entrenching environmental law and rights throughout international, regional and national law, it must be remembered that these cases would not be possible without the groundwork of the *Gabčíkovo-Nagymaros* decision. As cases continue to evolve along with the understanding of the contours for environmental law and related questions, the legacy and foresight of the *Gabčíkovo-Nagymaros* decision will continued to be reaffirmed for decades to come.

doi: 10.5553/HYIEL/266627012022010001005

Environmental Rights and Climate Rights

Erga Omnes Obligations in International Law and EU Law?*

*Ottavio Quirico***

Abstract

Is there an erga omnes right (and duty) to a sustainable environment in international law? Is an erga omnes right (and duty) to a sustainable climate developing within this framework? What is the contribution of EU law to this trajectory? This article explores the pace, nature and scope of application of the right to a sustainable environment as well as that of a possible right to a sustainable climate within this framework from the intertwined perspectives of international law and EU law. The article fundamentally claims that an erga omnes right and duty to a sustainable climate is developing in international law; EU law has largely contributed to this development and is currently essentially aligned with international law in this regard. By contrast, EU law seems to be more progressive than international law with respect to the development of the right to a sustainable climate as a specific erga omnes claim.

Keywords: environmental rights, climate rights, erga omnes obligations, sustainable development goals, EU Charter of Fundamental Rights.

1. Introduction

Environmental rights have undergone a significant development in international law, particularly since the 1970s. Regulatory instruments spanning the 1972 Stockholm Declaration of the UN Conference on Human Environment (UNCHE)[1] and the Convention on Biological Diversity[2] are key steps in the trajectory towards the establishment of environmental protection as a right, possibly having an *erga omnes* scope of application. Within this context, little attention has been devoted to the question of *climate rights* and, within this framework, to the possible development of the *right to a sustainable climate* as an *erga omnes* obligation. Nonetheless, at the normative level, the UN Framework Convention

* With the support of the Erasmus+ Program of the European Commission: 620604-EPP-1-2020-1-AU-EPPJMO-PROJECT. Contents reflect the view of the Author only.

** Ottavio Quirico: associate professor of law, University of New England, Australia and Australian National University, Centre for European Studies; Fernand Braudel Senior Fellow, European University Institute, Florence.

1 UNCHE, Report, UN Doc A/CONF 48/14/Rev 1 (16 June 1972).

2 Opened for signature 5 June 1992, 1760 UNTS 79, entered into force 29 December 1993.

doi: 10.5553/HYIEL/266627012022010001006

on Climate Change (UNFCCC)[3] clearly establishes certain principles and objectives in the matter that have attracted quasi-universal participation. This raises the question whether a right to a stable climate is emerging internationally, possibly as a universal duty.

Such developments are taking place not only at the global level, but also at the regional level. In particular, EU law has provided a meaningful contribution to the development of the right to a safe environment in international law, whereby the EU CFR[4] has played a key role, notably, in light of Article 37 on environmental protection. Significant developments are also taking place with respect to the possible recognition of the right to a safe climate, as the EU is adopting a progressive policy in the area, particularly *via* Resolution 2020/2134(INI) on the Effects of Climate Change on Human Rights and the Role of Environmental Defenders on This Matter.[5]

This article sets out to develop an essential analysis of the evolution of the right to a safe environment and the right to a safe climate as obligations *erga omnes* in international law and EU law as parallel and intertwined regulatory systems. Three perspectives are fundamental to the development of this research. *(i)* First, along the lines of the analysis developed by Hohfeld, it is considered that rights and duties are necessarily correlated notions and structures.[6] *(ii)* Secondly, the analysis develops against the background of the sources of international law, particularly as classified under Article 38 of the Statute of the ICJ, and, more specifically, the distinction between the general principles of international law, which have customary nature, under Article 38(1)(b), and the general principles of law inferred from domestic legal system under Article 38(1)(c). Indeed, although these sources are different, at least to a certain extent, by their very nature they create rights and duties that are *erga omnes* in scope.[7] *(iii)* Thirdly, it is necessary to consider the different meanings of the concept of an '*erga omnes* obligation'. Literally, the Latin expression '*erga omnes*' simply means '*vis-à-vis* everyone'.[8] Therefore, an *erga omens* obligation could simply be *regarded* as the duty of a legal person entailing the corresponding rights of all other legal persons under international law and EU law. According to the well-known *obiter dictum* of the ICJ in *Barcelona Traction*, *erga omnes* obligations are not only universal duties, but, more specifically, duties owed by a legal person to 'the international community as a whole', entailing a general interest in protection.[9] From this perspective, *erga omnes* obligations overlap with peremptory obligations (*jus cogens*), which are non-derogable universal rights and duties under Article 53 of the Vienna Convention on the Law of Treaties (VCLT) and the Vienna

3 Opened for signature 28 December 2009, 1771 UNTS 107, entered into force 21 March 1994.
4 Adopted 7 December 2000.
5 Res. 2020/2134(INI) of 19 May 2021.
6 Wesley Newcomb Hohfeld, 'Fundamental Legal Conceptions as Applied in Judicial Reasoning', *Yale Law Journal*, Vol. 26, 1916, p. 717.
7 Hugh Thirlway, *The Sources of International Law*, Oxford University Press, Oxford, 2019.
8 Britannica, *Erga Omnes*, at www.britannica.com/topic/erga-omnes.
9 ICJ, *Barcelona Traction, Light and Power Company, Limited (New Application: 1962) (Belgium v Spain) Second Phase (Judgment),* ICJ Reports 1970, p. 32, paras. 33-34.

doi: 10.5553/HYIEL/266627012022010001006

Convention on the Law of Treaties between States and International Organizations or between International Organizations (VCLTIO).[10]

The analysis is divided into two parts. The first part considers the evolution of the right to a sustainable environment as an *erga omnes* obligation under international law and subsequently deals with the right to a sustainable climate as an *erga omnes* one within this context. The second part focuses on the development of the right to a sustainable environment as an *erga omnes* one under EU law and considers, within this framework, the possible evolution of a separate right to a sustainable climate as an *erga omnes* obligation.

2. The Right to a Sustainable Environment and the Right to a Sustainable Climate: Erga Omnes Obligations in International Law?

2.1. The Right to a Sustainable Environment

Since the *Trail Smelter* arbitral award, the no-harm and polluter-pays rules, and thus, the right to a sustainable environment, are well-established in international law. Indeed, in the foundational *Trail Smelter* case, an Arbitral Tribunal, adjudicating upon the case of a lead and zinc plant located in Canada and emitting smoke causing damage to crops, livestock and timber across the border with the US held that "no State has the right to use or permit the use of its territory in such a manner as to cause injury by fumes in or to the territory of another or the properties or persons therein".[11] States are therefore internationally responsible for trans-boundary (air) pollution, and in *Nuclear Weapons*[12] the ICJ held that this duty is "part of the corpus of international law relating to the environment", implying that it has a customary nature and therefore a general scope of application.

At times, the *erga omnes* nature of the right to a sustainable environment has been explicitly affirmed in international law. Notably, in his dissenting opinion in *Gabcykovo-Nagymaros*,[13] Judge Weeramantry put forward the idea that the right to a safe environment is an *erga omnes obligation under customary international law*. Weeramantry indeed underscored the '*erga omnes* connotation' of environmental damage[14] and highlighted that "international environmental law will need to proceed beyond weighing the rights and obligations of parties within a closed compartment of individual State self-interest, unrelated to the global concerns of humanity as a whole."[15] This argument was later developed by the Inuit in their Petition against the US to the IACommHR for excessive GHG emissions, claiming

10 Thomas Weatherall, *International Law and Social Context*, Cambridge University Press, Cambridge, 2015, p. 351; Antônio Augusto Cançado Trindade, *International Law for Humankind*, Brill, Leiden, 2020, p. 291.

11 *Trail Smelter (US v Canada)*, 16 April 1938 and 11 March 1941, 3 *RIAA* p. 1965.

12 ICJ, *Legality of the Threat or Use of Nuclear Weapons (Advisory Opinion)*, ICJ Reports 1996, pp. 241-242, para. 29.

13 ICJ, *Case concerning the Gabčíkovo-Nagymaros Project (Hungary v Slovakia)*, judgment, ICJ Reports 1997, p. 7.

14 Id. Separate Opinion of Judge Weeramantry, p. 89.

15 Id. p. 118.

doi: 10.5553/HYIEL/266627012022010001006

that "[t]he right to a healthy environment is [...] a right of customary international law".[16]

More recently, the UN Human Rights Committee (HRC) adopted a Resolution acknowledging that "the right to a safe, clean, healthy and sustainable environment" *is 'a human right'*.[17] This is only a recognition of soft law and it is yet to be seen how the UN General Assembly will react to such an approach; however, the Resolution is particularly meaningful, as it allows the development of significant considerations on the *erga omnes* nature of the right to a safe environment. Indeed, besides being interdependent and indivisible, human rights are in principle universal,[18] and therefore, if the right to a safe environment qualifies as a fundamental one, it follows that it should also have a universal scope of application. In any case, the recognition of the right to a safe environment as a fundamental one would shift the focus from its interstate structure to a right primarily held by individuals *vis-à-vis* all other legal persons in the international community. Considering the duty-right to a safe environment from an intertemporal perspective,[19] some scholars have noted that the recognition of the human right to a healthy environment as an autonomous claim under general international law has a collective scope as a universal norm not only *vis-à-vis* present generations, but also the future ones.[20] To a certain extent, the obligation to protect the environment is also considered an *erga omnes* duty along the lines of the decision of the ICJ in *Barcelona Traction*,[21] thus approaching the notion of *jus cogens*. Indeed, scholars have noted that the duty to protect the environment should be equated to normative prohibitions, such as those against genocide and aggression.[22]

Having regard to the classification of the sources of international law under Article 38 of the ICJ Statute, it may be asserted that the right to safe environment could be emerging as an *erga omnes* obligation under Article 38(2)(c), rather than Article 38(c)(b), that is, *as a general principle of law*

16 IACommHR, *Inuit Petition to the Inter- American Commission on Human Rights, Seeking Relief from Violations Resulting from Global Warming Caused by Acts and Omissions of the United States*, P-1413-05, 7 December 2005, p. 74.

17 HRC, The Human Right to a Safe, Clean, Healthy and Sustainable Environment, UN Doc. A/HRC/48/L.23/Rev.1, 2021, p. 3, para. 1.

18 Mark Gibney & Sigrun Skogly (eds.), *Universal Human Rights and Extraterritorial Obligations*, University of Pennsylvania Press, Philadelphia, 2010.

19 Emily Grabham & Siân Beynon-Jones (eds.), *Law and Time*, Routledge, London, 2018.

20 Bridget Lewis, 'Human Rights as a Basis for Institutions for Future Generations', *in* Jan Linehan & Peter Lawrence (eds.), *Giving Future Generations a Voice: Normative Frameworks, Institutions and Practice*, Edward Elgar, Cheltenham, 2021, p. 62.

21 ICJ, *Barcelona Traction*, 1970, p. 32.

22 Alexander Orakhelashvili, *Peremptory Norms in International Law*, Oxford University Press, Oxford, 2006, p. 65. *See also* Mission of Colombia to the United Nations, Panel Discussion regarding Opinión Consultiva OC-23/17, 15 November 2017, Medio Ambiente y Derechos Humanos, 2018, p. 1.

doi: 10.5553/HYIEL/266627012022010001006

rather than a general principle of international law.[23] In other words, given that 178 States acknowledge the right to a sustainable environment *via* domestic regulation,[24] the right to a safe environment could be classified as a universal obligation recognized as such by most legal systems in the world. Moreover, in light of the fact that more than 100 States recognize the right to environmental sustainability at the constitutional level, it might be assumed that, also taken from the perspective of the general principles of law, it is evolving into a fundamental right.[25] For instance Section 112 of the Norwegian Constitution posits that "[e]very person has the right to an environment that is conducive to health and to a natural environment whose productivity and diversity are maintained", entailing a duty to manage natural resources on the basis of comprehensive long-term considerations that will also safeguard this right for future generations.

Overall, it is possible to consider that the right to a safe environment is evolving as an *erga omnes* right and duty under international law.[26] However, this approach is not yet clearly and fully established. Furthermore, it is not without systemic problems. Indeed, *(i)* first, there are different meanings of the notion of an '*erga omnes* obligation'.[27] *(ii)* Secondly, the right to environmental protection is quite general and encompasses a sub-set of rights, spanning biodiversity, the protection of forests and watercourses. Logically, if the right to a sustainable environment has an *erga omnes* scope of application, also the rights to the protection of forests and watercourses should be *erga omnes* in scope. In practice, declaring the *erga omnes* nature of the right to a sustainable environment would be tantamount to declaring the *erga omnes* nature of international environmental law as such.

2.2. The Right to a Sustainable Climate

The right to a sustainable climate is clearly affirmed in the Sustainable Development Goals, which acknowledge the necessity "to take action to combat climate change and its impacts" (Goal 13).[28] Within such a framework, the UNFCCC regime outlines an obligation to protect the environment from excessive GHG emissions.

Normatively, according to Article 2 UNFCCC, the parties to the Convention commit to the "stabilization of greenhouse gas concentrations in the atmosphere

23 Stefan Vogenauer & Stephen Weatherill, *General Principles of Law*, Hart, Oxford, 2017; Imogen Saunders, *General Principles as a Source of International Law: Art 38(1)(c) of the Statute of the International Court of Justice*, Hart, Oxford, 2020; Pierre-Marie Dupuy, *Customary International Law*, Edward Elgar Publishing, Northampton, 2021.

24 John Knox, *Preliminary Report on Human Rights and the Environment*, UN Doc A/HRC/22/43 5, 24 December 2012, para. 12.

25 David Boyd, 'The Right to a Healthy and Sustainable Environment', *in* Yann Aguila & Jorge Vinuales, A Global Pact for the Environment-Legal Foundations, University of Cambridge, Cambridge, 2019, p. 30.

26 *See* Maurizio Ragazzi, *The Concept of International Obligations Erga Omnes*, Clarendon Press, Oxford, 1997, p. 157.

27 *Cf.* the introductory section.

28 UN GA, Transforming Our Goals, RES/70/01, 2015, para. 59.

doi: 10.5553/HYIEL/266627012022010001006

at a level that would prevent dangerous anthropogenic interference with the climate system", aiming to ensure sustainable development. According to Article 3, the protection of the climate system should benefit both the present and future generations of humankind. This duty is reinforced by Article 4 UNFCCC, which compels the parties to implement national and regional programs, policies and measures to mitigate climate change, as well as adaptation measures. Along these lines, Article 2 of the Paris Agreement[29] provides that, within the context of sustainable development, the Parties aim to strengthen the response to climate change by, inter alia, keeping global average temperature increase well below 2°C above pre-industrial levels and pursuing efforts to limit such increase to 1.5°C, *via* adequate mitigation measures. These duties have been interpreted by scholars either as an obligation to prevent climate change[30] or as a recommendation belonging to soft law,[31] whereby an overall substantive duty of conduct to reverse the long-term trend of GHG emissions clearly emerges.[32]

Whether the right to a sustainable climate can also be regarded as an *erga omnes* obligation is a complex question. The UNFCCC and the Paris Agreement are subject to the relative effectiveness of treaties, according to Article 34 VCLT and VCLTIO; however, the UNFCCC has thus far been ratified by 197 Parties, while 192 parties have ratified the Paris Agreement.[33] Quasi-universal participation in these conventions could indicate the emergence of a universal duty and right to a safe climate, according to well-established international legal theory.[34] Meaningfully, in *Certain Activities carried out by Nicaragua in the Border Area*,[35] Judge Dugard noted that

> "the obligation not to engage in wrongful deforestation that results in the release of carbon into the atmosphere and the loss of gas sequestration services is certainly an obligation *erga omnes*."[36]

29 Opened for signature 12 December 2015, entered into force 4 November 2016.

30 Christina Voigt, 'State Responsibility for Climate Change Damages', *Nordic Journal of International Law*, Vol. 77, Issue 1-2, 2008, p. 5.

31 Malgosia Fitzmaurice, 'Responsibility and Climate Change', *German Yearbook of International Law*, Vol. 53, 2010, p. 106.

32 Daniel Bodansky, 'The Legal Character of the Paris Agreement', *Review of European, Comparative and International Environmental Law*, Vol. 25, Issue 2, 2016, p. 146; Benoît Mayer, 'Obligations of Conduct in the International Law on Climate Change: A Defence', *Review of European, Comparative and International Environmental Law*, Vol. 27, Issue 2, 2018, p. 135.

33 UNFCCC, Status of Ratification, at https://unfccc.int/process-and-meetings/the-convention/status-of-ratification/status-of-ratification-of-the-convention; Paris Agreement, Status of Ratification, at https://unfccc.int/process/the-paris-agreement/status-of-ratification.

34 Mark Villiger, *Customary International Law and Treaties*, Martinus Nijhoff, Dordrecht, 1985, p. 159.

35 ICJ, *Certain Activities carried out by Nicaragua in the Border Area (Costa Rica v Nicaragua), Compensation Owed by the Republic of Nicaragua to the Republic of Costa Rica,* ICJ Reports 2018, p. 15.

36 Id. Dissenting Opinion of *ad hoc* judge Dugard, p. 120.

doi: 10.5553/HYIEL/266627012022010001006

Some scholars have even sought to collect evidence that the duty to curb GHG emissions might be evolving as a peremptory obligation belonging to *jus cogens*.[37]

Considering human rights, while the obligation to curb GHG emissions is not qualified directly as a fundamental right in the UNFCCC regime, the Preamble to the Paris Agreement states that climate change is "a common concern of humankind" and the Parties should "respect, promote and consider their respective obligations on human rights" in "taking action to address climate change"' In 2019, the Special Rapporteur to the UN HRC on the Environment and Human Rights, Professor Boyd, considered that States have an obligation to respect, protect and fulfil "the right to a safe climate" through their own actions, including mitigation and adaptation measures.[38] Naturally, acknowledging the human rights nature of the right to a sustainable climate would also entail recognizing its *erga omnes* scope of application, given the universal nature of fundamental rights.[39] This would also entail a shift in focus from the interstate nature of the right and duty under the UNFCCC to a claim primarily addressing individuals as the right-holders, *vis-à-vis* not only present generations, but also future ones. Indeed, a Declaration on Climate Change and Human Rights recently adopted by the Global Network for Human Rights and the Environment (GNHRE) acknowledges that, within the context of the human right to a sustainable environment, '*everyone*' has "the right [...] to be free from dangerous anthropogenic interference with the climate system such that rising global temperatures are kept well below 2 degrees centigrade above preindustrial levels" [Principle I(5)].[40]

It cannot also be excluded that the right to safe climate emerges *de lege ferenda* as an *erga omnes* obligation under domestic constitutions. Some scholars have indeed underscored that fundamental norms provide "robust institutional structures to address climate change", as they protect the intrinsic value of environmental sustainability and guarantee procedural environmental rights.[41] Most significantly, in the case of *Juliana v US*, the US Court for the District of Oregon 'undoubtedly' affirmed that "the *right to a climate system capable of sustaining human life*" is "*fundamental* to a free and ordered society."[42] This statement entails the possibility of interpreting the right to a sustainable climate as a human right and therefore as an *erga omnes* obligation. However, in the

37 Ottavio Quirico, 'Towards a Peremptory Duty to Curb Greenhouse Gas Emissions?', *Fordham International Law Journal*, Vol. 44, Issue 4, 2021, p. 923.

38 David Boyd, Report of the Special Rapporteur on the Issue of Human Rights Obligations relating to the Enjoyment of a Safe, Clean, Healthy and Sustainable Environment, UN Doc A/74/161, 15 July 2019, p. 18, para. 65.

39 Gibney & Skogly, 2010.

40 Kirsten Davies *et al.*, 'The Declaration on Human Rights and Climate Change: A New Legal Tool for Global Policy Change', *Journal of Human Rights and the Environment*, Vol. 8, Issue 2, 2017, p. 250.

41 Samantha Julien, The Secretary-General Addressed the Role of Constitutions in Combating the Climate Crisis, IDEA, 2021, at www.idea.int/news-media/news/secretary-general-addressed-role-constitutions-combating-climate-crisis.

42 *Juliana v United States*, 217 F. Supp. 3d, D. Or. 2016, p. 1250. *See also* Valerie Brown, *Climate Change*, 2019, The Revelator, at https://therevelator.org/constitution-right-climate.

doi: 10.5553/HYIEL/266627012022010001006

absence of an explicit (constitutional) recognition of the right to a sustainable climate in most legal systems of the world, it would be difficult to assert that it is emerging as a general principle of law under Article 38(2)(b) of the ICJ Statute.

3. EU Law Developments

3.1. *An Erga Omnes Right to a Sustainable Environment? Lessons from Article 37 EU CFR*

Along the lines of the jurisprudence of the CJEU, EU law has developed a high level of environmental protection. Several rules within the EU system focus on the need to ensure sustainable development. Notably, the Preamble to the TEU establishes that the EU promotes economic and social progress, taking into account the principles of sustainable development and environmental protection. Along these lines, Article 3(3) TEU, which regulates the fundamental principles of the Union, establishes that the EU internal market promotes sustainable development and a high level of protection and improvement of the quality of the environment. Article 21(2)(f)-(g) TEU further transposes these principles within the sphere of the EU external action, aiming to preserve and improve the quality of the environment and the sustainable management of global natural resources. Moreover, within Title XX TFEU, which focuses on the 'Environment', Article 191 establishes that the Union acts to protect and improve environmental quality, particularly in its external action, with a focus on climate change. More specifically, Article 11 TEU posits that environmental protection must be integrated into the definition and implementation of Union policies and activities, with a view to promoting sustainable development. These rules are *summarized from a human rights perspective in Article 37 of the EU CFR* (Environmental Protection), which provides for the integration of a high level of environmental protection and the improvement of the quality of the environment into the policies of the Union, in accordance with the principle of sustainable development.

While this is not tantamount to establishing a right to a sustainable environment or better yet a right having an *erga omnes* scope of application, it indicates the centrality of environmental protection as a core value of the EU. Article 37 EU CFR tends to crystallize at the EU level a trend that is already embedded in regional instruments such as the African Charter on Human and Peoples' Rights, notably under Article 24. This approach has also developed within the Inter-American human rights protection system; notably, in November 2017, upon request by Colombia, the IACtHR adopted an advisory opinion that acknowledges the link between environmental protection and the rights to life and health.[43] The opinion states that *a decent environment is a necessary pre-condition for a decent life and health,*[44] and is thus indispensable to fulfil the general obligations to respect and ensure the rights to life and personal

43 IACtHR, *Advisory Opinion OC-23/17 of 15 November 2017 Requested by the Republic of Colombia on the Environment and Human Rights.*

44 Id. paras. 110-111.

doi: 10.5553/HYIEL/266627012022010001006

integrity.[45] Besides such implications, the opinion acknowledges the existence of a justiciable human right to a healthy environment, particularly in the light of Article 11 of the San Salvador Protocol to the American Convention on Human Rights,[46] as a claim distinct from other human rights.[47]

However, while environmental protection is already established as a fundamental right in the African human rights protection system and is being progressively established in the Inter-American system, it is unclear whether Article 37 EU CFR establishes a right rather than principle. Only if environmental protection qualifies as a right under Article 37 EU CFR, could its further nature as an *erga omnes* obligation be asserted. According to the majority of scholars, the wording of Article 37 EU CFR, focusing on the policies of the EU rather than individual rights, allows the *recognition of environmental sustainability as a principle, but not as an 'individual (human) right'* to a healthy environment.[48] However, the case law is more nuanced and, in a string of cases, *the CJEU has developed a right-oriented interpretation of Article 37 EU CFR.* Specifically, in *Romonta* the General Court mentioned the necessity of approaching Article 37 EU CFR in terms of 'rights and freedoms'.[49] In *European Air Transport*, Advocate General Villalón considered that Article 37 EU CFR "expressly recognizes the right to environmental protection".[50] In *Association de médiation sociale*, Villalón further determined that Article 37 EU CFR posits a "fundamental right".[51] Similarly, Advocate General Colomer considered that "[c]ommunity citizens are entitled to demand fulfillment of responsibility under Article 37 of the Charter of Fundamental Rights of the European Union."[52] Therefore, some scholars claim that Article 37 EU CFR might at least evolve into a right-duty relationship *de lege ferenda*.[53]

Of significance is the Resolution on the Effects of Climate Change on Human Rights and the Role of Environmental Defenders on This Matter recently passed by the European Parliament and Council.[54] The Resolution urges the European Commission to monitor the situation of human rights and climate change and to integrate the mainstreaming of human rights into all aspects of national and

45 Id. para. 243.

46 Opened for signature 22 November 1969, 1144 UNTS 123, entered into force 18 July 1978.

47 IACtHR, *Advisory Opinion OC-23/17 of 15 November 2017*, para. 63.

48 Elisa Morgera & Gracia Marin-Duran, 'Article 37', *in* Steve Peers *et al.* (eds.), *The EU Charter of Fundamental Rights: A Commentary*, Hart, Oxford, pp. 984, 995-96.

49 Judgment of 24 October 2014, *Case T-614/13, Romonta v Commission*, ECLI:EU:T:2014:835, para. 77.

50 Opinion of Advocate General Villalón Delivered on 17 February 2011, *Case C-120/10, European Air Transport SA*, ECLI:EU:C:2011:94, para. 78.

51 Opinion of Advocate General Villalón Delivered on 18 July 2013, *Case C-176/12, Association de Médiation Sociale*, ECLI:EU:C:2013:491, para. 44.

52 Opinion of Advocate General Colomel Delivered on 8 January 2004, *Case C-87/02, Commission v Italy*, ECLI:EU:C:2004:13, para. 36.

53 *See e.g.* Kristof Hectors, 'The Chartering of Environmental Protection: Exploring the Boundaries of Environmental Protection as a Human Right', *European Energy & Environmental Law Review*, Vol. 17, Issue 3, 2008, pp. 166 and 172.

54 European Parliament Resolution of 19 May 2021 on the Effects of Climate Change on Human Rights and the Role of Environmental Defenders on This Matter, 2020/2134(INI).

doi: 10.5553/HYIEL/266627012022010001006

international climate action, in cooperation with the UN HRC and High Commissioner on Human Rights (HCHR).[55] Within this framework, besides invoking full compliance with Article 37 EU CFR, the Resolution urges the EU to introduce "a right to a safe and healthy environment" in the Charter.[56] This is critical evidence in favor of the interpretation that *Article 37 EU CFR does not yet establish a human right to a safe environment,* which is nonetheless progressively developing in the EU legal system. It can therefore be assumed that for the time being, the right to a safe environment is not yet clearly established under EU law, neither at the interstate level, nor at the inter-individual level. However, it is evolving as such particularly from a human rights perspective and it should prospectively develop as an *erga omnes* obligation with regard to both state and non-state persons within the EU legal sphere.

3.2. An Evolving Erga Omnes Right to a Sustainable Climate?

There is no official recognition of the right to a sustainable climate as an *erga omnes* obligation in EU law. Nonetheless, there are significant initiatives where such a right emerges, possibly *via* a universal approach. Two recent regulatory instruments are particularly important: the Council and Parliament Regulation Establishing the Framework for Achieving Climate Neutrality (2021/1119)[57] and the above-mentioned European Parliament Resolution on the Effects of Climate Change on Human Rights and the Role of Environmental Defenders on This Matter.[58]

According to Recital (6), Regulation 2021/1119 operates within the framework of the EU CFR, particularly Article 37. Within this context, under Article 1 (Subject matter and scope), the Regulation establishes climate neutrality in the Union by 2050 as a "binding objective", aiming to achieve the long-term temperature goals and adaptation aims of the Paris Agreement. Consequently, Article 2 establishes that EU institutions and Member States take necessary measures to enable the achievement of neutrality, in light of relevant considerations of cost-effectiveness, which underscores the nature of the commitment as one of conduct rather than result. It can therefore be observed that EU law is fully aligned with the UNFCCC regime and does not allow the development of any additional insights as concerns the *erga omnes* nature of the obligation to curb GHG emissions. Essentially, this duty has a relative scope of application within the remit of the UNFCCC and the Paris Agreement, with the potential to develop into an *erga omnes* one in light of quasi-universal participation in these Conventions.[59]

By contrast, EU law seems to be particularly progressive from the standpoint of human rights, whereby Resolution 2020/2134 is a particularly meaningful instrument and has the potential to produce a significant impact on the

55 Id. para. 8.

56 Id.

57 Res. 2021/1119 of 30 June 2021.

58 Res. 2020/2134(INI) of 19 May 2021.

59 *See* Section 2.2 above.

recognition and shape of the fundamental right to a sustainable climate. Substantively, while it generally focuses on the intersection between climate change and first- and second-generation human rights, climate rights emerge in the text of the Resolution as a component of the broader third-generation right to a safe environment. The Resolution stresses the human rights impacts of climate change, *e.g.* in terms of biodiversity loss (Principle 2), water scarcity and peace (Principle 3). As a consequence, it underscores the necessity for the EU and its Member States to act as a reliable global partner supporting and implementing legislation inspired by a comprehensive human rights-based approach to climate action, with respect to both mitigation and adaptation (Principle 1). More generally, the Resolution commits the EU to supporting the mandate of the UN Special Rapporteur on Human Rights and the Environment in his endeavor towards the global recognition of the fundamental right to a safe, clean, healthy and sustainable environment, so that both the Union and its Member States foster the global recognition of such a right by the UN General Assembly, including relevant procedural implications, particularly access to information, public participation in environmental decision-making and access to justice (Principle 7).

Within this framework, while recalling the legal duty to respect 'the right to a safe, clean, healthy and sustainable environment' as a condition for sustainable economic activities, the Resolution notes that international human rights entail legal remedies to redress damage caused by climate change, thus holding not only States, but also businesses and individuals accountable for their actions (Principle 5). As a consequence, the European Parliament and the Council call on the Commission to ensure the concrete implementation of human rights in relation to the environment and climate change (Principle 6). In light of this, the Resolution underscores that *'all people'* should be granted the *"fundamental right to a safe, clean, healthy and sustainable environment and to a stable climate"*, without discrimination, which must "be delivered through ambitious policies" and must be *"fully enforceable through the justice system at all levels"* (Principle 9).[60] This is a significant acknowledgement, where the right to a safe climate emerges as a fundamental claim within the broader context of the human right to a safe environment. Furthermore, the fundamental right to a stable climate emerges as a universal one, and thus as an *erga omnes* right. In light of the necessary correspondence between rights and duties,[61] this entails the acknowledgment of the right to a stable climate as an *erga omnes* obligation.

On this basis, Resolution 2020/2134 reiterates the importance of protecting the Arctic from climate change and adopting an EU Arctic policy for this purpose (Principle 16). The Resolution also goes as far as to acknowledge the necessity of recognizing the crime of ecocide under the Statute of the International Criminal Court (Principle 11). As offences under the Preamble to the Rome Statute have, in principle, a peremptory nature, this approach might support the view that serious violations of the right to a sustainable climate entail peremptory implications.

60 Emphasis added.

61 Hohefeld 1916, p. 717.

Hungarian Yearbook of International Law and European Law 2022 (10) 1
doi: 10.5553/HYIEL/266627012022010001006

Procedurally, the Resolution calls for the establishment of climate focal points within the relevant services of the Commission and the European External Action Service (EEAS), aiming to climate-proof all EU external dealings (Principle 12).

4. Conclusion

International law has progressively developed, and is still developing, towards the recognition of the right to a *sustainable environment* as a universal (*erga omnes*) obligation. A decisive contribution to this development is coming from the progressive recognition of the human rights nature of such a claim, particularly upon the initiative of the HRC. EU law has contributed significantly to this evolution, notably through the EU CFR, and is developing at the same pace as international law. In this context, the right to a *sustainable climate* seems to sporadically emerge internationally as a parallel claim, possibly as a fundamental and universal (*erga omnes*) one, specifically *via* the jurisprudence of the ICJ and the initiative of some non-governmental organizations and scholarly work. In this respect, the EU provides a more holistic *de lege ferenda* framework for a fundamental right to a sustainable climate, hence an *erga omnes* duty, particularly via targeted regulatory initiatives, notably Resolution 2020/2134 of the Parliament and the Council. While affirming the peremptory (*cogens*) nature of the right to a safe environment seems to be logically impossible, it is not possible to exclude that the right to a safe climate evolves as such *de lege ferenda*: meaningful inferences can be developed in this respect from intersections with international criminal law under Resolution 2020/2134.

doi: 10.5553/HYIEL/266627012022010001006

Scientific Knowledge and the ICJ

Trends in the Judicial Handling of Science after the Gabčíkovo-Nagymaros Case

*Katalin Sulyok**

Abstract

This article maps current trends in the scientific engagement of the ICJ in environmental disputes. As a starting point, the analysis takes a closer look at the shortcomings in the ICJ's use of scientific knowledge and expertise in the Gabčíkovo-Nagymaros judgment. It argues that this decision marks the low-water mark of the ICJ's willingness to engage with the scientific aspects of environmental disputes, and details the direct and more subtle ways in which scientific authority was neglected and circumvented in the ICJ's inquiry. The article then points out three trends in more recent environmental decisions of the ICJ, which bespeak of a heightened judicial willingness to appreciate the scientific knowledge underlying environmental disputes. This paper examines how the ICJ now exerts greater control over the parties' negotiations in scientific matters, how it undertakes a more active role in the scrutiny of party-submitted evidence, and how recent disputes feature an extensive use of geospatial evidence. The article concludes by explaining the advantages of the ICJ's more thorough approach to science for the efficiency and legitimacy of environmental dispute resolution.

Keywords: science, scientific disputes, geospatial evidence, Gabčíkovo-Nagymaros judgment, ICJ.

1. Introduction

Perhaps the most disappointing aspect of the *Gabčíkovo-Nagymaros* judgment[1] lies in the visible efforts made by the ICJ to circumvent the apparent scientific dimensions of the parties' conflict regarding the damming of the Danube. The first contentious environmental case decided by the ICJ showcases several judicial maneuvers with which the bench sought to escape evaluating the highly technical party-submitted expert evidence, both at the stage of framing the legal dispute and during its scientific fact-finding procedure.

* Katalin Sulyok: senior lecturer, ELTE Law school, Budapest; chief legal advisor to the Hungarian Ombudsman for Future Generations, Budapest.

1 ICJ, *Case concerning the Gabčíkovo-Nagymaros Project (Hungary v Slovakia)*, judgment, ICJ Reports 1997, p. 7.

doi: 10.5553/HYIEL/266627012022010001007

The judgment marks a shaky start in the ICJ's history of deciding scientifically-loaded environmental disputes. Unsurprisingly, the decision was met with harsh criticism in contemporaneous scholarship for the many shortcomings in the ICJ's fact-finding technique and its lack of appreciation of the technical aspects of the case.[2] Since *Gabčíkovo-Nagymaros*, however, one may witness several welcome developments in the ICJ's case-law in terms of evaluating the scientific dimensions of disputes. The growing body of environmental disputes feature various techniques for the judicial framing of the scientific profile of disputes, the meaningful evaluation of expert evidence, and the use of technical evidence supplied by emerging Earth observation technologies.

This article first discusses, in Section 2, the deficiencies in the ICJ's scientific engagement in *Gabčíkovo-Nagymaros*. These shortcomings will be contrasted in Section 3 with more recent examples from the ICJ's environmental case-law, which reveal a more principled and thorough approach to scientific knowledge in several respects. First, the ICJ is now willing to exert greater control over the parties' negotiations whenever it mandates finding a mutually agreeable solution for science-heavy issues contested by the parties (Section 3.1). In addition, the ICJ has in recent cases shown openness towards taking on a more active role in the scrutiny of party-submitted evidence (Section 3.2.). Finally, recent disputes have seen an extensive judicial use of geospatial evidence (Section 3.3.). Section 4 explains the potential benefits this more transparent and hands-on approach to science for the efficiency and legitimacy of the ICJ's environmental jurisprudence.

2. The Gabčíkovo-Nagymaros Case as the Low-Water Mark of the ICJ's Engagement with Scientific Knowledge

In *Gabčíkovo-Nagymaros*, the ICJ famously held that "it is not necessary"[3] to take a position on the scientific points of contention between the parties. Hence, instead of examining the merits of the scientific evidence submitted by Hungary and Slovakia, the ICJ repeatedly urged the parties to find "an agreed solution"[4] with respect to virtually all science-heavy issues, such as specifying the volume of waters to be released to the old riverbed,[5] and concretizing the scope of environmental damage to be compensated by Slovakia.[6] The avoidance strategy of

2 Adriana Koe, 'Damming the Danube: The International Court of Justice and the Gabčíkovo-Nagymaros Project (Hungary v Slovakia)', *Sydney Law Review,* Vol. 20, Issue 4, 1998, p. 616; Stephen Stec & Gabriel Eckstein, 'Of Solemn Oaths and Obligations: The Environmental Impact of the ICJ's Decision in the Case Concerning the Gabčíkovo-Nagymaros Project', *Yearbook of International Environmental Law,* Vol. 8, Issue 1, 1997, pp. 41-57; Cesare PR Romano, *The Peaceful Settlement of International Environmental Disputes A Pragmatic Approach,* Kluwer Law International, 2000, pp. 259-260.

3 ICJ, *Gabčíkovo-Nagymaros,* judgment, para. 54. *see* in more detail in Chapter 3, Section 3.1.

4 Id. para. 142; and the same was mandated in para. 140: The parties "must find a satisfactory solution for the volume of water to be released into the old bed of the Danube."

5 Id. para. 140.

6 Id. para. 155, Section (2)D.

doi: 10.5553/HYIEL/266627012022010001007

the ICJ ultimately shaped the framing of the decisive legal issues in the case and the ICJ's approach to evidentiary assessment. These will be addressed in turn.

As to the framing of the relevant legal issues, it is salient how the ICJ simply carved out from the main thread of the judicial analysis those aspects that were most tainted with scientific complexities. Even though judicial economy, *i.e.* narrowing the scope of its judgments to the extent possible,[7] is an established feature of the ICJ's case law,[8] it is still striking how the ICJ 'minimized'[9] science in its inquiry. In the ICJ's reading, it was only asked to determine the basis of compensation but not the quantum of damages.[10] However, such a configuration of the judicial task in the case does not strictly follow from Article 2(2) of the Compromis of April 1993, which provides that "the Court is also requested to determine the legal consequences, including the rights and obligations for the Parties, arising from its Judgment". Arguably, even if the ICJ's mandate was indeed confined to ruling only on the legal basis but not the quantum of compensation, it should still have determined the basis and scope of compensation with more clarity. It appears that the ICJ made a strategic choice not to touch upon the science-intensive question of determining the quantum of compensation when it interpreted its mandate under the Compromis.

Such a narrow tailoring of the issues decided by the ICJ has come with a price, namely that the judgment was clearly unable to resolve the underlying conflict. The parties have failed to even begin a meaningful dialogue for over a decade after the judgment.[11] Subsequently, Slovakia filed a request for an additional judgment, asking the ICJ to determine the modalities for executing the original judgment.[12] Ever since, all attempts at engaging in meaningful negotiations have proven to be futile. Although the parties agreed to the formal discontinuance of the proceedings before the ICJ in 2017,[13] their protracted bilateral consultation did not reach a mutually agreeable solution in the scientifically-loaded issues. Tellingly, *Gabčíkovo-Nagymaros* has not been removed from the ICJ's list,[14] well illustrating the many questions that the judgment left unanswered.

7 Fulvio Maria Palombino, 'Judicial Economy and Limitation of the Scope of the Decision in International Adjudication', *Leiden Journal of International Law*, Vol. 23, Issue 4, 2010, p. 922.

8 Christine Gray, 'The 2016 Judicial Activity of the International Court of Justice', *American Journal of International Law*, Vol. 111, Issue 2, 2017, pp. 415-436.

9 Jorge E. Vinuales, 'Observations Sur Le Traitement Des Motifs Scientifiques Dans Le Contentieux Environmental International', *in* Couveinhes Matsumoto & Nollez-Goldbach (eds.), *Les motifs non-juridiques des jugements internationaux. Actes de la 1ére journée de droit international de l'ENS*, Pedone, 2016, pp. 114-116.

10 ICJ, *Gabčíkovo-Nagymaros*, judgment, para. 152.

11 Marcel Szabó, 'The Implementation of the Judgment of the ICJ on the Gabčíkovo-Nagymaros Dispute', *Iustum Aequum Salutare*, Vol. 5, Issue 1, 2009, p. 22. *See also* Marcel Szabó, 'A bős-nagymarosi vízlépcsőper és utóélete – két évtized távlatából', *in* Gábor Kajtár & Pál Sonnevend (eds.), *A nemzetközi jog, az uniós jog és a nemzetközi kapcsolatok szerepe a 21. században: tanulmányok Valki László tiszteletére*, ELTE Eötvös, Budapest, 2021, pp. 483-198.

12 Press release of the ICJ, No. 1998/28, 3 September 1998.

13 Press release of the ICJ, No. 2017/31 21 July 2017.

14 *See* the ICJ's list of pending cases at www.icj-cij.org/en/pending-cases.

doi: 10.5553/HYIEL/266627012022010001007

The *Gabčíkovo-Nagymaros* dispute also displayed a rather poor evidentiary assessment. In fact, the ICJ chose not to consider the abundant expert evidence submitted by the parties, and found the absence of an imminent environmental risk without evaluating any scientific data describing such peril.[15] This path has generated harsh criticism[16] given that solid and legitimate conclusions can hardly be drawn regarding matters of ecological risks without considering the substance of relevant scientific reports submitted by the parties. The ICJ's approach was in stark contrast with the position of the litigants, who regarded the issue of environmental risks as being primarily a scientific question, as evidenced by the sheer number of expert reports adduced. The Hungarian Reply alone included a 100-page long 'Scientific rebuttal,' in which it challenged the Slovakian scientific claims in detail.[17] Moreover, the scientific aspect of the conflict was thoroughly investigated by a fact-finding mission of the European Communities,[18] which also made express recommendations on the amount of water to be discharged into the Danube's old riverbed in order to prevent an irreversible adverse ecological impact. Nevertheless, the ICJ chose to circumvent the party-adduced evidence regarding environmental risks, and the plea of ecological necessity in particular, which led to an apparent inconsistency between "the strong environmentally-friendly language"[19] of the judgment and the conclusion reached therein.

Superficial evidentiary assessments are usually justified with reference to specialized State organs' superior epistemic capacity to make highly technical evaluations. This argument is often deemed as warranting an epistemically deferential review from international courts and tribunals.[20] However, a too deferential judicial review may easily undermine the exercise of the judicial function in science-heavy cases, as it leaves the parties' scientific narratives largely unchecked.[21] The dissenting opinion of Judge Herczegh pointed to a similar deficiency in the majority's position in *Gabčíkovo-Nagymaros*:

15 Koe 1998, p. 616.

16 Anna Riddell, 'Scientific Evidence in the International Court of Justice – Problems and Possibilities', *Finnish Yearbook of International Law,* Vol. 20, 2009, p. 242. *See* Joint Dissenting Opinion of Judge Al-Khasawneh and Judge Simma, Declaration of Judge Yusuf, Dissenting Opinion of Judge Vinuesa.

17 ICJ, *Gabčíkovo-Nagymaros*, Reply of the Republic of Hungary, Volume 2, Scientific Rebuttal, 20 June 1995, pp. 1-108.

18 Mission report of the Commission of the European Communities Czech and Slovak Federal Republic and Republic of Hungary, October 31, 1992, Bratislava (Annex 13 to the Memorandum of Republic of Hungary); Commission of the European Communities Republic of Hungary, Slovak Republic, Working Group of Monitoring and water management experts for the Gabčíkovo system of locks. Report on Temporary water management regime, December 1, 1993, Bratislava (Annex 19 to the Memorandum of Republic of Hungary).

19 James Crawford, 'In Dubio Pro Natura: The Dissent of Judge Herczegh', *in* Péter Kovács (ed.), *International law: a Quiet Strength. Miscellanea in memoriam Géza Herczegh,* Pázmány Press, Budapest, 2011, p. 268.

20 Esmé Shirlow, *Judging at the Interface - Deference to State Decision-Making Authority in International Adjudication,* Cambridge University Press, Cambridge, 2021, pp. 20-24.

21 Katalin Sulyok, *Judicial Deference and Science, Law and Proceedings of International Courts and Tribunals*, forthcoming in 2022, manuscript on file with the author.

doi: 10.5553/HYIEL/266627012022010001007

> "As a judicial organ, the Court was admittedly not empowered to decide scientific questions touching on biology, hydrology, and so on, or questions of a technical type which arose out of the G/N [Gabčíkovo-Nagymaros] Project; but it could – and even should – have ruled on the legal consequences of certain facts alleged by one Party".[22]

The ICJ indeed appeared to draw conclusions about Hungary's scientific arguments without making any transparent evaluation of the underlying facts. In particular, it dismissed Hungary's plea of ecological necessity by distinguishing "possible peril", described by uncertain scientific claims, from the "objective existence of a peril", which was to be supported by foreseeable future damage.[23] A slight majority found that the several hundred pages of scientific evidence only sufficed to suggest "serious uncertainties",[24] but could not establish an objective peril that justified a state of necessity. Choosing between these two legal scenarios, the factual bases of which run so closely together, without touching upon the scientific evidence submitted, let alone providing any transparent evaluation thereof, seriously undermines the legitimacy of the reasoning.

As a final note, the *Gabčíkovo-Nagymaros* judgment also proves that judges may sometimes react to the uncertainties in the underlying scientific knowledge in an asymmetric way. Not being familiar with the conventions and processes of scientific knowledge production, lawyers may often be skeptical about the reliable and unbiased nature of scientific arguments or tend to assume political considerations behind science-backed arguments. In the material case, Judge Oda in his dissenting opinion first asserted that "it cannot be said that the drafters of either the Treaty or of the Joint Contractual Plan failed to take due account of the environment".[25] This language suggests that Judge Oda did not question the credibility and scientific soundness of decisions made by the leaders of the Communist Parties, which negated all scientific concerns pertaining to the project when they concluded the treaty in 1977, despite having no detailed prior environmental impact assessment.[26] In the following sentence, the dissenting opinion voiced a "firm conviction" that concerns about environmental risks raised by environmental opposition groups in Hungary were without merit. Such a reasoning, which suspects political bias with regard to certain scientific claims but refutes those in relation to other scientific assumptions without any in-depth assessment of the scientific evidence can easily be vulnerable to criticism, as it appears to be arbitrary from an epistemic point of view.

In sum, *Gabčíkovo-Nagymaros* appears as the low-water mark of the ICJ's willingness to face, and openly deal with scientific complexities implicated in legal disputes referred to it. The ICJ was criticized for "acrobatically avoiding"[27] the ecological aspects of the dispute, for throwing the dispute "back into the lap of

22 ICJ, *Gabčíkovo-Nagymaros*, Dissenting Opinion of Judge Herczegh, p. 177.
23 ICJ, *Gabčíkovo-Nagymaros*, judgment, para. 54.
24 Id.
25 ICJ, *Gabčíkovo-Nagymaros*, Dissenting Opinion of Judge Oda, para. 12.
26 ICJ, *Gabčíkovo-Nagymaros*, judgment, para. 57.
27 Stec & Eckstein 1997, p. 42.

doi: 10.5553/HYIEL/266627012022010001007

the parties",[28] for deciding the dispute "solely on the law",[29] and also for "camouflaging" its factual evaluation in a suspicious manner.[30] There are indeed good reasons for regarding the *Gabčíkovo-Nagymaros* judgment as proof of the ICJ's "unwillingness or unsuitability"[31] at the time to deal with scientific disputes. Nevertheless, later cases attest a growing appreciation of the ICJ for the instrumental role that scientific knowledge plays in deciding environmental legal disputes.

3. Developments since Gabčíkovo-Nagymaros: the ICJ's Growing Appreciation for the Scientific Profile of Environmental Disputes

Ever since *Gabčíkovo-Nagymaros*, the number of scientific disputes referred to the ICJ has been on the rise.[32] These proceedings have seen considerable developments in how the ICJ approaches scientific knowledge embedded in the parties' arguments. Importantly, however, as the harsh criticism engendered by the majority's evidentiary findings in *Pulp Mills* shows, the ICJ's experiments with handling scientific evidence have not been without controversies.[33] Nevertheless, recent jurisprudence showcases a more direct and thorough engagement with science in the judicial inquiry. These developments include a judicial framing of disputes in a way as to include science-heavy aspects in the legally relevant ambit of cases (Section 3.1.), the use of geospatial data as persuasive evidence (Section 3.2.), and a closer judicial scrutiny of science-based positions (Section 3.3.).

3.1. Framing the Judicial Task to Reflect on the Scientific Dimensions of Disputes

In more recent environmental proceedings, the ICJ appears to frame environmental disputes in a way that allows scientific knowledge to enter the sphere of judicially relevant considerations. Such an approach is manifest, for instance, in the ICJ's more active involvement in the parties' negotiations regarding science-based, contested legal issues. Similarly, one may find occasions in more recent case-law when the ICJ is ready to follow the science-heavy pleadings of the parties, resulting in an equally science-intensive judicial inquiry. This is a marked improvement compared to *Gabčíkovo-Nagymaros*, where the ICJ

28 Romano 2000, p. 256.

29 Anna Riddell & Brendan Plant, *Evidence before the International Court of Justice*, British Institute of International and Comparative Law, 2016, p. 353.

30 Vinuales 2016, pp. 114-115.

31 Riddell & Plant 2016, p. 348.

32 ICJ, *Pulp Mills on the River Uruguay (Argentina v Uruguay)*, judgment, ICJ Reports 2010, p. 14; ICJ, *Aerial Herbicide Spraying (Ecuador v Colombia)*, Discontinuance, Order of 13 September 2013, ICJ Reports 2013, p. 278; ICJ, *Whaling in the Antarctic (Australia v Japan: New Zealand intervening)*, judgment, ICJ Reports 2014, p. 226; ICJ, *Certain Activities carried out by Nicaragua in the Border Area (Costa Rica v Nicaragua)* and *Construction of a Road in Costa Rica along the San Juan River (Nicaragua v Costa Rica)*, judgment, ICJ Reports 2015, p. 665; *Dispute over the Status and Use of the Waters of the Silala (Chile v Bolivia)*, filed in the Registry of the ICJ on 6 June 2016.

33 Riddell 2009, p. 242.

doi: 10.5553/HYIEL/266627012022010001007

refused to consider the scientific submissions of the parties in resolving the dispute. Lastly, the bench has now become more open to base findings on probabilistic scientific proof. Concrete examples of such framing techniques will now be addressed below.

First, the ICJ assumes a more active role in overviewing and supervising science-intensive negotiation processes. As addressed above, in *Gabčíkovo-Nagymaros*, the judgment outsourced the resolution of such questions to the parties in an open-ended negotiation process in which the ICJ had no role to play. In contrast, in *Certain Activities/Construction of a Road,* the ICJ set a deadline for the parties' consultation to determine the amount of compensation payable by Nicaragua for the environmental damage arising out of violating Costa Rica's territorial sovereignty. Importantly, the ICJ was ready to set the quantum of compensation in a separate judgment when the parties failed to find a solution of their own.[34] This judicial oversight of the consultation process therefore ensured an effective resolution of the disputed questions, even when the parties had reached a stalemate.

Moreover, the ICJ chose a fact-intensive argumentative path in the compensation judgment issued in *Certain Activities*. It was the first time that the ICJ adjudicated a compensation claim for environmental damage,[35] and it awarded compensation for the direct injuries resulting from the breach of territorial sovereignty. The parties could not agree on the quantum of reparation, as they disagreed about the appropriate scientific methods for valuing environmental damage.[36] Costa Rica put forward a 'value transfer approach', which accounted for both 'direct use value' of tradeable services (such as timber) and 'indirect use value' for non-tradeable ecosystem services (*e.g.* climate regulation services),[37] whereas Nicaragua preferred a valuation based on 'ecosystem service replacement costs'. Costa Rica therefore requested the ICJ's judgment to declare the amount of compensation.

It was in this context that the ICJ had to monetize the loss of ecosystem services provided by the wetland destroyed by Nicaraguan troops on Costa Rican territory.[38] The ICJ adopted an ecosystem services approach,[39] announcing that any "consequent impairment or loss of the ability of the environment to provide goods and services, is compensable under international law."[40] This approach yielded a particularly fact-intensive inquiry, where the ICJ had to engage closely with highly technical submissions. Even though the ICJ avowedly conducted an "overall valuation"[41] providing only a rather "opaque"[42] scientific assessment of

34 ICJ, *Certain Activities carried out by Nicaragua in the Border Area (Costa Rica v Nicaragua),* judgment on compensation, ICJ Reports 2018, p. 15.
35 Id. para. 41.
36 ICJ, *Certain Activities,* order of 18 July 2017, ICJ Reports 2017, p. 285.
37 ICJ, *Certain Activities,* judgment on compensation, para. 47.
38 Id. paras. 22-23, 27.
39 Id. para. 46.
40 Id. para. 42.
41 Id. paras. 80, 81, 83.
42 Id. Dissenting Opinion of Judge *ad hoc* Dugard, para. 22.

doi: 10.5553/HYIEL/266627012022010001007

the party-submitted evidence, it nevertheless conducted its own assessment regarding the valuation of various ecosystem services and did not accept any of the calculations offered by the parties in their entirety.[43] The bench took issue with the calculations offered by the parties when it had doubts regarding the reliability of the methodology used.[44] The ICJ therefore decided to make adjustments in its calculation of damages to "account for the shortcomings"[45] in the parties' methodologies, though without setting out the details of its own corrected analysis. All in all, the reasoning of the ICJ became remarkably science-heavy. This gives hope that the ICJ no longer shies away from crafting a legal argumentation that is essentially rooted in scientific evidence.

A final, noteworthy development in the ICJ's approach to science lies in how it approaches the problem of scientific uncertainty. The uncertain nature of scientific evidence means that scientific research can only provide probabilistic results as opposed to clear-cut certainties.[46] In *Gabčíkovo-Nagymaros,* scientific uncertainties in the underlying data essentially paralyzed the ICJ's analysis and prevented it from building the judicial evaluation on the expert evidence submitted. The ICJ firmly avoided confronting its evidentiary record by deeming it unnecessary[47] to comment on the evidence in rendering its judgment. In the compensation judgment issued in *Certain Activities*, however, the ICJ took an entirely different approach. It stressed that although the state of scientific knowledge relevant to a legal dispute may often be uncertain,

> "these are difficulties that must be addressed as and when they arise in light of the facts of the case at hand and the evidence presented to the Court. Ultimately, it is for the Court to decide"[48]

the relevant legal question rooted in scientific facts. This is indeed a laudable turn, as it ensures that science-heavy aspects will be deemed justiciable by the ICJ, and scientific arguments will not be carved out from the judicial analysis.

3.2. Use of Geospatial Evidence

The interpretation of highly technical scientific evidence often poses hurdles for judges without scientific training. Typically, the parties have been submitting maps, graphs, aerial photos and model calculations to the ICJ. Whereas highly technical modelling results have been dismissed by the ICJ on several occasions,[49]

43 Id. para. 52.

44 Id. para. 79.

45 Id. para. 86.

46 On the definition and various sources of scientific uncertainty *see* Katalin Sulyok, *Science and Judicial Reasoning – The Legitimacy of International Environmental Adjudication,* Cambridge University Press, Cambridge, 2021, pp. 32-36.

47 ICJ, *Gabčíkovo-Nagymaros,* judgment, para. 54.

48 ICJ, *Certain Activities,* judgment on compensation, para. 34.

49 ICJ, *Certain Activities/Construction of a Road,* judgment, paras. 203-204; ICJ, *Territorial and Maritime Dispute (Nicaragua v Colombia),* judgment, ICJ Reports 2012, p. 624, para. 36.

doi: 10.5553/HYIEL/266627012022010001007

a specific type of scientific evidence, namely geospatial data, is increasingly relied on by the ICJ as a basis for its findings.

In *Certain Activities/Construction of a Road*, for instance, Costa Rica submitted satellite images to prove the presence of Nicaraguan troops on its territory and to provide persuasive evidence on the extent of environmental damage caused to its territory. The ICJ found the imagery convincing evidence of the presence of Nicaraguan military groups on the territory, which led to the provisional measures being issued.[50] In the same proceedings, the high-resolution satellite imagery showed to the ICJ's satisfaction that the tree removal 'likely' occurred during the presence of the troops in the area.[51] The ICJ was also ready to find that remote sensing data was "strong evidence to suggest" that the channels in question were also constructed during the relevant period.[52]

These instances clearly illustrate the increasing penetration of geospatial information technologies into the sphere of international adjudication – a trend that will most likely continue in the future. Reliance on Earth observation technology is not confined to environmental disputes[53] and appears before several other international courts and tribunals as well.[54] One of the reasons for the influential nature of such data lies in that fact that satellite imaging techniques yield particularly powerful scientific proof. Satellite images are easily intelligible to laymen judges and provide an intuitively appealing and objective account of the factual circumstances. Geospatial evidence also allows environmental changes to be tracked over time, hence supplying information that may be relevant for a causal analysis. The rapid development and sophistication of remote sensing technology[55] means it can provide data even on nuanced environmental processes, such as gradually emerging or protracted pollution. Furthermore, Earth observation technologies can also provide high-resolution real-time data that may even substitute for site-visits by the ICJ, mimicking domestic environmental law developments, where national courts increasingly use such evidence as inspection tools.[56]

50 ICJ, *Certain Activities/Construction of a Road*, provisional measures, Order of 22 November 2013, ICJ Reports 2013, p. 354, para. 46.

51 ICJ, *Certain Activities*, judgment on compensation, para. 98.

52 Id. para. 98.

53 *E.g.* the applicant relied on satellite imagery in the Application instituting proceedings and the Request for the indication of provisional measures (11 November 2019), para. 11. in the case concerning *Application of the Convention on the Prevention and Punishment of the Crime of Genocide (The Gambia v Myanmar)*.

54 For the use of geospatial evidence by international criminal courts and tribunals, *see* Lindsay Freeman, 'The Impact of Digital Technologies on International Criminal Investigations and Trials', *Fordham International Law Journal*, Vol. 41, Issue 2, 2018, pp. 285-336.

55 For a recent report released by Group of Earth Observations detailing the recent application of remote sensing in environmental policy-making, *see* at https://eo4sdg.org/wp-content/uploads/2018/09/EO4SDG_for_GEO.Highlights.Report.pdf.

56 Katalin Sulyok *et al.*, *Summary Report of the European Forum of Judges for the Environment, Answers to the Questionnaire Concerning the Role of Science in Environmental Adjudication*, 2019, pp. 8-9, at www.eufje.org/images/docConf/hel2019/Summary_report_Questionnaire_EUFJE2019.pdf.

doi: 10.5553/HYIEL/266627012022010001007

Satellite imagery is supplied by commercial providers as well as international or state agencies. Litigants may feel encouraged to commission such imagery, as its costs have been deemed compensable by the ICJ. Also, a vast amount of geospatial data can be derived free of charge from international and national satellites, which may further foster their more frequent use in interstate disputes. The ICJ's reliance on geospatial data is an important development in buttressing the scientific bases of judgments. It ensures that the judicial analysis is informed by technical evidence and hence the legal assessment of the ICJ approximates the factual realities as closely as possible in disputes with a technically complex background.

3.3. Closer Scrutiny of Party-Submitted Scientific Evidence

While in *Gabčíkovo-Nagymaros*, a "factual anxiety"[57] was the hallmark of the ICJ's assessment of complex technical evidence, more recent environmental disputes attest to a greater willingness of the ICJ to take a closer look at the scientific record of such cases. This is manifest in the questioning of the experts and in the intrusive standard of review the ICJ has set for checking the scientific claims of the parties.

Expert evidence is now routinely presented by expert witnesses, who can be questioned by the ICJ and be cross-examined by counsels. The *Certain Activities/ Construction of a Road*[58] and the *Whaling in the Antarctic* cases both featured cross-examination, which allowed the ICJ to test the credibility and consistency of party-submitted scientific data. Importantly in *Whaling in the Antarctic*, the judges did not give "*carte blanche* acceptance of expert opinions",[59] nor did they use opposing scientific views as an excuse for disregarding the expert evidence. The active dialogue between the party-appointed experts and the bench during the fact-finding procedure[60] provided the ICJ with an in-depth understanding of the technical aspects of the dispute.

The ICJ's meaningful engagement with conflicting evidence in that case[61] also allowed the bench to craft a rather fact-intensive standard of review, which resulted in an intrusive scrutiny of the parties' scientific narratives. The legal controversy concerned the interpretation of the special permit procedure under the 1946 International Convention on the Regulation of Whaling (ICRW). Article VIII ICRW allows for Special Permit Whaling if it is conducted 'for purposes of scientific research'. Japan essentially claimed that its whaling program, JARPA II, pursued 'scientific objectives' and therefore fell under Article VIII of ICRW, whereas Australia argued that Japan relied on science only

57 Makane Moïse Mbengue, 'Scientific Fact-finding by International Courts and Tribunals', *Journal of International Dispute Settlement*, Vol. 3, Issue 3, 2012, p. 517.

58 ICJ, *Certain Activities/Construction of a Road*, judgment, para. 34.

59 Marc Mangel, 'Whales, Science, and Scientific Whaling in the International Court of Justice', *Proceedings of the National Academy of Sciences of the United States of America*, Vol. 113, 2016, p. 14526.

60 Id.

61 Philippe Sands, 'Climate Change and the Rule of Law: Adjudicating the Future of International Law', *Journal of Environmental Law*, Vol. 28, Issue 1, 2016, p. 29.

doi: 10.5553/HYIEL/266627012022010001007

as a pretext to mask its commercial whaling operations.[62] The parties offered rival definitions for the term 'scientific research'. In essence the ICJ was asked to decide whether Japan's appeal to scientific research could be seen as legitimate or rather a spurious claim of science. However, the ICJ geared its reasoning in such a way as to elegantly escape the difficult position of having to delineate (legitimate and valid) science from (spurious) non-science. Instead of choosing one from among the competing definitions of 'science' as advanced by the litigants, it decided not to become entangled in the definitional debate. Instead, it devised an objective standard of review, that of reasonableness, to assess Japan's claim of scientific research.

Under the reasonableness test, the ICJ assessed whether the whaling program's "design and implementation were reasonable in relation to its stated scientific objectives".[63] If JARPA II failed this reasonableness assessment; the ICJ held that it could not be regarded as being 'for purposes of' scientific research. The judgment listed several factors that were relevant to deciding whether the use of lethal methods was reasonable, such as the scale of lethal sampling, the methodology to select such sample sizes, the program's scientific output and the extent of scientific cooperation in relation to the program.[64] The judgment conducted a particularly science-intensive, 80-paragraph judicial inquiry into the design, methodology and implementation of the alleged research program,[65] which yielded an ambitious and intrusive standard of review.[66] This led the ICJ to conclude that JARPA cannot be deemed reasonable as to its design and implementation and declared a violation of ICRW.

In sum, the reasonableness standard of review was instrumental in enabling the ICJ to reflect closely on the scientific controversy between the parties while it also ensured that the expert opinions did not dictate the outcome of its inquiry. The bench formulated its own reading of the party-submitted scientific evidence and drew legal conclusions from the factual arguments.

4. Benefits of the ICJ's More Thorough Approach to Scientific Knowledge

The above discussed trends all provide grounds for optimism concerning the overall position of scientific knowledge before the ICJ. Litigants' prospects of successfully relying on scientific evidence have undoubtedly improved since the early environmental jurisprudence of the ICJ. As demonstrated above, the ICJ has made considerable headway in assessing and utilizing scientific input offered by the parties. Nevertheless, there are still open (and debated) questions pertaining to the ICJ's scientific fact-finding, including whether relying on *ex*

62 ICJ, *Whaling in the Antarctic*, judgment, para. 101.
63 Id. para. 88.
64 Id. para. 88.
65 Id. paras. 147-222.
66 Sulyok 2021, pp. 112-116.

Hungarian Yearbook of International Law and European Law 2022 (10) 1
doi: 10.5553/HYIEL/266627012022010001007

curia experts[67] or shadow experts[68] are desirable procedural avenues for buttressing the epistemic capacities of the bench. In any case, the currently pending *Waters of the Silala* dispute will put the ICJ's arguably more embracive approach towards science to the test, as the facts of the case rest on heavily contested scientific views between the parties.[69] We shall see in what ways the ICJ will gather expert advice and to what extent scientific input will drive its legal analysis.

Having surveyed the key respects in which the ICJ's approach has changed fundamentally towards a more transparent and direct assessment and reliance on scientific knowledge, this article concludes with offering some normative remarks on the benefits of the ICJ's growing appreciation for the scientific profile of disputes.

(i) First of all, considering science meaningfully by the ICJ levels the playing field for the party relying on scientific evidence. Evaluating technical scientific proof is often an obstacle to establishing environmental liability under international law.[70] Scientific arguments are typically invoked by those seeking to advance environmental protection measures or to challenge environmentally harmful practices. Treating uncertain and ambiguous scientific knowledge in an overly dismissive way disproportionately burdens these claims and reduces their chances of success in litigation.

(ii) Second, proper judicial engagement with scientific knowledge strengthens the binding force of environmental laws. Environmental rules cannot have a real 'bite' and be an effective deterrent if they cannot be enforced judicially. If environmental claims tend to fail for resting on uncertain scientific evidence, environmental litigation will remain ineffective. To guard against this, international courts and tribunals hearing science-heavy disputes ought to develop their *modus vivendi* with authoritative, complex, and ambiguous scientific evidence.

(iii) Third, duly considering scientific arguments can provide a response to the significant third-party effects of environmental disputes. Given the

67 Caroline E. Foster, 'New Clothes for the Emperor? Consultation of Experts by the International Court of Justice', *Journal of International Dispute Settlement*, Vol. 5, Issue 1, 2014, p. 139; Loretta Malintoppi, 'Fact Finding and Evidence Before the International Court of Justice (Notably in Scientific-Related Disputes)', *Journal of International Dispute Settlement*, Vol. 7, Issue 2, 2016, p. 421; James Devaney, *Fact-Finding before the International Court of Justice,* Cambridge University Press, Cambridge, 2016; Laurence Boisson de Chazournes *et al.*, 'One Size Does Not Fit All – Uses of Experts before International Courts and Tribunals: An Insight into the Practice', *Journal of International Dispute Settlement*, Vol. 9, Issue 3, 2018, p. 477.

68 Vinuales 2016, p. 120; Daniel Peat, 'The Use of Court-Appointed Experts by The International Court of Justice', *British Yearbook of International Law*, Vol. 84, Issue 1, 2014, p. 288; Riddell & Plant 2016.

69 ICJ, *Dispute over the Status and Use of the Waters of the Silala (Chile v Bolivia),* filed in the Registry of the ICJ on 6 June 2016.

70 Alexandre Kiss, 'Present Limits to the Enforcement of State Responsibility for Environmental Damage', *in* Francesco Francioni & Tullio Scovazzi (eds.), *International Responsibility for Environmental Harm*, Graham and Trotman, 1991, p. 5; Céline Négre, 'Responsibility and International Environmental Law', *in* James Crawford *et al.* (eds.), *The Law of International Responsibility*, Oxford University Press, Oxford, 2010, p. 805.

doi: 10.5553/HYIEL/266627012022010001007

considerable public interest involved in environmental litigation, environmental adjudication cannot be handled as a strictly *inter partes* matter.[71] Thorough investigation of the scientific facts in environmental conflicts 'should be seen as a public function of relevance to the international community as a whole',[72] for it represents the interests of affected third parties, such as the wider community, whose air is polluted, or future generations, whose resources are depleted on longer time scales by development projects pursued in the present.

(iv) Finally, evaluating the party-submitted evidence and feeding it into the judicial decision-making process in a transparent manner supports the legitimacy of the adjudicatory findings in the eyes of the parties. This is especially true in proceedings, where the litigants themselves deem the scientific dimensions of the dispute to be legally relevant or even decisive. The losing party and even the wider public will not accept a decision as just and appropriate if the underlying reasons are not clearly explained.[73] However, relying on expertise in a judgment only enhances the legitimacy of a decision if the scientific opinion is properly accounted for,[74] as judicial findings concerning techno-scientific complexities must be based on a "careful consideration of relevant facts"'.[75] This specific understanding of legitimacy, namely, epistemic legitimacy, requires that judgments duly respect the logic of scientific knowledge in the ways in which techno-scientific input is reflected on in the reasoning.

Securing the factual correctness of judgments in scientifically-loaded disputes is undoubtedly challenging for courts. It calls for innovative judicial solutions, both in terms of fact-finding and judicial reasoning, which may stretch beyond the epistemic comfort zone of international judges. Nevertheless, international fora should be cognizant of the consequential nature of the relationship between cognitively authoritative scientific knowledge and the convincing force of their own decisions in environmental disputes. As we have seen in the ICJ's practice, it depends on the conscious choices of the bench whether, and to what extent it reflects on pertinent scientific information when deciding such disputes. Considering how the ICJ essentially 'descienticized' its inquiry in early scientific cases, more recent trends give hope that it no longer seeks to distance itself from scientific considerations when hearing environmental disputes.

71 ICJ, *Gabčíkovo-Nagymaros*, Separate Opinion of Judge Weeramantry, para. 118.

72 Neil A. Craik, 'Recalcitrant Reality and Chosen Ideals: The Public Function of Dispute Settlement in International Environmental Law', *The Georgetown International Environmental Law Review*, Vol. 10, Issue 2, 1998, p. 572.

73 Yuval Shany, *Assessing the Effectiveness of International Courts*, Oxford University Press, Oxford, 2014, p. 37; Boisson de Chazournes *et al.* 2018, p. 487; Irmgard Griss, 'How Judges Think: Judicial Reasoning in Tort Cases from a Comparative Perspective', *Journal of European Tort Law*, Vol. 4, Issue 3, 2013, p. 250.

74 Jessica Lawrence, 'The Structural Logic of Expert Participation in WTO Decision-Making Process', *in* Mónika Ambrus *et al.* (eds.), *The Role of 'Experts' in International and European Decision-Making Processes*, Cambridge University Press, Cambridge, 2014, p. 173.

75 Daniel C. Esty, 'Good Governance at the World Trade Organization: Building a Foundation of Administrative Law', *Journal of International Economic Law*, Vol. 10, Issue 3, 2007, p. 517.

doi: 10.5553/HYIEL/266627012022010001007

ANNIVERSARY: THE 100TH ANNIVERSARY OF THE ESTABLISHMENT OF DIPLOMATIC RELATIONS BETWEEN THE US AND HUNGARY (1922-2022)

1956 and the US Legation in Budapest

Devoted, Enthusiastic Professionals Compelled to Act without Clear Instructions from Home and without Functioning Communication Devices in the Most Turbulent Historical Times[*]

Péter Kovács[**]

Abstract

It is well known that the academic literature on the 1956 Hungarian Revolution is enormous in Hungary and abroad and the analysis of the policy making within the main state-actors (Hungary, Soviet Union, US, Great Britain, Yugoslavia, etc.) and the UN is also abundant, filling long shelves in the libraries specialized in this field of research. Taking into account the Hungarian Yearbook's anniversary theme chosen for 2022, as well as the approximative length of the articles as established by the editorial board, I intend to cover the activity of the American Legation in Budapest during the Revolution. The article focuses on the activity of the American Legation and covers policy-making in Washington or in Budapest only to the extent that is strictly necessary to understand the background of the steps taken or omitted.

Keywords: 1956, revolution, US Embassy, US Legation, Imre Nagy.

1. Introduction and Personal Background

It is well known that the academic literature about the 1956 Hungarian Revolution is enormous in Hungary and abroad and the analysis of the policy-making within the main state-actors (Hungary, Soviet Union, US, Great Britain, Yugoslavia, *etc.*) and the UN is also abundant, filling long shelves in the libraries specialized in this field of research. Open-access electronic journals have also

* This contribution was written in my personal capacity, the thoughts expressed herein cannot be attributed to the ICC.

** Péter Kovács: professor of international law, Pázmány Péter Catholic University, Budapest; judge, International Criminal Court, the Hague (2015-2024).

doi: 10.5553/HYIEL/266627012022010001008

significantly contributed to a better and historically more and more accurate perception of these heroic and tragic events of the post-World War history.[1]

Taking into account the Hungarian Yearbook's anniversary theme chosen for this year as well as the approximative length of the articles as established by the editorial board, I intend to cover the activity of the American Legation in Budapest during the Revolution. In fact, I return to a topic that I treated in an article[2] commemorating the 50th anniversary of the Revolution. This article was followed by an annotated, footnoted interview[3] with Jordan Thomas Rogers[4] and Ernest Nagy, American diplomats serving in Hungary in 1956 with whom I lead a very intensive electronic correspondence. In these two papers, I used some previous scholarly articles, diplomatic documents published in the US[5] and in

1 *See e.g.* Charles Gáti, *Failed Illusions: Moscow, Washington, Budapest, and the 1956 Hungarian Revolution,* Woodrow Wilson Center Press, Washington DC, 2006. (In Hungarian: *Vesztett illúziók. Moszkva, Washington, Budapest és az 1956-os forradalom*, Osiris, Budapest, 2006.); Chris Tudda, '"Reenacting the Story of Tantalus" Eisenhower, Dulles and the Failed Rhetoric of Liberation', *Journal of Cold War Studies*, Vol. 7, Issue 4, 2005, pp. 3-35; Csaba Békés, 'The Neutrality of Hungary during the 1956 Revolution', *in* Mark Kramer *et al.* (eds.), *The Soviet Union and Cold War Neutrality and Nonalignment in Europe*, Lexington Books, London, 2021, pp. 324-343; Csaba Békés, 'The 1956 Hungarian Revolution and international politics', *Storia e Politica. Annali della Fondazione Ugo La Malfa*, Vol. XXX, 2015, September 2016, pp. 23-41; Csaba Békés *et al.* (eds.), *The 1956 Hungarian Revolution: A History in Documents (National Security Archive Cold War Readers)*, Central European University Press, Budapest, 2003.

2 Péter Kovács, 'Understanding or Misunderstanding? (About Diplomatic Telegrams sent from the American, British and Soviet Legations in Budapest between 23 October – 4 November 1956)', *Miskolc Journal of International Law*, Vol. 3, Issue 3, 2006, pp. 14-27, at http://mjil.hu/MJIL8/20063kovacs1.pdf.

3 Péter Kovács *et al.*, Forgotten or Remembered? – The US Legation of Budapest and the Hungarian Revolution of 1956 (A virtual and annotated conversation with Jordan Thomas Rogers, Ernest A. Nagy and Géza Katona serving at the American Legation in Budapest in 1956)', *Miskolc Journal of International Law*, Vol. 4, Issue 1, 2007, pp. 1-38, at http://mjil.hu/MJIL9/20071kovacs1.pdf.

4 I was particularly honored when the already 93-year-old Jordan Thomas Rogers came to New York during my campaign for being elected to the ICC. We met in the building of the Hungarian Mission to the UN, where we continued the discussion about his recollections, and I could personally thank him for all that he had done.

5 *Foreign Relations of the United States, 1955-1957, Eastern Europe. Volume XXV,* Washington DC, 1990 (FRUS or FRUS XXV), at https://history.state.gov/historicaldocuments/frus1955-57v25.

doi: 10.5553/HYIEL/266627012022010001008

Hungary[6] and interviews made by others.[7] Since then, plenty of new writings have been published, some of them also reflecting on my considerations or the views expressed by the interviewed veteran diplomats.[8] Later, Jordan Thomas Rogers gave some other interviews, as well.[9] Ernest Nagy earned his scientific degree on the basis of his dissertation written about 1956.[10] As it happens, I have since then discovered other papers[11] which I could have used, had I known about them or had I had access to them. Some other documents which also seem to be very pertinent to the subject were also published in the meantime.[12] However, the 'price' for granting access to some previously confidential documents was that the university database only received a 'heavily redacted' version, *i.e.* smaller or longer parts and personal names are omitted.[13] Naturally, I also relied on the writings of current Hungarian historians, experts of the Cold War and 1956.

With all the above in mind, I return to this topic focusing on the activity of the American Legation and covering the policy-making in Washington or in Budapest only to the extent strictly necessary to understand the background of the steps taken or omitted.

6 *Titkos jelentések 1956 okt. 23-nov. 4,* Hírlapkiadó, Budapest, 1989 (Secret Reports) The documents published in this book are the Hungarian translations of a good number of British and American cables, mentioning generally also their control numbers. Some of them are *verbatim* translations of those to be found in FRUS XXV. Other pieces have no equivalent in FRUS XXV, which is also only a selection. However, the most interesting is that the date of the 'Secret Reports' is prior to FRUS XXV. Moreover, the copyright page does not indicate the origin of the documents. I tried to find an explanation for the obscure origins of the Secret Reports in Kovács *et al.* 2007, pp. 31-32. Since then, the Secret Reports can be found at www.magtudin.org/Titkos_Jelentesek_56.pdf.

7 Martin Ben Swartz, *A new look at the 1956 Hungarian Revolution: Soviet opportunism, American acquiescence,* Ph.D. Fletcher School of Law and Diplomacy, 1989, at https://sites.tufts.edu/fletcherrussia/files/2018/09/1988-Martin-Ben-Swartz-A-new-look-at-the-1956-Hungarian-Revolution.-Soviet-opportunism-American-acquiescence.pdf; Géza Katona, Interviewed by Zsolt Csalog, 'A Major Oversight on Our Part', *The Hungarian Quarterly*, Vol. 47, Issue 182, Summer 2006, pp. 109-131, at www.ceeol.com/search/article-detail?id=15919.

8 Ronald D. Landa, *The 1956 Hungarian Revolution: A Fresh Look at the U.S. Response*, Draft, 2012, at www.esd.whs.mil/Portals/54/Documents/FOID/Reading_Room/MDR_Releases/FY12/12-M-1691.pdf.

9 Thomas J. Dunnigan, *Interview with Jordan Thomas Rogers. The Association for Diplomatic Studies and Training Foreign Affairs Oral History Project*, 2007, at http://lcweb2.loc.gov/service/mss/mfdip/2007/2007rog01/2007rog01.pdf.

10 Ernest A Nagy, *Crisis Decision Setting and Response: The Hungarian Revolution*, National Security Affairs Monograph 78-1, National Defense University, Washington DC, 1978.

11 *Clandestine Services History. The Hungarian Revolution and planning for the future, 23 October – 4 November 1956*, Volume I of II (1958), approved for release in 2005, the author's name is redacted. Available at https://nsarchive2.gwu.edu/NSAEBB/NSAEBB206/CSH_Hungarian_Revolution_Vol1.pdf. (In the followings: *The Hungarian Revolution* 1958). *See also* the interview with John R. Mapother in Swartz 1989, pp. 554-555.

12 *See especially* the extremely valuable collections of the National Security Archive: Malcolm Byrne (ed.), *A National Security Archive Electronic Briefing Book*, 2002, at https://nsarchive2.gwu.edu/NSAEBB/NSAEBB76/.

13 *See e.g.* the unreadable, whitened or blacked parts in Landa 2012, or in *The Hungarian Revolution* 1958.

doi: 10.5553/HYIEL/266627012022010001008

2. The Surprising Uprising

It is a common historical standpoint that the outbreak of the Hungarian Uprising, which soon turned into a Revolution, surprised all the important actors: the Hungarians (communists, whether Stalinist or moderate, non-communists and anti-communists), the Soviet Union, the US, Great Britain, France and Yugoslavia. Taking into account the subject of my article, let's take a look at the reasons why the US and its legation did not expect that the widely known political fermentation, closely followed by diplomats,[14] *i.e.* the debate in the communist party controlled Writers' Federation and the 'Petőfi Circle' as well as at the universities would suddenly turn into a mass demonstration on 23 October, the evening and night of which was already marked by armed fighting in Budapest, around the Radio Building and elsewhere.

Washington's surprise is mentioned *inter alia* by Kissinger,[15] Landau,[16] the 1958 CIA assessment,[17] the diplomats of the legation[18] and of the State Department,[19] *etc.* The unpreparedness was reflected first and foremost in the dilemma of "what to do" in the collision of the "roll back policy"[20] and the "liberation of the captive nations" in a situation where the imperative to avoid a direct military conflict with the Soviet Union prevailed.[21] The unpreparedness was also manifested *e.g. (i)* in the lack of an own radio-transmitting equipment at the legation, *(ii)* the replacement of the departing minister Ravndal by Wailes, his successor and the latter's belated arrival,[22] even if in the meantime, the Legation working with *cca.* 30 people had a *chargé d'affaires*, counsellor Spencer Barnes,[23] *(iii)* a long-term foreign mission assigned to Ernest Nagy, one of the three diplomats speaking Hungarian as their mother tongue.[24] On their own, each of

14 Kovács *et al.* 2007, pp. 4, 5, 12, and 13.

15 Henry Kissinger, *Diplomacy*, Simon and Schuster, New York, 1994, p. 557.

16 Landa 2012, pp. 84, and 85.

17 *The Hungarian Revolution* 1958, pp. 77, 89, 102, and 106.

18 Kovács *et al.* 2007, pp. 30, and 33; *see also* Katona in Swartz 1989, pp. 531-532.

19 Horace G. Torbert, in 1956 Officer-in-Charge in the office of Austrian-Italian Affairs, in the European Bureau of the State Department. *See* Swartz 1989, p. 598.

20 *See* Amory and Mapother in Swartz 1989, pp. 482, and 556; *see also* Rogers in Dunnigan 2007, p. 20.

21 Rogers in Kovács *et al.* 2007, p. 36 and in Swartz 1989, p. 587; *see also* Mapother in Swartz 1989, pp. 556, and 560; Landa 2012, pp. 32, and 49.

22 Christian Ravndal was sent as an Ambassador to Ecuador in August 1956 and Edwin Wailes, ambassador in South Africa succeeded him in Budapest. He arrived in Budapest only on 2 November. On his alleged hesitations, and the reasons of his late arrival due to a boat trip, a holiday and a French language course *see* Landa 2012, pp. 17-18.

23 The Legation was led during these weeks by *chargé d'affaires* Spencer Barnes. He had served formerly at the Moscow, Berlin and Tehran embassies. He was an excellent analyst but not an activist and rather "timorous" as characterized by Rogers and Katona. He was very active in collecting information, but he was not the one to take important, formal steps without instruction. Kovács *et al.* 2007, pp. 9, and 17; Landa 2012, p. 18; Csalog 2006, pp. 112, and 117; *see* Katona in Swartz 1989, p. 532; *see also* Rogers in Dunnigan 2007, p. 14.

24 Géza Katona, Ernest Nagy and Anton Nyerges. Some other diplomats, *e.g.* Jordan Thomas Rogers made efforts to learn Hungarian, but nevertheless, their language of communication was primarily English and eventually German. *See* Kovács *et al.* 2007, pp. 4-5.

doi: 10.5553/HYIEL/266627012022010001008

these problems could have been managed smoothly in normal times, but between 23 October and 4 November, their cumulative effect hindered the Legation's ability to reach real decision-makers in Washington with their thorough and accurate analysis and to receive appropriate instructions from them.

3. Communication, Information and their Limits

The lack of direct radio communication deserves an explanation. It was linked to the fact that some time before and upon the demand of the FBI, the Hungarian Legation in Washington was forbidden to use a radio-transmitting device and as a retaliation, the Hungarian authorities did the same *vis-à-vis* the American Legation. *Lacking a lawfully allowed transmitter, the coded communications went through the Hungarian Post,* but the service was often suspended due to alleged technical reasons.[25] The Legation had on the other hand a telex device but only an open communication version.[26] Since no such conflict emerged between London and Budapest concerning the use of own diplomatic radio devices, US diplomats occasionally asked their British counterparts for a favor to have their messages transmitted. However, due to capacity problems, the British legation sometimes asked Barnes and Rogers to shorten their reports considerably. Apparently, some of the reports that the US diplomats thought to have been sent by the British, never made it to Washington or at least cannot be found in the archives of the State Department or in the FRUS. Finally, Rogers and Gleason, the latter being one of the US military attachés, took all the reports – including the ones transmitted with the help of the British Legation and those which were sent through the occasionally functioning Hungarian Post Office – and drove to Vienna to transmit them from the US Embassy in Austria. They set off on 29 October but arrived in Vienna only on 30 October. They came back with a not too strong, but still functioning device that they used until it got identified by the Kádár puppet government, installed after 4 November by the Soviets.[27]

Under these circumstances, *the State Department and the White House were not informed directly by the Legation in Budapest* but *via* telegrams received from their embassies accredited in Vienna, Belgrade, Moscow, London, Paris, New York, *i.e.* capitals of neighboring countries or important actors in world policy, traditional stock exchange of diplomatic information, *etc.*

It is worth noting that even the CIA assessment paper was complaining – with a certain degree of self-criticism – about the *lack of adequate information seized directly in Hungary.* The collection of information mostly took place in Vienna or at the Austrian side of the border and in the latter case, essentially through intermediaries.[28] Their sources were generally returning journalists,

25 Kovács *et al.* 2007, p. 7; *see* Rogers in Dunnigan 2007, p. 26; *see also* Katona in Swartz 1989, p. 536.

26 Csalog 2006, p. 116; *see* Katona in Swartz 1989, p. 536.

27 *See* in detail Kovács *et al.* 2007, pp. 7, and 8; Landa 2012, p. 16; *The Hungarian Revolution* 1958, p. 85.

28 *The Hungarian Revolution* 1958, pp. 80, 81, 83, 84, *etc.*

doi: 10.5553/HYIEL/266627012022010001008

railroad workers, freedom fighters with the ambition to speak to the world from Vienna, and radio-amateurs able to catch broadcastings of city radios.[29] The report put a bitter emphasis on the fact that *there was only one agent under diplomatic immunity in Budapest* and only a few other staff members were present in Hungary during those days.[30] Some made their 'coming out' at an elderly age,[31] while some historians tried to identify others[32] even if according to the well-established custom, this may only be done after the person concerned has passed away.

The conditions were of course far from being optimal, even in an average, normal situation, but the members of the US Legation in Budapest felt themselves truly abandoned, when due to the lack of an own, direct and secure communication system, and to the repeated problems of the Hungarian Post Office (which surprisingly disappeared when the Revolution seemed to win at the end of October[33]) concerning not only telegrams but also open phone calls, the only source they could rely upon was public media broadcastings, newspaper coverage about Eisenhower's, John Foster Dulles's or, the ambassador to the UN, Henry Cabot Lodge's statements.

The talks with the staff of the US Embassy in Vienna on 30 October were certainly important for Rogers and Gleason. We also know that Minister Edwin Wailes was informed in detail by Ambassador Llewellyn Thompson. The briefing lasted a whole day and also contributed to his late arrival in Budapest, only on 2 November.

Between 23-29 October, conversations with British and other diplomats also working in Budapest could help somewhat, at least when the Foreign Office and the Quai d'Orsay could deal with other issues besides Suez. In the interviews with Rogers, apart from the British diplomats, Israeli and Yugoslav colleagues were mentioned as people helping or acting together with the American diplomats.[34] In this context, Géza Katona referred to contacts with the British, French, Italian, Egyptian, Turkish and Indian legations and, to a much lesser extent, with the Yugoslav legation.[35]

29 Id. pp. 96, 97, and 98.

30 Id. pp. 78, and 85; Mapother in Swartz 1989, p. 558.

31 "[...] Seymour Freidin, Vienna correspondent of the New York Post, confessed to being a CIA agent in 1973, and would presumably have been working for US intelligence in 1956 as well. There is no trace of such a suspicion in any Hungarian document [...]" János Molnár, *Foreign Correspondents in the 1956 Hungarian Revolution*, at http://server2001.rev.hu/msite/display_item.asp?id=2&act=tu&lang=e. *See also* Vienna based John R. Mapother in Swartz 1989, p. 555. On English side, *see* Anthony Cavendish, Inside intelligence, Granta, Cambridge, 1989. *See also* at https://en.wikipedia.org/wiki/Anthony_Cavendish.

32 CIA had a single officer in Hungary 1956, *see* at https://nsarchive2.gwu.edu/NSAEBB/NSAEBB206/index.htm.

33 Kovács *et al.* 2007, pp. 7-8.

34 Id. pp. 10, 15, and 16.

35 Csalog 2006, p. 127; The Yugoslav contact (by the way a next-door neighbor) is mentioned however also by Rogers in Swartz 1989, p. 586.

doi: 10.5553/HYIEL/266627012022010001008

4. Main Lines of the Few Instructions that the Legation Got and Had to Live with...

The US governmental (and of course the international) unpreparedness to a surprising Uprising and the already mentioned telecommunication problems explain that the staff of the Legation was suffering from the lack of reliable information from Washington[36] and had no other guideline than the traditional *'Wait and see! And please report!'*[37]

On 24 October, Imre Nagy was appointed as Prime Minister, and sometime later, the above-mentioned guideline was completed with the alleged instruction to keep a distance from him.[38] It is true that "Washington's instructions were not entirely explicit, not exactly precise."[39] (However, Géza Katona resolutely denied[40] having spoken about any instructions and having mentioned that at all to Csalog in his interview in 1984.)

What I could read as an instruction or at least as an official message having reached the Legation, is the following: *(i)* an empty expression of thanks and appreciation sent by J.F. Dulles to the Legation;[41] *(ii)* the advice that the only message that they can address to the crowds is the expression of sympathy and the promise to inform the US government in as much detail as possible;[42] *(iii)* a circular sent from Washington to all the US embassies and legations about the

36 Rogers: "And in any event, we felt very much on our own, having at best limited communications with Washington, and not receiving messages from Moscow and other posts, and so with little knowledge of the activities and attitudes in Washington. I would like to believe, that had we had a better comprehension of what was or was not taking place in Washington, our own communications would have been more useful. As you point out, this feeling of isolation is somewhat endemic to this profession. You are not told very much, but yet in times of stress you are expected to behave as though you have full knowledge not only of events but also of the thought processes of the Great Men at home!" Kovács *et al.* 2007, p. 8; *see also* Rogers in Swartz 1989, pp. 584, 585, 588-589, and 590.

37 *See* Jacob D. Beam, Deputy Assistant Secretary of State for Soviet and East European Affairs in 1956: "[...] Except for the Mindszenty problem, I do not recall sending special instructions to any of the missions in Eastern Europe, beyond keeping them informed of current developments and general policies. Our missions in the area were competently led and performed well, although in Budapest we didn't even have a Minister until well into the Revolution, and he was never able to present his credentials." Beam in Swartz 1989, p. 491; *see also* Katona in Swartz 1989, pp. 533, and 537.

38 *See* Katona in Csalog 2006, p. 126.

39 Id. *See also* the former consul Ernest Nagy's remarks: "The State Department was unhelpful and provided only minimal guidance to the Legation for the focus of its efforts." Kovács *et al.* 2007, p. 33; *see* Katona in Swartz 1989, p. 531.

40 Kovács *et al.* 2007, pp. 27-28. I have to add that Géza Katona gave his interview of 1984 to Zsolt Csalog apparently in Hungarian and it was translated into English by Tim Wilkinson and published in 2006. *See* Csalog 2006, pp. 109, and 131.

41 *108. Transcript of a Teletype Conversation Between the Legation in Hungary and the Department of State, October 25, 1956*, at https://history.state.gov/historicaldocuments/frus1955-57v25/d108. *See also* in Hungarian: 'Telegram of 25 October, Without numbering but with control number: 14835', *in Secret Reports* 1989, p. 49.

42 Id. *See also* in Hungarian: 'Telegram of 25 October, without numbering but with control number: 14853', *in Secret Reports* 1989, p. 51.

doi: 10.5553/HYIEL/266627012022010001008

Hungarian situation informing them that the US's standpoint is to encourage the Soviets to put an end to the use of their military troops in Hungary and to prepare to call back their troops. This is also the policy followed by the US in the UN. The promise of the Nagy-government to get rid of the Soviet troops is precarious, and it is too early to assess Imre Nagy' personality. The regime may cheat in order to break down the resistance. The US government is ready to send humanitarian aid, and the shipment of other items is still under consideration.[43]

As mentioned, Eisenhower's and J.F. Dulles's main concern was how to let things go, while avoiding a direct armed confrontation with Soviet Union.[44] Plenty of historical works have studied the brainstorming in the White House and the State Department. I do not want to enter into their presentation and analysis. However, one may assume that *the diplomats in Washington did not want to send any clear instructions* or answer the questions of their fellow diplomats working at the Legation concerning the proper course to be followed in the UN[45] *until a decision was taken at higher level.* Similarly, the question asked by military attaché Todd concerning the content of a reply if demand for assistance in weaponry were formulated by the Hungarian counterpart, was left deliberately without an answer.[46]

Although the intelligence branch kept complaining of the lack of reliable news on what was happening in Budapest,[47] the formal instruction or minimum guideline was the following: "we must restrict ourselves to information collection only, that agents sent to the border must not get involved in anything that would reveal US interest or give cause to claim intervention [...]"[48] and it was not permitted to send US weapons in.[49] The mistrust in Imre Nagy was also underlined, even though he seemed to be "daily gaining in stature and was acceding in giant steps to the increasingly radical demands [...]."[50]

The question whether the mistrust in prime minister Imre Nagy was well founded, was thoroughly examined by the diplomats of the Legation during our interview. They recognized their own responsibility in as much as *they realized too late that Nagy – even if a communist – was ready to go in another direction than the Moscovite dicta.*[51] They also emphasized that Nagy did not seem to be a strong

43 *143. Circular Telegram From the Department of State to All Diplomatic Missions,* at https://history.state.gov/historicaldocuments/frus1955-57v25/d143; *See also* in Hungarian: 'Telegram of 30 October, control number: 779/546', *in Secret Reports* 1989, pp. 82-83.

44 *See also* Katona in Swartz 1989, p. 535.

45 *See* Rogers in Kovács *et al.* 2007, p. 20. *See also* the cable 168, control number 17573, 27 October in *Secret reports* 1989, pp. 60-61.

46 Landa 2012, p. 41. Todd's telegram was written on 31 October but arrived in the Pentagon on 2 November.

47 *The Hungarian Revolution* 1958, p. 83.

48 Sent on 28 October. *The Hungarian Revolution* 1958, p. 91. *See also* instruction sent on 1 November. *The Hungarian Revolution* 1958, p. 95: "[...] Nothing must happen which would justify charge of intervention [...]."

49 Sent on 29 October. *The Hungarian Revolution* 1958, p. 92.

50 Sent on 31 October. Id. p. 93.

51 *See* Katona in Csalog 2006, pp. 125-126; and in Swartz 1989, pp. 532-533; *see* Rogers in Kovács *et al.* 2007, pp. 16, 18, 35, and 37.

doi: 10.5553/HYIEL/266627012022010001008

leader and it was always with hesitations that he went ahead alongside with the continuously radicalizing Revolution.[52] They confirmed that even now, looking back from the 21st century, this remains their professional conviction.[53] They pointed out, however, that the mistrust *vis-à-vis* the national communists was closely linked to the McCarthy legacy in the State Department,[54] led by John Foster Dulles, as well as in the intelligence, led by his brother, Allan Dulles. For J.F. Dulles, Cardinal Mindszenty was the potential focal point and not Imre Nagy, whom he felt weak.[55]

5. The Reporting Activity of the Legation

The following cables sent by the Legation became selected into the FRUS XXV: *(i)* a telegram about the demonstrations on 23 October;[56] *(ii)* a 23 October telegram about the continuation of the demonstration, the destruction of Stalin's statue, fights around the Radio;[57] *(iii)* a 24 October telegram suggesting the issuing of a solemn declaration in favor of the Hungarians and a strong protestation against Soviet military intervention;[58] *(iv)* telex-exchange of 25 October about shootings in Budapest, Imre Nagy's views and situation of Americans living or staying there;[59] *(v)* a 27 October telegram about the extension of the uprising to other cities; dilemma of insurgents whether to trust Imre Nagy; several suggestions *e.g.* issuing a presidential declaration in favor of the Hungarians, actions to be taken at the UN, *etc.*;[60] *(vi)* a 28 October telegram about the continuation of shootings; difficulties in communicating with Washington; query about eventual decision on previous suggestions; urging for

52 *See* Rogers and Nagy in Kovács *et al.* 2007, pp. 9-10, 17, 19, and 33.

53 Id.

54 *See* Rogers in Kovács *et al.* 2007, pp. 9, 17, and 37; and in Swartz 1989, p. 583; *see* Katona in Csalog 2006, p. 125; *see also* Torbert, speaking about the impact of ideology on contacts with communists at that time, in Swartz 1989, p. 600.

55 "[...] Mr. Dulles declared that the main problem facing us today in Hungary was the lack of a strong guiding authority to bring the rebels together. Nagy was failing to unite the rebels, and they were demanding that he quit. Somehow a rallying point must be found in order to prevent chaos inside of Hungary even if the Soviets took their leave. In such a heavily Catholic nation as Hungary, Cardinal Mindszenty might prove to be such a leader and unifying force. [...]" *152. Memorandum of Discussion at the 302nd Meeting of the National Security Council,* Washington DC, 1 November 1956, 9-10:55 am, FRUS XXV, at https://history.state.gov/historicaldocuments/frus1955-57v25/d152. *See* on that Rogers in Kovács *et al.* 2007, p. 9 and in Dunnigan 2007, p. 28.

56 *97. Telegram From the Legation in Hungary to the Department of State, Budapest, October 23, 1956, 2 pm,* at https://history.state.gov/historicaldocuments/frus1955-57v25/d97.

57 *98. Telegram From the Legation in Hungary to the Department of State, Budapest, October 23, 1956, midnight,* at https://history.state.gov/historicaldocuments/frus1955-57v25/d98.

58 *103. Telegram From the Legation in Hungary to the Department of State, Budapest, October 24, 1956, 3 pm,* at https://history.state.gov/historicaldocuments/frus1955-57v25/d103.

59 *108. Transcript of a Teletype Conversation Between the Legation in Hungary and the Department of State, October 25, 1956,* at https://history.state.gov/historicaldocuments/frus1955-57v25/d108.

60 *125. Telegram From the Legation in Hungary to the Department of State, Budapest, October 27, 1956, 11 am,* at https://history.state.gov/historicaldocuments/frus1955-57v25/d125.

doi: 10.5553/HYIEL/266627012022010001008

clear instructions;[61] *(vii)* a 29 October telegram about chaos in Budapest and suggestion that Washington should exercise real pressure on the Soviet Union in order to stop the military intervention;[62] *(viii)* a 30 October telegram about the situation in Budapest where insurgents demand free elections in return for stopping fighting. Imre Nagy's position is weakening but an agreement resulting in the withdrawal of Soviet troops can stabilize him. Beside him, two former peasant and small holder party politicians seem to emerge as a focal point. The Legation feels that the achievement of a status similar to Finland's could be a good solution.[63] *(ix)* A 31 October telegram about the Soviets' withdrawal from Budapest, even though there are some sporadic shootings. No sign of any antisemitic outbursts. Social-democrats reconstitute and can eventually enter Nagy's government. Prospects of good American-Hungarian relations. It would be useful to issue a presidential statement, a draft is attached.[64] *(x)* A 1 November telegram about Soviet critics on radicalization and about Nagy's strengthening Hungarian support. The Legation feels that Soviets and Nagy may be collaborating in order to stop the radical demands and suggests that the US should welcome the proclamation of Hungary's neutrality.[65]

As already mentioned, it is unclear (and the internet version of the FRUS XXV definitely doesn't contain any such indication) when the cables were received by Washington. The booklet entitled 'Secret Reports'[66] contains their Hungarian translation,[67] with two exceptions.[68] Moreover, it contains other telegrams as well, stating that they were sent from the Legation.

The cables that I sought to summarize from the 'Secret Reports' were as follows: *(i)* a telegram sent on 23 October about the continuing demonstrations;[69] *(ii)* a telegram of 24/25 October on the outbreak of armed clashes around the Radio Building. Participants of demonstrations were seen fraternizing with Hungarian soldiers coming with tanks. Arrival and intervention of Soviet tanks at different points of Budapest. Martial law is declared by the government.[70] *(iii)* A

61 *130. Telegram From the Legation in Hungary to the Department of State, Budapest, October 28, 1956, 2 pm*, at https://history.state.gov/historicaldocuments/frus1955-57v25/d130.

62 *135. Telegram From the Legation in Hungary to the Department of State, Budapest, October 29, 1956, 8 pm*, at https://history.state.gov/historicaldocuments/frus1955-57v25/d135.

63 *140. Telegram From the Legation in Hungary to the Department of State, Budapest, October 30, 1956, 2 pm*, at https://history.state.gov/historicaldocuments/frus1955-57v25/d140. The two people are Béla Kovács, having returned recently, former MP and charismatic general secretary and of the Smallholders Party who was kidnapped by Soviets in 1947 and sentenced to Gulag; and Zoltán Tildy, MP of the same party and former head of State between 1946-1948.

64 *148. Telegram from the Legation in Hungary to the Department of State, Budapest, October 31, 1956, 1 pm*, at https://history.state.gov/historicaldocuments/frus1955-57v25/d148.

65 *154. Telegram from the Legation in Hungary to the Department of State, Budapest, November 1, 1956, 9 pm*, at https://history.state.gov/historicaldocuments/frus1955-57v25/d154.

66 *See* the full reference of this booklet in the introductory footnotes of the article.

67 *See* according to the Roman numeration in the main text: the *i.* on pp. 26-28, the *ii.* on pp. 35-36, the *iv.* on pp. 43-51, the *v.* on pp. 60-61, the *vi.* on pp. 61-62, the *vii.* on pp. 70-71, the *viii.* on pp. 80-81, the *ix.* on pp. 98-99.

68 These are the *iii.* and the *x.*

69 'N°153, control n°13527', *in Secret Reports 1989*, p. 31.

70 'N°156, control n°14654', *in Secret Reports* 1989, pp. 36-37.

doi: 10.5553/HYIEL/266627012022010001008

telegram of 26 October about the situation and the fights during the previous night around the buildings where a number of US diplomats were living. Readiness of the Legation to arrange the evacuation of some US citizens. Heavy fights on the Buda side of the capital but also elsewhere.[71] *(iv)* Continuation of the telex-exchange of 25 October about shootings. Appreciation of Imre Nagy's and János Kádár's chances in the coming weeks. The State Department is ready to issue entry visa to the Hungarian delegation arriving soon at the General Assembly of the UN, no objection on behalf of the Legation.[72] *(v)* 26 October: Signs that some Hungarian army units are working together with, or in favor of the insurgents. Other units of the Hungarian army and of the security service and the Ministry of Defence are on the side of the Soviet army. Demand to receive urgently reliable information about the US position in the matter and the suggestion that the case should be brought before the UN and the insurgents' government should be recognized.[73] *(vi)* 26 October: a short report on a talk with an insurgent leader, informing them about their meeting with Imre Nagy, who asked for their support. It seems that this person would be ready to enter Nagy's government. The Legation is ready to maintain this contact without giving the impression of accepting the gentleman as its negotiating partner.[74] *(vii)* A 26 October telegram about another meeting with the same person, informing the Legation about Imre Nagy's views and relatively unsure position and Nagy's aspiration to arrange the withdrawal of the Soviet army if the insurgents surrender to his government.[75] *(viii)* A 27 October telegram about the nationwide repercussions of the fight for freedom and actions in different towns of the country. A larger overview of the considerations transmitted by an insurgent leader about Nagy.[76] The Legation urgently requests official information about the US standpoint when discussing the Hungarian situation in the UN.[77] *(ix)* A 27 October telegram about a visit two Hungarian ladies paid to a US diplomat's wife. (They are spouses of important Hungarian writers.[78]) The talk is about a cease-fire that the US Legation could propose and arrange between the insurgents and the government. The Legation asks for official position before giving an answer.[79] *(x)* A 29 October telegram about the continuous presence of Soviet troops in Budapest despite the official declaration that they would leave. The Legation is not convinced that the population has trust in Nagy's promises.[80] *(xi)* A 29 October telegram transmitting suspicions about the official news of the evacuation of Soviet troops. Different groups of the nationalist insurgents are not

71 'N°165, control n°17446', *in Secret Reports* 1989, p. 47.
72 'N°165, control n°14805', *in Secret Reports* 1989, p. 48.
73 'N°162, control n°17452', *in Secret Reports* 1989, pp. 57-59.
74 'N°163, control n°17435', *in Secret Reports* 1989, p. 59.
75 'N°166, control n°17548', *in Secret Reports* 1989, pp. 59-60.
76 Without giving the name, it seems that it is the same person as reported the day before.
77 'N°168, control n°17573', *in Secret Reports* 1989, pp. 60-61.
78 It is to be reminded that the debates organized by the Hungarian Writers' Federation played a very important role in the fermentation of the political climate turning into the Uprising and the Revolution.
79 'N°169, control n°17465', *in Secret Reports* 1989, p. 61.
80 'N°182, control n°17359', *in Secret Reports* 1989, pp. 71-72.

doi: 10.5553/HYIEL/266627012022010001008

cooperating with each other. The insurgents desperately need foreign assistance like *(a)* the setting up of an international commission representing their case in talks with the Hungarian communist government and the Soviets, *(b)* sending of military equipment.[81] *(xii)* A 30 October telegram about a new manifestation with the following claims: Cardinal Mindszenty for prime minister. Colonel Pál Maléter for minister of defense. Ceasefire and evacuation of Soviet troops. They ask for Western intervention in case of these demands are refused.[82] *(xiii)* A 30 October telegram about heavy fights at different points of Budapest after a relatively calm period. A demonstration arrived in front of the US Legation and asked for the US' intervention and assistance. Soviet troops are rather in the countryside, or in their barracks but not in the cities.[83] *(xiv)* A 31 October telegram suggesting the issuing of a presidential statement (draft attached), expressing joy over the independence and willingness to give economic assistance completing the already decided humanitarian assistance.[84] *(xv)* A 31 October telegram on calm conditions. Insurgents are controlling the surroundings of their positions and they arrange services. There is a cooperation between insurgents and the Hungarian army, namely, the insurgents do not oppose to the army entering former Soviet positions. According to the Radio, Soviets are leaving, but there are rumors about Soviets in Hungarian uniform.[85] *(xvi)* A 31 October telegram advising the State Department to use its press contacts to keep silent about the few atrocities and lynchings, and to emphasize instead the need to return to the rule of law and to show news on return to democracy, the new parties, *etc.*[86] *(xvii)* A 1 November telegram about the evacuation of Soviet troops from Budapest and also about news that they stopped in the countryside not too far from the capital. Insecurity in the streets especially at night. Evacuation of American families. Some exactions occurred against people who were presumed to be members of the former security services and there were also lynchings.[87] *(xviii)* A telegram of 1 November about the roots and perspectives of the uprising, dilemmas surrounding communist Imre Nagy's tactics, possible entry of former small holders' party leaders[88] in a diluted communist government. Complete return to private economy system is hardly possible.[89] *(xix)* A 1 November telegram about the proclamation of neutrality. The *chargé d'affaires* was invited to the Ministry for foreign affairs and the text was transmitted to him in the form of a *note verbale*.[90] *(xx)* A 1 November telegram about the necessity to restore law and order fully, in order to avoid whatever pretext for Soviets to come back. Imre Nagy's government seems to be accepted by the people and is ready to organize

81 'N°180, control n°17322', *in Secret Reports* 1989, pp. 72-73.
82 'Without N°, control n°18132', *in Secret Reports* 1989, p. 79.
83 'N° 197, control n°18530', *in Secret Reports* 1989, pp. 79-80.
84 'N° 201, control n°18984', *in Secret Reports* 1989, p. 99.
85 'N° 198, control n°19083', *in Secret Reports* 1989, p. 100.
86 'N° 203, control n°19176', *in Secret Reports* 1989, p. 100.
87 'N° 204, control n°422', *in Secret Reports* 1989, p. 103.
88 Béla Kovács and Zoltán Tildy, already mentioned in a previous telegram, *see* footnotes *supra*.
89 'N° 206, control n°1278', *in Secret Reports* 1989, pp. 104-105.
90 'N° 204, control n°208', *in Secret Reports* 1989, p. 106.

doi: 10.5553/HYIEL/266627012022010001008

free elections. The evacuated Soviet troops are still all around Budapest. Joy and pro-American feeling all over Budapest. A presidential statement or at least that of the Secretary of State is strongly advised by the legation, a draft is attached.[91] *(xxi)* A 1 November telegram about an alleged meeting between three members[92] of the government and cardinal Mindszenty, where the cardinal was asked to support Imre Nagy's government, but he seems to be reluctant and has conditions. The Legation feels that Mindszenty's standpoint is going against Hungary's prompt interests *i.e.* the re-establishment of law and order, the relaunching of the economy and the avoidance of anything that could be used by Russians as a pretext to return.[93] *(xxii)* A 2 November telegram about the relative calm in the capital, only some shootings at night. According to not fully confirmed information and rumors, Budapest is nearly encircled by Soviets and new motorized units are coming as well. The deputy minister for foreign affairs says that the Soviet ambassador[94] has not yet responded to the government's inquiry. Changes in government can be expected.[95] *(xxiii)* A 3 November telegram contains information about the military strength of the Soviet units surrounding Budapest. A Soviet ultimatum about the Warsaw Pact and recent changes in government can be expected, maybe the government will accept it, but the population will resist, and all this will turn into carnage. What about the UN? Rumors that a 16 member UN mission is allegedly on its way.[96] *(xxiv)* A 3 November telegram clarifies that the recent military information came from a very reliable Hungarian officer, high in the hierarchy. On the other hand, there are allegedly some talks about the complete withdrawal of Soviet troops. The Legation is in difficulty when evaluating the reliability of the different sources as the content of their information was rather contrary.[97] *(xxv)* A 4 November telex exchange between the Legation and the State Department about the outbreak of a massive Soviet attack. Tildy's secretary[98] called the Legation informing them about a general Russian attack all over the country and asked for help in the name of the government. The Legation begins to destroy all reports. Preparations for the evacuation of the families of US diplomatic staff. Cardinal Mindszenty arrived and asked for asylum and for American help and protection for Hungary, victim of the Soviet aggression. Exchange of impressions with the UK Legation about the Soviet military attack. Béla Kovács[99] was also present and asked for admission but finally left. The Hungarian delegation sent to negotiate with the Soviets about

91 'N° 210, control n°745', *in Secret Reports* 1989, pp. 111-112.

92 Béla Kovács and Zoltán Tildy and the newly appointed minister for defence, Pál Maléter.

93 'N° 212, control n°1123', *in Secret Reports* 1989, p. 115.

94 Youri Andropov.

95 'N° 217, control n°1670', *in Secret Reports* 1989, p. 119.

96 'N° 219, control n°2099', *in Secret Reports* 1989, p. 123. As an answer, the State Department informed the Legation about the content of not yet voted draft resolution submitted by the US in the UN and remarked that the arrival of whatever UN mission is a pure baseless gossip. Precisions are expected about evaluation of Soviets' troops. LEG-TEL 219, 3 November, *in Secret Report* 1989, p. 123.

97 'N° 224, control n°2258', *in Secret Reports* 1989, p. 123.

98 Zoltán Tildy was – at this time – State Minister *i.e.* deputy PM.

99 Béla Kovács, mentioned in the previous footnotes. *See* Katona in Swartz 1989, pp. 537-538.

doi: 10.5553/HYIEL/266627012022010001008

their withdrawal was most probably arrested. The State Department imparts some information about the current state of discussions in the UN on Hungary.[100] *(xxvi)* A 4 November telegram transmitting State Minister István Bibó's call upon the President to provide urgent help and to stop the Soviet aggression.[101] *(xxvii)* A 4 November telegram about the alleged establishment of a new government by the Soviets in Szolnok, led by János Kádár, qualifying Imre Nagy a counter revolutionary. Soviet ultimatum to Imre Nagy. Béla Kovács leaves and understands the consequences of refusing asylum. The Legation gives a presentation on the geographic location of Soviet attacks and popular resistance. Precise information on the number of Soviet tanks, soldiers, divisions already in Hungary and in some points in the neighboring countries. Estimation of Hungarian armed forces, freedom fighters, tanks, artillery. István Bibó's call to the peoples of the world to support Hungary and about the world-threatening danger of leaving Hungary to fend for itself.[102]

6. Secretary of State J.F. Dulles's Instruction to the Legation in Budapest on 3 November

Minister Edwin Wailes arrived in Budapest on 2 November but with the instruction to refrain from transmitting his credentials.[103] Suddenly, a telegram arrived from State Secretary Dulles which instructed the Minister to

> "act at once present credentials [...] and seek establish official contact highest levels Hungarian Government on urgent, close and continuing basis. [...] Factors dictating this action include: (1) Implications current Soviet military movements; (2) Hungarian Government's apparent acceptance and identification itself with popular demands and people's struggle freedom and independence; (3) Hungarian Government's forthright appeal US and UN for assistance in critical situation attended by its forceful protest against entrance new Soviet troops, its repudiation Warsaw Pact, its demand withdrawal all Soviet forces, and its proclamation neutrality. (4) Desirability that you enjoy proper formal access Hungarian authorities for prompt interchanges between Governments."[104]

The telegram contained also the text of the speech to be delivered before the Head of State with very warm words about heroism, friendship and the possibility

100 'Without number. Control n° 25.36', *in Secret Reports* 1989, pp. 135-141.

101 'Without number, "Document in the Eisenhower Library"', *in Secret Reports* 1989, p. 142.

102 'N° 231, control n°22881', *in Secret Reports* 1989, p. 143.

103 According to Swartz, the State Department followed here a proposal, submitted by the influential Ambassador Thompson leading the US Embassy in Vienna. Here, the American diplomacy lost precious time when being late in recognizing the nature of the events. Swartz 1989, pp. 355-358. Similarly, in Landa 2012, p. 66. *See also* Rogers in Kovács *et al.* 2007, p. 29.

104 *161. Telegram From the Department of State to the Legation in Hungary, Washington, November 3, 1956, 6:50 pm*, at https://history.state.gov/historicaldocuments/frus1955-57v25/d161.

doi: 10.5553/HYIEL/266627012022010001008

of cooperation and the promise to defend Hungary's independence at the UN.[105] The telegram added that upon transmittal of credentials, a press release should be published containing the text of the speech.

This was more or less close to the repeated suggestions made by the Legation about a solemn declaration recognizing the achievement of the government and expressing sympathy and willingness to provide assistance in economy and global politics. However, *the date and time of issuance (i.e. 3 November, 6:30 pm Washington D.C. time) meant 4 November, 12:30 am according to the Central-European time zone* applicable also in Budapest, and presumably the decrypting at the Legation also required a certain amount of time. In the meantime, *the Soviet offensive was launched at 04:15 am on 4 November* with the well-known tragic consequences and destruction all over Budapest. Under these circumstances, the credentials were not transmitted. After having sent a radio message to the Hungarian people and to the nations of the world,[106] Imre Nagy and some members of his government left the building of the Parliament and sought temporary refuge at the Yugoslav embassy of Budapest.

Finally, Wailes never transmitted his credentials when János Kádár and his government were installed by the Soviets in Budapest, the minister was once again instructed not to proceed with the transmittal, because it could be felt as a sign of recognition. As retaliation for withholding the transmittal of the credentials, Edwin Wailes was declared *persona non grata* and had to leave Hungary on 22 February 1957.

105 "Mr. President: In presenting the Letter accrediting me as Minister of the United States of America to the Government of Hungary, and the Letter recalling my predecessor, I express to Your Excellency, on behalf of the Government and people of the United States, warmest greetings to the people of Hungary. In this momentous hour of their national life, the Hungarian people have shown highest courage, integrity of purpose, and unfaltering spirit. Their just struggle for freedom and independence commands the sympathy and the admiration of the entire world. My Government understands and supports these aspirations of the people of Hungary. Deeply moved by the anguish and the heroic sacrifices which the Hungarian people have endured and honoring the traditional friendship which exists between the Hungarian and the American peoples, my Government is acting urgently at this time to espouse the cause of Hungarian freedom and independence before the United Nations and to contribute all possible assistance for the alleviation of human suffering in Hungary. In accordance with the clear purposes of my Government, I assure Your Excellency that I shall devote myself earnestly and unceasingly to the promotion of good will and friendly understanding between Hungary and the United States and to the advancement of those ideals and principles which inspire our two peoples, give rise to mutual interests, and ensure the welfare of both countries. It is my sincere hope that my efforts in this regard will engage the full cooperation of the Hungarian Government. I now present to Your Excellency my Letter of Credence as Envoy Extraordinary and Minister Plenipotentiary of the United States of America to the Government of Hungary and the Letter of Recall of my predecessor, Mr. Christian M. Ravndal." *See* at https://history.state.gov/historicaldocuments/frus1955-57v25/d161.

106 *See* the text here: *Hungarian Radio Broadcasts Speech Nagy Made in 1956*, at https://apnews.com/article/632e89b3416d1ac82bd9183a331b5a0e.

doi: 10.5553/HYIEL/266627012022010001008

7. The Contacts of the Legation with Hungarians

Former diplomats of the Legation were often asked about the quality and the depth of their relations with Hungary and the Hungarians whether representing the officialdom of Hungary, the politicians of the Revolution, the insurgents or civil society.

The diplomats admitted – not without a considerable amount of self-criticism – that *they did not have truly deep relations with the Hungarians.* As far as the underlying reasons were concerned, the following were said with special regard to the difference of approach in time *i.e.* before and during the uprising and the revolution.

(i) As to the official Hungary, the hostile attitude of the Hungarian ministry for foreign affairs made it *quasi* impossible to have whatever deep contact. During the events, the ministry stayed in the hands of hardliner communists until the end of October, and they refused to accept the good offices offered by the Legation concerning a cease-fire, suggested after the meeting with the already mentioned great writers' spouses. By the end of October, the foreign ministry was seized by a group of insurgents, which resulted in *cca.* two days of troubles in the connections. Finally, when Imre Nagy took over the ministership and conferred the bulk of the work on György Heltai, Pál Félix, *etc.* there were only a few days left until the uprising was quashed. The first real contact took place when Pál Félix called and received Spencer Barnes and transmitted the *note verbale* informing the US Legation on the proclamation of neutrality. As there was no indication before that from Nagy's team for a desire to establish contacts,[107] no other professional relations had been initiated prior to the transmission of the *note verbale* according to former US diplomats. They emphasized that without a fully empowered minister, when only a – rather timorous – *chargé d'affaires* led the Legation, taking action without instruction from Washington was out of question, contrary to Minister Ravndal's rather activist approach. In any case, they did not notice any steps taken in their direction from the side of the Hungarians.[108]

Current Hungarian historiography also takes it for granted that *Imre Nagy did not have and even did not want to have any serious contact with Western legations,*[109] except for a meeting with the Austrian ambassador. The only ministerial 'meeting' that occurred with the US Legation was the one with State Minister István Bibó, who went there in order to transmit his call for help: at the dawn of November 4, when the offensive had already started.

(ii) During the events, as mentioned in the diplomatic cables, the diplomats of the Legation made contact with the insurgents several times. The latter

107 *See also* Miklós Vásárhelyi in Swartz 1989, p. 603.

108 *See* Rogers in Kovács *et al.* 2007, pp. 8, 9, 14, 15, *etc. See also* Katona in Swartz 1989, pp. 532-533, and 537.

109 János Rainer M., 'The Development of Imre Nagy as a Politician and a Thinker', *Contemporary European History,* Vol. 6, Issue 3, 1997, pp. 263-277; János Rainer M., *Nemzeti függetlenség, semlegessség és dunavölgyi együttműködés, Nagy Imre külpolitikai nézetei,* at www.rev.hu/ords/f?p=600:2:::::P2_PAGE_URI:tanulmanyok/1956/nagyimre; Békés 2021.

doi: 10.5553/HYIEL/266627012022010001008

generally gathered in front of the building of the Legation or the condominium close to the Parliament accommodating most of the US diplomats and transmitted or left proclamations, demands for help, *etc.* As *per* usual, the US personnel tried to verify who was acting seriously, who acted *bona fide* but without any mandate or background and who was acting as an *agent provocateur*.

(iii) As to civil society, the Legation had some contacts in the fifties, but the diplomats apparently wanted to avoid creating situations which could serve as a pretext to initiate penal proceedings against these Hungarians, for this is what unfortunately happened with some of the Hungarian contracted employees of the Legation.[110] Sometimes, intelligence infiltration was also detected,[111] and some of the local employees informed the Hungarian secret services.[112] The negative consequences of McCarty's legacy[113] were also felt by diplomats who established – apparently *proprio motu* – contact with Miklós Gimes,[114] a close collaborator of Imre Nagy and they subsequently suggested to the State Department that he should be invited to the US together with other foreigners. However, he did not get the US visa because of his communist party membership.[115] It is true that there is no sign that Gimes wanted to revitalize this contact during the Revolution.

110 *See* Rogers in Kovács *et al.* 2007, pp. 14, 15, 30, and 31; Nagy p. 5.

111 *See* Rogers in Kovács *et al.* 2007, p. 30; *see also* Katona in Swartz 1989, p. 531.

112 As KGB general Serov reported on October 28, "from the observation of the American Legation, let us point out that some people are leaving the capital with parcels. Two Americans, Olivert and West told the secret informer of our friends that if the uprising is not crushed soon, UN troops will intervene, according to the proposal of the US, thus creating a second Corea." Serov's Report of October 28 to Mikoyan (Yeltsin-dossier, p. 55) cited in Kovács 2006, pp. 23-24. The so called 'Yeltsin-dossier' (*i.e.* a couple of Soviet documents transmitted to the new Hungary by Russian president Boris Yeltsin, were published in Hungarian as *A "Jelcin-dosszié" Szovjet dokumentumok 1956-ról*, Századvég, 1956-os Intézet, Budapest, 1993. About the story and the basic content of the Yeltsin-dossier, *see* www.rev.hu/ords/f?p=600:2:::::P2_PAGE_URI:tanulmanyok/1956/rmj2. It is to be noted that Landa could identify the real American persons concerned by this story: "The men, whose names were Oliveiras and Vest were not Legation employees but couriers responsible for carrying the diplomatic pouch between State and overseas posts. They could hardly be expected to reflect the Legation's views. Indeed, no mention has been found that it advocated or even discussed a possible armed UN intervention." Landa 2012, p. 53, and also endnote no. 107, at p. 102.

113 *See* Rogers in Kovács *et al.* 2007, pp. 9, and 6.

114 Miklós Gimes was condemned and executed together with Imre Nagy and Pál Maléter, on 16 June 1958.

115 "We had some contact with Miklós Gimes, whom we actually had recommended to visit the States as an observer of the US election (but a visa was denied him on the grounds that he was a communist. Still, we were very cautious: even in Gimes' case we did not seek to establish continuing contacts." Rogers in Swartz 1989, p. 585.

doi: 10.5553/HYIEL/266627012022010001008

However, according to Géza Katona the military branch of the Legation had allegedly some contacts with insurgents[116] (but as previously mentioned, he strongly denied[117] the accuracy of the words attributed to him in the Csalog-interview) as well as with high-ranking persons around the Hungarian government and in the Hungarian army when the Revolution seemed to be winning. (Nevertheless, a photo of this meeting has already been published[118] showing also the marines' names.[119])

Moreover, as Landa – recognizing the high value of the diplomats' reporting activity,[120] and finding unfounded the 1958 CIA's criticism as well as that of journalists[121] – puts it

> "the military attachés were active. On 30 October, Air Attaché Colonel Welwyn Dallam talked with the government's chief of military protocol, who said the government's aim was to establish an independent, socialist state similar to Yugoslavia. Dallam, pessimistic, felt that the Soviet Union would "settle for nothing less" than the complete crushing of the revolution, continued Communist political control of the government, and continued Soviet military occupation. He said that the Hungarian people "of both sides", apparently referring to government supporters and rebels, were "looking to UN for action"."[122]

It is worth recalling one of the cables already mentioned among those which are not on the Internet version of the FRUS XXV, but only in the 'Secret Reports': "*(xxiv)* A November 3 telegram clarifies that the recent military information came from a very reliable Hungarian officer, high in the hierarchy. [...]."

It is difficult to assess today the depth of information exchanges between diplomats and attachés but as Jordan Thomas Rogers noted:

> "In addition, there were the military attachés who sent their messages separately. However, during the period of the revolution, normal activities

116 "[...] The eight marines who did duty in the Legation couldn't wear their uniform, but that didn't stop them from going out into town in their civvies. There was no holding them back! They went off to the Kilian Barracks, even had themselves photographed with the freedom fighters, and they practically begged to be allowed to go off in uniform to help the Hungarians. "The Russians only need to give us Marines one look, and they'll be taking to their heels!" This spontaneous fervor obviously did not have much grounding in reality, but it was characteristic of the spirit of our military personnel. [....]" Katona in Csalog 2006, p. 124.

117 *See* Rogers, citing Katona's message in Kovács *et al.* 2007, p. 27. It is to be added that in the interview that Katona gave to Swartz, more or less at the same time when the Csalog-interview was made, the marines' visit is not mentioned.

118 Leo J. Daugherty III, *The Marine Corps and the State Department: Enduring Partners in United States Foreign Policy, 1798-2007*, McFarland, Jefferson, London, 2009, p. 118.

119 G. J. Bolick, Gene Comer and Edward Parauke. (Pages 114-120 show the 1956 Budapest events from their perspective and they contain also citations from their recollections.)

120 Landa 2012, pp. 19, and 22.

121 Id. pp. 15-16, 19, and 22.

122 Id. p. 21. Landa in his footnote no. 40 gives as source the Air Attaché's report (with precise numbering) and preserved on microfilm. *See* Landa 2012, p. 94.

doi: 10.5553/HYIEL/266627012022010001008

were put aside and the whole staff worked very much as a team, particularly by moving around the city (when it was possible to do so) to observe what was going on."[123]

The name of the "government's chief of military protocol" is not given by Landa and it is not clear whether he is the same person as the "very reliable Hungarian officer, high in the hierarchy" mentioned in one of the telegrams of 3 November.

On the other hand, there is a person who was not related to the military protocol but whose name appeared in a number of rumors and gossips[124] concerning his activity in 1956 and even before. He is colonel Ferenc Nándor, commandant of the Hungarian air force at the time. At the beginning of the Soviet invasion, he also took refuge at the Yugoslav Embassy and got accommodated in the flat of Vukmirovic, the Yugoslav deputy military attaché. Similarly to the other members of Imre Nagy's group, he also had to leave his refuge after a while and he was arrested and interrogated by KGB general Serov, the mastermind of the operations in Hungary. An already accessible report prepared by Serov to Nikita Khrushchev on 19 November 1956 about the results of some of the interrogations refers to previous meetings between Nádor and Dallam, namely on 2 November, when the American attaché allegedly asked for information *inter alia* about Soviet airplanes.[125] (Some contemporary Hungarian historians also confirm the relations between Dallam and Nádor while placing the date and place of the meetings differently, agreeing in substance, while differing in the perception of the outcome.[126]) Shortly afterwards, the new regime accused Welwyn Dallam of spying[127] and expulsed him from Hungary in 1957.[128] As to colonel Ferenc Nádor, he was not allowed to return to the Army but surprisingly, he completely avoided penal prosecution. He entered the Hungarian civil aviation

123 *See* Rogers in Kovács *et al.* 2007, p. 7.

124 Iván Dezső, 'A Magyar Néphadsereg légiereje 1956 októberében – novemberében', *Hadtörténelmi Közlemények*, Vol. 102, Issue 2, 1989, p. 215.

125 *Hiányzó lapok 1956 történetéből. Dokumentumok a volt SZKP KB levéltárából*, Móra Ferenc Könyvkiadó, Budapest, 1993, pp. 161-164. *See* the text in Hungarian also at www.rev.hu/sulinet56/online/szerviz/dokument/serov19s.htm.

126 *See* Krisztián Ungváry, 'A Kádár-rendszer kémelhárítása', *in* János Tischler (ed.), *Kádárizmus: mélyfúrások, Évkönyv XVI.*, 2009, p. 359. Ungváry accepts 2 November as the date and mentions the Air Force headquarters as the place where the meeting took place. Miklós Kun, the best Hungarian historian of Soviet and Eastern European secret services refers to a meeting which occurred on the premises of the Yugoslav embassy, already during the temporary asylum but with more or less the same content. Miklós Kun, *Rejtélyes XX. század/Nádor Ferenc ezredes és társai megpróbálnak elbujdosni*, at https://nava.hu/id/3118392/#. *See* in the film especially the sequences between 18:00-21:00 minutes. According to Professor Kun, who personally met Nádor, the colonel refused to transmit the information requested by attaché Dallam.

127 Released documents relating to Welwyn Dallam can be consulted in the Historical Archives of Former Hungarian Secret Services, *see* at www.abtl.hu/sites/default/files/raktari_jegyzekek/4_1.pdf, pp. 85 and 186, folders A-2126/138 and A-3209. It seems that a pedagogical 'case study' was also prepared by the Hungarian Secret Services of the time.

128 After Dallam's expulsion, Gábor Illési a food conservation technician, allegedly belonging to the attaché's network in 1955-1957, was arrested, condemned to death and executed. *See* Ungváry 2009, p. 360.

doi: 10.5553/HYIEL/266627012022010001008

where he got important positions and also served abroad as the representative of the MALÉV air company.

8. Conclusions

FRUS XXV and historiographic coverage makes give us insight into how the different options were elaborated, discussed, approved of or often postponed and even abandoned in the State Department, the National Security Council and the White House.[129]

These options concerned the policy in the UN (to seize the Security Council and the General Assembly and to proceed according to Resolution 377(V) "Uniting for peace"), the suggestion of military assistance (which was soon abandoned!) or the proposal to offer military concessions to the Soviet Union (*e.g.* reduction of US military presence in Italy), or to take demonstrative steps (*e.g.* highest alert of US troops in West Germany), ending in the repeated transmission of a speech President Eisenhower gave in Dallas to the Soviet leadership. This was intended as a message to calm hardliners in Moscow. Acknowledging at first sight the right of Hungary to freedom, it can also be interpreted as a tacit recognition of the fact that the Soviets have free hand in the matter, and they need not be afraid of a military or other, tougher type of retaliation.

> "The US has no ulterior purpose in desiring the independence of the satellite countries. Our unadulterated wish is that these peoples, from whom so much of our own national life derives, should have sovereignty restored to them, and that they should have governments of their own free choosing. We do not look upon these nations as potential military allies. We see them as friends and as part of a new and friendly and no longer divided Europe. We are confident that their independence, if promptly accorded, will contribute immensely to stabilize peace throughout all of Europe, West and East."[130]

Henry Kissinger writes in his *Diplomacy*:

> "A firmer, clearer American stance would have been essential to render the Soviet decision to intervene less calculable, or at least not quite so seemingly devoid of consequence. The Kremlin could have been warned that repression

129 *See* detailfully in Landa 2012, pp. 22-47; Békés 2016, pp. 31-34 and 34-37.

130 *134. Telegram From the Department of State to the Embassy in the Soviet Union, Washington, October 29, 1956*, at https://history.state.gov/historicaldocuments/frus1955-57v25/d134. *See also* these sentences before and after the Dallas speech excerpts in the instruction "Personal for Ambassador from Secretary. I call your attention to following language from my Saturday night speech at Dallas: [...] This paragraph resulted from intensive consideration here at highest level. We would like this to come to attention of highest Soviet authorities, including Zhukov, and to know that they appreciate it is a high level policy statement. Please use your discretion as to when and how to bring this about."

doi: 10.5553/HYIEL/266627012022010001008

> in Hungary would involve major political and economic costs and put a freeze on East-West relations for the foreseeable future. [...]"[131]

Compared with the US standpoint in the Suez crisis,

> "Hungary was a more complex case, for it would have required the application of power in some form. Yest, America's leaders were not willing to risk American lives for a cause which, however offensive to their consciences, involved no direct American security interest. [...] In Hungary, it acquiesced to *Realpolitik*, just as other nations do, because insistence on principle would have carried with the unavoidable risk of war, perhaps even nuclear war. The Soviet Union was clearly prepared to run bigger risks to preserve its position in Eastern Europe than the United States was willing to brave in order to liberate Hungary. Nothing could get around this equation. In terms of its rhetoric prior to the uprising, America's policy on Hungary was weak indeed; in terms of its interests, the refusal to run the risk of war was both inevitable and fitting – though it does not explain the reluctance to raise the cost of Soviet intervention by nonmilitary means. [...] The United States had left Hungary adrift in the sea of historical evolution, and American allies with a sense of their impotence."[132]

Kissinger continues as follows

> "A generation later, latent Soviet weakness would cast the Hungarian uprising as a harbinger of the ultimate bankruptcy of the communist system. Despite all that had happened, with ten years Hungary was to be internally freer than Poland and its foreign policy more independent of the Soviet Union. And thirty-five years later, in the next phase of Moscow's attempt at liberalization, the Soviets would entirely lose control over events."[133]

All this is true. In conclusion, the author would like to emphasize yet again that the aim of this short article was not to analyze the American policy, but to show how the people at the US Legation were working during those days and how they came to understand what was happening in Hungary. These devoted and enthusiastic professionals, compelled to act without clear instructions and without a functioning communication system deserve recognition for their efforts.

131 Kissinger 1994, p. 563.
132 Id. p. 566.
133 Id. p. 567.

doi: 10.5553/HYIEL/266627012022010001008

Ronald Reagan and International Law

Marcel Szabó[*]

Abstract

Doctrines always play an important law in US foreign relations and policy. Under the presidency of Ronald Reagan (1981-1989), international politics and the role of the US at the global level significantly changed. President Reagan firmly believed that the Soviets were weaker economically than the intelligence community believed – and from this point on, the US definitely won the Cold War against the Soviet Union. The US policy under President Reagan finally led to the fall of the Soviet bloc in 1989, and to the independence of the Central and Eastern European states, including Hungary. The article tries to evaluate the role President Reagan played at the level of international law in this period.

Keywords: US, Hungary, Soviet Union, Reagan doctrine, Reagan corollary.

1. Introduction

In his last debate with President Jimmy Carter in 1980, Ronald Reagan asked the US public: "Is America as respected throughout the world as it was? Do you feel that [...] we are as strong as we were four years ago?" Throughout the campaign, Reagan made clear his conviction that the international prestige and power of the US had declined under the previous presidents of the country. President Reagan particularly wanted to redefine US national policy towards the Soviet Union. On one hand, he had supported the fundamental policy of containing the Soviet Union that President Harry Truman adopted in 1947 and was subsequently followed by all presidents of the US. However, President Reagan believed that the Soviets had taken advantage of *détente*, as practiced by Presidents Nixon, Ford and Carter. Reagan was firmly convinced that the Soviets were economically weaker than the intelligence community believed. As early as 18 June 1980, Reagan underlined that "it would be of great benefit to the US if we started a buildup", because the Soviets would be unable to compete and would have come to the bargaining table.

The international law-related aspects of Ronald Reagan's presidency were discussed in several articles, and some of them display a rather critical attitude

* Marcel Szabó: professor of law, Pázmány Péter Catholic University, Budapest; justice, Constitutional Court of Hungary, Budapest.

Hungarian Yearbook of International Law and European Law 2022 (10) 1
doi: 10.5553/HYIEL/266627012022010001009

towards the Reagan Administration and its policy.[1] On the 100th anniversary of the beginning of the diplomatic relations between the US and Hungary, the time has come to evaluate the importance of President Ronald Reagan in public international law, because the US policy under President Reagan definitely led to the fall of the Soviet bloc in 1989, and to the independence of Central and Eastern European, former communist states, including Hungary.

2. International Law Issues under Reagan – An Overview

The Presidency of Ronald Reagan seriously influenced the development of public international law. As a non-exhaustive lists of the most important events, one can mention the invasion of Grenada in 1983,[2] the US standpoint concerning the draft of the International Convention on the Law of the Sea,[3] supporting the Nicaraguan contras, which, as is well-known, led to the *Nicaragua* case[4] before the ICJ. A detailed analysis of these cases is, however, beyond the scope of the present article.

During Reagan's presidency, the international law-related event with the greatest impact was the implementation of the so-called *Reagan doctrine* and the so-called *Reagan corollary*, since both bore on the foundations of international peace and security. The main object of the present article is therefore to demonstrate the lawfulness of these measures and to discuss considerations of international law with respect to their implementation. For the purposes of this article, a doctrine is defined as a prerogative in international public law that is successfully claimed by the state.[5] A doctrine is essentially a pre-issued statement specifying the response of the state to the behavior of other states. Insofar as other states are willing to accept that the doctrine specifies political consequences

1 *See e.g.* Burns H. Weston, 'The Reagan Administration versus International Law', *Case Western Reserve Journal of International Law,* Vol. 19, Issue 3, 1987, pp. 295-302; John King Gamble Jr., 'International Law in the Reagan Years: How Much of an Outlier", *Akron Law Review,* Vol. 23, Issue 3, 1990, pp. 351-370; Hauke Hartmann, 'US Human Rights Policy under Carter and Reagan, 1977-1981', *Human Rights Quarterly,* Vol. 23, Issue 2, 2001, pp. 402-430; Paul H. Kreisberg, 'Does the U.S. Government Think that International Law Is Important', *Yale Journal of International Law,* Vol. 11, Issue 2, 1986, pp. 479-491; Amy Young, 'Human Rights Policies of the Carter and Reagan Administrations: An Overview', *Whittier Law Review,* Vol. 7, Issue 3, 1985, pp. 689-696.

2 Grenada had gained independence from the United Kingdom in 1974. The situation in Grenada had been of concern to US officials since 1979, when the leftist Maurice Bishop seized power and began to develop close relations with Cuba. In 1983, another Marxist, Bernard Coard, had Bishop assassinated and took control of the government. On 25 October 1983, the US and a coalition of six Caribbean nations invaded Grenada, under 'Operation Urgent Fury'. The UN General Assembly condemned the invasion as "a flagrant violation of international law" on 2 November 1983, by a vote of 108 to 9.

3 George D. Haimbaugh Jr., 'Impact of the Reagan Administration on the Law of the Sea', *Washington & Lee Law Review,* Vol. 46, Issue 1, 1989, pp. 151-200.

4 ICJ, *Military and Paramilitary Activities in and against Nicaragua (Nicaragua v United States of America),* judgment, ICJ Reports 1984, p. 392.

5 Albert Bushnell Hart, *The Monroe Doctrine: An Interpretation,* Little Brown, 1916, pp. 80-81. The other meaning of the word 'doctrine' is the teachings of the science of international law.

doi: 10.5553/HYIEL/266627012022010001009

in response to the actions of the other members of the community bound by international law, those other states tacitly acknowledge the doctrine state's right to behave in accordance with the pre-announced course of action. In many cases, most of the actions specified by the doctrine in response to the behavior of other states cannot be categorized as friendly actions, but the edge of the behavior is dampened by the fact that it was announced before the event, thereby making it predictable. A more accurate classification defines doctrine as *an autonormative unilateral act* on the part of the state, announcing its intention to respond to behaviors exhibited by other international legal entities that infringe upon its interests.

The *Reagan doctrine* emerged in an unusual manner, as it was much rather discovered, than proclaimed. When President Reagan delivered his State of the Union address on 6 February 1985, he did not plan to announce a guiding principle of his administration's foreign policy. After he finished his address, no one recognized that the speech contained a doctrine until weeks later, when a political commentator declared that he had found a grand statement of foreign policy hiding in plain sight.[6] As a brief summary, the Reagan doctrine was used to characterize *the Reagan administration's policy of supporting anti-communist insurgents wherever they might be.*[7] A prominent example of implementing the Reagan doctrine is Nicaragua, where the US covertly assisted the Contra rebels fighting to oust the Cuban-backed Sandinista government, and Afghanistan, where the US provided material support to the Mujahideen rebels fighting to end the Soviet occupation of their country.

The *Reagan corollary* supplemented the Reagan doctrine in foreign affairs. The Reagan corollary is not merely a careless disregard for international law: *it was an attempt to pressure the international legal system into changing in a manner beneficial to US interests.* In order to orchestrate such change, the Reagan administration had proffered new rules of international law, relied on previous versions of existing rules, and reinterpreted existing rules and treaties by applying them in unprecedented contexts. The common threads connecting these practices are the assertion of unilateral state action and a broad right of self-defense, less reliance on international institutions such as the UN, and an emphasis on a state's right to pursue its national interest.[8]

6 Chester Pach, 'The Reagan Doctrine: Principle, Pragmatism, and Policy', *Presidential Studies Quarterly*, Vol. 36, Issue 1, 2006, p. 75.

7 As President Reagan summarized in his speech, "We must stand by our democratic allies. And we must not break faith with those who are risking their lives – on every continent, from Afghanistan to Nicaragua – to defy Soviet-supported aggression and secure rights which have been ours from birth."

8 Stuart S. Malawer, 'Reagan's Law and Foreign Policy, 1981-1987: The "Reagan Corollary" of International Law', *Harvard International Law Journal*, Vol. 20, Issue 1, 1988, pp. 85-86.

Hungarian Yearbook of International Law and European Law 2022 (10) 1
doi: 10.5553/HYIEL/266627012022010001009

3. US Policy and International Law – from Monroe to Reagan

The position of the US as a great power in the world was determined by the *Monroe doctrine* for almost a hundred years.[9] Secretary of State John Quincy Adams expressed his concerns to the President to the effect that Spain, being in the process of losing its American colonies, might receive assistance from other European powers. He was further concerned about the expansion of the Russian Empire in Alaska. The Secretary of State persuaded President Monroe to declare that the US ceased to regard the Americas as a destination of colonization by the great powers of Europe. As a part of the Monroe doctrine, it was further stated that with consideration to the differences in the political structures of the European states and the American states, any attempt to extend the European influence to the Americas was unwelcome. The Monroe doctrine was announced on 2 December 1823, in President James Monroe's seventh annual message to the Congress. *The European powers,* according to Monroe, *were obligated to respect the Western Hemisphere as the US' sphere of interest.* In simple terms, the Monroe doctrine is often summarized with the slogan *"America for the Americans."* In fact, President Monroe made four basic points: *(i)* the US would not interfere in the internal affairs of, or the wars between European powers; *(ii)* the US recognized and would not interfere with existing colonies and dependencies in the Western Hemisphere; *(iii)* the Western Hemisphere was closed to future colonization; and *(iv)* any attempt by a European power to oppress or control any nation in the Western Hemisphere would be viewed as a hostile act against the US.[10] The Monroe doctrine was invoked in 1865, when the US government exerted diplomatic and military pressure in support of the Mexican President Benito Juárez. This support enabled Juárez to lead a successful revolt against Emperor Maximilian, who had been placed on the throne by the French government. In 1904, President Theodore Roosevelt added an extension to the Monroe doctrine (the so-called *Roosevelt corollary*), which stated that in cases of flagrant and chronic wrongdoing by a Latin American country, the US could intervene in that country's internal affairs. In 1962, the Monroe doctrine was invoked symbolically when the Soviet Union began to build missile-launching sites in Cuba.

Although the Soviet administration greatly relied on the geostrategic considerations of the Russian Empire,[11] when, for instance, during discussions with the Allies Stalin repeatedly brought up his claims – inherited from the imperial foreign policy – in connection with Bosporus and the Dardanelles, the ports of Darien and Port Arthur, and free access for Soviet ships to the Mediterranean Sea,[12] *the Soviet Union's international visions were far more ambitious than the Russian Empire's most daring schemes had ever been.* The coat of arms of the Soviet Union depicted the entire globe for a reason. Its tendencies

9 Lassa Oppenheim & Ronald Roxbourgh, *International Law: A Treatise,* Clark, New Jersey, 2005, pp. 231-234.

10 *See e.g.* at www.americaslibrary.gov/aa/monroe/aa_monroe_doctrine_2.html.

11 Arthur H. Dean, 'Soviet Economic Penetration', *The Business Lawyer,* Vol. 14, Issue 1, 1958, p. 73.

12 Henry Kissinger, *Diplomacy,* Simon & Schuster, New York, 1994, p. 399.

doi: 10.5553/HYIEL/266627012022010001009

toward world revolution fired by the communist ideology meant that every country with a non-communist regime was effectively seen as a potential adversary, and generated ambitions of a scale that the Soviet Union could not meet in an economic sense and eventually not even in military terms. In the beginning, the policy achieved considerable success, however. Even so, Kissinger underlines that *Stalin immediately recognized the enormous potential military advantage of the US guaranteed by the possession of nuclear weapons, although he did not openly admit it.*[13] The forced Sovietization of the Eastern and Central European states had no other purpose than to equip Stalin with the strong trump cards needed in the bargaining process where the US had a military advantage and as a result of which, Kissinger believed, the Soviet Union would soon have to sacrifice Eastern and Central Europe to be able to preserve the Soviet Union's social structure and the Soviet State itself, under its post-1945 conditions. If Kissinger was right, the US missed a great opportunity when it failed to exploit its monopoly on nuclear weapons and coerce the Soviet Union into negotiations, since this was interpreted by the Soviet Union as a sign of international passivity on the part of the US. In the meantime, the agents of the US became engaged in some serious paperwork in connection with the internal crisis in Greece,[14] and soon the Korean War broke out.

The situation in Greece and Korea triggered the necessary response from the US. President Harry S. Truman set forth a policy of containment.[15] President Truman established that *the US would provide political, military, economic assistance to all democratic nations under threat from external or internal authoritarian forces.* The *Truman doctrine* effectively reoriented US foreign policy, away from its usual stance of withdrawal from regional conflicts not directly involving the US (as it followed from the Monroe doctrine), to one of possible intervention in far-away conflicts. In line with the Truman doctrine, the US mobilized substantial resources for both Greece and Korea: financial aid in the first case, and substantial military forces in the second in an effort to contain Soviet communist expansion around the world. According to Truman, the US could no longer stand by and allow the forcible expansion of Soviet totalitarianism into free, independent nations, because US national security depended upon more than just the physical security of US territory. Rather, in a sharp break with its traditional avoidance of extensive foreign commitments beyond the Western Hemisphere during peacetime, the Truman doctrine committed the US to actively offering assistance to preserve the political integrity of democratic nations when such an offer was deemed to be in the best interest of the US. On the other hand, by adopting the Truman doctrine, the US formally admitted that the states on which the Soviet Union had imposed its rule by military force during World War II

13 Id. p. 420.

14 During the Greek Civil War and War of Independence of 1942-1949, the Greek People's Liberation Army (ELÁS), supported by the Soviet Union, attempted to occupy the territory of the country by military force. The Greek government finally defeated the communist army with the help of Great Britain.

15 John Lewis Gaddis, 'Was the Truman Doctrine a Real Turning Point?', *Foreign Affairs*, Vol. 52, Issue 2, 1974, pp. 386-402.

doi: 10.5553/HYIEL/266627012022010001009

belonged to the Soviet sphere of influence. While there is no doubt that the *de facto* division of the world into spheres of influence had become clear to the world leaders participating in the Tehran, Yalta and Potsdam conferences, no legal documents to that effect had been drawn up.

The moral dilemma described above was recognized by President Eisenhower, as groups of Eastern European people living in exile in the US gave unequivocal signals to the President and his administration in the remote hope that with the help of the leading power of the world, they might one day return to their countries, as to those among the free nations and the community of democratic states. Succumbing to this political pressure and moral necessity, upon Secretary of State John Foster Dulles' advice *Eisenhower launched Operation Rollback, i.e.* a *policy of forcing retreat.* The policy of roll back was given due publicity by both the Voice of America and by Radio Free Europe,[16] which filled the nations of Eastern and Central Europe, including Hungary, with, unfortunately, unfounded hope.

The notion of "rollback" gained wider traction when the Truman administration approved a document known as NSC-68, just after the outbreak of the Korean War in 1950. NSC-68 had set rollback as an objective, but it failed to specify how to achieve that goal. In the Korean War, the US and the UN officially endorsed a policy of rollback – the destruction of the communist North Korean government – and sent UN forces across the 38th parallel. In the end, the rollback strategy caused Chine to intervene, and US forces were pushed back to the 38th parallel.

Following the 1952 presidential election, President Eisenhower adopted containment instead of rollback in October 1952 through National Security Council document NSC 162/2, effectively abandoning rollback efforts in Europe. In 1956, Eisenhower decided not to intervene during the Hungarian Uprising of 1956.[17] The Suez Crisis, which unfolded simultaneously, played an important role in hampering the US response to the crisis in Hungary. As Vice President Nixon later explained:

> "We couldn't, on one hand, complain about the Soviets intervening in Hungary and, on the other hand, approve the British and the French picking that particular time to intervene against [Gamal Abdel] Nasser."[18]

In 1956, President Eisenhower unequivocally returned to the Truman doctrine of respecting the spheres of influence. President Eisenhower addressed a message to

16 Peter Grose, *Operation Rollback: America's Secret War Behind the Iron Curtain,* New York, 2000, p. 164.

17 About the serious crimes committed during and after the 1956 uprising, *see e.g.* Réka Varga, 'A nemzetközi jog által büntetni rendelt cselekmények magyarországi alkalmazása (a Biszku-ügy margójára)', *Iustum Aequum Salutare,* Vol. 7, Issue 4, 2011, pp. 19-24. About the topic of war crimes and the application of international humanitarian law, *see e.g.* Réka Varga, 'Háborús bűncselekményekkel kapcsolatos eljárások nemzeti bíróságok előtt', *in* Eszter Kirs (ed.), *Egységesedés és széttagolódás a nemzetközi büntetőjogban,* Bíbor, Miskolc, 2009, pp. 91-111.

18 Interview with Richard Nixon concerning J.F. Dulles, NS Archive, Record No. 65 106.

doi: 10.5553/HYIEL/266627012022010001009

Nikita Sergeyevich Khrushchev, First Secretary of the Communist Party of the Soviet Union, in which he promised the Soviet Union to refrain from inviting Hungary to the Western military alliance, and that the US did not intend to develop close political ties with Hungary. It was all interpreted by Khrushchev and the Soviet leadership as a green light to Soviet intervention in Hungary. Khrushchev invoked the international obligation of the Soviet Union as justification for the Soviet intervention in Hungary, *i.e.* a principle requiring the leading power of the communist world to provide assistance to a sister country where workers, laboring peasants or communists were being hanged by counter-revolutionaries.

The Soviet Union did not invoke any formal ideology of international law or any doctrine of international relations in connection with the intervention in 1956. The reason may be that the Soviet Union contended that it had made its position clear whereby it expected every state to respect the spheres of influence established by the power balance and *status quo* developed at the end of World War II. A decade later, Professor Grigory Tunkin, the best-known scholar of international law in the Soviet Union, wrote in connection with the Soviet intervention in Hungary that a socialist intervention was an obligation to be fulfilled by the Soviet Union and accepted by international law in cases where socialist achievements, or the sovereignty or independence of socialist states had to be defended against an imperialist attack.[19]

The Soviet Union expected the world to fully respect its sphere of influence. Khrushchev was the one to announce the policy of *"peaceful coexistence"*, in the spirit of which the Soviet leadership envisioned a political and economic competition in place of a military conflict between the two opposing camps.[20] During the period of "peaceful coexistence" the Soviet Union did not stop adhering to the principle that anywhere around the world, it would give support to forces fighting for liberation from oppression if they were fighting for the true cause, but did not have the power to lead their cause to victory, and therefore needed international support. Encouraged by the successes of its international policy, the Soviet Union embarked on a new mission of territorial expansion, which reached the Americas following the revolution in Cuba. At this point the Soviet expansion crossed the forbidden demarcation line set by the Monroe doctrine, with the consequence that the presidents of the US regardless of party affiliation, took unanimous action against further gains by the Soviet Union in the Americas.

It is worth noting, that it was after the failed landing of Cuban exiles in the Bay of Pigs in 1961 that President Kennedy declared that the foremost national interest of the US was to prevent the intrusion of outside communist forces in the Americas.[21] Barely four years later, President Johnson stated in connection

19 Grigory Tunkin, *Theory of International Law*, Harvard University Press, Cambridge MA, 1974, pp. 435-436.

20 Adam Bromke, 'Ideology and National Interest in Soviet Foreign Policy', *International Journal*, Vol. 22, Issue 4, 1967, p. 556.

21 *Public Papers of the Presidents of the United States: John F. Kennedy*, 1961, pp. 304-306.

doi: 10.5553/HYIEL/266627012022010001009

with the US intervention in Dominica that the American action was unavoidable because some treacherous individuals had contrived to topple the lawful government of the Dominican Republic, and place the country under Soviet influence.[22]

The brutal crushing of the Prague Spring by Soviet troops was an enormous blow to the international reputation of the Soviet Union. For this reason, the Soviet Union felt the time had come to express its theoretical standpoint at an ideological level with regard to the international position of socialist countries and their margin for deviation. The detailed specification of the doctrine was made public in Sergei Kovalov's article titled *'Sovereignty and the International Duties of Socialist Countries'* dated 26 September 1968.[23] The ideas detailed in the article were adopted as the basic principles of the so-called *Brezhnev doctrine*, which was presented by First Secretary Leonid Brezhnev in his speech addressed to a socialist audience at the Fifth Congress of the Polish United Workers' Party on 13 November 1968.[24] The Brezhnev doctrine was also presented by Soviet Minister of Foreign Affairs Andrei Gromyko in his speech to the UN Assembly on 3 October 1968. According to the doctrine, while *socialist countries should be free to determine their path, "none of their decisions should damage either socialism in their country or the fundamental interests of other socialist countries."*[25]

In practice, the Brezhnev doctrine meant that only limited independence of the satellite states' communist parties was allowed, and that none would be allowed to compromise the cohesiveness of the Eastern Bloc in any way. That is, no country could leave the Warsaw Pact or disturb the ruling communist party's monopoly on power. Implicit in this doctrine was that the leadership of the Soviet Union, which reserved for itself the power to define 'socialism' and 'capitalism'. Following the announcement of the doctrine, numerous international treaties were signed between the Soviet Union and its satellite states to reassert these points and to further ensure inter-state cooperation. The Brezhnev doctrine stayed in effect until it was ended with the Soviet reaction to the Polish crisis of 1980-1981. In 1985 the Brezhnev doctrine was summarized by President Reagan as follows: *"once a country has fallen into communist darkness, it can never again be allowed to see the light of freedom."*[26]

The US intended to rely on peaceful means, agreements and a policy of *détente* in its efforts to halt the rather aggressive international expansion of the Soviet regime, President Nixon being the most important representative of this

22 52 Dept. St. Bull. 822 (1965).

23 The article was published in Pravda, the leading daily newspaper in the Soviet Union, which was also the official paper of Central Committee of the Communist Party of the Soviet Union until 1991. *See* Sergei Kovalov, 'Document 31 – Sovereignty and the International Duties of Socialist Countries', *Chronique de politique étrangére*, Vol. 23, Issue 1-2, 1968, pp. 247-250.

24 *See* the speech at https://loveman.sdsu.edu/docs/1968BrezhnevDoctrine.pdf.

25 *See* Stephen G. Glazer, 'The Brezhnev Doctrine', *The International Lawyer*, Vol. 5, Issue 1, 1971, pp. 169-179.

26 *Conservative Political Action Conference's Twelfth Annual Dinner*, 20 Weekly Comp. Pres. Doc. 243 (8 March 1985).

doi: 10.5553/HYIEL/266627012022010001009

policy.[27] The strategy of *détente* was based on the premise that the Soviet Union followed an expansionist policy because it felt threatened, and if it had assurances that the US and its allies had no ill intentions towards it, it would refrain from further aggressive expansionist policies. *Détente* achieved some undeniable success: it led to a number of agreements between Nixon and Brezhnev (including the Partial Test Ban Treaty, the Nuclear Non-Proliferation Treaty, and the Anti-Ballistic Missile Treaty), and later led to the Helsinki Process and the Helsinki Accords (1975). Nevertheless, it was another reinforcement of the recognition of the untouchable nature of the communist sphere of interest forcibly achieved at the end of World War II by the Soviet Union.

The Western world's expectations of the Helsinki Process and *détente* proved to be vain hopes. Following the invasion of Afghanistan in 1979, the Soviet Union continued to advance in Asia. It contributed to the overthrow of the Shah of Iran, and made preparations to undermine political stability in Saudi Arabia. These steps were clearly taken with the aim of further weakening the strategic power of the US in the region. The Soviet political and military advancement reached such a force, that President Carter was obliged to make an emphatic response declaring on 23 January 1980 that any attempt by an outside force to gain control of the Persian Gulf region would be regarded as an assault on the vital interests of the US, and would be repelled by any means necessary, including military force.[28] This emphatic response is referred to in the international political life as the *Carter doctrine*.

4. A Turn in the Reagan Era

Under the Presidency of Ronald Reagan, the US attempted to refashion the international legal system to loosen the restrictions that international law and international institutions placed on unilateral state action. The Reagan administration avoided the restrictions of international legal rules in three ways: *(i)* by 'bending' traditional rules or applying them to unprecedented situations; *(ii)* by interpreting treaty obligations; and *(iii)* occasionally, by advocating for new rules of international law.[29]

When he became President, Ronald Reagan added a clause to the Carter doctrine proclaiming that "We cannot permit Saudi Arabia to become Iran." This simple statement is known as the *Reagan corollary* to the Carter doctrine.[30] The

27 Josef Korbel, 'Detente and World Order', *Denver Journal of International Law and Policy*, Vol. 6, Issue 1, 1976, pp. 13-15.

28 *The State of the Union*, 16 Weekly Comp. Pres. Doc. 197 (23 January 1980). As President Carter underlined, "Let our position be absolutely clear: an attempt by any outside force to gain control of the Persian Gulf region will be regarded as an assault on the vital interests of the United States of America, and such an assault will be repelled by any means necessary, including military force."

29 Malawer 1988, p. 107.

30 George K. Walker, *State Practice Following World War II, 1945-1990*, US Naval War College, Vol. 65, p. 154, at https://digital-commons.usnwc.edu/cgi/viewcontent.cgi?article=1738&context=ils.

doi: 10.5553/HYIEL/266627012022010001009

Reagan corollary emphasized that the US would intervene to protect Saudi Arabia, whose security was threatened after the outbreak of the Iran-Iraq war. The reasoning of the Reagan corollary is significantly different from the view of the Carter doctrine. While the Carter doctrine pledged to defend the friendly governments of the Persian Gulf region against attacks by hostile outside forces, the Reagan corollary meant that the US was prepared to protect allied or friendly governments against hostile groups from within their states.

It is highly instructive and interesting to study the reception of the Reagan corollary by the community of international lawyers and politicians, including attempts to prove that the corollary seriously violated the rules of public international law. According to Reisman, the enormous nuclear power controlled by the US and the Soviet Union forced the two superpowers to come to a mutual agreement and to the establishment a system of some sort of minimum global order, which would reduce the chances of a conflict between them.[31] Reisman called these spheres of influence *critical defense zones*. Reisman believed that the international order may rely on the circumstance that both the US and the Soviet Union needed a zone of buffer states that, for fundamental reasons, remain loyal to one or the other superpower. Neither the US nor the Soviet Union had the right to interfere with the development of social order in their allied buffer states, but they may expect the states of the defense zones to align themselves with their respective superpowers in questions of foreign policy. Based on these arguments, Reisman concluded that the US had the lawful right to issue the Carter doctrine, since the state heading an alliance has a right to defend its allies against outside hostile intervention. He found the Reagan corollary dangerous, however, because in his opinion the states belonging to a defense zone only have the obligation to respect the authority and guidance of their leading superpower in matters of outside threats, but the superpowers cannot interfere with internal processes.[32]

Reagan's extension of the Carter doctrine may appear to be a small step, but it was a major departure from previous practices in US foreign policy and the beginning of a path that would lead to the collapse of the Soviet Union and the fall of communism. It is particularly interesting that while the Soviet international law community served the expansive policy of the Soviet Union and communist ideas in every respect, scholars of international law in the West urged their political leaders to maintain the *status quo* that emerged after World War II, even when there could have been room in international law for retaliation for the breaches of international law committed by the Soviet Union and thus, for the restoration of the international legal order. The Reisman argument – which was shared by a fair proportion of international law experts – rests on the premise that the tacit agreement between the great powers on the spheres of influence after World War II created an obligation in terms of international law that had to be respected by both the US and the Soviet Union. Although the 1969 VCLT only deals with written treaties, the rules it defines can be *mutatis mutandis* extended,

31 W. Michael Reisman, 'Editorial Comments: Critical Defense Zones and International Law: The Reagan Codicil', *American Journal of International Law*, Vol. 76, Issue 3, 1982, p. 589.

32 Id. p. 591.

doi: 10.5553/HYIEL/266627012022010001009

at least in the ambit of customary international law, to cases where the international binding force of unwritten agreements and the legal consequences of their violation are taken into account.[33]

Another basic document of international law is the UN International Law Commission's Draft Articles on the responsibility of states for internationally wrongful acts,[34] which codifies the legal consequences of behaviors in breach of international law. Article 22 states that

> "The wrongfulness of an act of a State not in conformity with an international obligation towards another State is precluded if and to the extent that the act constitutes a countermeasure taken against the latter State in accordance with chapter II of Part Three."[35]

As it was underlined by the Reagan administration, the US had a right to take such countermeasures.[36] The truth of this statement must be recognized by all those who took great pains to illustrate the importance of the US and the Soviet Union being surrounded by allied states loyal to them in the interest of maintaining international peace and security.

The constant redividing of the spheres of interest was a necessary consequence of the nature of the Cold War, but the unbroken Soviet ambition to re-write the spheres constituted the highest possible security risk for the world. It suffices to mention Cuba here. In this connection it is easy to accept that the Soviet acts in breach of international law were among the most serious wrongful acts after World War II.

Ronald Reagan's Secretary of State George Shultz made sure to clarify in his speeches the underlying principle of Reagan's foreign policy. Ronald Reagan recognized that Khrushchev's and Brezhnev's doctrines rested on the assumption that everything that belonged to the Soviet Union's sphere of influence was untouchable, while everything that was under the US sphere of influence was meant to be up for grabs.[37] President Reagan decided to abandon the old policy and pay the Soviet Union back with its own currency.[38] As was discussed above, he had every reason for that even in an international law sense. In his speech in October 1984, Reagan spoke of the fight between freedom and totalitarian dictatorship, which he correctly presented as a fight between good and evil. He

33 Xiaocheng Qin, 'Oral International Agreement and China's Relevant Practice', *Chinese Journal of International Law*, Vol. 4, Issue 2, 2005, p. 468.

34 Official records of the General Assembly, Fifty-sixth Session, Supplement No 10 and corrigendum (A/56/10 and Corr 1).

35 A/56/10 Report of the International Law Commission on the work of its fifty-third session, *Yearbook of the International Law Commission, 2001*, Vol. II, Part Two, pp. 75-76.

36 Francis Anthony Boyle, *World Politics and International Law*, Duke University Press, 1985, p. 268.

37 George Shultz's ideas were cited by Michael W. Reisman, 'The Brezhnev Doctrine and the Reagan Doctrine: Apples and Oranges', *American Society of International Law Proceedings*, Vol. 81, 1978, p. 565.

38 W. Michael Reisman, 'Old Wine in New Bottles: The Brezhnev Doctrines in Contemporary International Law and in Practice', *Yale Journal of International Law*, Vol. 13, Issue 1, 1988, p. 197.

doi: 10.5553/HYIEL/266627012022010001009

stressed that the free world cannot be content with just attempting to stop the Soviet threat. In 1985, Ronald Reagan declared that he did not recognize either the legitimacy or the finality of the Soviet occupation of Eastern and Central Europe. He also highlighted the importance of supporting forces fighting for freedom and democracy in any part of the world, which became known to the public as the Reagan doctrine.[39] Reagan did not simply mean this as a rhetorical statement: in September 1985, for instance, he signed National Security Decision Directive 166 ordering the continued exclusion of Soviet forces from Southeast Asia, now, by any available means.

Reagan did no more than turn the Soviet forces' own weapon against them, and promised to reciprocate by displaying the same international behavior that the Soviet Union had been exercising around the world. American experts of international law were engaged in a debate of several years over whether the Reagan doctrine and the Brezhnev doctrine could be equated. It was not until the first international successes of the Reagan doctrine that the American Society of International Law held a debate with the title "The Brezhnev Doctrine and the Reagan Doctrine: Apples and Oranges?"[40] During the debate, some of the participants defended the Reagan doctrine. The consistent policy of the Reagan administration supporting forces fighting against communist influence was subject to particularly strong attacks.

Since President Carter strove to create an image in the international arena as the leader of an US administration committed to human rights, a large share of his international actions were also aimed at the protection and reinforcement of human rights.[41] While President Carter was undoubtedly driven by good intentions, even his advocates noted that his human rights defense policy was noticeably incomplete, inconsistent and in many cases, selective.[42] With regard to human rights, President Ronald Reagan stressed that the most dangerous factors globally were activities of the subversive forces fighting to spread communism. These communist forces were simply labeled terrorists by the Reagan administration. The international fight against terrorism, which was later associated with the era of President George W. Bush, was a term used by the Reagan administration on a number of occasions referring to communist cells and forceful subversive acts carried out by groups in other countries.

President Reagan's activities in connection with the international support against communist subversive groups were heavily criticized by some of the US experts in international law, such as Francis A. Boyle.[43] The government of the US assisted the Nicaraguan *Contras* in their fight against the Sandinista government,

39 William D. Rogers *et al.*, 'The Brezhnev Doctrine and the Reagan Doctrine: Apples and Oranges: Remarks', *American Society of International Law Proceedings*, Vol. 81, 1987, pp. 561-570.

40 The debate was held on 11 April 1987, chaired by William D. Rogers.

41 John Murphy, 'Human Rights in United States Foreign Policy', *Houston Journal of International Law*, Vol. 4, Issue 1, 1981, pp. 133-136.

42 Robert A. Friedlander, 'Confusing Victims and Victimizers: Nicaragua and the Reinterpretation of International Law', *Denver Journal of International Law and Policy*, Vol. 14, Issue 1, 1985, p. 91.

43 Francis A. Boyle, 'Preserving the Rule of Law in the War against International Terrorism', *Whitter Law Review*, Vol. 8, Issue 4, 1986, p. 735.

doi: 10.5553/HYIEL/266627012022010001009

which led to a court case at the ICJ upon the initiative of the Nicaraguan government.[44] The ICJ's judgment was that the US intervention was unlawful. During the proceedings, however, the ICJ could not duly appraise the fact that the behavior of the US was very closely related to the global threat to security posed by the unstoppable expansion of the Soviet Union in the world.

President Reagan realized that the opportunities for US military development led to a new phase of the Cold War, a phase which was comparable to the unilateral possession of nuclear weapons in the mid-forties. The position of the US in the forties had offered significant, but regrettably unexploited opportunities against the Soviet Union. At the beginning of the Reagan Era, the vast majority of experts believed the Soviet Union to be a strong and unassailable state, but Reagan realized that the Soviet Union was a weak country struggling with several contradictions and could be forced to its knees given sufficiently decisive US actions. In terms of military policy, this implied two major elements. *(i)* One was the installation of medium-range missiles in Europe, which led to the military strategic result that the European allies were assured that these nuclear weapons would be deployed in case of a conflict between Western Europe and the Soviet Union. Western Europe had previously felt increasingly threatened as it had never been certain whether the US would be prepared to get involved in a nuclear war with the Soviet Union just to deflect an attack on Western Europe. The medium-range missiles, however, carried the risk of a nuclear war, should Western Europe suffer a Soviet attack, and this local, but nevertheless nuclear conflict between Western Europe and the Soviet forces would be followed by the deployment of untouched American nuclear forces against the Soviet Union. This risk was clearly too high to be ignored, and thus ensured that the Soviet Union would not risk a serious conflict in connection with the states of Western Europe once the missiles were based in Europe. *(ii)* The second idea, the Strategic Defence Initiative (SDI) was of even higher significance. The plan was to build a defense system around the US that would prevent any nuclear attack initiated from another country against the US.[45]

The relative security of the Cold War is essentially rooted in the notion of interdependence, *i.e.* the two-way dependence between the Soviet Union and the US, which rested on the principle of Mutually Assured Destruction (MAD).[46] If the US had succeeded in safeguarding itself against destruction, this would have secured a strategic advantage whereby it could have destroyed the Soviet Union without endangering its own existence. It is typical once again, that there were American experts in international law who emphatically argued that such

44 ICJ, *Military and Paramilitary Activities in and against Nicaragua.*

45 David Hodgkinson, 'The Reinterpretation of the ABM Treaty: Policy Versus the Law', *University of Western Australia Law Review*, Vol. 21, Issue 2, 1991, pp. 259-264.

46 Mark A. Clark, 'Directed-Energy Weapons on the High Frontier', *Denver Journal of International Law and Policy*, Vol. 13, Issue 1, 1983, p. 117.

doi: 10.5553/HYIEL/266627012022010001009

defensive military tools were contradictory to the international agreement on outer space.[47]

The general public and some political scientists found President Reagan to be a great communicator,[48] who used his exceptional acting skills to represent the strategic aims of the US in the international arena. The Strategic Defence Initiative, the so-called Star Wars plan, could only yield success in a very distant future given the enormous costs and the unprecedented challenge of technological development it called for. Ronald Reagan, however, was able to broadcast this threat to the Soviet forces with such credibility, that they perceived the implementation of the American plans for the SDI as an acute and immediate threat, which had a significant effect on the decisions of the Soviet leadership.

5. Conclusion

It was Ronald Reagan's tough policy that left no choice for the Soviet Union but to elect a leader like Gorbachev, who was prepared for compromises, and Reagan's well-timed change of direction and his ability to reach an agreement allowed him to prompt Gorbachev in order to keep his power and to launch reforms. This process gradually led to the peaceful dissolution of the Soviet regime and to the emergence of a new world, which was no longer characterized by a bipolar world order. For a long time, the US became the sole superpower of the world. During the Reagan Era, the US administration undeniably relied on a purposive interpretation of public international law to realize the goals of the US. Ronald Reagan firmly believed in the US being an exceptional nation, but he also believed in the moral obligation that this uniqueness carried with it. These beliefs gave him the power to rectify the mistakes of the post-war period and force the Soviet Union – whose aggressive foreign policy after World War II was at all times the greatest threat to international peace and security – to its knees with the help of assertive US policies. In the process of creating a new and more democratic world, where international law may apply more effectively, President Reagan's approach played a crucial role.

47 Treaty on the principles regulating the activities of states with regard to the exploration and use of outer space including the Moon and other celestial bodies. Allen Sultan, 'The International Rule of Law under the Reagan Administration', *University of Dayton Law Review*, Vol. 10, 1984, pp. 250-251.

48 Robert E. Denton Jr., *The primetime presidency of Ronald Reagan: the era of the television presidency*, Praeger Publishers, New York, 1988, pp. 1-15.

doi: 10.5553/HYIEL/266627012022010001009

DEVELOPMENTS IN EUROPEAN LAW

Expulsion of EU Citizens from Another EU Member State in the Recent Case Law of the CJEU*

*Laura Gyeney***

Abstract

The concept of a territorially united Europe is a necessary corollary to the completion of the Area of Freedom, Security and Justice (AFSJ). While the case law of the CJEU on EU citizenship in many respects aims to strengthen this status (and, at the same time, to weaken Member States' regulatory power) there is at least a partly opposite trend in the assessment of Member States' expulsion policy under EU law. This line of cases emphasizes not only the traditional role of the Janus-faced concept of social integration, which bolsters the exercise of rights, but also its role as a justification for the restriction of rights. This article examines how the CJEU can reconcile the federalizing concept of a new citizenship with an expulsion policy based on sovereignty and how all of this impacts the unifying and expanding concept of EU citizenship.

Keywords: EU citizenship, public security, social integration, good market citizen, Area of Freedom Security and Justice.

1. Introduction

The expulsion of EU citizens and their family members from an EU Member State other than their own Member State has always been a delicate issue of EU law. This is entirely understandable in a field of law which, although pertaining to the competence of the Member States, as part of the internal market, is in fact in the buffer zone between the Member States' values and European interests. The jurisdictional tension in this area, which has been well-defined from the outset, has only been exacerbated by the case law of the CJEU following the adoption of

* This article was written within the framework of "Programmes Aimed at Raising the Standard of Legal Education", founded by the Hungarian Ministry of Justice.

** Laura Gyeney: associate professor of law, Pázmány Péter Catholic University, Budapest.

doi: 10.5553/HYIEL/266627012022010001010

Directive 2004/38/EC[1] in which the concept of social integration is more pronounced in public policy and public security related decisions than before.

This case law, characterized as a restrictive one, is, from time to time, criticized in legal literature. This is because the CJEU, by blurring the previously clear boundaries of public policy and public security in its case law, and now requiring compliance with the host Member State's criminal law standards, as well as compliance with the category of good market citizen in order to enjoy enhanced protection against expulsion, not only undermines the previous system of protection for EU citizens, but also jeopardizes legal certainty.[2]

Critics rightly refer to the fact that, in addition to the classic grounds for expulsion under public policy, public security and public health laid down in Directive 2004/38/EC, the CJEU created another legal basis for expulsion in its 2014 *Dano* judgment.[3] According to this new doctrine, EU citizens who are essentially excluded from the scope and safety net of the Directive due to non-compliance with the condition of sufficient financial resources set out in Article 7 of the 2004/38/EC and their application for social assistance, are now vulnerable to expulsion.[4]

Indeed, it may be concluded from the CJEU's recent case law on expulsion that the main drivers of integration remain fundamentally economic in nature, centered on the idea of a good market citizen.[5] The CJEU's increased emphasis on the requirement of social inclusion merely reflects the fact that, due to its 'unfinished nature',[6] the legal institution of EU citizenship may not yet act as a catalyst in the field of expulsion policy. When adopting Directive 2004/38/EC, Member States made it clear that they did not wish to grant the right to absolute protection against expulsion even to EU citizens who are permanent residents.[7]

1 Directive 2004/38/EC of the European Parliament and of the Council of 29 April 2004 on the right of citizens of the Union and their family members to move and reside freely within the territory of the Member States.

2 Michal Meduna, 'Scelestus Europeus Sum: What Protection against Expulsion Does EU Citizenship Offer to European Offenders?', *in* Dimitry Kochenov (ed.), *EU Citizenship and Federalism*, Cambridge University Press, Cambridge, 2017, p. 405.

3 Judgment of 11 November 2014, *Case C-333/13, Dano*, ECLI:EU:C:2014:2358.

4 According to the CJEU's ruling in *Chenchooliah*, Article 15 of the Citizenship Directive serves as a legal basis for the expulsion of EU citizens for reasons other than public policy, public security or public health if the Union citizen no longer fulfills the conditions for residence under the Directive. Judgment of 10 September 2019, *Case C-94/18, Chenchooliah*, ECLI:EU:C:2019:693, paras. 74-75.

5 This suggestion is not entirely unfounded, given that the CJEU's case law on expulsion refers only once to EU citizenship as a fundamental status, and there are no indications yet as to why this would change in the future.

6 Meduna 2017, pp. 411-413; Sandra Mantu, 'Concepts of Time and European Citizenship', *European Journal of Migration and Law*, Vol. 15, Issue 4, 2013, p. 447.

7 According to the proposed directive, EU citizens and their family members who have acquired permanent resident status would still have enjoyed absolute protection against expulsion on grounds of public policy or public security. Although the European Parliament supported this absolute defense construct in its report on the draft, it failed in the Council in light of the almost unanimous opposition by the Member States. European Parliament, Report on the proposal for directive on the right of citizens of the Union and their family members to move and reside freely on the territory of the Member States, COM(2001) 257 final.

doi: 10.5553/HYIEL/266627012022010001010

The relative nature of the protection means that as one of the last bastions of national sovereignty Member States still retain their power of expulsion in case of the most serious breaches. This does not mean, of course, that the CJEU's recent case law does not take into account the long-term federalizing effect of the institutions of EU citizenship and free movement. As will be shown below, the emergence of common European values in the relevant CJEU case law, or the emphasis on the social rehabilitation of the Union citizen as a common European interest, may over time dilute the importance of sovereign state power.

Based on recent case law, this article seeks to unpack the long-term challenges that will shape the CJEU's jurisprudence on expulsion measures in the Member States. In this context, the theoretical issues and practical difficulties involved in the gradual establishment of an Area of Freedom, Security and Justice (AFSJ) will be discussed. If we consider the Union as a single area of freedom, security and justice, the expulsion of citizens who commit a criminal offence is nothing more than the 'transfer' of offending EU citizens from one corner of this borderless area to another.[8] If we accept that the Union is an area without frontiers, the open nature of the Union necessarily implies that the legal institution of expulsion is meaningless. In practice, expulsion decisions, or even entry bans in the Schengen area are difficult to enforce and apply. Even if a national of a Member State is expelled from the territory of a host Member State, there is no guarantee that he or she will not turn up later in the same Member State. A good example is the CJEU's 2021 ruling in *F.S.*[9] in which the CJEU examined the question when an expulsion decision of a Member State may be regarded as having been enforced and in which circumstances an actual departure from the territory of the Member State in question may be justified.

Ensuring the coherence of case law on the expulsion or residence of EU citizens[10] may be a similar challenge in the future. While the CJEU applies a typically restrictive approach to the expulsion of citizens moving within the EU, referring to the fundamental nature of the legal status, based on the *Zambrano* doctrine,[11] it already guarantees a very high level of protection where there is a risk that static citizens are forced to leave the EU. Although the difference between official decisions on expulsion from one Member State to another and forcing specific persons to leave the entire territory of the Union is clear, the case law is currently divergent on this point, which in my view is not in itself justified by the geographical difference between the two expulsions.

8 Elspeth Guild *et al.* (eds.), *The EU Citizenship Directive: A Commentary*, 2nd edition, Oxford University Press, Oxford, 2019, p. 289.

9 Judgment of 22 June 2021, *Case C-719/19, F.S.*, ECLI:EU:C:2021:506.

10 Meduna uses the term constructive deportation which is not entirely correct in law as the expulsion of one's own citizen is not legally possible under international law, and it is not the EU citizens themselves who are the subject of the dispute. However, this term makes it clear that a negative decision affecting parents also indirectly affects the residence of the EU citizen as there is the risk of leaving the territory of the Union.

11 As regards the EU citizenship under Article 20 TFEU, the CJEU ruled in *Zambrano* that EU law "precludes national measures which have the effect of depriving citizens of the Union of the genuine enjoyment of the substance of the rights conferred by virtue of their status as citizens of the Union". Judgment of 8 March 2011, *Case C-34/09, Zambrano,* ECLI:EU:C:2011:124.

doi: 10.5553/HYIEL/266627012022010001010

The article below provides a brief overview of the legal framework for the expulsion of EU citizens and their family members. It then outlines the main elements of the current case law, highlighting the emergence of the concept of social integration in expulsion policy. Finally, some of the future challenges of expulsion policy will be discussed.

2. The Relevant Provisions of Directive 2004/38/EC

The right of EU citizens to free movement is guaranteed by Article 21 TFEU. Although fundamental, this right is very limited and conditional. As Meduna puts it very aptly, free movement is neither free for all, nor free-for-all,' that is, free movement is not guaranteed to everyone, but it is not even free.[12] Primary law and Directive 2004/38/EC, on the one hand, lay down the conditions for residence and, on the other hand, give power to the Member States to expel nationals of other Member States and their family members on grounds of public policy, public security or public health.[13]

However, Directive 2004/38/EC has also reinforced the protection of EU citizens and their family members against expulsion by establishing a system of gradual protection proportionate to the length of stay.[14] Under this system, protection against expulsion will gradually increase depending on the degree of integration of the EU citizen concerned in the host Member State, as set out below.[15] *(i)* The first level of the system is the protection of EU citizens and their third-country family members without a right of permanent residence: Member States may, in addition to the protection provided for under Article 15 of the Directive,[16] restrict their entry or residence only on grounds of public policy, public security or public health. *(ii)* The second level of protection may be enjoyed by EU citizens and their third-country family members who have already acquired a permanent right of residence in the host state, since the ground for expulsion provided for in Article 15 of the Directive no longer applies to them. Under Article 28(2) of the Directive, the host state may decide to expel them only on the more serious grounds of public policy or public security. *(iii)* Finally, Article 28(3) of the Directive provides the highest, third level of protection as it only allows expulsion on the imperative grounds of public security. However, this 'enhanced

12 Meduna 2017, p. 395.

13 Since 2014 the CJEU has developed a new ground for expulsion under Article 15 of the Citizenship Directive which applies when an EU citizen no longer has a right of residence under the Directive in question.

14 As mentioned in the introduction, this protection is only relative as opposed to the original Commission draft.

15 As the CJEU has already stated in *Tsakouridis* in 2009, "the greater the degree of integration of Union citizens and their family members in the host Member State, the greater the degree of protection against expulsion should be." Judgment of 23 November 2010, *Case C-145/09, Tsakouridis*, ECLI:EU:C:2010:708, para. 25.

16 According to Article 15(1) of the Citizenship Directive, the procedures provided for by Articles 15 and 31 shall apply by analogy to all decisions restricting free movement of Union citizens and their family members on grounds other than public policy, public security or public health.

doi: 10.5553/HYIEL/266627012022010001010

protection' is only guaranteed to EU citizens who have been in the territory of the host Member State for 'the previous ten' years,[17] or to minors.

3. Some Elements of the CJEU's Restrictive Approach in its Recent Expulsion Case Law

In its case law following the entry into force of the Directive, the CJEU has sought to avoid, with regard to financial guarantees[18] even the impression that legislation may provide absolute or even close to absolute protection to citizens moving freely.

Thus, first, by blurring the previously seemingly clear boundaries between public policy and public security in *Tsakouridis* and *P.I.*,[19] the CJEU left it essentially up to the Member States to decide whether perpetrators of certain exceptionally serious offences could enjoy enhanced protection under the relevant provisions of the Directive. By further narrowing the potential scope of EU citizens under enhanced protection in *M.G.*,[20] the CJEU also ruled that the ten years required for such protection should be counted backwards from the expulsion decision[21] and that period of imprisonment interrupt the continuity of that stay as a general rule. With this, the CJEU essentially created a new qualitative condition not expressly provided for in the legislation. The CJEU took a similar view in *B. and Vomero*[22] when it stated that enhanced protection could only be obtained through the acquisition of permanent residence status, notwithstanding the fact that such a restriction is not provided for in the Directive.

Scholars trace this restrictive trend back to a wide variety of reasons. While some see the roots of this change in the changed political environment itself,[23] others see the CJEU's role in reversing the federal bargaining process behind the

17 This clause, which was inaccurately worded by the EU legislature, was subsequently the subject of the CJEU's interpretative decision in *M.G.*

18 The CJEU has still taken a strong position on the enforcement of the procedural guarantees provided for in the Directive.

19 Judgment of 22 May 2012, *Case C-348/09, P.I.*, ECLI:EU:C:2012:300.

20 Judgment of 16 January 2014, *Case C-400/12, M.G.*, ECLI:EU:C:2014:9.

21 Another condition is that these ten years must be continuous.

22 Judgment of 17 April 2018, *Joined cases C-316/16 and C-424/16, B. and Vomero*, ECLI:EU:C:2018:256.

23 The arguments for a changing political environment, which is closely linked to fears surrounding immigration, is clearly lending itself, as we tend to reinforce the distinction between 'we' and 'others' in a crisis situation. According to some authors, the expulsion of foreign offenders in this case is a kind of message from the Member States to their citizens that the government does control foreigners. This is especially true in a period of global crisis where nation-state frameworks are an essential source of security, reinforcing the importance of national affiliation and identity. Kathrin Hamenstadt, 'Expulsion and "Legal Otherness" in Times of Growing Nationalism', *European Law Review*, Vol. 45, Issue 4, 2020, pp. 453-470.

doi: 10.5553/HYIEL/266627012022010001010

jurisprudence.[24] Still others, with somewhat idealistic overtones, believe that national authorities have been applying EU law with such confidence for many decades of integration that the CJEU can be much more flexible in shaping EU rules.[25] Even if the reasons behind the CJEU's approach cannot be clearly identified, it is in any event certain that the CJEU has upheld the concept of social integration (rooted in the right to free movement) in its recent case law on expulsion.[26] The CJEU does all this in such a way that in its jurisprudence it now emphasizes not only the traditional role of this Janus-faced concept, which also strengthens the exercise of rights, but also its role both as a precondition for the exercise, and as a justification for the restriction of rights. This may even lead to keeping out or removing EU citizens from the territory of the Member State in question, instead of admitting them.

This approach also implies a sense of responsibility on the side of the citizens who move freely. While the traditional rights based approach[27] to the integration process treats the free mover as a passive actor in social inclusion,[28] the new case law of the CJEU imposes a much greater responsibility on the EU citizen by defining EU citizenship as a set of rights and obligations. Consequently, EU citizens must bear the consequences of a possible lack of social integration, including the loss of their right of residence and thus their expulsion from the territory of a Member State. This responsibility therefore imposes a double requirement on the EU citizen moving freely. On the one hand, the EU citizen must refrain from breaching the criminal law standards of the host Member State (moreover, in addition to the criminal law of the Member States, in its recent case law, the CJEU imposed this obligation also in respect of EU values). On the other hand, in order to enjoy enhanced protection through permanent residence, an EU citizen must also meet the economic criteria set out in the Directive.

3.1. Blending the Concepts of Public Order and Public Security

According to legal literature, the CJEU's decisions in *Tsakouridis* and *P.I.* were the first step in this restrictive interpretation and practice. In the cases in question, the national courts turned to the CJEU to interpret, inter alia, the concept of imperative grounds of public security within the meaning of Article 28(3) of the Directive.[29] *Tsakouridis* and *P.I.* were based on expulsion decisions adopted

24 *See also* Niamh Nic Shuibhne, 'Recasting EU Citizenship as Federal Citizenship: What Are the Implication for the Citizen When the Political Bargain Is Privileged?', *in* Kochenov (ed.) 2017, p. 153.

25 Dimitry Kochenov & Sir Richard Plender, 'EU Citizenship: From an Incipient Form to an Incipient Substance?', *European Law Review*, Vol. 37, Issue 4, 2012, p. 388.

26 Daniel Thym, 'The Evolution of Citizens' Rights', *in* Daniel Thym (ed.), *Questioning EU Citizenship*, Hart Publishing, 2017, p. 125.

27 According to that view, integration takes place essentially automatically by reason of the residence in the Member State concerned and the lapse of time.

28 Stephen Coutts, 'The Absence of Integration and the Responsibilisation of Union Citizenship', *European Papers*, Vol. 3, Issue 2, 2018, p. 765.

29 The two cases concerned EU citizens who had resided in the territory of the host Member State, Germany, for more than ten years, so that only an imperative ground of public security could justify their expulsion.

following convictions for particularly serious crimes committed by the individuals concerned (dealing in narcotics as part of an organized group and sexual exploitation of children).

It is apparent from the case file in *Tsakouridis* that the referring German court itself, regardless of the seriousness of the offence, did not consider it appropriate to establish a category of imperative public security, if any, which would otherwise have resulted from the relevant German legislation. The question was significant since Tsakouridis had resided in the territory of the host Member State for more than 10 years, so that only this legal ground could have served as a basis for expulsion. Based on the CJEU's earlier case law, the German judicial forum found that public security covered only the external and internal security of a Member State and was therefore narrower than the concept of public policy which included internal criminal law. Consequently, Tsakouridis might possibly represent a substantial threat to public policy, but not to the existence of the state and its institutions or the survival of the population.[30]

However, the CJEU did not share the German court's approach and departed from its own previous jurisprudence. While emphasizing that EU legislature intended to *limit measures based on Article 28(3) of the Directive to 'exceptional circumstances'*, the CJEU nevertheless ruled that the fight against crime in connection with dealing in narcotics as part of an organized group was capable of being covered by the concept of *'imperative grounds of public security'*, that is, the CJEU did not consider it necessary to separate the two concepts.[31] Moreover, the CJEU held that a threat to public security may be established in the event of any threat to the fundamental interests of society or to the host Member State that might directly threaten the calm and physical security of the population as a whole or a large part of it.[32] With this decision, the CJEU clearly intended to reflect its social value judgment in relation to certain exceptionally serious crimes. However, because of its devastating effect on society, dealing in narcotics may undoubtedly be particularly likely to *undermine the moral convictions of the population.*

30 *Case C-145/09, Tsakouridis*, para. 20.

31 Although there is some overlap between the concepts of public policy and public security, that is, the two concepts are not rigidly separated, public security usually constitutes an attack on state institutions or their basic infrastructure, or a significant security threat to the public due to the magnitude of the risk, for example in the form of a terrorist act. Public policy, on the other hand, is traditionally interpreted to involve the maintenance of peaceful social coexistence, and thus the protection of personal rights by criminal law.

32 Ultimately, however, the CJEU left it to the national court to decide whether Tsakouridis's conduct fell within the 'serious grounds of public policy or public security' or the 'imperative grounds of public security' within the meaning of Article 28(3) of the Directive.

doi: 10.5553/HYIEL/266627012022010001010

3.2. *Emphasizing the Exceptional Nature of an Act Committed in the Past rather than a Future Threat*

The CJEU followed the above logic also in *K. and H.F.*[33] in 2018 in which, in relation to the expulsion of persons convicted of war crimes[34] from the Netherlands and Belgium, set out the finding already well-known from *Tsakouridis* and *P.I.* According to this, internal security may be affected by the risk of a serious disturbance to the foreign relations of that Member State or to the peaceful coexistence of nations.[35] However, as long as dealers in narcotics or sex offenders may indeed have a tendency to perpetuate such behavior and thus pose a genuine and present threat to a fundamental interest of society, this is highly doubtful for war criminals. In *K. and H.F.*, however, the CJEU felt it necessary to reaffirm *the concept of a threat that passed from the past to the future,* that is, that an act committed in the past could, because of its exceptional gravity, pose a permanent threat to a fundamental interest of society in the future. Incidentally, the case is remarkable only because it is the first to deal with the relationship between EU refugee law and the free movement of EU citizens.[36] In my view, this approach of the CJEU is at least debatable: there is no threat to society years or decades after the commission of an earlier, serious crime. Nevertheless, the material gravity of the crime itself can be regarded as such that no immunity may be granted from the consequences of the commission of that crime. It therefore seems more appropriate to take into account both the risk of recidivism (which may be an assessment criterion for any offender, regardless of the material gravity of the offence) and the substantive weight of that offence, bearing in mind that *the mere fact of committing a particularly serious crime in itself creates the possibility of expulsion,* regardless of a possible risk of recidivism. This approach is essentially the same as when a convicted person cannot be absolved *ex post facto* from the adverse legal consequences of a conviction.

K. was a Croatian war criminal[37] living in the Netherlands since 2001, whose application for asylum was repeatedly rejected by the authorities under Article F(1) of the 1951 Geneva Convention on the grounds that he had been personally involved in war crimes and crimes against humanity in the former Yugoslavia. Subsequently, in view of these war crimes, the Dutch authorities

33 Judgment of 2 May 2018, *Joined cases C-331/16 and C-366/16, K. and H.F.*, ECLI:EU:C:2018:296.

34 About the relevance of war crimes at national level, *see e.g.* Réka Varga, 'Háborús bűncselekményekkel kapcsolatos eljárások nemzeti bíróságok előtt', *in* Eszter Kirs (ed.), *Egységesedés és széttagolódás a nemzetközi büntetőjogban,* Bíbor, Miskolc, 2009, pp. 91-111. From the Hungarian state practice, *see e.g.* Réka Varga, 'A nemzetközi jog által büntetni rendelt cselekmények magyarországi alkalmazása (a Biszku-ügy margójára)', *Iustum Aequum Salutare,* Vol. 7, Issue 4, 2011, pp. 10-24.

35 Id. para. 42.

36 Coutts 2018, p. 775.

37 About the violation of international humanitarian law during the Yugoslav wars, *see e.g.* Réka Varga, 'A nemzetközi humanitárius jog alkalmazhatósága a délszláv-válság idején: a horvátországi háború', *in* Vanda Lamm (ed.), *Dayton 10 év után,* MTA, Budapest, 2006. From the relevance of the Rome Statute of the ICC, *see e.g.* Réka Varga, 'A Római Statútum jelentősége a nemzetközi jogban és a nemzetközi büntetőjogban', *Iustum Aequum Salutare,* Vol. 2, Issue 1-2, 2006, pp. 95-98.

doi: 10.5553/HYIEL/266627012022010001010

declared K. to be an undesirable person on grounds of public policy and public security. The facts in *H.F.* were very similar to those in *K.* An Afghan national arrived in the Netherlands back in 2000 where his asylum application was rejected by the authorities. The applicant later settled in Belgium with his Dutch national daughter, where he wished to obtain a right of residence as a family member of an EU citizen. However, his application was rejected by the Belgian authorities on the grounds of his case file in the Dutch asylum procedure, namely because he was involved in war crimes or crimes against humanity. In both cases, the CJEU had to answer the question whether a restriction on freedom of movement based on acts or events that had occurred decades ago or in a specific historical or social context is compatible with EU law and unlikely to recur in the Member State in question.

In its judgment, the CJEU acknowledged, first of all, that the grounds relied on by a Member State, including the protection of fundamental values under Articles 2 and 3 TEU, may justify the application of the public policy and public security exception. However, it emphasized that *the refusal of asylum* by the authorities *alone could not automatically lead to a restriction on freedom of movement* in which case an individual assessment of the circumstances was required.[38] To that extent, the approach set out in the judgment cannot, in any way, be described as restrictive.

The real significance of the case consists in the CJEU's novel approach to how an act committed in the past is to be assessed, that is, whether a threat to a fundamental interest of society can be regarded as permanently immediate because of its particularly serious nature. Referring to its earlier decision in *Bouchereau*,[39] the CJEU confirmed that *the time elapsed* since the offence may indeed be *an important factor* in the assessment, but that the *exceptionally serious nature of a past act* (according to the CJEU's above-mentioned approach) may, even after a relatively long period of time, *justify such a risk.*[40]

It is surprising that an act committed in the past can in itself pose a threat to public order or public security, given that the concept of threat usually carries a risk for the future. While the finding of a risk of recidivism in relation to the perpetrator in question has been a particularly important element of the CJEU's earlier case law, according to the reasoning in *K. and H.F.* (questionable in my view), the mere physical presence, and therefore the presence in the same geographical and social area with the nationals of the host Member State, may jeopardize one of the fundamental interests of society owing to an act committed in the past.

By emphasizing the exceptional gravity of an act committed in the past, which does not necessarily jeopardize the physical security of the population but rather the moral order of the Member State or the Union as a whole and the fundamental interest of the peace of society, the exclusion of the application of

38 In that regard, the CJEU emphasized the different purpose of point F of the 1951 Geneva Convention and Article 27(2) of the Citizenship Directive. *K. and H.F.*, para. 48-64.

39 Judgment of 27 October 1977, *Case C-30/77, Bouchereau*, ECLI:EU:C:1977:172.

40 *Joined cases C-331/16 and C-366/16, K. and H.F.*, para. 58.

doi: 10.5553/HYIEL/266627012022010001010

public policy or public security becomes morally charged.[41] In addition to the CJEU's earlier and specifically forward-looking, harm-based case law,[42] there is now an *offence-based case law*[43] that focuses on past action and its compatibility with Member State and societal values.

3.3. Increased Importance of the Concept of Integration in the Field of Expulsion

The requirement of social integration in connection with expulsion is reflected in Directive 2004/38/EC itself, in the form of a proportionality test, which takes into account the degree of integration into the host Member State of the person to be expelled and even through the gradual system of protection against expulsion described above.[44] Under that system, therefore, protection against expulsion is progressively increased in the light of the length of residence by the EU citizen concerned in the host Member State and his or her parallel social integration. Although the conditions imposed by the Directive appear to be clear, the CJEU's recent case law that integration into the society of the host Member State is based not only on quantitative (temporal) but also on qualitative factors seems to rewrite the CJEU's earlier case law on expulsion. Thus, respect for the social values enshrined in the criminal law norms of the host Member State, and moreover, compliance with *the concept of good market citizen*, is now a precondition for obtaining enhanced protection against expulsion. Recent CJEU rulings therefore confirm the central nature of the two-faced concept of social integration in the field of expulsion, which no longer merely seeks to promote the exercise of rights deriving from EU citizenship but may also serve as a justification for restricting those rights where the citizen in question is unable, or does not want to integrate into the society of the host Member State.

3.3.1. Respect for Member States' Criminal Law Standards

The integration requirement in relation to the expulsion of EU citizens was first set out in *M.G.* in 2014 where the main question was whether the custodial sentence interrupts the continuity of the ten-year period of residence which is a condition for enhanced protection against expulsion.[45] In its judgment, the CJEU stated that

41 Stephen Coutts, 'The Expressive Dimension of the Union Citizenship Expulsion Regime: Joined Cases C-331/16 and C-366/16, K and HF', *European Papers*, Vol. 3, Issue 2, 2018, pp. 838-841.

42 Judgment of 26 February 1975, *Case C-67/74, Bonsignore*, ECLI:EU:C:1975:34; Judgment of 29 April 2004, *Joined cases C-482/01 and C-493/01, Orfanopoulos and Oliveri*, ECLI:EU:C:2004:262.

43 The value-based approach was already implicitly present in *Tsakouridis* and in *B. and Vomero* which will be described below.

44 In the Directive, integration emerged as a concept through the case law of the CJEU. This concept first appeared in case law in *Orfanopoulos and Oliveri*.

45 Judgment of 16 January 2014, *Case C-400/12, M.G.*, ECLI:EU:C:2004:9.

doi: 10.5553/HYIEL/266627012022010001010

> "the degree of integration of the persons concerned is a vital consideration underpinning both the right of permanent residence and the system of protection against expulsion measures established by Directive 2004/38."[46]

In its judgment on the concept of integration, the CJEU refers to the decision in *Onuekwere*,[47] delivered on the same day. The central issue in this case was the effect of the custodial sentence on the acquisition of permanent resident status in respect of which the CJEU briefly held that the custodial sentence reflected a lack of social integration. The CJEU ruled in the case serving also as a line of reasoning in *M.G.* that the penalty of imprisonment imposed by a national court demonstrates that the person concerned did not respect the values expressed in the criminal law of the society of the host Member State.[48] It has been argued by the CJEU that *a breach of the host country's criminal law constitutes a refusal of integration*. On that basis, the CJEU ruled in *M.G.* that the custodial sentence interrupted, as a general rule, the continuity of the stay and, where appropriate, the acquisition of the enhanced protection under Article 28(3) of Directive 2004/38/EC. Moreover, the CJEU stated in that judgment that *the duration of the custodial sentence could not be taken into account in calculating the period of residence*.

The decision cited by the CJEU is strongly criticized in scholarly literature given that most crimes involve imprisonment (or at least the threat of imprisonment), making it extremely easy to deprive EU citizens of effective protection against expulsion.[49] It is true that simplifying the requirement of social inclusion to comply with criminal law standards may easily be misleading. An expulsion decision based on public policy or public security is in most cases based on personal conduct which presupposes a breach of the host Member State's criminal law.

Therefore, the CJEU in *M.G.* left a loophole by imposing a comprehensive obligation to assess the extent to which the interruption of the continuity of residence by deprivation of liberty precluded the acquisition of enhanced protection. According to the CJEU, an overall assessment of the individual's situation is therefore necessary in each individual case where the question of expulsion arises. In making that overall assessment, which is therefore necessary in order to determine whether that person's social links and integration have in fact been interrupted, the national authorities may take into account both the relevant circumstances of the custodial sentence and the person's stay in the host Member State during the ten years preceding the custodial sentence.

In the above-mentioned *M.G.* case, the half sentences formulated by the CJEU raise very important questions about the definition of social inclusion, especially for persons who have lived in the territory of the host Member State for several decades. First of all, the question arises whether and how the time

46 Id. para. 32.

47 Judgment of 16 January 2014, *Case C-378/12, Onuekwere*, ECLI:EU:C:2014:13.

48 Id. para. 26.

49 Hamenstadt argues that if a violation of criminal law norms mediates a lack of integration, as the CJEU held in *M.G.*, the precondition for integration in order to obtain protection against expulsion has a Kafkian dimension. Hamenstadt 2020, p. 463.

doi: 10.5553/HYIEL/266627012022010001010

spent in the Member State before imprisonment should be assessed, if at all. Similarly, it must be raised whether periods spent in prison may be taken into account for social inclusion or excluded from the assessment, especially given that rehabilitation, which is closely linked to social reintegration, is the objective in the case of imprisonment. The CJEU answered just these questions in its 2018-year judgment in *B. and Vomero* which concerned two EU citizens who had lived in the host country for decades prior to their expulsion.

In *B. and Vomero* the CJEU confirmed the effect of the imprisonment on the relationship between the individual and the host State, namely that although prison years interrupt the continuity of residence as a general rule, an overall assessment of the individual's situation is required in each specific case when the issue of expulsion arises.[50] This assessment may cover, where appropriate, the fact that the person concerned has resided in the host Member State for the ten years preceding the custodial sentence. However, the CJEU emphasized, unlike in the past, that if a Union citizen has fulfilled the condition of ten years' continuous residence prior to the offence leading to his imprisonment, the custodial sentence shall not be deemed to automatically interrupt that person's integrative links previously forged with the host Member State and the continuity of his or her stay in the territory of that Member State. Thus, in *B. and Vomero*, the CJEU assessed the strict requirement of social integration in a much more balanced way, *rejecting* the view that *deprivation of liberty automatically and necessarily has a negative effect* on the relationship between the host state and a national of another Member State.

While the CJEU's earlier rulings focused on the conduct of the person concerned and the nature/circumstances of the act committed, the decision in *B. and Vomero* now places particular emphasis on consolidating the relationship with the host Member State in the period preceding the imprisonment. According to this approach, EU citizens may integrate into the society of the host Member State before their deprivation of liberty. The closer this relationship is in the pre-custodial period, the less likely it is to be broken by the custodial sentence. Focusing on the period prior to detention is thus in any case an innovative element of the CJEU's recent case law, as opposed to earlier case law where the act itself was sufficient evidence for a violation of the values of the host State to be established. Similarly, a novelty in the CJEU's decision in *B. and Vomero* is the answer to whether a Member State must also take into account the conduct followed by a prisoner during the period of imprisonment when assessing whether an EU citizen has finally moved away from social values by committing the offence or whether this connection may still be restored.[51] In essence, an answer is given also to the question of how the period before deprivation of liberty and the sentence itself should be taken into account when assessing the social integration of an EU citizen. By emphasizing the reintegrating role of deprivation of liberty in addition to the punitive nature of imprisonment in its

50 *Joined cases C-316/16 and C-424/16, B. and Vomero*, para. 70.
51 Id. para. 74.

doi: 10.5553/HYIEL/266627012022010001010

latest judgment in *B. and Vomero*, the CJEU clearly dampens the rigor of its earlier case law with regard to the requirement of social integration.

In my view, in cases where the EU citizen concerned has been in the territory of the Member State in question for several decades, it must be expressly acknowledged that the CJEU has shifted from its approach laid down in its earlier case law, in particular in *M.G.* which was strict and in many cases, albeit formally legitimate, in fact led to extremely unfair results.

3.3.2. *Meeting the Requirement of Good Market Citizen*

As we have seen in the recent case law of the CJEU on expulsion and EU citizenship in general, another national of a Member State, who is staying in the host state, is no longer merely an object but a subject of social inclusion, a responsible actor who shapes his or her personal destiny through his or her actions or omissions. This responsibility is not an abstract responsibility, but it imposes very specific obligations on citizens. EU citizens must therefore, above all, respect the fundamental social norms expressed in the criminal law of the host Member State, and even EU values according to *K. and H.F.* Moreover, not only the values expressed in criminal law but also economic activity itself plays a role in the CJEU's case law on the expulsion of EU citizens. That is, citizens must not only be law-abiding citizens but also 'good market citizens' in order to retain their right of residence. This is well reflected in the CJEU's statement in *B. and Vomero*, cited above, that enhanced protection under Article 28(3) of the Directive exists only if permanent resident status has been acquired. An interpretation to the contrary, at least according to the CJEU's reading, would lead to the paradoxical and incoherent conclusion that an EU citizen who does not yet have permanent resident status could be expelled only if he or she had committed an act against the imperative of public security. On the other hand, according to the case law of the CJEU, such an EU citizen may in fact be expelled if he or she becomes an unjustified burden on the social security system.

The CJEU adds to that the rule already well known from *Onuekwere* that integration, which determines the acquisition of the right of permanent residence under Directive 2004/38/EC, is based not only on territorial and time factors, but also *on qualitative elements, relating to the level of integration in the host Member State.*[52] It can be inferred from all this that enhanced protection against expulsion is granted only to those who fulfil the conditions laid down in Article 7 of the Directive, that is to say, are covered by the concept of good market citizen.[53]

52 Id. para. 58.

53 Myriam Benlolo Carabot, 'Citizenship, Integration, and the Public Policy Exception: B. and Vomero and K. and HF', *Common Market Law Review*, Vol. 56, Issue 3, 2019, p. 789.

doi: 10.5553/HYIEL/266627012022010001010

3.4. The Theoretical and Practical Considerations Behind the Case Law of the CJEU

As Coutts points out, the above-mentioned requirements actually meet the criteria of 'good citizen',[54] thereby placing normative expectations on EU citizens to be law-abiding, economically useful members of the society in the host state.[55]

I believe that the CJEU in its approach does not necessarily seek to establish some kind of ideal, but simply follows pragmatic considerations. The functioning of the internal market is much more served by economically active, law-abiding citizens than by those who do not work, even becoming a burden on the state budget (through the public authorities or the operation of the care system) with their unlawful behavior for example. Although a little exaggerated, the former is well illustrated by the position of Advocate General Rantos in *F.S.* which will be detailed below:

> "[...] the concept of 'social assistance' is broad and covers all the benefits that the Union citizen has not contributed towards and which are funded by the public purse. For instance, where a person [...] engages in repeated criminal conduct following his or her expulsion, that conduct could be relevant because it could reflect the risk of him or her representing an unreasonable burden on account of the mobilization, as a result of the conduct of the person in question, of a significant amount of police resources."[56]

However, the above approach is problematic[57] in that the mobilization of police resources for shoplifting and other petty crimes does burden the budget but in no way can it be considered to be aids meeting individual needs and, in the classical sense, putting a burden on the budget under 2004/38/EC Directive which may justify expulsion according to Article 15 of that Directive.[58] We must also not forget that the long-term goal of the Union is to create a general community of values and solidarity, even if this goal sometimes seems a little difficult to achieve due to the current political and economic circumstances.

However, in its recent case law, the CJEU has taken into account the *long-term federalizing effect of the institution of EU citizenship and freedom of movement:* for example, in *K. and H.F.*, in addition to the values of the Member States, it also referred to common EU values in relation to the commission of war crimes. Ideally, of course, national and supranational interests and values coexist and reinforce each other. These common values have already been referred to in the earlier case law of the CJEU, such as in *Tsakouridis* where the CJEU stated,

54 However, Coutts also emphasizes that there is already a serious risk of non-compliance with those criteria in this case, namely, the loss of the right of residence in the host state.

55 Coutts 2018, p. 779.

56 Opinion of Advocate General Rantos Delivered on 10 February 2021, *Case C-719/19, F.S.*, ECLI:EU:C:2021:104, para. 101.

57 In that case, the AG considered that Article 15 of the Directive was applicable even if there was merely a risk that the person concerned might place an unjustified burden on the social assistance system of the host Member State.

58 Even if it may have an indirect effect on the overall level of aid that may be granted by the state. *Case C-209/03, Bidar*, ECLI:EU:C:2005:169, para. 56.

doi: 10.5553/HYIEL/266627012022010001010

referring to Council Framework Decision 2004/757/JHA,[59] that illicit drug trafficking poses a threat to health, safety and the quality of life of citizens of the Union, and to the legal economy, stability and security of the Member States.[60] Similarly, in *P.I.* the CJEU also emphasized that, in accordance with Article 83(1) TFEU, the sexual exploitation of children is one of the areas of particularly serious crime with a cross-border dimension in which the EU legislature may intervene.[61] The CJEU's 'moralizing' practice of expulsion,[62] as described above, therefore not only serves as a means of expressing Member States' values, but increasingly also certain EU values.

At the same time, the CJEU's emphasis not only on common values but also on the social rehabilitation of a person serving a custodial sentence as a common European interest points towards federalization. The CJEU has already emphasized in its judgment in *Tsakouridis* that the perpetrator's social reintegration is not only in the interest of the Member State concerned but also of the EU in general.[63]

The gradual development of an AFSJ could lead to an even stronger emergence of EU interests, undermining the importance of Member States' borders and promoting the right to free movement beyond the concept of the internal market. This is likely to be exacerbated by the growing role of EU criminal law, which, in addition to sanctioning socially undesirable behavior, no longer necessarily requires the expulsion of EU citizens from the territory of the host state.[64] As the legal literature increasingly holds, Directive 2004/38/EC does not in any way prevent Member States from punishing serious crimes with imprisonment, but deportation does not have to be a necessary consequence of imprisonment.[65]

4. Future Challenges in Expulsion Policy

4.1. Challenges to the Development of AFSJ

As already mentioned in the introduction to this article, the development of an AFSJ will, over time, raise not only theoretical dilemmas but also serious practical difficulties. This includes the question of whether it is worth expelling citizens who can return to the host Member State without particular difficulty in a Europe of open borders.

All of this is well illustrated by *F.S.* rendered in 2021, which concerned a Polish national who was expelled from the Netherlands and returned there within

59 Council Framework Decision 2004/757/JHA laying down minimum provisions on the constituent elements of criminal acts and penalties in the field of illicit drug trafficking, as regards the definition of drug.

60 *Case C-145/09, Tsakouridis*, para. 46.

61 *Case C-348/09, P.I.*, para. 25.

62 Coutts 2018, p. 775.

63 *Case C-145/09, Tsakouiridis*, para. 50.

64 Dora Kostakopoulou, 'When EU Citizens Become Foreigners', *European Law Journal*, Vol. 20, Issue 4, 2014, p. 459.

65 Guild *et al.* 2019, p. 289.

doi: 10.5553/HYIEL/266627012022010001010

a month. In the context of that case, the national court (and ultimately the CJEU) had to consider how to assess the situation where a person expelled due to lack of sufficient resources formally leaves the country but also returns there shortly thereafter. In his Opinion, Advocate General Rantos stated that the case was based on a somewhat unusual factual background.[66] In reality, however, it is becoming increasingly common for foreigners to be expelled from the territory of a Member State, in this case the Netherlands, due to a lack of sufficient financial resources, especially if they also present some kind of 'inconvenience'.[67] It should be pointed out that the expulsion decision was issued against F.S. not on grounds of public policy but on the ground that he did not fulfil the conditions for a stay of more than three months. However, certain public policy considerations also arose in connection with the case.[68] This case focuses on how to deal with the internal contradictions of the federalized system of free movement, according to which the concept of free movement rights and open borders, widely granted to EU citizens, is accompanied by the prerogative of Member States to expel undesirable foreigners from their territories.[69]

In *F.S.*, the referring forum essentially asks the CJEU in case an expulsion decision is taken against an EU citizen for failing to fulfil the conditions for residence laid down in Article 7 of the Directive, it can be considered as enforced upon the demonstrable (physical) departure of the expelled person from the host Member State. If so, does the returning EU citizen have a three-month right of residence under Article 6 of the Directive, thus preventing the host state from expelling him or her again? If the answer is no, must the expelled EU citizen remain outside the territory of the host Member State for a certain period before returning, and if so, for how long.

In answering the first question, the CJEU concluded that if an EU citizen *had to cross only the border of the host Member State only to return immediately* to that Member State and invoke a new right of residence under Article 6 of the Directive, he or she could essentially circumvent the conditions set out in Article 7, *undermining the distinction between temporary and long-term residence.*[70] According to the CJEU, an interpretation to the contrary would jeopardize the dual purpose of the Directive: the exercise of the right to freedom of movement and residence and the protection of the social assistance systems of the Member States.

66 *Case C-719/19, F.S.*, AG Opinion, para. 34.

67 Dion Kramer, 'In Search of the Law': Governing Homeless EU Citizens in a State of Legal Ambiguity', *Access Europe Research Paper*, 2017/04.

68 According to Ristuccia, another implication of the ruling in *F.S.* is that it risks conflating the expulsion based on Article 15, for a citizen's illegal residence, and the deportation on grounds of public policy under Article 28 Directive 2004/38. Fulvia Ristuccia, '"Cause tramps like us, baby we were born to run": Untangling the effects of the expulsion of "undesired" Union citizens: FS', *Common Market Law Review*, Vol. 59, Issue 3, 2022, p. 909.

69 Dion Kramer, 'On the Futility of Expelling Poor Union Citizens in an Open Border Europe', *European Papers*, Vol. 6, Issue 1, 2021, p. 156.

70 Adopting that would allow such an EU citizen to rely on several consecutive temporary stays in that Member State in order to reside there permanently, while not fulfilling the conditions for the right of permanent residence laid down in that Directive. *Case C-719/19, F.S.*, para. 77.

doi: 10.5553/HYIEL/266627012022010001010

Consequently, physical departure from the territory of the host Member State is not in itself sufficient to fully enforce a return decision taken under Article 15 of the Directive. In order for an expelled EU citizen to be able to rely on a new right of residence under Article 6, his or her *previous residence must de facto end,* in such a way that his or her *return may not be considered as a continuation of his previous residence.* Although the CJEU left it to the Member State court to examine these aspects in an individual case, it sought to provide criteria for the national court to make an assessment. The CJEU stated, first of all, that the length of time an expelled citizen spends outside the territory of the host Member State is not in itself decisive but may be an important element in the overall assessment of whether the person concerned has actually ended his or her residence in that territory. In addition, the circumstances justifying the interruption of the relationship between the EU citizen in question and the host Member State must be taken into account. For the case-by-case assessment of the factors evidencing a break in the links between the citizen and the host member state, the following elements may be relevant: termination of a lease contract, removal from the population register, if any, and breaking off relationships that imply integration in the host State. In assessing these factors, particular attention shall be paid to the degree of integration of the EU citizen into the host Member State, the duration of the stay prior to his/her expulsion from the territory of the host Member State and his/her family and economic situation.[71] If the EU citizen has not actually terminated his/her stay in the host Member State, the expulsion decision cannot be considered enforced, so the EU citizen's stay remains unlawful and the host Member State is not obliged to issue a new expulsion decision to enforce the previous decision (again).

It is clear from the above that the issue of social integration also plays an important role in this case, only with the opposite effect to the earlier cases. It is, in essence, the 'flip side' of the integration criteria under Article 28(1) of Directive 2004/38/EC which must be considered in a decision on expulsion based on public policy or public security. In *F.S.*, the primary question is what may justify the actual termination of the links and factors indicating integration in the host Member State. These newly developed criteria do not serve integration, but serve as proof that the person concerned has taken all the necessary steps to terminate his or her relations with the host State. It is, of course, not an easy task to prove that an EU citizen has ceased to reside in the Member State concerned, especially in the case of a short stay where his or her relations with the host State have not yet deepened. According to Neier, it may therefore be particularly important to examine the duration of residence in another Member State in connection with the matter.[72] This brings us to the classic question, already raised by Advocate General Sharpston in her famous *Zambrano* opinion: what constitutes a genuine cross-border movement, the extent to which movement is

71 Id. paras. 91-93.

72 Christina Neier, 'New Clarifications on Ending the Union Citizen's Right of Residence: The Grand Chamber Decisions of the European CJEU of 22 June 2021 in C-718/19 and C-719/19', *European Papers*, Vol. 6, Issue 2, 2021, p. 953.

doi: 10.5553/HYIEL/266627012022010001010

required in order to be able to invoke EU citizens' rights of residence when crossing the border of another Member State.[73] Even if the legal situation is different in the two cases, the question is essentially the same: under what circumstances may residence in the territory of another Member State be regarded as genuine residence?[74] *Zambrano* also raises another, novel issue in case law, namely, ensuring the coherence of EU law with regard to the right of residence of EU citizens.

4.2. Ensuring the Coherence of EU Law in Respect of the Right of Residence

As we have seen in *F.S., B. and Vomero,* and *K. and H.F.*, the CJEU places particular emphasis on ensuring the coherence of the Directive in its interpretative work. Of course, legal certainty is not only based to the coherent interpretation of the Directive itself, but also the uniform interpretation by the CJEU of the EU citizens' right of residence enjoyed based on various legal bases, including Articles 20 and 21 TFEU.

However, in the present situation, cleavages are appearing, starting with the case law of the CJEU interpreting the impact of EU citizenship on the right of residence.[75] While the CJEU is not particularly determined to protect free-movers in the event of their expulsion within the Union, in its case law following *Zambrano*, envisioning a federal Union, it seeks to provide stronger protection against the 'expulsion' of static citizens from the Union. While it is clear that the impact of expulsion decisions on the fate of EU citizens cannot be equated,[76] it is questionable *how a coherent system can be established for EU citizens when case law in this area is highly fragmented.*[77] This question is increasingly thematized in light of the CJEU's recent case law on static citizens in which the CJEU places much greater emphasis on the application of fundamental rights.

In its early case law on the *Zambrano* doctrine, the CJEU even held that the desire to maintain family unity within the Union is not sufficient to obtain a derivative residence in accordance with Article 20 TFEU, however, in *Chavez Vilchez* it has already explicitly linked family life with Article 20 TFEU. In the above judgment, the CJEU emphasized that the question of whether the EU citizen concerned was in fact forced to leave the territory of a Member State depriving him of the enjoyment of the essence of the rights under Article 20 TFEU, must in all cases be assessed in the light of the right to family life, including Articles 7 and 24 EU CFR. The former provides for the right to respect for family life, the latter for the best interests of the child. Van Eijken concludes from this that Article 20 TFEU already includes the right to family life and to the

73 Opinion of Advocate General Sharpston Delivered on 30 September 2010, *Case C-34/09, Zambrano*, ECLI:EU:C:2010:560, para. 86.

74 Neier considers that these criteria, laid down by the CJEU, should be incorporated into the text of the Directive over time. Neier 2021, p. 952.

75 Dimitry Kochenov & Benedikt Pirker, 'Deporting EU Citizens: A Counter-Intuitive Trend', *Columbia Journal of European Law*, Vol. 19, 2013, p. 369.

76 The situation is different in the case of the expulsion of an offending EU citizen to another Member State, and again when the EU citizen is forced to leave the territory of the Union.

77 Meduna 2017, p. 407.

doi: 10.5553/HYIEL/266627012022010001010

best interests of the child, but at least the fundamental rights must be taken into account when assessing the right of residence under Article 20 TFEU in the Member States.[78]

The divergent nature characterizing the substance of the right of residence relating to the institution of EU citizenship has been somewhat mitigated by the CJEU in the interpretative decisions rendered in *Rendon Marin*[79] and *CS*.[80] In these cases it concluded that the rights of residence under Article 20 TFEU are not absolute rights, they may be restricted on grounds of public policy or public security like the rights ensured by Article 21 TFEU and the Directive. The CJEU, on the other hand, has already expressly ruled out such an analogous interpretation as regards the requirement of sufficient financial resources, when it stated in *RH*[81] that the requirement of sufficient financial resources could not be a condition for the application of Article 20 TFEU. In that judgment, the CJEU referred to the effectiveness of EU citizenship and the principle of proportionality, stating that a disqualification based solely on the objective to preserve public finances in the Member States (such as reference to the lack of necessary resources) cannot, because of its disproportionate nature, justify a serious breach of the substance of the rights attached to EU citizenship.

In its case law on Article 20 TFEU, the CJEU therefore relaxes the requirements of the internal market by removing both the requirement of the cross-border element and the economic aspects as obstacles to the exercise of EU citizens' rights. Moreover, in its related case law, the CJEU also confirms the exercise of fundamental rights, in particular the right to family life and the rights of the child. This could lead to a serious incoherence within the case law of the CJEU on EU citizenship on the long run.

5. Closing Remarks

Over the last decade, there has been significant criticism of the CJEU's case law on expulsion, mainly because it has put the interests of Member States ahead of the protection of the rights of individuals by gradually abolishing the earlier system of protection. In this way, EU citizens may feel that no matter how long they have lived in the host state, they will remain foreigners forever in the eyes of the authorities. This trend is essentially in line with the CJEU's general case law on EU citizenship in which *the cross-border element is increasingly being replaced by an additional requirement of social inclusion.*[82] However, while this requirement is only implicit in the right to equal treatment in relation to the right of residence

78 Hanneke van Eijken, 'Connecting the Dots Backwards, What did Ruiz Zambrano Mean for EU Citizenship and Fundamental Rights in EU Law?', *European Journal of Migration and Law*, Vol. 23, Issue 1, 2021, p. 66.

79 Judgment of 13 September 2016, *Case C-165/14, Rendon Marin*, ECLI:EU:C:2016:675.

80 Judgment of 13 September 2016, *Case C-304/14, CS*, ECLI:EU:C:2016:674, para. 36.

81 Judgment of 27 February 2020, *Case C-836/18, RH*, ECLI:EU:C:2020:119.

82 'Editorial Comments: EU Law as a Way of Life', *Common Market Law Review*. Vol. 54, Issue 2, 2017, p. 360.

and the related social benefits (*Dano*), it is already much more obvious in the field of expulsion.

It is often argued that freedom of movement comes at a price, so another important objective of EU law, namely, the security of the citizens of the host country must be weighed against this fundamental interest. That consideration should be based on nationality before all other aspects of belonging may, of course, seem a bit 'reactionist'[83] in the light of integration goals and the ideal of EU citizenship. At the same time, we need to see that expulsion policy is likely to remain one of the last bastions of national sovereignty for a long time to come. The vast majority of EU citizens feel that they are primarily citizens of a nation, and it seems that the social embeddedness of EU citizenship is not yet strong enough to have significant potential for federalization in this sensitive area. That is why, with one exception,[84] the CJEU does not refer to EU citizenship as a fundamental status in its case law on expulsion. A good example of this is the recent ruling of the CJEU in *Ordre des barreaux francophones et germanophone*[85] in which it ultimately intended to give a decisive role to the proportionality test in determining whether the detention of EU citizens to be expelled, as required by Belgian law, for a maximum period of eight months, which is the same as the period applicable to third-country nationals, is compatible with EU law. Although the CJEU made a distinction between the categories of EU citizens and third-country nationals in the reasoning for its decision, it was not the privileged status of the former and the exercise of the resulting rights that led the Luxembourg forum, but rather pragmatic considerations. The CJEU found that, as EU citizens are much easier to expel than third-country nationals, they cannot be subject to the same conditions of detention. At the same time, it is precisely these practical considerations that could lead to a future decline in the importance of state borders within the AFSJ. Not only can the expulsion of EU citizens from the territory of the host Member State be facilitated, but also their subsequent return to that Member State, as shown in *F.S.*

The concept of a territorially united Europe has already emerged in the case law on EU citizenship, at least as regards the risk of static citizens being forced out of the Union. Although the CJEU applies the *Zambrano* doctrine only in exceptional circumstances, it must also be seen that fundamental right considerations, in particular the need to respect family life and the protection of the best interests of the child, play an increasingly important role in these cases. The only question is how to ensure (or even whether to ensure) the coherence of these two sets of rules on EU citizenship in the future, depending on whether or not the citizen in question is exercising his or her right to free movement.

83 Katarina Hyltén-Cavallius, *EU Citizenship at the Edges of Freedom of Movement*, Hart Publishing, 2020, p. 54.

84 *Joined cases C-482/01 and C-493/01, Orfanopoulos and Oliveri.*

85 Judgment of 22 June 2021, *Case C-718/19, Ordre des barreaux francophones and germanophone and others*, ECLI:EU:C:2021:505.

doi: 10.5553/HYIEL/266627012022010001010

The Activation of the Temporary Protection Directive for People Fleeing from Ukraine

Ágnes Töttős[*]

Abstract

The Temporary Protection Directive (Council Directive 2001/55/EC) and especially its lack of previous activation has been widely criticized, therefore this study intends to highlight the reasons why it was ideal to finally use this tool for providing protection for those fleeing the war in Ukraine. This paper details how the EU activated the Directive and how its Member States implement its provisions for the first time, addressing legal issues such as the personal scope of implementation and operational aspects of the activation, including the solidarity measures offered by EU institutions and Member States. Finally, the wider implications of this activation and the solidarity measures related to it and already visible in the context of the reform of the Common European Asylum System shall also be discussed.

Keywords: Temporary Protection Directive, international protection, war in Ukraine, Common European Asylum System, solidarity.

1. Introduction

The Russian Federation launched a military offensive against Ukraine on 24 February 2022 that triggered the fastest growing refugee crisis since World War II. Following the invasion the European Council, in its conclusions of 24 February 2022,[1] condemned in the strongest possible terms Russia's unprovoked and unjustified military aggression against Ukraine, underlining the gross violation of international law and the principles of the UN Charter. The European Council demanded Russia's full respect for Ukraine's territorial integrity, sovereignty and independence within its internationally recognized borders, which includes Ukraine's right to choose its own destiny. The European Council also confirmed that the Russian government bears full responsibility for its act of aggression, causing human suffering and loss of lives, and that it will be held accountable for its actions. In solidarity with Ukraine, the European Council declared that the EU is united in its solidarity with Ukraine and will continue to

* Ágnes Töttős: visiting lecturer, Károli Gáspár University of the Reformed Church, Budapest; chief government counsellor, Cabinet Office of the Prime Minister of Hungary, Budapest.

1 European Council conclusions on Russia's unprovoked and unjustified military aggression against Ukraine, 24 February 2022, at https://consilium.europa.eu/en/press/press-releases/2022/02/24/european-council-conclusions-24-february-2022/.

doi: 10.5553/HYIEL/266627012022010001011

support Ukraine and its people together with its international partners, including through additional political, financial, humanitarian and logistical support and an international donors' conference.

Based on the experience gained from the aftermath of the 2014 Russian illegal annexation of the Autonomous Republic of Crimea and the city of Sevastopol, and from war in East Ukraine, EU Member States' expectation[2] was that half of the Ukrainians coming to the EU, benefitting from visa-free travel for short-stays, will join family members or seek employment in the EU, while the other half will request international protection. Nevertheless, the estimated numbers[3] were below the figures of those actually fleeing Ukraine.

> "The escalation of conflict in Ukraine has caused civilian casualties and destruction of civilian infrastructure, forcing people to flee their homes seeking safety, protection and assistance. In the first five weeks, more than four million refugees from Ukraine crossed borders into neighboring countries, and many more have been forced to move inside the country."[4]

According to UNHCR data,[5] from the start of the invasion on 24 February to 1 May 2022 more than 5.5 million people have been displaced from Ukraine.[6] Based on provisional estimates of the EU Asylum Agency[7] about 2.3 million persons fleeing Ukraine have been registered for temporary protection in the EU+ from the beginning of the war to 24 April 2022. A further 7.7 million people have been displaced internally within Ukraine. Some 13 million people in Ukraine are estimated to be stranded in affected areas or unable to leave due to heightened security risks, destruction of bridges and roads, as well as lack of resources or information on where to find safety and accommodation.

2 Council Implementing Decision (EU) 2022/382 of 4 March 2022 establishing the existence of a mass influx of displaced persons from Ukraine within the meaning of Article 5 of Directive 2001/55/EC, and having the effect of introducing temporary protection, ST/6846/2022/INIT, Recital (6).

3 According to Recital (6) of the Council Implementing Decision, depending on how the conflict evolves, based on current estimations, the EU is likely to be faced with a very large number of displaced persons, potentially between 2.5 million and 6.5 million as a consequence of the armed conflict, of whom it is anticipated that between 1.2 and 3.2 million would be persons seeking international protection. The UN High Commissioner for Refugees estimates that, under the worst-case scenario, up to 4 million people may potentially flee Ukraine. About the relevant case law of the CJEU, *see e.g.* Laura Gyeney, 'A családi élet tiszteletben tartásának követelménye az Európai Bíróság migrációs tárgyú döntéseiben a strasbourgi joggyakorlat fényében', *Iustum Aequum Salutare*, Vol. 3, Issue 3, 2007, pp. 95-113.

4 UNHCR, *Operational Data Portal: Ukraine Refugee situation,* at https://data2.unhcr.org/en/situations/ukraine.

5 Id.

6 Arrival statistics are compiled by UNHCR from a variety of sources, mainly data provided by authorities from official border crossing, yet figures on some arrivals represent an estimate.

7 Analysis on Asylum and Temporary Protection in the EU+ in the Context of the Ukraine Crisis Week 16 (18-24 April) 2022, 27 April 2022, at https://euaa.europa.eu/publications/analysis-asylum-and-temporary-protection-eu-context-ukraine-crisis-2.

doi: 10.5553/HYIEL/266627012022010001011

It seems more any more likely that the war and its consequences will not allow many Ukrainian nationals to return to their homeland for a longer time. Consequently, many of those fleeing Ukraine will eventually require a protection status from EU Member States, especially after the visa-free period that many of the Ukrainian nationals enjoy for 3 months in the Schengen area had lapsed. The specificities of the situation were recognized not only be individual EU Member States, but also by the whole of the EU and resulted in the first ever activation of Council Directive 2001/55/EC[8] (Temporary Protection Directive, Directive or TPD).

The Temporary Protection Directive and especially its lack of earlier activation has been widely criticized.[9] Therefore, this study intends to highlight the reasons why it was an ideal situation to finally use this tool for providing protection, how the EU had activated it and how the Member States implemented its provisions for the first time, both as regards legal issues such as the personal scope of implementation, as well as the operational aspects of activation, including the solidarity measures offered by EU institutions and the Member States. Finally, the wider implications of the activation and the solidarity measures related to it are already visible in the context of the reform of the Common European Asylum System (CEAS) that will also be discussed.

While the Temporary Protection Directive provides for a minimum harmonization of rights attached to the temporary protection status, the method and level of affording these rights differ in each Member State. Consequently, the study does not intend to provide an overview of these. Another specific aspect is the situation of those Ukrainian nationals, who also hold the citizenship of one of the EU Member States and therefore cannot be beneficiaries of temporary protection. They may also receive special help by the Member State of their nationality or other Member States, yet this is outside of the scope of the present study.

2. The Temporary Protection Directive

The asylum *acquis* of the EU was and still is based on the international obligations of its Member States and therefore the EU asylum policy "must be in accordance with the Geneva Convention of 28 July 1951 and the Protocol of 31 January 1967 relating to the status of refugees, and other relevant treaties."[10] Nevertheless, EU Member States gradually realized that apart from refugees

8 Council Directive 2001/55/EC of 20 July 2001 on minimum standards for giving temporary protection in the event of a mass influx of displaced persons and on measures promoting a balance of efforts between Member States in receiving such persons and bearing the consequences thereof.

9 *See e.g.* Meltem Ineli-Ciger, 'Has the Temporary Protection Directive become obsolete? An examination of the Directive and its lack of implementation in view of the recent asylum crisis in Mediterranean', *in* Celine Bauloz *et al.* (eds.), *Seeking Asylum in the European Union: Selected Protection Issues Raised by the Second Phase of the Common European Asylum System*, Brill, 2015, p. 234.

10 Article 78(1) TFEU.

doi: 10.5553/HYIEL/266627012022010001011

fulfilling the criteria set out in the Geneva Convention, there are other groups of people that may require different forms of international protection based on different types of recognition. This alternative protection may differ from refugee status either by it being subsidiary in terms of criteria or by being temporary as regards the duration of protection. It was during the Balkan wars that the need to regulate temporary protection was recognized at EU level.

After adopting a Council resolution in 1995 and a decision in 1996 related to burden-sharing in the admission and residence of persons displaced by the conflict in the former Yugoslavia on a temporary basis,[11] the Member States and the Commission expressed the need for the rapid adoption of minimum standards for giving temporary protection in the event of a mass influx of displaced persons from third countries who cannot return to their country of origin, as well as measures promoting a balance of effort between the Member States in receiving, and bearing the consequences of receiving displaced persons.[12]

As a result, Council Directive 2001/55/EC was specifically conceived to promote a balance of efforts to jointly manage intra-European displacements, by giving immediate protection to persons fleeing war, to avoid overwhelming Member States' asylum systems. The Directive establishes an extraordinary procedure as the existence of a mass influx of displaced persons should be established by a Council Decision adopted by qualified majority based on the proposal of the European Commission. This Decision shall be binding in all Member States in relation to the displaced persons to whom it applies. Once the Council Decision is adopted, Member States shall provide persons to be admitted to their territory for the purposes of temporary protection with every facility for entering, with formalities reduced to a minimum because of the urgency of the situation. After entering the EU, anyone belonging to the personal scope of the Council Decision enjoys temporary protection and has the right to ask for its attestation by the issuance of a document. This way, the lengthy application procedure that one is subject to in case of applying for asylum, can be omitted.[13]

Given the exceptional character of the provisions established by this Directive in order to deal with a mass influx or imminent mass influx of displaced persons from third countries who are unable to return to their country of origin, the protection offered should be of limited duration. Articles 12-16 TPD also set out a number rights in terms of which the Directive provides minimum harmonization. The Directive does not only set out obligations for Member States, but also facilitates their fulfillment by listing a number of solidarity measures in Chapter VI.

11 On 25 September 1995 the Council adopted a Resolution on burden-sharing, and, on 4 March 1996, adopted Decision 96/198/JHA on an alert and emergency procedure for the admission and residence of displaced persons on a temporary basis.

12 The Action Plan of the Council and the Commission of 3 December 1998; The European Council, at its special meeting in Tampere on 15 and 16 October 1999, acknowledged the need to reach agreement on the issue of temporary protection for displaced persons on the basis of solidarity between Member States.

13 Article 9 TPD.

doi: 10.5553/HYIEL/266627012022010001011

It should be noted that the TPD has never been activated before. The two institutions responsible for its activation, namely the Commission and the Council have often been blamed for missing the opportunity, while experiencing massive influxes of asylum-seekers. Scholars argue that excuses for the lack of willingness to activate, such as the fear of generating pull factors or the low scale of influx, cannot be justified. Thielemann notes that it is rather push factors than pull factors that shape migration flows,[14] while Ineli-Ciger argues that persons fleeing from armed conflict or violence are not necessarily looking for the best conditions, only a secure place to go to.[15] I do not wish to question these statements, instead, I would just simply point to the fact that they are characteristics of those who are in genuine need of protection. The fear of Member States from generating further influx of asylum seekers is not primarily related to those eligible for international protection, but rather to the massive influx of mixed migratory flows, which would overburden their asylum systems. As for the scale of influx required for the TPD's activation, Ineli-Ciger observes that even the 55,298 persons that had reached Lampedusa in eight months should have been defined as a large scale influx,[16] which is obviously far from the volume of inflow presently experienced.

Finally, even the Commission found the TPD obsolete and suggested restructuring the EU's response for cases of mass influx through its Asylum and Migration Pact. In its Communication[17] the Commission arrives at the conclusion that the existing measures to grant quick access to protection do not seem to be fit for purpose any more since they no longer respond to Member States' current reality and must be repealed. This conclusion is based on a study[18] in which stakeholders agreed that it has been near impossible to attain Member State agreement on the possible activation of the TPD. Nevertheless, the Pact recognizes that certain groups of third country nationals at a high risk must be granted protection on a quick – immediate – basis and therefore the legislative proposal, still under negotiation, addressing situations of crisis and *force majeure* in the field of migration and asylum[19] aims to ensure that the persons who are granted immediate protection benefit from equivalent economic and social rights that beneficiaries of subsidiary protection enjoy.

14 Eiko R. Thielemann, 'How Effective are National and EU Policies in the Area of Forced Migration?', *Refugee Survey Quarterly*, Vol. 31, Issue 4, 2012, p. 22.

15 Ineli-Ciger 2015, p. 234.

16 Id. p. 241.

17 Communication from the Commission to the European Parliament, the Council, the European Economic and Social Committee and the Committee of the Regions on a New Pact on Migration and Asylum, COM(2020) 609 final.

18 Hanne Beirens *et al.*, *Study on the Temporary Protection Directive*, Final report, 2016, at https://ec.europa.eu/home-affairs/system/files/2020-09/final_report_evaluation_tpd_en.pdf.

19 Proposal for a regulation of the European Parliament and of the Council addressing situations of crisis and force majeure in the field of migration and asylum, COM(2020) 613 final.

doi: 10.5553/HYIEL/266627012022010001011

3. Activation of the Temporary Protection Directive

Following the start of the Russian invasion of Ukraine millions of people, mainly women and children, arrived in the EU in the first few months. The focus of the four Member States bordering Ukraine (Poland, Slovakia, Hungary and Romania) together with Moldova was rightly on meeting the immediate reception and protection needs of those fleeing the war. Therefore, they opened their Eastern borders and ensured an unconditional but at the same time controlled inflow to their territory. The Commission also acknowledged their efforts after seeing first-hand the very substantial support programs these countries provided.[20]

Many of those arriving enjoyed visa free travel within the Schengen area, and national immigration laws of the relevant EU Member States also provided for various processes for gaining residence permits, either based on humanitarian or legal migration (*e.g.* employment or family reunification) bases. At an extraordinary meeting of the Justice and Home Affairs Council on 27 February 2022, Home Affairs Ministers took stock of the response to the consequences of the war in Ukraine.[21] In order to monitor the situation, coordinate solidarity measures and involve all relevant actors, following this exchange, the Presidency decided to fully activate the EU Integrated Political Crisis Response (IPCR) arrangements. The more people arrived, the more Member States welcomed people fleeing from the war in Ukraine while the capacities of the countries welcoming most of the people, especially Poland, gradually became saturated. Ministers also discussed the possibility of establishing an appropriate temporary protection mechanism for the reception of these nationals, which received broad support.

This gave the Commission the momentum to propose the activation of the TPD mechanism for the first time on 2 March 2022.[22] Shortly after this, Home Affairs Ministers during their Council meeting on 3 March[23] agreed officially on the activation of the Temporary Protection Directive by adopting a Council Decision.[24] The main purpose was to enable the EU Member States to provide people fleeing the conflict in Ukraine with an appropriate response for their situation by offering a status harmonized at EU level while also supporting Member States under pressure. Furthermore, this move also had a symbolic nature, demonstrating that Europeans are responding in unity and solidarity faced with this crisis ongoing in the heart of our continent. Consequently, from

20 Communication from the Commission to the European Parliament, the Council, the European Economic and Social Committee and the Committee of the Regions, European solidarity with refugees and those fleeing war in Ukraine, Strasbourg, 8 March 2022, COM(2022) 107 final, p. 4.

21 *See* at https://consilium.europa.eu/en/meetings/jha/2022/02/27/.

22 Proposal for a Council Implementing Decision establishing the existence of a mass influx of displaced persons from Ukraine within the meaning of Article 5 of Council Directive 2001/55/EC of 20 July 2001, and having the effect of introducing temporary protection, COM(2022) 91 final.

23 *See* at https://consilium.europa.eu/en/meetings/jha/2022/03/03-04/?utm_source=dsms-auto&utm_medium=email&utm_campaign=Justice+and+Home+Affairs+Council.

24 Council Implementing Decision (EU) 2022/382 of 4 March 2022 establishing the existence of a mass influx of displaced persons from Ukraine within the meaning of Article 5 of Directive 2001/55/EC, and having the effect of introducing temporary protection, ST/6846/2022/INIT.

doi: 10.5553/HYIEL/266627012022010001011

the first formulation of the idea on 27 February 2022 to its publication in the EU Official Journal on 4 March 2022 it only took five days to activate the TPD mechanism. This truly reflects the saying: if there is a will, there is a way. But it is also grounds for investigating what legal circumstances allowed for such a quick and unanimous activation of the Directive.

3.1. Scope of Activation

The Council decided to establish three different categories of eligibility for temporary protection. *(i)* There are categories to which the TPD shall be applied; *(ii)* in case of the second category the adequate level of protection may be ensured by either providing temporary protection set out in the TPD or under national law; and *(iii)* thirdly Member States may extend the application of the TPD to other categories. These categories shall be examined in comparison with the categories set out in the Commission's proposal in order to identify the justification behind their distinction

As regards the first, obligatory personal scope of the provision of EU temporary protection, the following categories of persons displaced from Ukraine on or after 24 February 2022, as a result of the military invasion by Russian armed forces that began on that date belong to this group: *(a)* Ukrainian nationals residing in Ukraine before 24 February 2022; *(b)* stateless persons, and nationals of third countries other than Ukraine, who benefited from international protection or equivalent national protection in Ukraine before 24 February 2022; and, *(c)* family members of the persons referred to in points *(a)* and *(b)*.[25]

Compared to the Commission's proposal, point *(b)* was narrowed to a great extent as it was originally proposed to cover all third-country nationals or stateless persons residing legally in Ukraine and who are unable to return in safe and durable conditions to their country or region of origin.[26] The requirement of inability to return in safe and durable conditions to their country or region of origin shall not apply to third-country nationals or stateless persons who have been legally residing on a long-term basis in Ukraine. It has been reported that the change was made at the request of Poland and several other countries[27] and narrowing down the personal scope through the Council Decision may be attributed to political and legal grounds. As regards applying the TPD to non-Ukrainian nationals, the issue may evoke recent grim recollections of illegal

25 For the purposes of paragraph 1*(c)*, the following persons shall be considered to be part of a family, in so far as the family was already present and residing in Ukraine before 24 February 2022: *(a)* the spouse of a person referred to in paragraph 1, point *(a)* or *(b)*, or the unmarried partner in a stable relationship, where the legislation or practice of the Member State concerned treats unmarried couples in a way comparable to married couples under its national law relating to aliens; *(b)* the minor unmarried children of a person referred to in paragraph 1*(a)* or *(b)*, or of his or her spouse, without distinction as to whether they were born in or out wedlock or adopted; *(c)* other close relatives who lived together as part of the family unit at the time of the circumstances surrounding the mass influx of displaced persons, and who were wholly or mainly dependent on a person referred to in paragraph 1*(a)* or *(b)* at the time.

26 COM(2022) 91 final, Article 2(1)(b).

27 *See* at https://politico.eu/article/eu-ministers-historical-deal-protect-ukraine-refugees/.

doi: 10.5553/HYIEL/266627012022010001011

migration having been instrumentalized by Belarus at the EU's Eastern borders.[28] This hybrid attack may have been behind the cautious approach of Member States when restricting the obligatory application of the TPD to those who had already benefited from international protection or equivalent national protection in Ukraine before 24 February 2022.

When carrying out this narrowing of scope in line with the EU *acquis*, the extent of harmonization could have been a useful guide. While the EU recognizes a number of international protection statuses, there is no harmonized status at EU level for tolerated stay that is to be provided to those who cannot be removed either because of the principle of *non-refoulement*[29] applies in their case or because certain factors delay their removal.[30] Consequently, in the Council Decision it was decided not to cover such persons with a harmonized status of temporary protection even if they are fleeing from Ukraine, but rather left it up to the Member States to decide. Nevertheless, the Council Decision even divides this category by setting out an obligation to protect those having permanently resided in Ukraine, while merely providing an opportunity to apply the TPD to those who only temporarily resided legally in Ukraine. Nevertheless, it should be noted that where the principle of non-refoulement applies, national law should allow those concerned to stay even if the Council Decision does not envision the obligatory or optional provision of EU harmonized temporary protection status for that specific category.

The second category, therefore, where the Council puts emphasis on the substance of the protection instead of its type, contains the category of stateless persons, and nationals of third countries other than Ukraine, who can prove that they were legally residing in Ukraine before 24 February 2022 on the basis of a valid permanent residence permit issued in accordance with Ukrainian law, and who are unable to return in safe and durable conditions to their country or region of origin. The third category to whom the TPD may optionally be applied includes stateless persons and nationals of third countries other than Ukraine, who were residing legally in Ukraine and are unable to return in safe and durable conditions to their country or region of origin.

3.2. Solidarity Measures

Chapter VI of the TPD sets out various forms of solidarity for the activation of the Directive. In the recent context of the reform of the CEAS that has been ongoing for several years, the main question was whether these solidarity measures shall be applied in an obligatory way or whether Member States may

28 European Council conclusions on Belarus, 24 May 2021, at https://consilium.europa.eu/en/press/press-releases/2021/05/24/european-council-conclusions-on-belarus-24-may-2021/.

29 Under international human rights law, the principle of non-refoulement guarantees that no one should be returned to a country where they would face torture, cruel, inhuman or degrading treatment or punishment and other irreparable harm. This principle applies to all migrants at all times, irrespective of migration status.

30 Responses to long-term irregularly staying migrants: practices and challenges in EU Member States and Norway, Common Template for EMN Study 2020, 17 July 2020, Final Version, at https://ec.europa.eu/home-affairs/system/files/2020-12/estonia_ltim_study_final_en.pdf.

doi: 10.5553/HYIEL/266627012022010001011

decide which ones to apply. In order to understand the legal context, it should be borne in mind that the TPD is the first EU Directive adopted in the field of asylum. As it is a Directive "belonging to a different era where the EU had different legal competences in the Treaties and migration priorities",[31] the formulation of the provisions of the Directive is rather vague. Nevertheless, it sets out a toolbox of solidarity measures that may be applied should the Member States decide to do so when activating the Directive. Consequently, the tools applied during a specific activation and the legal nature of those depend on the decision of the Council.

A number of helping tools are offered, including that of operational support by the relevant EU agencies. On 7 March 2022 the EU Agency for Law Enforcement Training (CEPOL) located in Budapest, Hungary, issued a statement[32] on behalf of the network of nine EU Agencies working on freedom, security and justice in the EU.[33] According to the statement the EU Justice and Home Affairs Agencies support the work of EU institutions and Member States as they help Ukraine and its people now that war once again reached Europe. By working together and utilizing each agency's particular expertise, they act as a matter of urgency to assist EU Member States in terms of humanitarian support, respect for fundamental rights, management of EU external borders, visa measures, anticipation of hybrid threats, and reception of people fleeing war.

In the following I would like to highlight three main types of assistance agreed on and provided at EU level, namely financial support, monitoring and coordination, as well as potential assistance regarding the intra-EU mobility of eligible persons.

3.2.1. *Financial Support*

First and foremost, Article 24 TPD provides for financial assistance to Member States. The Directive only refers to the then European Refugee Fund, now Asylum, Migration and Integration Fund (AMIF), yet this does not cover all the financial support available. It its Communication[34] the Commission set out the aim of helping Member States to use EU funds quickly and flexibly, so that tailor-

31 Sergio Carrera *et al.*, 'The EU Grants Temporary Protection for People Fleeing War in Ukraine', *CEPS Policy Insights*, No 2022-09, March 2022, p. 16, at https://ceps.eu/wp-content/uploads/2022/03/CEPS-PI2022-09_ASILE_EU-grants-temporary-protection-for-people-fleeing-war-in-Ukraine-1.pdf.

32 *See* at https://cepol.europa.eu/media/news/eu-justice-home-affairs-agencies-joint-statement-ukraine.

33 The nine agencies are: the European Institute for Gender Equality (EIGE), the European Monitoring Centre for Drugs and Drug Addiction (EMCDDA), the EU Agency for Asylum (EUAA), the EU Agency for the Operational Management of Large-Scale IT Systems in the Area of Freedom, Security and Justice (eu-LISA), the EU Agency for Criminal Justice Cooperation (Eurojust), the EU's Law Enforcement Agency (Europol), the EU Agency for Fundamental Rights (FRA), the European Border and Coast Guard Agency (Frontex) and the EU Agency for Law Enforcement Training (CEPOL).

34 Communication from the Commission to the European Parliament, the Council, the European Economic and Social Committee and the Committee of the Regions, Welcoming those fleeing war in Ukraine: Readying Europe to meet the needs, Brussels, 23 March 2022, COM(2022) 131 final.

doi: 10.5553/HYIEL/266627012022010001011

made funding can flow rapidly to support the efforts of Member States, key organizations and civil society to make the rights granted through temporary protection a reality. On 4 April 2022 the Council adopted legislative amendments[35] to EU funds as a clear evidence of the EU's continued solidarity with the refugees from Ukraine and with the Member States hosting them, in particular those sharing borders with Ukraine. This is an important step in ensuring that Member States have sufficient resources to meet the growing needs for housing, education and healthcare. The amendments provide for further flexibilities both as regards cohesion policy funds and home affairs funds and by redirecting resources to assist people escaping the Russian military aggression against Ukraine.

In the field of cohesion policy, the Council adopted the Regulation on Cohesion's Action for Refugees in Europe (CARE) amending the 2014-2020 legal framework governing the European Structural and Investment Funds (ESIF) and the Fund for European Aid for the Most Deprived (FEAD). The changes include exceptional flexibility to transfer resources between programs financed by the European Regional Development Fund and the European Social Fund to address the inflow of refugees, including the reallocation of resources earmarked for infrastructural projects to provide healthcare and education to persons fleeing from Ukraine. Member States can use overall up to EUR 9.5 billion under the 2022 tranche of REACT-EU, one of the largest post-pandemic EU public investment programs, as well as unallocated cohesion policy resources under the 2014-2020 budgetary period. CARE also extends the 100% financing from the EU budget for cohesion programs by one accounting year. The extension of the 100% financing, the unlocking of programmed 2014-2020 cohesion funding, and the 2022 React-EU tranche are estimated to release almost EUR 17 billion.

The Council also adopted an amendment to the 2014-2020 home affairs funds and to the 2021-2027 Asylum, Migration and Integration Fund. This amendment will provide extra resources for the reception of persons escaping the war in Ukraine. It will extend by one year the implementation period of the 2014-2020 home affairs funds and unlock access to unspent amounts in the Asylum, Migration and Integration Fund which had previously been earmarked for other purposes, such as for example relocation. This will enable Member States to urgently use the remaining funds to help address the mass inflow of persons, and it is expected to release an estimated maximum amount of EUR 420 million of additional support from unused funds.

While the adoption of these new measures were extraordinarily swift and the use of available resources is facilitated to a great extent, most of the resources offered by the Commission are already available, but unspent, for instance because they had been previously earmarked. This therefore raises the question whether all Member States affected the most by the inflow of persons fleeing

35 *See* at https://consilium.europa.eu/en/press/press-releases/2022/04/04/ukraine-council-unlocks-17-billion-of-eu-funds-to-help-refugees/?utm_source=dsms-auto&utm_medium=email&utm_campaign=Ukraine%3A%20%25u20ac17%20billion%20of%20EU%20funds%20to%20help%20refugees.

doi: 10.5553/HYIEL/266627012022010001011

from Ukraine have such unspent resources at hand or were they more successful in spending them earlier, therefore having less amounts available for coping with the present extraordinary situation. If so, will the European Commission be able to mobilize further financial support? The new generation of Home Affairs funds for 2021-27 opens the door to significant extra resources for Member States to provide effective reception facilities, including specialized support to vulnerable persons, and to manage asylum procedures.[36] Nevertheless, the adoption of many national programs is still ongoing, which does not allow for the swift use of such resources.

3.2.2. *Monitoring Member States' Capacity and the Task of Coordination*

Article 25 of the Directive puts much emphasis on the capacity of Member States to receive persons benefitting from the activation of the Directive. The TPD in theory requires the reception capacity of Member States to be set out in the Council Decision in figures or in general terms. According to the present practice it may be an impossible or useless exercise as certain Member States may mobilize further capacities should the situation so require, while the available capacities of other Member States may easily become occupied by non-Ukrainian asylum-seekers in the meantime. Therefore, instead of following the Directive word by word, the Council Decision chose a different approach. In order to allow the Union to coordinate and closely monitor the reception capacity of Member States so as to take action and provide additional support as needed, it creates a so-called 'Solidarity Platform' where Member States exchange information on their reception capacities and the number of persons enjoying temporary protection in their territories.

It should be noted that in recent years various platforms have been established with the aim of ensuring cooperation between Member States, of which the EU Migration Preparedness and Crisis Blueprint Network[37] (also called Blueprint Network) is the most recent one, initiated by the Commission in its Communication on the Asylum and Migration Pact. Its objective is to provide an operational framework for monitoring and anticipating migration flows and migration situations, building resilience, as well as organizing a situational response to a migration crisis. Member States should also contribute to a common situational awareness by sharing relevant information through the integrated political crisis response (IPCR) arrangements.

The new European response and the Solidarity Platform is meant to monitor the specific situation and the capacities of the Member States related to the war in Ukraine, while the Blueprint Network, as well as IPCR will also be used to collect information. The Solidarity Platform will collect information and examine the needs identified in the Member States and coordinate the operational follow-up in response to these needs. The Blueprint network will also continue to share situational information and consolidate all relevant information on migration

36 *See* Commission Communication, COM(2022) 107 final, para. 4.

37 Commission Recommendation (EU) 2020/1366 of 23 September 2020 on an EU mechanism for preparedness and management of crises related to migration, C/2020/6469.

doi: 10.5553/HYIEL/266627012022010001011

management related to the Russian invasion on Ukraine, including on the implementation of Directive 2001/55/EC. One may have the impression that the various networks existing in parallel and each having functions to collect and analyze information as well as coordinate may result in a duplication of certain exercises, but Member States' officials are definitely encouraged to share and assess information on a regular basis via these networks.[38]

3.2.3. *Intra-EU Movements*

It is also a key question why the capacities of certain Member States are exhausted. The answer may lie in the provision of Article 26 of TPD, which sets out that

> "for the duration of the temporary protection, the Member States shall cooperate with each other with regard to transferal of the residence of persons enjoying temporary protection from one Member State to another, subject to the consent of the persons concerned to such transferal."[39]

The Directive uses the term 'transferal of the residence of persons', which may be synonymous with the more recently used term relocation. In the ongoing debate on the CEAS reforms the key question is whether it is set out as an obligation or as an option. The Directive only imposes an obligation on Member States to communicate requests for transfers to the other Member States as well as the other Member States to inform the requesting Member State of their capacity for receiving transferees. While no distribution mechanism is envisioned by the Directive, yet it does not prohibit Member States from establishing one for this specific situation, either. Commissioner Johansson's speech at the Plenary Session on EU Protection of children and young people fleeing the war against Ukraine contained a reference to standard operating procedures for transferring unaccompanied minors between Member States, yet it still cannot be understood as a proposal for a relocation mechanism for this specific group of children.

While there may be several Member States opposing from a political perspective any form of obligatory relocation mechanism, there is a different legal context that needs to be taken into account. Ukraine is listed in Annex II to Regulation (EU) 2018/1806,[40] and nationals of Ukraine are exempt from the requirement to be in possession of a visa when crossing the external borders of Member States for stays of no more than 90 days in any 180-day period. Therefore, Ukrainian citizens in the possession of a biometric passport enjoy the right of visa free travel within the Schengen area for three months. Many of those fleeing from Ukraine can therefore practice short-term free movement within the

38 Article 3 of the Council Decision.

39 Article 26(1) TPD.

40 Regulation (EU) 2018/1806 of the European Parliament and of the Council of 14 November 2018 listing the third countries whose nationals must be in possession of visas when crossing the external borders and those whose nationals are exempt from that requirement.

doi: 10.5553/HYIEL/266627012022010001011

EU, furthermore, even those not enjoying such a right are allowed to enter Member States not bordering Ukraine.

The Commission Guidelines highlight that the beneficiaries of the activation of the TPD also enjoy the right to move freely after a Member State has issued a residence permit in accordance with Article 8 of the Directive as the person enjoying temporary protection has the right to travel to Member States other than the one issuing the residence permit for 90 days within a 180-day period. Yet, double statuses should be avoided and thus, where such a person subsequently moves to another Member State, the first residence permit issued and the ensuing rights must expire and be withdrawn, in accordance with the spirit of Articles 15(6) and 26(4) of Directive 2001/55/EC. While the Eurodac Regulation[41] does not extend to the collection and storage of the data of beneficiaries of temporary protection, Member States and the Commission have been working on creating an *ad hoc* scheme in line with EU data protection provisions that would allow for the regular exchange of such data in order to be able to identify potential double statuses.

In this context, it should also be highlighted that it is not the residence permit issued by Member States but the Council Decision that creates the right to temporary protection for those belonging to one of the categories of its personal scope (also depending on the choice of Member States as regards specific categories of persons). Consequently, while Article 11 of the Directive sets out that a Member State shall take back a person enjoying temporary protection on its territory, if the said person remains on, or seeks to enter without authorization onto, the territory of another Member State, this could hardly be implemented given the simple declarative nature of a residence permit issued by a specific Member State.

Therefore, it was a logical choice to apply the provision setting out that Member States may, on the basis of a bilateral agreement, decide that this Article should not apply. With a view to supporting Member States who are the main entry points of the mass arrival of displaced persons fleeing war from Ukraine, Member States also agreed not to apply Article 11 of the Directive on the margins of activating the TPD by adopting the Council Decision. This move seems practical from at least two viewpoints. Firstly, it allows Ukrainian nationals to find the most optimal Member State where they receive ideal support from their family, friends, employers or the state that is crucial for their integration should they need to or decide to stay for a longer period. Secondly, this also alleviates

41 Regulation (EU) No 603/2013 of the European Parliament and of the Council of 26 June 2013 on the establishment of 'Eurodac' for the comparison of fingerprints for the effective application of Regulation (EU) No 604/2013 establishing the criteria and mechanisms for determining the Member State responsible for examining an application for international protection lodged in one of the Member States by a third-country national or a stateless person and on requests for the comparison with Eurodac data by Member States' law enforcement authorities and Europol for law enforcement purposes, and amending Regulation (EU) No 1077/2011 establishing a European Agency for the operational management of large-scale IT systems in the area of freedom, security and justice.

doi: 10.5553/HYIEL/266627012022010001011

pressure from EU Member States bearing a disproportionate burden resulting from a mass influx of people fleeing from Ukraine.

Therefore, instead of an artificial relocation scheme where Member States and not the beneficiaries of temporary protection themselves decide on where to transfer, this scheme of simply disapplying Article 11 allows for a situation more focused on the needs of those fleeing from Ukraine. Nevertheless, it should be highlighted that such a move was only possible since it extends solely to those enjoying temporary protection from the moment they step onto the territory of the EU. This also distinguishes them from other persons requesting international protection from EU Member States.

4. Temporary Protection in Practice

Based on the input from Member States on the implementation of the Council Decision and the Temporary Protection Directive, the Commission has identified a number of issues on which it found it useful to provide guidance to the Member States in the form of operational guidelines.[42] The issues covered are mainly related to the scope of the Council Decision, including the issue of persons not covered by the Council Decision, how to handle children, particularly unaccompanied minors, and also questions on the right to move freely between Member States, registration and provision of information. At this point, I would just like to highlight a number of remaining practical issues.

According to the Commission Guidelines, no application process for temporary protection or adequate protection under national law should take place as the right to temporary protection of these persons is immediate. Therefore, the person concerned presenting themself to the authorities to avail of the rights attached to temporary protection or adequate protection, would only have to demonstrate their nationality, their international protection or equivalent protection status, residence in Ukraine or family link as appropriate.

However, there are several practical questions arising from the special legal nature of the Council decision. First and foremost, a declaratory document is practical and is also foreseen by Article 8 of the Directive so as to avoid questioning the eligibility of further rights deriving from the temporary protection. Secondly, requirements still exist, even if no application procedure is envisaged, such as presenting evidence that the person in question belongs to one of the categories specified in the Directive, as well as checking whether no exclusion criteria are applicable. Therefore, the proper administration and registration of the persons concerned shall be organized by the Member States.

Another challenge for national legislators is to decide on the personal scope of the application of the Council Decision. As it was discussed previously, the Council Decision allowed some room for maneuver for Member States as regards

42 Communication from the Commission on Operational Guidelines for the Implementation of Council Implementing Decision 2022/382 establishing the existence of a mass influx of displaced persons from Ukraine within the meaning of Article 5 of Directive 2001/55/EC, and having the effect of introducing temporary protection 2022/C 126 I/01, C/2022/1806.

doi: 10.5553/HYIEL/266627012022010001011

the second and third category of beneficiaries or potential beneficiaries. In the following I aim to show the reverse effect of EU harmonization on the scope of the temporary protection offered by Hungary. Furthermore, Denmark as a country not applying the TPD and the Council Decision as well as the no-longer EU Member State UK are interesting examples, since many of Ukrainians may also seek protection in these countries.

4.1. Temporary Protection in Hungary

There is a unique feature of the Directive as regards the division of competences. Article 7 TPD sets out that Member States may extend temporary protection as provided for in this Directive to additional categories of displaced persons over and above those to whom Article 5 of the Council Decision applies, where they are displaced for the same reasons and from the same country or region of origin. Member States shall notify the Council and the Commission immediately if this provision is applied. While Article 7 regulates the application of the temporary protection to categories not belonging to the non-obligatory personal scope, once the TPD is activated, there may be situations when Member States already activate in their national law the use of a similar temporary protection status as specified in the Directive.

According to Section 19 of Hungary's Act LXXX of 2007 on asylum, Hungary grants temporary protection not only on the basis of the TPD, but also on the basis of the Government's decision. It should be noted that before 2014 it was the Hungarian Parliament that had such a right, yet in 2014 – presumably as a result of the Crimean conflict – this competence was moved to the Government to establish a quicker activation procedure.[43] Nevertheless, just as in the case of the TPD, the national application process had not been activated before the Ukrainian war either. Yet, already on the eve of 24 February 2022 the Hungarian Government made an instant move, and by issuing a Government Decree[44] it activated the national temporary protection mechanism to those fleeing from Ukraine.

The personal scope of the national activation was surprisingly wide as it extended to all Ukrainian citizens who arrived from the territory of Ukraine and all the third-country nationals legally residing in Ukraine. The laconic Government Decree did not therefore exclude non-Ukrainian nationals, who only temporarily, but legally resided in Ukraine before having to leave the country. Nevertheless, following the activation of the TPD at EU level, a new Government Decree,[45] repealing the previous one, significantly narrowed down the categories

43 Act XVI of 2014, Section 277(2).

44 Government Decree No. 56/2022. (II. 24.) on the different application of the transitional rules of the asylum procedure set out in Act LVIII of 2020 on transitional rules and epidemiological preparedness related to the cessation of an emergency.

45 Government Decree No. 86/2022. (III. 7.) on the different application of the rules of the Act on the emergency rules related to persons recognized as entitled to temporary protection, as well as on the amendment of Act CVI of 2011 on public employment and amendments to other laws related to public employment.

doi: 10.5553/HYIEL/266627012022010001011

eligible for temporary protection in Hungary. Section 1 of the new Government Decree repeats the obligatory categories set out in the Council Decision.

As regards the second category of the personal scope discussed above, Section 2(2) declares the fact that Hungary chose not to apply the Council Directive, in accordance with its Article 2(2), to stateless persons and third-country nationals who can prove they held a valid permanent residence permit issued in accordance with Ukrainian law before 24 February 2022, who have resided legally in Ukraine on the basis of a residence permit and who are unable to return to their country or region of origin in safe and durable conditions. Section 2(3) merely adds that instead of the EU harmonized status of temporary protection, the immigration authority shall act in accordance with the general national rules. One may be puzzled by the interpretation and practical implementation of the consequence of choosing not to apply temporary protection to this category of persons. However, there are a number of specific rules that may apply in case of such humanitarian situations in Hungary that result in the ample protection which the Council Directive requires. For instance, Section 13(2) of Act II of 2007 on the entry and residence of third country nationals sets out that even in the absence of the conditions set out in this Act, entry and residence may be granted exceptionally, for the purpose of fulfilling an international obligation, for urgent humanitarian reasons or in the national interest.

It should also be noted that as regards a further, optional extension of the personal scope allowed by the Council Decision, although the national activation of the status covered this third category of persons with only a temporary legal status in Ukraine regardless of their ability to return to their country or region of origin, the Hungarian Government decided not to make such persons eligible for temporary protection at all. While this is not contrary to EU law, this will result in the rejection of applications for temporary protection by those falling within this category, who submitted their request between 24 February and 7 March 2022 based on the first Government Decree activating temporary protection in the national competence.[46] Nevertheless, the practice of the immigration authorities show that, by issuing certificates of temporary stay, they allow ample time for these people to make their decision on where to continue their stay and if they decide to reside in Hungary, to submit their application for their first residence permit on the territory of Hungary.

4.2. Other Forms of Temporary Protection

As regards the two countries, Ireland and Denmark that have an opt-out from the taking part in EU home affairs harmonization, Ireland is bound by the Temporary Protection Directive and therefore took part in the adoption of the Council Decision. Nevertheless, in accordance with Articles 1 and 2 of Protocol No 22 on the position of Denmark, annexed to the TEU and TFEU, Denmark is not taking

46 Section 12 of Government Decree No. 86/2022. (III. 7.) sets out that the provisions of this Decree shall also apply to proceedings concerning an application pending before the entry into force of this Decree.

doi: 10.5553/HYIEL/266627012022010001011

part in the adoption of the Council Decision and is not bound by it or is subject to its application. However, Denmark decided to unilaterally show solidarity by adopting a new special act[47] on temporary residence permits for persons displaced from Ukraine.[48]

The new Danish provisions make it possible for Ukrainians to apply for a residence permit in Denmark. One can be granted a temporary residence permit under the law on temporary residence permits for displaced persons from Ukraine, if one is staying in Denmark, and is either a Ukrainian citizen or recognized as a refugee in Ukraine. One can also be granted a residence permit, if they are a close family member to a person in Denmark, who has been granted a residence permit under this Special Act.

Before the withdrawal of the United Kingdom from the EU, the TPD was applicable to the UK as well. Although the United Kingdom had an opt-out,[49] it gave notice, by letter of 27 September 2000, of its wish to take part in both the adoption and application of this Directive. Nevertheless, as a non-EU Member State, the UK does not take part in the implementation of the TPD, although many Ukrainians were ready to choose it as their country providing protection. In order to fulfil these expectations and show solidarity, the United Kingdom started to offer on the one hand a Ukraine Family Scheme visa from 15 March 2022 in order to allow applicants to join family members or extend their stay in the UK,[50] and on the other hand a Ukraine Sponsorship Scheme (Homes for Ukraine) allowing Ukrainian nationals and their family members to go to the UK if they have a named sponsor under the Homes for Ukraine Scheme.[51]

To apply to the Ukraine Family Scheme, one must apply to join or accompany their UK-based family member, and be Ukrainian or the immediate family member of a Ukrainian national who is applying to the scheme, and have been residing in Ukraine on or immediately before 1 January 2022. Once an application is approved, such persons can stay in the UK for up to three years and will be able to live, work and study in the UK and access public funds. Since the introduction of this new scheme, both the category of family member as well as the scope of the UK-based family member had been expanded. For example, while originally the scheme only provided for family reunification with British nationals, now someone having settled or pre-settled in the UK may also be joined by their family members through this scheme.

To apply to the Ukraine Sponsorship Scheme one must be Ukrainian, or the immediate family member of a Ukrainian national, and have been residing in Ukraine on or immediately before 1 January 2022, be outside of the UK, and have

47 A bill on temporary residence permits for displaced persons from Ukraine (the Special Act) was adopted by the Danish Parliament on 16 March 2022 and is in force since 17 March 2022.

48 *See* at https://nyidanmark.dk/en-GB/Words%20and%20Concepts%20Front%20Page/Shared/Information%20Ukraine.

49 In accordance with Article 3 of the Protocol on the position of the United Kingdom and Ireland, annexed to TEU and to the Treaty establishing the European Community.

50 *See* at https://gov.uk/guidance/apply-for-a-ukraine-family-scheme-visa.

51 *See* at https://gov.uk/guidance/apply-for-a-visa-under-the-ukraine-sponsorship-scheme.

doi: 10.5553/HYIEL/266627012022010001011

an eligible UK-based sponsor. The UK-based sponsor does not need to register with the Homes for Ukraine Scheme if they are already in contact with the applicant, otherwise the applicant will be matched with people or organizations who have recorded their interest as ones wanting to offer a home to people fleeing Ukraine and become a 'sponsor' as part of the Homes for Ukraine scheme. Anyone in the UK with a spare room or home can become a sponsor as long as they can offer accommodation for at least six months and if they are not a British citizen, they have leave to remain in the UK for at least six months.[52]

5. Effect on the debate on the new EU Migration Pact

The New Pact on Asylum and Migration was initiated in a Commission Communication[53] on 23 September 2020 with another set of ideas and legislative proposals, with among others, the aims of giving a new impetus to reforming the CEAS. Although the newest reform proposals were prepared in rounds of consultation with the capitals and they aim at balancing the various interests of the different groups of like-minded countries, what has been proposed is a strange mixture of already existing elements of migration and asylum policy that have a questionable effect on their own, and when arranged into one set of rules, they do not necessarily create a truly operable system that is capable of resisting a crisis.

The main and almost exclusive form of reaction the Pact proposes to situations of disproportionate pressure is relocation or return sponsorship, the latter being in practice a delayed relocation after unsuccessful implementation of return decisions from the Member State of entry. Relocation has already proven to be an ineffective solution as it is neither capable of effectively alleviating the burden caused by constant inflows, nor is it capable of stemming further inflows of migrants. Those rescued and disembarked after a search and rescue (SAR) operation are handled as a separate category by the reform proposals, and the Pact envisions the automatic relocation of most of the rescued after a SAR operation, thus, it can generate further embarkations and increase the loss of lives, having the opposite effect of what is intended. While in 2020 the Commission was supportive of a quick adoption of the proposals, or at least those that have advanced well during the negotiations, the only reform element in which the co-legislators could reach an agreement was to turn EASO into a fully-fledged EU Asylum Agency.[54]

The protection provided by Central and Eastern European countries finding themselves on the frontline may raise two particular issues. *(i)* Firstly, the volatile situation of Ukraine has been in the spotlight in these countries for some time.

52 *See* at https://gov.uk/register-interest-homes-ukraine.

53 COM(2020) 609 final.

54 Regulation (EU) 2021/2303 of the European Parliament and of the Council of 15 December 2021 on the European Union Agency for Asylum and repealing Regulation (EU) No 439/2010, PE/61/2021/REV/1.

doi: 10.5553/HYIEL/266627012022010001011

As regards the migration crisis in 2015, Kowalski[55] pointed out that Polish authorities should have put their perception of the crisis in a broader context by highlighting the potential outflow of internally displaced persons in Ukraine after the annexation of the Crimean Peninsula by Russia in 2014 together with the tens of thousands of Ukrainian workers in Poland who could easily turn into refugees should the situation escalate further. *(ii)* Secondly, many regard the current action of solidarity towards Ukrainian refugees as a shift in the asylum policy of Central European states. The basis for this is the misperception that an anti-migration narrative means a complete denial of the international human rights of people in need of protection. The Greek Government has always been advocating for an automatic, wide-spread relocation mechanism with a compulsory nature that the Central European countries had collectively rejected.[56] The issue of changing the current outlook on the migration issue was raised during a recent meeting between Notis Mitarakis, Greece's Minister of Migration and Asylum, and his German counterpart Nancy Faeser.

> "While Greece is showing support for Ukrainians, the country's lawmakers are also hoping that Russia's invasion of Ukraine and the resulting refugee crisis will reopen the debate on a new EU Pact on Migration and Asylum that the government insists must now be completed. The prospect of a change in attitudes among the Visegrad countries, by far the toughest on migration issues, now seems to be on the agenda, given that those countries are now faced with the stark reality of increased migration flows. The goal of the Greek government, and the migration ministry in particular, according to local media reports, is for all EU countries to realize the value of the proportional relocation of refugees, a concept which until now had not gained traction among all of the EU partners."[57]

This interpretation simply ignores the position also highlighted by Visegrad countries that refugees should be supported in the region closest to their country of origin, and those who arrived during or after the 2015 migration crisis have either crossed several safe third countries or are not in genuine need of international protection. Therefore, being ready from the start to fulfil the protection needs of those now fleeing a war in our neighborhood is not only not contradictory to previous positions, in fact, quite the opposite is true: the new situation just provided an opportunity for them to confirm their position in practice by offering their help when it is primarily this region's duty to welcome these refugees. Even think tank CEPS acknowledges that triggering the temporary protection regime is fully consistent with the position held by some EU Member

55 Michałt Kowalski, 'From a Different Angle – Poland and the Mediterranean Refugee Crisis', *German Law Journal*, Special Issue on Constitutional Dimensions of the Refugee Crisis, Vol. 17, Issue 6, 2016, p. 968.

56 Joint Statement of the Prime Ministers of the Visegrad Group, 9 July 2021, at https://visegradgroup.eu/download.php?docID=461, p. 3.

57 *See* at https://infomigrants.net/en/post/39312/greece-ramps-up-measures-to-help-ukrainian-refugees.

doi: 10.5553/HYIEL/266627012022010001011

States, including that of the Visegrad countries.[58] CEPS nevertheless criticizes the *á la carte* nature of showing openness depending on the different origins of asylum-seekers arriving at the borders of the EU.[59]

6. Conclusions

Responding to the enormous numbers fleeing Russian military aggression, the EU made an unprecedented move by activating the Temporary Protection Directive on 4 March 2022, thereby offering a unified protection status for Ukrainian nationals and their family members. Nevertheless, it should also be highlighted that many of the Member States close to Ukraine already made a step towards providing national protection from the beginning of the war. For instance, the Hungarian Government already activated the national scheme of temporary protection on the eve of 24 February 2022, although as a result of EU harmonization this was followed by the narrowing of the scope of temporary protection to the minimum obligatory category set out by the Council Decision.

Ensuring an EU harmonized status for those fleeing Europe had a number of positive results. People fleeing from Ukraine may not only enter, but may also be sure of receiving legal protection the same way all over the EU. While the level of services provided in the areas specified by the Directive may differ across the Member States because EU law does not allow for the harmonization of social rights or educational systems, beneficiaries of temporary protection enjoy the same set of rights all over the EU. Nevertheless, if they find more ideal circumstances because of their family members, friends, employment or benefits provided by the state, they may choose to move on to the Member State of preference.

The Council Decision was also unique in terms of its adoption. While the TPD sets out a qualified majority requirement for the Council, all the Member States were on board as a result of negotiations focusing on the personal scope and the agreement on the disapplication of readmission rules between the Member States. Think tank CEPS found that

> "the decision-making strategy followed a long-standing malpractice in EU migration/asylum policy by both the previous and current European Commission which seeks to achieve an artificial need for a unanimous vote or 'consensus' among all EU Member States in this policy area."

I find calling the aim of full implementation and aiming for consensus a malpractice that is incomprehensible after the major tensions and failure of implementing the 2015 relocation schemes. Commissioner Ylva Johansson also defended the direction of negotiations "arguing that the unanimous decision on

58 CEPS 2022, p. ii.

59 Id. p. 3.

the ultimate product was more important than adopting the original proposal via a so-called qualified majority."[60]

The direction of negotiation and the final compromise reflected the wounds Member States suffered during the past couple of years. Whether these bruises were from the tensions and mistrust from the 2015 relocation quotas crossing the red lines of several Member States or the more recent hybrid attack generated by Belarus instrumentalizing illegally arriving migrants, Member States learned to be cautious. So especially in the midst of a war going on in our direct neighborhood, we should allow them to feel at peace with their decision when activating the EU-wide temporary protection for the first time in EU history.

The most recent tragic events in Ukraine and the millions of people fleeing also showed that even situations emerging in the direct neighborhood of the EU may require Member States to be prepared to provide instant help and protection. Central and Eastern European states were ready from the outset to mobilize their reception and protection systems. The large scale of the influx of Ukrainians in clear need of protection nevertheless raises the question for the rest of the EU as well, whether it can continue spending a huge part of its administrative and reception capacities on asylum-seekers not in genuine need of protection.

60 *See* at https://politico.eu/article/eu-ministers-historical-deal-protect-ukraine-refugees/.

doi: 10.5553/HYIEL/266627012022010001011

Rebooting US-EU Data Transfers in the Pipeline

The Resurrection of the Acclaimed Privacy Shield

István Sabjanics[*]

Abstract

On 25 March 2022 US President Biden and European Commission President von der Leyen announced that an agreement in principle had been struck by their negotiating representatives. This came two years after the CJEU declared invalid the Commission's Privacy Shield Decision regarding the adequacy of protection provided by the US. The joint announcement was welcomed with much anticipation. Economic and security concerns had been voiced on both sides of the Atlantic, while the desire to protect European privacy principles remain strong. Commission President von der Leyen underlined European hopes for a predictable and trustworthy data flow between the EU and the US, one that safeguards privacy and civil liberties. Not much has surfaced of the new deal. Still, with more than 20 years of experience in transatlantic data flow and two fatal decisions of the CJEU, we must assume that the proposal will yield more compliance with European data protection standards and less loopholes.

Keywords: data protection, Privacy Shield, GDPR, surveillance, Schrems.

1. Introduction

On 25 March 2022, Joe Biden and Ursula von der Leyen announced that their negotiating parties struck an agreement in principle on a refurbished data transfer agreement between the US and the EU.[1] It will be called Privacy Shield, according to the announcement. After more than a year of meticulous negotiations between the European and US delegations a common ground and a feasible proposal was reached. This breakthrough is crucial since the value of continued data flow produces more than USD 1 trillion in cross-border commerce on a yearly basis.[2]

The privacy law of the EU, the General Data Protection Regulation (GDPR) came into effect on 25 May 2018. It was considered a great achievement primarily in the eyes of supporters of privacy rights, but a contradictory decision at least, if not a Pyrrhic victory for those, who felt protective over the previously moderately

* István Sabjanics: senior lecturer, Pázmány Péter Catholic University, Budapest.

1 *See* at https://ec.europa.eu/commission/presscorner/detail/en/IP_22_2087.

2 *See* at www.whitehouse.gov/briefing-room/statements-releases/2022/03/25/fact-sheet-united-states-and-european-commission-announce-trans-atlantic-data-privacy-framework/.

doi: 10.5553/HYIEL/266627012022010001012

challenged economic and technological development in the field of data processing, and data fusion in particular. In July 2020 the CJEU invalidated Decision 2016/1250 on the adequacy of the protection provided by the previous EU-US Data Protection Shield. The decision of the CJEU put several global communication service providers operating in the EU in peril.

2. Beginnings: The Safe Harbor Agreement (2000-2015)

Personal data of EU citizens or personal data collected in the EU cannot be transferred to a third country unless the European Commission finds that this third country in question provides an 'adequate' level of personal data protection. Yet this adequacy requirement does not have a clear cut definition, for neither the Data Protection Directive, nor the GDPR succeeded in defining it.[3] According to the Commission: under EU law, an adequacy finding requires the existence of data protection rules comparable to the ones in the EU. This concerns both the substantive protections applicable to personal data and the relevant oversight and redress mechanisms available in the third country.[4] So far 14 countries[5] received this appreciation and recognition by the Commission for their data protection systems, including the UK after its recent departure from the EU. The US data protection system has never been recognized as an adequate system comparable to its European counterpart under the Data Protection Directive and the GDPR, which meant certain pre-approved mechanisms were necessary: previously the Privacy Shield and before that, the Safe Harbor. There are other so-called secondary mechanisms[6] that allow for the transfer of personal data. These were also updated and modernized as the GDPR came into force, albeit with certain exceptions.[7]

The 2013 Snowden revelations on surveillance activities carried out by US authorities on a global scale, targeting EU countries[8] and EU citizens in the

3 Regulated previously under Article 25 Data Protection Directive, and today under Article 45 GDPR.

4 Opinion: Exchanging and Protecting Personal Data in a Globalised World. European Economic and Social Committee (Rapporteur: Christian Pirvulescu), at https://webapi2016.eesc.europa.eu/v1/documents/EESC-2017-03365-00-01-AC-TRA-EN.docx/content.

5 These are Andorra, Argentina, Canada (only commercial organizations), Faroe Islands, Guernsey, Israel, Isle of Man, Jersey, New Zealand, Switzerland, Uruguay, Japan, United Kingdom, and South Korea.

6 These are the *(i)* Standard Contractual Clauses, sometimes referred to as Model Contracts, *(ii)* the Binding Corporate Rules, *(iii)* Passenger Name Records (PNR), and lastly *(iv)* the Terrorist Financing Tracking Program. The last two originating from obligations under international law.

7 Data controllers and processors can continue to rely on earlier forms of the Standard Contractual Clauses for contracts that were concluded before 27 September 2021, provided that the processing operations that are the subject matter of the contract remain unchanged. *See* at https://ec.europa.eu/info/law/law-topic/data-protection/international-dimension-data-protection/standard-contractual-clauses-scc_en.

8 The surveillance of elected members of parliaments and members of governments, most notably Angela Merkel, who was Germany's chancellor at the time, resulted in EU-US relations plummeting.

doi: 10.5553/HYIEL/266627012022010001012

process, played a crucial part in losing trust in the prevailing system, one, that was based on the presumption that data transfers over the Atlantic took place in compliance with the Privacy Principles.[9] Vivian Reding, Vice-President of the European Commission at the time, cunningly even said that 'The Safe Harbor agreement may not be so safe after all'.[10] The infamous PRISM program is the flagship of the American global surveillance initiative, which grants access for the National Security Agency (NSA) to the massive amount of data gathered by major US-based tech companies, such as Google, Yahoo, Apple, Microsoft and Facebook.[11] These companies had hundreds of millions of clients in Europe and transfer personal data for processing to the US on a scale which is practically inconceivable.[12]

On 25 June 2013 Maximilian Schrems, an Austrian national, made a complaint to the Data Protection Commissioner of Ireland, complaining that Facebook Ireland Inc. transfers his personal data to the US, where it can be automatically and secretly accessed by American authorities. Schrems also asked the Commissioner to exercise his statutory powers to prohibit Facebook Ireland from transferring his personal data to the US. Schrems, referring to the Snowden revelations earlier that year, contemplated that the law and practice applicable in the US did not ensure an adequate protection of the personal data held in its territory against the surveillance activities carried out by public authorities.[13] The Irish Data Protection Commissioner dismissed the complaint, on the grounds that Schrems did not prove that the NSA actually accessed his data, and regardless of the likelihood of any misconduct, the Commission had previously decided that the US provides an adequate level of protection.[14]

Schrems then appealed to the High Court, which after due consideration found that the electronic surveillance and interception of personal data transferred from the EU to the US serve necessary and indispensable objectives in the public interest, such as national security, counterterrorism, and complying with other international obligations. The High Court also added that the Snowden revelations, published earlier that year, have demonstrated a 'significant over-reach' on the part of US authorities, and in particular the NSA.[15] The High Court stated that Union citizens have no effective right to be heard in regard of the indiscriminate surveillance and interception carried out by US agencies and authorities on a large scale.[16] The High Court held that the mass and

9 These Privacy Principles were notice, choice, onward transfer, security, data integrity, access, and enforcement.

10 *See* at https://ec.europa.eu/commission/presscorner/detail/en/MEMO_13_710.

11 Section 702 of the Foreign Intelligence Surveillance Act of 1978 Amendments Act of 2008, at www.congress.gov/110/plaws/publ261/PLAW-110publ261.pdf.

12 Communication from the Commission to the European Parliament and the Council on the Functioning of the Safe Harbor from the Perspective of EU Citizens and Companies Established in the EU, COM/2013/0847, at https://eur-lex.europa.eu/legal-content/EN/TXT/?uri=CELEX%3A52013DC0847.

13 Judgment of 6 October 2015, *Case C-362/14, Schrems,* ECLI:EU:C:2015:650, para. 28.

14 Id. para. 29.

15 Id. para. 30.

16 Id. para. 31.

doi: 10.5553/HYIEL/266627012022010001012

undifferentiated access to personal data is clearly contrary to the principle of proportionality, should the case solely be decided on the basis of Irish national law, the fundamental values protected by the Irish Constitution.[17] The High Court stated that Schrems did not question the validity of the Safe Harbor decision, yet in reality this must come under due scrutiny eventually.[18]

Whether the Safe Harbor Decision precludes Member States' data protection authorities from assessing the adequacy decision on the level of protection afforded by the US or not, was one of the questions referred to the CJEU by the High Court. It was assumed unreasonable to allow Member States' institutions to investigate proceedings based on the decision of an EU institution, if meaningful evaluation is *ab ovo* out of the question, since such decisions cannot be found unlawful by Member States' institutions. It would take only one Member State's institution to find the protection provided by the US inadequate for it to automatically defeat the sole purpose of the Safe Harbor Decision. Measures of EU institutions are in principle presumed to be lawful and accordingly produce legal effects until such time as they are withdrawn, annulled in an action for annulment or declared invalid following a reference for a preliminary ruling or a plea of illegality.[19] For this reason it was no surprise that Advocate General Yves Bot advised the CJEU to find the Safe Harbor Decision all together invalid[20] with prevailing practices on international data transfers to be reviewed case-by-case by Member States' data protection authorities. Considering the apprehensive criticism voiced by European governments towards Washington following the Snowden-revelations, the lack of a Safe Harbor Decision meant that in due course the Member States' decision to suspend data flow became more than just a possibility, much rather a probability.

On October 2015 the Grand Chamber of the CJEU found the Safe Harbor Decision invalid based on the following four arguments. *(i)* The CJEU emphasized the importance of privacy and data protection, with reference to the freedom of thought, expression, and information under the EU CFR.[21] *(ii)* The exception for private companies meant that national security, public interest, or law enforcement requirements have primacy over the Safe Harbor Principles.[22] The CJEU further noted that US law did not contain any rule of exception for the surveillance of EU citizens,[23] which created a generalized process lacking any differentiation, limitation or exception, hence it was in clear violation of EU and Irish law regarding the essence of the fundamental right to respect for private

17 Id. para. 33.

18 Id. para. 35.

19 Id. para. 52; *see also* Judgment of 5 October 2004, *Case C-475/01, Commission v Greece*, ECLI:EU:C:2004:585.

20 Opinion of Advocate General Bot Delivered on 23 September 2015 (AG Opinion), *Case C-362/14, Schrems*, ECLI:EU:C:2015:627, paras. 183 and 216.

21 *See* Articles 7-8, and 10-11 EU CFR.

22 *Case C-362/14, Schrems*, para. 28.

23 Id. para. 88.

doi: 10.5553/HYIEL/266627012022010001012

life.[24] *(iii)* The US Federal Trade Commission (FTC) had the enforcement role over the Safe Harbor Principles, excluding the processing of personal data by public authority.[25] The legal safeguards in the system were incomplete in this regard, and in effect, EU citizens were left with no administrative or judicial means of redress,[26] resulting in a clear violation of the right to an effective remedy and to a fair trial under Article 47 EU CFR. *(iv)* Respect for fundamental rights is a condition for the validity of EU acts under the landmark *Kadi* decision.[27] Since the essence of these rights was violated, a more thorough examination of the legal act in question[28] or the assessment against the principle of proportionality was deemed unnecessary by the CJEU.[29]

3. Following Snowden and Schrems I: Privacy Shield (2016-2020)

Even before the Snowden-revelations, there were calls for a revision of the Safe Harbor Agreement as it contained a number of data protection loopholes, as certain European privacy advocates claimed.[30] Following the invalidation of the Safe Harbor decision the future of data flow between the US and the EU was uncertain, which was especially damaging for the economy reliant on data transfer. Discussions between EU and US officials on revising and updating the Safe Harbor Agreement began in late 2013,[31] partially in response to growing European concerns about surveillance programs carried out by US authorities and other subsequent allegations of US intelligence collection operations in Europe.[32] In addition, the Safe Harbor Agreement dated back to the beginning of the Internet, resulting in an unavoidable tension between the prevailing legal provisions and the existing technological advances. European criticism eventually had an effect on the FTC's approach to privacy claims against US companies.[33] Among other problems there were European concerns that some companies failed to completely implement Safe Harbor requirements, due to a lack of mandatory

24 Id. para. 94. *See also* Judgment of 8 April 2014, *Joined Cases C-293/12 and C-594/12, Digital Rights Ireland and others,* ECLI:EU:C:2014:238, para. 39.

25 *Case C-362/14, Schrems,* AG Opinion, para. 205, citing FAQ 11 in Annex II to Decision 2000/520 and Annexes III, V and VII. *See also C-362/14, Schrems,* judgment, para. 89.

26 *C-362/14, Schrems,* para. 94.

27 Judgment of 18 July 2013, *Joined Cases C-584/10 P, C-593/10 P, and C-595/10 P, Kadi,* ECLI:EU:C:2013:518, para. 66.

28 *C-362/14, Schrems,* para. 98.

29 Article 52(1) EU CFR.

30 Nikolaj Nielsen, 'Hundreds of U.S. Companies Make False Data Protection Claims', *EUobserver.com,* 8 October 2013, at https://euobserver.com/rule-of-law/121695.

31 The actions set out by the European Commission to restore trust in data flows between the EU and the US, were released on 27 November 2013.

32 European Commission, *First Vice-President Timmermans and Commissioner Jourova's Press Conference on Safe Harbor Following the Court Ruling in Case C-362/14 (Schrems),* Press release, 6 October 2015.

33 Wilson Sonsini Goodrich & Rosati, *FTC announces settlements for allegedly false Safe Harbor compliance claims,* 6 February 2014, at https://sites.law.berkeley.edu/thenetwork/2014/02/06/ftc-announces-settlements-for-allegedly-false-safe-harbor-compliance-claims/.

doi: 10.5553/HYIEL/266627012022010001012

annual compliance checks, which most probably induced companies to falsely claim they complied with requirements. This concern was deepened by the previous inactivity of the FTC in bringing actions against US companies. This omission was apparent, since only ten companies came under investigation during the first 13 years of the Safe Harbor Agreement.[34]

Criticism arose from European data protection officials and Members of the European Parliament, regarding specific major US based companies, such as Google and Microsoft, for their alleged involvement in the US surveillance program affected most citizens of the EU. This prompted a call for suspending the Safe Harbor Agreement. The proposal for suspension was eventually rejected, for the European Commission gave more weight to possible negative effects for EU business interests and overall, the Transatlantic economy on both sides. The negotiations between EU and US officials starting in November 2013 focused on key topics considered to be most problematic by European data protection officials: *(i)* enhancing transparency, *(ii)* ensuring redress, *(iii)* strengthening enforcement, and *(iv)* limiting the access of US authorities to dataflows under Safe Harbor.[35] All four topics purposely lacked detail, allowing representatives room for negotiation. The US' national security interests and European demands to ensure limited access seemed irreconcilable in practice, both before and after the CJEU judgment and all through the negotiations. On 2 February 2016 Penny Pritzker, the US Secretary of Commerce at the time, two days after the 31 January deadline established by the Article 29 Working Group, made the announcement that negotiations had been completed. The work-title Safe Harbor 2.0 previously in use was finalized as 'Privacy Shield' which also implied the intention of rebranding the outcome. On 29 February 2016, US and EU officials released the full text of the agreement and the supporting documentation. The Privacy Shield framework was substantially longer and encouragingly more detailed than the previous Safe Harbor.[36] The US Government noted that this

> "historic agreement is a major achievement for privacy and for businesses on both sides of the Atlantic. It provides certainty that will help grow the digital economy by ensuring that thousands of European and American businesses and millions of individuals can continue to access services online."[37]

The Privacy Shield principles covered seven distinct categories: *(i)* notice, *(ii)* choice, *(iii)* accountability for onward transfer, *(iv)* security, *(v)* data integrity and

34 Martin A. Weiss & Kristin Archick, *U.S.-EU Data Privacy: From Safe Harbor to Privacy Shield*, Congressional Research Service, 19 May 2016, at https://sgp.fas.org/crs/misc/R44257.pdf.

35 *See* European Commission, *European Commission Calls on the U.S. to Restore Trust in EU-U.S. Data Flows*, Press prelease, 27 November 2013, at http://europa.eu/rapid/press-release_IP-13-1166_en.htm; *see also* Communication from the Commission to the European Parliament and the Council on the Functioning of the Safe Harbor from the Perspective of EU Citizens and Companies Established in the EU, 27 November 2013.

36 Department of Commerce, EU-US Privacy Shield, Washington, DC, 29 February 2016.

37 Article 29 Data Protection Working Party, Minutes of the 103rd meeting of the Article 29 Data Protection Working Party.

doi: 10.5553/HYIEL/266627012022010001012

purpose limitation, *(vi)* access and recourse, and *(vii)* enforcement and liability. Essentially, the goal was to mirror, or at least attempt to mirror, the requirements of EU law. It was mandatory for all participants to comply with this new regime. The rules of conduct acted as a bridge between EU and US regulatory systems. The Privacy Shield regulation was in substance a softer version of EU data protection law. From the American perspective it was a reinforced US information privacy law. Provisions around sensitive data, secondary liability, the role of data protection authorities, human resources data, pharmaceutical and medical products, and publicly available data were also included in a supplemental set of principles in laid down in the Privacy Shield.

Addressing the foremost European concerns after the Snowden-revelations, the Privacy Shield accommodated five written commitments in the form of letters from US national security officials, about protection guaranteed under the Privacy Shield with regard to EU citizens' data. These letters from US institutions aimed at clarifying both parties' understanding and commitments from the US side. The letters were principally made up of *(i)* an International Trade Administration Letter[38] and the Arbitral Model, *(ii)* a letter from US Secretary of State John Kerry to Commissioner Jourova[39] and the Ombudsperson Mechanism,[40] *(iii)* a letter from FTC Chair Edith Ramirez to Commissioner Jourova,[41] *(iv)* a letter from the Director of National Intelligence (DNI) to the US Department of Commerce,[42] and *(v)* a letter from US Deputy Assistant Advocate General Bruce Schwartz to the Department of Commerce.[43] These letters are political commitments of the US Government by nature, reassuring the EU that US institutions will take the Privacy Shield's requirements seriously.

In 2018 the Report from the Commission to the European Parliament and the Council on the Second Annual Review of the Functioning of the EU-US Privacy Shield focused on two areas, to which certain recommendations were made: *(i)* the commercial aspects of the program, and *(ii)* the access by US authorities to data of EU citizens transferred through it.[44] As far as the commercial considerations were concerned, the report mostly focused on (re)-certification, compliance monitoring, enforcement, and complaint handling. In terms of numbers, Privacy Shield proved to be at least as attractive as the previous Safe Harbor Agreement, after its first two years in force, the amount of involvement remained practically unchanged, over 3,800 companies had signed-

38 *See* at www.privacyshield.gov/servlet/servlet.FileDownload?file=015t00000004q0M.

39 *See* at www.privacyshield.gov/servlet/servlet.FileDownload?file=015t00000004q0b.

40 *See* at www.privacyshield.gov/servlet/servlet.FileDownload?file=015t00000004q0g.

41 *See* at www.privacyshield.gov/servlet/servlet.FileDownload?file=015t00000004q0v.

42 *See* at www.privacyshield.gov/servlet/servlet.FileDownload?file=015t00000004q1F.

43 *See* at www.privacyshield.gov/servlet/servlet.FileDownload?file=015t00000004q0W.

44 Commission Staff Working Document Accompanying the Document Report from the Commission to the European Parliament and the Council on the Second Annual Review of the Functioning of the EU-US Privacy Shield, COM(2018) 860 final, at https://ec.europa.eu/info/sites/default/files/staff_working_document_-_second_annual_review.pdf.

doi: 10.5553/HYIEL/266627012022010001012

up and became certified under the program.[45] Additional elements were integrated into the certification procedure by the US Department of Commerce.

During the first annual review meeting it emerged that companies publicly referred to their adherence to the Privacy Shield even before their certification had been finalized by the US Department of Commerce. To avoid legal uncertainty and false claims, the Commission recommended that companies not be allowed to make public representations about their Privacy Shield certification before the US Department of Commerce had finalized the certification and included the company on the Privacy Shield list.[46] The US Government published an additional guidance on the Privacy Shield's website to clarify the procedure.[47] The report listed specific areas suggested by the Commission, that were in need of improvement, such as deeper engagement in awareness raising and cooperation between EU and US authorities. The report finally included a discussion on potential divergences in certain areas of data processing, that will need to be addressed in the future. These included automated individual decision-making and the definition of human resources data. It is obvious that US authorities can access data transferred to the US through the Privacy Shield, since protective orders were incorporated as approved procedures. Nonetheless, public authorities' access is regulated by law, specifically by the Foreign Intelligence Surveillance Act (FISA)[48] and the Stored Communications Act.[49] The US government made additional reassurances that bulk data collection is only an exceptional mechanism that in any case may never happen to personal data transferred under Privacy Shield.[50] The US Inspector General for the Intelligence Community "confirmed that any referral from the Privacy Shield Ombudsperson would receive his serious, timely and effective attention."[51]

On 6 July 2020 the CJEU delivered its decision on what is now referred to as *Schrems II*. Following the *Schrems I* judgment and the subsequent annulment by the referring court of the decision rejecting Schrems's complaint, the Irish supervisory authority asked Schrems to reformulate his complaint in the light of the ruling of the CJEU that Decision 2000/520 was invalid.[52] In his reformulated complaint lodged on 1 December 2015, Schrems claimed, *inter alia*, that US law requires Facebook Inc. to make the personal data transferred to it available to certain US authorities, such as the NSA and the Federal Bureau of Investigation. He submitted that, since that data was used in the context of various monitoring programs in a manner incompatible with Articles 7, 8 and 47 of the Charter, the

45 Id. p. 4.

46 Id. p. 6.

47 US Department of State Privacy Shield Ombudsperson, at www.state.gov/e/privacyshield/ombud/.

48 50 USC 36, para. 1081 *et seq*. Foreign Intelligence Surveillance Act (FISA).

49 18 USC ch. 121, Stored Wire and Electronic Communications and Transactional Records Access.

50 2nd Annual Review of the Functioning of the Privacy Shield, p. 25.

51 Maximin Orsero, *Understanding the data privacy divide between the United States and the European Union*, Lund University, 2019, p. 50.

52 *Judgment in Case C-311/18 Press and Information Data Protection Commissioner v Facebook Ireland and Maximillian Schrems,* CJEU Press release No 91/20, Luxembourg, 16 July 2020, p. 1.

doi: 10.5553/HYIEL/266627012022010001012

SCC Decision[53] cannot justify the transfer of that data to the US. On these grounds, Schrems asked the Commissioner to prohibit or suspend the transfer of his personal data to Facebook Inc.[54]

As Recital of the Privacy Shield Decision establishes, the US Foreign Intelligence Surveillance Court (FISC) does not authorize individual surveillance measures under Section 702 FISA. Instead, it authorizes surveillance programs[55] based on annual certifications prepared by the US Attorney General and the DNI. Since these operations usually lack the focus of an individual target, the certifications to be approved by the FISC contain no information about the individual persons to be targeted, but rather identify categories of foreign intelligence information. This way, the FISC does not assess under a probable cause or any other standard that individuals are properly targeted to acquire foreign intelligence information. However, it covers the purpose of the acquisition to obtain foreign intelligence information.[56] The FISA also claims to provide a number of remedies, available also to non-US citizens, when they challenge unlawful electronic surveillance. Individuals even have the right to challenge the legality of surveillance, and may seek to suppress the information in the event the US government intends to use or disclose any information obtained or delivered through electronic surveillance against the individual in judicial or administrative proceedings in the US.[57] Although the exception of national security purposes is regulated in this way,[58] it is also accepted by the Commission that not all legal bases that US intelligence authorities may use[59] are covered by the avenues of redress open for EU data subjects.

The High Court of Ireland found that Executive Order No. 12333 allows the NSA to access data *in transit* to the US by accessing underwater cables on the floor of the Atlantic, and to collect and retain such data before they arrive in the US and become subject there to the FISA. Thus, these activities conducted pursuant to Executive Order No. 12333 were not governed by statute.[60] In addition to this, the NSA's activities based on Executive Order No. 12333 were not subject to judicial oversight and were not justiciable.[61] Therefore, Executive Order No. 12333 did not confer rights which were enforceable against the US authorities in the courts.[62] The High Court of Ireland disputed that Section 702

53 The interpretation and validity of Commission Decision 2010/87/EU of 5 February 2010 on standard contractual clauses for the transfer of personal data to processors established in third countries under Directive 95/46, as amended by Commission Implementing Decision (EU) 2016/2297 of 16 December 2016.

54 Judgment of 16 July 2020, *Case C-311/18, Facebook Ireland and Schrems,* ECLI:EU:C:2020:559, para. 44.

55 Like the infamous PRISM and UPSTREAM

56 Commission Implementing Decision (EU) 2016/1250 (Privacy Shield Decision), Recital (109), at https://eur-lex.europa.eu/legal-content/EN/TXT/PDF/?uri=CELEX:32016D1250&from=EN.

57 Id. Recital (112).

58 Id. Recitals (113)-(114).

59 Like the ones covered by Executive Order No. 12333.

60 *Case C-311/18, Facebook Ireland and Schrems,* para. 63.

61 Id. para. 65.

62 Id. para. 182.

doi: 10.5553/HYIEL/266627012022010001012

of the FISA, Executive Order No. 12333, read in conjunction with Presidential Policy Directive No. 28, correlated to the principle of proportionality found in EU law. With that in mind, it could be doubted that the surveillance programs in question could be regarded as limited to what is strictly necessary.[63]

Judicial redress possibilities for surveillance under FISA offered limited causes of action and claims would be declared inadmissible where the individual cannot show standing which ultimately restricted access to ordinary courts.[64] The High Court of Ireland stated that EU citizens did not have the same remedies as US citizens in respect of the processing of personal data by US authorities. The Fourth Amendment to the US Constitution, which constitutes, in US law, the most important cause of action available to challenge unlawful surveillance, did not apply to EU citizens. There were substantial obstacles in respect of the causes of action open to EU citizens, in particular that of *locus standi*, which it considered to be excessively difficult to satisfy. Lastly, the Privacy Shield Ombudsperson did not qualify as a tribunal according to Article 47 of the Charter, therefore, the level of protection was essentially not equivalent to that guaranteed by the fundamental right enshrined in the Charter.[65]

Be that as it may, the Commission considered that the US ensured an adequate level of protection for personal data transferred from the EU to certain self-certified organizations in the US under the EU-US Privacy Shield Agreement.[66] The Advocate General in his opinion called into question the Commission's previous finding that the US provide an adequate level of protection of personal data transferred from the EU to the US, thus calling into question the validity of the Privacy Shield Decision.[67] The CJEU took the findings of the Commission and the opinion of the Advocate General into consideration,[68] and found that Article 1 of the Privacy Shield Decision was incompatible with Article 45(1) GDPR, read in the light of Articles 7, 8 and 47 of the Charter, and was therefore invalid.[69]

4. Hopes and Concerns Surrounding the Privacy Shield 2.0 Proposal (Announced in February 2022)

On 25 March 2022 US President Biden and European Commission President von der Leyen announced that the US and the EU have struck an agreement in principle on a revamped Privacy Shield data transfer agreement. Representatives of the US and the EU have been negotiating the agreement for almost two years now. Von der Leyen called the agreement a political breakthrough, responding to

63 Id. para. 184.

64 Privacy Shield Decision, Recital (115).

65 *Case C-311/18, Facebook Ireland and Schrems*, para. 65.

66 Privacy Shield Decision, Recital (136).

67 *Case C-311/18, Facebook Ireland and Schrems*, para. 160; Opinion of Advocate General Saugmandsgaard Øe Delivered on 19 December 2019, *Case C-311/18, Facebook Ireland and Schrems*, ECLI:EU:C:2019:1145, paras. 175-177.

68 *Case C-311/18, Facebook Ireland and Schrems*, judgment, paras. 191-193.

69 Id. para. 199.

doi: 10.5553/HYIEL/266627012022010001012

the hopes of Europeans for a predictable and trustworthy data flow between the EU and the US, one that safeguards privacy and civil liberties. Still, some issues are still on the table, such as effective legal redress from a European perspective, which still need resolving.[70]

In summary, we must take stock of certain issues, before we claim victory. *(i)* Firstly, there is an economic ambition that must be addressed. US President Biden stated that the framework would allow the authorization of Transatlantic data flows that facilitate USD 7.1 trillion in economic relations.[71] A relationship that is fruitful on both sides of the Atlantic and a lifeline for several businesses in areas from payroll processing to social media display. Lesser or ineffective regulatory limitation on data processing is obviously a goldmine for companies in the data processing business, but the threat of losing the European market is far too risky for them. Consequently, their willingness to comply with European data protection standards is almost certain. *(ii)* Secondly, public interests, namely national security is an acceptable exception recognized under the Charter and the GDPR. The US is the closest ally of its European partners with formidable intelligence capabilities. Thus, we can safely assume that the European counterparts of the NSA would graciously accept relevant information on counterterrorism. Should the opportunity present itself where illegally obtained data could prevent a terrorist attack, every European government would undoubtedly choose security over privacy. *(iii)* Thirdly, there are some legal issues that came to light in the CJEU's decision invalidating the Privacy Shield Decision of the Commission, to which no satisfying solution has been proposed as of yet. It is a well-known fact that the US's privacy regulation is best described as a patchwork consisting of state and federal level regulation. The lack of binding law, that provides a clear understanding of the principles of data protection, the rights of the data subject, the obligations of the data controller and the data processor unsurprisingly causes loopholes in the legal system. The method of self-certification used in the US under the Privacy Shield protocol provides even more opportunities for those who seek to bypass European data protection standards. The fact that there is a systematic discrimination by forums of possible remedies against those non-US citizens who do not reside within the US, raises some concerns. And *(iv)* lastly, from a European perspective at least, it is a wonder, how a relatively vaguely composed statute can endure a coexisting Executive Order that basically contradicts the essence of the statute in question, and eventually authorizes a public authority to pursue activities without any consideration to the statute or other legally binding documents.

Without wanting to sounding too pessimistic, we must hope for the best with the newly updated Privacy Shield in the pipeline, but trust is a two-way street. In light of the earlier conduct of the US public authorities, it is better to

70 Vincent Manancourt, 'EU, US strike preliminary deal to unlock transatlantic data flows', *Politico*, 25 March 2022, at www.politico.eu/article/eu-us-strike-preliminary-deal-to-unlock-transatlantic-data-flows/amp/.

71 Id.

doi: 10.5553/HYIEL/266627012022010001012

stay vigilant from the start and maintain a watchful eye on processes in the long run.

doi: 10.5553/HYIEL/266627012022010001012

Regulating the Unregulateable

Attempts at Crypto Regulation in Europe

Zsolt Halász[*]

Abstract

The regulation of virtual assets has been on the legislative agenda for many years. The elaboration of a user-friendly regulatory system, in particular, on a global (or at least in Europe) scale, is more than likely over the next few years. Virtual assets are a special, unprecedented category of assets, and their emergence and proliferation pose new regulatory challenges in several areas, such as their issuance, the supervision of operations and transactions related to them (e.g. stock exchange services, lending, and other financial activities), furthermore, important issues arise in the field of taxation, accounting, and securities law with the emergence of the blockchain and distributed ledger technology-based securities. In recent years, at the state level, one could also witness comprehensive regulatory efforts and innovative regulatory attempts in certain European countries in various related areas, particularly in Malta, France, Germany, Liechtenstein, and Switzerland. This study presents the key elements, objectives, and characteristics of regulatory solutions in selected European countries. In September 2020, the European Commission presented a six-element regulatory package for the uniform regulation of virtual assets and markets at EU level. Accordingly, this paper pays particular attention to the European Commission's regulatory package, reviewing and evaluating its solutions, main elements, and regulatory methods. Last but not least, I present some related issues that may be considered regulatory gaps that have been left unregulated in both national legislations and the European Commission's proposal.

Keywords: virtual assets, blockchain, tokens, financial services, securities.

1. Introduction

When examining the regulation of virtual assets, it is firstly necessary to answer the question what, and for which purpose the legislator intends to regulate. Once these questions have been answered, a further question may arise as to the details surrounding the operation of the specific regulation chosen by the legislator. The topic of virtual assets is still a very new subject of legislation, which, coupled with the rapid development of the sector and the outstanding interest in it, also raises

* Zsolt Halász: associate professor of law, Pázmány Péter Catholic University, Budapest.

doi: 10.5553/HYIEL/266627012022010001013

the need for regulation – even though it is its unregulated character which makes it so attractive for many potential users. At the moment, this area is still searching for its rightful place in the legal system,[1] and both the various regulatory solutions and their shortcomings show that when it comes to virtual assets, neither the exact scope, nor the method of regulation is fully developed.

2. Potential Scope of Regulation of Virtual Assets

There is a number of potential regulatory issues that may arise in the context of virtual assets. The most important question is whether it is necessary or appropriate to regulate virtual assets themselves, or does it suffice to merely regulate the various services associated with them.

If one compares the virtual assets with the fiat money issued by traditional central banks by analogy, it is apparent that laws do not regulate money in general, but the events, services, transactions and situations related to money (*e.g.* legal relations, contracts) instead. The concept of money is a subject of economics, left undefined by law. Law defines the concept of official currency or the requirements for providing financial services but *does not define what money is.* Therefore, it seems more expedient to approach the topic from this direction and examine the legal relationships and situations in which the emergence and spread of virtual assets require the supplementing and, in some cases, reform of existing regulatory frameworks.

It is also important to pay attention to fact that virtual assets are not a homogeneous conglomeration. Within this category, we can distinguish *(i) utility tokens,* that provide access to certain products or services; *(ii) payment tokens*, also known as virtual money (cryptocurrencies), which are intended for us as alternative means of payment; *(iii) security tokens,* which embody a membership right or a contractual claim, and are very similar in this regard to traditional equity or debt securities; and *(iv) hybrid tokens,* that show the combined features of utility and payment tokens.[2]

This brief categorization is the simplest portrayal of the complex picture that is today (in July 2022) made up of more than 23,300 different assets, with a total value of USD 1.05 trillion.[3] In terms of substance, it is clear that there are huge differences between even the best-known virtual assets (cryptocurrencies). This diversity poses a particular challenge for the legislator if it wants to develop an appropriate regulatory response to all relevant issues that may arise.

Keeping all of these in mind, if one tries to take stock of the topics that require a regulatory response, one will find a rather comprehensive list. The following may arise as relevant *regulatory topics: (i)* in the field of financial services: currency exchange (both in fiat/virtual and virtual/virtual pairs), deposit transactions, financing clients (P2P lending, collateral transactions), payment

1 Zoltán Nagy, 'A kriptopénzek helye és szerepe a pénzügyi rendszerben', *Miskolci Jogi Szemle*, 2019/2, p. 10.

2 Niklas Schmidt, *Kryptowährungen und Blockchains*, Linde, Wien, 2019, p. 61.

3 *See* at www.coinmarketcap.com.

doi: 10.5553/HYIEL/266627012022010001013

transactions; *(ii)* in the ambit of investment services: commercial transactions (operation of cryptomarkets), depository transactions, portfolio management, placement, issuance (initial coin offerings, ICOs, STOs); *(iii)* tax regulation (both in turnover, income and wealth taxation, and the possible authorization of the payment of taxes by virtual assets, tax procedure issues); *(iv)* the issues surrounding the proper categorization of virtual assets in accounting matters; *(v)* consumer protection, investor protection regulation, and related institutional issues; *(vi)* money laundering regulations; *(vii)* supplementing certain labor law rules (in particular: allowing for the payment of wages and other remuneration in a virtual asset); *(viii)* corporate and bankruptcy law issues (equity rules: virtual asset contribution for the equity, liquidation of assets, disposal of assets); *(ix)* certain securities law issues (issuance of blockchain-based securities); *(x)* data protection (GDPR[4] *versus* blockchain: data transfer, enforcement of the right to be forgotten); and the *(xi)* legal and technical feasibility of state coercive measures and enforcement actions.

This list could be continued and expanded. However, it is also important to point out that the basic purpose of the relevant regulation should be the clarification of what is to be considered a virtual asset, in particular, from the perspective of private law.

In the following sections, I present certain examples of European regulatory solutions that have already been adopted and had entered into force, which can serve, at least in some of their elements, as models for a comprehensive and harmonized set of global rules.

3. Complementing the Traditional System of Money and Capital Market Rules: the German Example

The German legislature laid down the foundations for the regulation of virtual assets by supplementing the national banking law [the *Kreditwesengesetz (KWG)*].[5] The KWG regulates both money and capital market service providers and the services they are permitted to provide. According to the law, credit institutions *(Kreditinstitute)* provide banking services, while the investment service providers *(Finanzdienstleistungsinstitute)* offer investment services *(Finanzdienstleistungen)* on a commercial basis. In the context of virtual assets, the law regulates two types of services: *(i)* the crypto-custody service (*Kryptoverwahrgeschäft*), and *(ii)* the crypto-securities register management (*Kryptowertpapierregisterführung*).

The KWG defines the assets that may be the subject of an investment service: these are financial instruments (*Finanzinstrumente*), which include in

4 *Cf.* Article 17 of Regulation (EU) 2016/679 of the European Parliament and of the Council of 27 April 2016 on the protection of natural persons with regard to the processing of personal data and on the free movement of such data (GDPR), on the right to erasure (right to be forgotten).

5 Gesetz über das Kreditwesen – Kreditwesengesetz in der Fassung der Bekanntmachung vom 9 September 1998 (BGBl. I S. 2776), das zuletzt durch Artikel 90 des Gesetzes vom 10 August 2021 (BGBl. I S. 3436) geändert worden ist.

doi: 10.5553/HYIEL/266627012022010001013

addition to traditional transferable securities, money market instruments, and also derivatives of the crypto-values (*Kryptowerte*). According to the KWG's definition, crypto-values are digital representations of value that are not issued or guaranteed by any central bank or government agency and do not have the legal status of currency or money, but are accepted by agreement or practice as means of exchange or payment instruments by natural or legal persons. Crypto-values can be used for investment purposes and they can be transmitted, stored, and distributed electronically. However, the law emphasizes that electronic money (which is subject to separate EU legislation) should not be considered a crypto/virtual asset.

It is clear from this regulatory solution that the German legislator has placed crypto-custody services *among investment services* and cryptocurrencies (virtual assets) as the financial instrument within the traditional money and capital market regulations. Furthermore, it introduced a new type of investment service (the crypto-securities register management) into the framework of the 2021 securities law reform.

Based on the KWG's supplemented regulatory framework, it should be emphasized that not all services related to crypto/virtual assets, but just the above-mentioned services forming the technical basis for crypto-services have come under the supervision of the German Financial Supervisory Authority (BaFin). Consequently, among others, rules on the acquisition of service providers, their reporting obligations to the supervisory authority, anti-money laundering and counter-terrorist financing laws have become applicable to entities providing regulated crypto-services. Their commercial market activities, just like those of other financial and investment service providers, have become subject to supervisory authorization and may be subject to supervisory action in case of an infringement of applicable laws.

At the same time, they have been exempted from certain requirements under the capital market regulation: they do not have to apply the EU's prudential rules (CRR[6]) or KWG's provisions on own funds, capital buffers, large exposures, internal credit and the establishment of a branch office as well as the cross-border services rules.

4. Is a Virtual Asset a Property or a Claim? – Answers from Austria, Germany, Switzerland and Liechtenstein

Defining and categorizing virtual assets – crypto-values – within the system of the private law is not an easy mission. A fundamental question is whether these instruments are to *be placed in property law or in the law of obligations.* Owing to the differences between virtual assets and traditional forms of property and claims, the private law definition and categorization may be solved by amending and/or supplementing the relevant rules of existing civil codes, which must be

6 Regulation (EU) No 575/2013 of the European Parliament and of the Council of 26 June 2013 on prudential requirements for credit institutions and investment firms and amending Regulation (EU) No 648/2012.

doi: 10.5553/HYIEL/266627012022010001013

preceded by a legislative decision on the legal treatment of these assets (whether they should be treated as property or claims). This question is of paramount importance, not only from a private law point of view, but also from an accounting and taxation aspect. There are some arguments in favor of considering virtual assets as receivables, namely, receivables without maturity. The complete lack of legal categorization of these assets poses serious difficulties also in the field of accounting.

Article 285 of the Austrian Civil Code (ABGB[7]) defines property in a legal sense as anything that is not a person and serves their benefit.[8] The ABGB distinguishes according to their nature between tangible and non-tangible property, including certain property rights, for example. Accordingly, in light of the ABGB concept of things, virtual assets and crypto-values must clearly be regarded as *things*. [In my opinion, a similarly clear statement cannot be made under the Hungarian Civil Code[9] (Ptk.) or under the civil codes of many other countries.]

Contrary to the concept of property under the Austrian ABGB, as a general rule, Section 90 of the German Civil Code (BGB[10]) regards only physical objects as property. However, the new Act on Electronic Securities[11] (eWpG) adopted in 2021 states that *electronic securities must be regarded as property* within the meaning of Section 90 BGB. The eWpG regulates two types of electronic securities: centrally registered – traditional – electronic securities and crypto-securities, which are registered in a separate crypto-security register. In respect of both types of electronic securities, the law clearly states that they must be regarded as property under Section 90 BGB.

The Swiss Civil Code (ZGB[12]) does not define the concept of property, however, it sets out the powers of the owner in Section 641, according to which "the owner of an object is free to dispose of it as he or she sees fit within the limits of the law". The ZGB distinguishes between ownership of immovable properties and ownership of chattel properties. The objects of chattel property are, by their nature, movable physical objects and forces of nature which may be the subject of legal rights, and do not form part of any immovable property (Section 713). The rules stipulated in Articles 20 and 171 of the Liechtenstein Law of Property (SR[13]) are almost identical to those applicable in Switzerland. Finally, according to the conceptual framework of Swiss private law, it is *difficult to extend the concept of things to virtual assets.*

7 Allgemeines bürgerliches Gesetzbuch für die gesamten deutschen Erbländer der Oesterreichischen Monarchie StF: JGS Nr. 946/1811.

8 Schmidt 2019, p. 118.

9 Hungarian Act V of 2013 on the Civil Code.

10 Bürgerliches Gesetzbuch in der Fassung der Bekanntmachung vom 2 Januar 2002 (BGBl. I S. 42, 2909; 2003 I S. 738), most recently amended by Section 2 of Act of 21 Dezember 2021 (BGBl. I S. 5252).

11 Gesetz über elektronische Wertpapiere vom 3 Juni 2021 (BGBl. I S. 1423)

12 Schweizerisches Zivilgesetzbuch vom 10 Dezember 1907 (as of 1 January 2022).

13 Sachenrecht (SR) 1922 vom 31 Dezember 1922, Liechtensteinisches Landesgesetzblatt, Jahrgang 1923 Nr. 4.

doi: 10.5553/HYIEL/266627012022010001013

5. Introduction of Dedicated Legislation in Malta and France

5.1 The Maltese Regulatory System

In 2018 Malta adopted three foundational laws underpinning the regulatory system for virtual assets, based on the National Blockchain Strategy: the Virtual Financial Assets Act[14] (VFA Act), the Innovative Technology Arrangements and Services Act[15] (ITAS Act), and the Malta Digital Innovation Authority Act[16] (MDIA Act). These statutory provisions are supplemented by guidelines of the Malta Financial Services Authority.

The provisions of the VFA Act shall apply to services, activities and institutions that arise out of, or are provided as services related to, a virtual financial instrument. According to the provision of the VFA Act, virtual financial asset or VFA means any form of digital medium recording that is used as a digital medium of exchange, a unit of account, or store of value and that is not *(i)* electronic money; *(ii)* a financial instrument; or *(iii)* a virtual token.

Electronic money is defined by the directive on electronic money institutions,[17] while financial instruments are listed in the MIFID2 directive.[18] Virtual token means a form of digital medium recording whose utility, value or application is restricted solely to the acquisition of goods or services, either solely within the DLT platform in relation to which it was issued, or within a limited network of DLT platforms (excluded DLT exchanges).

According to the VFA Act, activities related to virtual financial assets may be carried out under official supervision exercised by the Financial Services Authority of Malta. The VFA Act concerns the following activities related to virtual financial assets: *(i)* the initial virtual financial asset offering (a method for raising funds whereby an issuer issues virtual financial assets and offers them in exchange for funds); *(ii)* providing services related to virtual financial assets (VFA services).

The provision of VFA services is subject to the possession of a license to be granted under the VFA Act. These services are the following, when provided in relation to a virtual financial asset: *(i)* reception and transmission of orders; *(ii)* execution of orders on behalf of other persons; *(iii)* dealing on own account; *(iv)* portfolio management; *(v)* custodian services; *(vi)* investment advice; *(vii)* placement of virtual financial assets; *(viii)* operation of a VFA exchange; *(ix)* transfer of virtual financial assets.

14 Act XXX of 2018 as amended by Legal Notice 106 of 2021 and Act XLVI of 2021. (Virtual Financial Assets Act).

15 Act XXXIII of 2018 as amended by Legal Notice 389 of 2020 (Innovative Technology Arrangements and Services Act).

16 Act XXXI of 2018 (Malta Digital Innovation Authority Act).

17 Directive 2009/110/EC of the European Parliament and of the Council of 16 September 2009 on the taking up, pursuit and prudential supervision of the business of electronic money institutions amending Directives 2005/60/EC and 2006/48/EC and repealing Directive 2000/46/EC.

18 Directive 2014/65/EU of the European Parliament and of the Council of 15 May 2014 on markets in financial instruments and amending Directive 2002/92/EC and Directive 2011/61/EU.

doi: 10.5553/HYIEL/266627012022010001013

The basic requirements for issuing virtual financial assets are the preparation of a "White Paper" for introducing the issuer and the asset to be issued, its registration with the Financial Services Authority of Malta, and the appointment of a VFA agent for professional matters. The law stipulates the issuer's responsibility for misstatements in whitepapers, advertisements, and websites.

A VFA agent must be appointed in case someone either intends to issue virtual financial assets or provides a service related to these. A VFA agent is an individual advocate, accountant or auditor (or a relevant firm), registered with the supervisory authority, holding authorizations, qualifications, and/or experience deemed by the supervisory authority as possessing suitable expertise to exercise the tasks related to virtual financial assets issuance, or virtual financial asset related services). The role of the VFA Agent is to provide the appropriate professional background for VFA issuers and service providers. In addition to services related to virtual financial assets, the VFA Act also sets out rules for the prevention of market abuse.

Overall, as far as the regulation of the virtual financial assets in the Maltese legal system is concerned, there is *a regulatory framework similar to traditional capital market regulation*, where *(i)* the activities related to the issuance of virtual financial assets and the provision of related services must be authorized and supervised; *(ii)* similarly to investment services, the regulatory framework defines in an exhaustive manner which services must be considered virtual financial services; *(iii)* subject of the regulation are virtual financial assets, which are special financial instruments considered to be virtual financial services; *(iv)* the publication of a prospectus registered with the supervisory authority is mandatory when issuing virtual financial assets; *(v)* the regulation of prevention of market abuse is also a part of the regulatory system.

5.2 *A Comprehensive Legal Framework of Virtual Assets and the Utilization of the Shared Electronic Recording System in France*

In France, the very first step of the crypto-legislation was the application of anti-money laundering law in 2016, when cryptocurrency trading platforms and brokers became subject to the anti-money laundering legislation.[19]

One of the most significant parts of the French crypto-legislation is the legal framework related to the Action Plan for Business Growth and Transformation (PACTE), which allows for the use of blockchain for the registration of unlisted securities, crowdfunding and ICOs. The core element of the French crypto-legislation is the PACTE Act,[20] a dedicated legal framework, which aims at facilitating the growth of enterprises through several legislative measures,

19 Ordinance No. 2016-1635 of 1 December 2016, modifying Article L. 561-2 of the Code monétaire et financier (Monetary and Financial Code).

20 Act No. 2019-486 of 22 May 2019 on the growth and transformation of enterprises (PACTE: Plan d'Action pour la Croissance et la Transformation des Entreprises); Hubert de Vauplane & Victor Charpiat, 'The Virtual Currency Regulation Review: France', *in* Michael S. Sackheim & Nathan A. Howell (eds.), *The Virtual Currency Regulation Review*, 4th Edition, 2021, at https://thelawreviews.co.uk/title/the-virtual-currency-regulation-review/france.

doi: 10.5553/HYIEL/266627012022010001013

including rules governing ICOs and also intermediaries dealing with virtual assets. These rules were adopted by amending the existing *Code monétaire et financier* (Monetary and Financial Code) at several points.

The creation of a dedicated framework for the financing of SMEs through crowd-lending platforms in 2016 was the first appearance of blockchain in French law.[21] According to the relevant provisions, financial securities, issued on French territory and subject to French legislation, are registered either in a security account held by the issuer or by one of the intermediaries, or in a shared electronic recording system.[22] The French law makes it possible to use a distributed ledger (a shared electronic recording system) for the issuance, registration, and transfer of unlisted securities (securities which are not admitted to the operations of a central depository).[23] The shared electronic recording system must guarantee the identification of the owners of the securities, as well as the nature and number of securities held.[24]

These securities issued, registered, and transferred by using a distributed ledger must not be confused with security tokens, since according to the Monetary and Financial Code, tokens issued under ICOs cannot be regarded as securities.[25]

Distributed ledgers (including public and private blockchains) can be used for the registration of securities, if *(i)* they are conceived and implemented in a way that preserves the integrity of the information recorded; *(ii)* they directly or indirectly allow the identification of the securities owners and the nature and number of securities held; *(iii)* they include a business continuity plan; and *(iv)* the owners of the securities registered on them are able to access their statements of transactions.[26]

The French legal framework became a viable background for the issuance of bonds, covered bonds, and shares on the Ethereum blockchain. In France, the Central Bank (*Banque de France*, BdF) started working on developing a *central bank digital currency* (CBDC), to ensure the safe development of tokenized financial markets and to improve cross-border and cross-currency payments, in line with ECB's project on digital euro issuance.

As one of the first occasions of using a CBDC in practice, in April 2021, the European Investment Bank (EIB), in collaboration with commercial banks, launched a digital bond issue, intending to use distributed ledger technology for the registration and settlement of digital bond securities.[27] The issuance was settled with a CBDC issued by the BdF on the blockchain. According to the Monetary and Financial Code, a token is an intangible asset representing, in digital form, one or more rights that can be issued, registered, retained or

21 Ordonnance n° 2016-520 du 28 avril 2016 relative aux bons de caisse.
22 Article L. 211-3 of the Code monétaire et financier.
23 Articles L. 211-3, L. 211-7, L. 211-15 and L. 211-17 of the Code monétaire et financier.
24 Article R. 211-9-7 of the Code monétaire et financier.
25 Article L. 552-1 of the Code monétaire et financier.
26 Vauplane & Charpiat 2021.
27 *See* at www.eib.org/en/press/all/2021-141-european-investment-bank-eib-issues-its-first-ever-digital-bond-on-a-public-blockchain.

doi: 10.5553/HYIEL/266627012022010001013

transferred through a shared electronic recording system that identifies, directly or indirectly, the owner of said property.[28]

ICOs are explicitly separated from securities offerings. The French supervisory authority of financial markets (*Autorité des Marchés Financiers,* AMF) supervises and authorizes the initial coin offerings (ICOs) and grants approval to those ICOs that comply with the requirements set out by the Monetary and Financial Code. Any issuer who makes a public offering of tokens (ICOs) may request authorization from the AMF. Nevertheless, obtaining the AMF's approval is optional for all token issuers.[29] ICOs without formal approval are subject to marketing restrictions only, by contrast, the AMF's approval serves as a sort of quality seal. For approval, ICO issuers must file an information document (white paper) containing various details of the offer and the issuer.[30]

French legislation also regulates the digital asset service providers (DASPs), who are entities providing services related to digital assets. Digital assets include: *(i)* the tokens defined in the ICO framework, except those qualifying as financial instruments; *(ii)* any digital representation of value which is not issued or guaranteed by a central bank or by a public authority, which is not necessarily attached to a currency having legal tender nature and which does not have the legal status of a currency, but which is accepted by natural or legal persons as means of exchange and which can be transferred, stored or exchanged (traded) electronically.[31]

The legal framework and definition of digital asset services is based on traditional investment services: *(i)* the custody service of digital assets or access to digital assets (private cryptographic keys) on behalf of third parties; *(ii)* buying or selling digital assets for fiat money (legal tender); *(iii)* exchanging digital assets for other digital assets; *(iv)* the operation of a digital asset trading platform; *(v)* various other investment-type services, such as the reception and transmission of orders on digital assets on behalf of third parties, portfolio management of digital assets on behalf of third parties, advice to subscribers of digital assets, underwriting of digital assets, placement of digital assets.[32]

For service providers established in France or providing these services in France, who are custodians of digital assets, providers of the service of purchase or sale of digital assets against legal currency and other digital assets, and those operating a digital asset trading platform, a registration with the AMF is mandatory before starting their activity. For any other service provider, registration is optional.[33]

28 Article L. 552-2 of the Code monétaire et financier.
29 Article L. 552-4 of the Code monétaire et financier.
30 Article L. 552-4 of the Code monétaire et financier.
31 Article L54-10-1 of the Code monétaire et financier.
32 Article L54-10-2 of the Code monétaire et financier.
33 Article L54-10-4 of the Code monétaire et financier.

doi: 10.5553/HYIEL/266627012022010001013

6. A Possible Precursor to an EU Regulatory Proposal: the Liechtenstein Example

The regulatory system for virtual assets was conceived in the Principality of Liechtenstein in 2019: the Act on Token and TT Service Providers (TTTL[34]) and the Regulation on Token and TT-Service Providers (TTTR[35]). The TTTL sets out the legal framework for trusted technology (hereinafter: TT) based transaction systems, regulating in particular: *(i)* the principles of private law governing tokens, the representation of rights by tokens and their transfer; *(ii)* the rules governing the supervision of trusted technology providers and TTP's rights and obligations.

The Act doesn't specify trusted technologies (consequently, it is exclusively applicable to distributed ledger technology and blockchain). It considers those technologies to be trusted technology that ensure the integrity of tokens, the clear assignment of tokens to TT IDs, and the availability of tokens. The law defines *token as a piece of information* on a TT system that: *(i)* may represent a claim or rights of membership against a person, a right to property or any other absolute or relative right; and *(ii)* is assigned to one or more TT IDs.

The law does not specify whether to treat tokens as property or a claim. However, from a private law perspective, it regulates the owners of the tokens and considers the owner of a token to be the person who possesses the access keys (TT keys) to a token. Access to the token creates the possibility of disposing of the right embodied by the token.

TT services include token issuance, token creation, TT key and token custody, TT token commission service, token/money exchange service, token alienation verification service, price information service, ownership adequacy/verification service, TT agency services (intermediation of foreign services).

In the case of domestic services, the condition for the operation of TT service providers is registration with the Liechtenstein Financial Market Authority (*Finanzmarkt Aufsicht* – FMA), which also supervises the operation of TT service providers (similarly to other traditional financial institutions). In its supervisory competence, the FMA carries out *(i)* the registration of TT service providers; *(ii)* provides information on the applicability of the TVTG and other legislation on trusted technologies; *(iii)* keeps the register of TT service providers; *(iv)* prosecutes violations of the law, inspects TT services and service providers, and applies the measures specified by law where necessary.

The service is considered to be subject to Liechtenstein law if the service provider or token issuer has headquarters or a place of residence in Liechtenstein, or parties declare its provisions to expressly apply in a legal transaction over tokens. The condition for registration is that the applicant is *(i)* has legal capacity; *(ii)* reliable; *(iii)* technically suitable; and has *(iv)* its headquarters or place of

34 Gesetz vom 3 Oktober 2019 über Token und VT-Dienstleister (TVTG), Liechtensteinisches Landesgesetzblatt Jahrgang 2019, Nr. 301.

35 Verordnung vom 10 Dezember 2019 über Token und VT-Dienstleister (TVTV), Liechtensteinisches Landesgesetzblatt, Jahrgang 2019, Nr. 349.

doi: 10.5553/HYIEL/266627012022010001013

residence in Liechtenstein; *(v)* the necessary minimum capital (depending on the service provided) is between CHF 30,000 and 250,000; *(vi)* suitable organizational structure with defined areas of responsibility and a procedure to deal with conflicts of interest; *(vii)* written internal proceedings and control mechanisms that are appropriate in terms of the type, scope, complexity, and risks of the TT Services provided, including ensuring sufficient documentation of these mechanisms; *(viii)* special internal control mechanisms, where appropriate; *(ix)* authorization pursuant to the Trustees Act if they intend to act as a TT Protector; and *(x)* if they intend to conduct activity that is subject to an additional authorization obligation according to the Financial Market Supervision Act, for which the corresponding authorization is available.

A characteristic feature of Liechtenstein legislation is that it allows TT services not only to be provided by companies, since private individuals may also carry out this activity. Overall, the Liechtenstein regulation differs in many aspects from the legislative solutions presented above. It is not constructed simply by analogy to traditional money and capital market regulations. Instead it defines – in the view of the specificities of the regulated technological innovation – the relevant concepts and the tasks, rights, and obligations of the issuers, service providers, and supervisory authorities. For this reason, it is appropriate to use it as a model for developing a future common European, and possibly global regulatory system.

7. EU Legislation: Proposal for a Regulation on Markets in Crypto-Assets (MICA)

In September 2020 the European Commission published its proposal for a regulation on markets in crypto-assets[36] (MICA proposal), which seeks to fill a long-standing regulatory gap. Until now, relevant provisions in the EU legislation can almost exclusively be found among the provisions combatting money laundering,[37] and there are no specific rules on this topic in other areas of the EU law.

The scope of the EU's Anti-Money Laundering Directive[38] (AMLD) was extended in 2018 by an amendment[39] (Fifth Money Laundering Directive) to

36 Proposal for a Regulation of the European Parliament and of the Council on Markets in Crypto-assets, and amending Directive (EU) 2019/1937 COM/2020/593 final (MICA proposal).

37 Péter Bálint Király, 'A kriptovaluták pénzügyi fogyasztóvédelmi aspektusai', *Iustum Aequum Salutare*, Vol. 16, Issue 4, 2020, p. 50.

38 Directive (EU) 2015/849 of the European Parliament and of the Council of 20 May 2015 on the prevention of the use of the financial system for the purposes of money laundering or terrorist financing, amending Regulation (EU) No 648/2012 of the European Parliament and of the Council, and repealing Directive 2005/60/EC of the European Parliament and of the Council and Commission Directive 2006/70/EC.

39 Directive (EU) 2018/843 of the European Parliament and of the Council of 30 May 2018 amending Directive (EU) 2015/849 on the prevention of the use of the financial system for the purposes of money laundering or terrorist financing, and amending Directives 2009/138/EC and 2013/36/EU.

doi: 10.5553/HYIEL/266627012022010001013

include virtual currency and fiat money exchange services providers and custodian wallet providers for which the amendment made their registration compulsory. This amendment was the first legislative act, where EU law defined the concept of virtual currency:

> "a digital representation of value that is not issued or guaranteed by a central bank or a public authority, is not necessarily attached to a legally established currency and does not possess a legal status of currency or money, but is accepted by natural or legal persons as a means of exchange and which can be transferred, stored and traded electronically."

By preparing and presenting a proposal for a MICA regulation the Commission acknowledges the regulatory shortcomings outlined above. The proposal attempts to regulate the at EU level hitherto unregulated crypto-assets and the relevant service providers by defining the requirements for issuing and trading different types of crypto asset tokens and providing services with them.

The proposal is part of the *Digital Finance Package*, which sets out a new digital financial services strategy[40] for the EU's financial sector, as well as a proposal for the regulation of a pilot regime for market infrastructures based on distributed ledger technology (DLT),[41] a proposal for an EU regulatory framework on digital operational resilience[42] ("DORA"), as well as a proposal to clarify or amend certain related EU rules on financial services.[43]

The main rules of MICA cover *(i)* the transparency and disclosure requirements for the issuance and admission to trading of crypto-assets; *(ii)* the authorization and supervision of crypto-asset service providers and token issuers; *(iii)* the operation, organization and governance of token issuers and crypto-asset service providers; *(iv)* consumer protection rules for the issuance, trading, exchange, and custody of crypto-assets; *(v)* measures to prevent market abuse in order to ensure the integrity of crypto-asset markets.

This Regulation applies to persons that *(i)* are engaged in the issuance of crypto-assets or *(ii)* provide services related to crypto-assets in the EU (such services include custody and administration of crypto-assets on behalf of third parties, the operation of a trading platform, the exchange of services for fiat currencies or other crypto-assets, the execution of orders on behalf of third

40 Communication from the Commission to the European Parliament, the Council, the European Economic and Social Committee and the Committee of the Regions on a Digital Finance Strategy for the EU, COM(2020) 591 final.

41 Proposal for a Regulation of the European Parliament and of the Council on a pilot regime for market infrastructures based on distributed ledger technology COM(2020) 594 final.

42 Proposal for a Regulation of the European Parliament and of the Council on digital operational resilience for the financial sector and amending Regulations (EC) No 1060/2009, (EU) No 648/2012, (EU) No 600/2014 and (EU) No 909/2014 COM(2020) 595 final.

43 Proposal for a Directive of the European Parliament and of the Council amending Directives 2006/43/EC, 2009/65/EC, 2009/138/EU, 2011/61/EU, EU/2013/36, 2014/65/EU, (EU) 2015/2366 and EU/2016/2341 COM(2020) 596 final.

doi: 10.5553/HYIEL/266627012022010001013

parties, placing of crypto-assets, the reception and transmission of orders on behalf of third parties, providing advice).

According to the proposal, separate rules will apply to asset and electronic money-based tokens as well as other tokens (non-stable coins) that do not fit in these categories. One can discover many similarities in the proposed regulatory system with the solutions of traditional money and capital market regulation.

By analogy with securities law, the draft identifies the drafting, notification, and publication of the *White Paper* (like a *prospectus*) as the essential requirement for the issuance of a cryptocurrency, which, in addition to identifying the issuer and presenting the project to be financed, also details the risks and technological requirements involved. Similarly to securities legislation, the draft prescribes a supervisory license requirement as a precondition for the issuance of asset referenced and electronic money-based tokens. The definition of the obligations and responsibilities of the issuer, the requirement to ensure the consumer's right of withdrawal , and the definition of the rules on market abuse are of paramount importance for the protection of customers and consumers.

The proposal requires cryptocurrency service providers to be licensed to enter the market, to operate in line with certain prudential rules and the detailed rules for services, and to operate a complaint handling system. The regulation sets out the tasks, powers, and possible actions of the competent supervisory authorities and the *European Banking Authority* (EBA).

The Commission proposal contains a number of elements that are justified in the regulatory framework of the new instruments, however, there are several issues that are not covered by the proposal, even though appropriate regulation in these areas would be more than justified and necessary. Examples for such 'missing' elements include: *(i)* the private law categorization of crypto assets (defined as property or claim); *(ii)* the regulation of crypto asset loans and the use of crypto assets as credit collaterals by creating the private law foundations of these activities, as well as the collection of crypto-asset deposits; *(iii)* the extension of the scope of the proposed regulation to existing instruments (which raises several questions, should this be the case, but also in case this regulatory solution is not pursued); *(iv)* the establishment of institutions similar to traditional deposit insurance and investor-protection funds, the definition of the services and damages they cover, and the extent and method of compensation for claims incurred; *(v)* regulating the application of state coercive measures (enforcement, seizure of assets in the framework of an official procedure) to be able to take enforcement action or other action in respect of crypto-assets; *(vi)* adaptation of company law in the field of rules on equity (definition of the rules for the contribution of cryptocurrencies as equity); *(vii)* harmonization of the proposal with the requirements of the *General Data Protection Regulation*[44] (GDPR) in particular, with the technological characteristics of distributed ledger technology (in particular, data transfer, the right to forgotten and the right to privacy).

44 Articles 16, 17, and 18 GDPR.

8. Summary

Looking at the regulatory solutions of certain European countries, it is apparent at first glance that European countries use different regulatory solutions (stand-alone, separate regulation vs incorporating new rules into traditional money and capital market laws), yet the relevant laws put in place do not differ greatly. EU legislation is currently lagging far behind the regulatory progress of individual Member States; only the relevant provisions of the Anti-Money Laundering Directive are in force, but a more comprehensive regulation is yet to be adopted.

In general, the obligation to register (license) for the issuance of virtual assets appears everywhere (both in the already adopted national regulations and in the proposal of the European Commission). The concept of services related to virtual assets is very similar to the concept of investment services, the provision of services falls under financial supervision and the operation of service providers is subject to rules similar to those for money and capital market institutions.

In addition to regulatory similarities, regulatory gaps cover nearly identical areas. Except for the Austrian example (which may be considered a random exception), *the private law definition of virtual assets* (the definition of assets as property or claim) *does not appear in any legislation.* A deficiency is, that in addition to services similar to traditional investment services, the rules applicable to services such as financial services (lending, deposit-taking, money substitutes, *i.e.* the issuance of cards) do not appear in the regulation, although these services are becoming more and more widespread. There is also a *lack of an institutional protection system* (*e.g.* investor protection) similar to the relevant institutions in traditional money and capital markets. Finally, among these shortcomings, one must also highlight the *lack of a system of legal and technological requirements for the enforceability of state coercive measures.*

All in all, a long-needed legislative process has begun in many countries and also in the EU, with elements that seem fruitful and promising. However, due to the technological possibilities, it would be expedient to regulate this topic – or at least its basic elements – at global level, and the establishment of this regulatory framework should take place as soon as possible. Contrary to the endeavors of several states and the EU, there are more and more countries around the globe, that are not in favor of the proliferation of crypto-assets and consequently, a user-friendly legislation to govern them.

Hungarian Yearbook of International Law and European Law 2022 (10) 1
doi: 10.5553/HYIEL/266627012022010001013

Reconciling Jurisdictions in the European System of Constitutional Adjudication

Reform Proposals for the CJEU

Márton Csapodi[*]

Abstract

Several authors have concluded that an institutional reform of CJEU is necessary, with some putting forward reform proposals accordingly. This paper briefly recounts the reasons why such a reform may be indeed necessary, with due attention to the fact that national constitutional resistance to the Luxembourg court seems to be occurring with increasing frequency. In what follows, I present some of the institutional reform proposals that appeared in the academic discourse and make some critical observations in respect of these ideas. These proposals include: the introduction of a reverse preliminary reference procedure for cases related to national identity; a political override mechanism; a proposal for limiting preliminary reference rights to high courts (albeit with exceptions); and finally, the idea to establish a new court specialized in competence issues. Perhaps the latter proposal is the most popular, although various authors propose substantially different constructions. I conclude that a Subsidiarity Court specialized in competence issues could be an effective instrument for a better representation of national constitutional perspectives at the EU level, which would be essential, should open non-compliance be avoided. I also propose a complementary mechanism to the preliminary reference procedure, which would allow constitutional courts to participate in the European constitutional dialogue.

Keywords: CJEU, constitutional courts, reform, preliminary reference, subsidiarity court.

1. Why Should We Think about Reforming the CJEU?

During the last decade, there have been three occasions where a national constitutional court or supreme court ruled that the CJEU exceeded the competences conferred on it: first in the Czech Republic, then in Denmark, and finally in Germany.[1] In the same vein, the Polish Constitutional Court's *K 3/21*

* Márton Csapodi: PhD student, Pázmány Péter Catholic University, Budapest; junior research fellow, MCC Center for Constitutional Politics, Budapest. The author would like to thank Prof. Balázs Schanda and Kálmán Pócza for their guidance and support.

1 PL. ÚS 5/12.; Danish Supreme Court (Højesteret) Case no. 15/2014; BVerfGE 2 BvR 859/15.

doi: 10.5553/HYIEL/266627012022010001014

decision can be understood as an attempt of resistance against the integrationist role of the CJEU.[2] Even if we cannot speak of a coherent process, this series of *ultra vires* judgments is certainly spectacular, considering that this kind of resistance was previously completely unheard of. Although the resistance of the Czech and Polish Constitutional Courts or the Danish high court could have been seen as isolated cases, the *PSPP* decision of the *Bundesverfassungsgericht* raises the possibility that other constitutional courts may follow suit.[3] Of course, when national constitutional resistance emerges, its form and rationale may differ, nevertheless is possible that the underlying problems are intrinsic features of the system.

The case-law of the CJEU and the doctrines it has developed (in particular the principles of direct effect and primacy) have played a prominent role in the creation of the 'ever closer union', the current integrated legal system of the EU.[4] The preliminary reference procedure has played a crucial role in this process, in the framework of which the CJEU has developed intensive and mutually beneficial relations with the lower courts of the Member States.[5] The relationship between the CJEU and the constitutional courts of Member States, on the other hand, is not always amicable and is sometimes embittered by two interlocking problems. *(i)* First, the preliminary reference procedure can be used by ordinary courts to challenge the practice of the constitutional courts and, *in extremis*, even to question their role in the constitutional system, all with the CJEU's assistance.[6] *(ii)* Secondly, the control and delimitation of powers of the EU

2 Trybunał Konstytucyjny K 3/21.

3 Arthur Dyevre, 'Domestic Judicial Defiance in the European Union: A Systemic Threat to the Authority of EU Law?', *Yearbook of European Law*, Vol. 35, Issue 1, 2016, pp. 4-5. *Cf.* Arthur Dyevre, 'How Europe's legal equilibrium unraveled', at www.arthurdyevre.org/2020/05/19/how-europes-legal-equilibrium-unraveled/. About the PSPP decision, *see e.g.* Robert Böttner, 'The First Ever Ultra Vires Judgment of the German Federal Constitutional Court: PSPP – Will the Barking Dog Bite More Than Once', *Hungarian Yearbook of International Law and European Law*, Vol. 9, 2021, pp. 168-192; Maria Kordeva, 'The PSPP Judgment of the German Federal Constitutional Court – The Judge's Theatre According to Karlsruhe', *Hungarian Yearbook of International Law and European Law*, Vol. 9, 2021, pp. 193-211.

4 Joseph H. H. Weiler 'The Transformation of Europe', *The Yale Law Journal*, Vol. 100, Issue 8, 1991, pp. 2413-2418; Alec Stone Sweet, *The Judicial Construction of Europe*, Oxford University Press, New York, 2004, p. 53; Jean-Michel Josselin & Alain Marciano, 'How the court made a federation of the EU', *Review of International Organizations*, Vol. 2, Issue 1, 2007, pp. 67-73; Anne-Marie Burley & Walter Mattli, 'Europe Before the Court: A Political Theory of Legal Integration', *International Organizations*, Vol. 47, Issue 1, 1993, pp. 41-42.

5 Luigi Corrias, *The Passivity of Law – Competence and Constitution in the European Court of Justice*. Springer, New York, 2011, p. 15; Karen J. Alter, *The European Courts Political Power: Selected Essays*, Oxford University Press, New York, 2009, p. 32; Morten Broberg & Niels Fenger, *Broberg and Fenger on Preliminary References to the European Court of Justice*, 3rd edition, Oxford University Press, New York, 2021, p. 2; Ernő Várnay, 'Az Európai Bíróság és az aktivizmus délibábja', *Állam- és Jogtudomány*, Vol. 58, Issue 2, 2017, p. 94.

6 Michal Bobek, 'The Impact of the European Mandate of Ordinary Courts on the Position of Constitutional Courts', *in* Monica Claes *et al.* (eds.), *Constitutional Conversations in Europe*, Intersentia, Mortsel, 2012, pp. 291-292; Jan Komárek, 'National constitutional courts in the European constitutional democracy', *International Journal of Constitutional Law*, Vol. 12, Issue 3, 2014, pp. 526-528.

doi: 10.5553/HYIEL/266627012022010001014

institutions (including the CJEU) is sought by both the Luxembourg court and the national constitutional courts reserving their right of *ultra vires* review (competence-problem).[7]

The prevalence of these problems is well illustrated by the responses given by the Czech and Polish Constitutional Courts to the *Landtová* and *A.B. and others* decisions.[8] In both cases, the supreme administrative court made a preliminary reference with the aim of challenging the practice or decision of the national constitutional court. In both cases, the CJEU was open to furthering this initiative.[9] The Czech Constitutional Court, defending its own reputation, declared the CJEU's judgment *ultra vires*, stating that it overstepped the powers conferred on the EU by the Czech Constitution.[10] The Polish Constitutional Court did not rule on the applicability of the specific CJEU judgment, but on the relationship between EU law and the Constitution in the context of an abstract constitutional interpretation upon the Prime Minister's motion. However, the Polish Constitutional Court made very clear that it did not consider the CJEU's

7 Joseph H. H. Weiler & Ulrich R. Haltern, 'The Autonomy of the Community Legal Order – Through the Looking Glass', *Harvard International Law Journal,* Vol. 37, 1996, pp. 445-446. *Cf.* Theodor Schilling, 'The Autonomy of the Community Legal Order: An Analysis off Possible Foundations', *Harvard International Law Journal,* Vol. 37, 1996, pp. 406-407; Takis Tridimas, 'The ECJ and National Courts – Dialogue, Cooperation and Instability', *in* Anthony Arnull & Damian Chalmers (eds.), *The Oxford Handbook on European Union Law,* Oxford University Press, New York, 2015, pp. 417-419.

8 Judgment of 22 June 2011, *Case C-399/09, Landtová*, ECLI:EU:C:2011:415; Judgment of 2 March 2021, *Case C-824/18, A.B. and others*, ECLI:EU:C:2021:153

9 In *Landtová*, the CJEU has ruled that the practice of the Czech Constitutional Court regarding the so-called Slovak pensions is discriminatory and contrary to EU law. Judgment of 22 June 2011, *Case C-399/09, Landtová*, ECLI:EU:C:2011:415, paras. 41-54. In the Polish case, the question is more complex: the CJEU ruled that the referring court can continue to exercise its jurisdiction, which has been terminated by an 'amendment' of national law. It should be added that the legal provision on which the jurisdiction was based has been repealed by the Polish Constitutional Court. Judgment of 2 March 2021, *Case C-824/18, A.B. and others*, ECLI:EU:C:2021:153, paras. 26, and 71. More recently, the CJEU reached a similar conclusion in the Romanian *Euro Box* case. It stated that the primacy of EU law precludes "national rules or a national practice under which national ordinary courts are bound by the decisions of the national constitutional court and cannot, by virtue of that fact and without committing a disciplinary offence, disapply, on their own authority, the case-law established in those decisions, even though they are of the view, in the light of a judgment of the Court of Justice, that that case-law is contrary to" the law of the EU. Judgment of 21 December 2021, *Case C-357/19, Euro Box Promotion and Others*, ECLI:EU:C:2021:1034, para. 262.

10 Ústavni soud PL. ÚS 5/12.

doi: 10.5553/HYIEL/266627012022010001014

judgment and the judicial development of European integration to be compatible with Poland's sovereignty.[11]

Although the displacement of constitutional courts and the conflict of jurisdiction, both separately and together, may pose a serious challenge to the proper functioning of the rule of law, the EU does not have an adequate response. In response to the German *PSPP ruling*, the European Commission launched infringement proceedings. The proceedings were due to end in December 2021, when the new German government promised the Commission that it would do everything to ensure that such judgments would not be taken by the Constitutional Court in the future. If they keep their promise, it will be most regrettable, representing a painful blow to the principle of the separation of powers.[12]

Recently, some have expressed concerns about the jurisprudence of the CJEU, calling *e.g.* for national constitutional resistance or institutional reforms.[13] However, the possible reform of the Luxembourg court has been a topic of academic debate for decades and there have also been political proposals from the Member States.[14] This paper aims to summarize reform proposals that could offer some solution to the problems described above. These include a reverse preliminary ruling procedure, limiting the preliminary reference right to higher courts, a political control mechanism for the jurisdictional review of CJEU judgments, and the establishment of a new court or chamber for competence review. Naturally, this paper does not aim to cover all existing proposals. It is also important to note that the ideas presented here are in part very general, sometimes lacking important details and leaving many questions open. In what follows, I critically assess these reform proposals and make some suggestions towards reconciliation by ensuring that Member States' constitutional concerns are properly addressed at EU level.

11 "Article 1, first and second paragraphs, in conjunction with Article 4(3) of the Treaty on European Union – insofar as the European Union, established by equal and sovereign states, creates 'an ever closer union among the peoples of Europe', the integration of whom – happening on the basis of EU law and through the interpretation of EU law by the Court of Justice of the European Union – enters 'a new stage' in which: *a)* the European Union authorities act outside the scope of the competences conferred upon them by the Republic of Poland in the Treaties; *b)* the Constitution is not the supreme law of the Republic of Poland, which takes precedence as regards its binding force and application; *c)* the Republic of Poland may not function as a sovereign and democratic state – is inconsistent with Article 2, Article 8 and Article 90(1) of the Constitution of the Republic of Poland." Trybunał Konstytucyjny K 3/21.

12 *See* Márton Sulyok, 'Is This Loyalty In Fact Disloyalty? On the Remarks of the German Government to the Commission after PSPP', *Constitutional Discourse,* 12 January 2022, at www.constitutionaldiscourse.com/post/marton-sulyok-is-this-loyalty-in-fact-disloyalty.

13 Roman Herzog & Lüder Gerken, 'Stop the European Court of Justice', *EUobserver,* 10 September 2008, at https://euobserver.com/opinion/26714; Agustín José Menéndez, 'The Existential Crisis of the European Union', *German Law Journal,* Vol. 14, Issue 5, 2013, pp. 525-526; Jan Komárek, 'National constitutional courts in the European constitutional democracy: A rejoinder', *International Journal of Constitutional Law,* Vol. 15, Issue 3, 2017, p. 825.

14 Alter 2009, pp. 129-130.

doi: 10.5553/HYIEL/266627012022010001014

2. Reversing the Preliminary Reference Procedure

2.1. Making Two-Way Traffic Compulsory

According to Christoph Grabenwarter *et al.*, in order for their relationship to be a two-way traffic rather than just a one-way street, the CJEU should be obliged to refer a question to the national constitutional court for constitutional interpretation, when the case enters the sphere of national identity.[15] This way, the CJEU and the respective constitutional court would reach a joint conclusion, while at the same time taking decisions of binding force as independent courts.[16] Without invoking the concept of a reverse preliminary reference, the Hungarian Constitutional Court's *Decision No. 2/2019. (III. 5.) AB* also reflects the idea of harmonizing independent binding decisions. The authentic interpretation of the Constitutional Court cannot be impaired by any other body (including the CJEU), and the acting judicial fora must take into account each other's authentic interpretations.[17]

Considering the fact that the CJEU does not show openness to involve constitutional courts in the judicial process in cases concerning national constitutional identity, and that the treaties do not explicitly oblige the CJEU to do so, Grabenwarter *et al.* propose a treaty amendment. This would add an Article 267a to Article 267 TFEU, which would oblige the CJEU to refer a question to the competent constitutional court for a preliminary ruling when a case potentially affects the concept of national identity enshrined in Article 4 TEU.[18]

Other authors also argue that a reverse preliminary reference procedure would be in line with the bottom-up legitimacy structure of the EU and would also allow constitutional courts to regain their position in the national judicial hierarchy (and the position they would deserve in the European judicial system), that had been eroded by lower courts taking recourse to the preliminary reference procedure.[19]

15 Christoph Grabenwarter *et al.*, 'The Role of the Constitutional Courts in the European Judicial Network', *European Public Law*, Vol. 27, Issue 1, 2021, p. 51.

16 According to Grabenwarter *et al.*, a further advantage would be that the reverse preliminary reference procedure would better integrate the CJEU into the EU system of checks and balances.

17 Decision No. 2/2019. (III. 5.) AB, Reasoning [37]-[38]. About the decision, *see e.g.* Marcel Szabó, 'Practical Questions Concerning the Relationship Between a Member State's Constitution, EU Law and the Case-Law of the CJEU. Decision No. 2/2019. (III. 5.) AB of the Constitutional Court of Hungary', *Hungarian Yearbook of International Law and European Law*, Vol. 8, Issue 1, 2020, pp. 383-392.

18 They add that there are certainly other ways to involve the constitutional courts, and they also argue that the constitutional courts could at least be involved as interveners in cases involving constitutional identity, similarly to the European Commission or national governments in any case.

19 Denis Preshova, *On the Rise while Falling – The New Roles of Constitutional Courts in the Era of European Integration*, Inaugural-Dissertation zur Erlangung der Doktorwürde einer Hohen Rechtswissenschaftlichen Fakultät der Universität zu Köln, 2019, pp. 157-158.

doi: 10.5553/HYIEL/266627012022010001014

2.2. *The Significance of Having the First Say*

The purpose of the reverse preliminary reference procedure is that the substance of national identity can thus be fleshed out by the constitutional courts, upon request of the CJEU. This will, however, give much more importance to the 'right of the first word' than to the 'right of the final say'. The CJEU can decide for itself which issues fall within the scope of national identity and then require a reverse preliminary reference. The effect is that, although the constitutional courts would have the final say on national identity, it is the CJEU that would determine which issues involve national identity at all. In effect, this renders the procedure itself pointless. The above proposal is therefore unlikely to achieve its objective without some additional mechanism that would allow constitutional courts to determine not only the substance of national identity in the questions asked by the CJEU, but also to determine which questions fall under the national identity clause.

3. Involving the High Courts through the Exclusion of Lower Courts

3.1. *Limitation of Preliminary Reference Rights to High Courts*

Jasaron Bajwa proposes that, as a general rule, only national courts of last instance should be authorized to refer preliminary questions to the CJEU. He would make three exceptions: *(i)* a lower court must refer a case for a preliminary ruling if it finds that EU law is unlawful or invalid; *(ii)* a lower court can refer a case for a preliminary ruling if it can show that its inability to interpret a provision of EU law reaches a level that it renders the court unable to rule on the case in a reasonable way; *(iii)* a court of appeal must refer a case for a preliminary ruling if it reaches a different conclusion on the interpretation of EU law than the lower court.[20]

3.2. *Exceptions to the Limitation – What Would Change?*

The author justifies the first exception by arguing that it follows from the practice of the CJEU that national courts cannot decide on the invalidity of EU law, yet lower courts cannot be expected to apply EU law despite their conviction of its invalidity.[21]

Under the second exception, the lower court would have to show that its doubts regarding the interpretation are so serious that it is unable to decide the case – and the CJEU would obviously decide whether to admit the question.[22] However, this exception would in fact render the whole proposal pointless. The author also argues that the CJEU simply distrust the application of EU law by ordinary courts and prefers to keep it under as close scrutiny as possible. In this situation, it is difficult to imagine a scenario in which the CJEU, faced with the uncertainties of a national court, would not decide the question of interpretation itself, but would conclude that the doubts raised are not serious enough, and that

20 Jasaron Bajwa, '"Grow Up!": Rethinking the Preliminary Reference Procedure from the Perspective of Maturity', *LSE Law Review*, Vol. 6, Issue 2, 2020, p. 93.

21 Id.

22 Id.

doi: 10.5553/HYIEL/266627012022010001014

the national court could then decide the question. The exact opposite is likely to happen: the CJEU would in fact accept any question that would fall within the scope of this exception rule. It should also be borne in mind that the lower courts frequently make preliminary references, and it is conceivable that with this exception rule the restriction would only serve to turn even minor difficulties of interpretation into serious, undecidable questions for them. Although I cannot provide a comprehensive European analysis of this issue, such a solution does not exist in the Hungarian judicial system either: the judge decides the case even if his interpretation is uncertain, and if his decision is wrong, the appellate forum has an opportunity to course-correct.

The third exception is also based on interpretative uncertainty: according to the author, it can be assumed that the interpretation causes serious problems for national courts if they reach conflicting conclusions in the interpretation of EU law, and therefore the intervention of the CJEU is immediately necessary. However, the conclusion is overreaching: the presence of two conflicting interpretations does not mean that the task of interpretation is intolerably difficult. It can mean that at least one of the two interpretations is wrong, but two different interpretations may be correct in a legal system, depending on the circumstances of the case.[23] A lower court's incorrect interpretation may occur even if the correct interpretation, based on the CJEU's case law, has already been adopted by the courts. This exception rule is therefore contrary to the purpose of the proposal, as it could allow for a preliminary reference even in clear-cut situations.

On the whole, it may be concluded that the author's proposal would not result in a significant change in the current system due to the application of the last two exceptions. It is important to point out that the preliminary references in the *Landtová* and *A.B. and others* cases, which led to the conflict between the constitutional courts and the CJEU, were made by courts of last instance. It would therefore not in itself solve the problem if only supreme/constitutional courts could initiate preliminary reference procedures. It seems, it is the question asked, not the court who asks, that is of decisive nature.

4. A Political Override Mechanism to Curb the CJEU

4.1. Giving the Final Say to the Masters of the Treaty

Fritz W. Scharpf believes that the European Council is an institution whose members are both sensitive to the problems caused by the implementation of European law in the Member States and to *e.g.* the dangers of protectionist national measures. More importantly, he says, the members of the European Council are in fact the 'masters of the treaties' and are therefore best placed to determine whether the CJEU is interpreting EU law in a way that is more expansive than intended. Scharpf argued in 2009 that there was a lack of political

23 This is well illustrated in the Hungarian case law by the BH 2013.276. "The existence of two possibly conflicting decisions of lower courts does not justify the lack of unity of the case-law as a whole on a given law."

doi: 10.5553/HYIEL/266627012022010001014

will to adopt a reform that would require treaty change, but this could change in the event of open opposition from a Member State – an event that would strike at the very foundations of the EU legal system, as the latter relies heavily on voluntary compliance.[24] Scharpf argued that it would be more appropriate if *ultra vires* complaints were not simply declared by a Member State, but they would be addressed to the European Council, with the promise that in the event of confirmation of the CJEU's judgment by a simple majority of the European Council, the complainant Member State would fully implement the judgment. He added that such a procedure would, on the one hand, absolve the Member State concerned from any accusation of disloyalty to the EU and, on the other hand, the potential political veto alone would encourage the CJEU to take into account the possible interests of Member States in the process of delivering judgments.[25]

4.1. Dangers of Political Override

Scharpf's proposal offers a practical solution with a number of arguments to consider. While a court can always develop rigid, rock-solid doctrines on competences, a political settlement mechanism may be able to offer a more flexible, adaptable solution. A criticism of Scharpf's proposal may be that it offers a political response to a legal dispute or that it makes the decision of the highest legal forum overridable for political reasons. However, the division of competences between Member States and the EU is also a political issue, and it is not unknown in different constitutional systems for the *e.g.* the legislature as a political actor to be able to override the highest legal forums decision.[26] It is not inconceivable, therefore, that the masters of the Treaty should have a say in the interpretation of competences.

The question is to what extent the constitutional basis of European integration can be ignored. The transfer of powers from a Member State to the EU is of constitutional nature. The jurisprudence of the CJEU has very quickly moved beyond the limits set by the contracting parties. Without going into detail, it can be said that what the practice of the CJEU stands for in relation to certain doctrines (*e.g.* the primacy principle) is accepted only with reservations by many Member States. Thus, some of the jurisprudention 'inventions' of the CJEU reaching beyond the treaties may be embraced by the majority of Member States, but not entirely by the rest. Bearing this in mind, Scharpf's proposal can be viewed from both an optimistic and a pessimistic perspective. Optimistically, this proposal means that a simple majority of European Heads of State and Government could decide that the mandate given to the CJEU has been exceeded. But from a pessimistic perspective, it could also mean that a simple majority of European Heads of State or Government could decide that a doctrine of the

24 Fritz W. Scharpf, 'Legitimacy in the multilevel European polity', *European Political Science Review*, Vol. 1, Issue 2, 2009, pp. 198-200.

25 Id. p. 200.

26 For instance, in Canada, the legislature can override the court's decision, after the latter repeals a law. *See* Kálmán Pócza, 'Többségi demokrácia és gyenge alkotmánybíráskodás: egy elszalasztott lehetőség', *in* Fruzsina Gárdos-Orosz & Zoltán Szente (eds.), *Jog és politika határán – Alkotmánybíráskodás Magyarországon 2010 után*, HVG-ORAC, Budapest, 2015, pp. 200-201.

doi: 10.5553/HYIEL/266627012022010001014

CJEU, that goes beyond the Treaty framework should be accepted as if it had been laid down in the Treaty through the consensus of all Member States. Also, the proposed procedure entails the risk that the vote on jurisdictional and competence issues may be subject to political bargaining on quite different matters.

5. A Special Court for Competence Review

5.1. A Constitutional Council for Europe

In 1995, Joseph Weiler *et al.* proposed the creation of an EU court specialized in competence matters, which would give a binding interpretation of the Treaty on the question of competence.[27]

In 1995, Weiler argued that the problem of competences could be solved in the long term through the creation of an EU Constitutional Council (modeled on the French namesake), which would deal with specific competence issues, including subsidiarity. This forum would decide on the quasi-constitutionality of any European legal act even before it enters into force (*i.e.* whether it exceeds the competences laid down in the Treaty). The review process could be initiated by any EU institution (including the European Parliament, with a majority of votes) or by any Member State. The Constitutional Council would be composed of delegated judges from the national constitutional courts (or equivalent high courts) and chaired by the current President of the CJEU. Member States would not have veto power and its composition would, according to Weiler, also symbolize that, although the settlement of competences is a matter of national constitutional arrangements, it should be subject to an EU solution. He argues that the Constitutional Council, which he believes would enjoy far greater public confidence than the CJEU, could protect the integrity of EU law by channeling problems and conflicts surrounding competences.[28]

5.2. New Proposal: a Mixed Grand Chamber

Interestingly, a quarter of a century later, Weiler would propose a different composition for the court that decides on EU competences. By declaring a CJEU judgment *ultra vires* in the *PSPP* case, the *Bundesverfassungsgericht* has apparently turned the tide of academic opinion against itself.[29] This is also true of Weiler, who, maintaining that if more constitutional courts follow this example, the integrated legal system, the rule of law, and the single market will all be lost, believes that *ultra vires* rulings should be avoided at all costs. To that end, Weiler and Daniel Sarmiento have yet again proposed the creation of a judicial forum

27 Joseph H. H. Weiler *et al.*, 'European Democracy and its Critique – Five Uneasy Pieces', *Florence: European University Institute Working Paper*, 1995/11, p. 43; *See also* Weiler & Haltern 1996, pp. 447-448.

28 Joseph H. H. Weiler *et al.*, 'European Democracy and its Critique', *West European Politics*, Vol. 18, Issue 3, 1995, p. 38.

29 *See e.g.* Pavlos Eleftheriadis, 'Germany's Failing Court', *Verfassungsblog*, 18 May 2020, at https://verfassungsblog.de/germanys-failing-court/.

that would decide on competence conflicts between the EU and the Member States.[30] This forum would operate strictly within the institutional framework of the CJEU, more specifically the Grand Chamber. The composition they put forward is the following: six judges of the CJEU, six constitutional judges from a constitutional court of a Member State according to a pre-defined order, and the President of the CJEU as the President of the panel (but no judge who was involved in the original CJEU judgment). The new body, to be known as the Mixed Grand Chamber, would have the power to annul EU acts (including judgments of the CJEU) that constitute a *serious breach* of conferred competences. They argue that if all the constitutional judges on the panel believe that the challenged act is *ultra vires*, it would be inappropriate for it to be adopted by seven judges of the CJEU, and therefore they would prefer a vote of eight or nine judges to validate an EU act from the point of view of competences. The review could be initiated by national constitutional courts, supreme courts, or even governments and parliaments, within one year of a CJEU judgment validating an EU act under scrutiny becoming final. The President of the court (or Member State) with which the appeal is lodged would participate in the Mixed Grand Chamber's section for national constitutional judges, otherwise, the national delegates would sit in a rotational order. In addition, Member States and EU institutions would be allowed to intervene.[31]

Important differences can be outlined between Weiler's 1995 Constitutional Council blueprint and his 2020 Mixed Grand Chamber proposal. At first glance, the most striking is the question of composition: while the Constitutional Council would have been composed of only the national judges of the Member States (aside from the President), the Mixed Grand Chamber, which already refers to the composition in its name, would be composed of a larger proportion of European judges. Although the proposal explicitly states that it would not be a good solution if the Luxembourg judges were to decide the issue alone, the difference is still striking, since in this case, it would be sufficient for one or two constitutional judges to vote with the European judges. While the Constitutional Council is described as having the distinctive function of *ex ante* review of European norms, the Mixed Grand Chamber, although not precisely delineated, is described as a

30 Joseph H. H. Weiler & Daniel Sarmiento, 'The EU Judiciary After Weiss: Proposing A New Mixed Chamber of the Court of Justice', *EU Law Live*, 1 June 2021, at https://eulawlive.com/op-ed-the-eu-judiciary-after-weiss-proposing-a-new-mixed-chamber-of-the-court-of-justice-by-daniel-sarmiento-and-j-h-h-weiler/#.

31 The proposal also includes minor additions, such as the idea that hearings should be broadcast live for transparency, or that the dissenting opinions should not be made public (but should be made public if the re-election of judges is excluded). On the issue of dissenting opinions, Roland Vaubel notes that, in the case of the CJEU, making public which judge voted which way in a case may encourage judges to take due account of national interests. They would then not only be biased towards the EU, but also to some extent towards the Member States, but he says the aim is not to make judges more biased, but not to make them biased at all. He himself suggests that the judges of the CJEU should be chosen from among the judges of the constitutional courts/ higher courts of the Member States. *See* Roland Vaubel, *The European Institutions as an Interest Group – The Dynamics of Ever-Closer Union*, The Institute of Economic Affairs, London, 2009, p. 80.

doi: 10.5553/HYIEL/266627012022010001014

forum for ex-post review. While the Constitutional Council could decide on the validity of all legal acts (and thus certainly on the validity of CJEU judgments), the Mixed Grand Chamber would only examine European norms that have been validated by the CJEU after they had been challenged. This probably implies that before the Mixed Grand Chamber, judgments of the CJEU could not be challenged in general, but merely other European legal acts validated by the CJEU. In the case of the Constitutional Council, it is explicitly mentioned that the application of the subsidiarity principle would also be a task in connection with questions of competence, but in the case of the Mixed Grand Chamber, this is no longer explicitly mentioned by Weiler.[32] He does, however, explicitly mention that, in his view, the Mixed Grand Chamber should not repeal or declare inapplicable all EU acts that exceed the conferred competences, but only those that would constitute a serious infringement.

5.3. A "Sequential Model" to Soften the Mixed Grand Chamber

Władysław Jóźwicki would add to Weiler and Sarmiento's proposal, as he believes that the mere fact that an EU legislative act infringes the national identity of one (or more) Member State(s) does not justify a prohibition of its use in every other Member State. In such cases, therefore, the review forum should not declare an EU legal act completely inapplicable because of the constitutional identity of one Member State but should merely exempt that Member State from its obligation to apply it. According to Jóźwicki, this would not mean that the EU act in question would lose its harmonizing function. This solution, which he calls the 'sequential model', is only inapplicable if not applying it in one Member State is incompatible with the purpose of the EU legal act in question. In this case, the court has two options: either annul the challenged EU act or uphold it (in the latter case still at the risk of opposition from the national constitutional court).[33]

32 Nevertheless, it can be assumed that the Mixed Grand Chamber would also have jurisdiction to interpret the principle of subsidiarity, as this is inseparable from competence disputes.

33 Władysław Jóźwicki, 'Ultra vires and constitutional identity control – apples and oranges or two drops of water? Some remarks on the possible role of the New Mixed Chamber of the Court of Justice in the context of the "sequential" model of adjudication on art. 4(2) TEU', *Verfassungsblog*, 15 June 2020, at https://verfassungsblog.de/ultra-vires-and-constitutional-identity-control-apples-and-oranges-or-two-drops-of-water/. In a somewhat similar vein, Oliver Garner also proposes the use of the preliminary reference procedure. Here, the constitutional courts would have to make a second preliminary reference after an unfavorable judgment of the CJEU, and the CJEU could then reconsider its previous decision. If it does not reconsider, then legislative methods would have to be used to resolve the conflict. Oliver Garner, 'Squaring the PSPP Circle: How a 'declaration of incompatibility' can reconcile the supremacy of EU law with respect for national constitutional identity', *Verfassungsblog*, 22 May 2020, at https://verfassungsblog.de/squaring-the-pspp-circle/. What is somewhat overlooked is that the CJEU does not necessarily pay enough attention to answering the questions of the constitutional courts, and its answers are not sufficiently thorough. *See* Grabenwarter *et al.* 2021, p. 58. Maduro draws attention to the same point. Miguel Poiares Maduro, 'Some Preliminary Remarks on the PSPP Decision of the German Constitutional Court', *Verfassungsblog*, 6 May 2020, at https://verfassungsblog.de/some-preliminary-remarks-on-the-pspp-decision-of-the-german-constitutional-court/.

doi: 10.5553/HYIEL/266627012022010001014

5.4. Advocates of the Neglected Subsidiarity Principle

The establishment of a court for competence review has also been suggested by other authors.[34] Although most of the proposals are either not detailed in this respect or would adopt a similar solution as Weiler in terms of organization and composition, interestingly, the proposed review forum is mostly referred to as a "subsidiarity court".[35] This points to a fundamental conceptual difference: subsidiarity court proposals tend to emphasize that the case law of the CJEU is constantly expanding and overstepping EU competences, with the Court being biased towards the EU institutions in its judgments, with a tendency to depart from *e.g.* the subsidiarity principle. The subsidiarity court is thus explicitly called upon to uphold the principle of subsidiarity in competence disputes, a task for which its own name will always be a reminder. By contrast, Weiler's Constitutional Council or Mixed Grand Chamber is not functionally intended to defend subsidiarity, but only to settle potential conflicts and to avoid situations of open non-compliance.[36]

6. Considerations for a Subsidiarity Court

The key question surrounding the proposals to set up a judicial forum for competence review is, of course, whether they can achieve the desired result. The aim is twofold: *(i)* to avoid the proliferation of *ultra vires* judgments endangering the integrated European legal system; *(ii)* to bring the CJEU's activism under control and to give greater weight to the principle of subsidiarity in EU case-law.

The first goal can be achieved through the competence review court but cannot be guaranteed. The existence of such a court would not in itself change the fact that the EU system of competences is based on the principle of conferral: integration clauses would therefore remain a legal 'bridge' through which national constitutional courts could claim to guard over the competences. Ultimately, *ultra*

34 Herzog & Gerken 2008; As early as 1993, Vaubel *et al.* as the European Constitutional Group proposed, for example, the creation of a separate court for competence review in a possible European constitution. *See* Roland Vaubel, 'Constitutional courts as promoters of political centralization: lessons for the European Court of Justice', *European Journal of Law and Economics*, Vol. 28, Issue 3, 2009, p. 218.

35 Pieter Cleppe, 'An EU Subsidiarity Court as a means to keep the ECJ in check', *BrusselsReport.eu*, 1 February 2016, at www.brusselsreport.eu/2016/02/01/an-eu-subsidiarity-court-as-a-means-to-keep-the-ecj-in-check/; Vaubel 2009, pp. 80-81; Lars P. Feld, 'The European constitution project from the perspective of constitutional political economy', *Public Choice*, Vol. 122, Issue 3-4, 2005, p. 440; Peter Kurrild-Klitgaard, 'The constitutional dilemma of European integration', *MPRA Paper*, No. 35437, 1998, at https://mpra.ub.uni-muenchen.de/35437/1/MPRA_paper_35437.pdf, p. 16; Steven Blockmans *et al.*, 'From Subsidiarity to Better EU Governance: A Practical Reform Agenda for the EU', *CEPS Essay*, No. 10, 2014, at https://papers.ssrn.com/sol3/papers.cfm?abstract_id=2429252, p. 10.

36 Weiler himself stresses that it is not that the review is needed because the CJEU's practice takes away national powers or erodes the authority of national constitutional courts, but that the creation of a review forum would be useful to avoid open non-compliance to CJEU rulings, and an ensuing collapse of the EU legal system, which he thinks would be the result of *ultra vires* judgments. *See* Weiler & Sarmiento 2020.

doi: 10.5553/HYIEL/266627012022010001014

vires control could only be ruled out if the treaty explicitly excluded it. However, if it did, Member States would lose control over the remaining part of their sovereign statehood – which would be contrary to the purpose of the proposal. Whether the establishment of a competence review court will indeed minimize the likelihood of *ultra vires* decisions depends only on the seriousness with which this forum takes the task entrusted to it. The fulfillment of the first of the two objectives of the proposal therefore depends on the extent to which the second is fulfilled, *i.e.* how effectively it can safeguard the Member States' perspective and the principle of subsidiarity in matters of competence.

In Weiler's Mixed Grand Chamber proposal, the CJEU, the supranational level, and the national constitutional courts, the national level, are in fact equal forces. This design gives the impression of a dispute settlement forum where the collective will of the Member States and the will of an EU institution are almost equally balanced. The court that would determine the competences should reflect the will of the Member States, not a compromise between the Member States as a whole and an EU institution that cherishes the dream of an ever closer integration. Such a court should therefore have room only for delegates from the Member States.[37] Indeed, it is worth considering that such an institution could be called a Subsidiarity Court, ensuring that the principle of subsidiarity is not lost sight of. It would also be essential for this Subsidiarity Court to have the right to review all EU legal acts at the request of a Member State or an EU institution – not only legislative acts but also judgments of the CJEU. As the CJEU has been a flagship institution in the process of integration, there is no reason to exempt its activities from under constitutional scrutiny in these terms.

It is also important to avoid the concern that the review process could in fact become a mere instrument to strengthen the activism of the CJEU if a simple majority is sufficient for validation. Of course, unanimity cannot be expected, nor is it appropriate for two or three closely cooperating Member States to be able to block EU adjudication. The right balance could be found between the two, for example by relying on the analogy of qualified majority voting (and the blocking minority) in the Council of the EU. For example, if a Member State (or a national constitutional court) considers an act of an EU institution (*e.g.* a judgment of the CJEU) to be *ultra vires*, a blocking minority of the members of the Subsidiarity Court would be sufficient to repeal the EU act in question.[38] Accordingly, the consensus of members of the court representing more than 35% of the EU population plus one member could repeal a legislative act or CJEU judgment.

It is clear that this Subsidiarity Court would differ significantly from the conventional concept of adjudication both in its composition and in its decision-

37 It could be of symbolic importance if the President of the CJEU could be present at the review court, maybe even presiding, but there is no reason to give them voting rights. It could also mean that, if Member States disagree on whether a particular competence has been conferred on the EU, the question could be decided by a vote of the President of the CJEU in favor of a 'yes' answer, whereas conceptually, in case of doubt, a 'no' answer would be appropriate.

38 Article 238(3)(a) TFEU: "A blocking minority must include at least the minimum number of Council members representing more than 35% of the population of the participating Member States, plus one member, failing which the qualified majority shall be deemed attained."

doi: 10.5553/HYIEL/266627012022010001014

making process. It should not be seen strictly as an EU constitutional court but as the highest forum of judicial dialogue defending the constitutional perspective of the Member States. The Subsidiarity Court could be an institution of high legitimacy, with members who are perfectly aware of the importance of the uniform application and enforcement of EU law, yet it is their loyalty to the national constitutional systems that ultimately influences their decision-making.

7. A Supplementary Mechanism to the Preliminary Reference Procedure

As Jan Komárek pointed out, the separate treatment of issues falling within the scope of constitutional law is of particular importance in preserving the role of constitutional courts.[39] Therefore the issue of primary importance is whether a question referred to the CJEU by an ordinary court enters the *'domaine réservé'* of the constitutional court, that of constitutional adjudication and interpretation. A solution to the problem, that national constitutional courts are left out of the European constitutional dialogue, could be found if questions of a constitutional nature were to be raised by the constitutional courts.

In this context, I suggest distinguishing three categories. The first category is where a preliminary reference of an ordinary court raises the question of whether the constitutional court's decision is compatible with EU law. The second category is where the preliminary reference concerns the interpretation of EU primary law. The third category would include questions concerning the interpretation of secondary law which is also reflected in primary law or otherwise has constitutional relevance.[40] I propose that the preliminary reference procedure could be restructured in a way that the questions raised, if they are of constitutional relevance (as outlined above), would enter the European scene through the constitutional courts. More precisely, this would mean that all questions raised by lower courts would reach the CJEU, but the references would first go through the constitutional court. It would be at the discretion of the constitutional court to decide whether the question raised falls into one of the three categories above. If it falls outside these categories, it would simply forward the question to the CJEU unchanged. If it finds that the question falls within the three categories, it would have the opportunity (but not an obligation) to supplement the referral with its own views within a specified time limit, drawing attention to the specific features of the constitutional system and its own views, to which the CJEU would be subsequently obliged to respond in substance. This procedure is designed to ensure that the constitutional courts are not left out of the decision-making process on constitutional questions and that the CJEU cannot establish doctrines concerning the relationship between EU law and national law without giving serious consideration to national constitutional aspects in the process. Ultimately, if this mechanism fails to lead to consensus, the constitutional court could turn to the Subsidiarity Court as outlined above.

39 Komárek 2017, p. 825.

40 The prohibition of discrimination, for example, appears in secondary law and also in the Charter.

doi: 10.5553/HYIEL/266627012022010001014

8. Summary and Conclusions

Several authors have concluded that a comprehensive institutional reform of the relationship between the CJEU and the constitutional courts is needed, and some have proposed reforms accordingly. This paper started with briefly reviewing the reasons why a reform of the CJEU may be needed, with particular attention to the fact that national constitutional resistance to the CJEU seems to occur with increasing frequency. Aiming to provide concise but thorough summaries, I presented some of the institutional reform proposals that have appeared in the academic discourse and expressed some concerns about these ideas. Perhaps the proposal for a new court specialized in competence issues is the most popular idea. I arrived at the conclusion that a Subsidiarity Court specialized in competence issues could be an effective instrument for a better representation of national constitutional perspectives at EU level, which would be essential, if open non-compliance is to be avoided. I also proposed a complementary mechanism to the preliminary ruling procedure, which would allow constitutional courts to participate in the European constitutional dialogue. Together, these solutions could ensure that national constitutional aspects are sufficiently taken into account at European level, providing an institutionalized system of prevention and reconciliation.

Of course, a crucial issue is whether an institutional reform of the CJEU is politically feasible? An analysis of the attitudes and possible intentions of Member States and various political actors is, of course, not possible here. But in general, the reform of the CJEU is not on the European political agenda. However, this does not mean that there would be an absolute lack of political will to reform the CJEU. The proposals described above would require an amendment of the Treaties, which would need the support of all Member States. The likelihood of a Treaty amendment is very low: hitherto, all efforts to this end have failed.[41] Nevertheless, as Roman Herzog has put it, in terms of protection of national interests and subsidiarity, the CJEU is not up to the task of being the last instance forum.[42] Therefore, Member States should seek a more suitable solution.

41 Alter 2009, pp. 129-130.

42 Herzog & Gerken 2008.

doi: 10.5553/HYIEL/266627012022010001014

DEVELOPMENTS IN INTERNATIONAL LAW

One Hundred Years of International Copyright

*Anett Pogácsás**

Abstract

The Berne Convention (BC or Convention) celebrates its one hundred and thirty-sixth birthday this year, but for Hungary, 2022 marks a milestone anniversary, as the country joined the BC exactly a hundred years ago. Considerations taken into account at the time of becoming a party to the Convention, and the circumstances now, a century later, are in many ways different. An important question is whether the Convention still conforms to our sense of justice. For Hungary in the early 1900s, this dilemma was effectively a matter of weighing up the principle of formality-free protection. Originally required as a corrective rule in BC, automatic protection has grown into a fundamental principle since then. It was to be expected from the outset that the principle would not only have its benefits, but also its side effects. One hundred years of international copyright has taught us to insist on what BC has earned for right holders, but to strive for BC-compatible, efficient and modern solutions. How far we can go in doing so will be one of the most important questions of the near future.

Keywords: Berne Convention, revision, copyright, formalities, legal certainty.

"It is only to be wished that the Berne Convention continues to flourish and further expand as a most efficient basis of up-to-date implementation of the protection of authors' rights on a worldwide scale." (György Boytha)[1]

1. Introduction

International treaties are of paramount importance in narrowing the gap between countries' different speeds of development. This is a very complex task since different countries face different problems, they have divergent goals and efforts, therefore, the Berne Convention (BC or Convention), dealing with the protection of literary and artistic works and the rights of their authors,[2] could only attempt

* Anett Pogácsás: associate professor of law, Pázmány Péter Catholic University, Budapest; member of the Hungarian Council of Copyright Experts.

1 György Boytha, 'The Berne Convention and the Socialist Countries with Particular Reference to Hungary', *Columbia-VLA Journal of Law & the Arts*, Vol. 11, Issue 1, 1986, pp. 57-72.

2 Berne Convention for the Protection of Literary and Artistic Works, 9 September 1886.

doi: 10.5553/HYIEL/266627012022010001015

to define common principles and set minimum standards. But these principles have been of great value to copyright law and therefore, to the entire creative sector.

> "What is the reason for which governments give rights to authors that allow them to derive material benefits from the use of their works by others and make any unauthorized distribution of their works illegal? And, what is the reason for which countries are ready to undertake the obligation, as they do under the Berne Convention, to give such rights to foreigners?"[3]

As the Hungarian-born Árpád Bogsch,[4] former Director General of World Intellectual Property Organization (WIPO) stated in response to his own questions above, it is believed that the underlying reason is *a sense of justice*.[5] The Berne Convention celebrates its one hundred and thirty-sixth birthday this year, but for Hungary, 2022 marks a milestone anniversary, as it joined the BC exactly a hundred years ago. Considerations taken into account at the time of becoming a party to the Convention, and the circumstances now, a century later, are in many ways different. A valid question is whether Berne Convention still conforms to our sense of justice.

2. Pros and Pressures

2.1. International Difficulties

It is well-known that it has been a bumpy road towards the Berne Convention's worldwide acceptance. As Sam Ricketson pointed out in 1986, the birth of the BC can be seen as a manifestation of a period when human society was attempting, in a *high-minded but practical* spirit, to bring about change and development across a whole range of matters through international cooperation.[6] The whole Berne Union, of course, served as the *focal point* "for the comparison, confrontation and, if possible, reconciliation of the official policies of the various countries in matters of international copyright relations."[7]

One of the biggest dichotomies was on the question of formalities. Under the original text of the Berne Convention, authors who are subjects or citizens of any of the countries of the Union shall enjoy in the other countries for their works the rights which the respective laws do grant to their own nationals. And the enjoyment of these rights shall be subject to the accomplishment of the

3 Árpád Bogsch, *The First Hundred Years of the Berne Convention for the Protection of Literary and Artistic Works*, International Bureau of Intellectual Property, Geneva, 1986, p. 5.
4 Árpád Bogsch was born in Hungary in 1919, and was the Director General of WIPO from 1973 to 1997. The WIPO main building in Geneva was named after him (Árpád Bogsch Building) out of respect for him.
5 Bogsch 1986, p. 5.
6 Sam Ricketson, 'The Birth of the Berne Union', *Columbia-VLA Journal of Law & the Arts*, Vol. 11, Issue 1, 1986, pp. 9-32.
7 Árpád Bogsch, 'Opening Speech of Arpad Bogsch at the Conference Celebrating the Centenary of the Berne Covention', *Columbia-VLA Journal of Law & the Arts*, Vol. 11, Issue 1, 1986, p. 5.

doi: 10.5553/HYIEL/266627012022010001015

conditions and formalities prescribed by law in the country of origin of the work.[8] This meant that among the countries of the Union, foreign authors were treated equally to domestic authors, moreover, they could even be in a better position than domestic authors if their national laws do not prescribe any formalities. Later on, *automatic protection* was worded differently, namely that the extent of protection shall be governed exclusively by the laws of the country where protection is claimed.[9] This rule was clearly directed against the Anglo-American registration system, but this restriction was not an end in itself. The BC established a system of equal treatment of foreign right holders with own nationals, which is maybe the most important rule of the Convention, yet under this rule, the level of protection depends on the law of the country affording the protection. This formal equality can conceal a profound inequality: a country that applies formal reciprocity with the US protects the works of a US citizen author free of any formalities (as a matter of fact of creation) under its own rules, while its own authors can only obtain protection in the US if they have complied with the costly and burdensome formalities required there.[10] For this reason, beside the principle of equal treatment with own nationals the principle of informality is a kind of *corrective rule*, similarly to the minimum standards for the substance of the protection to be granted by the countries of the Union.[11]

The BC has steadily developed and strengthened international copyright law, but the Universal Copyright Convention (UCC), established under the auspices of the UN, caused some initial confusion and stalling. The different needs of developing countries and the resistance of the US, including on the issue of formalities,[12] led to the launch of this competing international cooperation.[13] The UCC offered a kind of compromise between the high level of automatic protection typical of the European *droit d'auteur* system and those Anglo-American countries where "where copyright is viewed as a privilege obtainable only upon compliance with certain statutory formalities."[14] However, it later became clear that the UCC

8 BC (1886), Article 2.

9 BC (1908), Article 4(2).

10 István Tímár, 'Nemzetközi egyezmény-rendszerek', *in* Aurél Benárd & István Tímár (eds.), *A szerzői jog kézikönyve*, Budapest, 1973, pp. 382-383.

11 Id.

12 This topic has been widely discussed in scientific literature, and remains so today. As Michael L. Lovitz summed up in 1989, there were five major and nine minor areas in US copyright that were in conflict with the BC (differences in notice requirements and other formalities, recognition of moral rights, retroactivity, duration, jukebox license and other points of concern). *See* Michael L. Lovitz, 'Copyright Protection in the United States: It's All Berned Up', *Temple International and Comparative Law Journal*, Vol. 3, Issue 1, 1989, pp. 38-43.

13 Tímár 1973, p. 389.

14 Hamish R. Sandison, 'The Berne Convention and the Universal Copyright Convention: The American Experience', *Columbia-VLA Journal of Law & the Arts*, Vol. 11, Issue 1, 1986, pp. 89-90.

doi: 10.5553/HYIEL/266627012022010001015

was more of a stepping stone for US law in the direction of the Berne Convention,[15] a 'bridge', rather than an alternative to it.[16]

Despite the detour, the BC ended up having a major impact on US copyright law.[17] Eliminating copyright formalities prescribed by the Berne Convention represented the most significant barrier to adherence to the Convention.[18] In 1989, after the US also become a signatory, some authors stated that the price of Berne membership was relatively low.[19] However, its copyright system is often criticized for not fully complying with the principle of protection without formalities. As David R. Carducci emphasizes, "unfortunately, though the relaxation of formalities was a goal of the current Copyright Act, certain formalities remain."[20] Although registration is not a condition of copyright protection,[21] copyrights are not self-enforcing, copyright owners must act to guarantee their exclusive rights. In cases where this rule affects foreign right holders, under the BC's rules on formality, a pre-suit obligation on foreign copyrighted works is precluded.[22] A recent court decision has also made it clear that this rule is also applicable if a work is published on a foreign website accessible also in the US,[23] since this kind of 'simultaneous publication' does not make the work a 'United States work', therefore it is not subject to the US registration formality. As Jane Ginsburg put it, this was an – albeit unsuccessful – attempt to extend the pre-suit registration requirement to foreign works first published on a non-US website.[24] In this case the US District Court, D. Delaware emphasized that

> "[If] such publication transformed the work into a United States work, plaintiff would be subjected to the very formalities that the Berne

15 Eric Stenshoel, 'From Berne to Madrid and Beyond: The road to international copyright and trademark protection in the United States', *Entertainment, Arts and Sports Law Journal*, Vol. 24, Issue 1, 2013, p. 2.

16 Carol A. Motyka, 'Effects of U.S. Adherence to the Berne Convention', *Rutgers Computer & Technology Law Journal*, Vol. 16, Issue 1, 1990, p. 201.

17 David M. Spector, 'Implications of United States Adherence to the Berne Convention', *AIPLA Quarterly Journal*, Vol. 17, 1989, pp. 100-121.

18 Richard J. Inglis, 'The United States Legislates Its Way into Berne', *Suffolk Transnational Law Journal*, Vol. 13, Issue 1, 1989, p. 282.

19 Id. p. 315. "Congress introduced a two tier approach to the provision governing registration as a prerequisite to an infringement suit which maintained previous law as applied to United States citizens and eased requirements for foreign nationals."

20 David R. Carducci, 'Copyright Registration: Why the U.S. Should Berne the Registration Requirement', *Georgia State University Law Review*, Vol. 36, Issue 3, 2020, p. 873.

21 17 US Code § 408 – Copyright registration in general. *(a)* Registration Permissive "[...] the owner of copyright or of any exclusive right in the work may obtain registration of the copyright claim by delivering to the Copyright Office the deposit specified by this section, together with the application and fee specified by sections 409 and 708. Such registration is not a condition of copyright protection."

22 17 US Code § 101, § 411

23 *Moberg v 33T LLC et al.*, Civil No. 08-625(NLH)(JS) (D. Del. 6 October 2009).

24 Jane C. Ginsburg, 'The US Experience with Copyright Formalities: A Love/Hate Relationship', *Columbia Journal of Law & the Arts*, Vol. 33, Issue 4, 2010, p. 311.

doi: 10.5553/HYIEL/266627012022010001015

> Convention eschews. To hold otherwise would require an artist to survey all the copyright laws throughout the world, determine what requirements exist as preconditions to suits in those countries should one of its citizens infringe on the artist's rights, and comply with those formalities, all prior to posting any copyrighted image on the Internet. The Berne Convention was formed, in part, to prevent exactly this result."[25]

Stepping back in time again to the beginning of the Convention's history, some of the countries, not unlike Hungary, faced exactly the same problem when considering accession to the BC.

2.2. Hungarian Dilemmas

For Hungary, accession to BC was a long process, mainly because of historical circumstances and adversities, analyzed and discussed in detail by Péter Munkácsi in his recent essay.[26] As Jose Bellido recalls, there was no common framework – neither on the global level, nor in Europe – legally or philosophically, therefore each country had specific political and legal ambitions.[27]

In this paper, however, I would like to focus on the impact of the principle of automatic protection for foreigners, and one particular aspect of that was significant for Hungarians, among many other countries, in terms of accession to the BC.

It is the fourth copyright act that is currently in force in Hungary.[28] The first Hungarian copyright act came into force on 1 July 1884, which is a particularly important date because the first diplomatic conference of the BC began shortly afterwards, on 8 September 1884. No wonder the Hungarian position was quite clear:

> "the Hungarian government has come to the realization, on the basis of its completely new legislation, that the country's cultural characteristics do not allow foreigners' works, especially their translations, to enjoy more extensive protection in general than that granted to its citizens by Hungarian law, and has therefore refused to participate in the conference."[29]

25 *Moberg v 33T LLC et al.*, p. 14. The court notes in a footnote to this statement that "[a]ll informed intellectual property regimes recognize that unduly complicated protection prerequisites are likely to chill artistic expression."

26 Péter Munkácsi, 'Stuck in a Waltz: The Austro-Hungarian Monarchy and Its Imperial Approach to the Berne Convention', *in* P. Sean Morris (ed.), *Intellectual Property and the Law of Nations, 1860-1920*, Brill, Nijhoff, 2022.

27 Jose Bellido, 'Colonial Copyright Extensions: Spain at the Berne Convention (1883-1899)', *Journal of the Copyright Society of the USA*, Vol. 58, Issue 2, 2010-2011, p. 264.

28 Act LXXVI of 1999 on Copyright.

29 The words of Emil Steinbach, who was one of the Austro-Hungarian ministerial advisers with voting rights at the conference. Cited by Péter Munkácsi, 'Osztrák-Magyar Monarchia, Ausztria, Magyarország: csatlakozás a Berni Egyezményhez?', *in* Anett Pogácsás (ed.), *"Intellectual Creations in the Service of Mankind": Study Volume of the Memorial Conference in Honor of Professor Dr. Levente Tattay*, Pázmány Press, Budapest, 2022, p. 176.

doi: 10.5553/HYIEL/266627012022010001015

This completely new legislation stipulated that the translation of an original work without the author's consent shall be considered an infringement of copyright, if the author has retained the right of translation on the title page or at the beginning of the original work, provided that the publication of the translation had begun within one year of the publication of the original and completed within three years. Protection shall cease in respect of languages for which translation had not begun within the first year.[30] At the diplomatic conference it became clear that one of the main aims of the proposed convention is to ensure that the enjoyment of the rights should be subject to the accomplishment of the conditions and formalities prescribed by law in the country of origin of the work.[31] The problem was similar to the US one mentioned above, namely that foreign authors shall not simply be treated equally, but they may have been in a more favorable position than their own national authors.

According to Article 2(2) BC, to enjoy the exclusive right of translation, authors had to comply with the conditions and formalities laid down for the original work, however, they were exempted from any special formalities which related to exercising the translation right, such as that contained in German law, for example.[32]

Nevertheless, for the sake of completeness, it is also necessary to mention that even contemporaries themselves reported that the Hungarian provisions, inspired by the German model, required "excessive and unjustified formalities" for the validity of copyright.[33] Viktor Ranschburg, for example, was of the opinion that it will therefore be in our own interest, in the event of accession to the Berne Convention, to free our law of those formalities, which were introduced in order to reduce the protection afforded to foreign authors.

> "Indeed, our law, modelled on the now obsolete German law, requires excessive and unjustified formalities for the validity of copyright, formalities which make the protection given by the law almost illusory, especially with regard to the right of translation."[34]

While some authors argued that it would be in our own interest to abolish domestic formalities in the event of accession to the Convention, others thought that accession could be risky for Hungarian authors. As Eva Hemmungs Wirtén put it, referring to Sweden, the rationales of so-called user-nations and the strategies and responses deployed by 'minor' languages[35] have put the issue of

30 Act XVI of 1884 on Copyright, Section 7(3).

31 Article 2 BC (1886).

32 Louis Renault, 'Report Presented on Behalf of the Committee by the French Delegation', *in* Árpád Bogsch (ed.), *The First Hundred Years of the Berne Convention for the Protection of Literary and Artistic Works*, International Bureau of Intellectual Property, Geneva, 1986, p. 139.

33 Viktor Ranschburg, *A szerzői jog nemzetközi védelmére alkotott Berni Egyezmény, vonatkozással Magyarországra*, Eggenberger-féle Könyvkereskedés, Budapest, 1901, p. 44.

34 Id.

35 Eva Hemmungs Wirtén 'A Diplomatic Salto Mortale: Translation Trouble in Berne, 1884-1886', *Book History*, Vol. 14, Issue 1, 2011, p. 90.

doi: 10.5553/HYIEL/266627012022010001015

translation and formalities in a different light. Also in the Hungarian scientific literature, some authors made a precise attempt to weigh up the economic consequences of making translation more expensive, particularly in the light of the fact that domestic literature was less important in terms of exports.[36] Based on our position in international literature, they did not hope to benefit from accession, but feared its impact on Hungarian culture and cultural economy. In order to ensure not only formal reciprocity, but also a situation corresponding to material reciprocity, *i.e.* where countries concerned apply the same substantive law in relation to each other,[37] Hungary had no interest in maintaining its rules on formality. Finally, the issue was decided for Hungary on rather pressing grounds. The Treaty of Trianon, which concluded World War I, signed by representatives of Hungary on the one side and the Allied Powers on the other, also contained obligations for accession to the Berne Convention.[38] However, as Péter Munkácsi recalled the statements made in the National Assembly in 1921, although we were obliged to join this Union within twelve months of the entry into force of the Treaty of Trianon, our accession was not based on the peace treaty. Because there was an intention to join long before the world war, it was not real pressure, but it rather happened under the influence of the fact that we had a great deal of interest to do so. Take, for example, the enthusiastic words of Viktor Ranschburg from 1901:

> "We do not believe that the Hungarian government and legislature can permanently refrain from imposing the principles of equity and justice of the Berne Convention, even if it were to be shown that its adoption would entail cultural and economic sacrifices."[39]

It was strongly emphasized by contemporaries that we were entering the Union of our own free will.[40] Although there were opponents to accession, it was a more

36 Péter Munkácsi & Zoltán Kiss, 'Magyarország 1922-es csatlakozása a Berni Egyezményhez', *in* Anett Pogácsás (ed.), *Quaerendo et Creando, Ünnepi kötet Tattay Levente 70. születésnapja alkalmából*, Szent István Társulat, Budapest, 2014, pp. 285-308.

37 György Boytha, 'Reciprocity in International Copyright Law', *in* György Haraszti (ed.), *Questions of International Law*, Hungarian Branch of the International Law Association, Budapest, 1968, p. 42.

38 Treaty of Trianon (Treaty of Peace between the Allied and Associated Powers and Hungary), Versailles on 4 June 1920, Article 222: "Hungary undertakes, within twelve months of the coming into force of the present Treaty, to adhere in the prescribed form to the International Convention of Berne of September 9, 1886, for the protection of literary and artistic works, revised at Berlin on November 13, 1908, and completed by the Additional Protocol signed at Berne on March 20, 1914, relating to the protection of literary and artistic works. Until her adherence, Hungary undertakes to recognize and protect by effective measures and in accordance with the principles of the said Convention the literary and artistic works of nationals of the Allied and Associated Powers. In addition, and irrespective of the above-mentioned adherence, Hungary undertakes to continue to assure such recognition and such protection to all literary and artistic works of the nationals of each of the Allied and Associated Powers to an extent at least as great as upon July 28, 1914, and upon the same conditions."

39 Ranschburg 1901, p. 22.

40 Munkácsi & Kiss 2014, p. 305.

doi: 10.5553/HYIEL/266627012022010001015

pronounced position that we can "safely accept this agreement based on mutual equity, without any fear that our statehood or our culture will be harmed in any way."[41] A hundred years on, it is worth wondering whether we could still make this statement with the same confidence and calm.

3. 'Resilient Character'

The inherent stability of a hard-achieved international treaty is a success in itself. It has been repeatedly pointed out that the BC has remained intact through all the political and economic upheavals that had taken place since its creation.[42] As Peter Burger put it very aptly,

> "the Berne Union has developed its own resilient character – a character that has helped it overcome conflicts caused by different copyright philosophies and different levels of economic development. This resilience has given the Union the strength to survive two world wars, the development of new technologies, and the pressures of decolonization. Through all of these changes, the Union has continued to further its goal of increasing international copyright protection."[43]

On the one hand, therefore, its resilience is a huge advantage. It attempted to serve both the authors and the interests of the public by resisting "the occasional temptation to adopt opportunistic solutions"[44] for more than a hundred years. The main question, however, is which of the proposed solutions would be opportunistic, which would be harmful in the long term, and which are the situations where change is needed to meet the original purpose of the convention. The BC has undergone a number of substantial revisions and modernizations since its birth, and this is why most of the authors evaluated its first hundred years as a success story, in which it served both the authors and the interests of the public. Even Árpád Bogsch emphasized that from its rudimentary provisions at the very beginning (the original text from 1886), the BC has become, "through its several revisions during the century, a detailed and refined legal instrument that obliges the Member States to provide for a protection of a high level."[45] Between 1886 and 1967[46] there were several topics that did not prove to be too opportunistic reasons for amendment. Then, more than half of our Berne Union membership has passed without the BC changing. Yet these last fifty-plus years have not exactly been uneventful, especially as far as the

41 Ranschburg 1901, p. 44.

42 *See e.g.* Jack Black & Gerald Dworkin, 'Foreword', *Columbia-VLA Journal of Law & the Arts*, Vol. 11, Issue 1, 1986, pp. 1-2.

43 Peter Burger, 'The Berne Convention: Its History and Its Key Role in the Future', *Journal of Law and Technology*, Vol. 3, Issue 1, 1988, p. 1.

44 Bogsch 1986, p. 5.

45 Id.

46 Revised at Stockholm on 14 July 1967, and concluded at Paris on 24 July 1971.

doi: 10.5553/HYIEL/266627012022010001015

technological background of the copyright industry and the creator-user relationship are concerned.

The original text of the BC itself provided that the Convention may be submitted to revisions for the purpose of introducing amendments therein intended *to perfect* the system of the Union.[47] The current text also provides that the Convention shall be submitted to revision with a view to introduce amendments designed *to improve* the system of the Union.[48] It seems that while there is a strong need for continuous improvement in international copyright, the BC has indeed proven to be resilient – mostly to time and change. Some authors argue that this *unchangeability* must be seen as the true merit of the Convention, since if a revision of the Berne Convention was to take place in our day, it is clear from the current political and economic pressures that the interests of the authors would be sacrificed.[49]

The question is whether this advantage outweighs the drawbacks of immutability, or, ultimately, the authors themselves will be adversely affected.

4. The Next Hundred Years

As Peter Burger underlined in his paper from 1988, the BC must remain true to its original goal, which means that it must continue to focus on the protection of authors.[50] This protection can be best achieved through the principle of national treatment, at least "until a common substantive law will have been created."[51] As we pointed out earlier, the principle of automatic protection, *i.e.* that protection does not require any formalities or notifications, was created precisely 'to correct' the principle of national treatment. In his opening speech at the centenary celebrations[52] of the Convention, Numa Droz also raised the question of formalities to be complied with for the recognition of rights. As he emphasized, writers and artists are demanding the utmost simplification in this connection, because if an author has to comply with the formalities of registration and deposit in each country in order to obtain protection, the whole operation becomes overly intricate and costly. However, he also expressed the belief that if a work is once duly secured in the country of origin, it can without any difficulty be

47 Article 17 BC (1886), which also stated that questions of this kind, as well as those which are of interest to the Union in other respects, shall be considered in Conferences to be held successively in the countries of the Union by delegates of the said countries.

48 Article 27 BC (1979).

49 Georges Koumantos, 'The Future of Berne Convention', *Columbia-VLA Journal of Law & the Arts*, Vol. 11, Issue 1, 1986, p. 236.

50 Burger 1988, p. 1.

51 György Boytha, *Selected Essays of György Boytha*, Gondolat, Budapest, 2014, p. 316.

52 This ceremony took place in *Stationers' Hall*, which was the very place in which Registry of published books was established. The Statute of Anne made the register book at the Stationers' Company the official record of book authors' ownership, and it also created a right for anyone to search the register book and obtain a certificate of entry, or proof of copyright registration. *See* in details Edward L. Carter, '"Entered at Stationers' Hall": The British Copyright Registrations for the Book of Mormon in 1841 and the Doctrine and Covenants in 1845', *Brigham Young University Studies*, Vol. 50, Issue 2, 2011, p. 79.

doi: 10.5553/HYIEL/266627012022010001015

accepted as being valid in all the other countries. "You will determine, Gentlemen, whether it is possible to accede to this desire which, for my part, I consider to be a legitimate one."[53]

During its first hundred years, automatic protection has been cemented into a *fundamental principle*, backed by important considerations such as the need for uncensored protection, artistic freedom and the personal nature of the relationship between authors and their works.[54] The natural law concept of copyright has let us forget the pragmatic roots of the prohibition on formalities, prioritizing other benefits. It is therefore no longer sufficient, when examining whether the prohibition is still necessary, to look at whether a change in the circumstances existing at the time of the Convention's conclusion still justifies this legal instrument. Today, the question is more about how to make the copyright system effective in the framework of the existing international rules, which have not changed for a long time.

4.1. And What About Efficiency?

Although the rules laid down in the BC are almost 'untouchable', international copyright law is very much alive. The principles of the Convention have been 'carried forward' by other legal instruments (*e.g.* TRIPS Agreement[55] or WCT,[56] and the legal sources of the EU[57]) over the last century.

According to its preface, the countries of the Berne Union, "being equally animated by the desire to protect, in as effective and uniform a manner as possible, the rights of authors in their literary and artistic works."[58] The vast majority of the world accordingly considers it to be a starting point, a governing convention. Only in 2022 two new member states joined this Union – Cambodia in March, and Uganda in April –, bringing the total number of contracting parties

53 Bogsch 1986, p. 88.

54 Stef van Gompel, *Formalities in Copyright Law. An Analysis of their History, Rationales and Possible Future*, Wolters Kluwer, Amsterdam, 2011, p. 283.

55 Agreement on Trade-Related Aspects of Intellectual Property Rights, Annex 1C of the Marrakesh Agreement Establishing the World Trade Organization, signed in Marrakesh, Morocco on 15 April 1994.

Article 9 [Relation to the Berne Convention] "1. Members shall comply with Articles 1 through 21 of the Berne Convention (1971) and the Appendix thereto. However, Members shall not have rights or obligations under this Agreement in respect of the rights conferred under Article 6*bis* of that Convention or of the rights derived therefrom."

56 WIPO Copyright Treaty (WCT) adopted in Geneva on 20 December 1996, Article 1 [Relation to the Berne Convention]: "(1) This Treaty is a special agreement within the meaning of Article 20 of the Berne Convention for the Protection of Literary and Artistic Works, as regards Contracting Parties that are countries of the Union established by that Convention. This Treaty shall not have any connection with treaties other than the Berne Convention, nor shall it prejudice any rights and obligations under any other treaties. (2) Nothing in this Treaty shall derogate from existing obligations that Contracting Parties have to each other under the Berne Convention for the Protection of Literary and Artistic Works."

57 The EU is not a party to the Berne Convention, nevertheless obliged under Article 1(4) of the WIPO Copyright Treaty, to which it is a party, to comply with Articles 1 to 21 of the Berne Convention.

58 BC (1979), Preface.

doi: 10.5553/HYIEL/266627012022010001015

to 181. Their reasons for joining are obviously different from the reasons Hungary had, one hundred years ago. Since then, the factors to be taken into account have changed, and the stakeholder structure has become very complex. Nevertheless, it is still a fact that Hungarian authors (and other right holders) are working (creating works) in a relatively small country, using a unique language. These factors are still decisive for their role in the international cultural market. It can be a major challenge to help authors effectively in today's context in the framework of a convention that has been 'entrenched' for a hundred – or at least fifty – years.

The stability and universality of the Convention is in itself a value that is indispensable for the protection of authors' rights, and its importance is stressed in the literature even if the protection could be more effective under today's circumstances. "The advent of digital technology has rejuvenated the formalities debate, which has been rather well settled in the international community following the United States' accession to the Berne Convention."[59] But this debate is not all about whether to eliminate the principle of automatic protection, other options have also been raised.

Although BC contracting states are allowed to impose formalities on domestic works,[60] as Stef van Gompel stressed, from an international point of view, reintroducing copyright formalities limited to domestic works would have a "fairly marginal impact."[61] He argues however, that in the digital era the no-formalities rule no longer appears to be necessary to guarantee an efficient protection of copyright at the international level.[62] Instead, he considers a uniform formality rule to be effective. But considering the possibilities for change from the perspective of international law, it is not surprising that many scholars and experts have tended to focus on developing BC-compatible solutions. These ideas seek to increase the effectiveness of regulation by leaving the hard-won common ground intact.

Some authors argue that recordation of transfers (back to the original author) can be desirable and a Berne-permissible solution,[63] others assert that any formality that focuses on varying available remedies can also be defended as Berne-compliant.[64] We also find authors who argue that 'new-style formalities' could be the solution, providing the filtering and information-creation benefits of traditional formalities, but leaving behind the bureaucratic difficulties of 'old-

59 Peter K. Yu, 'Tales of the Unintended in Copyright Law', *Studies in Law, Politics, and Society*, Vol. 67, Issue 1, 2015, p. 14.

60 Rebecca Giblin, 'A Future of International Copyright? Berne and the Front Door Out', *in* Graeme Austin *et al.* (eds.), *Across Intellectual Property: Essays in Honour of Sam Ricketson*, Cambridge University Press, Cambridge, 2020, p. 127.

61 Gompel 2011, p. 291.

62 Id. p. 292.

63 Daniel Gervais & Dashiell Renaud, 'The Future of United States Copyright Formalities: Why We Should Prioritize Recordation, and How To Do It', *Berkeley Technology Law Journal*, Vol. 28, Issue 3, 2013, p. 1496; Daniel J. Gervais, *(Re)structuring Copyright: A Comprehensive Path to International Copyright Reform*, Edward Elgar Publishing, Cheltenham-Northampton, 2019.

64 Christopher Jon Sprigman, 'Berne's Vanishing Ban on Formalities', *Berkeley Technology Law Journal*, Vol. 28, Issue 3, 2013, p. 1581.

doi: 10.5553/HYIEL/266627012022010001015

style formalities'.[65] The voluntary use of the benefits of formality is also considered by some authors as a viable option.[66]

According to scientific literature, there is a growing conviction that, although there is little chance of revising the BC in the near future, we may not need to, as its rules are flexible enough to allow us to find *alternative solutions compatible with the BC*.[67]

4.2. The Future of Formality-free Protection

The future of formality-free protection is also a good indicator of the future of international copyright law and copyright harmonization. There are also less optimistic views on the latter issue. Clark D. Asay is of the opinion that although copyright harmonization had been the norm between Europe and the US for decades, currently this process is stalled, because "copyright's once predictable international political economy has splintered with new technological entrants."[68] But he takes the view that the EU Copyright Directive can be a good example of one of the possible ways forward, namely, as covert harmonization efforts disguised as go-it-alone copyright law and policy-making. Which means that these kind of significant legal sources may have a harmonization effect, as other countries apply similar rules and adapt to them without being bound by international law.[69]

But the CJEU also seems to consider the no-formality rule of the BC in a 'flexible' way. In *VG Bild-Kunst* the CJEU emphasized, referring to *Soulier and Doke,*[70] that in a situation where an author gives *prior, explicit and unqualified* authorization regarding the publication of their articles on the website of a newspaper, *without* making use of technological measures restricting access to that work from other websites, that author may be regarded, in essence, as having authorized the communication of that work to all Internet users. Therefore, by adopting, or by obliging licensees to employ, technological measures limiting access to their works from websites other than that on which they had authorized communication to the public of such works, the copyright holder is *to be deemed to have expressed their intention* to attach qualifications to their authorization to communicate those works to the public by means of the Internet, in order to confine the public in respect those works solely to the users of one particular website.[71] This kind of 'opt-in' solution is necessary "in order to ensure legal

65 Christopher Sprigman, 'Reform(aliz)ing Copyright', *Stanford Law Review*, Vol. 57, Issue 2, 2004, pp. 485-568.

66 Yu 2015, p. 8.

67 Sam Ricketson, 'The International Framework for the Protection of Authors: Bendable Boundaries and Immovable Obstacles', *Columbia Journal of Law & the Arts*, Vol. 41, Issue 2, 2018, p.

68 Clark D. Asay, 'Rethinking Copyright Harmonization', *Indiana Law Journal*, Vol. 96, Issue 4, 2021, p. 1058.

69 Id.

70 Judgment of 16 November 2016, *Case C-301/15, Soulier and Doke,* ECLI:EU:C:2016:878, para. 36 and the cited case law.

71 Judgment of 9 March 2021, *Case C-392/19, VG Bild-Kunst,* ECLI:EU:C:2021:181, paras. 38 and 42.

doi: 10.5553/HYIEL/266627012022010001015

certainty and the smooth functioning of the internet".[72] As Eleonora Rosati draws attention to the fact that the list of prohibited formalities is open-ended. And in this case the CJEU has, not unprecedentedly, chosen the path to consider this kind of 'formality' to be justified by the *objectives to be achieved*.[73]

Mihály Ficsor highlights that Article 10*bis* of the BC[74] itself is a "harmless exception to the principle of formality-free protection."[75] In addition to this particular rule of the BC, it can be concluded that the CJEU also considers certain forms of formality to be compatible with the principle of automatic protection in cases where its application appears not only harmless but also expressly necessary to achieve the objective pursued by the Convention. However, not everyone agrees with this teleological method. Maciaj Szpunar, Advocate General in *VG Bild-Kunst*, warns that

> "the solution of linking the scope of the author's exclusive rights to the application not of technological measures to restrict access but of technological measures to protect against certain practices on the internet would, in my view, push EU copyright in a dangerous direction. Such a solution would in fact mean that the application of technological protection measures would be a prerequisite for the legal protection conferred by copyright and would run counter to the principle that the protection conferred by copyright is unconditional. [...] In my view, it is preferable to delimit with certainty the scope of the author's exclusive rights and to permit opt-out solutions, [...] rather than to transform the copyright system, as far as online uses are concerned, into an opt-in system subject to the application of technological protection measures."[76]

Nevertheless, we can observe that the Member States of the BC and the EU consider solutions that do not conflict with the objectives of the principle of

72 *Case C-392/19, VG Bild-Kunst*, para. 46.

73 Eleonora Rosati, 'Linking and Copyright in the Shade of VG Bild-Kunst', *Common Market Law Review*, Vol. 58, Issue 6, 2021, p. 1875.

74 BC (1979), Article 10*bis* [Further Possible Free Uses of Works: 1. Of certain articles and broadcast works; 2. Of works seen or heard in connection with current events]: "(1) It shall be a matter for legislation in the countries of the Union to permit the reproduction by the press, the broadcasting or the communication to the public by wire of articles published in newspapers or periodicals on current economic, political or religious topics, and of broadcast works of the same character, in cases in which the reproduction, broadcasting or such communication thereof is not expressly reserved. Nevertheless, the source must always be clearly indicated; the legal consequences of a breach of this obligation shall be determined by the legislation of the country where protection is claimed."

75 Mihály Ficsor, *Guide to the Copyright and Related Rights Treaties Administered by WIPO, and Glossary of Copyright and Related Rights Terms*, WIPO, Geneva, 2003, pp. 65-66.

76 Opinion of Advocate General Szpunar Delivered on 10 September 2020, *Case C-392/19, VG Bild-Kunst*, ECLI:EU:C:2020:696, paras. 130-131.

doi: 10.5553/HYIEL/266627012022010001015

formality-free protection to be acceptable, even if they may formally conflict with Article 2 of the BC.[77]

5. 'Suum cuique tribuere'

'May all get their due'. Hundred years ago it was a huge dilemma for Hungary whether the BC would actually be able to fulfil this wish, *i.e.* whether the often mentioned balance between the stakeholders would actually be properly achieved in the event of our accession to the Convention. Will it bring about effective regulation for the domestic creative community, the users and the public? For Hungary in the early 1900s, this dilemma was effectively a matter of weighing up the principle of formality-free protection. Originally required as a corrective rule in the BC, automatic protection has grown into a fundamental principle since then. It was to be expected from the outset that the principle would not only have its benefits, but also its side effects. But the BC rule on regular revisions provided a guarantee that side effects could be avoided by reviewing the effects from time to time.

But the last fifty years have shown that there must be another way to ensure that the Convention continues to serve its purpose in the context of today's demands. There is a need for the BC to be compatible with modern solutions. The only question is where the limits will be for solutions that are still considered 'compatible'.

Many authors, and it seems the CJEU itself, are increasingly focusing on the purpose of the no-formality protection in today's context. As we have seen, it was originally intended to prevent the use of formality as a tool, or loophole against foreign authors. Hungarian authors argued one hundred years ago that our accession is necessary in order to prevent 'being fish in troubled water'.[78] And today, we hear the same argument in favor of possibly introducing formalities.

György Boytha, in his paper on the protection of computer programs, argues that the advantage of copyright protection is that it is instantaneous and immediately available, but the disadvantage is that its existence cannot be proven *a priori*. Either automatic protection or legal certainty. "Everything is not given."[79]

Or could it be done? One hundred years of international copyright has taught us to insist on what the Berne Convention has earned for right holders, but at the same time to strive for BC-compatible, efficient and modern solutions. How far we can go in doing so will be one of the most important questions of the near future.

77 *See also* ALAI Report and Opinion on a Berne-compatible reconciliation of hyperlinking and the communication to the public right on the internet, adopted by the Executive Committee on 17 June 2015.

78 Munkácsi & Kiss 2014, p. 285.

79 Boytha 2014, p. 178.

doi: 10.5553/HYIEL/266627012022010001015

The Human Rights Diplomacy of Regional and Political Groups within the UN Human Rights Council*

*István Lakatos***

Abstract

The article provides a comprehensive picture of the human rights diplomacy of the five most important groups of states (sub-Saharan African states, Asian states, Muslim states, the EU, and Latin American and Caribbean states) in the UN Human Rights Council (UN HRC). This paper intends to debunk the myth that the UN HRC has become a platform for the "clash of civilizations". An analysis of bloc behavior proves that the dividing lines are not between civilizations, but within each group, between governments aiming at establishing a strong global human rights regime and those, seeking to undermine it.

Keywords: UN Human Rights Council, human rights diplomacy, clash of civilizations, regional and political groups, UN HRC.

> *"The ideal subject of totalitarian rule is not the convinced Nazi or the convinced Communist, but people for who the distinction between fact and fiction and the distinction between true and false no longer exist." (Hannah Arendt, German-American philosopher and political theorist)*[1]

1. On Human Rights Diplomacy

Human rights diplomacy has gone through substantial changes since the end of the Cold War, not just in its acceptance, but also its means and participants. Despite the permanent tension that exists between the principle of sovereignty and respect for human rights, human rights issues have become an integral part of a state's foreign policy. The obvious consequence of the collapse of the Berlin Wall was the replacement of the East-West confrontation by conflicts in North-South relations. The political changes at the end of the 80s made the differences between the European approach to human rights and that of the US more visible.

* The opinions expressed herein are strictly personal and do not necessarily reflect the position of the Hungarian MFAT.

** István Lakatos: career diplomat, former human rights ambassador of the Ministry of Foreign Affairs and Trade of Hungary, current senior adviser of the Ministry of Human and Minority Rights of Montenegro.

1 Hannah Arendt, *The Origins of Totalitarianism*, Harcourt, San Diego, 1951, p. 474.

doi: 10.5553/HYIEL/266627012022010001016

Although states remained the most important players in shaping the human rights diplomacy of the international community, in the post-Cold War period new actors appeared, such as civil society and the business community. The role of international organizations has increased since the 90s, as for many states they proved to be much more suitable forums, for both political and economic reasons, to highlight human rights concerns in third countries. The establishment of the position of the UN High Commissioner for Human Rights brought new quality to the international fight against human rights violations. Human rights NGOs have become one of the most important sources of information regarding the human rights situation in the world, while big multinational companies are more and more involved in human rights debates, by realizing their corporate social responsibility in this field. The use of the different means of human rights diplomacy, starting with diplomatic steps, through economic sanctions to the use of military measures very much depends not only on the human rights problems of a given state, but on *realpolitik* considerations, such as the size, and the economic and military power of the given country, not forgetting bilateral diplomatic and trade relations as well.

The last few decades have brought several completely new challenges for mankind, such as the impacts of climate change, environmental degradation, and biodiversity loss, and the development and use of digital technologies, artificial intelligence, and the phenomenon of transnational crime, targeted killings by drones, mass migration, the growing power of multinational corporations, and global inequality. The World Wide Web and social media platforms such as Facebook, Twitter, and YouTube have substantially changed the lives of billions of people around the world, resulting in a more democratic information age, but also allowing dictators and cynical governments to manipulate more people with their massive misinformation campaigns. Addressing the above mentioned new human rights challenges of our globalized age is vital for international human rights diplomacy to remain relevant in the future.

Despite all the controversies surrounding human rights diplomacy, it has become an important reference point in international relations, having a strong legitimizing power. Not surprisingly, according to research based on data collected during the period between 1976 and 2002, regimes with negative human rights records are signing and ratifying international human rights treaties at similar rates to pro-human-rights governments, exploiting the low-cost legitimizing power of ratification in the absence of an effective implementation and monitoring system.[2] Consequently, the international community should focus on reinforcing these mechanisms to make human rights diplomacy more efficient. The importance of the moral and legitimizing power of human rights is also well demonstrated by the fact that many governments are trying to manipulate international human rights diplomacy, by allowing their

2 Emilie M. Hafner-Burton *et al.*, 'International Human Rights Law and the Politics of legitimation', *International Sociology*, Vol. 23, Issue 1, 2008, p. 115.

doi: 10.5553/HYIEL/266627012022010001016

public to hear criticisms of them only from rival powers and not from neutral or friendly states or organizations.[3] As noted by Pease:

> "Human rights and humanitarian diplomacy is not about reaching some Western European social ideal about the relationship of the state to its citizens, but rather constructing a home where everyone can comfortably live while preserving human dignity and respecting cultural differences."[4]

2. About the Most Important Regional and Political Groups within the UN Human Rights Council

This article intends to introduce the main priorities and characteristics of the human rights diplomacy of those regional/cultural/political groups, which are the major actors within the most important intergovernmental human rights body of the UN, namely the HRC. The five groups (the EU, Latin American and Caribbean states, sub-Saharan African states, Asian states, and Muslim states) chosen as the subject of this exploration are not identical to the regional groups working within the UN system [Western European and Others Group (WEOG), Group of Latin America and Caribbean (GRULAC), African Group, Asia-Pacific Group, Eastern-European Group (EEG)] as certain groups, such as the EEG, cannot be considered as a separate entity in this context. In addition, while the states belonging to the Organization of Islamic Cooperation (OIC) share many common elements in their human rights diplomacy, they can be found in three UN regional groups. As a result, sub-Saharan states are considered a separate grouping, while North African states are discussed as part of the group of Muslim states. The EU also forms a particular entity considering its active and sophisticated internal and external human rights diplomacy, even though its members belong to three regional groups within the UN system. Besides the group of Sub-Saharan African states, the Asian-Pacific Group is where certain overlapping with the Muslim states could not be avoided, as Asian Muslim states have certain features in their human rights diplomacy linking them to other Asian states, while others are similar to other Muslim states.

The most appropriate forum to demonstrate the main features of the human rights politics of the five regions selected is the politically most important universal human rights body of our days, the UN Human Rights Council (HRC), which, in 2006, replaced the Commission on Human Rights (CHR) established in 1946. The three 2017 sessions of the HRC are studied in detail; this was the last full year before the preparation of this study started – as part of a doctoral thesis – and therefore all details were readily available. It was also the last year before the COVID-19 pandemic, that the US was still a member of the HRC. In 2018,

3 Jamie J. Gruffydd-Jones, 'Citizens and condemnation: Strategic uses of international human rights pressure in authoritarian states', *Comparative Political Studies*, Vol. 52, Issue 4, 2019, p. 589.

4 Kelly-Kate Pease, *Human Rights and Humanitarian Diplomacy*, Manchester University Press, Manchester, 2016, p. 180.

Hungarian Yearbook of International Law and European Law 2022 (10) 1
doi: 10.5553/HYIEL/266627012022010001016

upon the decision of President Donald Trump, the US delegation resigned from the Council. (It was one of the first decisions by the Biden Administration to re-join the HRC.) Several people may raise the question whether the sections dealing with the 2017-year sessions of the HRC will become obsolete in the short term. It is important to know that about 80% of the HRC resolutions are the same every year and even the content does not change much, so 'unfortunately' the vast majority of the findings for 2017 will not lose their relevance by 2022. However, given the importance of certain developments during the last few years of the HRC, at the end of the article I summarize the new trends appeared during the COVID-19 Pandemic, and compare the voting results of 2017 with the ones of 2021/22 regarding a few important resolutions.

The sequence of the five groups is based on their size, starting with the smallest, the EU (27 in 2017), followed by the Latin American and Caribbean states (33), sub-Saharan African states (46), Asian states (55), and ending with the largest group, the Muslim states (57). This order also follows a logic in the sense that a grouping based on religious belief is aligned with the four geographical regional groups.

3. The EU

The EU has developed a highly sophisticated coordination system at the multilateral human rights forums, where it acts as a unified block, voting together in most cases. However, it may at the same time strengthen the group dynamics in relation to other regional groups, which are in many instances under the influence of states with radical human rights agendas, not allowing smaller, more moderate states to follow their own path. The new members of the EU, mostly from Central and Eastern Europe, belong to the EEG, which serves only technical/electoral purposes. They cannot attend WEOG meetings, which are the main venues of trans-Atlantic human rights policy discussion and cooperation. This collaboration is, however, essential for the success of the EU in the HRC or in the UNGA. Practice has shown that the most sensitive political problems should be solved in Brussels and not in Geneva or in New York. There is no point in pushing for their solution during EU coordination meetings at UN headquarters. Moreover, there are too many EU priorities to be implemented at multilateral human rights forums, like the Third Committee or the HRC sessions. The US, which is a more efficient lobbyist in this field, usually has two to three priorities per session. The EU Delegation (EUDEL) should consult more often and with substantially smaller UN member states than with the large, powerful countries, as they are more likely to become allies in many issues.

The strength of EU external human rights policy lies in its multilayered and multifaceted character. The EU has a wide range of tools at its disposal to influence other states. There is a need to achieve more coherence in coordinating and calibrating these tools to find the best solutions in a given human rights situation, involving the local heads of missions (HOMs) to obtain the optimal outcome. Finally, I should mention the looming effects of BREXIT on the external

doi: 10.5553/HYIEL/266627012022010001016

human rights diplomacy of the EU, as some of the most professional human rights diplomats with an extensive diplomatic network left the EU, seriously diminishing its lobbying force. Regarding the substantial work of the EU, it may have more profound effects on country-specific situations than on thematic issues. The special relationship of the UK with several countries in Africa and Asia was a great asset for the EU; its leverage will be missed in the future during sensitive negotiations or human rights crises. As a result of Brexit, a stronger US-UK cooperation can be predicted, and we cannot exclude the involvement of London in JUSCANZ (Japan, US, Canada, Australia and New Zealand), which would become an even more effective informal information-sharing group. Continued strong cooperation with the UK is needed to minimize the backlash for EU human rights diplomacy. An important consequence of Brexit will be that one of the most vocal internal critics of the EU will disappear from the picture, which may have both positive (smoother EU coordination meetings) and negative effects (diminishing state contribution to the work of EUDEL, including certain controlling elements).

3.1. The Operation of the EU in the HRC under its Current Treaty Framework

The establishment of the EEAS certainly marked a different chapter in the representation of the EU on the UN HRC. The EEAS was considered a strange animal by most of the delegations outside the EU. In 2011, the EUDEL human rights team contained five experts, which was certainly not sufficient to run the show in the HRC, so EUDEL still had to rely on the rotating presidency to carry out its work. In the first few years, many states still considered the EU member states as their key partners and not the EEAS officers, so during this transition period the rotating EU Presidency had an important role to play.

As mentioned above, the entry into force did not automatically change the status of the EU at the UN. In the HRC, the EU enjoys observer status. This means that the EU is not in the position to submit resolutions or to participate actively in their adoption. It can only speak as an observer, after the HRC members. Therefore, the rotating presidency speaks on behalf of the EU in plenary debates and introduces resolutions. The EEAS can only speak on behalf of the EU during the interactive debates with mandate holders, where there is no distinction between members and observers. The other challenge of the representation of the EU in Geneva was that the staff members of the EEAS were recruited from three sources, which required the successful linking of different working methods and working cultures. The fourth challenge was that the EU had to build up its profile and credibility and had to gain the confidence of EU member states and that of third countries. The last challenge was the communication of the human rights policy of the EU. The importance of that was recognized by the appointment of a media officer to EUDEL in mid-2011.

The presence of a permanent EEAS team helped to establish a professional diplomatic leadership during the HRC sessions, but several member states felt it also had a negative effect on the creativity of the EU, as the new ideas and energy

doi: 10.5553/HYIEL/266627012022010001016

brought by each rotating presidency was now missing from the system.[5] However, the very effective burden-sharing system established among member states helps to use the creative energy of the almost 200 human rights diplomats of EU member states present during the HRC sessions. Every human rights resolution on the agenda of the Council is followed by either EUDEL or an EU Member State, which represents the position of the EU during the negotiations and keeps the other delegations in the loop. This is complemented with an organized outreach system in Geneva where EU member states help EUDEL to transmit the EU's messages to the UN missions of HRC member states and observers. The most important political messages are forwarded by démarches to the capitals, mostly by the local EUDELs, but also by EU Member States that have special relations with the country concerned. Experience has shown that the US can be an extremely useful partner in lobbying and that good personal relations can make this cooperation very successful, like it was the case during the review of the HRC's work, or regarding country situations, as was the case with the special session on Libya in 2011. The latter case was the first occasion that the HRC recommended to the UNGA to suspend the membership of an HRC member as a consequence of gross and systematic human rights violations.

As a logical reaction to the decreased voting force of the EU within the HRC, the number of *cross-regional alliances* initiated by the EU has increased. By 2018, a large part of the resolutions was run by cross-regional Core Groups. For example, those initiatives where at least one EU member was part of the main sponsoring cross-regional Core Group during the thirty-seventh session of the HRC in March 2018 included the one *(i)* on the right to privacy (Austria, Germany); *(ii)* on adequate housing (Germany, Finland); *(iii)* on the role of good governance (Poland); *(iv)* on human rights and the environment (Slovenia); *(v)* on persons belonging to national or ethnic, religious and linguistic minorities (Austria, Slovenia); *(vi)* on the right to work (Greece, Romania); *(vii)* on cultural rights (Cyprus, Greece, Ireland, Italy, Poland); *(viii)* on the promotion of human rights through sport (Cyprus, Greece); *(ix)* on the implementation of the 2030 Agenda for Sustainable Development (Denmark, Luxembourg, Portugal); *(x)* on the human rights situation in the Syrian Arab Republic (France, Germany, Italy, UK); *(xi)* on the human rights situation in the Islamic Republic of Iran (Sweden); *(xii)* on the situation of human rights in South Sudan (UK); and *(xiii)* on the world drug problem (Greece, Portugal).[6]

3.2. The Human Rights Diplomacy of the EU in Light of the Main Sessions of the HRC in 2017

It is worth analyzing in detail the three HRC sessions of the year 2017 (being the last full year before the US decided to withdraw from the Council in June 2018) with respect to the resolutions run by the EU or the EU Member States. It gives

5 Hanna Tuulia Tuominen, *The role of the European Union at the United Nations Human Rights Council*, Academic Dissertation, Lund University, 2016, p. 74.

6 Universal Rights Group, Report on the 37th Session of the Human Rights Council, 27 March 2018, at www.universal-rights.org/blog/report-37th-session-human-rights-council/.

also a clear indication that by now, EU Member States are running most of their traditional resolutions by a cross-regional core group, garnering stronger support from among the UN membership.

The EU like in the previous years sponsored four resolutions during the March session (34th session). Two country initiatives were submitted: the "Situation of human rights in the Democratic People's Republic of Korea" (sponsored together with Japan) and the "Situation of human rights in Myanmar". The two traditional thematic resolutions were the ones on the "Freedom of religion or belief" and on the "Rights of the Child: protection of the rights of the child in the implementation of the 2030 Agenda for Sustainable Development" (sponsored together with the GRULAC). All four resolutions were adopted by consensus, without a vote, which should be considered a success for the EU.

It is interesting to note that besides the four EU sponsored resolutions, EU Member States were participated in 11 core groups submitting resolutions to the 34th session of the HRC, but there were only two EU Member States (Denmark and Portugal) running a resolution alone and not by a core group.[7] In this context, we should keep it in mind that two of the resolutions ("Mandate of the special rapporteur on minority issues" – Austria; "Regional arrangements for the promotion and protection of human rights" – Belgium) submitted during this session on behalf of a core group were previously run by a single EU Member State.

During this session, there were four splits within the EU Member States, which were members of the HRC in 2017. Concerning the "Human rights in the Occupied Syrian Golan", which was finally adopted by 26 votes to 3, with 18 abstentions, the UK voted against the resolution, together with the US and Togo, while the other EU Member States abstained. The EU also failed to achieve a consensual position regarding "Ensuring accountability and justice for all violations of international law in the OPT, including East Jerusalem", which was supported by Slovenia, while the other EU member states abstained. *The EU was also divided* on the resolution on "Israeli settlements", as Belgium, Germany, the Netherlands, Portugal, and Slovenia supported it, while Croatia, Hungary, Latvia and the UK abstained during the vote.[8] In conclusion, it may be established that *issues in the Middle East remained the weakest point of EU human rights policy*, as three of the four splits within the EU which occurred during this session were related to resolutions dealing with this region. The resolution on the "Elaboration of International Complementary Standards to the International Convention on the Elimination of all Forms of Racial Discrimination", presented by the African Group was adopted by 31 to 4, with 12 abstentions.[9] This resolution even led to a three-way split within the EU, as Germany and the UK voted against the

7 Universal Rights Group, Report on the 34th Session of the Human Rights Council, pp. 12-15, at www.universal-rights.org/urg-human-rights-council-reports/report-34th-session-human-rights-council/.

8 Report of the Human Rights Council on its 34th Session, A/HRC/34/2, 14 June 2017, pp. 124-127.

9 Id. pp. 133-134.

doi: 10.5553/HYIEL/266627012022010001016

resolution, while Portugal supported it; the other EU HRC members abstained. The majority position of the EU regarding this issue was that the international community should focus on the implementation of the ICERD, as there is no evidence that the Convention is not addressing all contemporary forms of racism, therefore, there is no need for complementary standards at this stage. It did not exclude however, the option of non-legally binding instruments.

The EU like in the previous years sponsored one resolution during the June session (35th session). The traditional EU resolution on the situation of human rights in Belarus was adopted by 18 to 8, with 21 abstentions, which was a little better result than last year (3 more yes votes and 1 less no votes).[10] It was China, which asked for a vote as Russia was not a member of the Council. The resolution had 42 co-sponsors, including the 28 EU Member States.

EU Member States participated in 12 core groups submitting resolutions to the 35th session of the HRC, but similarly to the March session there were only two EU Member States (Sweden and Portugal) running a resolution alone and not by a core group.[11] In this context, we should keep it in mind that three of the resolutions ("Mandate of the special rapporteur on the independence of judges and lawyers", the "Independence and impartiality of the judiciary, jurors and assessors", and the "Independence of lawyers" – Hungary, "Internally displaced persons" – Austria) submitted during this session on behalf of a core group were previously run by a single EU Member State.

During this session the EU could not achieve a common position concerning three resolutions. The resolution on the "Right to peace", submitted by Cuba was adopted by 32 to 11, with 4 abstentions. Portugal abstained, while the other EU Member States voted against the resolution. The EU expressed its position in its explanation of vote, that *there is a lack of legal basis in international law for the existence of the right to peace.*[12] The resolution on the "Enhancement of international cooperation in the field of human rights", submitted by Venezuela on behalf of NAM, was adopted by 32 to 3, with 12 abstentions. From the EU, Hungary voted against the resolution (together with the US and the Republic of Korea) while the other EU Member States abstained. The EU was of the view in its explanation of vote that *the promotion and protection of human rights cannot rely only on the enhancement of international cooperation;* the EU stressed the primary responsibility of states in this regard.[13] The third resolution on the "Protection of the family: role of the family in supporting the protection and promotion of human rights of older persons" was adopted by 30 to 12, with 5 abstentions.[14] The EU Member States voted against the resolution, with the exception of

10 Report of the Human Rights Council on its thirty-fifth session, A/HRC/35/2, 14 June 2017, pp. 59-60.

11 Universal Rights Group, Report on the 35th Session of the Human Rights Council, 2017, pp. 9-12, at www.universal-rights.org/urg-human-rights-council-reports/report-35th-session-human-rights-council/.

12 Report of the Human Rights Council on its thirty-fifth session, A/HRC/35/2, 14 June 2017, pp. 27-28.

13 Id. p. 30.

14 Id. pp. 33-35.

doi: 10.5553/HYIEL/266627012022010001016

Hungary, which abstained during the vote. Before the final vote, the EU introduced an amendment, which would have recognized that in different cultural, political and social systems, various forms of the family exist. This amendment did not receive sufficient support within the Council (19 to 22, with 5 abstentions), therefore the EU could not support this initiative, emphasizing that the resolution put the emphasis on the protection of the family, rather than on the international law obligations of states regarding the protection and promotion of the human rights of individual family members.

During the 36th session of the HRC there were two initiatives on behalf of the EU. *(i)* Estonia presented a resolution on behalf of the EU on the "Renewal of the mandate of the Commission of Inquiry on Burundi", which was finally adopted by 22 to 11 with 14 abstentions.[15] *(ii)* The second initiative put forward by the EU was a short decision in order to extend the mandate of the independent international fact-finding mission on Myanmar.[16] It was the first time that a mandate had been extended by a procedural decision and not by a resolution. The decision was adopted without a vote.

Besides the two EU led initiatives, EU Member States participated in 10 core groups submitting resolutions to the 36th session of the HRC, but there was only one EU Member State (Austria) running a resolution alone and not by a core group.[17] In this context, we should keep in mind that three of the resolutions ("Enforced or involuntary disappearances" – France, "Conscientious objection to military service" – Croatia, "Cooperation with the UN, its representatives and mechanisms in the field of human rights" – Hungary) submitted during this session on behalf of a core group were previously run by a single EU Member State.

The most controversial initiative of the session was submitted by the African Union (AU) entitled "From rhetoric to reality: a global call for concrete action against racism, racial discrimination, xenophobia, and related intolerance."[18] The major difference between the positions of the AU and the EU was that the African states were not willing to delete a reference to the commencement of the negotiations of a new additional protocol on the criminalization of acts of racist and xenophobic nature. The EU asked for a vote and the African resolution was adopted by 32 to 5, with 10 abstentions. The delicate nature of the issue was well demonstrated by the fact that even the EU states were divided and while Germany and the UK rejected the resolution, the other EU Member States of the HRC abstained.

15 Report of the Human Rights Council on its thirty-sixth session, A/HRC/36/2, 2018, pp. 48-49.

16 Id. pp. 49-50.

17 Universal Rights Group, Report on the 36th Session of the Human Rights Council, pp. 12-16, at www.universal-rights.org/urg-human-rights-council-reports/report-36th-session-human-rights-council/.

18 Id. pp. 159-160.

doi: 10.5553/HYIEL/266627012022010001016

4. Latin American and Caribbean States

The particular situation of this region, containing 33 members of the Group of Latin American and Caribbean States (GRULAC) was aptly described by Ted Simon:

> "The Latin American has no tribe to fall back on, as the African does, no reliable judiciary to defend his rights as the European does, no social ideal or sacred constitution as the North American does, no pervasive mythology to soften life as it does in Asia, and not even an ideology to subscribe to, as does the Russian or Chinese. Without wealth, what is there left to him but his manhood, to be flaunted and defended at every occasion?"[19]

In line with Simon's assessment, in the absence of strong traditions, external validation is necessary for any reform project to be successful in the region. The clear orientation of Latin America towards modernity is therefore unsurprising. In his well-known book, entitled 'Latin America. A New Interpretation', Whitehead describes the region as a "mausoleum of modernities."[20]

4.1. The Human Rights Diplomacy of the GRULAC in Light of the Main Sessions of the HRC in 2017

During the 34th session of the UN HRC (held between 27 February and 24 March 2017) there were five resolutions on the human rights situation in the Middle East ("Human rights in Syrian Golan", "Human Rights in the OPT", "Accountability in the OPT", "Self-determination", and "Israeli settlements"). The Latin American states followed a unanimous voting pattern, as six of the eight Council members supported all five resolutions, while Panama and Paraguay abstained. *EU Member States voted the same way,* except for the resolution on human rights in the Syrian Golan, where part of the EU voted against, and others abstained.[21]

The situation was a bit different in the case of the resolution on "Iran", which was supported only by El Salvador, Panama, and Paraguay, while Bolivia, Cuba, and Venezuela voted against it. Brazil and Ecuador abstained. Similarly, the Latin American states were divided on the issue of the resolution on "Syria", which was supported by Brazil, El Salvador, Panama, and Paraguay, while Bolivia, Cuba, and Venezuela voted against it. Ecuador abstained.[22]

There were three resolutions that are traditionally voted on according to a North-South division line. The first on "Foreign debt" was tabled by Cuba and supported by the whole GRULAC except Brazil, who voted against the resolution. The second on "Human rights and unilateral coercive measures" was tabled by

19 *See* at www.azquotes.com/quote/736878.

20 Laurence Whitehead, *Latin America. A New Interpretation,* Palgrave Macmillan, Basingstoke, 2010, p. 4.

21 Report of the Human Rights Council on its 34th Session, A/HRC/34/2, 14 June 2018, pp. 124-127.

22 Id. p. 58.

doi: 10.5553/HYIEL/266627012022010001016

Venezuela on behalf of NAM and was supported by the whole group. The third on "Illicit funds" was tabled by Egypt, Libya, and Tunisia on behalf of the African Group and where Panama and Paraguay abstained, the others supported the resolution.[23]

During the 35th session of the UN HRC (6-23 June 2017) the resolution on "Syria" was adopted by 27 to 8, with 12 abstentions. The Latin American states were quite divided concerning this initiative, as Bolivia, Cuba, and Venezuela voted against it, while Brazil, El Salvador, Panama, and Paraguay supported it. Ecuador abstained.[24]

It was not surprising that GRULAC members were also divided concerning the resolution on "Belarus", which was finally adopted with a vote of 18 to 8, with 21 abstentions. It was not supported by Bolivia, Cuba, and Venezuela. Brazil, Panama, and Paraguay voted yes on the resolution. Ecuador and El Salvador abstained.[25] Regarding the other Eastern European country initiative, namely the resolution on "Ukraine", which was adopted with a vote of 22 to 6, with 19 abstentions, GRULAC was also divided. Ecuador and Panama supported it. Bolivia, Cuba, and Venezuela voted against it.[26]

During this session, most of the controversial thematic resolutions were strongly influenced by North-South political differences, and the GRULAC members of the Council, almost unanimously, supported all of them ("International solidarity", "Right to peace", "International cooperation", "Protection of family", and "Contribution of development"). The two exceptions were the resolution on the "Protection of family", where Brazil and Panama abstained, and the resolution on the "Contribution of development", where Panama abstained, and Paraguay was absent. The role of Latin American states was quite remarkable. The first two were submitted by Cuba, and the third by Venezuela. Besides these two resolutions, Cuba was the main sponsor of the resolution on the Social Forum, which was adopted by consensus.[27]

During the 36th session of the UN HRC (11-29 September 2017), GRULAC members of the Council were divided on three of the four country-specific resolutions adopted by the HRC by a vote. As far as the resolution on "Syria" is concerned, as usual Bolivia, Cuba, and Venezuela voted against the resolution, while Brazil, El Salvador, Panama, and Paraguay supported the initiative. Only Ecuador abstained.[28]

The Council renewed the mandate of the "Commission of Inquiry on Burundi" for one year by a voted (22 to 11, with 14 abstentions) resolution submitted by the EU.[29] The resolution was not supported by Bolivia, Cuba, and

23 Id. pp. 39-46.

24 Report of the Human Rights Council on its 35th Session, A/HRC/35/2, 14 June 2018, pp. 58-59.

25 Id. pp. 59-60.

26 Id. p. 79.

27 Universal Rights Group, Report on the 35th Session of the Human Rights Council, p. 9, at www.universal-rights.org/urg-human-rights-council-reports/report-35th-session-human-rights-council/.

28 Report of the Human Rights Council on its 36th Session, A/HRC/36/2, 2018, pp. 48-49.

29 Id. pp. 47-48.

doi: 10.5553/HYIEL/266627012022010001016

Venezuela, while Brazil, El Salvador, Panama, and Paraguay supported it. Ecuador abstained.

Tunisia, on behalf of the African Group, submitted a competing resolution on the "Mission by the Office of the UN High Commissioner for Human Rights" to improve the human rights situation and accountability in Burundi (23 to 14, with 9 abstentions) which was supported by most of the Latin American states; only Panama and Paraguay abstained.[30]

GRULAC members of the Council voted in a quite coherent way concerning most of the sensitive thematic resolutions ("Mercenaries"; "Democracy and equitable international order"; "Right to development"; "Rights of peasants"; "Composition of the staff of the OHCHR"; "Unilateral coercive measures"; "From rhetoric to reality"). They supported all of these resolutions. Panama was missing from the room for the vote on the "Right to development" and on "Unilateral coercive measures".[31] The resolutions on "Mercenaries", on the "Composition of the Staff of the OHCHR", and on "Democracy and equitable international order" were submitted by Cuba. The resolution on the "Right to development" and on "Unilateral coercive measures" was tabled by Venezuela on behalf of NAM. The resolution on the "Right of peasants" was tabled by Bolivia, Cuba, Ecuador, and South Africa. Consequently, *GRULAC states played a determining role regarding all sensitive thematic resolutions,* except for the last one, entitled "From rhetoric to reality", which was an initiative by the African Group.

GRULAC members of the HRC were divided during the vote on the resolution on "Reprisals", which was critical of the support of those who want to cooperate with the UN. The resolution, which was adopted by 28 to 0, with 19 abstentions, was supported by most GRULAC states; however, Bolivia, Cuba, and Paraguay were among those 19 states that abstained.[32] However, before this final vote, there were 19 hostile amendments; three of them were adopted by the Council. Venezuela was one of the key players in this attack against the resolution, besides Russia, Egypt, China, and India.

GRULAC states were not as divided as other regional groups – like the Asia-Pacific or the African Group – in the case of the resolution on the "Death penalty", tabled by a Core Group containing Costa Rica and Mexico, alongside other countries. Only Cuba abstained during the vote on the resolution, which was finally adopted by 27 to 13, with 7 abstentions.[33]

5. Sub-Saharan African States

The social and political concerns of Africans are shaped mainly by the legacy of colonialism and the memory of the instability in the post-colonial era. Together, these concerns are also shaped by the severe socio-economic challenges the continent faces, including huge international debt, the highest number of

30 Id. pp. 14-15.
31 Id. p. 35.
32 Id. pp. 54-63.
33 Id. pp. 38-42.

doi: 10.5553/HYIEL/266627012022010001016

refugees in the world, and widespread famine. In this context, many Africans still consider human rights as a Western-inspired imperialist notion. The fact that Western powers supported African dictators in the past raised suspicions about the intentions of the West. The inability of the international community to stop the genocide in Rwanda further discredited human rights in the region.

Cultural nationalists argue against the applicability of a human rights doctrine that is based on the notion of the individual, a notion which does not exist in Africa, where the worth of the individual can be found only in the context of the community. Therefore, Africans traditionally prioritize duties and obligations over rights. Another common understanding of why human rights are inapplicable in Africa is the well-known argument that human rights in the West developed over a long period of struggle for democracy and that Africa has yet to go through this stage.

Despite this resistance to human rights, the emerging African human rights system clearly indicates the political will of more and more African countries to establish a solid foundation guaranteeing the rights and fundamental freedoms of the peoples on the continent. However, besides the lack of necessary financial preconditions for a sufficient regional protection system, the lack of political will frequently results in a poor implementation of the highly sophisticated African human rights instruments. The public frustration caused by this deficiency means that civil society often turns towards UN mechanisms as a real solution.

5.1. The Human Rights Diplomacy of Sub-Saharan African States in Light of the Main Sessions of the HRC in 2017

During the 34th session of the UN HRC a strong resolution was adopted on "South Sudan" without a vote, which extended and strengthened the mandate of the UN Commission on Human Rights on South Sudan to "determine and report the facts", and make all information and evidence about alleged human rights violations available to all transitional mechanisms, including the Hybrid Court for South Sudan, should one be established in cooperation with the AU.[34] The report by the Commission affirmed that there was a deliberate targeting of civilian populations by the government based on the victims' ethnic identity.

The HRC adopted a resolution without a vote on the "Technical assistance and capacity-building for Mali in the field of human rights", which welcomed the close cooperation between the Independent Expert, the implementation of the Peace Agreement, and legal reform, and it also renewed the Mandate of the Independent Expert.[35]

During the interactive dialogue with the Commission of Inquiry on Burundi, the Chair of the Commission underlined that they had decided to focus their investigation on those human rights violations which may amount to crimes against humanity. The Commission regretted that Burundi was not willing to

34 Report of the Human Rights Council on its Thirty-Fourth Session, 27 February to 24 March 2017, UN Doc. A/HRC/34/2, 14 June 2018, p. 60.

35 Id. p. 141.

doi: 10.5553/HYIEL/266627012022010001016

cooperate with them and that there was almost complete impunity for the serious human rights violations in the country.

It is also interesting to *analyze the voting behavior of the 11 sub-Saharan members of the Council regarding country situations.* The sub-Saharan countries typically ally with their North African Muslim neighbors and support the resolutions condemning Israel. While this was the case with most of the sub-Saharan members, there was one remarkable exception, namely Togo, which was the only member of the HRC (other than the US) to vote against all five resolutions. However, this is not surprising in light of the close cooperation between the Togolese government and Israel in the last few years. Israeli Prime Minister Benjamin Netanyahu met Togolese President Faure Gnassingbé twice in 2017. It was very indicative of their relationship that the Togolese President wrote the following in the guestbook during his visit: "I dream of Israel's return to Africa and Africa's return to Israel."[36] The Togolese Minister of Foreign Affairs Robert Dussey's opinion is also very telling in this regard: "The African continent is booming and Israel holds the solution for African development."[37] Besides establishing strong political and economic ties with Israel, the Togolese government, despite the questions about the legitimacy of the president and the serious human rights violations, still receives a significant amount of development aid from the US (over USD 13 million in 2016).[38]

It was also notable that, regarding resolutions involving the Middle East, Botswana abstained in the case of one, Congo in the case of two, and Rwanda in the case of four, indicating a small shift in the Middle East policy of sub-Saharan African states.[39] The fact that the members of the African Group did not condemn Israel en bloc was not in line with their historical heritage established in the early post-Colonial period when the sub-Saharan countries used to unanimously support all the initiatives condemning Israel in solidarity with their North African partners.

As far as voting on the "Human rights situation in Iran" is concerned, there were significant discrepancies among the positions of the different sub-Saharan HRC members. While Botswana and Rwanda supported the US-led resolution, Burundi and Kenya voted against it and Congo, Côte d'Ivoire, Ethiopia, Nigeria, Ghana, and Togo abstained.[40] The situation was quite similar to the resolution on "Syria", where Botswana, Côte d'Ivoire, Ghana, Rwanda, and Togo supported the resolution while Burundi voted against it, and the others abstained.[41] The sub-Saharan HRC members were even divided regarding the resolution on the "Cooperation with Georgia", where Botswana, Ghana, and Togo supported the

36 Simon Hooper, 'Togo: How a repressive West African state built close ties with Israel', *Middle East Eye*, 22 December 2017, at www.middleeasteye.net/news/togo-how-repressive-west-african-state-built-close-ties-israel-1894664807.

37 Id.

38 Id.

39 Report of the Human Rights Council on its Thirty-Fourth Session, 27 February to 24 March 2017, UN Doc. A/HRC/34/2, 14 June 2018, pp. 124-127.

40 Id. pp. 58-59.

41 Id. p. 60.

doi: 10.5553/HYIEL/266627012022010001016

resolution submitted by the country concerned, and Burundi, in line with its firm policy opposing all country resolutions, voted against it. The other sub-Saharan African states abstained.[42]

The African Group submitted its three customary resolutions on racism, namely on the "Mandate of the Intergovernmental Working Group on the Effective Implementation of the Durban Declaration and Programme of Action"; the "Mandate of the Special Rapporteur on Contemporary Forms of Racism, Racial Discrimination, Xenophobia, and Related Intolerance"; and the "Elaboration of International Complementary Standards to the ICERD". It submitted a new one on the establishment of a "Forum for People of African Descent". The latter, together with the resolution on the Special Rapporteur's mandate, was adopted without a vote, while the other two were voted on. From a legal standpoint, the most interesting vote was on the resolution of the ICERD, which resulted in a three-way split within the EU.[43]

A fifth resolution submitted by the African Group was on the "Negative Impact of Non-Repatriation of Funds of Illicit Origin on the Enjoyment of Human Rights and the Importance of Improving International Cooperation". The US voted against this resolution, and 16 other countries abstained. The West's major point of contention was that the resolution focused on non-repatriation of illicit funds to countries of origin rather than focusing on the obligation of states to prevent this illegal activity. Furthermore, they were not convinced about the link between the repatriation of illicit funds and the right to development. They did not consider that problem a human rights issue.[44]

During the 35th session, the Council adopted a resolution on the "Human rights situation in Eritrea" without a vote. The resolution was submitted by Djibouti and Somalia, and it reflected the recommendations of the Special Rapporteur and encouraged the establishment of an OHCHR presence in the country.

One of the most chaotic procedures surrounded the adoption of the resolution on the DRC. The essence of the problem was that, despite all efforts during the review of the HRC in 2011, the Council still lacks a sufficient toolkit to address the situations of individual countries. The African Group emphasized that the Council should engage constructively with the DRC by providing technical assistance and capacity-building. The EU, on the other hand, highlighted the need for a proper balance between international support and the DRC's obligation to address the serious human rights violations in certain parts of the country.[45] This disagreement led to the tabling of two resolutions, one by the EU and another by the AU. After lengthy and last-minute negotiations, the EU agreed to merge the two resolutions. The result was a resolution that looked more like a technical assistance resolution but included an accountability mechanism, which is more typical for resolutions of human rights situations that

42 Id. p. 140.
43 Id. pp. 132-134.
44 Id. p. 49.
45 Id. p. 80.

doi: 10.5553/HYIEL/266627012022010001016

require the Council's attention. Finally, the resolution on the "Technical Assistance to the DRC and Accountability Concerning the Events in the Kasai Regions" led by the African Group was adopted by the Council without a vote.[46]

During the interactive dialogue with the "Commission of Inquiry on Burundi", the Chair of the Commission regretted that there was no cooperation from the side of the government and that, unfortunately, the human rights crises had not seemed to improve over the previous two years.[47]

Like in the case of the thirty-fourth session of the Council, the voting behavior of the 11 sub-Saharan African members of the Council regarding country situations was far from uniform. On the resolution on "Syria", Burundi voted negatively, as usual, while Botswana, Côte d'Ivoire, Ghana, Rwanda, and Togo supported the text, and Congo, Ethiopia, Kenya, Nigeria, and South Africa abstained.[48] African states were seemingly more cautious regarding the two East European country situations. Regarding the EU initiative on "Belarus", only Ghana supported the resolution, Burundi voted no, and all others abstained.[49] Given the hostilities between Ukraine and Russia, and thus the more politically charged nature of the resolution on "Ukraine", Côte d'Ivoire and Rwanda joined Ghana in support of it, while the rest of the African Group voted as they had for the "Belarus" resolution.[50]

Since most of the controversial thematic resolutions were strongly influenced by North-South political differences during this session, the African members of the Council voted unanimously on all of them (international solidarity, right to peace, international cooperation, protection of the family, and contribution of development).

During the 36th session the Council voted to renew the mandate of the Commission of Inquiry on Burundi for one year, a resolution submitted by the EU.[51] Although there were neither comments by Burundi nor by the African Group on the EU resolution, the African Group started parallel negotiations with Burundi and, as a result, Tunisia (on behalf of the African Group) submitted a competing resolution on "Technical assistance and capacity-building to Burundi".[52] The resolution of the African Group was largely based on the EU draft, but it replaced the renewal of the Commission of Inquiry with a request to send an expert team to reinforce the OHCHR office in Bujumbura, by making suggestions for technical assistance and by collecting and preserving information. However, the African Group did not agree to grant this new mechanism the same

46 Id.

47 Universal Rights Group, Report on the 35th Session of the Human Rights Council, p. 5, at www.universal-rights.org/urg-human-rights-council-reports/report-35th-session-human-rights-council/.

48 Report of the Human Rights Council on its 35th Session, A/HRC/35/2, 14 June 2018, p. 50.

49 Id. pp. 50-51.

50 Id. p. 65.

51 It was interesting to note that among the sub-Saharan African States only Burundi, Congo, Ghana, and South Africa rejected the EU-led resolution, while Côte d'Ivoire, Ethiopia, Kenya, Nigeria, and Togo abstained, and Botswana supported the text.

52 Report of the Human Rights Council on its Thirty-sixth Session, 11-29 September 2017, UN Doc. A/HRC/36/2, 14 June 2018.

doi: 10.5553/HYIEL/266627012022010001016

investigative power and independence as the Commission of Inquiry had under the original resolution. It is significant to note that Botswana and Rwanda did not join the African Group in submitting the draft, nor when the EU asked for a vote regarding the text, which was adopted by 23 to 14, with 9 abstentions. Botswana abstained, and Rwanda did not participate in the voting.[53] As a result of the adoption of two competing resolutions on "Burundi" in 2018, there were a total of six debates on Burundi in the HRC in this session.

The HRC adopted a strong resolution on the "Technical Assistance and Capacity-Building in the Field of Human Rights in the CAR" without a vote.[54] The resolution was submitted by the African Group and the CAR, and the President of the CAR, speaking to the HRC on 27 September 2017, confirmed his country's commitment to fight impunity and to work towards justice.

The African Group presented a resolution on the "Technical Assistance and Capacity-Building to Improve Human Rights in Sudan", which renewed the Mandate of the Independent Expert for one year. The resolution, which was adopted without a vote, focused on the positive developments in the country, and it was mainly the result of bilateral negotiations between the US and Sudan with the aim, which was finally achieved, of preventing the transfer of the role of the Independent Expert to an OHCHR Office.[55]

Similar to the previous sessions of the Council, the voting behavior of the members of the African Group was not uniform when it came to the human rights situation in "Syria". While Burundi voted against the resolution, as usual, five African states (namely Botswana, Côte d'Ivoire, Ghana, Togo, and Rwanda) supported it. The other sub-Sharan African states (Congo, Ethiopia, Kenya, Nigeria, and South Africa) abstained.

The African Group submitted four thematic resolutions during the session. One of the resolutions, adopted without a vote, renewed the Mandate of the Working Group of Experts on People of African Descent. Another one established a new Intergovernmental Working Group to elaborate the content of an international regulatory framework on the regulation, monitoring, and oversight of the activities of private military and security companies. The latter was also adopted without a vote as the EU, despite its concerns, finally joined the consensus. South Africa expressed its gratitude for this gesture exercised by the EU. The most controversial initiative by the AU was entitled "From Rhetoric to Reality: A Global Call for Concrete Action against Racism, Racial Discrimination, Xenophobia, and Related Intolerance." The major difference between the positions of the AU and the EU on this resolution was that the African states were not willing to delete a reference to the negotiations' commencement of an additional protocol on criminalizing acts of racist and xenophobic nature. The EU eventually asked for a vote and the African resolution was adopted by a vote of 32 to 5, with 10 countries abstaining. The delicate nature of the issue was demonstrated by the fact that even the EU Member States were divided, and

53 Id. pp. 14-15.
54 Id. p. 161.
55 Id. p. 167.

doi: 10.5553/HYIEL/266627012022010001016

while Germany and the UK rejected the resolution, the other EU Council members abstained. The fourth initiative brought forward by the AU was on the renewal of the Mandate of the Special Rapporteur on the Implications for Human Rights of the Environmentally Sound Management and Disposal of Hazardous Substances and Wastes. This resolution was adopted without a vote although the EU was not supportive of a reference to the Declaration on the Right to Development in the text.[56]

In respect of most of the sensitive thematic resolutions, the African members of the Council voted in a coherent way. However, it is interesting to note that, regarding the Cuban resolution on the "Composition of the Staff of the OHCHR", Togo abstained as it did on the resolution on "Human Rights and Unilateral Coercive Measures". It was not the first time that the position of Togo was completely different from the rest of the group, as in the case concerning the Middle East resolutions earlier that year. The African states were strongly divided during the vote on the resolution on "Reprisals", which was critical for the support of those who want to cooperate with the UN.[57] While Botswana, Congo, Côte d'Ivoire, Ghana, and Rwanda supported this initiative, the other African states abstained. The African states were even more divided in the case of the "Death penalty" resolution, where Congo, Ghana, Rwanda, South Africa, Togo, and Côte d'Ivoire supported the initiative; Botswana, Burundi, and Ethiopia rejected it; and Kenya and Nigeria abstained.[58]

6. Asia-Pacific States

The fact that except for Thailand, China, and Japan, all countries of the region were colonies in some period of their history, resulted in a strong adherence to the principles of sovereignty and non-interference. This phenomenon, combined with nationalism and the decision by most states to choose economic modernization without Westernization, has deeply shaped the human rights diplomacy of Asia. After careful examination of the three dominant religions of the region, it seems that the teachings of Confucianism, Buddhism, and Hinduism are also reconcilable with the notion of human rights.

The promotion of so-called Asian values in the 90s was a reaction to Western pressure to comply with international human rights standards and served to challenge the moral foundations of the West, contributing to the nation-building efforts of the political elite which also used this concept to safeguard its position. Their argument emphasizing the primacy of economic development over the protection and promotion of human rights was seriously undermined during the Asian financial crisis of 1997. Those values promoted under the 'Asian' label can also be found in Europe and have an important place in European conservative traditions. It is not a coincidence that in Europe, the concept of human rights and sovereignty developed in parallel, and as a result, the sovereign state was not just

56 Id. p. 37.
57 Id. pp. 47-54.
58 Id. pp. 32-36.

doi: 10.5553/HYIEL/266627012022010001016

the potential violator, but also a powerful protector of human rights. It also protected the weaker states against their hegemonic neighbors. This did not happen in Asia, where they adopted the European concept of sovereignty without reservation, and without the human rights component.

These developments shaped the human rights diplomacy of most Asian states. This has resulted in the reserved position of most Asian states towards international judicial organs, based on their conservative understanding of the principles of non-interference and national sovereignty. Similar factors contributed to the fact, that presently Asia is the only continent without a regional human rights organization.

6.1. The Human Rights Diplomacy of Asian States in Light of the Main Sessions of the HRC in 2017

During the 34th session of the UN HRC there were five resolutions on the human rights situation in the Middle East ("Human rights in Syrian Golan"; "Human Rights in the OPT"; "Accountability in the OPT"; "Self-determination", and "Israeli settlements"). All were submitted by Pakistan on behalf of the OIC. The Asian countries usually allied with the OIC's position and supported these resolutions condemning Israel, which is not surprising as influential members of the Group are also members of the OIC. Only Japan abstained on two occasions ("Human rights in Syrian Golan"; "Accountability in the OPT"), India once ("Accountability in the OPT"), and the Republic of Korea once ("Human rights in Syrian Golan").[59]

The resolution on the situation of "Human rights in Myanmar" was tabled by the EU and adopted by consensus. With this resolution, the Council decided to dispatch an international fact-finding mission to be appointed by the President of the HRC, as Myanmar did not accept the original solution to entrust this investigative task to the existing Special Rapporteur. The resolution extended the mandate of the Special Rapporteur, welcomed the positive developments that happened since the new government took office in April 2016, but also expressed concerns over several issues, including the situation in the Rakhine State. During the adoption of the resolution, Myanmar, China, India, and Venezuela dissociated from the whole text, while the Philippines dissociated only from the paragraphs regarding the fact-finding mission.[60]

The resolution on the "Situation of human rights in the DPRK" submitted by Japan and the EU was adopted without a vote. Besides Japan, the Republic of Korea and the Maldives also co-sponsored the resolution which strengthened the capacity of the OHCHR and its field office in Seoul, to enhance the current monitoring and documentation efforts to prepare the ground for future accountability processes.[61]

59 Report of the Human Rights Council on its 34th Session, A/HRC/34/2, 14 June 2018, pp. 137-140.

60 Id. p. 64.

61 Id. pp. 65-66.

doi: 10.5553/HYIEL/266627012022010001016

A short procedural resolution was adopted by consensus on "Promoting reconciliation, accountability, and human rights in Sri Lanka". The text presented by a Core Group [US, UK, Macedonia (now North Macedonia), and Montenegro] and co-sponsored by Sri Lanka, requested the OHCHR to continue reporting on the implementation of HRC Resolution 30/1 of 2015.[62]

Regarding the voting on the resolution concerning the "Human rights situation in Iran", submitted by a Core Group [Sweden, US, Macedonia (now North Macedonia) and Moldova] the Asia-Pacific Group was completely divided. Japan, Qatar, the Republic of Korea, Saudi Arabia, and the United Arab Emirates (UAE) supported it. Mongolia and the Philippines abstained. Bangladesh, China, India, Indonesia, Iraq, and Kyrgyzstan voted against the resolution. This voting pattern reflects the complex relationship the Arab world has with Iran.[63]

The situation was quite similar in case of the resolution on "Syria", submitted by a Core Group (US, France, UK, Germany, Italy, Kuwait, Morocco, Jordan, Saudi Arabia, and Turkey) where Japan, Qatar, the Republic of Korea, Saudi Arabia, and the UAE supported it; Bangladesh, Indonesia, Mongolia, and the Philippines abstained; while China, Iraq, and Kyrgyzstan voted against the resolution.[64]

The Asian HRC members were evenly divided in the case of the resolution on "Cooperation with Georgia", where only Japan could support the text, enjoying the consent of the concerned country as well. Meanwhile, except for China, all other members of the Asia-Pacific Group abstained. *China following its traditional policy on country situations voted against the resolution.*[65]

The most divisive thematic resolution for the Asia-Pacific Group during this session was the one submitted by Egypt, Saudi Arabia, Jordan, Morocco, and Algeria on the "Effects of terrorism on the enjoyment of all human rights".[66] The resolution requested the Advisory Committee of the HRC to prepare a report on the negative effects of terrorism on the enjoyment of all human rights and fundamental freedoms, with a particular focus on economic, social, and cultural rights. The EU could not support the text because it believes that the discussion on the impact of terrorism on the economy is not within the mandate of the HRC. Japan and Korea supported the EU's position, while Kyrgyzstan and Mongolia abstained. The other members of the Asia-Pacific Group supported the resolution.

Three resolutions are traditionally voted on along a North-South division line. The first on "Foreign debt" tabled by Cuba was supported by the whole Asia-Pacific Group except Japan and Korea, who voted against the resolution. For the second on "Human rights and unilateral coercive measures", tabled by Venezuela on behalf on NAM, besides the objection of Korea and Japan, the other Asian members of the HRC supported the initiative. The third was on "Illicit funds"

62 Id. p. 18.
63 Id. pp. 64-65.
64 Id. pp. 66-67.
65 Id. pp. 153-154.
66 Id. pp. 43-44.

doi: 10.5553/HYIEL/266627012022010001016

tabled by Egypt, Libya, and Tunisia on behalf of the African Group. Japan and Korea abstained, while the others supported the resolution.[67]

The resolution run by Norway on the "Mandate of the Special Rapporteur on the situation of human rights defenders" still provokes heated discussions within the HRC, as it concerns the philosophy of the member states regarding civil society. Only Japan, Korea, and the Maldives became co-sponsors of the resolution. The level of tension about the question was well illustrated by the fact that there were five amendments to the resolution tabled by Russia, China, Cuba, and Pakistan. They intended to delete any reference to the term "human rights defenders" and downgrade the reference to the work of the Special Rapporteur. China, India, Qatar, Saudi Arabia, and the UAE supported the amendments, while Indonesia, Iraq, Japan, Kyrgyzstan, Mongolia, and Korea voted against them. The Philippines and Bangladesh abstained.

During the 35th session of the UN HRC the resolution on "Syria" was adopted by 27 to 8, with 12 abstentions. It was not a surprise that China, Iraq, Kyrgyzstan, and the Philippines did not support the initiative submitted by a Core Group, (US, France, UK, Germany, Italy, Kuwait, Morocco, Jordan, Saudi Arabia, and Turkey) while Japan, Qatar, Korea, Saudi Arabia, and the UAE supported it. The other members of the Asia-Pacific Group abstained.[68]

It was also not surprising that the Asia-Pacific Group was divided concerning the resolution on "Belarus", which was finally adopted with a vote of 18 to 8, with 21 abstentions. Japan and Korea supported the resolution submitted by the EU, while China, India, and the Philippines voted against it. The other members of the group abstained.[69]

It was more interesting that almost the same division existed in case of the resolution on "Ukraine", which was submitted by Ukraine. China and the Philippines voted against it, while only Iraq, Japan, and the Republic of Korea supported it. The other members of the Asia-Pacific Group abstained. This resolution on technical assistance was adopted with a vote of 22 to 6, with 19 abstentions.[70]

It was not surprising that because most of the controversial thematic resolutions during this session reflected North-South political differences, the Asian members of the Council voted almost unanimously in all of them ("International solidarity", "Right to peace", "International cooperation", "Protection of family", and "Contribution of development"). It was no coincidence that Japan and the Republic of Korea were the only two states not to support these initiatives. Japan voted against four resolutions and abstained in the case of the one regarding international cooperation. Korea voted against three initiatives and abstained from the ones on "Protection of family" and the "Contribution of development".

67 Id. pp. 153-154.
68 Report of the Human Rights Council on its 35th Session, A/HRC/35/2, pp. 58-59.
69 Id. pp. 59-60.
70 Id. p. 79.

doi: 10.5553/HYIEL/266627012022010001016

During the 36th session, the HRC extended the mandate of the independent international fact-finding mission on "Myanmar" without a vote.[71] It was the first time that a mandate was extended by a procedural decision and not by a resolution. During this same session, the Chair of the independent fact-finding mission presented an oral update on the situation in Myanmar. Marzuki Darusman reported mass killings, excessive use of force, torture, ill-treatment, sexual and gender-based violence, and landmine-killings in his verbal update.[72]

The *Asia-Pacific Group was divided on all the four country-specific resolutions* adopted by the Council by a vote. On the resolution on "Syria", as usual, China, Iraq, and the Philippines voted against, while Japan, Qatar, the Republic of Korea, Saudi Arabia, and the UAE supported it. The other members of the group (Bangladesh, India, Indonesia, Kyrgyzstan, and Mongolia) abstained.[73]

The Council renewed the "Mandate of the Commission of Inquiry on Burundi" for one year by a voted resolution (22 to 11, with 14 abstentions) submitted by the EU.[74] From the Asia-Pacific Group, Japan, Mongolia, and the Republic of Korea supported the renewal of the mandate; China, Saudi Arabia, and the UAE were against it; while the others abstained. Tunisia, on behalf of the African Group submitted a competing resolution on the "Mission by the Office of the UN High Commissioner for Human Rights to improve the human rights situation and accountability in Burundi" (23 to 14, with 9 abstentions). Not surprisingly, this resolution received broader support from the Asia-Pacific Group as Bangladesh, China, India, Iraq, Saudi Arabia, and the UAE supported it, while only the Republic of Korea voted against it. The other members, including Japan, abstained during the vote.

The last country-specific resolution adopted by a vote (45 to 1, with 1 abstentions) during this session was the one on "Technical assistance and capacity-building in the field of human rights in the DRC". Besides the one "no" vote cast by the US, the Republic of Korea alone abstained from among the HRC members.[75]

The Asian members of the HRC voted in quite a coherent way concerning most of the sensitive thematic resolutions: "Mercenaries"; "Democracy and equitable international order"; "Right to development"; "Right of peasants"; "Composition of the staff of the OHCHR"; "Unilateral coercive measures"; "From rhetoric to reality". Eleven members of the Asia-Pacific Group supported all of the initiatives; only Japan and the Republic of Korea voted differently. Japan objected to all the resolutions, except for the one entitled "From rhetoric to reality: a global call for concrete action against racism, racial discrimination, xenophobia, and related intolerance" and the one on the "Rights of peasants", where Tokyo abstained. The Korean voting pattern was almost identical with the

71 Id. pp. 49-50.
72 Id.
73 Id. pp. 48-49.
74 Id. pp. 47-48.
75 Id. pp. 168-169.

doi: 10.5553/HYIEL/266627012022010001016

Japanese one, with the sole exception that Seoul also abstained concerning the resolution on the "Right to development".[76]

There were two resolutions where the Asia-Pacific Group was even more divided for obvious reasons, as these were not issues based on North-South ideological differences. These were the one on the "Death penalty" and the resolution on "Cooperation with the UN, its representatives, and mechanisms in the field of human rights".[77] On the first one, tabled by a Core Group including Mongolia from the Asia-Pacific Group, Bangladesh, China, India, Iraq, Japan, Qatar, Saudi Arabia, and the UAE voted against the resolution, while Kyrgyzstan and Mongolia supported it. Indonesia, the Philippines, and the Republic of Korea abstained during the vote (27 to 13, with 7 abstentions). According to Johnson and Zimring, political evolution and not cultural factors led many countries in Asia to follow an abolitionist policy.[78] They rejected the common argument which attributed the refusal to abolish the death penalty to Asian values. In their view, democratic governance and the promotion of human rights have an important role in this process.

7. Muslim States

States discussed here are members of the Organization of Islamic Cooperation (OIC). The Muslim world is much more diverse than it is often considered by the general public and it is time to overcome the rigid portrayal of this religion and the region as "hot, bearded camel riders, desert-like, poor, underdeveloped, backward, governed by Muslim fanatics and tyrants, characterized by rich Arabs in London and Arab terrorists blowing up planes."[79]

It is important to search for proper answers to the question of the compatibility between Islam and the international human rights regime, which is vital for the life of the 1.5 billion believers of the world's fastest-growing religion. The problem is even more complex because Islam never treated religion and politics as two separate institutions.

Those answers to the challenging question of compatibility which result in the dilution of human rights to legitimize the opposition of the Muslim elite to human rights cannot be supported. Finding a solution is even more pressing due to the "increasing role of Islam in world politics and the increased presence of Muslims in Europe and in North America" which makes interactions between the two civilizations/cultures more intense.[80] This struggle is not just between civilizations; it is also ongoing within the civilizations themselves, for in both

76 Id. pp. 30-42.
77 Id. pp. 54-62.
78 William Schabas, 'Is Asia the last bastion of capital punishment?', *Asia Policy*, No. 10, July 2010, pp. 198, 200.
79 Beverly Milton-Edwards, *Contemporary Politics in the Middle East*, Polity Press, Cambridge, 2018, p. 3.
80 Bassam Tibi, 'Islamic Law/Shari'a, Human Rights, Universal Morality and International Relations', *Human Rights Quarterly*, Vol. 16, Issue 2, 1994, p. 298.

doi: 10.5553/HYIEL/266627012022010001016

Islam and Christianity there are forces who oppose, and forces who support the extension of human rights.[81] In Islam, this means that the old traditionalists are usually trying to "Islamize modernity", while the reformers are trying to modernize Islam. The most pressing human rights problems faced by Muslim societies today are not related to "cultural preferences or religious-cultural authenticity", but the serious human rights violations committed by their governments, regardless of their cultural or ideological facade.[82]

7.1. *The Human Rights Diplomacy of Muslim States in Light of the Main Sessions of the HRC in 2017*

During the 34th session of the UN HRC there were five resolutions on the human rights situation in the Middle East ("Human rights in Syrian Golan"; "Human Rights in the OPT"; "Accountability in the OPT"; "Self-determination"; and "Israeli settlements"). All of them were submitted by Pakistan on behalf of the OIC. Both the sub-Saharan and Asian countries in this question usually ally with the OIC position and support these resolutions condemning Israel, which is not surprising, as influential members of these groups are also members of the OIC. There was a remarkable exception, however: Togo. Togo was the only member of the HRC together with the US voting against all five resolutions.[83]

Regarding voting on the resolution on the "Human rights situation in Iran", submitted by a Core Group (Sweden, US, North Macedonia, and Moldova), the OIC members of the African Group almost unanimously abstained during the vote, except for Egypt, which voted against the resolution. The Asia-Pacific OIC members were more significantly divided, as their voting pattern was shaped by the Sunni-Shiite rivalry and regional security policy considerations. As a result, while Qatar, Saudi Arabia, and the UAE supported the resolution, Bangladesh, Indonesia, Iraq, and Kyrgyzstan voted against the it.[84]

In the case of the resolution on "Syria", Cote d'Ivoire and Togo supported it, while the other African OIC members abstained. The resolution submitted by a Core Group (US, France, UK, Germany, Italy, Kuwait, Morocco, Jordan, Saudi Arabia, and Turkey) was supported by Qatar, Saudi Arabia, and the UAE among the Asia-Pacific OIC members, while Bangladesh, and Indonesia abstained, and Iraq and Kyrgyzstan voted against.[85] Albania, as usual, voted with the EU and supported the resolution.

The OIC members of the HRC were divided in the case of the resolution on "Cooperation with Georgia", where Togo and Albania supported the resolution submitted by the country concerned, and the other OIC member states abstained.

The resolution submitted by Egypt, Saudi Arabia, Jordan, Morocco, and Algeria on the "Effects of terrorism on the enjoyment of all human rights" was

81 Sayed Khatab & Gary D. Bouma, *Democracy in Islam,* Routledge, Abindon, 2007, p. 3.

82 Reza Afshari, 'An essay on Islamic cultural relativism in the discourse of human rights', *Human Rights Quarterly*, Vol. 16, Issue 2, 1994, p. 249.

83 Report of the Human Rights Council on its 34th Session, A/HRC/34/2, 14 June 2018, pp. 137-140.

84 Id. pp. 64-65.

85 Id. pp. 66-67.

doi: 10.5553/HYIEL/266627012022010001016

even divisive within the Asia-Pacific Group, but the OIC members of the HRC were relatively unified on that issue as 11 OIC members supported it, with the only abstention by Kyrgyzstan and the negative vote by Albania aligned with the EU's position.

The resolution run by Norway on the "Mandate of the Special Rapporteur on the situation of human rights defenders" always provokes heated discussions within the HRC as it concerns the philosophy of the member states on civil society. Quite a few OIC member states have become co-sponsors of the resolution, such as the Maldives, Albania, Benin, Cote d'Ivoire, Djibouti, Guinea, the State of Palestine, Indonesia, and Togo. The level of tension about the issue in this session was well marked by the fact that there were five amendments to the resolution tabled by Russia, China, Cuba, and Pakistan. They intended to delete any reference to the term "human rights defenders" and to downgrade the reference to the work of the Special Rapporteur. Egypt, Nigeria, Qatar, Saudi Arabia, and the UAE supported the amendments; Bangladesh supported most of the amendments, while Albania, Cote d'Ivoire, Indonesia, Iraq, Kyrgyzstan, Togo, and Tunisia voted against them.[86]

During the 35th session, the resolution on "Syria" was adopted by 27 to 8, with 12 abstentions. It was no surprise that Iraq and Kyrgyzstan did not support the initiative submitted by a Core Group (US, France, UK, Germany, Italy, Kuwait, Morocco, Jordan, Saudi Arabia, and Turkey) while Albania, Qatar, Saudi Arabia, the UAE, Cote d'Ivoire, and Togo supported it. The other members of the OIC abstained.[87]

It was also unsurprising that the OIC member states were a little divided concerning the resolution on "Belarus", which was finally adopted with a vote of 18 to 8, with 21 abstentions. Albania supported the resolution submitted by the EU, while Egypt voted against it. The other members of the OIC abstained.[88]

It was more interesting that certain divisions existed in the case of the resolution on "Ukraine", which was submitted by Ukraine. Only Iraq and Albania supported it. The other members of the OIC abstained. This resolution on "Technical assistance" was adopted with a vote of 22 to 6, with 19 abstentions.[89]

It was not surprising that because during this session most of the controversial thematic resolutions were strongly influenced by North-South political differences, the OIC members of the Council voted unanimously in all of them ("International solidarity"; "Right to peace"; "International cooperation"; "Protection of family"; and "Contribution of development"). Only Albania supported the EU line regarding these five resolutions, with three negative votes and two abstentions.[90]

During the 36th session of the UN HRC, the OIC members of the Council were divided on three of the four country-specific resolutions adopted by the

86 Id. pp. 39-42.

87 Report of the Human Rights Council on its 35th Session, A/HRC/35/2, pp. 58-59.

88 Id. pp. 59-60.

89 Id. p. 79.

90 Id. pp. 27-45.

doi: 10.5553/HYIEL/266627012022010001016

HRC by a vote. On the resolution on "Syria", Iraq as usual voted against it, while Albania, Qatar, Saudi Arabia, Cote d'Ivoire, Togo, and the UAE supported it. The other members of the OIC Group (Bangladesh, Indonesia, Kyrgyzstan, Nigeria, Egypt, and Tunisia) abstained.[91]

The Council renewed the "Mandate of the Commission of Inquiry on Burundi" for one year by a voted (22 to 11, with 14 abstentions) resolution submitted by the EU.[92] Albania of course, as an EU candidate country supported the initiative, while Egypt, Saudi Arabia, and the UAE were against it. The other OIC members of the HRC abstained.

Tunisia, on behalf of the African Group, submitted a competing resolution on the "Mission by the Office of the UN High Commissioner for Human Rights to improve the human rights situation and accountability in Burundi" (23 to 14, with 9 abstentions). Not surprisingly, this resolution received broader support from the OIC members as Egypt, Cote d'Ivoire, Nigeria, Togo, Tunisia, Bangladesh, Iraq, Saudi Arabia, and the UAE supported it, while only Albania voted against it. The other OIC members abstained.[93]

The OIC members of the Council voted in a quite coherent way concerning most of the sensitive thematic resolutions. ("Mercenaries"; "Democracy and equitable international order"; "Right to development"; "Right of peasants"; "Composition of the staff of the OHCHR"; "Unilateral coercive measures"; "From rhetoric to reality"). Only Albania, in complete harmony with the EU's position, voted against five of them and abstained regarding the resolutions on the "Right to development" and on the "Right of peasants". Regarding the Cuban resolution on the "Composition of the staff of the OHCHR",[94] Togo alone abstained, just like in case of the resolution on "Unilateral coercive measures".[95]

The OIC members of the HRC were also divided during the vote on the resolution on "Reprisals", which was critical for the support of those who want to cooperate with the UN. While Albania, Cote d'Ivoire, Tunisia, and Iraq supported this initiative, the other OIC member states abstained (28 to 0, with 19 abstentions). However, before this final vote, there were 19 hostile amendments; three of them were adopted by the Council. Egypt was one of the key players in this attack against the resolution, besides Russia, Venezuela, China, and India.[96]

The OIC states were even more divided in the case of the resolution on the "Death penalty", tabled by a Core Group containing Benin. It was Egypt who asked for a vote on this initiative. Albania, Togo, Kyrgyzstan, and Cote d'Ivoire supported the initiative, while Bangladesh, Iraq, Qatar, Saudi Arabia, Egypt, and the UAE rejected it. The other members of the OIC abstained.[97]

91 Report of the Human Rights Council on its 36th Session, A/HRC/36/2, pp. 48-49.
92 Id. pp. 47-48.
93 Id. p. 42.
94 Id. pp. 13-14.
95 Id. p. 35.
96 Id. pp. 54-63.
97 Id. pp. 38-42.

doi: 10.5553/HYIEL/266627012022010001016

8. Most Recent Developments in the HRC during the COVID-19 Pandemic

It is worth looking at cases of cross-regional cooperation and divisions among the different regional groups during the first pandemic in the history of mankind which effected every single corner of our Globe. The 43rd session of the HRC was held in two segments, as due to the pandemic it had been suspended on 13 March 2020 and resumed on 15 June. An important initiative of cross-regional cooperation was launched by Switzerland, Norway, Sierra Leona and Uruguay, aimed at highlighting the central role the HRC should play regarding the preventive agenda of the UN. This cross-regional group clearly indicated that they would like to achieve a general consensus within the international community regarding the importance of the preventive mandate of the HRC.[98] There was another important issue during this session where HRC member states managed to reach a consensus, namely on the resolution addressing the human rights violations by law enforcement officers against people of African descent.[99]

During the 45th session of the HRC there were heated debates about the importance of traditional family roles and hierarchies. Russia "attacked" the resolution on the "Rights of the child" with several hostile amendments aimed at strengthening the rights of parents over their children, making their participation "in decision-making conditional upon the permission/direction of parents and other adults". Most of the proposed amendments were finally withdrawn, and the two remaining ones were rejected by 13 to 27, with 6 abstentions.[100] In the course of this session, the core group which was already mentioned with regard to their statement on the importance of prevention within the mandate of the HRC, managed to submit a resolution on this topic and it was finally adopted by 32 to 3, with 11 abstentions.

During the 46th session of the HRC (22 February – 24 March 2021) there were a few important statements made by groups of states strongly supporting China and attacking the practice of Western states to criticize the internal human rights diplomacy of other governments. It was a clear massage addressed to Washington that they do not want to accept the *status quo ante* when the US delegation dominated the agenda and the work of the HRC.[101] China has started to become increasingly active over the last few years of the Council, however the return of the US to the HRC after the Trump Administration made the clashes between the 2 superpowers unavoidable. The Chinese statement – on behalf of a group of states – criticizing the operation of Australian offshore detention centers and the alleged war crimes committed by Australian overseas military personal certainly represents a new phase in the Chinese external human rights

98 Universal Rights Group, Report on the 43rd Session of the Human Rights Council, at www.universal-rights.org/blog/report-on-the-43rd-session-of-the-human-rights-council/.

99 Id.

100 Universal Rights Group, Report on the 45th Session of the Human Rights Council, at www.universal-rights.org/urg-human-rights-council-reports/report-on-the-45th-session-of-the-human-rights-council/.

101 Universal Rights Group, Report on the 46th Session of the Human Rights Council, at www.universal-rights.org/blog/report-on-the-46th-session-of-the-human-rights-council/.

doi: 10.5553/HYIEL/266627012022010001016

diplomacy, making it as visible as their economic and trade diplomacy.[102] A statement with a similar underlying philosophy was delivered by Belarus on behalf of a group of states, including Iran, China, Burundi, Russia, Syria or Venezuela, criticizing the human rights situation of EU member states and the UK. Cuba managed to get 64 states to join a statement, which defended the Chinese "people-centered philosophy" and asked the international community to stop interfering into the internal affairs of China.[103] The response by the US to the above-mentioned attacks arrived during the same session, and in a statement on behalf of 53 states, these governments made it very clear that the human rights violations by a state cannot be considered as an internal affair and those states which committed them must be held accountable.[104] In order to reinforce its position, Washington also joined the statement delivered by Finland on behalf of 31 states on the human rights situation in Egypt,[105] and the statement delivered by Poland on behalf of 44 states on the human rights situation in Russia.[106]

An important feature of the session was that many states – especially with poorer human rights records – criticized the practice of human rights sanctions. The traditional resolution tabled by the Non-Alligned Movement on unilateral coercive measures was adopted by 30 to 15, with 2 abstentions.[107] The resolution certainly neglected the fact that most of the new sanction regimes adopted recently by the international community were so called smart sanctions targeting only the leading figures of a regime, trying to avoid their negative effects on society as a whole. It was also very telling that China tabled a hostile amendment to the resolution on Belarus, which was critical about the sanctions imposed against Minsk, and it was almost adopted by the HRC (12 to 18, with 17 abstentions).[108]

It was the first time that a specific COVID-19 focused resolution was adopted by the HRC on ensuring equitable, affordable, timely and universal access for all countries to vaccines. Although this resolution was adopted by consensus, it made it very clear that the pandemic made the inequalities among states even greater, and this was also reflected in their access to vaccination.

102 Joint Statement Delivered by China on Behalf of a Group of Countries at Item 4 General Debate, 46th Session of the Human Rights Council, 12 March 2021, at www.china-un.ch/eng/dbdt/t1860569.htm.

103 64 countries voice opposition to unfounded allegations against China on human rights, Xinhua, 1 March 2021, at www.xinhuanet.com/english/2021-03/13/c_139807296.htm.

104 Joint Statement under Item 8 at the 46th Session of the United Nations Human Rights Council, at https://geneva.usmission.gov/2021/03/19/joint-statement-under-item-8/.

105 Joint Statement by Finland on behalf of a group of countries on Egypt, 12 March 2021, at https://geneva.usmission.gov/2021/03/12/joint-statement-on-human-rights-in-egypt/.

106 Cross-regional joint statement, 12 March 2021, at https://geneva.usmission.gov/2021/03/12/joint-statement-on-the-deteriorating-situation-of-human-rights-in-russia/.

107 The negative impact of unilateral coercive measures on the enjoyment of human rights Human Rights Council resolution No. A/HRC/46/L.4, at https://documents-dds-ny.un.org/doc/UNDOC/LTD/G21/061/10/PDF/G2106110.pdf?OpenElement.

108 Universal Rights Group, Report on the 46th Session of the Human Rights Council, at www.universal-rights.org/blog/report-on-the-46th-session-of-the-human-rights-council/.

doi: 10.5553/HYIEL/266627012022010001016

Finally, it should be mentioned in relation to the developments prompted by the pandemic, that by that session the HRC became the first UN body using digital voting technology.[109]

From the 47th session of the HRC – taking place between 21 June and 13 July 2021 – the interactive debate between member states and the High Commissioner, Michelle Bachelet should be highlighted. During this debate the High Commissioner underlined the importance of respecting civil, political and socio-economic rights during the pandemic, and that vaccines should be considered a public good, and states should guarantee equitable access to them. Madame Bachelet expressed the wish to create a "human rights economy" through measures like progressive taxation, efficient and equitable allocation of resources, fighting corruption, and enhanced international cooperation.[110] An important cross-regional statement was delivered by Denmark on behalf of 46 states, suggesting a "Sustainable Recovery Pledge", according to which human rights should be put at the heart of efforts to "build back better" following the pandemic through the promotion of democratic principles, ensuring effective civil society participation, fighting inequalities and discrimination, and adopting an environmentally sensitive approach to recovery efforts.

Regarding country situations we can start with the resolution on the "Situation of human rights in Belarus", which was adopted by 21 to 7 with 19 abstentions. This result is somewhat worse than in 2017 (18 to 8, with 21 abstentions), but still there are supporters from each regional group, not just from Europe (Argentina, Bahamas, Brazil, Fiji, Japan, Malawi, Marshall Islands, Mexico, Republic of Korea, Uruguay). The resolution on "Syria" was adopted by 26 to 6 with 15 abstentions, which is however a somewhat better result than in 2017 (27 to 8, with 12 abstentions). Besides the supporters of the Belarusian resolution, we can find Cote d'Ivoire, Gabon, Libya, Somalia and Togo in the group. Compared with 2017, there were two new country resolutions submitted by the EU, on "Eritrea" and on the "Tigray region of Ethiopia". The first one was adopted by 21 to 13 with 13 abstentions, with almost the same supporters as in the case of the resolution on "Belarus". The only difference was that Armenia supported it (and did not abstain), in addition, Malawi abstained (and didn't support) the resolution on "Eritrea". The resolution on "Tigray region of Ethiopia" was adopted by 20 to 14 with 13 abstentions, with all African members of the Council either voting against it or abstaining. Finally, the voting result of the last country situation, namely on the "Cooperation with and assistance to Ukraine in the field of human rights" was somewhat worse than 5 years ago (22 to 6 with 19 abstentions), as it was adopted by 19 to 8 with 20 abstentions.[111]

Among the most divisive thematic resolutions we can mention the one on the "Enhancement of international cooperation in the field of human rights"

109 Id.

110 Universal Rights Group, Report on the 47th Session of the Human Rights Council, at www.universal-rights.org/nyc/uncategorized-nyc/report-on-the-47th-session-of-the-human-rights-council/.

111 Id.

Hungarian Yearbook of International Law and European Law 2022 (10) 1
doi: 10.5553/HYIEL/266627012022010001016

which was adopted by 30 to 14 with 3 abstentions. The resolution had almost the same number of supporters than 5 years ago, (32 to 3 with 14 abstentions) but the number of "no" votes significantly increased, indicating a growing polarization within the Council. Those who voted "no" were all European states, plus Japan and Korea. The other divisive resolution was the one on "Human rights and international solidarity" which was adopted by 32 to 14 with 1 abstention, which is almost the same result as it was in 2017 (32 to 15, without any abstentions).[112]

The 48th session of the HRC took place between 13 September and 11 October 2021.[113] There are 4 country situations we have to mention in respect of this session. The resolution on the "Situation of human rights in Syria" which was adopted by 23 to 7 with 17 abstentions, indicated a little less support than during the 47th session of the Council. The resolution on "Yemen" submitted by a core group headed by the Netherlands had been defeated by 18 to 21, with 7 abstentions, which was an unprecedented event. It was a success story for the EU in 2017, as the resolution adopted then established a mandate for a Group of Eminent Experts on Yemen. It was renewed in 2018, 2019, and in 2020. The third resolution is on "Burundi", which was adopted by 21 to 15, with 11 abstentions, which is a somewhat less promising result than the one achieved 5 years ago (22 to 11, with 14 abstentions). The last country initiative did not exist 5 years ago: it was tabled by the EU on the "Situation of human rights in Afghanistan" and was adopted by 28 to 5, with 14 abstentions. The initiative was supported by Argentina, Armenia, Bahamas, Brazil, Cote d'Ivoire, Fiji, India, Japan, Malawi, Mexico, Namibia, the Philippines, the Republic of Korea, Sudan, Togo and Uruguay besides the European members of the HRC.[114]

From among the thematic resolutions, the one entitled "From rhetoric to reality: a global call for concrete action against racism, racial discrimination, xenophobia and related intolerance" should be mentioned, which was submitted by the African Group and adopted by 32 to 10, with 5 abstentions, which indicates that more members voted "no" than those who abstained, unlike 5 years ago (32 to 5, with 10 abstentions). The resolution submitted by China on the "Negative impact of the legacies of colonialism on the enjoyment of human rights" was a clear sign of the increasingly active role Beijing intends to play within the Council, trying to counterbalance Washington. There were 3 "hostile" amendments tabled by the UK to the draft (one of them was subsequently withdrawn) and were adopted (16 to 13, with 16 abstentions, and 15 to 13, with 17 abstentions). The amended draft was finally adopted by 27 to 0, with 20 abstentions. This was a clear failure for China, who decided to withdraw its other initiative on "Realizing a better life for everyone". The traditional divisive resolutions of the session were on "Right to development" (29 to 13, with 5 abstentions) on "The use of mercenaries as a means of violating human rights and

112 Id.

113 Universal Rights Group, Report on the 48th Session of the Human Rights Council, at www.universal-rights.org/blog/report-on-the-48th-session-of-the-human-rights-council/.

114 Id.

doi: 10.5553/HYIEL/266627012022010001016

impeding the exercise of the right of peoples to self-determination" (29 to 14, with 4 abstentions) and on "The promotion of a democratic and equitable international order" (30 to 14, with 4 abstentions). The results were more or less the same 5 years ago: countries voted along the lines of the North-South division, just like in 2017. The resolution on the question of the "Death penalty" (29 to 12, with 5 abstentions) was supported by members of all regional groups and received more support than 5 years ago (27 to 13, with 7 abstentions).[115]

The last, 49th session of the HRC before I closed this paper took place between 28 February and 1 April 2022.[116] Starting with the traditionally controversial resolutions on the Middle East we can mention the one on the "Right of the Palestinian people to self-determination". This was adopted by 41 to 3, with 3 abstentions, with a "no" vote by US, UK and Marshall Islands and an abstention by Cameroon, Lithuania, and Honduras. The result was almost the same 5 years ago (43 to 2, with 2 abstentions). The second one was on the "Israeli settlements in the Occupied Palestinian Territory, including East Jerusalem, and its occupied Syria Golan", which was adopted by 38 to 4, with 5 abstentions. The voting result was 36 to 2, with 9 abstentions in 2017. The third one was on the "Human rights in the occupied Syrian Golan", which was adopted by 29 to 15, with 3 abstentions. In 2017 this resolution was adopted by 26 to 3, with 18 abstentions. The fourth one was on the "Human rights situation in the Occupied Palestinian territories", which was adopted by 31 to 14, with 2 abstentions. In 2017 it was adopted by 41 to 2, with 4 abstentions, which indicates a significant decrease in the support of that initiative by the OIC.[117]

The most important and new country initiative was on the "Situation of human rights in Ukraine stemming from the Russian aggression". This resolution which was submitted by Ukraine was adopted by 32 to 2, with 13 abstentions. Only Eritrea and Russia voted against the initiative. There was an old, traditional resolution on the "Human rights situation in the Islamic Republic of Iran" on the agenda of the session, which was adopted by 19 to 12, with 16 abstentions. The result of the adoption of that resolution in 2017 was 22 to 12, with 13 abstentions. There was a new resolution compared to 2017, namely the one on the "Protection and promotion of human rights in Nicaragua", which was submitted by a core group of American states and was adopted by 20 to 7, with 20 abstentions. Latin American members of the HRC were completely divided during the vote, as 4 of them supported the initiative (Argentina, Brazil, Mexico and Paraguay) while 4 were against it (Bolivia, Cuba, Honduras, and Venezuela). The resolution on the "Cooperation with Georgia" was adopted by 19 to 6, with 20 abstentions. Five years ago, the HRC adopted this initiative by 18 to 5, with 24 abstentions. Due to serious human right violations in connection with the presidential elections in Belarus the EU submitted a resolution entitled "Situation of human rights in Belarus in the run-up to the 2020 presidential election and its

115 Id.

116 Universal Rights Group, Report on the 49th Session of the Human Rights Council, at www.universal-rights.org/blog/report-on-the-49th-session-of-the-human-rights-council/.

117 Id.

doi: 10.5553/HYIEL/266627012022010001016

aftermath". The resolution was adopted by 22 to 6, with 19 abstentions. The last divisive country specific resolution of the session was on "Advancing human rights in South Sudan", which was submitted by a cross-regional core group and was adopted by 19 to 11, with 17 abstentions.[118] Five years ago the resolution on South Sudan was adopted without a vote.

Among the divisive thematic resolutions, we have to mention the traditional one on the "Negative impact of unilateral coercive measures on the enjoyment of human rights", which was tabled by NAM and was adopted by 27 to 14, with 6 abstentions. Five years ago, the result was 32 to 14, without abstentions. The traditional initiative submitted by Cuba on the "Effects of foreign debt" was adopted by 29 to 14, with 4 abstentions. In 2017 this resolution was adopted by 31 to 16, without abstentions. The last resolution to be mentioned in this context is the initiative on "Promoting and protecting economic, social and cultural rights within the context of addressing inequalities in the recovery from COVID-19 pandemic", which was submitted by Bolivia, China, Egypt, Pakistan and South Africa and the HRC adopted it by 31 to 14, with 2 abstentions. This resolution created an almost full North-South divide. Only Honduras, and Marshall Islands rejected the resolution from the South.[119]

9. Conclusion

Based on the main findings of this research, we can safely state that *the HRC did not become a platform for the clash of civilizations.* It does not mean, however, that there are no issues sharply dividing the HRC membership and that there are easy solutions to overcome these debates. However, most of these are not civilizational issues, but related to the existing economic, social, and political problems of the Global South, which are abused by several HRC member states to escalate tensions between the North and the South.[120] If we look at the sensitive human rights issues, such as country situations, or the question of civil society, or the prevention of reprisals against those who cooperate with the UN in the field of human rights, we find that the *dividing lines are not among civilizations.* Instead, they are between those countries that consider the protection and promotion of human rights worldwide to be an important political aim, and those that are interested in the weakening of the international human rights monitoring system, to be able to continue their policy of abusing human rights without any serious international consequences. When comparing the voting results of 2017 with 2021/22, we can see that *most of the dividing lines remained the same* and there were no significant differences between the voting patterns of the two periods. However, we can see that polarization has grown among member states, which is illustrated by the increasing proportion of "no" votes instead of abstentions, as reflected in the case of several resolutions.

118 Id.
119 Id.
120 István Lakatos, *Comparative Human Rights Diplomacy*, Palgrave Macmillan (e-book), 2022, p. 362.

doi: 10.5553/HYIEL/266627012022010001016

Questions of General International Law with Special Regard to the Security Council's Competence

Mohammad Alipour & Anikó Szalai[*]

Abstract

Based on Article 1 of the UN Charter, the Security Council (SC) shall act in accordance with international law to prevent and remove threats to international peace and security. Even though Article 103 of the UN Charter confers some sort of supremacy on the decisions of the SC, there are nevertheless certain fundamental norms in international law that restrict the SC's powers from which no derogation is permitted. These are referred to under the heading General International Law (GIL). Principles of GIL are classified into two types: axiomatic and axiological. The former consists of rational principles developed from the logic of nature and the structure of international law and society, and the latter are derived from the values of the international community. GIL does not require the consent of states and impacts the freedom of all subjects of international law, including the UN and its organs. Throughout the course of performing its tasks under the UN Charter, the SC must adhere to the requirements of GIL.

Keywords: Security Council, UN Charter, general international law, jus cogens, erga omnes.

1. Introduction

Once the Security Council ascertains that the commission of mass atrocities by a state is a threat to peace, it can apply a wide range of powers conferred upon it by the UN Charter. The scope of this wide competence makes it necessary to examine whether the SC's competence is limited by general international law when it comes to maintaining international peace and security. The first paragraph of Article 1 of the UN Charter is the point where further elaboration is justified. Due to the ambiguity in the Article's language, the question has been raised as to whether the UN Charter grants certain exemptions to the SC when it comes to implementing international law.

Several commentators have interpreted the Article as giving the SC *carte blanche* to disregard the mandatory aspects of international law whenever

* Mohammad Alipour: PhD student, University of Szeged. Anikó Szalai: associate professor of law, University of Szeged.

doi: 10.5553/HYIEL/266627012022010001017

maintaining peace and security is the focus[1] *(exceptional interpretation)*. This paper will critically evaluate their contentions and argue that all bodies of the UN, including the SC, must adhere to general international law *(integral interpretation)*.

As a consequence of integral interpretation, certain rules of international law are binding without exception, on all subjects of international law.[2] They are known as GIL. Due to the fact that scholars use the term GIL in various contexts with different meanings, there is no general definition or consensus regarding its concept, and each author provides evidence to support their argument. In some cases, GIL is regarded as a customary rule of international law, in others as a synergy of customary and general principles of law, and the last group of scholars places emphasis on the number of subjects of a rule, namely, if all or a large number of states are members of a treaty or are involved in a customary rule, the relevant rule becomes a GIL. The authors argue that GIL is used in contemporary international law as an indication of the basic norms of international law in a novel concept. The concept of GIL was applied in this sense in Article 53 VCLT as well as in the practice of certain international courts and tribunals. In this context, GIL cannot be equated with the main sources of international law, as reflected in Article 38 ICJ Statute, but is much rather an *infra* legal issue. Essentially, it refers to the principles that are the pillars upon which modern international law is based and developed. These principles are rooted in the realities of international relations and were developed in response to the requirements of the collective life of states. If states resolve to form an international community, as they do, inevitably they must be conscious of the requirements of building a society. The principles of GIL are dynamic in nature,

1 David Schweigman, *The authority of the Security Council under Chapter VII of the UN Charter: legal limits and the role of the International Court of Justice*, Kluwer Law International, The Hague, 2001, p. 29; Hans Kelsen, *The law of the United Nations: a critical analysis of its fundamental problems: with supplement*, Stevens & Sons, London, 1951, p. 730; Bernd Martenczuk,'The Security Council, the International Court and judicial review: what lessons from Lockerbie?', *European Journal of International Law*, Vol. 10, Issue 3, 1999, pp. 544-545; Devon Whittle, 'The Limits of Legality and the United Nations Security Council: Applying the Extra-Legal Measures Model to Chapter VII Action', *European Journal of International Law*, Vol. 26, Issue 3, 2015, p. 680; Leland M. Goodrich *et al.*, *The Charter of the United Nations*, Columbia University Press, London, 1969, pp. 27-28; Miguel Lemos, 'Jus Cogens Versus the Chapter VII Powers of the Security Council: With Particular References to Humanitarian Intervention and Terrorism', *Chinese Journal of International Law*, Vol. 19, Issue 1, 2020, pp. 31-32; Stefan Talmon,'The Security Council as world legislature', *American Journal of International Law*, Vol. 99, Issue 1, 2005, p. 184.

2 Simon Chesterman, 'The UN Security Council and the Rule of Law', UN General Assembly Security Council, Doc. A/63/69-S/2008/270, 2008, p. 10; Ramses A. Wessel, 'The UN, the EU and Jus Cogens', *International Organizations Law Review*, Vol. 3, Issue 1, 2006, p. 3; Matthew Saul & Nigel D. White. 'Legal means of dispute settlement in the field of collective security: The quasi-judicial powers of the Security Council', *in* Duncan French *et al.* (eds.), *International Law and Dispute Settlement: New Techniques and Problems*, Hart, Oxford, 2010, p. 206; Rosalyn Higgins, 'The place of international law in the settlement of disputes by the Security Council', *American Journal of International Law*, Vol. 64, Issue 1, 1970, p. 9; Terry D. Gill, 'Legal and some political limitations on the power of the UN Security Council to exercise its enforcement powers under Chapter VII of the Charter', *Netherlands Yearbook of International Law*, Vol. 26, 1995, pp. 78-79.

doi: 10.5553/HYIEL/266627012022010001017

for society is also a dynamic phenomenon. Therefore, GIL is the legal manifestation of international community requirements.

This article begins by discussing GIL as a novel concept. In this context, we discuss whether GIL should be viewed as an independent concept or as an equivalent to treaties, customs, general principles of law, or as a synthesis of the same. Next, we discuss Article 1 of the Charter as a point of disagreement between two interpretative approaches: the exceptional and the integral approach, and finally, the last section is devoted to the limitations placed on the SC by GIL.

2. General International Law in Positive International Law

Article 53 VCLT stipulated that "[a] treaty is void if, at the time of its conclusion, it conflicts with a peremptory norm of general international law. [...]" and Article 64 provided that "[i]f a new peremptory norm of general international law emerges, any existing treaty which is in conflict with that norm becomes void and terminates."

The 2001 Draft Articles on Responsibility of States for Internationally Wrongful Acts (DARSIWA) in Articles 26, 40 and 50 mentioned the "obligation arising under a peremptory norm of general international law". Articles 26, 41 and 53 of the 2011 Draft Articles on the Responsibility of International Organizations enshrined the same discourse and in both drafts, peremptory norms are considered to be rooted in general international law. In *Pulp Mills*, the ICJ held that,

> "[...] the obligation to protect and preserve, under Article 41(a) of the Statute, has to be interpreted in accordance with a practice, which in recent years has gained so much acceptance among States that it may now be considered a requirement under general international law to undertake an environmental impact assessment when there is a risk that the proposed industrial activity may have a significant adverse impact in a transboundary context."[3]

While in the *Certain Activities carried out by Nicaragua in the Border Area*, the ICJ, with finely tuned nuances, considered an obligation to conduct an environmental impact assessment under a treaty or customary law, rather than GIL.[4] In *Iron Rhine*, arbitration pointed out, that

> "where development may cause significant harm to the environment there is a duty to prevent, or at least mitigate, such harm [...] This duty, in the

3 ICJ, *Pulp Mills on the River Uruguay (Argentina v Uruguay)*, judgment, ICJ Reports 2010, pp. 14, and 83, para. 204.

4 ICJ, *Certain Activities carried out by Nicaragua in the Border Area (Costa Rica v Nicaragua)*, judgment, ICJ Reports 2015, pp. 708-710, paras. 108, and 112.

doi: 10.5553/HYIEL/266627012022010001017

opinion of the Tribunal, has now become a principle of general international law."[5]

In the *Indian Waters Kishenganga* arbitration, environmental impact assessment was considered under general international law and the ICJ's approach was reaffirmed once again.[6] In *Chagos*, in the same vein as the ICJ, the tribunal constructed its reasoning about international environmental law on the basis of general international law. The arbitration held that

> "[a]s a general matter, the Tribunal has little difficulty with the concept of procedural constraints on State action, and notes that such procedural rules exist elsewhere in international environmental law, for instance in the general international law requirement to carry out an environmental impact assessment in advance of large-scale construction projects."[7]

It is noteworthy that in all these cases, instead of considering the relevant rules from the perspective of treaties or customary law, the international courts and tribunals addressed them under the chapeau of GIL.

3. Distinction Between GIL and Sources of International Law

The sources of international law establish one of the most important patterns that provide the framework for international legal discourse as well as legal claims.[8] It has long been agreed by scholars that sources of international law are causes of disagreement and the controversies surrounding the sources of international law will prevail.[9] The latter are taken here to refer to recognized formal sources, since there is a fundamental rule, that only those recognized sources may be referred to, or relied upon, as creative sources of international law. Hence, an allusion to Article 38 of the ICJ Statute is inevitable in this context.[10] As to the Article, it should be stressed that it outlines the legal framework for the judicial function of the ICJ through which disputes should be resolved. Consequently, it is therefore not an exhaustive list of international law sources as such. As Pellet noted, the list of Article 38 is undoubtedly incomplete and with time, its lacunae emerged, hence, it is argued that "general reference to international law in the opening sentence suffices to enable the Court to have

5 PCA, *Iron Rhine (Belgium v Netherlands)*, Case 2003-2, Award of 24 May 2005, p. 29, para. 59.

6 PCA, *Indian Waters Kishenganga (Pakistan v India)*, Case 2011-01, Award of 20 December 2013, p. 291, paras. 450-451.

7 PCA, *Chagos Maritime Protected Area Arbitration (Mauritius v United Kingdom)*, Case 2011-03, Award of 18 March 2015, p. 129, para. 322.

8 Jean d'Aspremont & Samantha Besson (eds.), *The Oxford Handbook of the Sources of International Law*, Oxford University Press, Oxford, 2017, p. 2.

9 Samantha Besson & Jean D'Aspremont, 'The Sources of International Law', *in* d'Aspremont & Besson (eds.) 2017, pp. 6-7.

10 Hugh Thirlway, *The Sources of International Law*, 2nd edition, Oxford University Press, Oxford, 2019, p. 8.

doi: 10.5553/HYIEL/266627012022010001017

recourse to other sources of international law whenever it deems this necessary."[11] Crawford wrote that

> "[i]n the context of international relations, however, the use of the term 'formal source' is misleading since it conjures up notions associated with the constitutional machinery of law-making within states. No such machinery exists for the creation of international law."[12]

Klabbers pointed out, that "this already suggests that the list is not exhaustive; it is possible that there are sources of law not mentioned in Article 38 Statute ICJ."[13] Tomuschat contended that "even by simple logical inference, one can conclude that Article 38 does not set forth an exhaustive regulation of all and any conceivable sources of international law."[14]

Regarding the interaction between the sources of international law and GIL, the latter is another whole level, and should be assessed in accordance with the nature of the international legal system and the requirements of the international community. The axiomatic (rational) principles arise from the structure of the international legal system, which is an indivisible component of the legal system like *pacta sunt servanda*. In essence, these principles are legal fictions that serve as the basis for a legal system to operate and make sense. As a result of the evolution of a community based on the axis of humanity, the international community develops axiological principles. Article 53 VCLT, in which GIL is described as the source of peremptory norms, makes reference to this concept.

In this vein, Tomuschat analyzed whether the concept of GIL could be equated with the three aforementioned sources, or whether it requires its own consideration. He started with the presumption that "[t]he concept of GIL presupposes that there exist legal rules which address every subject of international law."[15] Regarding the treaties, in constructing his argument, he relied on the principle of *pacta tertiis nec nocent nec prosunt*, which has application even to conventions whose implementation serves the interest of the entire international community.[16]

According to the principle of equality of sovereignty, a treaty cannot confer rights or impose obligations without the consent of the states.[17] Moreover, the rejection of a treaty is not always due to the incompatibility of a norm with the

11 Alain Pellet, 'Article 38', *in* Andreas Zimmermann *et al.* (eds.), *The Statute of the International Court of Justice: A Commentary*, Oxford University Press, Oxford, 2012, pp. 1421-1422.

12 James Crawford, *Brownlie's principles of public international law*, 8th edition, Oxford University Press, Oxford, 2012, p. 20.

13 Jan Klabbers, *International law*, Cambridge University Press, Cambridge, 2017, p. 24.

14 Christian Tomuschat, 'General International Law: A New Source of International Law?', *in* Riccardo Pisillo Mazzeschi & Pasquale De Sena (eds.), *Global Justice, Human Rights, and the Modernization of International Law*, Springer, 2018, p. 188.

15 Id. p. 189.

16 Id.

17 Id. p. 190.

doi: 10.5553/HYIEL/266627012022010001017

national interest.[18] It could be the case that states may not be willing to subject themselves to the mechanism of the treaty concerned, while agreeing with its norms.[19] Therefore, international treaties cannot be classified as GIL.[20] Similarly, Thirlway believed that the rules of *jus cogens* are principally outside the purview of treaties.[21] As an example, let's say that most members of the international community have ratified a treaty on certain human rights. Would it be possible to consider the concomitant norms as GIL in this case? There answer would be in the negative. Because in lack of third-party consent, it is not possible to bind that third party. In light of the presumption outlined above, the given norm cannot be considered a rule of GIL, because it does not apply to all subjects of international law. In another possible scenario, all members have ratified a treaty in which a withdrawal clause had been inserted. In this case, at the time of membership of all parties, the norm may be considered as GIL, but what if some of the parties withdraw from the accord? Due to the fact that they no longer adhere to the rule of the norm, the treaty does not apply to them either as GIL or any other title, and the given norm would cease to be GIL due to the loss of universal membership. It is possible to argue that a state is bound by the given rule, since the latter had become a customary rule of international law. If the state was not a persistent objector, this argument would be valid. The majority of the members of the international community, but not all, ratified the 1948 Convention on the Prevention and Punishment of the Crime of Genocide. If a non-party, who is also a persistent objector, violates the Genocide Convention, then no one has the right to interrogate the state concerned,[22] while in *Genocide*, the ICJ held that the norms of the Genocide Convention are binding upon states, even in the absence of any conventional obligations.[23] In addition, South Africa's claim that it was a persistent objector to the prohibition of racial discrimination and apartheid was universally rejected on the grounds that a persistent objector is not exempt from peremptory norms.[24]

The same point was made by Byers, who argued that treaties merely generate obligations between parties and do not have the capability of establishing a rule of GIL. This is because firstly, it is impossible for treaties to compel parties to modify them in the future or to release them from their obligations thereunder,

18 Id.

19 Id.

20 Id.

21 Hugh Thirlway, *The Sources of International Law*, 2nd edition, Oxford University Press, Oxford, 2019, p. 176.

22 By referring to *jus cogens*, one can provide another argument for neutralizing the legal effect of persistent objectors. Due to the fact that genocide is prohibited under *jus cogens*, the persistent objector norm is irrelevant in this instance. Report of the International Law Commission on the Work of Its Seventy-First Session, UN GAOR, 74th Sess., Supp. No. 10, pp. 1-2, paras. 1, and 3, UN Doc. A/74/10, 16 September 2019, pp. 144-145.

23 ICJ, *Reservations to the Convention on the Prevention and Punishment of the Crime of Genocide (Advisory Opinion)*, ICJ Reports 1951, p. 23.

24 Jure Vidmar, 'Norm Conflicts and Hierarchy in International Law: Towards a Vertical International Legal System?', *in* Erika de Wet & Jure Vidmar (eds.), *Hierarchy in International Law: The Place of Human Rights*, Oxford University Press, Oxford, 2012, p. 26.

doi: 10.5553/HYIEL/266627012022010001017

and secondly, despite the fact that *jus cogens* norms are universally applicable and binding, none of the international treaties that include *jus cogens* have been universally ratified.[25] Articles 53 and 64 VCLT would appear to indicate that GIL does not fall within the customary rules of international law since it does not recognize practice as an essential component of *jus cogens*, and that the consensus of the international community as a whole determines which norm should be considered *jus cogens*.[26] Thirlway raised an intriguing question in this regard, namely, "[i]f jus cogens norms exist without the custom-generative process being followed, then why class them as custom at all: why not recognize them as something different?"[27]

Lastly, with respect to General Principles of Law, Tomuschat maintained

> "general principles of law and GIL remain alien to one another. In all the cases that constitute the testing ground for the present considerations, where the concept of GIL was resorted to, the requisite broad scope of the norm concerned as a 'principle' was visibly absent. In the *Pulp Mills* case, the concept of environmental impact assessment denotes a complex procedure with well-known specificities, the fruit of some environmental principles whose legal nature has not yet been fully established under international law, the principle of prevention and the precautionary principle. Accordingly, to range an environmental impact assessment among the general principles of law pursuant to Article 38(1)(c) ICJ Statute would amount to a misleading systematization of that procedure, hardly compatible with the original understanding of general principles."[28]

Relying on the ICJ's methodological approach in *Bosnia-Herzegovina v Serbia and Montenegro* and *Croatia v Serbia*, he reinforced his argument. In fact,

> "rules on interpretation of treaties, on State responsibility and on succession in respect of obligations that have arisen as a consequence of the commission of an internationally wrongful act [...] are in principle straightforward rules that do not require lengthy deductions from a general principle"

and therefore, the ICJ's method implied a specific place for general international law.[29] He noted that, in practice, the ICJ often used GIL and customary law interchangeably, for example in *Fisheries (UK v Norway)*, but at other times, it used GIL in a manner that did not correspond to customary law, like in *Pulp Mills*.

25 Michael Byers, 'Conceptualising the relationship between Jus Cogens and Erga Omnes Rules', *in* Koen De Feyter (ed.), *Globalization and Common Responsibilities of States*, Routledge, London, pp. 220-221.

26 Tomuschat 2018, p. 195.

27 Thirlway 2019, pp. 178-182.

28 Id. p. 193.

29 Id. p. 194.

doi: 10.5553/HYIEL/266627012022010001017

> "The rule proclaimed [in these cases] is not inferred from the accumulation of practice by way of induction but is deduced from axiomatic premises of the international legal order. ICJ preferred [...] to invoke GIL without attempting to show that its approach was supported by that kind of consistent practice which, in theory, it views as a condition for the existence of a rule of customary law."[30]

Additionally, since there is no hierarchy between the formal sources of international law (treaties, customary law, and general principles of law), if one considers GIL to be equivalent to any of these sources, then two or more subjects of international law may conclude a treaty or establish a customary rule inconsistent with GIL, which is the birthplace of peremptory norms.[31]

4. Nature of General International Law

In the wake of the treaties of Westphalia, the face of the world changed and classical international law emerged as the minimum legal order to govern relations between sovereigns. States were not forced into such a legal order by a powerful state or a super-state entity, it was much rather the result of the requirements of living together in an international society.

As Stephan wrote, "[t]he international order insists that states bear certain duties by their very nature of existing in an international system, independent of any manifestation of assent to the obligation."[32] It was a matter of facts and circumstances that prompted the states to adopt a legal mechanism to control the absolute will of international actors, or otherwise no sovereignty would be immune from the other's aggression or interference, and consequently, nobody would be safe. The states submitted to international law not out of courtesy or true belief in the common good, but rather because they had no other alternative to pursue their interests. Thus, after many years, the international forum evolved into an international society based on two constituent elements: state and law.[33] Although this order is significant, it should not be overstated. The fact that international society was governed by law does not mean that states did not rebel against it. As long as their interests so require, they disregard the law. Further, classical international law was a kind of private law, meaning the states did not engage with the international society in order to advance a common good, but rather to safeguard and defend their national interests. Accordingly, international law was informed by reciprocity, and provided a mechanism for

30 Id. p. 200.

31 Report of the International Law Commission Fifty-seventh session (2 May-3 June and 11 July-5 August 2005), Supplement No. 10 (A/60/10), p. 223, para. 487. However, some commentators believed that peremptory norms are the basis of hierarchy in international law. This approach can be justified under the category of material hierarchy in international law.

32 Paul B. Stephan, 'The political economy of jus cogens', *in* Alberta Fabbricotti (ed.), *The Political Economy of International Law*, Edward Elgar Publishing, Northampton, 2016, p. 1078.

33 Hermann Mosler, *The international society as a legal community*, Sijthoff & Noordhoff, Alphen aan den Rijn, 1980, pp. 18-19.

doi: 10.5553/HYIEL/266627012022010001017

organizing the freedom to act, the distribution of responsibilities, and the corresponding obligations.[34]

The aftermath of classical international law has left its mark on world history through regional wars, colonialism, and most notably, two destructive World Wars. The negative impact of the private law nature of classical international law was experienced with all its inevitable ramifications. The international community responded to these facts by revising and rearranging international law to meet the requirements of collective life. Hence, the Members moderated the private nature of international law by incorporating the common good as a new element of international law. During this phase, international law underwent a dramatic transformation from classical to modern international law. This, however, was not an easy task. Unlike in national societies, where unifying elements are already in place as a result of a historical common ground, international societies lack both of these factors, as well as the willingness of its members to sacrifice their own interests for the benefit of the international community.[35] For this reason, modern international law was developed to achieve the common good by unifying members of the international community. Toward this end, the international community is perceived as a fiction and its realization relies on the fulfillment of the requirement of collective life. These requirements are reincarnated as general principles, which are distinct from general principles of law. As regards the former, it is one of the sources of international law, while the latter is an *infra*-legal principle and a constituent element of General International Law. According to Judge Cancado Trindade, international law has certain principles "pertaining to the *substratum* of all international legal norms, and, accordingly, to the very foundations of the international legal system."[36] These principles are characterized as

> "fundamental principles of law which identify themselves with the very foundations of the legal system, revealing the values and ultimate ends of the international legal order, guiding it, protecting it against the incongruencies of the practice of States, and fulfilling the necessities of the international community."[37]

GIL consists of two types of principles: those derived from rational requirements associated with membership in the international community *(axiomatic)*, and those rooted in values *(axiology)*. The principles of GIL apply to every subject of international law who aspires to become a member of the fiction of international community. As Mosler pointed out, "[p]rinciples and Rules Derived from the Specific Nature of the International Community."[38] States shall accept the

34 Hedayatollah Falsafi, *International law of Treaties*, Nashr Now publications, Tehran, 2016, p. 28.

35 For instance, nuclear states are reluctant to achieve an agreement in order to nuclear weapon disarmament.

36 Antonio Augusto Cançado Trindade, *International law for humankind: towards a new jus gentium*, Brill/Nijhoff, Leiden, 2010, p. 63.

37 Id. p. 59.

38 Mosler 1980, p. 130.

doi: 10.5553/HYIEL/266627012022010001017

requirements of an international community governed by the rule of law if they assume such a community. Hence, the term "general" signifies the potentiality embodied in the content of these principles as well as their status, namely the basis, rank, and importance of these principles in the international legal system.[39] A broad scope of application is not a constituent element of GIL, but much rather an inevitable consequence of the same. Due to the importance of GIL and its function as a fundamental pillar of international law and a guarantee of collective life, it must be applicable to all subjects of international law. As Tunkin wrote, "[...] general international law, which is the foundation of the whole system of international law."[40]

What differentiates GIL from other sources of international law is the states' will. In contrast with obligations arising from other sources, obligations originating from GIL do not require the consent of states. An opponent of positivism might argue that such an interpretation of GIL is contrary to the positive nature of international law, since there is no evidence of consent. In response, the practice of ICJ may be instructive. As previously mentioned, the axiomatic principles of GIL are *a priori* principles that enable the establishment and formation of a society. Hence, they directly originate from societal requirements. In *Reparation for Injuries Suffered in the Service of the UN*, the ICJ's argument concerning the determination of the legal personality of the UN is noteworthy. The ICJ shed light on the impact of the requirements of international life on the development of international law, and confirmed that international law evolves together with social change. The ICJ held that

> "[t]he subjects of law in any legal system are not necessarily identical in their nature or in the extent of their rights, and their nature depends upon the needs of the community. Throughout its history, the development of international law has been influenced by the requirements of international life, and the progressive increase in the collective activities of States has already given rise to instances of action upon the international plane by certain entities which are not States."[41]

In addition, the ICJ illustrated the basis for the international legal personality of the UN by arguing that

> "the Court's opinion is that fifty States, representing the vast majority of the members of the international community, had the power, in conformity with international law, to bring into being an entity possessing objective international personality, and not merely personality recognized by them alone, together with capacity to bring international claims."[42]

39 Falsafi 2016, p. 45.

40 Grigory Tunkin, 'Is general international law customary law only', *European Journal of International Law,* Vol. 4, Issue 4, 1993, p. 538.

41 ICJ, *Reparation for Injuries Suffered in the Service of the United Nations (Advisory Opinion)*, ICJ Reports 1949, p. 178.

42 Id. p. 185.

doi: 10.5553/HYIEL/266627012022010001017

At first glance, one may be inclined to question that the UN Charter is a treaty, and under the principle of *res inter alios acta alteri nocere non debet*, it cannot affect third states and be construed as being applicable to them. The ICJ, however, ruled that UN has objective international personality, which entitles it to exercise its duties and rights even against non-member parties. It is noteworthy that the ICJ did not tie the establishment of legal personality to the will of the states parties, that is, since they constitute a majority, they can grant a new entity legal personality. Even though fifty states have established the UN, its personality is not a result of their will. Only through independent personality will the UN be able to fulfill its vocations. Given that the UN is the defender of common good for all members of the international community, it must necessarily enjoy rights and duties under international law and must be opposable to all. Therefore, the common good, for which the UN is responsible, necessitates objective personalities, and the will of fifty states, as representatives of the international community, is evidence of such a personality.

As an example of GIL being applied to a dispute by the ICJ, *Nicaragua* is another case. As part of its allegations, Nicaragua accused the US of violating the UN Charter and customary rules of international law and general international law by use of force. The US claimed that the ICJ cannot proceed under the Charter, due to the Vandenberg Amendment. This reservation excluded

> "disputes arising under a multilateral treaty, unless *(i)* all Parties to the treaty affected by the decision are also Parties to the case before the Court, or *(ii)* the United States of America specially agrees to jurisdiction."[43]

Regarding the reservation, the US claimed that the ICJ is not permitted to proceed under the Charter because the affected states, as Charter members, have not accepted the compulsory jurisdiction of the ICJ in this case.[44] Despite accepting the defense, ICJ proceeded to the charge in accordance with customary international law. To determine whether prohibition of use of force is a customary international law rule, the ICJ considered *opinio juris* and practice. According to ICJ, the US *opinio juris* exists through consent to conventions and numerous resolutions that prohibit the use of force.[45] But, the approach of the ICJ is intriguing in terms of identifying the practice. There was no recognition of any practice by the US. In principle, identifying a specific act as a customary rule is not an easy task,[46] let alone identifying an omission of act as a constituent element of customary law, particularly as far as the use of force is concerned, since there has been a proliferation of such incidents since the adoption of the

43 Declaration of the United States of America recognizing as compulsory the jurisdiction of the court, in conformity with Article 36, para. 2, of the Statute of the International Court of Justice, UN Treaty Series, Vol. I, 1946-1947, p. 10.

44 ICJ, *Military and Paramilitary Activities in und against Nicaragua (Nicaragua v US)*, judgment, ICJ Reports 1986, p. 92, para. 173.

45 Id. pp. 99-100, paras. 188-189.

46 Martti Koskenniemi, 'General principles: reflections on constructivist thinking in international law', *in* Martti Koskenniemi (ed.), *Sources of International Law*, Routledge, London, 2000, p. 397.

doi: 10.5553/HYIEL/266627012022010001017

UN Charter. However, the ICJ's approach was innovative. Rather than focusing on practice, it focused again on *opinio juris*. The ICJ held that

> "[t]he Court does not consider that, for a rule to be established as customary, the corresponding practice must be in absolutely rigorous conformity with the rule. In order to deduce the existence of customary rules, the Court deems it sufficient that the conduct of States should, in general, be consistent with such rules, and that instances of State conduct inconsistent with a given rule should generally have been treated as breaches of that rule, not as indications of the recognition of a new rule. If a State acts in a way prima facie incompatible with a recognized rule, but defends its conduct by appealing to exceptions or justifications contained within the rule itself, then whether or not the State's conduct is in fact justifiable on that basis, the significance of that attitude is to confirm rather than to weaken the rule."[47]

The ICJ's reasoning regarding this practice is ambiguous. It found that if state conduct generally complies with the rule, it can be regarded as practice, whereas it is unclear which practice the ICJ was referring to, despite the fact that it did not address or identify "practice". One might argue that if the ICJ was seeking to identify practice, the international society is replete with war, although not on the scale of the two World Wars, thus, it is most likely that there is no customary rule prohibiting the use of force. Although the ICJ brought attention to practice, it shed light on the claim of the states that they always justified their use of force under the exceptions contained within the rule. Once again, the ICJ focused on the states' *opinio juris*, not their practice.

Regarding the *axiological principles of GIL*, this paper claims that it revolves around the axis of humanity. In the case concerning the *Genocide Convention*, the ICJ affirmed that adherence to the principles underlying the Genocide Convention is not contingent upon the states' consent. The ICJ held that

> "[t]he first consequence arising from this conception is that the principles underlying the Convention are principles which are recognized by civilized nations as binding on States, even without any conventional obligation. A second consequence is the universal character both of the condemnation of genocide and of the co-operation required 'in order to liberate mankind from such an odious scourge' (Preamble to the Convention)."[48]

4.1. General International Law: The Provenance of Jus Cogens and Erga Omnes

Legal literature also refers to GIL under the title of *jus cogens* and *erga omnes*. Article 53 VCLT identifies the provenance of peremptory norms in general international law. In the same vein, Article 40 DARSIWA, declares that the

47 ICJ, *Certain Activities carried out by Nicaragua in the Border Area (Costa Rica v Nicaragua)*, judgment, ICJ Reports 2015, p. 729, para. 186.

48 ICJ, *Reservations to the Convention on the Prevention and Punishment of the Crime of Genocide (Advisory Opinion)*, ICJ Reports 1951, p. 23.

doi: 10.5553/HYIEL/266627012022010001017

peremptory norms of international law are derived from general international law. The concept of *erga omnes* was introduced to the international society by the ICJ[49] as a judicial body of the UN. Thereafter, legal literature revolved around the judgment to deliver clearer concepts of *erga omnes*.[50]

As *erga omnes* pertains to the common interest of the international community, its obligations are enforceable against any subject of international law, regardless of whether the consent of the subject has been expressed or not.[51] *Erga omnes* norms are derived from GIL[52] and for this reason they are associated with *jus cogens*. While the latter protects GIL norms within the context of treaties, the former seeks to do so in other areas of international law by bringing up the issue of responsibility for violation of correlative obligations. In its effort to codify articles related to the DARSIWA, the ILC did not refer ro the term *erga omnes*, but discussed it in the Commentary under Articles 40 and 48.[53] These Articles are included in Chapter three, titled "serious breaches of obligations under peremptory norms of general international law". The ILC did not add any new insights on *erga omnes*, but rather highlighted the practice of the ICJ by citing the ICJ's opinion regarding this issue.[54] Although the ILC's work appears not to add any new insight on *erga omnes* norms, their inclusion as particular consequences of a serious breach of an obligation under international law implies a subtle message. In the opinion of the ILC, the breach of peremptory norms and *erga omnes* norms have the same consequences.

5. Article 1 of the UN Charter, Place of the Dispute: Is International Law Applicable to the Security Council?

The competence of the SC has been a contentious issue since the San Francisco negotiations. The principal concern is whether, when the SC acts to maintain international peace and security, it is subject to any limitations. In *Lockerby*, Judge Shahabuddeen, in his separate opinion wrote that

> "In the equilibrium of forces underpinning the structure of the UN within the evolving international order, is there any conceivable point beyond which a

49 ICJ, *Barcelona Traction, Light and Power Company, Limited (Belgium v Spain)*, Merits, Second Phase, judgment, ICJ Reports 1970, p. 32, para. 33.

50 Christian J. Tams, *Enforcing obligations erga omnes in international law*, Cambridge University Press, Cambridge, 2005, p. 100.

51 Gaetano Arangio-Ruiz, *Fourth Report on State Responsibility*, Vol. II(1), Year book of ILC 34, 1992, para. 92; Robert Ago, Fifth Report on State Responsibility, Vol. II(1), Yearbook of ILC 29, 1976, para. 89; Thomas Weatherall, *Jus Cogens: International Law and Social Contract*, Cambridge University Press, Cambridge, pp. 352-353; Antonio Augusto Cançado Trindade, 'Jus Cogens: The Determination and The Gradual Expansion of Its Material Content in Contemporary International Case-Law', p. 6, at www.oas.org/en/about/who_we_are.asp.

52 Tams 2005, pp. 100, 114, and 121-122.

53 Draft articles on Responsibility of States for Internationally Wrongful Acts, with commentaries 2001, PP112-128

54 Id. pp. 112, 115, 116, and 127.

doi: 10.5553/HYIEL/266627012022010001017

legal issue may properly arise as to the competence of the Security Council to produce such overriding results? If there are any limits, what are those limits and what body, if other than the Security Council, is competent to say what those limits are?"[55]

In the same vein, Judge Weeramantry raises this issue in his dissenting opinion. He wrote "does [...] the Security Council discharge [...] its variegated functions free of all limitations, or is there a circumscribing boundary of norms or principles within which its responsibilities are to be discharged?"[56] To answer this question, naturally, but not exclusively, the Charter is the primary source. Article 1 provided that

> "To maintain international peace and security, and to that end: to take effective collective measures for the prevention and removal of threats to the peace, and for the suppression of acts of aggression or other breaches of the peace, and to bring about by peaceful means, and in conformity with the principles of justice and international law, adjustment or settlement of international disputes or situations which might lead to a breach of the peace;"

With regard to this paragraph, there are two opposing interpretative approaches: exceptional interpretation and integral interpretation.

5.1. Exceptional Interpretation

Based on the UN Charter, certain scholars believe that while the SC strives to maintain international peace and security, it is not subject to any limitations imposed by international law and is given *carte blanche* authority. Their argument rests on paragraph 1 of the UN Charter. They argue that the first part of the Article, which concerns collective measures, specifies the competence of the SC when acting for international peace and security, and the second segment refers to the duty of the Members and Organs, including the SC, to pursue peaceful

55 ICJ, *Questions of Interpretation and Application of the 1971 Montreal Convention arising from the Aerial Incident at Lockerbie (Libyan Arab Jamahiriya v United Kingdom)*, Order of 14 April 1992, Provisional measures, Separate Opinion of Judge Shahabuddeen, at p. 33.

56 Id., Dissenting Opinion of Judge Weeramantry, p. 61.

doi: 10.5553/HYIEL/266627012022010001017

settlement of disputes, in compliance with justice and international law, but the latter condition does not apply to collective measures.[57]

In short, they hold that if the international community is in a normal state, relations are governed by justice and international law, but when international peace and security are in danger, the SC may disregard justice and international law in order to restore or maintain peace and security. Therefore, extraordinary situations call for extraordinary measures.

In the context of exceptional interpretation, one approach classified the SC's actions into two clusters, namely those aimed at the peaceful resolution of disputes and those directed toward the maintenance and restoration of international peace and security. As far as the former is concerned, the SC is required to observe justice and international law, while regarding the latter, it is not, and such a derogation is justifiable under the theory of the extra-legal model.[58]

According to this approach, a connection was made between prevailing circumstances and the powers of the SC. Under normal circumstances, the SC is subject to international law, while when an abnormal situation arises, the SC enjoys freedom in the name of peace. Whittle acknowledged that such a scenario is clearly beyond the realm of the law, and therefore invoked the doctrine of mitigation.[59]

As per this doctrine, normal law applies in all situations, including an emergency, a violation of law by the executive may be ratified after a political, moral, and non-legal assessment which exempts the executive from the usual legal consequences of the unlawful action.[60] Such subsequent ratification does not modify the existing legal order, nor is it a derogation, but it exempts the executive from responsibility for wrongful actions taken in the event of an emergency.[61] The extra-legal measures model justifies unlawful action in light of

57 David Schweigman, *The authority of the Security Council under Chapter VII of the UN Charter: legal limits and the role of the International Court of Justice*, Kluwer Law International, The Hague, 2001, p. 29; Hans Kelsen, *The law of the United Nations: a critical analysis of its fundamental problems: with supplement*, Stevens & Sons, London, 1951, p. 730; Bernd Martenczuk, 'The Security Council, the International Court and judicial review: what lessons from Lockerbie?', *European Journal of International Law*, Vol. 10, Issue 3, 1999, pp. 544-545; Devon Whittle, 'The Limits of Legality and the United Nations Security Council: Applying the Extra-Legal Measures Model to Chapter VII Action', *European Journal of International Law*, Vol. 26, Issue 3, 2015, p. 680; Leland M Goodrich *et al.*, *The Charter of the United Nations*, Columbia University Press, London, 1969, pp. 27-28; Miguel Lemos, 'Jus Cogens Versus the Chapter VII Powers of the Security Council: With Particular References to Humanitarian Intervention and Terrorism', *Chinese Journal of International Law*, Vol. 19, Issue 1, 2020, pp. 31-32; Stefan Talmon, 'The Security Council as world legislature', *American Journal of International Law*, Vol. 99, Issue 1, 2005, p. 184.

58 Whittle 2015, p. 680.

59 Id. p. 681.

60 Oren Gross, 'Chaos and rules: Should responses to violent crises always be constitutional', *Yale Law Journal*, Vol. 112, Issue 5, 2002, pp. 1096-1106.

61 Oren Gross, 'Extra-legality and the ethic of political responsibility', *in* Victor V. Ramraj (ed.), *Emergencies and the Limits of Legality*, Cambridge University Press, Cambridge, 2008, p. 62.

doi: 10.5553/HYIEL/266627012022010001017

the values deemed to be protected by the law.[62] In the same vein, Whittle wrote that

> "[w]hen the UNSC acts under the Chapter VII, it could be argued that it enters an 'exceptional' phase of action, governed by a limited form of law different to the normal legal order."[63]

Taking precautions to avoid leaving the SC in a state of absolute freedom, he conditioned the SC's extralegal measures taken under Chapter VII on two requirements: *(i)* first, the SC must explicitly acknowledge the extra-legal nature of the action; and *(ii)* second, the action must be evaluated and adjudged by the international community.[64]

Rosand argues that the Charter's principles and purposes do not apply to the actions of the SC when it acts under Chapter VII, including the principles that prohibit the UN from interfering with matters that are essentially within the domestic jurisdiction of any state, as well as the need to act in conformity with the principles of justice and international law.[65] He went on to explain that international law merely restricts the actions of the SC under Chapter VI with regard to the exercise of its dispute resolution powers and concluded that

> "the measures the Council seeks to impose to address threats to peace and security need not be consistent with existing international law and may touch upon issues of largely domestic concern."[66]

The most radical opinion was taken by Miguel Lemos, who argued that when the SC acts to maintain or restore international peace and security, not only it is not obliged to observe justice and international law, but is also free to disregard *jus cogens* as well.[67] Otherwise, the measures for maintaining international peace and security would not be "effective" (according to Article 1) or "prompt and effective" (according to Article 24).[68]

In response to the argument that Article 53 VCLT (which states that any international agreement in conflict with the peremptory norm of general international law is void) has changed the classical legal order and appears as a limit on the SC,[69] he made the counterargument that *(i)* firstly, according to Article 103 of the UN Charter, obligations arising from the UN Charter take precedence over other international obligations, as reflected most prominently in

62 Gross 2002, pp. 1096-1106; Nomi Claire Lazar, *States of emergency in liberal democracies*. Cambridge University Press, Cambridge, 2009, p. 5.

63 Whittle 2015, p. 686.

64 Id.

65 Eric Rosand, 'The Security Council as Global Legislator: Ultra Vires or Ultra Innovative', *Fordham International Law Journal*, Vol. 28, Issue 3, 2005, p. 556.

66 Id.

67 Lemos 2020, p. 36.

68 Id. p. 32.

69 Id.

doi: 10.5553/HYIEL/266627012022010001017

Articles 30, 52 and 75 VCLT; *(ii)* secondly, Article 4 of the Convention provided that it "applies only to treaties which are concluded by States after [its] entry into force". Hence, VCLT *per se* is not sufficient to strengthen the idea that the SC is bound by *jus cogens*.[70] Regarding the relationship between the UN Charter and *jus cogens* he wrote that

> "[t]his suggests that the superiority of any jus cogens norm – irrespective of whether such norm was already in existence at the time of the adoption of the Charter or it was created only at a later stage – has to be reconciled with the superiority of Chapter VII decisions of the SC. Reconciliation is easy: as jus cogens norms exist in an international system the primordial objective of which is the maintenance of international peace and security, their superiority is only absolute to the extent that such superiority does not conflict with the primordial objective."[71]

Finally, Lemos and scholars sharing the same point of view, in order to reinforce their argument, invoked in preparation for the UN Charter given that the drafters deliberately failed to restrict the SC to act in compliance with justice and international law.[72] As Schweigman observed

> "[t]he obligation to act in conformity with international law is only prescribed for the latter category, and the negotiating history of the Charter reveals that this was done deliberately. An amendment that would have extended the obligation to act in conformity with the principles of justice and international law to measures taken by the Council pursuant to its responsibility for the maintenance of international peace and security, was rejected by the major powers as curtailing the Council's freedom of (swift) action."[73]

5.2. Integral Interpretation

The UN Charter is first and foremost an international treaty and should be interpreted in light of the rules of the law of the treaties. Regarding the general rule of interpretation, Article 31(1) VCLT provided "[a] treaty shall be interpreted in good faith in accordance with the ordinary meaning to be given to the terms of the treaty in their context and in the light of its object and purpose" and Article 31(3)(c) stated that "[t]here shall be taken into account, together with the context: [...] *(c)* any relevant rules of international law applicable in the relations between the parties." According to these Articles, any interpretation shall be done in the context of international law.

Although Article 4 VCLT provided that it is binding only on the parties of the Convention and does not have retroactive effect, a set of rules for interpretation

70 Id. pp. 32-33.

71 Id.

72 Id.; Schweigman 2001, p. 29.

73 Id.

doi: 10.5553/HYIEL/266627012022010001017

is also contained in customary law, which operates in conjunction with the rules of interpretation outlined in Articles 31, 32 and 33. These rules of international custom are identical to those specified in the VCLT.[74] Therefore, Articles 31-33 VCLT should be considered as evidence of both the rules of interpretation applicable under the convention between its parties, as well as the rules that apply under customary international law.[75] The authors argue below that an integral interpretation of Article 1(1) is consistent with the context of international law.

6. Interaction Between the Security Council and General International Law

We now move on to analyze the interaction between the SC and GIL. The GIL, as discussed above, is a response to the needs of collective life and constitutes the foundation of an international legal order that is binding on all.[76] Therefore, the SC as an organ of the UN is subject to GIL.[77] The SC was established in order to maintain international peace and security in light of international order.

In the aftermath of World War II, *opinio juris* became the legitimate basis for conduct and as such, the absolute will of the state was replaced by the rule of law. Rule of law has the effect of distributing competence between subjects of international law and limiting uncontrolled freedom of action. The SC is not an exception and must adhere to the legal order upon which it came to exist. As the International Criminal Tribunal for the Former Yugoslavia (ICTY) held

> "[t]he Security Council is an organ of an international organization, established by a treaty which serves as a constitutional framework for that organization. The Security Council is thus subjected to certain constitutional limitations, however broad its powers under the constitution may be. Those powers cannot, in any case, go beyond the limits of the jurisdiction of the Organization at large [...]."[78]

Considering this scenario, it is difficult to accept the conclusion that the SC has the authority to disturb the international legal order for the maintenance of international peace and security, which in turn is directly related to the international legal order. There appears to be an obvious contradiction in such an approach. The proposition that the SC is not bound by international law amounts to the denial of the rule of law and the establishment of international law, while

74 Ulf Linderfalk, *The Modern International Law as Expressed in the 1969 Vienna Convention on the Law of Treaties*, Springer, Netherlands, 2007, p. 7.

75 Id. *See* more about the existence of agreements on the customary character of Articles 31-33 among states, scholars, and international courts in Linderfalk, 2007, endnotes 21, 22, 23, p. 24.

76 Josef L. Kunz, 'General International Law and the Law of International Organizations', *The American Journal of International Law*, Vol. 47, Issue 3, 1953, p. 456.

77 Id. p. 458.

78 ICTY, *Prosecutor v. Dusko Tadic aka "Dule"*, Trial Chamber in the Trial Chamber Decision on the Defence Motion on Jurisdiction, Case No. IT-94-1-T, 10 August 1995, para. 28.

doi: 10.5553/HYIEL/266627012022010001017

at the same time turning the Council into a super-state – a view that was explicitly rejected by the ICJ. The Court held that

> "[s]till less is it the same things as saying that it is "a super-State", whatever that expression may mean. It does not even imply that all its right and duties must be upon the international plane, anymore that all the rights and duties of a State must be upon that plane. What it does mean is that it is a subject of international law and capable of possessing international rights and duties [...]."[79]

Last but not least, the commentators who support the SC's freedom from compliance with international law, cite the preparatory work of the UN Charter at San Francisco. According to them, Norway's government proposal to incorporate certain rules of conduct for the SC in the Charter was rejected, and this rejection implies that the drafters did not intend to limit the SC by international law. Nevertheless, no consensus has been reached concerning such an understanding of the preparatory work. As noted by some commentators, the legislative history of the SC leaves some doubt as to whether the SC can adopt measures that are contrary to international law.[80] Furthermore, Norway's primary concern was the political independence and equality of states, and its amendment was tailored to provide some assurance regarding "independence, territorial integrity [and] of their continued existence as political entitles".[81] The Norwegian government sought to ensure that the SC would not act as a superstate. If rejection of the amendment is considered to imply that the SC can disregard international law, they must accept *contrario* the argument, that the SC has the power to target the independence and territorial integrity of a state. Such an interpretation runs counter to both the Charter and the foundations of international law.

In addition, one may also refer to Article 32 VCLT. The Article considered preparatory work of the treaty as a supplementary means of interpretation (not primary) when the interpretation according to Article 31 VCLT would be ambiguous, obscure, or manifestly absurd or unreasonable, while Article 1(1) of the UN Charter is clear, calling for all actions to maintain international peace and security to be carried out in accordance with justice and international law.

As to the exception interpretation, it remains unclear why states attempt to form relations based on the rule of law to ensure social order, while at the same time establishing the SC with unlimited power, capable of violating any order, norm, or rule in the interest of peace and security.

The findings of this study suggest that the phrase "in conformity with justice and international law" in Article 1 of the UN Charter applies to the SC, and since GIL is a component of international law, the SC is subject to it.

79 ICJ, *Reparation for Injuries Suffered in the Service of the United Nations (Advisory Opinion)*, ICJ Reports 1949, p. 179.

80 Rüdiger Wolfrum, 'Purposes and Principles, Article 1', *in* Bruno Simma *et al.* (eds.), *The Charter of the United Nations: A Commentary*, Vol. I, Oxford University Press, Oxford, 2012, p. 114.

81 *See* at https://archive.org/details/documentsoftheun008818mbp/page/n395/mode/2up.

doi: 10.5553/HYIEL/266627012022010001017

6.1. Article 103 of the UN Charter and Jus Cogens

It is important to analyze the conflict between the SC decision and *jus cogens*. Which obligation has supremacy? Article 103 of the UN Charter provided that

> "[i]n the event of a conflict between the obligations of the UN Members under the present Charter and their obligations under any other international agreement, their obligations under the present Charter shall prevail."

The main question that may arise is whether the term "obligations under any other international agreement" also encompasses *jus cogens*. It is contended that the article is primarily directed "to secure the efficacy of UN action in the maintenance of peace"[82] and according to Article 25 of the UN Charter the Members undertake to carry out the decisions. Regarding Article 103, it should be noted that it is not only related to the decisions of the SC, but also to all the norms listed in Articles 1 and 2. Therefore, any interpretation of the Article relating to the SC should be consistent with other Charter norms. The issue of a possible conflict between Article 103 and *jus cogens* has been debated in the Repertory of practice of UN organs and the Article was mostly discussed in the light of Articles 1 and 2 of the UN Charter. According to the delegations, the above Articles are "uncontestable norms of international public law", and Article 103 was designed to neutralize the legal effects of subsequent treaties which may override the Charter's norms.[83] The necessity of Article 103 in international law was justified in terms of the dignity and importance of the Preamble, Articles 1 and 2.[84] The Charter does not generate these norms, rather, they already exist in international law. Hence, "the rules of *jus cogens* undoubtedly included the purposes and principles set forth in Articles 1 and 2 of the Charter and in its Preamble."[85] Under these circumstances, the SC has primary responsibility to maintain international peace and security in order to safeguard all norms and its measures must abide by *jus cogens* otherwise it would defeat the purpose. Hence, it is generally acknowledged that a conflict between Charter Law and *jus cogens* would result in the nullification of the Charter Law.[86] As Tomuschat wrote,

> "[Article 103] does not refer to general international law. General international law reflects the consensus of the international community. On the other hand, Article 103 is designed to override specific national

82 Robert Kolb, 'Does Article 103 of the Charter of the United Nations Apply only to Decisions or also to Authorizations Adopted by the Security Council?', *Zeitschrift für ausländisches öffentliches Recht und Völkerrecht*, Vol. 64, Issue 1, 2004, p. 21.

83 Repertory of practice of United Nations organs. Supplement no. 4, Vol. 2, Articles 55-111 of the Charter, covering the period 1 Sept. 1966 to 31 Dec. 1969, p. 368, at 17.

84 Id. p. 369, at 27.

85 Id.

86 Johann Ruben Leiß & Andreas Paulus, 'Article 103', *in* Simma *et al.* (eds.) 2012, p. 2119.

doi: 10.5553/HYIEL/266627012022010001017

> peculiarities. It has a totally different purpose and would be used contrary to its meaning if applied against general international law."

Judge Lauterpacht in his separate opinion in *Genocide* asserted, that

> "[t]he concept of jus cogens operates as a concept superior to both customary international law and treaty. The relief which Article 103 of the Charter may give the Security Council in case of conflict between one of its decisions and an operative treaty obligation cannot – as a matter of simple hierarchy of noms – extend to a conflict between a Security Council resolution and *jus cogens*. Indeed, one only has to state the opposite proposition thus – that a Security Council resolution may even require participation in genocide – for its unacceptability to be apparent."[87]

Therefore, Article 103 should be interpreted in favor of *jus cogens*. The purpose of the Article is to protect the norms of *jus cogens* that are included in the Charter, not to grant the SC the authority to override them. The Article is to guarantee efficiency of the Charter and to eliminate barriers in "ordinary treaty norms" for the implementation of obligations arising under the Charter,[88] not standing against *jus cogens*.

6.2. Different Function

Through subsequent legal action, states can neutralize the legal effects of the UN Charter norms or the SC decisions[89] and, in this way, weaken the UN system and lead it to the fate of the League of Nations. For this reason, in order to ensure the successful implementation of the Charter, the drafters have given primacy to its obligations. The ILC clarified that

> "[t]he lower-ranking rule is merely set aside to the extent that it conflicts with the obligation under Article 103. [...]. [T]he very language of Article 103 makes it clear that it presumes the priority of the Charter, not the invalidity of treaties conflicting with it."[90]

Article 103 is, therefore, a rule of conflict and cannot be invoked to nullify other legal actions in conflict with the UN Charter.[91] It merely indicates primacy. Not

87 ICJ, *Application of the Convention on the Prevention and Punishment of the Crime of Genocide (Bosnia and Herzegovina v Serbia and Montenegro)*, Order of 13 September 1993, Separate opinion of Judge ad hoc Lauterpacht, para. 100.

88 Leiß & Paulus 2012, p. 2123.

89 Andreas L. Paulus, 'Jus cogens in a time of hegemony and fragmentation-an attempt at a re-appraisal', *Nordic Journal of International Law*, Vol. 74, Issue 3, 2005, p. 319.

90 International Law Commission, Report on the Fragmentation of International Law: Difficulties Arising from the Diversification and Expansion of International Law (2006) UN Doc. A/CN.4/l. 682, p. 170, para. 333.

91 Paulus 2005, p. 317; Leiß & Paulus 2012, pp. 1297-1298; Rain Liivoja, 'The scope of the supremacy clause of the United Nations Charter', *International & Comparative Law Quarterly*, Vol. 57, Issue 3, 2008, p. 584.

doi: 10.5553/HYIEL/266627012022010001017

only does the Article not grant *carte blanche* to the SC but neither does it confer upon the SC the power to annul agreements between states, while *jus cogens* is a matter of merit and voids any legal action that conflicts with the fundamental values of international law, including the UN system. The UN's fundamental norms are enshrined in the Preamble, Articles 1 and 2, which provide authority for Article 103. In the preamble 'faith in fundamental human rights' was reaffirmed. As part of the UN's purposes, Article 1 defines 'equal rights', 'self-determination of peoples' and respect for 'freedoms for all without distinction as to race, sex, language, or religion'. As a prerequisite to achieving the purposes of the UN, Article 2 stipulated the prohibition of use of force. All of these norms are *jus cogens* and *erga omnes* in nature.[92]

Furthermore, the primacy conferred by Article 103 on the SC's decision rests on the common presumption that the SC acts within its remit and "if the Security Council adopts a resolution in excess of its competence (*ultra vires*), then no obligation arises under the resolution."[93] As a result, there is no clash between Article 103 and *jus cogens*, and any action by the SC must be crystallized through filter of *jus cogens*. As Kitharidis pointed out,

> "where the UNSC breaches a permissive norm, there can be no conflict capable of allying under Article 103; ultra vires resolutions cannot exist within obligations that may fall under the scope of Article 103. Ultra vires resolutions cannot authorize states to violate their other international law obligations [...]."[94]

6.3 *Article 103 and the Principle of Nemo Dat Quod Non Habet*

As a final point, the question of whether, in principle, states can endow the SC with the power to override *jus cogens* is worth analyzing. An answer to this question is tied to the issue of whether states in turn may override *jus cogens*. ILC discussed the issue at its fifty-eighth session and concluded as follows:

92 The following norm was included in the list of non-exhaustive jus cogens provided by the ILC at its seventy-first session: "*(a)* The prohibition of aggression; *(b)* The prohibition of genocide; *(c)* The prohibition of crimes against humanity; *(d)* The basic rules of international humanitarian law; *(e)* The prohibition of racial discrimination and apartheid; *(f)* The prohibition of slavery; *(g)* The prohibition of torture; *(h)* The right of self-determination". Report of the International Law Commission on the Work of Its Seventy-First Session, UN GAOR, 74th Sess., Supp. No. 10, at 1-2, paras. 1, 3, UN Doc. A/74/10, 2019, p. 147; also in Draft Articles on State Responsibility, Commentary on Article 40, paras. 4-6 in Official Records of the General Assembly, Fifth-sixth Session (A/56/10), pp. 283-284.

93 Kjetil Mujezinović Larsen, *The human rights treaty obligations of peacekeepers*, Cambridge University Press, Cambridge, 2012, p. 323; Alexander Orakhelashvili, 'The impact of peremptory norms on the interpretation and application of United Nations Security Council resolutions', *European Journal of International Law*, Vol. 16, Issue 1, 2005, p. 69.

94 Id.; Sophocles Kitharidis, 'The Power of Article 103 of the un Charter on Treaty Obligations: Can the Security Council Authorise Non-Compliance of Human Rights Treaty Obligations in United Nations Peacekeeping Operations?', *Journal of International Peacekeeping*, Vol. 20, Issue 1-2, 2016, p. 1229.

doi: 10.5553/HYIEL/266627012022010001017

> "[i]f United Nations Member States are unable to draw up valid agreements in dissonance with *jus cogens*, they must also be unable to vest an international organization with the power to go against peremptory norms. Indeed, both doctrine and practice unequivocally confirm that conflicts between the United Nations Charter and norms of *jus cogens* result not in the Charter obligations' pre-eminence, but their invalidity."[95]

There is no norm of *jus cogens* contained in Article 103 of the UN Charter, it merely indicates that the Charter, including the decisions of the SC, has precedence over other international agreements. Here, the key question is whether the decision of the SC qualifies as *jus cogens*. There is no doubt that the SC is not "the international community of States as a whole", because it involves fifteen members and even to reach a decision, participation of all members is not mandatory.[96] Moreover, during the discussion on identifying specimens of *jus cogens*, the ILC assigned to states the responsibility "to establish or recognize peremptory norms".[97] Thus, the SC is not qualified to introduce *jus cogens*.

The SC may be argued to be a representative of the international community of states, therefore, it may transgress *jus cogens* in accordance with Article 103 on their behalf. It is not clear, however, how states can confer powers on the SC when they are deprived of them in substance. It was noted by the ILC that even though international organizations possess independent legal personality, they are created by states, so it is difficult to accept the idea that states are permitted to disregard *jus cogens* by establishing international organizations.[98] A presumption must exist that an international organization may not deviate from peremptory norms, and any contravention would be *ultra vires*.[99] The UN and its members are equally bound by the norms of international law, and are required to comply with its obligations.[100] In the same vein, Liivoja aptly held that

> "if jus cogens norms are, by definition, norms from which no derogation is possible, it would be nonsensical to stipulate that Security Council resolutions are an exception - this argument would involve a complete discarding of the very concept of *jus cogens*."[101]

Judge Fitzmaurice, in his dissenting opinion in the *Namibia Advisory Opinion* reckoned that "the Security Council is as much subject to it (for the UN is itself a

95 International Law Commission, Fifty-eighth session, Geneva, 1 May-9 June and 3 July-11 August, 2006, A/CN.4/L.682, p. 176, para. 346.

96 UN Charter, Article 27.

97 The United Nations Conference on the Law of Treaties between States and International Organizations or between International Organizations, Vol. II, 1986, p. 39.

98 Id.

99 Orakhelashvili 2005, p. 68.

100 Dapo Akande, 'The International Court of Justice and the Security Council: Is There Room for Judicial Control of Decisions of the Political Organs of the United Nations?', *International & Comparative Law Quarterly*, Vol. 46, Issue 2, 1997, p. 320.

101 Liivoja 2008, p. 610.

doi: 10.5553/HYIEL/266627012022010001017

subject of international law) as any of its individual members are".[102] In *Kadi* the CJEU spelled out that

> "[i]nternational law thus permits the inference that there exists one limit to the principle that resolutions of the Security Council have binding effect: namely, that they must observe the fundamental peremptory provisions of *jus cogens*. If they fail to do so, however improbable that may be, they would bind neither the Member States of the United Nations nor, in consequence, the Community."[103]

7. Conclusion

By adopting the UN Charter following World War II, a new legal order was established. The international legal order is founded on the assumption of the rule of law, which settles the relationships between all subjects of law in the international society.

In this regard, the SC, following the legal personality of the UN, is bound by the requirements of the rule of law. The first paragraph of Article 1 endorses this assumption and states that in order to maintain international peace and security, international law and justice must be observed and on the other hand, Article 103 of the UN Charter denotes the primacy of SC decisions over other international agreements. There are, however, certain principles in international law, known as GIL, that limit the jurisdiction of the SC, and in the event of a conflict, GIL will prevail over Article 103. GIL is not derived from the will of states, as is the case with the sources of international law, but rather stems from the necessities of collective life. GIL includes two clusters of principles: axiomatic and axiologic principles. The former is derived from the structure of international society and law; salient examples are the prohibition of use of force or *pacta sunt servanda*. The latter originated from values of the international community which revolve around the axis of humanity. In this line of arguments, one could say that *jus cogens* and *erga omnes* originate from GIL and almost all norms identified as *jus cogens* and *erga omnes* are related to humanity. When the SC acts to maintain international peace and security, it must adhere to limits set by GIL. The crucial responsibility of maintaining international peace and security does not alter the status of the SC as a *sui generis* organ. The SC, as an organ of the UN, shall fulfill its mission according to the fundamental norms of the international legal order.

102 ICJ, *Legal Consequences for States of the Continued Presence of South Africa in Namibia (South West Africa) notwithstanding Security Council Resolution 276 (1970) (Advisory Opinion),* ICJ Reports 1971, p. 294, para. 115, Dissenting Opinion by Judge Gerald Fitzmaurice.

103 Judgment of 21 September 2005, *Case T-315/01, Kadi,* ECLI:EU:T:2005:332, para. 230.

doi: 10.5553/HYIEL/266627012022010001017

HUNGARIAN STATE PRACTICE

The Ups and Downs of Hungarian Administrative Law's Europeanization in the Field of Environmental Protection

Krisztina F. Rozsnyai[*]

Abstract

The article gives an overview of the influence of European law on Hungarian administrative law in the field of environmental protection. It briefly discusses new institutions that were introduced with the implementation of the acquis communautaire and the Aarhus Convention. There were quite a few developments in general administrative law dealt with in the article that can even be labelled as spill over or gold-plating effects in connection with public participation. The analysis shows that following a good start in Hungary both case law and legislation became somewhat less favorable to public participation in matters relating to the environment. After procedural backlogs, the abolishment of independent environmental administrative authorities in 2015 on territorial and in 2016 on national level hindered environmental protection. Nevertheless, the CJEU's case law also had an important influence on the codification of some Hungarian administrative court procedure rules, such as the loosening of the causality link requirement in the ambit of procedural errors or the creation of rules for mass procedures. Some signs give reason for hope in a gradual change of legal culture, such as the activity of the deputy ombudsman for the protection of the interests of future generations, the resilience of environmental NGOs as well as the rise of environmental law as a core subject in graduate legal studies.

Keywords: Aarhus Convention, access to environmental information, access to justice in environmental cases, public participation in matters relating to the environment, EIA.

* Krisztina F. Rozsnyai: professor of administrative law, ELTE Law School, Budapest. ORCID: 0000-0002-1494-5051.

doi: 10.5553/HYIEL/266627012022010001018

1. Hungary's Basic Attitude towards Union Law in the Field of Environmental Protection

The Environmental Protection Code (EPC) of 1995 opened a new chapter in environmental protection law in Hungary.[1] This act laid down for the first time and in an integrated manner the general rules of environmental protection. In 1976 thus, a comprehensive set of rules on the protection of the environment had been created comprising many important principles, yet this was rarely directly applicable.[2] The regulation that prevailed for a long time was characterized by government and ministerial decrees, unrelated to other areas of legal regulation. The depth of the regulation was quite variable and mostly low. Instead of prevention, the focus was on repression. After the fall of communism in 1990, the situation did not change immediately; environmental protection was seen more as an obstacle to the development of the new economic order. Although there were individual areas where important progress was made, a new era dawned with the EPC. At the time, the influence of European law was already noticeable in the anteroom of the forthcoming European integration.

The preamble of the EPC radiated this European influence across national constitutional law, taking the shape of constitutional principles.[3] The influence of European law was also tangible in some special fields, such as water management and nature protection. The harmonization of Hungarian legislative provisions applicable in the field of environmental protection was among the preconditions for accession to the EC. Hungary transposed the *acquis communautaire* through a series of implementing government Decrees, in addition to amending the EPC and specific laws governing the protection of individual elements of the environment. The promulgation of the Aarhus Convention also formed part of this harmonization endeavor.[4]

The new Fundamental Law of 2011 refers to environmental protection in various aspects.[5] Compared to the previous constitution, these fundamental rights have been reformulated as state goals and duties. However, if we analyze the jurisprudence of the Constitutional Court, the fundamental rights were

1 The EPC was promulgated as Act LIII of 1995 on 22 June 1995 and came into force 180 days later on 19 December 1995.

2 Act II of 1976.

3 Article P) of the Hungarian Fundamental Law, as well as Articles XXI and XX. *See e.g.* Katalin Sulyok, 'Az egészséges környezethez való jog' and 'Az egészséghez való jog', *in* Lóránt Csink (ed.), *Alapjogi kommentár az alkotmánybírósági gyakorlat alapján,* Novissima, Budapest, 2021, pp. 259-269, and 251-258, as well as Katalin Sulyok, 'The Public Trust Doctrine, the Non-Derogation Principle and the Protection of Future Generations', *Hungarian Yearbook of International Law and European Law*, Vol. 9, Issue 1, 2021, p. 360. *See also* Marcel Szabó, 'The Precautionary Principle in the Fundamental Law of Hungary: Judicial Activism or an Inherent Fundamental Principle? An Evaluation of Constitutional Court Decision No. 13/2018. (IX. 4.) AB on the Protection of Groundwater', *Hungarian Yearbook of International Law and European Law,* Vol. 7, Issue 1, 2019, pp. 67-83.

4 Act LXXXI of 2001.

5 Gyula Bándi, 'Környezetvédelmi igazgatás', *in* András Lapsánszky (ed.), *Közigazgatási jog. Fejezetek szakigazgatásaink köréből,* Vol. II., Complex, Budapest, 2013, pp. 373-374.

doi: 10.5553/HYIEL/266627012022010001018

already interpreted in this sense before the Hungarian Fundamental Law came into force.[6]

2. New Institutions for the Implementation of European Law

2.1. Access to Environmental Information

Administrative bodies were faced with some new legal institutions. One of these was access to environmental information, which is based on three pillars. *(i)* Firstly, Article VI(3) of the Fundamental Law of Hungary states that everyone has a right to know and disseminate data of public interest. The enforcement of this right is controlled by an independent authority and shaped by the Law on Informational Self-Determination and Freedom of Information.[7] The latter regulates the scope of data of public interest and applications for access to data. *(ii)* The second pillar is made up of the provisions of the EPC. The introductory provisions enshrine the principle that everyone has a right to know environmental information. Environmental information is qualified as data of public interest in the EPC, establishing the link to the Data Protection Act.[8] In order to implement the Information Directive, the EPC prescribes on the one hand the comprehensive provision of environmental information to the public through a public information platform accessible *via* the Internet. This platform and the data stored there can be accessed and viewed by anyone without restriction and free of charge. The public platform must publish the environmental information specified in a law or government Decree that belongs to the information system or is derived from this data. The Information Directive was further implemented by amending the EPC rules on environmental information at the end of 2005. Obligations to provide environmental information are imposed not only on public authorities and other public bodies, but also on persons under private law who perform public functions. The EPC also stipulates that any person using the environment must, upon request, provide anyone with information on the environmental pollution or environmental stress they had caused, as well as the data associated with the related environmental hazard. Should this duty to provide information be infringed, action may be taken by the competent supervisory body. Another duty related to data of public interest is the obligation to make public permits and other official decisions affecting the environment. Furthermore, a database was set up in which NGOs active in environmental protection can register. Here, relevant decisions are made known directly and automatically to the registered NGOs. *(iii)* The third pillar is Government Decree 311/2005. (XII. 25.) on Access to Environmental

6 For example, the Constitutional Court stated that "the right to the environment is a fundamental right, but not a subjective right", and that "the subject of the right to the environment in fact is humanity and nature". The Constitutional Court also stated that the constitutional rules ensure the guarantees of the exercise of state functions in the field of environmental protection.

7 Act CXII of 2012.

8 Act CXII of 2011 on Informational Self-Determination and Freedom of Information.

doi: 10.5553/HYIEL/266627012022010001018

Information.[9] This contains detailed rules on the implementation of the provisions of the EPC.

Interestingly, already six months before the amendments to the ECP at the end of 2005, the Code of Civil Procedure (CPR) was amended in line with the Aarhus Convention, granting standing in administrative court procedures to persons who requested environmental information under international treaties and did not receive it. Additionally, this amendment to the CPR also created a possibility to sue for disclosure of information without party capacity under the CRP. This rule was repealed in 2009, meanwhile, the obligation to publish all substantive decisions of the environmental authorities was formulated in the EPC.[10]

The Data Protection Act grants access not to administrative, but to civil courts in the event of a denial of data of public interest, which must decide as promptly as possible in special proceedings. Case law interprets exceptions to the obligation to disclose restrictively.[11] There was also an important organizational change. Relying on the Tromsø Convention,[12] in 2012 the Data Protection Act replaced the Data Protection Supervisor with the Hungarian National Authority for Data Protection and Freedom of Information.[13] According to the former act, the erstwhile supervisor was a special commissioner to whom the rules on the ombudsman applied, whereas the data protection authority was set up as an autonomous administrative agency. The institution of ombudsman was also amended to a significant degree: whereas in the previous act on the Parliamentary Commissioner for Civil Rights[14] there were three special ombudsmen (special commissioners) with the independent competence to request norm control procedures and to conduct investigations, under the new act adopted in 2012[15] there are now two deputy ombudsmen with no independent competence to request norm-control from the Constitutional Court or the Supreme Court.

Similarly to the deputy ombudsman of future generations in judicial disputes concerning the environment, the data protection authority may, in addition to its administrative competences join the plaintiff in court actions for the disclosure of data.

9 Government Decree No. 152/1995. (XII. 12).

10 Section 67(5) and Section 71(3).

11 *E.g.* Decision No. 2.Pf.20.169/2009/3 of the Metropolitan Regional Court, which declared the denial of data on the grounds of them being business secrets to be unlawful.

12 Council of Europe Convention on Access to Official Documents of 18 June 2009.

13 There were even infringement procedures against Hungary launched by the European Commission ending with the finding of infringement: Judgment of 8 April 2014, *Case C-288/12, European Commission v Hungary*, ECLI:EU:C:2014:237.

14 Act LIX of 1993.

15 Act CXI of 2011.

doi: 10.5553/HYIEL/266627012022010001018

2.2. The Environmental Impact Assessment

Environmental impact assessment (EIA) was first regulated in an overarching manner in 1993.[16] The most important rules were enshrined in the EPC two years later, while other rules were laid down in the Government Decree implementing the EIA.[17] After an intermediate stage[18] a new Government Decree was issued,[19] regulating not only the EIA but also the Integrated Environmental Permit.[20] This regulation is still in force today, the procedures are handled according to the general rules of administrative procedure with additional rules contained in this regulation. The integrated procedure only exists since September 2011, that is a novelty of procedural law with its only counterpart in the field in construction law.[21]

A special feature of the EIA Decree is that it transposes both the EIA Directive 2011/92/EU and the IPPC Directive 2010/75/EU into Hungarian law. Annex 1 is based on Annex I of the EIA Directive. Annex 2 of the EIA Decree adopts Annex I of the IPPC Directive. In Annex 3 we find the requirements of Annex II of the EIA Directive. This regulation has received much criticism from the European Commission because Hungary did not transpose the EIA Directive correctly into national law, especially when it comes to the rules on project screening. Certain exclusion thresholds and criteria were set out in such a way that not all relevant selection criteria of Annex III of the Directive were taken into account. This resulted in a restrictive application of the Directive. The issue was raised in a letter of formal notice sent to Hungary in May 2009, followed by another letter in January 2010. As a result, Hungary made some changes to its legislation to bring it in line with the provisions of the Directive. While the Commission welcomed these changes, it nevertheless found that there were still shortcomings in relation to the screening of some projects. Therefore, it issued a new reasoned letter in June 2012, following which[22] the regulation was amended again.

Striving to avoid the obligation of EIA is a general endeavor of investors throughout Europe. Perhaps the most well-known such strategy is the splitting

16 Government Decree No. 86/1993. (VI. 4.). Beforehand, there were initial rules, such as the Council of Ministers' Decree 46/1984. (XI. 6.) for major projects, but still without detailed rules and specifications. It was only the Directive on the Rules of EIA of the Minister for Environmental Protection (MI-13-45-1990) which had a normative content. In the early 1990s, sector-specific regulations were also issued, such as Government Decree No. 146/1992. (XI. 14.) in connection with projects in the energy sector.

17 Government Decree No. 152/1995. (XII. 12.).

18 The EIA and IPPC Directives were transposed together in Government Decree No. 20/2001. (II. 14.). This particularity was also retained in the new regulation in Government Decree No. 314/2005. (XII. 25.) after Hungary's accession to the EC.

19 Government Decree No. 314/2005. (XII. 25.).

20 *See* István Hoffman, 'Environmental assessment in Hungary', *in* Veronika Tomoszková (ed.), *Implementation and Enforcement of EU Environmental Law in the Visegrad Countries*, Olomouc, 2014, p. 207.

21 Only, if the project falls under the 3rd Annex of the EIA Government Decree and if it does not have a significant effect on the environment.

22 *See* at http://europa.eu/rapid/press-release_IP-12-656_en.htm. There were mainly problems with the special regulations on EIA.

doi: 10.5553/HYIEL/266627012022010001018

up of projects into smaller independent projects, to avoid falling within the scope of the EIA Regulation. This avoidance strategy was opposed by the CJEU in *Paul Abraham.*[23] While the Curia of Hungary (the Hungarian Supreme Court) quoted this decision *verbatim* in a similar Hungarian case at the end of 2012, this did not affect the merits of the case: the Supreme Court dismissed the appeal. This decision followed from the system of national regulation of the EIA and the Supreme Court's Uniformity Decision No. 4/2010,[24] an aspect that was also addressed in the amendment of the EIA Decree, which explicitly states that cumulative effects must be considered when deciding on the need for an environmental impact assessment. Several provisions of the Construction Code were also amended: the integration of building permit procedures[25] was intended to promote public participation. Nevertheless, since the cited decision of the Curia of Hungary was published as a fundamental decision, and its ratio decidendi was taken from the *Paul Abraham* case, this CJEU judgment has since influenced the case law in a positive way, namely through its *ratio decidendi* in connection with the amendment of the EIA Decree.[26]

Unfortunately, another avoidance strategy has been developed in Hungary since then, that of qualifying a project as a 'project of special national economic interest'. Special procedural rules apply to such projects in order to be realized promptly. This solution was partly due to the fact that these projects are usually co-financed by European funds, and the realization of the project must therefore be secured in a timely manner, and in this regard, the EIA and the associated public participation may significantly prolong these procedures. Since the introduction of this institution, the number of projects qualified by the government to be of such an interest, is growing dynamically year by year.

3. Administrative Procedure

3.1. The Beginnings

In general administrative procedural law, the right to public participation in administrative procedures have brought about important changes. The Hungarian Act on the General Rules of Administrative Procedure of 1957 (HuAPA1957), in its Section 3(4), granted the status of party to, among others, organizations whose functions were affected by the administrative matter, but did not participate in the proceedings as an authority or special authority (so-

23 Judgment of 28 February 2008, *Case C-2/07, Abraham and others*, ECLI:EU:C:2008:133.

24 Decision for the Uniform Interpretation of Law No. 4/2010 KJE of the Supreme Court (now Curia of Hungary). The cited case law of the CJEU could of course have justified a different decision, or at least a preliminary reference procedure, as is evident from the Judgment of 21 March 2013, *Case C-244/12, Salzburger Flughafen*, ECLI:EU:C:2013:203. *See* Krisztina F. Rozsnyai & László Szegedi, 'A Kúria ítélete a repülőtéri postai üzem építési engedélyének jogszerűségéről: A környezeti hatásvizsgálat-köteles jelleg és az önkormányzat kvázi-ügyféli jogállása a közigazgatási hatósági eljárásban', *Jogesetek Magyarázata,* Vol. 4, Issue 4, 2013, p. 48.

25 Construction Act Section 30/B. Unfortunately, the integrated plant approval procedure is only an option, not an obligation.

26 *E.g.* Curia of Hungary, Decision No. Kfv. III. 37.385/2012/7.

doi: 10.5553/HYIEL/266627012022010001018

called *quasi*-parties). This provision may be traced back to the socialist ideology of the unity of power and offered the possibility of direct political control over administrative procedures. After the fall of communism, however, it took on an entirely new meaning with the emergence of civil society in Hungary. NGOs began to make use of this clause. Local self-government bodies increasingly took recourse to it to oppose large-scale projects. Even professional chambers sought to assert the particular interests of their members this way.

This development was triggered in environmental law by Section 98(2) of the EPC, which allowed for an action by associations in matters relating to the environment through the granting of the status of party – already from the promulgation of the act, several years before the adoption of the Aarhus Convention:

> "Civil organizations founded for the protection of environmental interests, which qualify neither as political parties nor as organizations for the representation of interests, have the status of parties in the administrative proceedings under environmental protection law in their functional area."[27]

This paragraph was an icebreaker and induced changes far beyond the realm of public participation in environmental protection cases. It had a gold-plating effect, as it became a parallel provision to Section 3(4) of the HuAPA1957 and resulted in the case law expanding the scope of 'organization' in this section so as to encompass both NGOs and administrative bodies. This was not the only aspect of public participation where the ordinary courts in this first period were open to the impulses of EU law and the Aarhus Convention: they interpreted the concept of 'matters relating to the environment' generously,[28] thereby encouraging public participation, in an effort to preserve the original meaning of the implemented regulations.[29]

3.2. *Transplanting Institutions of Public Participation into General Administrative Procedural Law*

Quite unexpectedly, the promulgation of the Aarhus Convention with Act CXXXI of 2001 brought about a narrowing of this case law formerly favorable to public participation. This development was owed to legislative changes, namely the recodification of general administrative procedural law. In the autumn of 2004, the new Act on the General Rules of Administrative Procedure (HuAPA2004) was passed, which diversified the rules on the status of parties and established a set of rules for the affected public. In this piece of legislation, the Europeanisation of

27 Gyula Bándi, 'A környezetvédelmi közigazgatási hatósági eljárás fogalmáról', *Közigazgatási Szemle*, Vol. 1, Issue 3, 2007, pp. 90-97.

28 As mentioned above, the Decision for the Uniform Interpretation of Law No. 1/2004. KJE was a milestone in this development, applying the Aarhus Convention already for the interpretation of the notion of an administrative matter relating to the environment enshrined in Section 98(1) EPC.

29 *See generally* Krisztina Rozsnyai, 'Public Participation in Administrative Procedures', *Curentul Juridic*, Vol. 58, Issue 3, 2014, p. 50.

doi: 10.5553/HYIEL/266627012022010001018

administrative procedural rules was quite apparent, especially when it comes to public participation. The new concept split up the notion of '*quasi*-parties' which included on the one hand the administrative bodies with duties affected by the administrative matter, unless proceeding as an authority or special authority in the procedure [Section 15(4) HuAPA2004]. On the other hand, NGOs safeguarding a fundamental right or a public interest affected by the case could also enjoy a quasi-party status, but only where sectoral law *expressis verbis* foresaw this.[30] The HuAPA2004 merely contained this possibility and did not grant any rights to NGOs.

Thus, it was the model of Section 98 of the Environmental Act that was followed.[31] Instead of the general status of NGOs as parties under Section 3(4) of the HuAPA1957, Section 15(5) of the HuAPA2004 only empowered the special legislator to grant NGOs parties' rights, but no longer directly granted NGOs any rights as parties. For the third category of the interested public, this way the developments at the national level in connection with the EIA unfortunately led to a narrowing of the possibility of public participation. The sectoral legislator was reluctant to use this form of public participation; the public was only involved where there was an external obligation to do so, primarily arising from EU law. Accordingly, NGOs have been given the position of party in administrative proceedings, apart from matters relating to the environment in some nature conservation and consumer protection issues, as well as in the anti-tobacco regulation (*e.g.* advertising and promotion of tobacco).

The quasi-party status of Section 15(4) HuAPA2004 granted to administrative bodies whose area of responsibility was affected was mainly used by local self-government bodies. This possibility neatly complemented the actions of NGOs. The local governments had this party status without limitation in all administrative matters, not only in environmental law, with the unique requirement that their area of responsibility be affected by the administrative matter. Since the local governments have a competence to act in all local public matters not falling within the competence of another state organ, establishing such a connection did not seem particularly complicated. However, according to the Decision for the Uniform Interpretation of Law No. 2/2004 KJE, case law required for standing that the area of responsibility be directly affected, which usually consisted in concrete duties like the initiation of a planning procedure, the introduction of traffic control measures, *etc.*

The HuAPA2004 also contained a special rule for the second category of the affected public: they were parties in mass proceedings[32] regulated with an irrefutable presumption: anyone who had a right registered in the land register within the impacted spatial area of a future facility was a party to the procedure for the (mostly planting) permission. Despite some uncertainties it was a great

30 István Hoffman, 'Access to justice in environmental matters in Hungary', *in* Tomoszková (ed.) 2014, p. 273.

31 And with this, Recommendation No. R (87) 16 of the Council of Ministers of the Council of Europe on administrative procedures affecting a large number of persons, at https://rm.coe.int/cmrec-87-16-on-administrative-procedures-affecting-a-large-number-of-p/1680a43b59.

32 Section 15(2) HuAPA2004.

doi: 10.5553/HYIEL/266627012022010001018

achievement of the new general regulation that it combined the special rules of mass proceedings into one initial, but important type of procedure. Spill-over effects of the EIA regulation were two institutions integrated into the general administrative procedure law: the public hearing and the so-called administrative mediator, whose task was to mediate between opposing interested parties, or between the parties and the authority.

3.3. Erosion

In 2008, a major amendment of the HuAPA2004 took place, which also influenced the provisions on party status and thereby also the possibilities of judicial review. The new wording of the provisions of Section 15(3) HuAPA2004 made it clear that the general concept of party may not be restricted by the specialized legislator.[33] Here, the legislator followed the case law and in essence, codified it.[34] The concept of party in mass procedures was diluted, and transformed into an authorization for the sectoral legislator to create such a special rule in the sectoral regulation. Several government decrees had made use of this authorization and granted automatic party status to landowners in the area affected by the facility in various permission procedures.[35]

The legislator also decided to amend the provisions on the possible participation of NGOs in administrative procedures and to introduce a new three-fold rule. According to the first layer, all NGOs had a right to be heard – in any administrative matter. The second layer was to authorize the sectoral legislator to grant individual rights of participation to NGOs. The original text of the HuAPA2004 became the third layer, *i.e.* the authorization of the sectoral legislator to grant the right to be a party. This change can only be interpreted as a weakening of public participation, intended to deprive NGOs of the right of access to court while further granting them other – "less dangerous" – procedural rights. This is all the more the case if we take into account the newly introduced subsequent paragraph which made it possible to preclude the rights of parties in certain cases. Accordingly, remedies – including the appeal procedure – could be precluded by the sectoral legislator in the case of the party concerned not participating in the original first instance procedure despite having been notified of the procedure. The same applied if the party did not express objections in the procedure – if he did not make use of his procedural rights in the first instance, the law presumed he did not want to do so later neither and precluded him from

33 Section 15(3) HuAPA2004 read until the end of September 2009: "A more detailed definition of parties may be determined by act or government decree."

34 This was also formulated as a general guiding principle in Opinion 1/2007. KK of the Administrative Law College of the Supreme Court from 2007, in addition to concrete judgments (reprinted in BH 2008/3.).

35 Thus, Government Decrees No. 289/2012. (X. 11.) on railway construction, No. 159/2010. (V. 6.) on airports, as well as the Road Transport Act I of 1988.

doi: 10.5553/HYIEL/266627012022010001018

remedy procedures. The restriction of individual participation rights was only a first step to be followed by further restrictions in 2013.[36]

This stricter perspective gradually took hold in the case law as well. The Curia confirmed its Decision for the Uniform Interpretation of Law No. 1/2004. KJE in the new, already mentioned Decision for the Uniform Interpretation of Law No. 4/2010 with the clarification that it is not sufficient for the environmental protection authority (at that time the National Inspectorate for Environment, Nature Conservation and Water Management) to act as an authority or special authority in the procedure to qualify as 'matters relating to the environment'. Additionally, it must be a case within the scope of application of the EPC as it is only through Section 98 of this act that NGOs are granted the status of party and thus access to court. In all other cases where this authority proceeds and in cases that touch upon environmental elements but fall under the jurisdiction of other authorities (*e.g.* forestry), the NGOs only have participation rights in case the sectoral legislator expressly so provides. But apparently sectoral legislation hardly does provide for such rules.

This Decision for the Uniform Interpretation of Law became obsolete in 2015 (*cf.* Section 5.1.). It is a strong sign of backsliding, that the Curia of Hungary was not willing to revoke or alter its decision ever since, notwithstanding the fact the underlying regulatory concept was completely changed.

In 2015, work began on the creation of a Code of Administrative Court Procedure which strengthened 'recodificationalist' voices and finally resulted in a new Administrative Procedure Act, the Code on the General Rules of Administrative Procedure (HuAPA2016). The two new acts entered into force on 1 January 2018.[37]

Looking at the trends of the previous years, it was no great surprise that the HuAPA2016 did not bring any positive changes to the rules of public participation. On the contrary, related provisions were all omitted, as the concept of the new, general code was to regulate only those institutions that were actually relevant to all procedures. According to this concept, rules that cannot be applied in all procedures do not belong in the code on general rules of administrative procedure but must be transferred to sectoral law. Therefore, not only institutions such as the public hearing and the authoritative mediator were omitted, but also the rules on the quasi-party status, as well as the rules on mass

36 Participation in the first instance procedure could be circumscribed by the sectoral legislator: it could even establish substantive criteria which declarations or applications submitted in the administrative procedure had to meet [Section 15(6) HuAPA2004]. Furthermore, the sectoral legislator was also empowered to establish substantive criteria for the appeal in the appellate procedure. It was even allowed to stipulate that no further parties were allowed to join the proceedings at least six months after the decision had become final and thus, they could not claim legal protection even if they had not been informed of the proceedings [Section 15(6a) HuAPA2004]. The sectoral legislator had made use of these possibilities in the area of building permits, which is most affected by remedies [Section 53/A(11) and (12) Construction Act, and Government Decree No. 312/2012. (XI. 8.) on Construction law procedures].

37 Act CL of 2016 and Act I of 2017. *See* a detailed summary of the two acts in Krisztina F. Rozsnyai, 'Administrative Law Hungary – Chronicle for 2016 and 2017', *European Review of Public Law*, Vol. 29, Issue 4, 2017, pp. 1373-1394.

doi: 10.5553/HYIEL/266627012022010001018

proceedings. This concept was flawed, as the sectoral legislators did not follow this concept and – with a few exceptions – did not regulate these institutions. For example, public consultation is only regulated in detail in the Nuclear Energy Act, but the mediator is not regulated in any of the sectoral acts, although it is mentioned, or even foreseen in several sectoral procedures. The sectoral rules promulged under the HuAPA2004 however remain in force, so that the affected public or NGOs still have the right to participate in some procedures. This represents a significant step backwards as regards the general procedural rules.

4. The Influence of EU Law on Administrative Court Procedure

The new Code of Administrative Court Procedure (CACP) tried to follow some trends of Europeanisation. On the one hand, section 17 CACP regulates four categories of so-called privileged plaintiffs. Thus, on the one hand, administrative bodies are entitled to file an action if they did not participate in the preceding administrative procedure as an authority or special authority, but their area of responsibility is affected by the administrative action of another administrative body. This is particularly important for local governments, primarily in cases with a great impact on the local environment. The public prosecutor's office has this power within the scope of its non-criminal area of responsibility, supervising the lawfulness of the decisions of public administration. Similarly to the previous rules of the HuAPA2004, the CACP only empowers the sectoral legislator in Section 17 points *c)* to *e)*: NGOs in operation for at least one year and having the protection of public interest or human rights as their objective may be authorized by law to file an action if the administrative act is realized in their territorial area of activity, in case the act affects their field of responsibility. Although this provision follows the case law of the CJEU[38] as regards the criteria NGOs have to comply with, it precludes newly set up NGOs from access to court through the requirement of at least one year of operation. Yet it should not affect and narrow the rule of Section 98(1) EPC, as sectoral law can contain rules that depart from the CACP. This was a legislative response to some abusive practice.

Further rules in connection with collective actions are contained in the CACP for actions filed by more than four persons, as well as for notification in mass proceedings. A so-called model procedure was also introduced, which is meant to relieve courts in parallel actions. This institution is not so much to decide a pilot case, but to help the court cope with lots of similar actions (*e.g.* actions filed by persons directly affected living in the impacted area) – once a case is decided, the other cases with the same legal and similar factual grounds can be decided without a hearing. This is only a possibility for the court, not an obligation.

The concept of the serving or secondary role of procedural rules is also an important element of the doctrine of consequences of procedural vices in Hungarian administrative procedure. This concept finds its most important

38 *Cf.* Judgment of 15 October 2009, *Case C-263/08, Djurgården-Lilla Värtans Miljöskyddsförening*, ECLI:EU:C:2009:631.

doi: 10.5553/HYIEL/266627012022010001018

consequence in the thesis that violations of procedural rules have no effect on the existence of decisions if they do not affect the decision on the merits. Accordingly, the previous Hungarian CPR stated that the court shall set aside the unlawful administrative decision – with the exception where a violation procedural rules that had no effect on the merits. According to the case law, a procedural error has an impact on the merits if there is at least a theoretical possibility that without the procedural error the administrative decision could have been different. This principle was developed by the courts and finally incorporated into the rules of administrative court procedure in 2004.[39] Thus, the court should not overrule administrative decisions in the case of irrelevant errors.

This approach is at odds with the view of the intrinsic value of procedural rules and guarantees, foremost the assumption that if procedural rules are followed, it is likely that the decision will be lawful and just. This approach is also found in Hungarian law, where a regulation states that discretionary decisions can only be reviewed for procedural errors or errors of consideration and for misuse of discretion. The two approaches contradict each other to a certain extent. The CJEU accepted the concept of the serving role of procedural law in principle in *Gemeinde Altrip*, but at the same time narrowed its scope of application.[40] This decision influenced the new rules, which also reflect a growing appreciation of procedural rules. On the one hand, the previously cited rule was retained in a new version of Section 88(1) CACP:

> "(1) The court shall dismiss the claim, if
> a the claim is unfounded,
> b no direct violation of the right or legitimate interest of the claimant can be established,
> c the procedural infringement did not have a relevant impact on the evaluation of the case on the merits."

On the other hand however, Section 92 CACP regulates a ground for mandatory annulation if "*b)* the infringement caused by the violation of substantial rules of the preceding administrative procedure cannot be remedied in the action."

This mandatory annulation practically reflects on the third answer of the CJEU in *Gemeinde Altrip*. If the case law will use this clause properly, it may help in upholding the constitutional guarantee of good administration contained in Article XXIV of the Fundamental Law of Hungary – based on Article 41 EU CFR. This could somewhat mitigate the consequences of the regression with regard to procedural guarantees in general and also with regard to public participation.

This new concept was followed – only punctually yet – by the Constitutional Court, which declared the doctrine of irrelevance of procedural errors in the case

39 Section 339(1) of the (previous) CPR as until the end of 2017, administrative proceedings were governed by the CPR. *See* Krisztina F. Rozsnyai, 'The Procedural Autonomy of Hungarian Administrative Justice as a Precondition of Effective Judicial Protection', *Studia Iuridica Lublinensia*, Vol. 30, Issue 4, 2021, pp. 491-492.

40 Judgment of 7 November 2013, *Case C-72/12, Gemeinde Altrip and others*, ECLI:EU:C:2013:712.

of a serious procedural error to be unconstitutional.[41] In the newest case law of the highest courts on unlawful silence of administration we can also see the causation link requirement being left aside. The Curia of Hungary annulled already several decisions because of the administration exceeding procedural time limits[42] and the Constitutional Court also stated a constitutional requirement of the reduction of the sanction to be imposed in the case of a delay in the decision-making of the tax authority.[43]

5. Changes in the Administrative Organization Hindering Compliance with EU Law

5.1. Integration of the Territorial State Administration

In the last years the most significant problems of environmental authorization procedures were connected to the vast changes of administrative organization. For a long time, the Hungarian organizational setup was quite in line with Union law. There had been a ministry responsible for the protection of the environment since 1987, with subordinated territorial authorities acting as legal units with own competences.[44] There were some competences (*e.g.* forestry) that belonged to other authorities and thus to the field of competence of other ministries.

Since 2010, however, there has been a very strong tendency of centralization in Hungary. On the one hand, the number of ministries had been significantly reduced, integrating environmental protection into the Ministry for Rural Development. On the level of territorial public administration, administrative bodies operating at the county level were integrated into the County Government Offices set up by the new constitution, the Fundamental Law of Hungary. These Offices act as the territorial body of the Government with general competence. This meant a shift into the direction of the French 'prefecture' model. The National Inspectorate for Environment and Nature Conservation was among the few central administrative authorities that had been allowed to keep their territorial units. This was primarily owed to their regional territorial competence which differed from that of the county-based administrative bodies.

The next step of integration, however, also reached these administrative bodies. At this point in 2014, integration did not affect the material competences of the environmental authorities: integration was initially carried out in such a way that the substantive competence of the environmental protection authorities was conferred upon a unit of the Government Office. This unit was not an independent administrative body regarding its organization, but disposed of own competences free from the instructive powers of the Government Commissioner. Nevertheless, this situation did not last for long. In the next wave of integration, already in early 2015, all substantive competences were conferred from the

41 Constitutional Court Decision No. 3311/2018. (X. 16.) AB.

42 Curia of Hungary, Kfv.I.35.760/2016/6, Reasoning [64].

43 Constitutional Court Decision No. 25/2020. (XII. 2.) AB.

44 A central administrative agency for the Protection of the Environment and Nature Conservation had already been established in 1977, and successively transformed to a ministry in 1987.

doi: 10.5553/HYIEL/266627012022010001018

individual units of the County Government Office to its head, the Government Commissioner. This was a momentous step: the devolution of all competences did not only involve a transfer of competences for conducting environmental protection procedures and issuing decisions from the unit to the Government Commissioner, but it also "simplified" all (typical) procedures in which the environmental protection authority participated as a special authority. As a result, with the exception of municipal authorities' procedures, special authority procedures in the field of environmental protection became obsolete, since the Government Commissioner obtained the competences of all units. In effect, the legal construction of procedural integration was replaced by organizational integration.[45]

Since the integrated units of the County Government Office no longer had own competences, they could not proceed as special authorities. However, units of the County Government Office concerned with the special questions retained some consultative functions: instead of special authorizations they now give opinions on the special issue.

In connection with the Decision for the Uniform Interpretation of Law No. 4/2010 KJE,[46] however, this meant that public participation was only ensured in cases where the County Government Office acted as an environmental protection authority. In all other procedures, where the environmental protection authority was only responsible for enforcing environmental protection as a special authority and the NGOs enjoyed the party status because of the special authority involvement of the environmental protection authority, this guarantee was no longer available. Section 66/A, inserted into the Environmental Protection Act (EPA) at the end of 2015 states that in an authorization procedure of an activity resulting in the use of environment, the enforcement of environmental protection aspects is examined as a special issue. In Section 98(1a) the EPA states that if the opinion of the unit on the special issue must be obtained, this procedure is considered to be an environmental matter and thus the party status of NGOs is ensured. However, there are no further procedural rules that clarify whether and how environmental organizations are to be involved in these proceedings. It was suggested by lower courts that the Decision for the Uniform Interpretation of Law No. 4/2010. KJE should be amended or replaced in light of this development in order to reflect the new legal situation and to better guarantee the status of party. Yet this request was not followed by the Curia of Hungary, and none of the persons who could have filed a motion for a procedure for the uniform interpretation of law have made use of this right so far. Thus, the cited KJE decision does not include such participation involving the provision of an opinion on a special issue.

The Constitutional Court examined this rule in light of the dissolution of environmental protection authorities. Although it examined the differences between the two types of environmental protection authority involvement at

45 The authorities for water protection being separate authorities still proceed in numerous cases as a special authority.

46 This decision upheld Decision No. 1/2004. KJE, *see* above, at Section 3.3.

doi: 10.5553/HYIEL/266627012022010001018

length and found that the new regulation lacked any procedural guarantees, it held that the substantive guarantee of Section 66/A(2), which states that the authority may not authorize the planned activity if it would endanger or harm an environmental element, was not contrary to the non-derogation principle. Instead of annulling the contested provision, the Constitutional Court only established an unconstitutional omission on the side of the legislator, on the grounds that the administrative body is not bound by the opinion given on the special issue, *i.e.* the environmental impact of the matter in the administrative decision.

The Constitutional Court also established the constitutional requirement[47] that environmental concerns must not be subordinated to any other considerations in the decision-making of authorities.[48] However, this requirement is formulated very vaguely and cannot heal the unconstitutional regulation. A substantive legal duty governing decision-making without procedural guarantees is not sufficient to allay environmental law concerns. If we compare this new form of participation of the County Government Office's Unit of Environmental Protection following the transfer of responsibilities to the Government Commissioner with the model of participation as special authority, that is, the former territorial authority for environment and nature conservation as an independent authority, it is striking, that in the latter case, there are strict procedural guarantees, through which the failure to take account of environmental law concerns also has an effect on the validity of the decisions. Where the special authority was not involved in the procedure or it was involved, but its opinion was not taken into account, the decision of the authority conducting the procedure was null and void. Although the new rule of the EPC states that the 'opinion on the special issue' is binding on the authority conducting the proceedings, and the authority may not grant the permit in case the activity to be authorized would endanger or harm an element of the environment, in case it nevertheless unlawfully grants the permit, this shall not entail nullity of the decision. As of yet, it is unclear how the Curia of Hungary will deem such errors.

The new rule in Section 66/A(3) EPC is a step in the right direction. With this provision, the legislator fulfilled the legislative obligation imposed upon it by the Constitutional Court with a one-year delay in 2020. Just like the constitutional requirement itself, this provision also focuses on formal aspects. It obliges the authority to establish in the operative part of its decision that the special issue was assessed, what the result of the examination was and what special

47 This is a special power of the court to spare the legal norm, where instead of annulment the Constitutional Court merely sets for the constitutional interpretation of the norm. In recent years the Constitutional Court has resorted to this type of decision instead of annulment. *See* generally Eszter Bodnár, 'Disarming the Guardians', *in* Martin Krygier *et al.* (eds.), *Anti-Constitutional Populism,* Cambridge University Press, Cambridge, 2022, pp. 279-286.

48 Constitutional Court Decision No. 4/2019. (III. 7.) AB. *See generally* Katalin Sulyok, '4/2019. (III. 7.) AB határozat – Zöldhatóságok integrációja', *in* Fruzsina Gárdos-Orosz & Kinga Zakariás (eds.), *Az Alkotmánybírósági gyakorlat: Az Alkotmánybíróság 100 elvi jelentőségű határozata,* (Vol. 1.), HVG-ORAC, Budapest, 2021, p. 955.

doi: 10.5553/HYIEL/266627012022010001018

requirements, if any, were set forth on this basis. The statement of reasons must contain the detailed results of the assessment of the special issue. This rule is very helpful in one respect: it renders the already mentioned rule in Section 98(1a) ECP, inserted in 2017, applicable, stating that where there is an opinion on a special issue, is to be considered an administrative procedure for the protection of the environment. With this regulatory link, in such cases the ECP now grants party status and thus also access to court to NGOs, overriding the Legal Uniformity Decision No. 4/2010 of the Supreme Court. Coming back to the first part of this article, in such cases the NGOs must be notified of the launch of a procedure, as well. Meanwhile, other procedural guarantees are, of course, still very much lacking.

5.2. Centralization at the State Level

The integration of territorial administrative organization was followed by the centralization and the abolishment of the majority of the central agencies in 2016. These agencies all functioned in hierarchical subordination to the different ministries with the main profile of handling second instance and special first instance administrative cases. The National Inspectorate for the Environment and Nature Conservation as a central agency was no exception: the agency was dissolved and its competences were conferred upon the County Government Office of the Central Hungarian Province of Pest almost without exception. This change diminished the level of environmental protection. Firstly, the lack of a central agency means that the task of governing territorial environmental administration was split up between two bodies: the supervisory authority responsible for managing the professional work is the Ministry of Agriculture (from May 2022 on the Ministry for Technology and Industry[49]). However, this authority does not deal with appeals; instead, a designated County Government Office acts as the appellate body over other County Government Offices. This artificial separation the function of managing professional work creates both lacunes and superfluous, overlapping activities, by far not enhancing the authorities' effectivity. At the same time, first-instance competences were transferred to the subordinate territorial units of the County Government Offices: the district offices.[50] This way, at least for a transitional period, the County Government Office of Pest County (the Central Hungarian County

49 This reorganization well illustrates the level of importance accorded to environmental issues in the present governmental structure.

50 Competences were transferred only to selected district offices which proceeded this way with a territorial competence not for a district, but at least for one county (or even several counties).

doi: 10.5553/HYIEL/266627012022010001018

around Budapest) acted both as a first-instance authority and as an appellate body.[51]

In addition, the County Government Offices are subject to a twofold, hierarchical management: the supervision of professional activities lies in the hands of the ministry responsible for that specific field of administration, meanwhile, organizational matters such as structure, finances, personnel, *etc.* are managed by the Chancellor's Office. This double subordination weakens professional supervision to a certain extent, and in the concrete case, the control of administrative activities of the government office as environmental protection authority.

The other negative consequence of this restructuring is that the organizational structure of the County Government Offices is determined by the Chancellor's Office. Thus, it may be the case that in some County Government Offices there is no independent environmental protection unit, but instead, these issues are put together in one unit with other, often competing areas (*e.g.* transport) – a situation which is difficult to reconcile with Union law.

6. Conclusion

Apparently, the transposition of EU law did not achieve lasting change in Hungarian administrative culture. The changes in case law also proved to be ephemeral. Unfortunately, the analyzed developments show that following a good start, where European law had a strong influence on Hungarian law in the field of environmental protection, and even spill-over effects were recorded in both administrative procedure and administrative court procedure, Hungarian courts' case law as well as legislation tried to hinder public participation in matters relating to the environment. In more recent legislation, the level of protection already achieved was not maintained owing to changes on the level of both the organization of public administration and general administrative procedural law. The institutions that had been transplanted to general administrative procedural law especially with regard to procedures relating to the environment were undermined or abolished. Unfortunately, we can still, or rather, increasingly report implementation concerns in this area.[52]

However, there are some developments that give reasons for hope. NGOs try to maintain their positions, as does the deputy ombudsman elected by Parliament

51 This problem was also the subject of an application for a review of the act by the Budapest-Capital Administrative and Labor Court. Here, too, the Constitutional Court, in its *Decision No. 12/2019. (IV. 8.) AB* did not actually remedy the unconstitutionality by annulling the Decree with a retroactive effect, but only annulled it *ex nunc*. It stated in an undogmatic way that the court should handle this situation breaching the right to effective remedy as if the Government Commissioner had not proceeded as a second instance authority, but had amended its own first-instance decision (to which authorities are entitled in certain circumstances under the rules of administrative procedure).

52 László Szegedi, 'The Eastern Way of Europeanisation in the Light of Environmental Policymaking? Implementation Concerns of the Aarhus Convention-related EU Law in Central and Eastern Europe', *ELTE Law Journal*, Vol. 2, Issue 1, 2014, p. 134.

doi: 10.5553/HYIEL/266627012022010001018

to protect the interests of future generations, colloquially known as the 'Green Ombudsman'. This deputy-ombudsman has few powers of his own, but he can still do a lot to protect the environment. To challenge legal acts before the Constitutional Court he must naturally involve the ombudsman, the Commissioner for Fundamental Rights, who rarely makes use of this competence. One such occasion though was the *ex post* constitutional challenge brought against the amendment of the Forest Act by the Ombudsman, upon which the Constitutional Court annulled several amendments for infringing the right to a healthy environment and the environmental interests of future generations as enshrined in Article P of the Fundamental Law.[53]

Another important instrument is publicity. The Green Ombudsman is very active in raising his voice against 'constitutional inconsistencies' in the field of environmental protection. He regularly publishes statements of position, for example, against the integration and centralization of the administrative organization of environmental protection,[54] or against the dysfunctions of waste management,[55] the rules of which do not comply with the basic principles of environmental law. These statements of position are his most important instrument. For example, an earlier opinion against the planned abolishment of the requirement to obtain a permit for private well drilling played a major role in the Constitutional Court annulling the new regulation based on the non-derogation principle.[56]

What we can identify as a first sign of a more lasting change in legal culture is that environmental law is becoming an independent subject taught at almost all Hungarian law faculties, in some cases taking the place of the former subject 'agricultural law' or gradually reshaping its content. This may lay the groundwork for the new generations of lawyers to be more inclined to foster public participation in favor of future generations.

53 Constitutional Court Decision No. 14/2020. (VII. 6.) AB. *See* its analysis in Sulyok 2021, p. 360.

54 *See* at www.ajbh.hu/documents/10180/2762244/Elvi_%C3%A1ll%C3%A1sfoglal%C3%A1s_Fel%C3%BCgyel%C5%91s%C3%A9gek_integr%C3%A1ci%C3%B3ja_2018.05.08.pdf/f7b76ffa-f01a-3b8c-aaf0-ed6948efe5b7.

55 *See* at www.ajbh.hu/documents/10180/2896961/a_hulladekgazdalkodasi_kozszolgaltatas_mukodesi_problemairol.pdf.

56 Constitutional Court Decision No. 13/2018. (IV. 9.) AB. However, with the state of emergency regulation, the government then implemented this change with a much wider scope causing possibly much more harm: dwells for irrigation purposes can be drilled without any permission with effect from 1 January 2021. The Green Ombudsman yet again published a statement of position at www.ajbh.hu/documents/10180/3310290/k%C3%B6zlem%C3%A9ny+a+v%C3%ADzjogi+enged%C3%A9lyez%C3%A9si+szab%C3%A1lyok+enyh%C3%ADt%C3%A9s%C3%A9vel+kapcsolatos+alkotm%C3%A1nyos+agg%C3%A1lyokr%C3%B3l/8d836651-cafd-0539-ef8e-c9872adfc894.

doi: 10.5553/HYIEL/266627012022010001018

60 Years of the New York Convention in Hungary

A Formalistic, Yet Pro-Arbitration Approach*

*Richárd Schmidt***

Abstract

The New York Convention on the Recognition and Enforcement of Foreign Arbitral Awards celebrates the 60th anniversary of its entry into force in Hungary in 2022. After being hibernated for nearly three decades, the Convention has become an essential source of Hungarian lex arbitri since the political-economic transition of the country from socialism to market economy in 1989-1990. Given that the Convention celebrates its 'diamond anniversary' in Hungary this year, the time is ripe to review its application by domestic courts over the last decades, by focusing on the recognition and enforcement of international arbitration agreements and foreign arbitral awards in Hungarian judicial practice. This study aims at verifying whether the approach of Hungarian state courts is in line with, or at least converging towards the dominant pro-arbitration bias of the Convention. On the other hand, it is worth identifying those domains, where national judicial practice departs from the mainstream tendencies, and to shed light on those fields, where the risk of divergence from the arbitration-friendly orientation arises.

Keywords: New York Convention, recognition and enforcement of foreign arbitral awards, Hungary, lex arbitri, arbitration.

1. Introduction

It can be hardly disputed that the 1958 New York Convention on the Recognition and Enforcement of Foreign Arbitral Awards[1] (Convention) is a key legal source in the field of international commercial arbitration. According to a renowned English judge and arbitrator, the Convention is probably *"the most effective*

* The author would like to thank Dr. Katalin Raffai for her support and advice. The author is responsible for all errors and omissions.

** Richárd Schmidt: managing partner, SMARTLEGAL Schmidt & Partners law firm, Budapest; guest lecturer of international dispute resolution at the Department of Private International Law at the Pázmány Péter Catholic University, Budapest.

1 UNTS, Vol. 330, Issue 4739. Convention on the Recognition and Enforcement of Foreign Arbitral awards, done at New York on 10 June 1958.

doi: 10.5553/HYIEL/266627012022010001019

instance of international legislation in the entire history of commercial law".[2] Besides having almost 170 signatories at the time of writing this article, due to its impact on the UNCITRAL Model Law on International Commercial Arbitration,[3] chosen as the foundation for the modernization of national arbitral laws by more than 80 countries worldwide, the Convention may be characterized as the 'alpha and omega' of international commercial arbitration. Besides its symbolic meaning, the above-mentioned expression well illustrates the main purpose of the Convention, *i.e.* to regulate the first and the last stage of arbitration: the beginning of the dispute, where the recognition and enforcement of the arbitration agreement by state courts is a crucial issue, and the very end of the arbitral process, which materializes in the recognition and enforcement of the foreign arbitral award by states. Given that the Convention celebrates its 60th anniversary of entering into force in Hungary, the time is ripe to review the case law of Hungarian courts over the last decades to verify whether the approach of domestic courts is in line with, or at least converging towards, the dominant pro-arbitration bias of the Convention. On the other hand, it is worth identifying those fields, where national judicial practice is diverging from this direction, or at least where there is a risk of such divergence. The second section of this article presents the place of the Convention in the Hungarian legal system, discusses the reasons for its marginal role until the '90s, explains how its principles and provisions have become an essential part of Hungarian arbitration law and summarizes the case law relating to commercial reservation. The third section examines the judicial practice of domestic courts regarding the recognition and enforcement of international arbitration agreements. Finally, in the fourth section, I analyze the case law of Hungarian courts on the recognition and enforcement of foreign arbitral awards.

2. The Convention in the Hungarian Legal Order

2.1. Accession and Hibernation until the '90s

Together with other states from the so-called Eastern bloc, who joined the Convention in the late 50's and early 60's, Hungary joined the Convention on 5 March 1962, by making both reciprocity and commercial reservations. The Convention entered into force in Hungary on 3 June 1962,[4] and the Ministry of Justice even issued a decree, in order to clarify some issues in respect of the Convention's implementation.[5] It should be noted that regardless of Hungary's early accession, *the Convention could play only a marginal role in the international*

2 Michael John Mustill, 'Arbitration: History and Background', *Journal of International Arbitration*, Vol. 6, Issue 2, 1983, p. 43.

3 UN Doc. A/40/12, annex I as adopted by the UN Commission on International Trade Law on 21 June 1985, and as amended by the UN Commission on International Trade Law on 7 July 2006.

4 Legislative Decree No. 25 of 1962 on the promulgation of the Convention on the Recognition and Enforcement of Foreign Arbitral awards, done in New York on 10 June 1958.

5 Decree of the Hungarian Ministry of Justice No. 12/1962. (X. 31.) (Ministerial Decree).

doi: 10.5553/HYIEL/266627012022010001019

commercial relations of our country before 1990, since behind the iron curtain cross-border business activities were carried out exclusively via state-owned companies, and mainly among countries belonging to the Council for Mutual Economic Assistance (Comecon).[6] It is hardly surprising that the only Hungarian treatise on international arbitration from this era dedicates a whole chapter to the rules of procedures of the various arbitration institutions of the Comecon countries, while presenting the Convention quite sketchily.[7] At the same time, the marginal role played by the Convention in Hungary in the first three decades after its entry into force was not based on purely economic or political considerations, but it was justifiable on pragmatic grounds, too. Indeed, the Moscow Arbitration Convention, adopted with a view to resolve cross-border commercial disputes between the companies of the Comecon member states, set forth more favorable award enforcement provisions than the Convention.[8] Furthermore, the Hungarian implementation of the Convention introduced a blanket rule that could be invoked by the Hungarian award-debtor to resist the enforcement of the foreign arbitral award, which amounted to a significant risk for foreign parties outside the iron curtain.[9] Based on the above, the domestic application of the Convention could only really gain momentum after the political and economic transition in 1990, which brought the fall of the iron curtain, and the opportunity for Hungarian private market actors to conduct cross-border commercial activities.[10]

2.2. *'Indirect Effect' on Hungarian Arbitration Laws from '90s*

Before delving into the case law analysis, it is worth recalling the impact of the Convention on the current arbitral laws of Hungary. Given that the Hungarian legislator used the Model Law as a starting point for reforming the Hungarian *lex arbitri* both in 1994 and 2017, *the Convention had significant 'indirect effect' on both*

6 The Comecon had been set up in 1949 by the Soviet Union in Moscow, in response to the Marshall Plan, to facilitate the economic reconstruction and progress by mutual assistance, cooperation and trade behind the iron curtain. Vast majority of Eastern European Countries participated in the Comecon.

7 László Faragó, *Nemzetközi választottbíráskodás*, Közgazdasági és Jogi Kiadó, Budapest, 1966, pp. 193-215, and 227-323.

8 Convention on the Settlement by Arbitration of Civil Law Disputes Resulting from Relations of Economic and Scientific-Technical Cooperation, Done at Moscow, 26 May 1972. Article V of the Moscow Arbitration Convention includes fewer grounds for refusing the recognition and enforcement of the arbitral award.

9 Section 5 of the Ministerial Decree, which has been repealed in 1994, provided that the recognition and enforcement of the foreign award could be refused, in case the Hungarian party entered into the arbitration agreement or the underlying legal relationship, without being entitled to do it, or without having the necessary administrative permit.

10 Katalin Raffai, 'Interpretation and Application of the New York Convention in Hungary', *in* George Bermann (ed.), *Recognition and Enforcement of Foreign Arbitral Awards. The Interpretation and Application of the New York Convention by National Courts*, Springer, 2017, p. 444.

doi: 10.5553/HYIEL/266627012022010001019

the former and on the current Hungarian Arbitration Act.[11] In this way, Article II of the Convention, defining the concept, form and 'negative effect' of arbitration agreements, had been reflected in Article 7 (Option I) and Article 8(1) of the Model Law and these provisions were essentially adopted by Sections 8 and 9 of the Hungarian Arbitration Act. Probably the most important innovation of the Model Law was the unification of the grounds for annulment of the arbitral award, by mirroring the grounds for refusing the recognition and enforcement of foreign awards of Article V of the Convention.[12] These unified grounds for setting aside arbitral awards in Article 34(2) of the Model Law were taken over verbatim by Section 47(2) of the Hungarian Arbitration Act. Last, but not least, when it comes to the grounds for refusal of the recognition and enforcement of arbitral awards set forth in Article V of the Convention, these were taken over by Article 36(1)(a) and (b) of the Model law,[13] and the grounds for refusal in point (b) (infringement of public policy, lack of arbitrability) were regulated in Section 54 of the Hungarian Arbitration Act. Based on the above, due to the Convention and the Model Law, when it comes to the most important milestones of arbitral proceedings, namely the enforcement of arbitral agreements, the setting aside of arbitral awards, and the enforcement of the latter abroad, a harmonized legal framework was born in the field of international arbitration, which was entirely taken over by the Hungarian legislator in the '90s. At the same time, given that the line of demarcation between purely domestic and international arbitrations is unclear in the Hungarian practice,[14] this harmonized legal framework can be characterized as constituting both a risk and a potential at the same time. On the one hand, given that Hungarian courts face grounds for not enforcing arbitration agreements and arbitral awards most frequently in purely domestic settings, there is a real risk that judges, wearing the 'same glasses', apply the standards crystallized in these national proceedings in international cases, as well. On the other hand, the reception of the dominant pro-arbitration interpretation of the Convention by other jurisdictions may have a positive effect on the application of national arbitral laws in domestic cases as well. While this study focuses mainly on the domestic judicial practice forged during the application of the provisions of the Convention, given the possible interplay between the above regimes, where it is relevant, I will also refer to the

11 The former Hungarian Arbitration Act was Act LXXI of 1994 on Arbitration. The current Hungarian Arbitration Act ("Hungarian Arbitration Act") is Act LX of 2017 on Arbitration. The provisions of the current Hungarian Arbitration Act entered into force gradually, starting with 16 June 2017. The provisions governing arbitral proceedings entered into force with effect from 1 January 2018, and these are applicable to arbitral proceedings that were commenced after this date.

12 Explanatory Note by the UNCITRAL secretariat on the 1985 Model Law on International Commercial Arbitration as amended in 2006 (Explanatory Note), Sections 46-47.

13 Explanatory Note, Sections 49-51.

14 The Hungarian Arbitration Act governs both purely domestic and international arbitral proceedings. Section 1(1) of the Hungarian Arbitration Act provides as follows: "The provisions of this Act shall apply if the place of the arbitration is in Hungary." The case law of Hungarian courts has started to show some differentiation in the last two decades in relation with public policy, *see* Section 4.2.7.

doi: 10.5553/HYIEL/266627012022010001019

court practice applying the respective provisions of the Hungarian Arbitration Act.

2.3. Subject Matter Scope, Commercial Reservation

When it comes to subject matter scope, in accordance with the Hungarian implementation of the Convention, the provisions of the latter shall be applied on the one hand, to awards made outside the territory of Hungary, and on the other hand, to awards made in Hungary, provided that these were made in proceedings where the seat of arbitration was abroad and the majority of the arbitral tribunal members or the sole arbitrator was a foreign national.[15] While the application of the above provisions had not caused debates in practice, the commercial reservation had often been invoked by award debtors over the last decades. Given that since the mid '90s *the concept of "commercial dispute" has not been defined by domestic law*, this legislative gap gave an interpretative task to the courts.[16] For example, in a case, where the award debtor resisted the enforcement of an award delivered by the arbitral tribunal of the Austrian Chamber of Commerce, the first instance court wrongly concluded that the transfer of ownership would be a relevant factor when assessing the commercial nature of the relationship. The second instance court corrected this decision by establishing that a lease agreement with an option for the subsidiary of the tenant to enter into a leasing agreement with the landlord shall be considered a commercial relationship.[17] In another case, a commercial agency contract that was subject to Swiss law had to be interpreted by the Hungarian court, since the award debtor contended that he had been in an employment relationship with the award creditor. The courts rightly concluded that an agreement between two independent persons, without subordination, could not be qualified as an employment relationship, since by setting common business goals, the parties strived for gaining individual profit, based on which the legal relation was qualified as commercial.[18] Another award-debtor called into question the commercial nature of the legal relationship on the grounds that his electricity network development contract concluded with the Kingdom of Belgium was governed by Belgian administrative law. However, the Hungarian courts pointed out that even if electricity supply has some connection with the public powers of the state, by entering into the network contract at hand, the foreign state had not exercised its public powers *(acta iure imperii)*, but acted as a private market actor *(acta iure gestionis)*, therefore, the commercial reservation was not applicable.[19] In

15 Section (1)(a) and (b) of the Ministerial Decree.

16 Article 2 of the Ministerial Decree defined the concept of commercial dispute by referring to Decree No. 1/1960. (V. 10.) PM of the Minister of Transportation, Media and Energetics, which was repealed in 1994, with the entering into force of the former Arbitration Act. *See* Raffai 2017, p. 435.

17 Hungarian Supreme Court, Case No. BH2004.369.

18 Hungarian Supreme Court, Case No. BH 2007.130.

19 Regional Court of Appeal of Budapest, Case No. 2201-3. Pfk.27.107/2015/10. Cited by Anikó Bajcsy, 'Külföldi választottbírósági ítélet elismerése megtagadásának magyar bírósági gyakorlata', *Kúriai Döntések*, 2017/2, pp. 275-280.

doi: 10.5553/HYIEL/266627012022010001019

the international practice of the Convention *the commercial nature of the dispute is usually interpreted broadly,* and refusal of enforcement for lack of commerciality is rather exceptional.[20] Based on the above case law, we can conclude that in this respect, the Hungarian judicial practice is in line with the dominant approach. At the same time, the author of this study agrees with the opinion of several scholars, that the commercial reservation should be withdrawn, to avoid causing any complications in the future.[21]

3. Enforcement of Arbitration Agreements

At the outset, it should be highlighted that Article II of the Convention is rarely invoked directly before Hungarian courts, because *the Hungarian Arbitration Act adopted verbatim the respective provisions of the Model Law mirroring the above provisions of the Convention*, therefore, it is more convenient for parties to rely on the provisions of domestic law.[22] Yet, there are some court decisions which merit attention in relation to the formation of the arbitration agreement, where the issues of incorporation by reference, and contract conclusion through an agent revealed some inconsistencies in addressing conflict of laws issues by domestic courts. In addition, besides giving an overview of the issue of arbitrability in the pre-award phase, I draw attention to some negative tendencies regarding arbitration agreements in domestic arbitral practice, which may pose a risk for future cases falling under the Convention.

3.1. Incorporation by Reference – Tacit Approval

When it comes to issues of consent under Article II(1) of the Convention, it is illuminating how the coincidence of the legislative gap of the Convention regarding the determination of the law governing arbitration agreements in the pre-award phase, and domestic tendencies, such as the so-called *Heimwärtsstreben,*[23] *i.e.* the leaning of national courts to apply *lex fori,* and the parochial practice of domestic courts on contract formation is capable of undermining the efficiency of international arbitration agreements. According to Hungarian contract law, general terms and conditions (GTCs) become an integral part of the contract only in case the party using them made it possible for the other party to familiarize themselves with the content of these terms prior to the conclusion of the contract. Furthermore, unusual GTCs, often referred to in legal practice as 'surprise clauses', must be expressly accepted by the other party following a notification drawing attention to these and made by the party using them.[24] The above substantive law provisions, applicable even in business to

20 Emanuelle Gaillard & George Bermann (eds.), *The UNCITRAL Secretary Guide on the New York Convention*, Brill, Nijhoff, 2017, p. 39.
21 Raffai 2017, p. 434.
22 Article 7 (Option I) and Article 8 of the Model law are reflected in Section 8 and 9 of the Hungarian Arbitration Act.
23 Arthur Nussbaum, *Deutsches Internationales Privatrecht*, J.C.B. Mohr, 1932, p. 384.
24 Section 6:78 (1)-(3) of the Hungarian Civil Code.

doi: 10.5553/HYIEL/266627012022010001019

business (B2B) cases, can be relevant in arbitration, because the outdated judicial practice developed in domestic arbitral proceedings considers arbitration clauses incorporated into GTCs as 'surprise clauses', which are enforceable only in case of express consent.[25] This line of thought is reflected in the first instance decision rendered in a recent case involving a legal dispute between an Austrian seller and a Hungarian buyer, where the seller's GTCs stipulated Austrian law as the law governing the contract, and an ICC arbitration clause with a seat of arbitration in Innsbruck (Austria). Despite the above circumstances, the court of first instance accepted the argumentation of the buyer, relying on Hungarian contract law as *lex fori*, according to which in the absence of express acceptance of such a 'surprise clause' like the arbitration agreement, that clause did not come into existence. Hopefully, the court of second instance took a different view and applied Austrian law as *lex causae* to the existence of the arbitration clause, according to which, in case the parties do business in the same sector, or they have an ongoing business relationship, the provisions of the GTCs become part of the contract if one of the parties intends to use them, and the other party is aware of this fact.[26] Even if the provisions of the Convention have not been invoked directly, the solution of the court of second instance is in line with the dominant approach under Article II(1) of the Convention, according to which the conclusion of the arbitration clause shall be governed by the same law as its validity, and the uniform conflict of law rule of Article V(1)(a) shall be applied *mutatis mutandis* in respect of the arbitral agreement in the pre-award phase, in order to ensure a coherent standard during all stages of arbitration.[27] Yet, *the first instance decision perfectly illustrates the traditional approach of Hungarian courts,* and it reveals how a flaw in the application of the proper connecting factor accompanied by an unfortunate domestic case law on the formation of contracts can undermine the parties' agreement to arbitrate in international matters.

3.2. Issues of Representation

The issue of consent can be a delicate one, in case the arbitration agreement is concluded *via* an agent, whose authority of representation is challenged later, calling into questions the existence of the arbitral agreement in the meaning of Article II(1) of the Convention. One particular case, involving a share purchase contract in relation to the business shares of a Hungarian limited liability company, merits attention in this context.[28] The above contract had been entered into by a Cyprian company as the seller and a Swiss company as the buyer in Budapest, and it contained an arbitration clause in favor of the Arbitration Court of the Russian Chamber of Commerce and Industry. The seller sued the buyer before the Hungarian courts, by challenging the existence of the share purchase contract and the arbitration clause, arguing that it was concluded on its behalf by

25 Hungarian Supreme Court, Case Nos. EH2003.875 and BH2001.131.

26 Regional Court of Appeal of Győr, Case No. Gf.20.108/2020/5.

27 Reinmar Wolff (ed.), *New York Convention – Article-by Article Commentary,* 2nd edition, C.H. Beck, München, 2019, p. 104; Gary B. Born, *International Commercial Arbitration,* 2nd edition, Kluwer Law International, 2014, p. 566.

28 Regional Court of Appeal of Budapest, Case No. 10.Gf.40.417/2011/12.

doi: 10.5553/HYIEL/266627012022010001019

a false representative, who acted based on a power of attorney, given to him in Cyprus 5 years before the sales transaction. The buyer disputed the jurisdiction of Hungarian courts based on the arbitration clause. However, in the opinion of the Hungarian courts, the power of attorney issued in Cyprus and the share purchase contract concluded 5 years later in Budapest had to be considered as one transaction. According to the courts, this transaction had the closest connection with Hungary, so they applied Hungarian law in the case. Since the sale of the target company did not fall into the subject matter scope of the power of attorney, the Hungarian courts ruled that the false representative could not enter into a binding arbitration agreement on behalf of the seller. The above decision can be criticized mainly for *ignoring the principle of separability of the arbitration agreement*, which prevented the court from examining the issue of representation, and the existence of the arbitration clause in the light of any other law than the *lex fori*, which is further 'evidence' for the disadvantageous effects of the above-mentioned phenomenon of *Heimwärtsstreben* of domestic courts in the field of cases involving matters of international commercial arbitration.

3.3. *Arbitrability in the Pre-Award Phase*

Since unlike Article V(1)(a) of the Convention, Article II(1) fails to specify which law governs the issue of arbitrability in the pre-award phase, there are diverging views on this issue. Some courts apply *lex fori*, other courts apply *lex causae*,[29] while in the opinion of some courts and commentators the abovementioned laws should be applied cumulatively.[30] Developed jurisdictions distinguish between purely domestic and international matters, and based on the *pro-arbitration* approach, they interpret the arbitrability exception narrowly in the latter cases.[31] Hungarian courts are mainly faced with the issue of inarbitrability in company law matters, where two court decisions merits the attention. In the first case, the defendant raised an *exceptio arbitri* relying on the arbitration clause of a share purchase contract, but the claimant argued that his claim is directed towards the establishment of the nullity of the entire contract, which could concern the Hungarian company register in which the defendant had been already registered. For this reason, the claimant held that the plea of the defendant was inadmissible on grounds of objective inarbitrability, since in his opinion, only state courts were allowed to make any decision modifying the content of Hungarian public registers. However, the courts rightly made a difference between claims directly or indirectly concerning the register of companies as a public register, ruling that the legal dispute was theoretically arbitrable in the latter case, since the eventual establishment of nullity of a contract would have only *inter partes* effect, without directly affecting the content of the public register.[32]

29 Gaillard & Bermann 2017, pp. 56-57.
30 For the cumulative approach *see e.g.* Wolff 2019, p. 150.
31 Born 2014, pp. 957, 964, and 969.
32 Regional Court of Appeal of Budapest, Case No. 10.Gf.40.417/2011/12. (ÍH 2012.82.).

doi: 10.5553/HYIEL/266627012022010001019

In another corporate law case, where the articles of association of a Hungarian company provided for arbitration at a Belgian arbitral institution in case of shareholder disputes, a Belgian minority shareholder intended to appoint an *ad hoc* auditor, to examine some dubious action of the management, however, this motion was not upheld at the shareholders' meeting. When the minority shareholder turned to the Hungarian company court, seeking negative declaratory relief for the lack of competence for the above shareholder dispute because of the arbitral clause, the second instance court came to the conclusion that under Hungarian company law an *ad hoc* auditor can be appointed only in the framework of supervisory proceedings, belonging to the exclusive competence of company courts, therefore, the arbitration clause was unenforceable in this case.[33]

The above decisions illustrate that Hungarian courts apply *lex fori* when evaluating arbitrability in the pre-award phase. While a differentiation of arbitrability in domestic and international cases is missing from domestic practice, it can be concluded that the narrow interpretation of the concept objective inarbitrability in the first case, and the non-arbitrability of certain company matters involving regulatory and controlling functions of the state was not incompatible with the pro-arbitration bias of Convention.

3.4. Negative Effect of Arbitration Agreements

Article II(3) of the Convention *requires national courts to refer the parties to arbitration, if it is requested by at least one party, unless the court finds that the agreement is null, void, inoperative, or incapable of being performed.* When it comes to the standard of review applied by Hungarian courts in the context of Article II(3), instead of conducting a mere *prima facie* inquiry, like in France, the domestic practice follows rather German standard of full review instead.[34] They conduct a comprehensive evidentiary procedure, if needed, to decide on the existence and validity of the arbitration agreement in the pre-award phase. However, in domestic matters, there is an alarming phenomenon in case one of the parties becomes insolvent after the conclusion of the arbitration agreement. A series of first instance and appellate court decisions established in these cases that the arbitration agreement has become "incapable of being performed" by reason of the very fact of the commencement of liquidation proceedings against one of the parties.[35] Even if this issue is polarizing on the international level, since German courts seem to accept a similar approach, while English and Portuguese courts have not considered the lack of financial resources as a factor

33 Regional Court of Appeal of Budapest, Case No. 16.Cgtf.43.178/2017. (BDT2017. 340.). It must be noted that the court of second instance considered the arbitration clause "incapable of being performed", however the court actually decided that such a supervisory proceeding cannot be subject of arbitration, which practically means the objective inarbitrability of the subject-matter.

34 Gaillard & Bermann 2017, pp. 70-71.

35 Curia of Hungary, Case No. EBD2014.11.4.G; Regional Court of Appeal of Pécs, Case No. Gf. 40.041/2014/11; Budapest-Capital Regional Court, Case No. G.42.087/2016/31; Debrecen Regional Court, G.40.169/2015/42.

doi: 10.5553/HYIEL/266627012022010001019

which renders the agreement for arbitration incapable of being performed,[36] the tendency of Hungarian courts to make a *prima facie* decision of not enforcing the arbitration agreement, without verifying the actual financial status of the party concerned, received strong criticism from domestic practitioners.[37] Indeed, the Curia, that is, the Hungarian supreme court has not yet had a chance to address this issue, and the author of this article hopes that the above questionable case law will be not be carried over to the international level, since this approach could erode the *Kompetenz-Kompetenz* principle and the efficiency of arbitration agreements in Hungary.

4. Enforcement of Arbitral Awards

From the perspective of the court seized by an award creditor with an application to recognize and enforce a foreign arbitral award under the Convention, the procedure can be broken down into two phases. In the 'formal phase', the court examines whether the practitioner fulfilled its obligations under Article IV, while in the 'substantive phase', the court deals with the case on the merits, by examining whether the grounds for refusal under Article V of the Convention are applicable. Under Hungarian procedural law, *the formal and substantive phases are conducted by the judge in the same non-litigious proceeding*, at the end of which the court either dismisses the application, or issues the so-called *'exequatur'* certificate. In the absence of clear legal provisions, some Hungarian courts conducted this proceeding on *ex parte* basis, in which case the award debtor became aware of the award enforcement only when the first instance decision on 'exequatur' was served upon him. As one commentator rightly pointed out, an *inter partes* procedure can be better reconciled with basic procedural principles, since in case of an *ex parte* first instance proceeding, the award debtor can put forward his arguments only in the appeal. These arguments are only considered for the first time by the court of second instance, so the right to a fair trial and the right to an effective remedy, enshrined by Article 6 ECHR may be jeopardized.[38]

4.1. Compliance with Formalities

When it comes to compliance with formalities under Article IV, there are two paradigms among national courts worldwide. While a minority of courts, in particular, in Italy and Spain, held that *Article IV contains mandatory procedural prerequisites, in the absence of which the application shall be dismissed*, the majority of jurisdictions construed Article IV as a provision merely concerning evidence.

36 Wolff 2019, p. 195; *ICCA's Guide to the Interpretation of the 1958 New York Convention – Handbook for judges*, International Council for Commercial Arbitration, 2011, p. 117.

37 Miklós Boronkay, 'A fizetésképtelenség hatása a választottbírósági szerződésre', *in* János Burai-Kovács (ed.), *A Kereskedelmi Választottbíróság Évkönyve 2018*, HVG-ORAC, Budapest, 2019, pp. 222-239; Zsolt Okányi, 'Fizetésképtelen társaságok a választottbírósági eljárásban: a választottbírósági kikötés betar(ta)tása és a törvényes bíróhoz való jog', *in* Burai-Kovács 2019.

38 Bajcsy 2017, pp. 272-273.

According to the latter approach, non-compliance with all of the formalities did not amount to an automatic dismissal of the application, which is more in line with the spirit of the Convention.[39] The approach of Hungarian courts is closer to the first paradigm, therefore, in case the applicant fails to comply with all of the necessary formal obligations, the first instance court usually orders the completion of documents *ex officio*, or the court of second instance orders new proceedings. Except for a few cases, where, in accordance with Article VII of the Convention, bilateral treaties take priority over the provisions of the Convention,[40] non-compliance with Article IV(1)-(2) leads to the rejection of the application seeking the recognition of foreign awards. For example, Hungarian courts did not grant recognition where the arbitration agreement was missing, or in cases where it was submitted as a simple photocopy, without legalization by a notary public.[41]

In one particular case, the Supreme Court stressed that in the recognition procedure, the arbitration agreement shall be submitted and its existence cannot be established on the basis of other evidence, *e.g.* on the grounds that the award debtor acknowledged the existence of the arbitration clause in its request for arbitration.[42] The same approach was taken in those cases where petitioners submitted the arbitral award in a simple copy, without legalization.[43] When it comes to translations, although in some countries the translation of the award and the arbitration agreement is not always requested,[44] Hungarian courts are conservative in this regard and recognition was not granted in cases where the arbitral award was submitted in a simple translation, or without an attestation clause from the translator.[45] The *excessive formalism of Hungarian courts* is well characterized by a recent decision, according to which, despite electronic communication applicable to all civil proceedings with effect from 1 January 2018 in Hungary, besides submitting the arbitration agreement and arbitral award as an e-document, signed by the legal representative *via* a qualified electronic signature within the meaning of the eIDAS Regulation,[46] the applicant had to submit these documents in hard copy, as well.[47] From the perspective of award creditors, the formalistic approach of Hungarian courts which is capable of prolonging the enforcement proceeding can be a major risk, since award debtors

39 Maxi Scherer, 'Article IV', *in* Reinmar Wolff (ed.), *New York Convention – Article-by Article Commentary*, 2nd edition, C.H. Beck, München, 2019, p. 224; Gaillard & Bermann 2017, p. 109.

40 Hungarian Supreme Court, Case No. BH2004.416.

41 Hungarian Supreme Court, Case Nos. BH1999.270.; BH2004.19. and BH2002.582.

42 Hungarian Supreme Court, Case No. BH2004.285.

43 Hungarian Supreme Court, Case No. BH1999.223.

44 *ICCA's Guide* 2011, p. 77.

45 Hungarian Supreme Court, Case Nos. BH2004.19. and BH1999.223.

46 Regulation (EU) No 910/2014 of the European Parliament and of the council of 23 July 2014 on electronic identification and trust services for electronic transactions in the internal market and repealing Directive 1999/93/EC.

47 Regional Court of Appeal of Budapest, Case No. 2201-7. Pkf.25558./2019/4. Cited by Dániel Gelencsér & Sándor Udvary (eds.), *A bírósági végrehajtásról szóló törvény és a kapcsolódó jogszabályok kommentárja*, HVG-ORAC, Budapest, 2021, p. 713.

doi: 10.5553/HYIEL/266627012022010001019

can use the extra time generated by the requirement of full compliance with formalities to frustrate the successful enforcement of the arbitral award.

4.2. Grounds for Refusal

4.2.1. Governing Principles

Before examining the domestic court practice regarding the grounds for refusal of the recognition and enforcement of foreign arbitral awards, set forth in Article V(1)-(2) of the Convention, it is worth analyzing the application of the general principles governing this phase by national courts. When it comes to the general prohibition of the *'révision au fond'* which ensures that the court acting in the recognition and enforcement phase does not become an 'appellate forum' reviewing yet again the merits of the case, this principle has been confirmed by several Hungarian decisions.[48] The same is true in relation to the *exhaustive character* of the grounds under Article V of the Convention, based on which domestic courts rejected the award creditors' objections relying on the decrease of the claim, or invoking ongoing litigation with third parties, clarifying that these defenses may not be invoked under the said provision.[49] When it comes to the *burden of proof*, it is also well-settled case law in Hungary that the award debtor shall expressly invoke and substantiate the grounds mentioned in Article V(1) of the Convention.[50]

4.2.2. Incapacity, Invalid Arbitration Agreement – Article V(1)(a)

According to the first prong of Article V(1)(a) of the Convention the recognition and enforcement of the arbitral award can be refused in case *one of the parties of the arbitration agreement was under some incapacity.* Since Convention-related domestic case law does not yield any results in respect of this ground for refusal, it is worth mentioning two relevant cases from the domestic practice on setting aside arbitral awards. In one case, an embassy of a foreign state in Hungary signed a lease contract with a local lessor, despite the relative provisions of the Vienna Convention on Diplomatic Relations of 1961,[51] according to which the lessee did not have legal personality.[52] In another case where the condominium representative signed a loan contract with an arbitration clause on behalf of the condominium in the absence of specific legal provision or condominium resolution. In both cases the lack of legal capacity led to the setting aside of the arbitral awards, at the same time, these cases illustrate that this ground may be invoked only under very exceptional circumstances before of Hungarian courts.

When it comes to the *invalidity of the arbitration agreement* under the second prong of Article V(1)(a) of the Convention, this ground for refusal is often invoked, but it is rarely successful in practice. In a case where the award debtor

48 Hungarian Supreme Court, Case Nos. BH+ 2015.5.209. and BH1998.184.

49 Hungarian Supreme Court, Case Nos. BH2007.130 and BH1996.375.

50 Hungarian Supreme Court, Case No. BH1997.34.

51 Vienna Convention on Diplomatic Relations, Done at Vienna on 18 April 1961. Entered into force on 24 April 1964. UN Treaty Series, Vol. 500, p. 95.

52 Curia of Hungary, Case No. BH2014.154; Hungarian Supreme Court, Case No. BH2009.252.

doi: 10.5553/HYIEL/266627012022010001019

invoked Article V(1)(a) and tried to question the formal validity of the arbitration agreement by pretending that a separate written agreement to arbitrate was not entered into between the parties, the Hungarian courts rightly pointed out that the sales confirmation signed by him included an arbitration clause in favor of an arbitral institution seated in Hamburg, which was an arbitration agreement under the Convention.[53] In another case, where the parties entered into a bill of lading through the exchange of telex messages, which contained an English choice-of-law clause and an arbitral agreement in favor of an arbitral institution in London, the award debtor could not successfully resist enforcement, because in the court's view, it was governed by English law as *lex causae*, and the award debtor could not invoke any specific legal provision that would have rendered the arbitration clause invalid.[54] Finally, in another case involving the transfer of rights and obligations arising out of a shareholders' agreement and an option agreement, both including an ICC arbitration clause, the award-debtor unsuccessfully invoked Hungarian civil law, which at the time of the transfer did not allow for the transfer of an entire contractual position. The courts did not question the findings of the arbitral tribunal in relation to the transmission of the arbitral clause together with the main contracts.[55] The above examples illustrate the pro-arbitration approach of Hungarian courts when ruling on the validity of arbitration agreements in the award-enforcement phase.

4.2.3. Lack of Notice and Due Process Violations – Article V(1)(b)

The first prong of Article V(1)(b) of the Convention covers cases, where the award debtor can invoke the *lack of his notification about the arbitral appointment or arbitral proceedings*. Hungarian courts interpret this ground for refusal narrowly. For example in one particular case, the debtor returned the mail to the arbitration tribunal with the indication 'refused', but later, in the enforcement phase he acknowledged that the summons was duly received by him, therefore, the courts did not accepted his complaint regarding the 'lack of notice' about the arbitral proceedings.[56] In another case, the franchise contract of the parties included an arbitration clause and the next clause provided for a quite detailed regulation of the service of written communication between the parties. When the award debtor tried to resist the enforcement inter alia by relying on the improper service of documents during the arbitral proceedings, the Hungarian courts granted enforcement, highlighting that the documents of the arbitral proceedings were duly delivered to the representative of the losing party at the front desk of a restaurant, indicated in the service clause of the franchise contract.[57]

The second prong of Article V(1)(b) on the basis of which award debtors can resist enforcement by pretending that *they were unable to present their case* is not frequently applied either in domestic practice. For example a losing party, who

53 Raffai 2017, pp. 437-438.

54 Hungarian Supreme Court, Case No. BH1997.34.

55 Curia of Hungary, Case No. BH+2015.5.209.

56 Hungarian Supreme Court, Case No. BH2004.416.

57 Regional Court of Appeal of Budapest, Case No. 2201-3. Pkf.25.561/2019/2. (ÍH2019.94).

doi: 10.5553/HYIEL/266627012022010001019

actually participated in the arbitral proceedings, by being present at the oral hearing and sending written submissions to the tribunal could not successfully rely on this ground for refusal.[58] In the same way, the award debtor unsuccessfully tried to invoke the said provision, when during the arbitral proceedings the service of documents took place by courier service, and the arbitral award failed to give an exhaustive list about successful deliveries of all correspondences between the tribunal and the parties.[59] Award debtors often tried to invoke *due process violations* by relying on language barriers, like the conduct of arbitral proceedings in a foreign language, or the lack of correspondence in their mother tongue. These arguments, in the absence of a clear stipulation of the language of communication between the parties in the underlying commercial contract, were not successful.[60] Similarly, the sole fact that the Hungarian translation of the arbitral award had not been served upon the award debtor was not qualified as a violation of due process.[61] At the same time, it must be pointed out that in the domestic setting aside practice the reference to due process violations was generally successful in cases, where the arbitral tribunal requalified factual or legal issues, which prevented the party from presenting its case and the tribunal issued a 'surprise award'.[62] This latter domestic approach is generally in line with international case law on the Convention according to which surprise decisions are considered as a particular case of due process violations.[63]

4.2.4. Excess of Jurisdiction or Competence – Article V(1)(c)

Article V(1)(c) of the Convention allows national courts to *refuse the recognition and enforcement of the foreign arbitral award or the part of it,* where the award decides matters *"beyond the scope of the submission to arbitration"*. While the theory differentiates between excess of jurisdiction, which focuses on the issues that the arbitral tribunal was not authorized to consider, and excess of competence, which refers to the substance of the decision instead,[64] in practice, the difference between the above categories is often blurred. In relation with this ground for refusal in the Convention, Hungarian case law is quite meagre, but the domestic practice yields some useful analogies in connection with the standard approach of judges regarding the scope issues of the arbitration agreement.

For example, in a case, where the commercial agent asserted a claim relying on statutory legal basis before of the arbitral tribunal after the termination of his

58 Regional Court of Appeal of Budapest, Case No. 7. Pkf.26.013/2017/3. Cited by Gelencsér & Udvary (eds.) 2021, p. 718.

59 Regional Court of Appeal of Budapest, Case No. 2201-3. Pkf.25.561/2019/2. Cited by Gelencsér & Udvary (eds.) 2021, p. 718.

60 Regional Court of Appeal of Budapest, Case No. 3. Pkf.26.476/2015/2. Cited by Gelencsér & Udvary (eds.) 2021, p. 718.

61 Regional Court of Appeal of Szeged, Case No. Gpkf.II.30.001/2008/2. Cited by Gelencsér & Udvary (eds.) 2021, p. 718.

62 Hungarian Supreme Court, Case Nos EH 2011.2421 and EH 2008.1794.

63 Maxi Scherer, 'Article V', *in* Wolff (ed.) 2019, p. 320.

64 Christian Borris & Rudolf Hennecke, 'Article V', *in* Wolff (ed.) 2019, p. 324.

doi: 10.5553/HYIEL/266627012022010001019

agency contract including an arbitration clause, the court held that the claim was contractual, since relevant statutory provisions became an integral part of the parties' commercial contract, and it could be pursued via arbitration even after the expiration of the contract. Thus, the court concluded that the arbitrators had not exceeded their jurisdiction neither *rationae materiae*, nor *rationae temporis*.[65] In another case, where the claimant's first relief sought was the returning of certain work tools (*rei vindicatio*) or, alternatively the payment of damages, and as a secondary injunction, he asked for the payment of non-pecuniary damages, the courts referred the dispute to arbitration, since in their opinion the arbitration clause covered these claims, arising out of the underlying commercial contract.[66] Finally, in another case the Supreme Court laid down that the concept of 'legal dispute' cannot be interpreted narrowly to cover only disputes arising out of a given contract, in case the parties concluded further contracts, with the aim to remedy the breach of the first one, including the arbitration clause.[67] The above broad interpretation of the subject-matter scope of the arbitration agreement by Hungarian courts is undoubtedly in line with the general limited standard of review, and the pro-arbitration approach of the Convention.

4.2.5. Improper Composition of the Tribunal or Flawed Arbitral Proceedings – Article V(1)(d)

By confirming the primacy of the parties' private autonomy in international arbitration, Article V(1)(d) of the Convention allows for the refusal of the recognition and enforcement of a foreign arbitral award in case *the composition of the tribunal or the arbitral procedure was not in accordance with the parties' agreement, or with the law of the country where the arbitration took place.* Since the domestic case law in relation to this provision of the Convention is quite scarce, it is worth recalling how Hungarian courts approached these issues in domestic setting aside proceedings. Hungarian courts rightly prevented the defendant from raising the issue of the irregular composition of the tribunal at a later stage of the proceedings, when he declared at the first hearing that he did not have any objection against the arbitral tribunal.[68] This approach is in line with the *'doctrine of preclusion' or 'waiver'* applied by most developed jurisdictions in similar cases.[69] However, regarding procedural irregularities, sometimes the Supreme Court took a perhaps too conservative approach, *e.g.* in a case when it annulled the arbitral award made by two arbitrators, after the third withdrew from office during the deliberation, reproaching the truncated tribunal that it failed to wait for a new arbitrator's appointment.[70] Some years later, the highest judicial forum went even further by annulling an arbitral award because of a failure to observe the

65 Hungarian Supreme Court, Case No. BH2007.411.

66 Hungarian Supreme Court, Case No. BH2009.186.

67 László Kecskés & Katalin Murányi, 'A hazai és a külföldi választottbírósági ítéletek végrehajtásának elrendelésével kapcsolatos gyakorlati tapasztalatok Magyarországon', *Magyar jog*, 2013/03, p. 135.

68 Hungarian Supreme Court, Case No. BH2006.218.

69 Gaillard & Bermann 2017, p. 216.

70 Hungarian Supreme Court, Case No. BH2010.96.

doi: 10.5553/HYIEL/266627012022010001019

deliberation in 'closed session' rule set forth under the rules of procedure of an arbitral institution.[71] Even if it is well established case law in Hungary that absent express parties' agreement to the contrary, the provisions of the Civil Code of Procedure are not applicable in arbitral proceedings,[72] the above decisions indicate an overly strong formalism when it comes to compliance with procedural rules. This is hardly reconciliable with the pro-arbitration spirit of the Convention, demonstrated by the case law of most arbitration-friendly jurisdictions, where only substantial defects in the arbitral procedure and/or a causal nexus between the procedural defect and the award can be considered as a procedural irregularity within the meaning of Article 5(1)(c).[73] Hopefully, this strong formalism regarding procedural irregularities in domestic matters will not be transplanted to the judicial practice related to the Convention.

4.2.6. *Non-Binding Award – Article V(1)(e)*

According to Article V (1) (e) of the Convention, the recognition and enforcement of the award can be refused, if *it has not yet become binding on the parties or it has been set aside or suspended in the country of origin.* While Hungarian court practice has not yet produced any decision in relation to the enforcement of annulled awards, which is one of the most interesting and polarizing issues of the Convention, the domestic courts had the opportunity to address the issue of non-binding and suspended awards.

In a recent enforcement procedure, where the award debtor invoked Article V(1)(e) by pretending that in the country of origin the award had not been properly served to him, the court highlighted that "binding" nature shall mean either that there is no ordinary legal remedy available against the award, which can have suspensory effect, or that the award has been declared immediately executable by the arbitral tribunal. These questions are independent from the issue whether the award has been served upon the debtor, which fact can be relevant only from the perspective of the performance deadline. However, this issue falls outside the scope of the recognition of the award under the Convention.[74] The case law of Hungarian courts confirms that the sole fact of instituting setting aside proceedings against the award in the country of origin does not justify the application of Article V(1)(e) of the Convention.[75] However in a case, where the award had been suspended in the country of origin, the Hungarian courts refused recognition and enforcement.[76]

4.2.7. *Inarbitrability, Violation of Public Policy – Article V(2)*

While Article V(1) of the Convention sets forth the grounds for refusal to be invoked by the party resisting the enforcement of the arbitral award, Article V(2)

71 Curia of Hungary, Case No. BH2017.126.
72 Hungarian Supreme Court, Case No. 1999/9. VBH I (Gfv. VI. 30.111/1999).
73 Gaillard & Bermann 2017, p. 212.
74 ÍH2021.22.
75 Curia of Hungary, Case No. BH+2013.1.31.
76 Regional Court of Appeal of Debrecen, Gpkf.III.30.289/2007./4. Cited by Gelencsér & Udvary (eds.) 2021, p. 723.

doi: 10.5553/HYIEL/266627012022010001019

includes two further grounds for refusal that may be observed by the state courts absent any award debtor reference, *ex officio*. When it comes to Article V(2)(a) of the Convention, allowing courts to refuse the award recognition or enforcement in case *the matter was not capable of being settled by arbitration, there is no available decision in Hungary.* Given that in accordance with the Convention, the issue of objective arbitrability shall be evaluated under the *lex fori*, it is worth mentioning that the current Hungarian Arbitration Act[77] renders only the following three categories of disputes to be not arbitrable: *(i)* the disputes arising out of consumer contracts, with the exception of trusts contracts; *(ii)* the disputes which are regulated as special proceedings under the Code of Civil Procedure;[78] and *(iii)* the proceedings falling under the scope of the Code of Administrative Court Procedure. At the same time, it is doubtful whether this is an exhaustive list, because the case law presented in relation with the enforcement of arbitration agreements above indicated that certain company matters could also be considered as ones that cannot be resolved by arbitration. As regards Article V(2)(b) of the Convention, there is an abundance of cases where award debtors invoked the violation of public policy to resist the enforcement of the foreign award in Hungary.

It is well-settled case law in Hungary that recognition may be refused on the basis of the *violation of public policy* in accordance with Article V(2)(b), if the recognition of the foreign award would have consequences beyond the legal relationship of the parties and it would manifestly or severely violate fundamental rights, domestic social values and the socio-economic order.[79] Based on the above, in line with the above narrow interpretation of public policy violation, the Hungarian courts were reluctant to refuse award recognition *inter alia*, when the award debtor referred to the failure of the arbitral tribunal to postpone the hearing despite its request,[80] or when the debtor relied on ongoing criminal procedures against its former managing director.[81]

While scholars and developed jurisdictions differentiate between the violation of domestic public policy and international public policy, conceiving the second one as a smaller set, and arguing that the recognition of the foreign arbitral award should be refused only in case of a violation of the latter, such a sophisticated distinction was missing for a long time from the domestic practice of the Convention. However, in the last decades, the case law produced some signs of development in this field. Regarding substantive public policy, Hungarian case law sheds some light on the line of demarcation between domestic and international public policy, by holding in an annulment case that *the unusually*

77 Section 1(3)-(4) of the Hungarian Arbitration Act.

78 Act CXXX of 2016 on the Civil Procedure Code regulates the following litigations as special proceedings: disputes concerning civil status, guardianship, matrimonial cases, disputes concerning origin, actions for custody of a child; action for the dissolution of adoption; actions for child maintenance; certain actions for personality rights; labor disputes; enforcement actions; actions in relation to notary decisions.

79 Curia of Hungary, Case No. BH+2015.209.

80 Hungarian Supreme Court, Case No. BH2003.505.

81 Curia of Hungary, Case No. BH+2015.209.

doi: 10.5553/HYIEL/266627012022010001019

high attorney's fees could be grounds for setting aside a domestic award, while the same reason could not serve as grounds to refuse the recognition of a foreign arbitral award.[82] When it comes to procedural public policy, two recent appellate court decisions merit attention. In the first case, the appellate court firmly rejected to examine the issue of delivery of documents and its alleged consequences for the procedural rights of the losing party under the lens of public policy. It thereby limited the examination of the losing party's allegation of the potential violation of the due process principle set forth in Article 5(1)(b) of the Convention.[83] In the other case,[84] where the award debtor invoked the violation of public policy because the arbitral award had allegedly not been served upon him, the appellate court referred to the judgment of the Hungarian Supreme Court,[85] delivered under similar factual circumstances but in an enforcement procedure of a foreign state court judgment under the Brussels I Recast Regulation.[86] While in domestic cases the Hungarian courts exhibit a tendency to set aside arbitral awards on purely procedural grounds,[87] the decisions rendered in the two above-mentioned international cases indicate a more restrained attitude. According to this latter approach, the party resisting the enforcement of a foreign court judgment or arbitral award must show some serious procedural irregularity and the real effects of the alleged procedural breach on the merits of the case, in the absence of which the violation of procedural public policy cannot be invoked with success to refuse recognition and enforcement. In this vein, the two Hungarian appellate courts showed in the above-mentioned cases that they interpret Article V(2)(b) of the Convention narrowly when it comes to the public policy exception on procedural grounds. In addition, by applying the same procedural public policy test under two different supranational legal sources, the two above-mentioned court decisions demonstrate that Hungarian higher courts have started to adopt a unified approach to this concept in international cases.

5. Conclusions

As mentioned above, the Convention was in the state of 'hibernation' in the first three decades after its entry into force in Hungary. The domestic judicial practice forged from the '90s onwards shows a somewhat mixed picture, where arbitration-friendly tendencies and some parochial trends can be discerned at the same time.

Regarding the subject-matter scope of the Convention, the arbitration-friendly approach of Hungarian courts is demonstrated by the narrow application

82 Hungarian Supreme Court, Case Nos. BH.2003.127. and BH 2007.130, respectively.

83 Regional Court of Appeal of Budapest, Case No. 2201-3. Pkf.25.561/2019/2. (ÍH2019.94).

84 Regional Court of Appeal of Szeged, Case No. Gpkf.III.30.174/2020/2. (ÍH2021.22).

85 Curia of Hungary, Case No. BH 2012.98.

86 Regulation (EU) No 1215/2012 of the European Parliament and of the Council of 12 December 2012 on jurisdiction and the recognition and enforcement of judgments in civil and commercial matters.

87 Curia of Hungary, Case Nos. BH2016.122. and EH 2010.2150.

doi: 10.5553/HYIEL/266627012022010001019

of the commercial reservation. When it comes to the recognition and enforcement of arbitration agreements, domestic insecurity in the field of applicable law can be explained partially by the absence of a conflict of laws rule in Article II of the Convention, which creates room for the 'traditional' *lex fori* approach. Since the latter can coincide with parochial domestic case law on contract creation where GTCs are present, the domestic 'climate' is capable of undermining the efficiency of international arbitration agreements. While the case law of objective arbitrability is in line with the general standards, the *prima facie* approach, taken in the bad sense, in case of insolvency of one of the parties is a telling sign of formalism. This can be a further obstacle to enforce the parties' agreement to arbitrate in international matters. In the award enforcement stage, some formalistic tendencies may be discerned as well, which risk the successful enforcement of the award: the orthodox interpretation of Article IV of the Convention and the rigid adherence to full compliance with all formal requirements by award creditors can give a significant advantage to award-debtors to frustrate enforcement in Hungary. Hopefully, as regards the substantive issues, it is the pro-arbitration approach of the courts that is dominant: the general governing principles for refusal under Article V are widely respected and applied, therefore, foreign awards were not reviewed on the merits by Hungarian courts, and award-debtors were unsuccessful in invoking grounds not listed by the Convention, as well as in their attempts to reverse the burden of proof. Furthermore, the grounds for refusal of recognition and enforcement in Articles V(1)-(2) were interpreted narrowly, in line with the dominant approach in other jurisdictions.

While the legislative gap in Article II of the Convention was a contributing factor to some unfortunate decisions in the pre-award stage, threatening the efficiency of arbitration agreements, the same problems were not detectable in the context of Article V(1)(a) of the Convention, and Hungarian courts enforced arbitral awards by applying foreign law to the arbitration agreement in the post-award phase. In addition, there are promising developments in the context of Article V(2)(b) of the Convention, when it comes to distinguishing between domestic and international public policy, both on a substantive and procedural level. This sophisticated approach sends the positive message that Hungarian courts understand the difference between domestic and international arbitration. Overall, the balance of the application of the Convention is positive, and with the exception of the above issues, we can conclude that Hungarian courts adopt mostly a pro-arbitration approach when recognizing and enforcing arbitration agreements and foreign arbitral awards.

doi: 10.5553/HYIEL/266627012022010001019

The Protection of Privacy During the Covert Collection of Information for National Security Purposes

Findings of an Ex Officio Investigation

Attila Péterfalvi[*]

Abstract

In 2021 the Hungarian news portal Direkt36 published an article entitled "A tough Israeli spyware was exposed to have been used to target critics of the Orbán government and Hungarian journalists." In the article, Direct36 discovered that "'Pegasus', the spyware of an Israeli cyber company called NSO, suitable for jailbreaking smart phones, was used against targeted Hungarian persons years ago; investigative journalists and wealthy businessmen owning media companies and their close contacts were among the persons targeted. In the course of this research, we found a number of indirect evidence indicating that Hungarian state bodies may be behind the secret surveillance." Based on this information, the Hungarian National Authority for Data Protection and Freedom of Information (Authority) launched an ex officio examination. The article summarizes the findings of this examination, with due regard to the question whether according to the laws of Hungary and the EU, privacy shall be protected during the covert gathering of information.

Keywords: data protection, privacy, Pegasus, national security, external authorization.

1. Introduction

In 2021, the Hungarian news portal Direkt36 published an article entitled "A tough Israeli spyware was exposed to have been used to target critics of the Orbán government and Hungarian journalists." As a part of an international investigative project, Direct36 discovered that

> "Pegasus', the spyware of an Israeli cyber company called NSO, suitable for jailbreaking smart phones, was used against targeted Hungarian persons years ago; investigative journalists and wealthy businessmen owning media

* Attila Péterfalvi: president, Hungarian National Authority for Data Protection and Freedom of Information, Budapest; honorary professor of law, ELTE Law School & Pázmány Péter Catholic University, Budapest.

doi: 10.5553/HYIEL/266627012022010001020

> companies and their close contacts were among the persons targeted. In the course of this research, we found a number of indirect evidence indicating that Hungarian state bodies may be behind the secret surveillance."[1]

In early July, a journalist of the French *Le Monde* newspaper, also taking part in the investigative project asked Minister of Justice Judit Varga in an interview whether she would authorize the monitoring of a journalist or a member of the opposition. She indignantly answered: "What a question! This is in itself is a provocation!" Varga said that only surveillance requests in compliance with the law may be authorized, adding that "there are so many threats to the state all over". Following the article mentioned above, the Hungarian National Authority for Data Protection and Freedom of Information (the Authority) ordered an *ex officio* investigation.

The article gives an overview of how the Hungarian legislation concerning the protection of privacy during the covert collection of information for national security purposes has changed since the change of political system (1989) and what role the Authority plays in facilitating the exercise of data subjects' rights, in view of the fact that in the course of data processing for national security purposes, the data subject's ability to enforce their rights under the Hungarian Privacy Act[2] is limited.

2. The Transformation of Relevant Hungarian legislation since the Change of Political System

2.1. *Act X of 1990 on the Transitional Regulation for Authorizing Special Secret Service Means and Methods*

At its session on 25 January 1990, shortly after the change of regime in 1989, the Hungarian Parliament adopted Act X of 1990 on the Transitional Regulation for Authorizing Special Secret Service Means and Methods. This legislation classified the application of every means and methods as special means if they were applied without the knowledge of the person concerned and whose use infringed the rights to the inviolability of private homes, private secrets, confidentiality of correspondence and the protection of personal data. It was stipulated already in this act that special means may only be applied in case the data cannot be obtained in any other way.

The legislation distinguished between cases in which special means can be applied for criminal acts or for national security purposes even though this term is not used. However, in terms of substance, it listed cases corresponding to national security interests. It was the competence of the Minister of Justice to

1 *See* (in Hungarian) at www.direkt36.hu/leleplezodott-egy-durva-izraeli-kemfegyver-az-orban-kormany-kritikusait-es-magyar-ujsagirokat-is-celba-vettek-vele/. Translation is provided by the author.

2 Act CXII of 2011 on the Right to Informational Self-Determination and the Freedom of Information.

doi: 10.5553/HYIEL/266627012022010001020

authorize the collection of information. The act included a safeguard clause providing that

> "where the application of special means does not give rise to a penal procedure against the person under surveillance, the entity requesting the authorization shall notify the person under surveillance of the measures applied and the data obtained in the course of the surveillance will subsequently be destroyed."[3]

2.2. Act CXXV of 1995 on the National Security Services

Act X of 1990 was repealed by Act CXXV of 1995 on the National Security Services (National Security Services Act). The regulation in force distinguishes between the *covert information gathering authorized (i) by a judge; and (ii) by the Minister of Justice.* In relation to the authorization powers of the minister, the question arises, whether locating the authorization competence within the executive power is appropriate from the viewpoint of protecting privacy. Where a judge authorizes the gathering of information this issue does not arise, since the judge is located in a branch of power separate from the executive.

With regard to the protection of privacy, in addition to the protection afforded by the EU Member States' constitutional, civil and penal law, it is equally important to take into account the ECHR as another source of international obligations, in particular, Article 8. With due regard to the jurisprudence of the ECtHR, *Decision No. 32/2013. (XI. 22.) AB* of the Constitutional Court of Hungary declared that:

> "As the secret gathering of intelligence by necessity excludes the possibility of effective legal remedy, it is of vital importance that procedural arrangements enabling its application provide sufficient guarantees to protect the individual's rights. In view of all this, the application must be subject to three-stage control: when the intervention is mandated, during the implementation of the intervention and following the completion of the intervention. Control will be carried out by bodies that are independent from the executive power. It is first and foremost the permanent and mandatory control that guarantees that the requirement of proportionality is observed in specific cases."[4]

As far as the constitutionality of the secret gathering of intelligence was concerned, the reasoning in *Decision No. 2/2007. (I. 24.) AB* of the Constitutional Court of Hungary gives important guidance:

> "In a democratic constitutional state, the circumstance that traditional means do not prove to be sufficient for successfully combating certain

3 Section 5(2) of Act X of 1990 on the Transitional Regulation of Authorization of Special Secret Service Devices and Methods.

4 Decision No. 32/2013. (XI. 22.) AB, Reasoning [72].

doi: 10.5553/HYIEL/266627012022010001020

> criminal acts severely violating or jeopardizing the order of society is grounds for making use of the secret gathering of intelligence and the secret collection of data employed as instruments of criminal law. Hence, the restriction of the fundamental rights under scrutiny by way of methods applied in secret procedures cannot be considered as a constitutionally unnecessary means. The protection of the constitutional state and fundamental rights, however, require that the law regulate the procedure for using such instruments in detail and in a differentiated manner. Since the use of secret means and methods constitutes a severe intervention into the life of the individual, they may be applied only exceptionally, as a transitional and last resort."[5]

The ECtHR underlined that

> "precisely because the intervention in fundamental rights is secret and the use of such instrument provides imponderable opportunities to the executive power, it is indispensable that the procedures themselves provide sufficient guarantee for the enforcement of the rights of the individual."[6]

2.3. Bill to Amend the Law

Taking into account that the ECtHR in *Szabó and Vissy* did not consider the external authorization regime of the covert information gathering to be appropriate and declared that Hungary violated Article 8 ECHR, the Ministry of the Interior prepared a proposal to amend the law and issued it for public debate. *This proposal would have institutionalized the power of the Authority to override the authorization of the Minister of Justice*. According to the draft, journalists, Members of Parliament and clerics could be intercepted in the future only if approved by the Authority. The Authority could have monitored the lawfulness of data collection subject to external authorization. The Minister of Justice would have had to forward its decision granting authorization within 48 hours of signing and the Authority would have had 72 hours to render a decision on the issue. Had the Authority deemed that the gathering of information unlawful, and it would have been able to instruct the given entity to stop data collection and erase the data gathered. Whoever would have learned or suspected that an agency conducted covert data collection against him unlawfully, would have had the right to turn to the Authority, which would have had three months to investigate the complaint. If a person was put under surveillance unlawfully, the Authority would have been able to put a stop to this (provided that surveillance was still in progress), and in case it suspected a criminal act, it could file charges as well.

As the President of the Authority, I sent the recommendations of the Authority to improve the external authorization system of covert information collection for national security purposes to the Legislative Committee of the Parliament. In my point of view, the ECtHR judgment cited above, which found that Hungary infringed Article 8 ECHR, in a wider context called

5 Decision No. 2/2007. (I. 24.) AB, ABH 2007, 65, 100.

6 ECtHR, *Szabó and Vissy v Hungary*, No. 37138/14, 12 January 2016.

Hungarian Yearbook of International Law and European Law 2022 (10) 1
doi: 10.5553/HYIEL/266627012022010001020

> "attention to the fact that the rapid development of info-communication technology implies dangers also in addition to countless favorable effects: it renders the mass application of secret surveillance increasingly easy, which may be concomitant with other unfavorable social impacts in the longer term beyond intervention in the privacy of citizens. The attention of the public in advanced democratic constitutional states was directed to these problems first and foremost by the documents disclosed by Edward Snowden. Indirectly, the leakage led to the annulment of the Safe Harbor Convention regulating the Trans-Atlantic transfer and use of personal data. The Privacy Shield, which replaced Safe Harbor, reinforced the protection of the personal data of European citizens against secret surveillance by the intelligence agencies of the US and authorized the data protection authorities of the EU Member States to collaborate in the remedy procedures related to these data collections by secret services with a view to protecting the rights of citizens. Beyond this, the Privacy Shield[7] is essential from the viewpoint of our subject matter because the data protection expectations set against the US expressed common European fundamental values, which are naturally governing for European countries when the legislatures of the Member States decide under what conditions secret surveillance is possible and what safeguards are needed to protect the rights of the citizens."

The court procedure did not extend to obtaining the opinion of the Authority resulting in numerous legally and factually incorrect statements which remained unscrutinized in the course of litigation on the external control over the ministerial authorization in the Hungarian regulation. Thus, the ECtHR did learn of the experiences made by the Authority in the course of the independent external monitoring of the covert information gathering activities of the National Security Services.

Pursuant to Article VI(3) of the Fundamental Law, the enforcement of the right to the protection of personal data and access to data in the public interest shall be supervised by the Authority, an independent authority established by a cardinal law, *i.e.* the Privacy Act.[8] Based on the provisions of the Privacy Act, the Authority is an independent supervisory body responsible for the protection of personal data. The scope of the Privacy Act extends to *all the covert information gathering activities carried out by the National Security Services in the territory of Hungary and the Authority is authorized to supervise these activities.* Pursuant to Section 52(1), anyone may turn to the Authority, if in their view any of the Hungarian National Security Services has conducted or is conducting unlawful covert gathering of information, or there is a direct threat of unlawful covert gathering of information.

7 Judgment of 16 July 2020, *Case C-311/18, Schrems II,* ECLI:EU:C:2020:559. The CJEU declared Commission implementing decision (EU) 2016/1250 of 12 July 2016 on the adequacy of the protection provided by the EU–US privacy shield under Directive 95/46/EC of the European Parliament and of the Council invalid.

8 *See* especially Sections 1, 2(1), 38(2), 38(5), and 52(1) of the Privacy Act.

doi: 10.5553/HYIEL/266627012022010001020

The Privacy Act provides adequate instruments to the Authority to explore possibly unlawful covert information gathering and to take action against any infringement. The rules of the investigative procedure[9] grant authorization to inspect, ask for copies, access data, entry, request information and initiate inquiries similarly to the Hungarian commissioner for fundamental rights' procedure. Section 71 of the Privacy Act sets forth rules which provide access to the necessary data for the Authority in case of procedures expressly affecting the National Security Services.

In addition, the Authority may use the data, including national classified data, accessed in the course of the investigative procedure also in its data protection procedure. As a result, for instance, it may prohibit the unlawful processing of personal data, order the erasure of unlawfully processed personal data, order that information be provided to the data subject, in case the controller had denied disclosure unlawfully, and it may impose fines. These are much stronger powers than that of the commissioner's procedure referred to as independent external control invoked in the ECtHR's judgment.

In its practice of applying the law, the Authority's point of departure is that covert surveillance by its very nature deprives the data subject from recourse to direct legal remedy, hence, independent external data protection control is the key element to the protection of informational privacy in this area. Accordingly, the Authority investigates every complaint or notification concerning covert surveillance received from citizens irrespective of whether the circumstances described in the submission referred to covert gathering of information, or whether the data subject can be informed of the results of the procedure. Annually, the Authority receives roughly 10-20 notifications with this subject matter.

In my opinion I also underlined that

> "Decision No. 32/2013. (XI. 22.) AB and the judgment focus on the preliminary supervision of covert information gathering, *i.e.* external authorization. Preliminary external authorization is one of the elements of the set of guarantees protecting informational privacy, which is important, but insufficient in itself. The procedural order of preliminary external authorization is characterized by tight timeframes, a rather tied supply of evidence (decision has to be made on the basis of a documentation selected, edited and formulated by the entity submitting it), the full exclusion of the public and the absence of the adversary procedure. Because of this, in accordance with the guidance of Decision No. 2/2007. (I. 24.) AB, it is expedient to look at the entire system of control over covert information gathering jointly and in context and seek a legal regulatory solution, which, overall, allows adequate protection against unlawful (unnecessary, disproportionate) surveillance of citizens by the secret services. In other words, a multi-stage (preliminary, interim and subsequent) and multi-agency (internal controls by the National Security Services, supervision by the

9 Sections 52-58 Privacy Act.

doi: 10.5553/HYIEL/266627012022010001020

> parliamentary committee, the entity entitled to external authorization and the data protection authority) control system has to operate adequately in total to achieve the above-mentioned goal."

It follows from its function stipulated in the Fundamental Law and its responsibilities set forth in the Privacy Act that the Authority is responsible for the subsequent control of covert information gathering, including the investigation of complaints and notifications, taking or initiating the necessary measures in relation to covert information gathering whether subject to external authorization or not. According to the Authority's position, therefore, the unity of the subsequent data protection supervisory system should not be disrupted, thus, the investigation of citizens' complaints concerning covert information gathering subject to external authorization should not be delegated to another entity. The safeguard role of subsequent control was reinforced through the amendment of the Privacy Act, on the basis of which the Authority may launch also *ex officio* investigations in relation to covert information gathering.

Several types of regulatory models can apply when the preliminary external authorization system of covert information gathering is transformed. In terms of the independence of external control and the principles of the separation of powers and public law, the transfer of external authorization powers, currently vested in the Minister of Justice, to the court of justice would be an unacceptable solution.

The judgment of the ECtHR, however, allows for an interpretation according to which the preliminary authorization powers of the Minister would be retained. In relation to this, the Authority's recommendations sent to the Legislative Committee of the Parliament in 2016 underlined the following:

> "The results of an earlier data protection investigation carried out using a statistical analysis of several years of data from external authorization procedures for covert information gathering indicated that, in the case of the external authorization powers of the Minister of Justice, single-person decision-making authority may clash with the requirement of informed decision-making. Every year, the directors-general of the National Security Services submit such a large number of submissions that a single person, the Minister, cannot possibly review in sufficient depth before making a decision on authorization. For this reason, should these powers remain within the ministerial framework, in the Authority's opinion, the establishment of a committee should be considered which should be entrusted with the task of screening submissions for lawfulness and necessity, and to put forward recommendations as to whether they can be authorized, prior to ministerial decision-making. The members of this committee would include experts with the necessary special national security knowledge, delegated by government agencies with an interest in the lawfulness of covert information gathering (such as the Ministry of the Interior, National Security Services). This committee would, therefore, not carry out independent external control, instead its role would be to facilitate the lawfulness and the informed

doi: 10.5553/HYIEL/266627012022010001020

character of ministerial decisions to be made concerning external authorization, thereby fulfilling its role in protecting rights. The regulatory framework for establishing the committee can be created by amending the Act on National Security Services.

In view of the provisions of the judgment, should the minister's external authorization powers be upheld, it is inevitable to subject it to independent external control. From a public law point of view, there is nothing to impede the Authority from fulfilling this role, as it is an independent data protection supervisory authority as specified in the Fundamental Law, and whose powers in any case include the subsequent control of the lawfulness of covert information gathering. The Privacy Act provides the appropriate regulatory framework for the performance of this task, including the investigative authorizations needed to establish the facts of the case and to take the necessary measures in the event of a ministerial decision infringing informational privacy. Essentially, it would suffice to supplement the Privacy Act with the statement that the Authority continuously supervises the lawfulness of the ministerial authorization of covert information gathering."[10]

3. Comprehensive Data Protection Audit of the Covert Information Gathering Activities of National Security Services[11]

The Authority also conducts procedures aimed at facilitating the lawfulness of data processing related to the special activities of the National Security Services. In 2016, upon the initiative of, and in cooperation with one of the National Security Services, the Authority carried out a data protection audit whereby it supervised the lawfulness of the application of the individual means and methods for covert information gathering through practical tests. This activity by the Authority was based on a novel data protection supervisory method unprecedented even in international comparison.

The core of the method developed for the data protection audit of covert information gathering is that in the experimental situations designed by the Authority, National Security Services should carry out their service provider activities related to covert information gathering under circumstances as close to reality as possible.

The Authority examined the entire process of the procedures related to covert information gathering by the National Security Services under circumstances close to reality. Every test started off with the Authority handing over the documentation of the order corresponding to the fictitious facts of the text case to the National Security Services on behalf of the non-existent Civil Surveillance Service, including the service notes completed with fictitious data and the fictitious external authorization in the case of covert information

10 Case No. NAIH/2016/6396/3/J.

11 *See* in detail: Attila Péterfalvi, *25 éves az NBSZ*, Budapest, 2021, pp. 79-86.

doi: 10.5553/HYIEL/266627012022010001020

gathering subject to external authorization. In the course of preparing and implementing the tests, the National Security Service acted in every respect as a service provider within the meaning of Section 8(1)(a) of the National Security Services Act.

The implementation of the test was documented by a designated staff member of the National Securities Service in a protocol. (Incidentally, this would be the Authority's task, but this was the only way for us not have access to information to which the Authority is not authorized pursuant to the provisions of Section 71 of the Privacy Act and which was in any case not indispensable for the implementation of the tests.) At the same time, the staff members of the Authority documented in a memo drafted on the given test whether, as officers of the Civic Surveillance Service, they consulted the staff members of the National Security Service or, for instance, received extraordinary 'operative information' on the fictitious covert information gathering. In this way, the communication and interaction between the National Security Service and the commissioning organization became fully verifiable.

The National Security Service gathered, recorded and processed information in the course of the tests as if it was providing services 'in live mode'. The nature of the documentation handed over to the Authority as a result of the secret information gathering tests (*e.g.* protocol, video recording, sound recording, expert opinion, *etc.*), as well as the degree of information processing, their data content and format were the same as in the case of an actual gathering of covert information. In the period between April 2016 and February 2017, 34 covert information gathering tests were implemented.

The audit clearly confirmed the commitment of the National Security Services for the lawfulness of data processing, at the same time, the tests explored a few details of the activities related to covert information gathering, in relation to which the Authority made observations and recommendations with a view to ensure the enforcement of the data protection requirements at the highest standard.[12]

4. Evaluation of the Hungarian Legislation in Force from the Viewpoint of Safeguards – Investigation of the Use of the 'Pegasus' Spyware in Hungary

Let us now examine whether the authorization of covert information gathering for national security purposes as set forth in the Hungarian legislation in force meets the above criteria and provides sufficient guarantees for the protection of the privacy of the person under surveillance.

Based on the effective legislation applicable to covert information gathering for national security purposes, it can be established that as far as the authorization powers of the Minister of Justice are concerned, there have been

12 Report of the Authority on its activities in 2016, at www.naih.hu/eves-beszamolok?download=22:naih-beszamolo-a-2016-evi-tevekenysegrol.

doi: 10.5553/HYIEL/266627012022010001020

no amendments to the legislation, thus, the rules in force at present are the same as those on account of which the ECtHR had condemned Hungary.

I, however, find it important to stress that when aligning the Privacy Act[13] with the GDPR[14] the Authority was authorized to initiate an investigation or data protection procedure *ex officio*. This empowers the Authority to launch investigations or data protection procedures to audit covert information gathering for national security purposes *ex officio*. This is the case also in relation to the use of the 'Pegasus' spyware.

From the perspective of the Privacy Act, covert information may be gathered for the purposes of *law enforcement* (prevention, investigation and detection of criminal acts) or for the purposes of *national security*. Pursuant to Section 2(3) of the Privacy Act, the substantive and procedural rules of the Privacy Act shall apply in both cases to these data processing operations and their supervision. It is, however, important to note that whereas data processing for the purposes of law enforcement is subject to EU law, *i.e.* the Criminal Justice Directive[15] transposed into Hungarian law by the provisions of the Privacy Act, data processing for national security (and defense) purposes is outside the scope of EU law and it is within the regulatory and administrative competence of the Member States. Both Article 2(2)(a) and Recital (16) of the GDPR and Recital (14) and Article 2(3)(a) of the Criminal Justice Directive are unambiguous on the fact that the processing of personal data carried out in the course of activities related to national security falls outside the scope of EU law. This means that national security as the subject matter of legislation and the application of the law in this field is, according to EU law, within the exclusive scope of authority of the Member States.

I would not venture to predict how the ECtHR would assess the legislative amendments since 2016 with regard to external control over authorization within the executive power (by the Minister of Justice). However, I find it important to note the depth of the supervision carried out in relation to the use of the 'Pegasus' spyware and the types of documents the had Authority checked.

Pursuant to Section 54(1) of the Privacy Act, in the course of its investigation, the Authority has access to and may make copies of all data processed by the controller subject to the inquiry that are presumed to relate to the case at hand and it has the right of access to, and may request copies of such documents, including documents stored in an electronic data storage medium. The Authority may learn about the data processing associated with the case under

13 Sections 20 and 23 of Act of XXXVIII of 2018, in force from 26 July 2018.

14 Regulation (EU) 2016/679 of the European Parliament and of the Council of 27 April 2016 on the protection of natural persons with regard to the processing of personal data and on the free movement of such data and repealing Directive 95/46/EC (General Data Protection Regulation – GDPR).

15 Directive (EU) 2016/680 of the European Parliament and of the Council of 27 April 2016 on the protection of natural persons with regard to the processing of personal data by competent authorities for the purposes of the prevention, investigation, detection or prosecution of criminal offences or the execution of criminal penalties and on the free movement of such data and repealing Council Framework Decision 2008/977/JHA.

doi: 10.5553/HYIEL/266627012022010001020

investigation, it may enter the premises serving as the place of processing, it has access to the tools used for performing the processing operation and it may request written or verbal information from the controller subject to the inquiry and from any employee of the controller. These investigative powers, however, are not limited to the controller, as the Authority may request written information and copies of any data associated with the case under investigation, including data stored in an electronic data storage medium not only from the controller, but also from any organization or person associated with the case subject to the inquiry. The controller subject to the inquiry and any other organization or person associated with the case under investigation shall comply with the instruction of the Authority within the period specified by the Authority. (It was on the basis of this provision that the Authority contacted the Amnesty International Magyarország Egyesület, as well as the Amnesty International Secretariat, however, unfortunately they declined to cooperate.)

The Authority's responsibilities and powers for the supervision of data processing by the National Security Services and, within that, the control of the lawfulness of the covert information gathering is rather wide also by international comparison. In the course of its investigation, the Authority contacted the data protection authorities of the EU Member States and requested information concerning their responsibilities and powers to take action to control data processing for national security purposes. It transpires from the responses of the data protection authorities of the EU Member States that the supervisory authorities of numerous Member States do not have supervisory or controlling powers with regard to data processing by the National Security Services, in particular, their covert information gathering. In addition, the majority of the Member States' authorities, which, according to their national law are authorized to supervise data processing for national security purposes, have never carried out an investigation of this kind.

In the course of controlling the lawfulness of external authorization by the Minister of Justice, the Authority examined the submissions in every single case to see whether these complied with the formal and procedural requirements set forth in the legislation.

In this procedure, the Authority examined whether the submission for covert information gathering came from the director general of the National Security Service authorized to covertly gather information and whether it contained all the data set forth in Section 57(2) of the National Security Services Act. The submission must include the location of the covert information gathering, the name(s) or scope of the person(s) concerned, and the available data suitable for identification, as well as the description of the covert information gathering (*i.e.* the means and methods to be applied) and the justification of its necessity and the start and end dates of the activity (and in the case of a submission related to an exceptional authorization according to Section 59 of the National Security Services Act, justification that it was indispensably necessary in the given case for the successful operation of the National Security Service).

When investigating the lawfulness of external authorization, the Authority examined whether there was adequate substantiation of the fact that the covert

doi: 10.5553/HYIEL/266627012022010001020

information gathering was necessary in the interest of national security. The Authority's investigation therefore extends to the existence and the nature of the *interest of national security*. Section 74(a) of the National Security Services Act defines the interpretation of '*interest of national security*'; by comparing it with the facts of the case, to established or exclude that the interest of national security prevails. The Authority may investigate with regard to every data processing operation whether it restricts the right of the data subjects to informational self-determination to the necessary and proportionate extent, even where no interest of national security is invoked. Therefore, it must be examined whether the enforcement of the interest of national security in a given case restricts the right of the data subjects concerned to informational self-determination and the right to privacy to a necessary and proportionate extent in the course of covert information gathering.

The Authority also examined whether there was sufficient substantiation in the submission concerning the external authorization of covert information gathering, that the purpose of data processing cannot be achieved without such intervention, and whether the requested use of the means and methods is necessary. The submission must also to substantiate whether the covert information gathering is indispensably necessary for the requested period, and the Authority examines whether the authorization was requested for a maximum of ninety days, or if that period was extended by another ninety days, *via* a new submission and justification as required by law.

The Authority is also responsible for examining whether the decision of the Minister of Justice reasonably follows from the facts set forth in the submission. The Minister brings the decision on whether to approve the submission or to reject it if it is unfounded within 72 hours from its receipt. This means that the Authority examines not only the formal and procedural requirements of the submission, but also the decisions made by the Minister of Justice on the individual submissions.

It is important to examine in the case of every decision whether the Minister of Justice justifies the granting of the external authorization in view of the facts and circumstances detailed in the given submission. *Decision No. 32/2013. (XI. 22.) AB* of the Constitutional Court referred to the obligation to provide justification for the external authorization as a precondition to the enforcement of *ex post* external control by specifying a constitutional requirement. Consequently, the justification must be sufficiently detailed and individualized so that it should enable the control of the facts and circumstances taken into account in making the decision and the adequacy of the content of the decision made on the basis of these facts and circumstances in the course of *ex post* external control.

On the basis of the legal provisions mentioned, the Authority carried out its examination of the lawfulness of the external authorization in relation to the conformity of nearly one hundred submissions and related decisions of the Minister of Justice. The examination took place along the following questions: *(i)* Were the submissions compliant with formal and procedural rules? *(ii)* Was the submission received from the director general? *(iii)* Did the submission include all the data specified in Section 57(2) of the National Security Services Act? *(iv)* Was the authorization granted within the time limit? *(v)* Did the validity of the authorization exceed 90 days? *(vi)* Was the justification attached to the authorization? *(vii)* In case of exceptional authorization, were the relevant rules complied with? *(viii)* Did the submission substantiate that the covert information gathering was necessary in the interest of national security? *(ix)* Did the submission substantiate that the purpose of data processing could not be achieved without covert information gathering? *(x)* Did the submission substantiate that the use of all the means and methods requested were necessary? *(xi)* Did the submission substantiate that the duration of covert information gathering requested was necessary? *(xii)* Did the decision of the Minister of Justice reasonably follow from what was proposed in the submission? *(xiii)* Did the Minister of Justice justify the granting of the external authorization with sufficient detail reflecting on the facts and circumstances presented in the submission?

The procedure of the Authority is of outstanding significance also because data subjects have a limited opportunity to exercise their rights in the course of data processing for national security purposes, therefore, the Authority can exercise the rights according to the Privacy Act instead of, and on behalf of the data subjects.[16]

As regards processing for law enforcement purposes, Article 17 of the Criminal Justice Directive obliges Member States to adopt provisions where national law provides for the delay, restriction or suspension of the exercise of the rights of the data subject,[17] whereby "*the rights of the data subject may also be exercised through the competent supervisory authority*".

Since the rules on data processing for law enforcement purposes laid down in the Privacy Act,[18] pursuant to the Criminal Justice Directive, apply with regard to data processing for law enforcement purposes (with some exceptions expressly provided for in the Privacy Act), in the event of a refusal to provide information pursuant to Section 48 of the National Security Services Act, the data subject may exercise his rights in accordance with the above provisions of the Privacy Act[19] with the assistance of the Authority. Accordingly, the Authority will have to conduct an *ex officio* investigation in the case of every data subject appearing in the news, even if the data subjects do not wish to make use of the enforcement possibilities afforded to them.

16 According to Section 48 of the National Security Services Act, the director general of the National Security Service may refuse to provide information on data processed by the national security services or to erase personal data at the request of the data subject, on grounds of national security or in order to protect the rights of others, and the director general may restrict the right of access of the data subject in connection with the classified data of the national security services, as provided for in Act CLV of 2009 on the Protection of Classified Data, on grounds of national security. As a safeguard the National Security Services have the obligation to keep records of requests received from data subjects, the mode of their adjudgment and the reasons for their refusal. The Services must report on these annually to the Authority.

17 *Cf.* Criminal Justice Directive, Articles 13(3), 15(3), 16(4).

18 Section 2(3) Privacy Act.

19 Sections 22, 51/A(2), and 60(1) Privacy Act.

doi: 10.5553/HYIEL/266627012022010001020

In the course of the Authority's investigation, no information was found that the bodies authorized to covertly gather information subject to external authorization according to Section 56 of the National Security Services Act would have used the spyware for any purpose other than those specified by the manufacturer (prevention and detection of criminal acts and acts of terrorism), and the discharge of their duties specified by law. According to the information made available to the Authority in the course of its investigation, the Specialized National Security Service used the technical tool subject to its investigation in the course of the provision of its services in the field of the covert surveillance of information systems and premises.

The Authority also established that the contractual conditions concerning the use of the technical tool stipulate that the contracting party is to take all the measures to prevent access by any unauthorized external party to the personal data affected by the use of the tool. According to the position of the Authority, the data protection provisions of the contract provide the requisite guarantees for this purpose. No data was found in the course of the Authority's investigation that would cast doubt on whether the Specialized National Security Service has acted, and is acting, when using the technical tool, in accordance with the relevant legal regulations, the provisions regulating the organization of public administration and, in the case of contractual relationships, its obligations undertaken in the contract.

With respect to the conditions of using covert information gathering subject to external authorization, it is important to underline that the Hungarian law in force does not differentiate between vocations or professional activities, *i.e.* it does not restrict the authorization of the National Security Services to carry out the activities under Section 56 of the National Security Services Act in respect of any profession (*e.g.* journalist, human rights activist, opposition politician, lawyer and businessman).

In the course of its procedure, the Authority had to clarify how personal data indicating that covert information gathering took place against the data subjects were published. Unfortunately, the Authority's investigation failed to clarify how the phone numbers that may be linked to Hungarian individuals, which Amnesty International's Security Lab unit found to have been infected by the spyware, could have been disclosed during the so-called Pegasus Project fact-finding investigation. At the same time, it can be clearly established that such data should not have been disclosed because according to the principles of personal data processing as set forth in Section 4(1)-(3) of the Privacy Act, personal data can be processed only for clearly specified and legitimate purposes in order to exercise certain rights and fulfil obligations. Data processing must comply with the purpose of processing in all its stages; data shall be collected and processed fairly and lawfully. Only personal data that is essential and suitable for achieving the purpose of processing may be processed. Personal data may be processed only to the extent and for the period of time necessary to achieve its purpose. The personal data will retain this quality during processing as long as the relationship with the data subject can be re-established. The link with the data subject can be

doi: 10.5553/HYIEL/266627012022010001020

re-established if the controller has the technical conditions necessary for the re-establishment.

Pursuant to Section 4(4a) of the Privacy Act, the controller shall ensure adequate security of personal data by applying appropriate technical or organizational measures during processing, in particular measures to protect against unauthorized or unlawful processing, accidental loss, destruction of, or damage to data. The controller shall ensure an adequate level of security of the personal data processed and the fundamental rights of the data subjects by implementing technical and organizational measures appropriate to the extent of the risks represented by the processing. In designing and implementing the technical and organizational measures, the controller shall take into account all the circumstances of the processing, in particular the state of science and technology at all times, the cost of implementing the measures, the nature, scope and purpose of processing and the risks of varying likelihood and severity to the rights of data subjects presented by the processing. The use of the technical tool under investigation requires respect for the principles of integrity and confidentiality, including protection against unauthorized or unlawful processing and accidental loss, destruction or damage, by applying appropriate technical and organizational measures.

Pursuant to Section 3(26) of the Privacy Act

> "personal data breach means a breach of security leading to the accidental or unlawful destruction, loss, alteration, unauthorized transfer or disclosure of, or unauthorized access to, personal data transferred, stored or otherwise processed."

The Authority's investigation therefore also covered whether a personal data breach could have occurred in the context of the use of the technical tool by the data controllers investigated by the Authority. The Authority's investigation did not identify any information indicating that such a personal data breach had occurred. In the course of its procedures, the Authority made use of an expert in information security, who explained that in his opinion the circumstances of the data leakage are not known, it can, however, be assumed that data security was breached in some way, as presumably an unauthorized access to personal data took place, so it cannot be excluded that there was a personal data breach. In the event that there was no data breach but an unauthorized third party had unauthorized access to the personal data processed, it is punishable according to Act C of 2012 on the Criminal Code, several criminal offences may have been committed.[20] In view of the above, it cannot be ruled out that a criminal offence has been committed, therefore the Authority initiated criminal proceedings with the investigating authority pursuant to Section 70(1) of the Privacy Act.

20 *E.g.* Section 219: misuse of personal data; Section 265: misuse of classified data; Section 261: spying; Section 423: information system or data breach; Section 424: circumvention of a technical measure to protect an information system.

doi: 10.5553/HYIEL/266627012022010001020

5. Annex – Facts about the 'Pegasus' Spyware

Presentation of the 'Pegasus' spyware based on the analysis of the expert in information security invited by the Authority.

5.1. The Leaked List Containing Phone Numbers

A "leaked" list containing some 50,000 phone numbers is a key element of the Pegasus Project. According to the Pegasus Project, the phone numbers in the list have been involved in the activities of the Pegasus spyware in one way or another since 2016. The data included the time and date of the selection of the numbers and their entry into the system. The source of the list is unknown and there is no information available about the circumstances of the leakage. It is not known who compiled the list on what basis and how the list was obtained by the Pegasus Project umbrella organization or Amnesty International, nor is it known what other data are included in the list in addition to the phone numbers and dates.

Based on the data in the list, the media partners of the Pegasus Project identified ten governments, which are believed to be responsible for selecting the targets.[21] There is a great deal of uncertainty surrounding the list. The statements related to the list can be misinterpreted and do not necessarily match their direct or underlying meaning. NSO Group firmly denied[22] that the list could be connected to their activities or the activities of their clients; according to their position, the list is not a list of the targets or potential targets of NSO clients. NSO's response included an allusion to the fact that the phone numbers in the list may come from public services, including among others Home Location Register (HLR) search service, which is not connected to NSO or the services of the company. It can be concluded that inclusion in the list means specific surveillance activity only if coupled with a positive result of the examination and digital trace analysis of the device (this however was established only in the case of 37 phone numbers according to the investigative report). In such a case it may become apparent that there is a connection between the time and date of the inclusion in the list and the specific infection.

In relation to the leakage of the list containing the phone numbers, it was raised on several occasions that the data were leaked from a Cyprus server. NSO claimed that it had no servers in Cyprus, and they checked several data in the list and none of them are connected to any of their clients. The list included 300 Hungarian phone numbers. The appendix to the digital trace analysis report issued by Amnesty International shows only two Hungarian data subjects, but the Direkt36 investigative portal, the Hungarian partner of the Pegasus Project identified several phone numbers and continues to publish materials related to the Hungarian persons concerned. Direkt36 published materials in relation to several persons concerned, whose devices could not be examined, but whose phone number was included in the original list. According to the terminology

21 Azerbaijan, Bahrein, Kazakhstan, Mexico, Morocco, Rwanda, Saudi-Arabia, Hungary, India and the United Arab Emirates.

22 *See* at www.theguardian.com/news/2021/jul/18/response-from-nso-and-governments.

doi: 10.5553/HYIEL/266627012022010001020

used by Direkt36, the persons in the list were "targeted". This, however, did not mean that the device of the person concerned was actually infected and/or wiretapped.

Direkt36 published some material also about a person, whose phone number was not included in the leaked list, but he had earlier initiated an examination by the staff of Citizen Lab and Amnesty International, who did find the traces of Pegasus generated in 2021 on the device handed over for examination.

5.2. Pegasus Agent (The 'Spyware' Application)

Following successful infection, a 'spyware' application is installed on the device. Installation does not require the users' authorization; it takes place without the user noticing it. The application running on the infected device provides full authorization to the attacker for the device and the data stored on it. The Pegasus agent is integrated between the kernel of the device's operating system and the legitimate applications running on the device. This ensures that the agent can access the system functions and legitimate applications, as well as the data stored in them. The agent "sees into" the operation of the applications (*e.g.* phone calls, text messages, chat, *etc.*), which means that even though a chat application may use encryption from endpoint to endpoint, the attacker is able to access the data, which are yet unencrypted. Pegasus uses the vulnerabilities of the devices or the applications running on the devices to install the application.

5.3. Hiding, Survivability and Self-Destruction

Once installed, the Pegasus agent hides its operation as it functions at the kernel level of the operating system, its activity is virtually imperceptible to the user, at most the increased data traffic may betray that a fairly substantial exfiltration is taking place in the background. The Pegasus agent contains self-destructive mechanisms in the event the agent is unable to communicate with its control server. In such cases, it automatically removes itself after the default 60 days, this time interval, however, can be set freely.

5.4. The Compromising Process and the Underlying Infrastructure

NSO firmly stated on several occasions that they only sell the technology, its use and operation are the responsibility of the client. However, according to WhatsApp, NSO operated the infrastructure through which the earlier "zeroday-zeroclick" attack took place affecting 1,400 users. The accessible court material reflects the wording that according to WhatsApp, the attacking activity was carried out by NSO, thus, it cannot be clearly determined, based on the contradictory and somewhat vague information what the rolc the NSO and the client played in the hacking process. This issue is of outstanding importance, because if devices centrally operated by NSO also participate in the hacking processes, NSO can have access to information about the activities carried out by the operator, such as the persons under surveillance or even the data collected by them.

Based on these two documents, the servers responsible for the installation of the agents operate on the client's side and the direction, configuration and

doi: 10.5553/HYIEL/266627012022010001020

updating of the agents is also implemented from these servers. The servers, which receive the data obtained from the infected devices, the GSM communications modules or text message gateways that store the collected data and the operator work stations enabling the operation of the system, also operate at the client's side.

Based on the details of the various support levels and debugging activities, it may be assumed that NSO's support engineers get remote access to the systems operating at the client or already have such access in order to carry out these activities. In relation to this, the question may arise whether NSO may have access to the data stored in the system through the deep-level technical support and the necessary access (whether temporary or periodic). This is the case when it comes to traditional external corporate IT support, and that is why such access is controlled by the security-minded organizations that are more mature from the viewpoint of IT security, for instance, by monitoring support activities even by recording such activities on video.

The Transparency Report issued by NSO contains a statement, which according to the Darknet Diaries professional podcast raises the possibility that NSO may have insights into the data of the clients under certain circumstances. The host of the podcast and John Scott-Railton, the head of Citizen Lab's NSO research, discussed that clients are under an obligation to provide data to NSO on the use of the product. The transparency report indeed includes such a statement but in the context that NSO may launch an investigation against the given client, if suspicion of an unlawful use of the product arises. In such cases, the client must provide information, for instance, the data of the system log files, or even data related to targeting specific targets. Refusal to provide this information leads to the immediate suspension of the right to use the system.

5.5. Anonymizer and Proxy Network

Once the Pegasus agent is successfully installed at the target (or it is already launched), the Pegasus agent begins to communicate with the control server and the surveillance and interception, the forwarding and processing of the data begins.

5.6. The Possibility to Intercept and Detect 'Pegasus'

Already installed (or launched), the activity of the Pegasus agent is virtually imperceptible for users. However, iOS devices carry out system logging, in which signs of Pegasus activity can be detected by digital trace analysis and, it is possible to detect some of the signs, indicative of infection in the case of Android devices as well.

Digital trace analysis is a complex technical and administrative process based on documented and attested examination methodology, which consists of recording the digital traces, exploring the digital traces (activity, event data, logged data, process information, file characteristics, data content, transaction data, traffic data, dates, *etc.*), searching for connections between the information collected, their analysis and evaluation and the preparation of the report on digital trace analysis. In other words, digital trace analysis is the reconstruction

doi: 10.5553/HYIEL/266627012022010001020

and technical/scientific examination of past digital events that have already taken place, providing answers and evidence as to whether or not an event or activity has taken place, why, when and how it took place, what was its extent, what processes were affected, *etc.* It is an important criterion that the examination can be reproduced, thus, it can provide attested evidence whether the activity or event under scrutiny has taken place.

Citizen Lab confirmed the results of the research by Amnesty International; based on the document they published, they found Amnesty International's methodology to be sound and the results of their examination correct, and both organizations found the same results in the course of their examinations independently of one another. Although neither the Pegasus Project, nor Amnesty International disclosed the source through which they had access to the list containing 50,000 phone numbers, or the list itself, the independent investigations of the French and the Belgian governments confirmed the results of Amnesty International's investigation in relation to Belgian and French data subjects.

doi: 10.5553/HYIEL/266627012022010001020

CASE NOTES

The CJEU as a Guarantor of Judicial Independence in the EU?

An Analysis of Case C-564/19, IS*

*Nasiya Daminova***

Abstract

The recent Hungarian C-564/19 IS (Illegality of the order for reference) case suggests that the interpretation of the principle of judicial independence in EU law precludes the possibility to launch disciplinary proceedings against a judge for submitting a request for preliminary ruling to the CJEU, thereby adding a new angle to the discussion on the substance of Article 47 EU CFR, Article 19 TEU and Article 267 TFEU. The aim of this case note is to shed light on the reasoning of the IS AG's Opinion and the CJEU's judgment, given their possible impact on the Luxembourg and Strasbourg Courts' jurisprudence concerning the 'rule of law backsliding' and the AFSJ. The main argument presented is that the IS judgment may be seen as a further development of the previous CJEU's Associação Sindical dos Juízes Portugueses (ASJP)/Miasto Łowicz lines of cases which perceive the judicial independence of the EU Member States' courts [Article 19(1) TEU] as one of the key guarantees for the enforcement of Union values (Article 2 TEU). Apart from this important premise, the IS judgment evidently reinforced several aspects of the suspect's rights to interpretation and information in criminal proceedings within the meaning of the Interpretation and Translation Directive (2010/64/EU) and the Information Directive (2012/13/EU). Hence, the IS line of reasoning can presumably lead to the formation of 'EU-specific' procedural guarantees in these areas, which may be considered an upgrading of the standards of protection articulated by parallel developments in the ECtHR's case law.

Keywords: judicial independence, rule of law backsliding, CJEU, Directive 2010/64/EU, Directive 2012/13/EU.

* This contribution was produced thanks to the Alexander von Humboldt Research Fellowship for Postdoctoral Researchers (December 2019-November 2021), and is current as of 15 April 2022. The author would like to thank Prof. Marten Breuer, Prof. Marcel Szabó, Dr. Laura Gyeney and the anonymous reviewers for the constructive comments on the earlier version of the contribution.

** Nasiya Daminova: postdoctoral research fellow, 'Just recovery from Covid-19? Fundamental rights, legitimate governance and lessons learnt' (JuRe) project, University of Tampere.

doi: 10.5553/HYIEL/266627012022010001021

1. Introduction

Considering the wave of the preliminary reference requests following the 2016-2018 reforms concerning the Polish judiciary, the CJEU became the key defender of judicial independence in national legal systems – using Article 47 EU CFR and Article 19 TEU as the main legal tools for this intervention.[1] It will be argued that the recent Hungarian *IS (Illegality of the order for reference)* case adds a new angle to the discussion, suggesting an interpretation of the principle of judicial independence in EU law as precluding the possibility to launch disciplinary proceedings against a judge for submitting a request for the CJEU's preliminary ruling (Article 267 TFEU). Moreover, the facts of the case required clarification of the scope of the right to interpretation and information within the context of the ongoing reform of the Area of Freedom, Security and Justice (AFSJ), in particular, the implementation of the so-called Stockholm Roadmap Directives.[2] The aim of this article is to shed light on the reasoning of the AG's Opinion and the CJEU's judgment in *IS*, given their possible impact on the Luxembourg and Strasbourg Courts' jurisprudence concerning the 'rule of law

1 Laurent Pech *et al.*, 'Poland's Rule of Law Breakdown: A Five-Year Assessment of EU's (In)Action', *Hague Journal on the Rule of Law*, Vol. 13, 2021, p. 26.

2 The adoption of the so-called 'Roadmap for strengthening procedural rights of suspected or accused persons in criminal proceedings' (Resolution of the Council of 30 November 2009) – later included in the 'Stockholm Program – An open and secure Europe serving and protecting citizens' (The conclusions of the European Council, 10/11 December 2009, EUCO 6/09) – was aimed at increasing the responsibility of the CJEU and the national courts in overseeing the protection of EU *due process* rights and helping individuals enforce their rights in the course of national proceedings. In this sense, *see e.g.* Lorena Bachmaier Winter, 'New Developments in EU Law in the Field of *in Absentia* National Proceedings. The Directive 2016/343/EU in the Light of the ECtHR Case Law', or Stefano Ruggeri, 'Participatory Rights in Criminal Proceedings. A Comparative-Law Analysis from a Human Rights Perspective', *in* Serena Quattrocolo & Stefano Ruggeri (eds.), *Personal Participation in Criminal Proceedings: A Comparative Study of Participatory Safeguards and in absentia Trials in Europe*, Springer, 2019. To date, the realization of the Resolution of the Council of 30 November 2009 on a Roadmap for strengthening procedural rights of suspected or accused persons in criminal proceedings includes the implementation of six basic Directives covering a wide range of procedural rights in criminal proceedings: *(i)* Directive 2010/64/EU of the European Parliament and of the Council on the right to interpretation and translation in criminal proceedings; *(ii)* Directive 2012/13/EU of the European Parliament and of the Council on the right to information in criminal proceedings; *(iii)* Directive 2013/48/EU of the European Parliament and of the Council on the right of access to a lawyer in criminal proceedings and in European arrest warrant proceedings, and on the right to have a third party informed upon deprivation of liberty and to communicate with third persons and with consular authorities while deprived of liberty; *(iv)* Directive (EU) 2016/343 of the European Parliament and of the Council on the strengthening of certain aspects of the presumption of innocence and of the right to be present at the trial in criminal proceedings; *(v)* Directive (EU) 2016/800 of the European Parliament and of the Council on procedural safeguards for children who are suspects or accused persons in criminal proceedings; *(vi)* Directive (EU) 2016/1919 of the European Parliament and of the Council on legal aid for suspects and accused persons in criminal proceedings and for requested persons in European arrest warrant proceedings.

doi: 10.5553/HYIEL/266627012022010001021

backsliding'[3] and the Area of Freedom, Security and Justice (AFSJ). The main argument presented is that the *IS* judgment may be seen as a further development of the CJEU's previous *Associação Sindical dos Juízes Portugueses (ASJP)/Miasto Łowicz* line of cases which perceive the judicial independence of the EU Member States' courts [Article 19(1) TEU] as one of the key guarantees for the enforcement of Union values (Article 2 TEU). Apart from this important premise, the *IS* judgment evidently reinforced several aspects of the suspect's rights for an interpretation and information in criminal proceedings within the meaning of the Interpretation and Translation Directive (Directive 2010/64/EU, Articles 2 and 5) and the Information Directive (Directive 2012/13/EU, Articles 4 and 6). Hence, the *IS* line of reasoning can presumably lead to the formation of *EU-specific procedural guarantees* in these areas, which may be considered an upgrading of the standards of protection articulated by the parallel developments in the ECtHR's case law.

2. Background of the Case

The *Criminal proceedings against IS* case originated from the Hungarian criminal proceedings against a Swedish national of Turkish origin, who was arrested in Hungary on 25 August 2015 due to an alleged infringement of the law on firearms and ammunition. While the assistance of a lawyer and an interpreter was requested before questioning, the defense counsel was unable to participate and the accused person (*IS*) was informed through the interpreter of the suspicions against him. Hungary does not have an official register of translators and interpreters to be appointed in criminal proceedings, and there are no formal criteria for the appointment of an *ad hoc* translator or interpreter in criminal proceedings with a cross-border element. Hence, neither the lawyer, nor the court assessing the case are capable of verifying the quality of the interpretation provided within the context of criminal proceedings.[4] The accused person refused to testify because he could not consult his lawyer, and was then released after questioning. An act of prosecution was issued on 26 February 2018 for an alleged

3 Within the given context, this phenomenon – sometimes also referred to as 'systemic deficiencies' – is often defined as the governmental strategy aimed at the weakening the state's internal checks and balances system, and undermining key *rule of law* components (such as the access to justice and judicial review, legal certainty, and transparency). In this sense, *see e.g.* Kim Lane Scheppele & Laurent Pech, 'What is Rule of Law Backsliding?', *Verfassungsblog*, 02 March 2018, at https://verfassungsblog.de/what-is-rule-of-law-backsliding; Armin von Bogdandy, 'Principles and challenges of a European Doctrine of systemic deficiencies', *MPIL Research Paper No. 2019-14, Vol. 14*, 2019, pp. 10-11; Veronika Bilkova, 'The Council of Europe and the Rule of Law – The Venice Commission', *in* Stefan Kadelbach & Rainer Hofmann (eds.), *70 Years of Human Rights and the Rule of Law in Europe*, Nomos Verlag, 2021, pp. 130-132; Barbara Grabowska-Moroz & Dimitry Vladimirovich Kochenov, 'EU Rule of Law: The State of Play Following the Debates Surrounding the 2019 Commission's Communication', *in* Giuliano Amato & Benedetta Barbisan (eds.), *Rule of Law vs Majoritarian Democracy*, Bloomsbury Publishing, 2021, p. 73.

4 Opinion of Advocate General Pikamäe Delivered on 15 April 2021, *Case C-564/19, Criminal proceedings against IS*, ECLI:EU:C:2021:292, paras. 16-17.

doi: 10.5553/HYIEL/266627012022010001021

infringement of the law on firearms and ammunition. Since the accused currently lives outside Hungary and the summons to appear before the court was returned marked as 'unclaimed', the referring court was required under national law to continue proceedings *in absentia*.[5]

In view of the substance of the questions submitted for the CJEU's preliminary ruling, the broader Hungarian legal and social context shall also be taken into consideration. After the Hungarian judicial reform (2012), the President of the *Országos Bírósági Hivatal* (National Office for the Judiciary, NOJ) obtained broad discretion in deciding on judicial appointments and commencing disciplinary proceedings against judges. A particular example for such appointments was the President of the *Fővárosi Törvényszék* (Budapest High Court) which was an appellate court for the referring court in the *IS* proceedings, namely a single judge at *Pesti Központi Kerületi Bíróság* (Central District Court of Pest).[6] In 2018, a legislative amendment established an additional remuneration of prosecutors, while the rules on the remuneration of judges remained unchanged. Consequently, the salaries of judges were generally lower than those of prosecutors of the same level and with the same grade and duration of service. Nonetheless, the distribution of bonuses and rewards to the Hungarian judges by the NOJ President was also allowed at that point in time.[7]

The single judge of the Central District Court of Pest made a reference for the CJEU's preliminary ruling (Article 267 TFEU) upon the request of the IS's defense counsel. The Prosecutor General brought an extraordinary appeal before the *Kúria* (Curia of Hungary, *i.e.* the Hungarian Supreme Court) on 19 July 2019, directed against the initial request for a preliminary ruling, which was made possible under Article 668 of the Hungarian Code of Criminal Procedure. The Curia of Hungary held on 10 September 2019 that the initial request for a preliminary ruling was unlawful since the questions referred were presumably irrelevant for the resolution of the dispute. As a consequence of the declaration of illegality, disciplinary proceedings were initiated against the referring judge by the President of the Budapest High Court – which were however terminated on 22 November 2019.[8]

Considering these premises, the Hungarian judge firstly felt it necessary to refer the question to the CJEU as to *(i)* whether a Member State was obliged to create a register of properly qualified independent translators and interpreters, in order to comply with the requirement of a fair trial stemming from Article 6(1) TEU and Article 5 ('Quality of the interpretation and translation') of the Interpretation and Translation Directive. *(ii)* Secondly, he also found it crucial to clarify whether the NOJ President's powers in the allocation of cases, the commencement of disciplinary procedures against judges, and the assessment of judges were compatible with the principle of judicial independence as captured by the joint reading of Article 19(1) TEU and Article 47 EU CFR. *(iii)* Thirdly, the

5 Id. paras. 6, 15.
6 Id. para. 18.
7 Id. paras. 19, 24.
8 Id. paras. 22-23.

doi: 10.5553/HYIEL/266627012022010001021

referring court asked for the CJEU's interpretation of the latter provisions to explain whether it precludes a situation where, by law, Hungarian judges receive lower remuneration than prosecutors, notwithstanding the fact that they are professionals of the same level and with the same grade and duration of service. *(iv)* Fourthly, the Central District Court judge submitted a procedural question as to whether a national practice, whereby the court of last instance declares unlawful a decision by which a lower court makes a request for a preliminary ruling, is compatible with the interpretation of Article 267 TFEU. *(v)* Fifthly, the referring court questioned the compatibility of the disciplinary proceedings brought against a judge for having made a request for a preliminary ruling with the principle of judicial independence, reaffirmed by Article 19(1) TEU and Article 47 EU CFR read in conjunction with Article 267 TFEU.[9]

3. Advocate General's Opinion

In his Opinion, Advocate General Pikamäe assessed the Hungarian legislation on the right to interpretation and information in criminal proceedings and on the preliminary reference procedure, in light of the right to an effective remedy and to a fair trial under Article 19 TEU and Article 47 EU CFR, as well as the CJEU's case law on the principles of judicial independence and the primacy of EU Law. In order to analyze the questions submitted by the Central District Court of Pest in accordance with Article 267 TFEU, AG Pikamäe clearly aimed at defining the degree of national judges' discretion in submitting a request for a preliminary ruling. Since the 'rule of law backsliding' context presumably adds a new angle to the ongoing discussion on the substance of judicial independence as a concept of EU law, the facts of the *IS* case shall be interpreted in light of pertinent CJEU's jurisprudence. The earlier *Miasto Łowicz* formula – which was also reiterated in the subsequent *Commission versus Poland (Disciplinary regime for judges)*[10]– where the CJEU underlined that a possibility of the disciplinary proceedings for making a request for a preliminary ruling could discourage the EU Member States' national judges from using the Article 267 TFEU mechanism (*chilling effect*)[11] paved the way to the *IS* findings.[12]

The appraisal of admissibility laid the foundation for the substantive analysis of the questions submitted for the CJEU's preliminary ruling. In light of the introductory remarks, it comes as no surprise that the suggested order of the questions' assessment in the Opinion was the following: the fourth, the first, the

9 Id. para. 24.

10 Judgment of 15 July 2021, *Case C-791/19, Commission v Poland (Disciplinary regime for judges)*, ECLI:EU:C:2021:596. In this sense, *see also* Laurent Pech, 'Protecting Polish Judges from Political Control: A Brief Analysis of the ECJ's Infringement Ruling in Case C-791/19 (Disciplinary Regime for Judges) and Order in Case C-204/21 R (Muzzle Law)', *Verfassungsblog*, 21 June 2021, at https://verfassungsblog.de/protecting-polish-judges-from-political-control.

11 Petra Bárd, 'Jeopardizing Judicial Dialogue is Contrary to EU Law: The AG Opinion in the IS case', *Verfassungsblog*, 20 April 2021, at https://verfassungsblog.de/jeopardizing-judicial-dialogue-is-contrary-to-eu-law.

12 *Case C-564/19, IS*, AG Opinion, paras. 26-27.

doi: 10.5553/HYIEL/266627012022010001021

second and third (in conjunction) concluded by an analysis of the fifth question. Importantly, the emphasis was placed on the role of the preliminary reference procedure within the 'rule of law backsliding' context, and in particular the Hungarian legislation allowing for the possibility to declare the preliminary ruling request unlawful and to initiate the disciplinary proceedings against the national judges for making such a reference to the Luxembourg Court.[13]

The recourse was made to the reasoning presented in earlier CJEU's case law, which was summarized in the *Miasto Łowicz* judgment: questions on the interpretation of EU law referred by a national court enjoy a presumption of relevance, and it is only for the CJEU to make decision(s) on their admissibility. At the same time, the preliminary reference procedure of Article 267 TFEU is an instrument of direct cooperation between the CJEU and the national courts, aimed at providing an interpretation of EU law provisions for the effective resolution of the pending dispute. Hence, within the context of the CJEU's assessment, no general or hypothetical questions shall be considered admissible, but only those necessary to *'give judgment'* within the meaning of Article 267 TFEU. This implies the requirement of a connecting factor – *either direct or indirect* – between that dispute and the EU law provisions whose interpretation is sought.[14]

Starting with the fourth question, AG Pikamäe suggested to find it admissible considering an *indirect but real link* between the main proceedings and Article 267 TFEU (*Miasto Łowicz*). The fourth question is presented as a procedural issue which must be solved before deciding the case on the merits – contrary to the Hungarian Government's claim to find the issue irrelevant to the outcome of the main proceedings. The Curia's judgment declaring the initial order for the preliminary reference to be unlawful was seen as requiring the CJEU's intervention, as the interpretation of Article 267 TFEU was crucial to choose one of two legal tracks under Hungarian law, namely, deciding the dispute only on the basis of national legislation, or applying EU law to the circumstances of the case.[15]

While turning to the substantive analysis of the fourth question submitted by the Pest court, the Advocate General shed light on the possibility of extraordinary appeals (or the *'appeals in the interests of the law'*) following the request of the national court for a preliminary ruling. The importance of a free dialogue between independent national courts and the CJEU was underlined in four points. *(i)* Firstly, the preliminary ruling system remains a key tool to guarantee the uniform application of EU law within the context of the Union's multilevel judicial system (Article 19 TEU). The system created by Article 267 TFEU does not frame a triangular relationship, but rather creates a link between the national court(s) and the CJEU, since the EU legislator has not intended other courts to participate in this construct.[16] *(ii)* Secondly, the EU law principle of

13 Id. paras. 27-30.
14 Id. paras. 32-33.
15 Id. paras. 34-39.
16 Id. paras. 44-47.

effectiveness would presumably be questioned if the appeal system under national law (even in case of the highest national court) could limit the discretion of national judges to forward preliminary reference requests under Article 267 TFEU.[17] *(iii)* Thirdly, considering the *erga omnes* legal force of the CJEU's judgments – comprising ones given in the preliminary ruling proceedings – the Curia's final declaration of unlawfulness under national law of an order for such a ruling made prior to the substantive decision in the main proceedings potentially undermines the *primacy* of EU law.[18] *(iv)* Fourthly, the national courts not only have the power to apply EU law, but also have the power to disapply the conflicting provisions of national legislation.[19]

After having examined the issue of the Curia's extraordinary appeal, AG Pikamäe moved to the analysis of the first question, which formed the core of the original criminal proceedings against *IS* at the Hungarian court. It should be mentioned that the AG proposed to broaden the scope of the originally submitted question(s), proposing to focus on the systemic interpretation of the provisions of the Interpretation and Translation Directive, the Information Directive and the Presumption of innocence Directive (Directive 2016/343/EU) in conjunction with Article 47 EU CFR ('Right to an effective remedy and to a fair trial'). Since the criminal proceedings *in absentia* were pending and gave rise to several questions clearly connected to the application of the Interpretation and Translation Directive and the Information Directive, the CJEU's response was considered to be crucial for deciding the case on the merits. Hence, this question cannot be considered irrelevant or hypothetical, having no relation to the case facts, and shall thus be admissible.[20]

The Advocate General focused on the first part of the question, concerning the scope of the EU Member States' obligation to create a register of properly qualified independent translators and interpreters, in order to comply with the requirements of Article 2 'Right to interpretation', Article 3 'Right to translation of essential documents' and Article 5 'Quality of the interpretation and translation' of the Interpretation and Translation Directive. He reiterated that linguistic assistance in criminal proceedings shall be provided both in the form of oral interpretation and the written translation of certain essential documents, shall be free and of 'adequate' quality, sufficient to safeguard the fairness of the proceedings.[21]

The benchmark for the assessment of the interpretation and translation of the 'sufficient quality' is established by Article 5(1) of Directive 2010/64/EU which – read in conjunction with Article 2(8) and Article 3(9) of that Directive – requires that the suspected or accused persons shall *(i)* have knowledge of the case against them, and *(ii)* to exercise their rights of defense. At the same time, AG Pikamäe acknowledged that the EU Member States had broad discretion in

17 Id. paras. 48.
18 Id. paras. 49-50.
19 Id. para. 51.
20 Id. paras. 53-55.
21 Id. paras. 59-62.

doi: 10.5553/HYIEL/266627012022010001021

means of guaranteeing this quality of linguistic assistance. While Article 5(2) of Directive 2010/64/EU clearly encourages the Member States' authorities to create the 'register or registers of independent translators and interpreters who are appropriately qualified', the existence of such a register cannot be considered mandatory. However, a procedural law framework shall be created for the quality control of interpretation and translation in the criminal procedure, comprising the possibility to complain that the quality of interpretation provided was not sufficient [Article 2(5) and Article 3(5) of Directive 2010/64/EU].[22]

Advocate General then moved to the second part of the first question, attempting to discuss the possibility of *in absentia* proceedings against an accused person *(i)* who does not speak or understand the language of the criminal proceedings and *(ii)* who cannot be established to have been informed of the suspicions or accusation against him or her *(iii)* owing to a lack of adequate interpretation – in view of holistic interpretation of Directives 2010/64, 2012/13 and 2016/343, in conjunction with Article 47 of the EU Charter. He underlined that the legal constructs of Article 1 'Subject matter', Article 3 'Right to information about rights' and Article 6 'Right to information about the accusation' of the Information Directive 2012/13 captured two separate rights of suspects or accused persons, namely the right to be informed of their procedural rights and the right to information about the accusation as such. He also noted that the applicable provisions of the Presumption of Innocence Directive 2016/343 (Article 1 'Subject matter' and Article 8 'Right to be present at the trial') established the following conditions for the substantive assessment of guilt or innocence in *in absentia* trials: *(i)* the suspect or accused person has been informed, in due time, of the trial and of the consequences of non-appearance or *(ii)* alternatively, they are represented by a mandated lawyer, having been informed of the trial.[23]

Thus, AG Pikamäe did not seem to discard completely the possibility for the EU Member States to remedy a breach of the right to information about the accusation during the investigation stage during a subsequent *in absentia* trial, even in light of Article 47 EU CFR guarantees. He noted however that the disclosure of detailed information on the charges shall take place *no later* than when the hearing of the argument on the merits begins (*Kolev and Others*).[24] Moreover, the adversarial principle and the principle of equality of arms require that the accused and/or his defense counsel shall be provided with sufficient time to become acquainted with that information, in order to enable a suspected/accused person or, alternatively, his lawyer to effectively prepare the defense. This requirement allows that, in case of necessity, such (*in absentia)* proceedings can be stayed, with the case hearing being postponed to a subsequent date (*Moro*).[25]

22 Id. paras. 63-66.
23 Id. paras. 67-76.
24 Id. para. 80-81.
25 Id. para. 82.

doi: 10.5553/HYIEL/266627012022010001021

Further, the Advocate General approached the second (NOJ President's powers) and third (judges' remuneration) questions in conjunction. Since general or hypothetical questions are directly excluded from the scope of Article 267 TFEU, only relevant questions shall be answered by the CJEU within the framework of the preliminary reference procedure. The *IS* case concerns an *in absentia* trial within the context of the application of the Interpretation and Translation Directive), the Information Directive and the Presumption of Innocence Directive. Hence, the questions concerning the peculiarities of the Hungarian judicial system – such as the remuneration scales and appointment of members of the judiciary – are of a general nature and shall be considered inadmissible.[26]

Finally, he elaborated on the fifth question concerning the possibility of initiating disciplinary proceedings against judges for making a request for a preliminary ruling. Since the said disciplinary procedure has already been discontinued, the fifth question was rendered hypothetical and irrelevant for the solving of the *IS* case – at least from a purely legal point of view.[27] However, AG Pikamäe suggested the second line of reasoning allowing for finding the fifth question admissible – by considering the fourth and fifth questions as an indivisible whole.

Referring to the *Miasto Łowicz* premises, he underlined that even the mere existence of a possibility of bringing disciplinary procedures against a judge for making a preliminary ruling request could be seen as grounds for the CJEU's prevention of any recurrence of actions of this type. The suggestion was therefore made for a corresponding reformulation,[28] in order to apply the *'procedural questions of national law' (Miasto Łowicz)* approach which allows for a significant degree of flexibility in the interpretation of Article 267 TFEU. Within the margin allowed for this approach, the conditions for continuing the main criminal proceedings – such as the possible disciplinary investigation against the referring judge even if it does not relate to the substantive resolution of the dispute – may be considered such a question.[29]

4. The Judgment of the CJEU

The *IS* judgment seems to have adopted a less straightforward approach than the AG Pikamäe Opinion, while *generally following the key suggestions of the Advocate General.* It is quite interesting that the AG Opinion's human rights-based argument primarily revolves around Articles 47-48 EU CFR – both in the sections containing the analysis of the matters related to the peculiarities of the Hungarian judicial system and the scope of application of the Stockholm Roadmap Directives' procedural rights. As far as the first question is concerned, the CJEU's judgment places a strong emphasis on the correspondence between

26 Id. paras. 85-92.
27 Id. paras. 93-97.
28 Id. para. 98.
29 Id. paras. 98-100.

doi: 10.5553/HYIEL/266627012022010001021

the standard of protection afforded by the EU CFR and the one articulated by the ECHR. Meanwhile it approaches the substance of other questions related to the various aspects of judicial independence under EU law primarily through the lens of Article 47 EU CFR and/or Article 267 TFEU. The CJEU starts the analysis from the fourth and the fifth question, then moves to the first one, to then conduct the admissibility assessment of the second and third question (read in conjunction).

The request for an expedited procedure submitted by the referring judge was declined by the Luxembourg judges, since this route is reserved only for matters of exceptional urgency. The disciplinary investigation against the referring judge was withdrawn during the preliminary reference proceedings, and the case did not involve an individual deprived or subjected to deprivation of liberty. Moreover, the sensitive and complex issues raised by the *IS* case required a thorough and detailed analysis, which could not be conducted properly in course of an requested expedited procedure.[30]

The Grand Chamber, first, reformulated the fourth question, having made a special emphasis on the principle of the *primacy* of EU Law as a possible ground for the national court to disregard a decision of the supreme court declaring unlawful a request for the CJEU's preliminary ruling made by that lower court. The Luxembourg judges underlined the gravity of possible consequences of the Curia decision for the development of the *IS* proceedings, as the referring judge still had to make further decisions concerning the relaunch of the proceedings and the willingness to maintain the questions submitted for a preliminary ruling.[31]

After noting that Article 267 TFEU remains a keystone of the EU judicial system established by the Treaties, the CJEU stated that the effectiveness of EU law would be questioned if an appeal to the Curia would *de facto* limit the discretion of the lower court – which was clearly precluded by the earlier *Melki/Abdeli* case law. The CJEU also underlined that if the pending preliminary reference request is not answered properly, this Curia precedent could become typical for the Hungarian legal system. The Grand Chamber judges also noted that this would be contrary to the *Van Gend en Loos 'vigiliance of the EU individual'* approach – and would hence undermine the principle of the *primacy* of EU law– a situation for which even the national constitutional provisions cannot serve as an acceptable justification. Hence, the CJEU concluded that the *primacy of EU law requires a lower court to disregard a decision of the supreme court of the Member State* in question, and the provisions of national law which undermine the *effectiveness* of Article 267 TFEU shall be set aside.[32]

The CJEU followed the suggestions of AG Pikamäe and found the fifth question admissible after the proposed reformulation. Thus, the Grand Chamber addressed the question whether the referring judge would still be able to refrain

30 Judgment of 23 November 2021, *Case C-564/19, Criminal proceedings against IS (Illegality of the order for reference)*, ECLI:EU:C:2021:949, paras. 52-56.

31 Id. paras. 58-66.

32 Id. paras. 67-82.

doi: 10.5553/HYIEL/266627012022010001021

from complying with the Curia decision when solving the dispute in the main proceedings without having to be concerned about the reopening of the disciplinary proceedings that were brought against him (for submitting the request for a preliminary ruling).[33] Therefore, the referring judge is faced with a procedural obstacle, arising from the application of national legislation against him, which he must address before solving the main case on the merits without external interference. While underlining the crucial significance of the *external* aspect of judicial independence in EU law, the CJEU made reference to Article 47 EU CFR and the earlier *Governo della Repubblica italiana* and *Miasto Łowicz* cases. At the same time, the Grand Chamber judges prominently made a distinction from *Miasto Łowicz* where the similar issue had not been discussed substantively.[34]

Despite the strong message sent on admissibility, the substantive analysis seems to be rather brief. The CJEU skipped the direct analysis of the combined reading of Article 19 TEU, Article 47 EU CFR and Article 267 TFEU (just like in the original question submitted), and – since the *Miasto Łowicz* 'procedural questions' approach was chosen – preferred to examine the matter only in light of Article 267 TFEU. The EU Member State judges are responsible for the application of EU law, comprising the effective exercise of their discretion to make a reference to the CJEU. Therefore, any provision of national law exposing national judges to disciplinary proceedings for making such request are disallowed for undermining their role as judges responsible for the application of EU law on the national level (*Miasto Łowicz, CommissionversusPoland/Disciplinary regime for judges*). Such disciplinary proceedings are capable of discouraging all national courts from making Article 267 references, which in itself could jeopardize the uniform application of EU law. Thus, the construct of Article 267 TFEU as such comprises the guarantee to be free from any disciplinary proceedings for making the preliminary reference request to the CJEU.[35]

The CJEU then turned to the scope of the EU Member States' discretion in creating a register of qualified translators and interpreters and the obligation to control the quality of language interpretation in criminal proceedings, which gave rise to the dispute pending before the national court. The Grand Chamber had no issue with finding the first question admissible, since the main proceedings concerned an investigation in the course of which the accused person had been questioned by the police in the presence of a Swedish-language interpreter and without the assistance of a lawyer, which was therefore clearly related to the application of the Interpretation and Translation Directive and Information Directive.

During the course of the national trial, the issue of the possibility of continuing criminal proceedings *in absentia* arose, hence the CJEU's answer was obviously necessary for the resolution of the dispute in the main proceedings.[36]

33 Id. paras. 83-85.
34 Id. paras. 86-88.
35 Id. paras. 89-93.
36 Id. paras. 94-97.

Hungarian Yearbook of International Law and European Law 2022 (10) 1
doi: 10.5553/HYIEL/266627012022010001021

However, the Luxembourg judges found Article 6(1) TEU – apart from the general reference to the EU CFR – irrelevant for answering the first question. Hence, the issue was solved solely on the basis of the pertinent Charter provisions. In particular, the CJEU took recourse to Article 48 EU CFR ('Presumption of innocence and right of defense') and underlined the pre-eminence of the scope and standard of protection under the ECHR [Article 52(3) EU CFR] in the case of the corresponding rights, namely Articles 6(2) and (3) ECHR.[37]

In light of these premises, the Grand Chamber then reformulated the first part of the question in order to establish whether Article 5 of Directive 2010/64 creates an obligation *(i)* to create a register of independent translators and interpreters and *(ii)* to establish procedural mechanisms to review the quality of the interpretation in criminal proceedings. The Directive's objectives and the legal context shall be considered for interpretation (*Surmačs, DHL Express*), as well as the fact that this EU law instrument lays down *common minimum rules,* with a wide margin of discretion granted to the EU Member States in their implementation. Article 5(2) of the Interpretation and Translation Directive ('Member States shall endeavor to establish a register or registers') presents the creation of a register of independent translators or interpreters as the desirable situation and the mean to ensure the 'sufficient quality' of interpretation provided. However, the Directive's wording ('*endeavor*') does not create a (directly effective) obligation to achieve a certain result, therefore, the establishment of such a register cannot be regarded as a requirement towards the EU Member States.[38]

Nevertheless, the State shall still adopt *'concrete measures'* to ensure the *'sufficient quality'* of interpretation, and a complaint procedure shall be established to control the quality of the translation provided in accordance with Article 5 of the Interpretation and Translation Directive. This statement was supported by reference to the earlier CJEU's case law which clarified that the *sufficient quality* of interpretation meant that the suspected or accused persons were provided with the sufficient information on the charges, putting them into a position where they could arrange for defense (*Covaci*).[39] Furthermore, the Strasbourg Court's case law also provided empirical backing to the CJEU's reasoning: the requirements relating to a fair trial stemming from Article 6 ECHR comprise not only the interpreter's appointment but the subsequent control over the interpretation quality as well (*Hermi, Knox*).[40] While it is still for the Member States to take concrete measures to comply with the abovementioned criteria, it is crucial that the national judges are provided with sufficient information on the interpreters' selection and appointment procedures in order to conduct the required assessment.[41]

37 Id. paras. 98-101.
38 Id. paras. 103-106.
39 Id. para. 113.
40 Id. para. 114.
41 Id. paras. 115-117.

doi: 10.5553/HYIEL/266627012022010001021

With regard to the second part of the question, the Grand Chamber aimed to clarify whether – in the absence of a register of interpreters, and when it is impossible to verify if the suspect or accused person has been informed of the suspicions or accusation against him or her – the combined reading of Articles 4(5), 6(1) of Information Directive and Article 48(2) EU CFR precludes the continuation of the criminal proceedings *in absentia*.[42] The Grand Chamber judges, again, demonstrated the loyalty to the ECHR standards of protection and referred to Article 6(1)-(3) ECHR which require that the information on the nature and cause of the accusation shall be delivered in the language the accused or suspected person understands (*Pélissier/Sassi, Sejdovic, Simeonovi*).[43]

The Grand Chamber judges underlined that providing full, detailed information concerning the charges and procedural rights was crucial for the effective realization of the accused's right to prepare their defense, and thus for the compliance with the Information Directive requirements. In accordance with Articles 4 'Letter of Rights on arrest' and 6 'Right to information about the accusation' of Directive 2012/13, the accused or suspected persons shall be provided with both oral interpretation without delay and the written translation of essential documents – as a minimum, in the form of a *'Letter of Rights'* in a language that they understand (Article 4). While the Information Directive does not establish an exact procedure for providing information on the criminal charge, the EU legislators underline that it shall be done *promptly* and in sufficient detail to enable the suspect/accused person to exercise defense rights effectively (Article 6).[44]

The CJEU addressed this construct from the perspective of an *in absentia* trial situation: if the quality of interpretation/translation was not appropriate and the substance of charge was not communicated (which is for the national court to verify), the *in absentia* proceedings would infringe the right to a fair trial and – at the later date – be contrary to the objectives of Article 6 of the Information Directive. In order to provide additional backing to this conclusion, the CJEU took recourse to Articles 8 'Right to be present at the trial' and 9 'Right to a new trial' of the Presumption of Innocence Directive. These provisions make an *in absentia* trial possible only in case the suspected/accused persons were informed of the trial and the consequences of non-appearance in due time – with the possibility of a new trial, or an access to other legal remedy, allowing a new determination of the merits of the case if these conditions were not met. In light of this systemic approach to the Stockholm Roadmap Directive, the trial *in absentia* in the given case would potentially constitute an infringement not only of the Interpretation and Translation Directive [Article 2(5)] and of the Information Directive [Articles 4(5) and 6(1)], but of Article 8(2) of the Presumption of Innocence Directive as well.[45]

42 Id. para. 118.
43 Id. paras. 121-122.
44 Id. paras. 125-128.
45 Id. paras. 129-137.

Hungarian Yearbook of International Law and European Law 2022 (10) 1
doi: 10.5553/HYIEL/266627012022010001021

Finally, the CJEU considered the second and third questions in conjunction, finding both of them inadmissible. The Grand Chamber judges followed the AG Opinion's reasoning and underlined that only the questions which were necessary to allow the national court to give a judgment in the case should be considered. With reference to the *Miasto Łowicz* formula, the CJEU elaborated on the lack of a connecting factor between the dispute in the main proceedings and EU law.[46] Since the dispute pending before the national court did not concern the Hungarian judicial system as a whole, a material connection between the substance of the main proceedings and Article 47 EU CFR and – more broadly – Article 19 TEU was not sufficient. The *Miasto Łowicz* 'procedural questions of national law' criterion was not applied either, since the interpretation of Article 19 TEU and Article 47 EU CFR was not required to enable the referring national court to rule on the substance of the *IS* pending dispute.[47]

5. Comments

The judgment of the CJEU in *Criminal proceedings against IS* raises many interesting questions, especially with respect to the CJEU's increasing role in framing the guarantees of judicial independence within the EU Member States' legal systems. Moreover, the *IS* judgment sheds light on several aspects of the right to information and interpretation in criminal proceedings, which could be of importance for the implementation of the Interpretation and Translation Directive, the Information Directive and the Presumption of Innocence Directive. This comment first addresses the CJEU's interpretation of Article 267 TFEU, whereby the supreme courts of the EU Member States are precluded from declaring a request of the national courts for a preliminary ruling unlawful (Section 5.1). After discussing the Grand Chamber's approach to the disciplinary proceedings against the national judges for submitting such a request (Section 5.2), it will examine the potential significance of the *IS* outcomes for the further development of the CJEU's jurisprudence on the Stockholm Roadmap Directives (Section 5.3).

5.1. (Further) Limiting the Procedural Autonomy of the EU Member States?

Before moving to the substantive analysis of the Grand Chamber approach to the fourth question submitted by the Central District Court of Pest, one shall shed light on the broader context of the case, namely the earlier Luxembourg Court's case law on national remedies '*sufficient to ensure effective legal protection in the fields covered by Union law*' [Article 19(1) TEU] and the newly formed body of the CJEU/ECtHR 'rule of law backsliding' jurisprudence. Early CJEU's case law, through the *direct effect* and *primacy* doctrines, created a two-level system of EU law adjudication with the CJEU and the EU Member States courts, acting as an integral part of the EU legal system (*Foto-Frost*).[48] In *Van Gend en Loos*, the CJEU

46 Id. paras. 139-143.

47 Id. paras. 144-147.

48 Judgment of 22 October 1987, *Case C-314/85, Foto-Frost*, ECLI:EU:C:1987:452, para. 16.

doi: 10.5553/HYIEL/266627012022010001021

was concerned that a different outcome 'would remove all direct legal protection' of the individual rights of the Union's nationals:

> "[t]here is the risk that recourse to the procedure under [EU law] would be ineffective if it were to occur after the implementation of a national decision taken contrary to the provisions of the Treaty".[49]

In accordance with Article 19(1) TEU, it is for the national courts – and therefore not in principle for the EU – to provide 'remedies sufficient to ensure effective legal protection in the fields covered by Union law'. Indeed, as the CJEU famously put in *Rewe*, in the absence of Union rules, it was for the domestic legal systems to designate courts with jurisdiction and to lay down procedural rules governing actions before those courts (*national procedural autonomy*)[50] for the purpose of safeguarding the rights stemming from EU law, provided that the rules are no less favorable than those governing similar domestic actions (*equivalence*), and do not render virtually impossible or excessively difficult the exercise of rights conferred by EU law (*effectiveness*).[51]

The model of decentralized judicial review chosen by the Union favored the development of the 'EU-specific' principle of effective judicial protection (review) fulfilling the two-fold task of: *(i)* the effective protection of the rights of individuals stemming from EU law and *(ii)* the effective enforcement of EU law within national legal systems.[52] In view of these premises, the issue of remedies before national courts within the CJEU's jurisprudence was traditionally addressed from two perspectives, namely the principle of effective judicial protection (the *Johnston* case law) and the *Rewe effectiveness.* The *Johnston* line of reasoning found its origins in Articles 6 and 13 ECHR and gave rise to the cluster of procedural guarantees enhancing individuals' access to the national courts acting within the scope of EU law.[53] On the contrary, the *Rewe* effectiveness jurisprudence was formulated negatively, fulfilling the task of precluding EU Member States from introducing laws that make the exercise of rights under EU law '*excessively difficult*'.[54]

It will be argued that the *IS* case significantly develops the *Rewe* line of reasoning: both AG Pikamäe and the Grand Chamber judges built the analysis

49 Eyal Benvenisti & George Downs, 'The Premises, Assumptions, and Implications of Van Gend en Loos: Viewed from the Perspectives of Democracy and Legitimacy of International Institutions', *European Journal of International Law*, Vol. 25, Issue 1, 2014, p. 86.

50 Judgment of 16 December 1976, *Case C-33/76, Rewe-Zentralfinanz*, ECLI:EU:C:1976:188, para. 5. Diana-Urania Galetta, *Procedural Autonomy of EU Member States: Paradise Lost? A Study on the 'Functionalized Procedural Competence' of EU Member States*, Springer, 2010, pp. 1-8.

51 Gunnar Beck, *The Legal Reasoning of the Court of Justice of the EU*, Bloomsbury Publishing, 2013, p. 228.

52 Christoph Görisch, 'Effective Legal Protection in the European Legal Order', *in* Zoltán Szente & Konrad Lachmayer (eds.), *The Principle of Effective Legal Protection in Administrative Law: A European Perspective*, Routledge, 2016, pp. 29-33.

53 Monica Claes, *The National Courts' Mandate in the European Constitution*, Hart, 2006, p. 138.

54 Judgment of 5 March 1996, *Joined Cases C-46/93 and C-48/93, Brasserie du Pêcheur*, ECLI:EU:C:1996:79, para. 83.

doi: 10.5553/HYIEL/266627012022010001021

primarily around *effectiveness*-related arguments. Comparing the Opinion with the judgment, the main difference that stands out is that the Advocate General approached the issue of admissibility primarily from the perspective of the 'indirect but real link' between the main proceedings and Article 267 TFEU (*A.K. and Others*), enabling the national judge to resolve 'a procedural question of national law' before being able to rule on the substance of the main case before him (*Miasto Łowicz*).[55] By contrast, the CJEU primarily examined the admissibility of the fourth question in light of the more traditional *'relevance'* (*Omni Metal Service, Openbaar Ministerie*) and seemed to avoid references to the '*backsliding*' Polish jurisprudence, presumably due to the sensitivity of the matter. At the same time, the Grand Chamber judges emphasized that the CJEU's answer was crucial not only for the development of the main proceedings, but also for the referring judge's decision on whether or not to maintain his questions submitted for a preliminary ruling.[56]

While the judgment's reasoning reflected four main points made by the Advocate General, with the analysis revolving primarily around the principle of the *primacy* of EU law and the (ensuing) *effectiveness* principle, the references to the case law providing empirical backing to the conclusions seem to be quite different. The Grand Chamber judges took recourse to the premises of *Opinion 2/13* (*'the keystone of the judicial system established by the Treaties'*)[57] and – with an additional reference to the recent *A.B. and others* case – underlined that Article 267 TFEU had established a direct system of cooperation between the EU Member States' courts and the CJEU, in order to enable the national judges to ensure the consistency of EU law, its full effect and its autonomy.[58] Mirroring *PFE* – one of the cases concerning the concept of 'court or tribunal' within the meaning of Article 267 TFEU[59] – the Luxembourg judges emphasized the wide discretion of ordinary national courts in referring questions to the CJEU, and the importance of the obligation for the courts of last resort to make such references.[60]

The CJEU underlined that even though Article 267 TFEU did not exclude the possibility for the reference to be subject to the national remedies (*Cartesio*),[61] the possible outcome of the national practice of declaring requests for preliminary ruling unlawful could have the effect of discouraging national courts from making such requests, and, as a consequence, undermining the *effectiveness* of EU law (*Melki and Abdeli*).[62] Therefore, the Grand Chamber elaborated on the so-called '*chilling effect*' concept, which, following *Miasto Łowicz/Commission versus Hungary (Transparency of Associations)* has given a new impetus to the

55 *Case C-564/19, IS*, AG Opinion, paras. 39, 98-100.
56 *Case C-564/19, IS*, judgment, paras. 58-66.
57 Id. para. 72.
58 Id. para. 64.
59 Sacha Prechal, 'The Many Formations of the Court of Justice: 15 Years After Nice', *Fordham International Law Journal*, Vol. 39, Issue 5, 2016, p. 1282.
60 *Case C-564/19, IS*, judgment, paras. 68-70.
61 Id. para. 72.
62 Id. para. 73.

doi: 10.5553/HYIEL/266627012022010001021

Luxembourg Court's 'EU values' jurisprudence.[63] Within the given context, this doctrine is understood as the 'national measures which are adopted and/or applied with the aim to dissuade natural persons from fulfilling their professional obligations' related to EU law (in this case, the EU Member States' judges) and shall therefore be precluded by EU law.[64]

The CJEU thus connected the *Van Gend en Loos 'vigiliance of individuals'* premise with the limitations on the exercise by national courts of the discretion conferred upon them by Article 267 TFEU, which would potentially *(i)* restrict the *effective judicial protection* of the rights deriving from EU law and *(ii)* the *effectiveness* of cooperation established by the preliminary ruling mechanism (*Ognyanov*). The reference to *Ognyanov* may possibly indicate a potential welcoming of further *strategical* requests for preliminary references on national rules undermining the effectiveness of the preliminary reference system established by the EU Treaties.[65] The further sequence of the judgment seems to confirm this idea, for apart from elaborating on the key CJEU's primacy cases (*Van Gend en Loos, Cartesio, Melki*) the Grand Chamber judges also incorporated the very recent jurisprudence on the issues of judicial independence in Romania (*Asociația 'Forumul Judecătorilor din România'*).[66]

Finally, the strong statement was made by the Grand Chamber, namely the new obligation of the EU Member State courts to *disregard* the decision of the national supreme court declaring unlawful the request for a preliminary ruling submitted to the CJEU under Article 267 TFEU by a lower court. This finding derived from the principle of EU law *primacy*, and seems to reflect the ongoing judicial dialogue between the two European Courts and the Polish Constitutional Tribunal. It should be mentioned here that the legitimacy of the latter court was recently questioned by both the CJEU (*A.B. and others*) and the ECtHR (*Xero Flor*).

In *A.B. and others* the Grand Chamber judges emphasized that *"maintaining ... independence is essential [for the national courts] as confirmed by the second paragraph of Article 47 [EU Charter of Fundamental Rights]"*, so they could realize the principle of effective judicial protection of the rights stemming from EU law. Therefore, the CJEU used the principle of *primacy* of EU law as a tool to set aside a decision of the Polish Constitutional Tribunal, which *de facto* limited the discretion of the national courts in submitting requests for preliminary rulings. This underlined that the abovementioned principle is binding on all the bodies of the Member States, and even the reliance on the constitutional provisions cannot

63 Laurent Pech, *The Concept of Chilling Effect: Its Untapped Potential to Better Protect Democracy, the Rule of Law, and Fundamental Rights in the EU*, Open Society European Policy Institute, 2021, p. 2.

64 Id. pp. 4-6.

65 Jesse Claassen, 'Assessing the strategic use of the EU Preliminary Ruling Procedure by National Courts', *in* Alicia Köppen *et al.* (eds.), *Cynical International Law? Abuse and Circumvention in Public International and European Law*, Springer, Berlin, Heidelberg, 2020, p. 181.

66 *Case C-564/19, IS*, judgment, paras. 78-79.

doi: 10.5553/HYIEL/266627012022010001021

prevent that.[67] In *Xero Flor,* the Strasbourg judges described the independence and impartiality of the court members (*'very close interrelationship'*) as one of the key components of the notion of *'court or tribunal'* within the meaning of Article 6 ECHR.[68] Consequently, a violation of the right to a fair trial was established, since the breaches in the procedure for electing three judges of the Constitutional Tribunal were of such gravity as to undermine the very essence of the right to a *'tribunal established by law'*, with no remedies available.[69]

The Polish Constitutional Tribunal responded to these statements in its *K3/21* judgment (7 October 2021), aimed at examining the conformity of several provisions of the TEU with the Polish Constitution.[70] The Tribunal judges found that Article 1 TEU (*competences*) in conjunction with Article 4(3) TEU (*the principle of sincere cooperation*), and Article 19 TEU (*the principle of effective judicial review*) are incompatible with the Constitution of the Republic of Poland seeing that the CJEU uses these provisions to review the various aspects of national judicial independence, in particular the procedures for the judicial appointments (pertaining to the powers of the President of the Republic of Poland as well of the National Council of the Judiciary).[71]

Hence, the subsequent *IS* judgment seems to respond to the arguments in *K3/21*, claiming the EU's authority in guaranteeing judicial independence in the EU Member States. Given that the national judges are acting within the scope of EU law, the CJEU relies on the *primacy* of EU law and the ensuing *Rewe effectiveness* as bases for this interference. At the same time, insofar as the Grand Chamber judges found the second and third questions inadmissible (concerning, among other issues, the powers of the Hungarian National Office for the Judiciary in judicial appointments), the *IS* ruling also defines the limits for possible EU intervention in the traditional area of national procedural autonomy, namely the organization of the Member States' judicial systems.

5.2. Disciplinary Investigations against Judges and the Preliminary Ruling Procedure

The status as a court or tribunal is perceived by the CJEU as 'a self-standing concept of EU law',[72] since the CJEU systematically interprets any reference to these notions in light of Article 267 TFEU (*i.e.* a body authorized to submit a

67 Judgment of 2 March 2021, *Case C-824/18, A.B. and others*, ECLI:EU:C:2021:153, paras. 140-150. In this sense, *see e.g.* Marcjanna Dębska *et al.*, 'You Cannot Change the Rules in the Middle of the Game" – An Unconventional Chapter in the Rule of Law Saga (Case C-824/18, *A.B. and others v. the KRS*)', at https://europeanlawblog.eu/2021/04/22/you-cannot-change-the-rules-in-the-middle-of-the-game-an-unconventional-chapter-in-the-rule-of-law-saga-case-c-824-18-a-b-and-others-v-the-krs.

68 ECtHR, *Xero Flor w Polsce sp. Zoo. v. Poland,* No. 4907/18, 7 May 2021, para. 247.

69 Id. paras. 288-291.

70 Polish Constitutional Tribunal, Decision K *3/21*, 7 October 2021, at https://trybunal.gov.pl/en/hearings/judgments/art/11662-ocena-zgodnosci-z-konstytucja-rp-wybranych-przepisow-traktatu-o-unii-europejskiej.

71 Id. para. 3.

72 Information note No. 2009/C 297/01 on references from national courts for a preliminary ruling, para. 9.

request for a preliminary ruling).[73] Hence, the notion of judicial independence could appear in the CJEU's case law on the admissibility of the national body – not formally belonging to the judicial system of the EU Member State – to the preliminary reference system.[74] The independence of the national judiciary as such has not been questioned by the Luxembourg Court for a long time since, from the 1970s, all the EU Member States remained simultaneously ECHR signatories and were bound by the Strasbourg standards of protection in this area.[75]

Indeed, the ECtHR's early jurisprudence in this area was rather profound, with properly conducted disciplinary proceedings as one of the key components of judicial independence within the system of the administration of justice (*'internal independence'*),[76] finding Article 6(1) ECHR (*'civil limb'*) guarantees applicable in this category of cases.[77] According to the Strasbourg Court, disciplinary proceedings against judges shall be conducted with a high degree of care, due to the gravity of the possible consequences for the individual judges and their careers and for society in general, as the public confidence in the functioning of the judiciary is at stake while *"in a democratic State, this confidence guarantees the very existence of the [rule of law]."*[78] The Strasbourg Court also responded to the reform of the Polish judiciary with a series of judgments elaborating on the standard of protection afforded by Article 6 ECHR in these cases, addressing the issue of disciplinary proceedings against judges either directly or indirectly (*Reczkowicz,*[79] *Dolińska-Ficek/Ozimek,*[80] *Grzęda).*[81]

The *'rule of law backsliding'* has given a new impetus to the CJEU's jurisprudence in this area as well: in *ASJP*, the Luxembourg judges demonstrated a clear intention to consider the judicial independence of the EU Member States' courts [Article 19(1) TEU] as one of the key guarantees of Union values (Article 2 TEU).[82] In order to justify this intervention and the development of an EU-specific principle of effective judicial review, the Luxembourg Court referred to the EU Member States courts competence to apply and/or interpret EU law, and

73 Judgment of 19 September 2006, *Case C-506/04, Wilson,* ECLI:EU:C:2006:587, paras. 51-62.

74 Koen Lenaerts, 'New Horizons for the Rule of Law Within the EU', *German Law Journal*, Vol. 21, Special Issue 1, 2020, p. 30.

75 Laurent Pech & Angela Ward, 'Effective Judicial Remedies before the Court of Justice', *in* Steve Peers *et al.* (eds.), *The EU Charter of Fundamental Rights: A Commentary*, Hart Publishing, 2014, p. 1251.

76 Joost Sillen, 'The concept of 'internal judicial independence' in the case law of the European Court of Human Rights', *European Constitutional Law Review*, Vol. 15, Issue 1, 2019, pp. 104-106. In this sense, *see* ECtHR, *Parlov-Tkalčić v Croatia*, No. 24810/06, 22 December 2009, para. 86; ECtHR, *Agrokompleks v Ukraine*, No. 23465/03, 6 October 2011, para. 137; ECtHR, *Moiseyev v Russia*, No. 62936/00, 9 October 2008, para. 182.

77 ECtHR, *Olujić v Croatia*, No. 22330/05, 5 February 2009, paras. 39-44.

78 ECtHR, *Ramos Nunes de Carvalho e Sà v Portugal*, Nos. 55391/13, 57728/13 and 74041/13, 6 November 2018, para. 196.

79 ECtHR, *Reczkowicz v Poland*, No. 43447/19, 22 July 2021.

80 ECtHR, *Dolinska-Ficek and Ozimek v Poland*, Nos. 49868/19 and 57511/19, 8 November 2021.

81 ECtHR, *Grzęda v Poland*, No. 43572/18, 15 March 2022.

82 Judgment of 27 February 2018, *Case C-64/16, Associação Sindical dos Juízes Portugueses*, ECLI:EU:C:2018:117, paras. 32-35.

doi: 10.5553/HYIEL/266627012022010001021

the deriving right (or duty) to submit requests for the CJEU's preliminary rulings (Article 267 TFEU).[83] The similar reasoning prominently appeared in the subsequent Polish *Miasto Łowicz* and *Commission versus Poland (Disciplinary regime for judges)* cases where the CJEU approached Article 19 TEU and Article 267 TFEU within the context of the possibility of initiating disciplinary proceedings against national judges for submitting a request for the CJEU's preliminary ruling.

In *Miasto Łowicz*, the CJEU found the questions of two Polish judges inadmissible, as the answer would not have had any impact on the solution of the dispute in the main proceedings and the disciplinary investigations had already been closed. However, it was the first occasion where the CJEU underlined that, considering the crucial importance of the effective exercise of the discretion granted by Article 267 TFEU, the

> "provisions of national law which expose national judges to disciplinary proceedings as a result of the fact that they submitted a reference to the Court for a preliminary ruling cannot therefore be permitted."[84]

The Luxembourg Court also attempted to extend the scope of the Article 267 TFEU application by incorporating the *'procedural questions of national law'* clause, in order to render admissible those preliminary questions which are not directly linked to the facts of the case, but should be answered to enable the referring national courts to rule on the substance of the disputes before them.[85] This extended the scope of the 'necessity' criterion of Article 267(2) TFEU, *"a [CJEU's] decision on the question is necessary to enable it to give judgment."*[86]

In *Commission versus Poland (Disciplinary regime for judges)*, the CJEU took a step further and conducted the substantive assessment of the Commission's claim concerning a possible restriction of the right of national courts to submit requests for a preliminary ruling and of their obligation to do so by ensuing disciplinary proceedings under Article 267 TFEU. Referring to the above-mentioned *A.B. and others/Miasto* Łowicz arguments, the CJEU concluded that such provisions of national law are contrary to Article 19(1) TEU,

> "since they give rise to the risk that the disciplinary regime at issue might be used for the purpose of creating, in respect of judges of the Polish ordinary courts, pressure and a deterrent effect which are likely to influence the content of the judicial decisions which those judges are called upon to give."[87]

It will be argued that the *IS* judgment is based on and developed these premises: the CJEU has followed the *ASJP* institutional perspective and applied the *Miasto Łowicz/Commission versus Poland (Disciplinary regime for judges)* formulae to the

83 Id. paras. 42-44.

84 Judgment of 26 March 2020, *Case C-558/18, Miasto Łowicz (Disciplinary regime applicable to national judges)*, ECLI:EU:C:2020:234, para. 58.

85 Id. para. 51.

86 Id. para. 45.

87 *Case C-791/19, Commission v Poland (Disciplinary regime for judges)*, judgment, para. 229.

doi: 10.5553/HYIEL/266627012022010001021

Hungarian 'backsliding' context. In both the AG's Opinion and the Grand Chamber judgment, the emphasis was put on the crucial importance of the proper functioning of the judicial cooperation system embodied by the preliminary ruling mechanism under Article 267 TFEU for the uniform application of EU law, its full effect and its autonomy. The CJEU clearly made a distinction with the *Miasto Łowicz* facts, where the criterion of *'necessity'* was not satisfied, despite the strong message sent to the Polish government.[88] In order to find the question admissible and to apply the *'procedural questions of national law'* formula, the Grand Chamber judges turned to the EU concept of judicial independence, and in particular, the guarantee to decide the main proceedings without external interference (*Governo della Repubblica Italiana*).[89]

Hence, Article 19(1) TEU, Article 47 EU CFR and Article 267 TFEU were interpreted as giving rise to the EU-specific guarantee of judicial independence of the EU Member States' judges, namely the freedom from being exposed to disciplinary proceedings or measures for having exercised a discretion (or a duty) to bring a matter before the CJEU within the framework of the preliminary reference procedure.[90] The references (*Miasto Łowicz, Disciplinary regime for judges)* arguably seem to demonstrate the pre-eminence of the Polish *'rule of law backsliding'* jurisprudence (judicial reform), sending a message to both the Hungarian and Polish legislators. The reasoning adopted by the Grand Chamber seems to reflect the *Rewe* line of arguments, with a focus on the *effectiveness* of EU law within national legal systems.

The principle of *'effective judicial protection'* was not discussed in the section of the judgment devoted to the fifth question, and the references to Articles 6 and 13 ECHR were missing from both the AG's Opinion and the *IS* judgment. This could be explained by two possible reasons: *(i)* firstly, the issue is directly related to the peculiarities of the EU's judicial system, namely the preliminary reference procedure, and the CJEU could avoid references to the Strasbourg case law while discussing the *'EU-specific'* guarantee of judicial independence. *(ii)* Secondly, even though the *IS* outcome seems to be identical to the one reached by the Strasbourg Court in similar cases (*Reczkowicz, etc.*), the reasoning of the European Courts differs significantly. The ECtHR discusses the facts of the case from the *perspective of the individual right* of the judge(s) to have sufficient guarantees of internal independence within the context of disciplinary proceedings.[91] The CJEU has taken an *institutional perspective*: the earlier *ASJP* formula was applied in light of Articles 2 and 19 TEU as precluding the EU Member States from amending their legislation in such a way as to bring about a reduction in the protection of the rule of law, by refraining from adopting rules negatively affecting the

88 *Case C-558/18, Miasto Łowicz (Disciplinary regime applicable to national judges),* judgment, para. 60.

89 *Case C-564/19, IS,* judgment, paras. 86-87.

90 Id. paras. 89-93.

91 In this sense, *see e.g.* Mathieu Leloup, 'Who Safeguards the Guardians? A Subjective Right of Judges to their Independence under Article 6(1) ECHR', *European Constitutional Law Review,* Vol. 17, Issue 3, 2021, pp. 394-421.

doi: 10.5553/HYIEL/266627012022010001021

organization of justice, and in particular ones undermining the independence of judges.[92]

5.3. *Directive 2010/64/EU, Directive 2012/13/EU and In Absentia Trials*

Besides elaborating on the guarantees of the EU Member State judges' independence, the *Criminal proceedings against IS* seems to make several important clarifications regarding the substance of Articles 2(5), 5 of the Interpretation and Translation Directive and Articles 4(5), 6(1) of the Information Directive. From this perspective, the IS case complements the developing body of the CJEU's Roadmap Directives case law: *e.g.* Directive 2010/64/EU provisions have been substantively assessed in five cases,[93] while Directive 2012/13/EU already appeared in 16 CJEU's judgments.[94]

Just like the Interpretation and Translation Directive, the Information Directive is primarily aimed at following or upgrading the existing Strasbourg standard of protection where the right to information arises from Articles 5(4), 6(1) and 6(3) ECHR.[95] The ECtHR traditionally approaches the abovementioned ECHR provisions in light of the *effectiveness* of the potential defense strategy:

> "[...] the accused must at any rate be provided with sufficient information as is necessary to understand fully the extent of the charges against him with a view to preparing an adequate defense",

being afforded necessary time and facilities for such a familiarization.[96] In general, the reasoning taken by the CJEU in *IS* seems to be in line with the developing body of the Roadmap Directives jurisprudence, where the Luxembourg Court interprets the procedural rights of Articles 47-50 EU CFR, paying however particular attention to the consistency with the standard of protection afforded by the Strasbourg case law.[97]

Firstly, the CJEU provided the EU Member States with a long-awaited answer to the question concerning the margin of discretion in establishing the register or registers of independent translators and interpreters, in order to guarantee the translation or interpretation services of sufficient quality in national criminal proceedings. Recital (31) and Article 5(2) of Directive 2010/64/EU proclaim that the EU Member States shall endeavor to establish a register or registers of independent translators and interpreters who are appropriately

92 In this sense, *see e.g.* Aida Torres Pérez, 'From Portugal to Poland: The Court of Justice of the European Union as watchdog of judicial independence', *Maastricht Journal of European and Comparative Law,* Vol. 27, Issue 1, 2020, pp. 105-119.

93 The statistics of the Directive 2010/64/EU usage in the CJEU's judgments, *via* the website search form of the homepage of the CJEU (curia.eu).

94 The statistics of the Directive 2012/13/EU usage in the CJEU's judgments, *via* the website search form of the homepage of the CJEU (curia.eu).

95 Directive 2012/13/EU of the European Parliament and of the Council of 22 May 2012 on the right to information in criminal proceedings, Recital (14).

96 ECtHR, *Mattoccia v Italy*, No. 23969/94, 25 July 2000, paras. 60-65.

97 In this sense, *see e.g.* Elaine Fahey, *The Global Reach of EU Law*, Routledge, 2016, pp. 68-89.

doi: 10.5553/HYIEL/266627012022010001021

qualified. These provisions were considered problematic since the time of drafting, in view of the high costs of interpretation and translation services, the lack of common standards for quality assessment – or review procedures – in case of interpretation/translation of insufficient quality in criminal proceedings, and the lack of equivalent national registers of the properly qualified interpreters and translators. In view of these conditions, some authors considered the compulsory creation of the register as a necessary step for compliance with Directive 2010/64/EU requirements.[98] Others elaborated on the wide margin of appreciation in providing interpretation/translation services in criminal proceedings, considering the establishment of such a register a final rationale of Article 5(2) of the Interpretation and Translation Directive.[99]

The approach and reasoning of the AG Opinion and the *IS* judgment differ significantly: Advocate General Pikamäe's analysis of Article 5 of the Interpretation and Translation Directive (in conjunction with Articles 2 and 3) seems rather modest, while the Grand Chamber reasoning appears to be very rich and profound. The Advocate General applies the textual approach to the Directive's provisions (the verb *'endeavor'*) and makes a brief reference to *Covaci* (one of the leading CJEU cases defining the scope of the right to interpretation and written translation within the meaning of Directive 2010/64) to substantiate the finding that establishing the register is not mandatory, if the proper review procedures for the quality of the interpretation and translation are ensured.[100]

By contrast, the Luxembourg Court's judges turned to the contextual interpretation of Article 5 and suggested the consideration of the broader context and the objectives of the Interpretation and Translation Directive, referring to the earlier comparably simple and non-controversial *Surmacs* (retail depositors protection) and *DHL Express* (postal services in the EU) cases.[101] The CJEU emphasized that it may also be necessary to consider EU law provisions, to which the national court has not referred to in its questions (*Smith*).[102] Unlike the Advocate General, the Grand Chamber made extensive references to Article 48(1) ('presumption of innocence') and 48(2) ('the rights of the defense') of the EU Charter. Moreover, the *harmonizing clause* of Article 52(3) EU CFR and the reference to *Gambino and Hyka*, which underlined that the standard of protection afforded by Article 48 should be consistent with one stemming from Article 6(2) and (3) ECHR, were used as a connecting link to the pertinent Strasbourg Court's jurisprudence.[103] From the ECtHR's perspective, not only the appointment of the interpreter but, if necessary, subsequent control over interpretation quality is included in the scope of Article 6 ECHR, and the failure of national courts to

98 Carmen Valero-Garcés, 'Navigating between theory and practice. Design and implementation of a continuous training course for interpreters and translators of the administration', *Lingua Legis*, Vol. 27, 2019, p. 13.

99 Michał Hara, 'Ensuring quality in legal translation by 3 parties – governments, courts and translators', *The Journal of Specialised Translation*, Vol. 27, 2017, p. 15.

100 *Case C-564/19, IS*, AG Opinion, para. 62.

101 *Case C-564/19, IS*, judgment, para. 104.

102 Id. para. 99.

103 Id. paras. 100-101.

doi: 10.5553/HYIEL/266627012022010001021

examine the complaints regarding the inadequate quality of interpretation can amount to the infringement of defense rights.[104]

Importantly, the CJEU responded not only to the earlier ECHR standard of protection (*Hermi*), but also demonstrated its loyalty to the newly-formed body of the Strasbourg Court's jurisprudence with the Roadmap Directives component. The reference was made to *Knox*, one of the leading ECtHR's cases where the provisions of Directive 2010/64/EU had been used as the criterion of the developing European consensus and which has had a significant impact on the outcome of the case (the so-called *spill-over* effect of EU law on the Strasbourg doctrines).[105] The CJEU reiterated that Directive 2010/64/EU laid down the *common minimum rules* on interpretation and translation in criminal proceedings. Therefore, the Grand Chamber judges concluded that the wording of Article 5 of ('*endeavor*') indeed defined the creation of the register as the final objective of Directive 2010/64, and not as an obligation.[106] In view of these premises, the CJEU underlined the role of EU Member States' courts in the assessment of the proper quality of interpretation, and the need to guarantee the access of national judges to the information on the selection and appointment procedures for independent interpreters and translators within this context.[107]

As regards the second part of the first question, the AG Opinion suggested the lowest level of the guarantee in case of the *in absentia* trials, following the minimum harmonization approach of the Interpretation and Translation Directive, the Information Directive and the Presumption of innocence Directive.[108] While addressing one of the widely criticized legal gaps of Directive 2012/13 – namely the fact that it does not regulate the procedures whereby information on charges must be communicated to the suspected or accused person[109] – the Advocate General built his analysis around the interpretation of Article 47 EU CFR in the light of Directive 2012/13/EU (*Kolev, Moro, Lom*). Special emphasis was placed on the non-absolute nature of the right to be present at the trial within the meaning of the Presumption of Innocence Directive 2016/343 [Recital (35)], and the diligence exercised by the accused or suspected person in order to receive information on the trial and the nature of the accusation [Recital (38)],[110] in order to suggest the possibility to continue the proceedings *in absentia* in accordance with Article 2(8) of Directive 2010/64, Article 6(3) of Directive 2012/13, and Article 8(2)(b) of Directive 2016/343.

However, the CJEU took another perspective and preferred to focus on the analysis of Articles 4 ('Letter of Rights on arrest') and 6 ('Right to information

104 Id. paras. 113-114.

105 In this sense, *see e.g.* Tobias Lock, 'The Influence of EU Law on Strasbourg Doctrines', *European Law Review*, Vol. 41, Issue 6, 2016, pp. 804-825.

106 Id. paras. 105-107.

107 Id. paras. 105-109, and 115-117.

108 In this sense, *see e.g.* Thomas Elholm & Renaud Colson, 'The Symbolic Purpose of EU Criminal Law', *in* Renaud Colson & Stewart Field (eds.), *EU Criminal Justice and the Challenges of Diversity*, Cambridge University Press, 2016, p. 153.

109 *Case C-564/19, IS,* AG Opinion, para. 80.

110 Id. para. 77.

doi: 10.5553/HYIEL/266627012022010001021

about the accusation') of Directive 2012/13 in light of Article 48 EU CFR, in order to preclude the possibility of an *in absentia* trial in cases where – on account of inadequate interpretation – it did not seem possible to establish whether the suspected/accused persons have been informed of the accusations against them.[111] The ECtHR's autonomous concept of *criminal charge* seems to have played a significant role in the Grand Chamber reasoning, as its flexible interpretation allowed for the potentially broad range of situations falling within the scope of the Interpretation and Translation Directive and the Information Directive. This is because the ensuing Article 6 ECHR guarantees shall apply from the moment *(i)* that an individual is officially notified by the competent authority or *(ii)* their situation has been substantially affected by actions taken by the authorities following from the accusations (*Simeonovi*), for instance arrest (*Brusco*),[112] questioning about the degree of their involvement in the acts constituting a criminal offence (*Schmid-Laffer*),[113] or – under certain conditions – even questioning as a witness (*Kalēja*).[114]

Just like in the previous section, the Grand Chamber judges took into account the pertinent developments in the Strasbourg Court's case law, starting the assessment from another *spill-over* effect judgment, namely *Simeonovi*, where the provisions of the Information Directive and Access to a Lawyer Directive (Directive 2013/48/EU) seem to have had a significant impact on the outcome of the proceedings.[115] While defining the standards of protection afforded by Article 48 EU CFR under the given circumstances, the Grand Chamber also elaborated on such seminal ECtHR cases as *Pelissier/Sassi* and *Sejdovic*, in order to underline *(i)* the close connection between being informed properly of the accusation and the effective realization of the defense rights and *(ii)* the necessity of the procedural and substantive safeguards of the right to be informed, considering its crucial importance for the further development of the criminal proceedings.[116] The CJEU then partly followed the suggestions of the Advocate General and referred to *Moro*, placing an emphasis on enabling suspects to prepare their defense for the safeguarding of the overall fairness of the trial.[117]

The arguments of AG Pikamäe on the possibility of an *in absentia* trial on the condition that the suspected/accused person is represented by the lawyer of their choice or appointed by the state, were disregarded in light of the overriding need for the proper enforcement of the Article 48(2) EU CFR guarantees. The Grand Chamber judges took the opposite view: further grounds for precluding the *in absentia* trials under the given circumstances were found in Article 8 of the Presumption of innocence Directive. This makes the conviction *in absentia*

111 *Case C-564/19, IS*, judgment, paras. 118-120.

112 ECtHR, *Brusco v France*, No. 1466/07, 14 October 2010, paras. 47-50.

113 ECtHR, *Schmid-Laffer v Switzerland*, No. 41269/08, 16 June 2015, paras. 30-31.

114 ECtHR, *Kalēja v Latvia*, No. 22059/08, 5 October 2017, paras. 36-41.

115 In this sense, *see e.g.* Nasiya Daminova, 'The European Court of Human Rights on the "Access to a Lawyer" Directive 2013/48/EU: the Quest for a Coherent Application of the Right to a Legal Assistance in Europe?', *European Criminal Law Review*, Vol. 11, Issue 2, 2021, pp. 211-241.

116 *Case C-564/19, IS*, judgment, paras. 121-122.

117 Id. para. 128.

possible only when the suspected/accused person has been informed, in due time, of the trial and the consequences of non-appearance. The CJEU seems to have included the right to be informed about the 'criminal charge' in the scope of the right to be informed of the trial within the meaning of the latter provision.[118] Therefore, the failure to inform the person involved of the charges as a result of an interpretation of inappropriate quality does not seem compatible with the systemic interpretation of the Interpretation and Translation Directive and Information Directive, which cannot be compensated for even by the possibility of the new trial prescribed by Article 9 of Presumption of Innocence Directive, or another legal remedy which allows for a fresh assessment of the case on its merits.[119]

6. Conclusion

The CJEU's judgment in the *Criminal proceedings against IS* case clearly develops the earlier *ASJP* approach, *i.e.* interpreting the judicial independence of EU Member States' courts [Article 19(1) TEU and Article 47 EU CFR] as one of the key guarantees of the Union values (Article 2 TEU). By doing so, the Grand Chamber made two key findings concerning the notion of judicial independence within the meaning of EU law.[120] *(i)* Firstly, the Luxembourg judges transposed the more recent (Polish) *Miasto* Łowicz formula precluding EU Member States from conducting disciplinary proceedings following the submission of the request for a preliminary ruling (Article 267 TFEU) to the Hungarian context, demonstrating the aspiration to develop a consistent jurisprudence on *'rule of law backsliding'*. *(ii)* Secondly, the *IS* judgment significantly developed the *primacy* of EU law doctrine, as the latter notion served as a basis for enabling national courts to *disregard* national judicial practice (comprising the decisions of supreme courts) which limits their discretion in making references to the Luxembourg Court.

Moreover, apart from elaborating on the substance of the notion of judicial independence within the meaning of Articles 2 and 19 TEU, the Luxembourg judges made several important clarifications on the scope of the rights of accused persons to information and interpretation in criminal proceedings in the EU. The Strasbourg Court's case law on Article 6 ECHR (*Hermi, Knox*) played a decisive role in the CJEU's assessment of the scope of the right to interpretation as captured by Article 48(2) of the EU Charter in conjunction with the provisions of the Interpretation and Translation Directive and the Information Directive. This 'Strasbourg-friendly' attitude is predictable as two European Courts are now actively developing the Stockholm Roadmap Directives' jurisprudence, and the

118 Id. paras. 134-136.

119 Id. para. 135-138.

120 Petra Gyöngyi, 'IS (Illegality of the order for reference) (C-564/19): A ground-breaking judgment but an uncertain outcome on the ground', *EU Law Live*, 30 November 2021, at https://eulawlive.com/op-ed-is-illegality-of-the-order-for-reference-c-564-19-a-ground-breaking-judgment-but-an-uncertain-outcome-on-the-ground-by-petra-gyongyi.

doi: 10.5553/HYIEL/266627012022010001021

mutual references are a typical feature of this developing body of CJEU/ECtHR case law. From this perspective, *IS* seems to be in line with this trend, demonstrating a strive towards a consistent application of *new* procedural rights in Europe, given that 27 EU Member States make up the majority of the 46 Council of Europe States.

In view of these premises, the reasoning of the Luxembourg judges differs significantly in the sections dealing with the various aspects of judicial independence and procedural rights in EU law. While the Luxembourg Court underlined the importance of the coherent application of corresponding EU Charter/ECHR rights in accordance with Article 52(3) of the EU Charter in cases involving the application of the Stockholm Roadmap Directives,[121] the issue of disciplinary proceedings following the request for a preliminary ruling was scrutinized in light of the *Rewe effectiveness* principle. This is presumably due to the specificity of the matter, namely, the role of the preliminary reference procedure in EU law: by reiterating the *Opinion 2/13* orthodoxy, the CJEU connected the notion of judicial independence with the *effectiveness* of the Article 267 TFEU mechanism, hence demonstrating awareness of its own preliminary ruling jurisdiction, and the *unity* and *autonomy* of EU law.

121 *Case C-564/19, IS*, judgment, para. 101.

doi: 10.5553/HYIEL/266627012022010001021

Mutual Constitutional Tolerance in the EU, with Special Emphasis on the Recent Case Law of the Polish and the Hungarian Constitutional Court

György Kovács[*]

Abstract

For more than five decades, the constructive and responsible judicial dialogue concerning the primacy of EU law over the national constitutions, have significantly contributed to the creation of a more democratic EU, with a strong and efficient, multi-level fundamental rights protection. For five decades, national constitutional courts and the CJEU have avoided encroaching upon each other's powers and inflicting lasting damage on the European integration and on the rule of law itself. In recent years, however, we have witnessed the worrying signs of a profound defiance towards the supremacy of EU law by some national constitutional courts, particularly in Germany, Romania and in Poland. As it became clear from the consequences of these decisions, defiance of national constitutional courts regarding their obligations based on EU law does not pay off. Namely, national courts and authorities will be under the legal obligation based on EU law to ignore such a decision brought by the national constitutional court, which renders an EU legal act inapplicable; and – as it happened in case of Germany and Poland - it will most likely result in infringement proceedings. The right approach instead, is to continue an open and direct judicial dialogue, as long as it is necessary, to find a solution for domestic constitutional concerns, which is in compliance with the legal obligations under EU law of the Member State in question.

Keywords: constitutional tolerance, constitutional court, judicial dialogue, supremacy, constitutional reservations.

1. Background

More than 50 years have passed, since the CJEU has developed its activist and revolutionary, but for the future of the European integration inevitable case law on the autonomous, directly applicable and directly effective character of the EU law, which requires supremacy in case of conflict with national law, even in respect of national constitutional law.

* György Kovács: attorney-at-law, Budapest; visiting lecturer, Pázmány Péter Catholic University, Budapest; president, Hungarian Fulbright Association, Budapest.

doi: 10.5553/HYIEL/266627012022010001022

Equally, a long time has passed since for the first time, the German Constitutional Court, elaborated its fundamental rights-based reservations, which were later followed by competence-based, sovereignty-based and constitutional identity-based reservations to defeat the requirement of unconditional acceptance of the supremacy of EU law over national constitutional law.

The above case law of the German Constitutional Court was followed by other European constitutional courts, and the German Constitutional Court became the leading and most influential national constitutional court, in – at least at the beginning – a very productive constitutional dialogue, between the CJEU and national constitutional courts.

The legitimate concerns expressed by national constitutional courts have contributed to major changes in EU law. Whether the increased role of the European Parliament until it became co-legislator, or the involvement of the national Parliaments in EU legislation, these changes made the operation of the EU more democratic.[1]

In the area of the protection of fundamental rights, concerns expressed by the German Constitutional Court and later other European constitutional courts, forced the CJEU to clarify what it considers to be a part of the EU fundamental rights framework. The Member States, in turn, have made the decision, that the EU shall join the ECHR, meanwhile, the Lisbon Treaty rendered the EU CFR a part of primary law, with both vertical and horizontal direct effect. In effect, the judicial dialogue between national constitutional courts and the CJEU was constructive and successful.

For almost five decades the above-described constitutional dialogue has proved to be beneficial and greatly contributed to the further development of European integration. For almost five decades, the CJEU and also national constitutional courts avoided encroaching upon each other's powers and inflicting a lasting damage on the common European project. The various reservations, developed by national constitutional courts, following the path trodden by their German counterpart, in the area of fundamental rights, competences, sovereignty and constitutional identity, were not only used carefully, but the dialogue itself helped shape the European integration in a great extent.

There was probably only one instance, when the constitutional court of a recently joined Member State applied the *ultra vires* control over a CJEU decision,[2] however, this was widely condemned in scholarly literature[3] and

1 There are still democratic shortcomings, which gives reason to remain critical. *See e.g.* Joseph H. H. Weiler, 'Epilogue: Living in a Glass House: Europe, Democracy and the Rule of Law', *in* Carlos Closa & Dimitry Kochenov (eds.), *Reinforcing Rule of Law Oversight in the European Union*, Cambridge University Press, 2016, pp. 313-326.

2 As a reaction to the *Landtová* judgment (Judgment of 22 June 2011, *Case C-399/09, Landtová*, ECLI:EU:C:2011:415), the Czech Constitutional Court declared an EU act *ultra vires*, in its decision of 31 January 2012, *Pl. ÚS 5/12 Holubec*.

3 Jan Komarek, 'Playing with matches: the Czech Constitutional Court's Ultra Vires Revolution', *UK Constitutional Law Association*, 2012.

doi: 10.5553/HYIEL/266627012022010001022

considered as a misstep from a relatively new Member State's constitutional court. It remained an isolated case. Apart from this singular incident, however, for almost five decades, national constitutional courts continued to acknowledge the ultimate and immense responsibility of declaring an EU act inapplicable, continuing to avoid applying the *Damocles' sword* and inflicting unrepairable damage, *not only on the European integration, but on the rule of law itself.*[4]

The above described cautious approach of national constitutional court radically changed in 2015,[5] when the German Constitutional Court decided for the first time to ignore its obligation to send a preliminary reference to the CJEU in a European arrest warrant case.[6] Instead, it declared the matter *acte claire*, and refused to execute the European arrest warrant in question, citing a violation of Article 1 of the *Grundgesetz*. This approach was further escalated, in the summer of 2020, when the German Constitutional Court declared a CJEU decision and a decision of the European Central Bank to be *ultra vires* and not applicable. As a result, the German Federal Bank was under a legal obligation on the basis of EU law, to ignore the judgment of the Federal Constitutional Court, and at the same time it was under the legal obligation on the basis of German constitutional law, to ignore the relevant decisions of the ECB and the CJEU.[7] The German Constitutional Court not only ignored its obligation to send a preliminary reference to the CJEU, but also created the possibility for infringement proceedings against Germany,[8] and showed a less positive example to other constitutional courts, by breaching the practice of great and well respected predecessors, followed for five decades.

2. Decision No. K 3/21 of the Polish Constitutional Tribunal

The example set by the German Constitutional Court was quickly followed, when on 7 October 2021, the Constitutional Tribunal of Poland (PCT), upon a request for interpretation by the Prime Minister of Poland with respect to the compatibility of Articles 1, 2, and 19 TEU with the Constitution of Poland, declared, that the cited provisions of the TEU are partly unconstitutional.[9]

4 András Jakab & Pál Sonnevend, 'The Bundesbank is under a legal obligation to ignore the PSPP Judgment of the Bundesverfassungsgericht', *Verfassungsblog*, 25 May 2020.

5 On the possible causes and outcomes, *see* Franz C. Mayer, 'Defiance by a Constitutional Court – Germany', *in* András Jakab & Dimitry Kochenov (eds.), *The Enforcement of EU Law and Values: Ensuring Member States' Compliance*, Oxford University Press, 2017.

6 BVerfG 2 BvR 2735/14 15 December 2015 – EAW II.

7 *See* Mayer 2017.

8 Ingolf Pernice, 'Sollte die EU-Kommission Deutschland wegen des Karlsruher Ultra-Vires-Urteils verklagen? PRO', *Verfassungsblog*; *see also* Judgment of 30 September 2003, *Case C-224/01, Köbler*, ECLI:EU:C:2003:513; Judgment of 13 June 2006, *Case C-140/09, Traghetti*, ECLI:EU:C:2010:335; Judgment of 9 September 2015, *Case C-160/14, Ferreira da Silva e Brito*, ECLI:EU:C:2015:565; Judgment of 28 July 2016, *Case C-168/15, Tomásová*, ECLI:EU:C:2016:602.

9 Decision No. K 3/21 (X. 7.) by the Constitutional Court of Poland.

doi: 10.5553/HYIEL/266627012022010001022

2.1. Context of the Decision

Based on the questions raised by the Prime Minister of Poland before the PCT, it is not difficult to find connections, with the already ongoing infringement proceedings and the rule of law procedure, lunched by the European Commission against Poland, mainly centering around the issue of judicial independence, and the existence of the disciplinary chamber at the Supreme Court.

As it is known, the CJEU passed important rulings with regard to judicial independence in Poland, in its judgments in *C-585/18, C-624/18 and C-625/18.* These CJEU judgments were not well received by the Polish government and the Polish Constitutional Tribunal. The Parliament adopted a new law at the end of 2019, which introduced a new disciplinary offence punishable with dismissal from office, for those cases, where a judge challenges the existence, legitimacy or the effect of a judicial appointment, and the PCT suspended the decision of the Polish Supreme Court, which wanted to give effect to the CJEU rulings by hearing challenges from judges with regard to the existence, legitimacy, or the effect of judicial appointments. With this approach, the PCT was not only defying the enforcement of EU law, but it also blocked the Supreme Court from fulfilling its duties under EU law.

The CJEU ruling on 2 March 2021, in case *C-824/18*[10] on the judicial control over judicial appointment procedures is of a paramount importance from the aspect of strengthening judicial independence within the EU. The CJEU held that Articles 19(1) and 267 TFEU, as well as Article 4(3) TEU preclude the application of national law, which, deprive a national court of its jurisdiction to rule on appeals in judicial appointment cases (in particular, the Polish Supreme Court, against decisions of the Polish National Council of the Judiciary) or which declare such appeals to be discontinued by law while they are still pending, ruling out the possibility of being continued or lodged again, and which thereby also deprive a national court of the possibility of obtaining an answer to the questions that it has referred to the CJEU for a preliminary ruling.

In particular, the CJEU pointed out that Article 267 TFEU and Article 4(3) TEU preclude the application of national law, which have the effect of preventing the CJEU from ruling on questions referred for a preliminary ruling, and Article 19(1) second subparagraph TEU precludes the application of national law, which gives rise to legitimate doubts, as to the independence and neutrality of the judges appointed. Article 19(1) second subparagraph TEU also precludes the application of national law, which would have the effect, that the outcome of appeals in judicial appointment cases are ignored.

No wonder, that the Prime Minister's questions targeted the very same provisions of the TEU, which were referenced in the above case law of the CJEU.

2.2. Legitimacy of the PCT

Well before the judgment in question, serious legitimacy issues were raised with regard to the appointment of five judges of the PCT, due to the fact that in 2015

10 Judgment of 2 March 2021, *C-824/18, A.B. and Others* (nomination of Supreme Court judges, Poland), ECLI:EU:C:2021:153.

doi: 10.5553/HYIEL/266627012022010001022

the President of Poland refused to swear in five justices elected by the Polish Parliament to the Constitutional Tribunal, only because parliamentary elections were to be held that year, and he expected that his party (PiS) will win the elections. Following the elections that the PiS had in fact won, the newly elected Parliament elected five new justices, who were sworn in by the President. However, in its May 2021 judgment in *Xero Flor*[11] the ECtHR declared, that the judges sworn in in 2015 were not legitimately elected judges (the decision focused in particular on one of these judges, Mariusz Muszinsky), and Article 6 ECHR (the right to a tribunal established by law/the right to a fair trial) had been violated. It follows from the above, that if the PCT itself is not elected entirely legitimately, then its judgment will not be legitimate either.

2.3. *Critique of the Decision*

Constitutional courts are the institutions responsible for interpreting the national constitution with *erga omnes* effect, but not the TEU, therefore the Constitutional Tribunal of Poland should have at least submitted a preliminary reference to the CJEU, to clarify the interpretation of the respective provisions of the TEU. Ignoring its obligation to submit a preliminary reference is in itself a breach of EU law under Article 267 TEU.

There are however stronger arguments[12] that the PCT should have instead refused to rule on the matter, as the PCT has already issued a ruling on the compatibility of the respective provisions of the TEU with the Constitution of Poland, in its well-known *Accession Treaty Judgment No. 18/04*[13] (passed in 2005, following accession).

In its *Accession Treaty Judgment* the PCT already gave clear guidance for national courts and authorities on how to reconcile the supremacy of the Polish Constitution declared in Article 8 of the Constitution with the principle of supremacy of EU law. As the PCT back in 2005 pointed out, Article 9 of the Constitution declares the principle of the respect for international law by the State. Poland mainly follows a dualist approach to public international law.[14] Even if the Constitution is the supreme law of Poland, it must respect its international commitments according to the earlier case law of the PCT. Where there is a conflict between the Constitution and the international commitments of the state, then it is the duty of the Constitutional Tribunal to call upon the legislator if necessary, to find a way to resolve the conflict. The above logic was reflected in the earlier case law of the Polish Constitutional Tribunal. According to the *Polish Accession Treaty Judgment*, since the constitution declares itself to be the supreme law of the land, the legislator must resolve all conflicts that may

11 ECtHR, *Xero Flor (dec.)*, No. 4907/18, 7 May 2021.

12 Statement of Retired Judges of the Polish Constitutional Tribunal, *Verfassungsblog*, 11 October 2021, at https://verfassungsblog.de/statement-of-retired-judges-of-the-polish-constitutional-tribunal/.

13 Decision No. 18/04. (V. 11.) of the Constitutional Court of Poland.

14 *See also* Anna Wyrozumska, *Transnational Judicial Dialogue on International Law in Central and Eastern Europe*, Łódz, 2017, pp. 20-23.

doi: 10.5553/HYIEL/266627012022010001022

arise between the Constitution and the international commitments of the state to ensure compliance with international commitments.

In its *Accession Treaty Judgment*, the Constitutional Tribunal suggested *three scenarios* to resolve a possible conflict between EU law and the Polish Constitution, which can also be very helpful in the current situation: *(i)* Scenario one refers to the amendment of EU law, in order to ensure compliance with the Polish Constitution – this scenario seemed less realistic for the Constitutional Tribunal judges in 2005, and it is still less realistic. *(ii)* Scenario two would be to amend the Polish Constitution[15] to ensure its compliance with EU law, which seems to be the most realistic way to solve such a conflict. *(iii)* Last, but not least, scenario three, the least plausible option is to withdraw[16] from the EU.

Even if the PCT has referenced the case law of its German counterpart several times, it should be seen clearly, that there is not much similarity between the German *PSPP* ruling and the *PCT* ruling in case *K 3/21*. Whereas the German Constitutional Court declared a ruling of the CJEU *ultra vires*, primarily because it lacked an appropriate assessment of proportionality, an issue that has later been resolved, in the Polish cases, the EU law provisions found *ultra vires* by the PCT are not about technicalities in a CJEU decision. Instead, these provisions are some of the most fundamental and most important provisions of the TEU, which, as noted above, already passed the constitutional review of the PCT in 2005, following Poland's accession to the EU.

Finally, it must be emphasized, that constitutional reservations, expressed in the form of a cooperative judicial dialogue by constitutional courts towards the unconditional supremacy of EU law over national constitutions is a practice by the majority of constitutional courts in Europe. As underlined earlier, this dialogue was a constructive contribution to the development of European integration. Meanwhile, ignoring legal obligations under EU law, and openly defying the supremacy of EU law can likely result in infringement proceedings and will not further the long term goal of protecting the national constitution either.

2.4. Consequences

Based on the earlier cited case law of the PCT, the Polish government maneuvered itself into a dead-end, with two remaining options (since an amendment of the TEU as a result of the *K 3/21 PCT* judgment is not a realistic scenario): *(i)* either to amend the constitution of Poland, to ensure its compliance with EU law, or *(ii)* to withdraw from the EU. Since EU membership within the population in Poland

15 This happened as a result of the European Arrest Warrant decision of the PCT, in its *P1/05* judgment, where the Constitutional Tribunal declared the EAW FD unconstitutional to the extent that the surrender of a Polish citizen is prohibited by the Constitution. This provision was repealed in order to comply with EU law.

16 Withdrawal from the EU is regulated with the Treaty of Lisbon in Article 50 TEU. Even in the case of withdrawal, the withdrawing state would be responsible for compliance with its legal obligations under EU law for a minimum of two years from the date of notification of withdrawal from the EU.

doi: 10.5553/HYIEL/266627012022010001022

is still supported by a large majority,[17] scenario *(ii)* seems less feasible from the perspective of the political future of the ruling party. Given the history of the governing coalition since 2015 in Poland, scenario *(ii)* seems to be equally unlikely. As a result, the PCT decision seems to have led to a dead-end for the government of Poland. Probably with two tangible results: *(i)* first, the EUR 1 million daily penalty payment imposed on Poland, for not complying with the CJEU order in *C-204/21 R*, in particular for not suspending the operation of the disciplinary chamber at the Supreme Court (failure to fulfil obligations), where it would be a naivety to think, that even if the two cases were not directly related, the PCT decision did not have an impact on the amount of the penalty; *(ii)* infringement proceedings launched on 22 December 2021.

3. Decision No. 32/2021. (XII. 7.) AB of the Hungarian Constitutional Court

Following the above decision of the PCT, there were great expectations how the Hungarian Constitutional Court will respond to a question of interpretation of the Europe clause in the Fundamental Law posed by the Minister of Justice in February 2021.[18] The Minister's question concerned the enforcement of CJEU judgment *C-808/18*,[19] which required Hungary to allow a foreign national staying illegally in the territory of Hungary to stay for the period until the migration control procedure is conducted, or if they submitted an application for asylum, until the asylum procedure is concluded. The concern raised by the Minister was, that given the lack of efficiency of the EU migration control mechanism, only one third of those whose return is ordered actually leave the territory of the Member States. As a result, the persons concerned could well remain in the territory of Hungary and become part of the Hungarian population, which however would violate national sovereignty and Hungarian constitutional identity.

The Hungarian Constitutional Court however, opted not to follow the example set by the German Constitutional Court in the PSPP judgment and the Polish Constitutional Tribunal. Instead it ruled, that as the Minister requested an interpretation of the Fundamental Law, it can only give an interpretation of the respective provisions of the Fundamental Law, and the Hungarian Constitutional Court can neither rule on the constitutionality of a CJEU judgment, nor on the primacy of EU law. In connection with the interpretation of the Europe clause in the Fundamental Law, the Hungarian Constitutional Court pointed out, that in line with the doctrine of pre-emption under EU law,[20] where the joint exercise of competences is incomplete, Hungary may exercise the relevant non-exclusive EU competence, until the EU institutions take the necessary measures to ensure the effectiveness of the joint exercise of competences.

17 *See* at www.bankier.pl/wiadomosc/Ponad-80-proc-Polakow-za-pozostaniem-w-Unii-Sondaz-Kantar-8186349.html.

18 The question of interpretation was related to Articles E(2) and XIV(2) of the Fundamental Law.

19 Judgment of 17 December 2020, *Case C-808/18, Commission v Hungary*, ECLI:EU:C:2020:1029.

20 *See also* Decision No. 32/2021 (XII.7.) AB, Concurring opinion by Marcel Szabó.

doi: 10.5553/HYIEL/266627012022010001022

The decision was largely positively received in literature,[21] mainly because the Hungarian Constitutional Court did not follow the defiant tendencies of its German and Polish counterparts, avoiding a direct conflict with the CJEU. There were however also arguments, that with this decision the Hungarian Constitutional Court practically empowered the government to ignore EU law, by partially handing over constitutional control to the government.[22] This latter interpretation doesn't seem to be supported by the text of the decision, nor its reasoning, on the contrary, on para. 28 for instance it is noted, that:

> "the institutions and bodies of the Hungarian State have a duty under Article E(2) of the Fundamental Law to ensure that, when drawing up national legislation on asylum applications and asylum seekers, these provisions are formed in accordance with the principles of solidarity and sincerity laid down in Article 4(3) TFEU."

The above decision by the Hungarian Constitutional Court seems to be consistent with its earlier approach, particularly its *Decision No. 2/2019. (III. 5.) AB*, where the Constitutional Court pointed out, that the Constitutional Court interprets the Fundamental Law in conformity with EU law, in the vein of *Europafreundlichkeit*, and with due respect to the European constitutional dialogue. As far as the identity review is concerned, the Hungarian Constitutional Court also pointed out that constitutional identity is not a list of static values, it includes the fundamental freedoms, division of competences, republic as form of government, respect for autonomies under public law, freedom of religion, parliamentarism, equality, acknowledging judicial power, protection of nationalities, altogether the achievements of the Hungarian Historical Constitution upon which the entire Hungarian legal system is based. All these must be safeguarded in the framework of a constitutional dialogue[23] with the CJEU and other European constitutional courts, based on the principles of collegiality, equality and mutual respect.

21 Kim Lane Scheppele, 'Escaping Orbán's Constitutional Prison: How European Law Can Free a New Hungarian Parliament', *Verfassungsblog*, 21 December 2021, at https://verfassungsblog.de/escaping-orbans-constitutional-prison/; Nóra Chronowski & Attila Vincze, 'Full Steam Back: The Hungarian Constitutional Court Avoids Further Conflict with the ECJ', *Verfassungsblog*, 15 December 2021, at https://verfassungsblog.de/full-steam-back/.

22 László Blutman, 'Az uniós jog elsőbbsége: alkotmánybíróságok lázadása', *Közjogi Szemle*, 2022/1, p. 6.

23 For more on the notion and forms of a judicial dialogue in this context, *see* Tímea Drinóczi, 'Alkotmányos párbeszéd-elméletek', *Jura*, 2012/2, pp. 60-72; on the distinction between monologues and real dialogues *see also* Attila Vincze & Nóra Chronowski, *Magyar alkotmányosság az európai integrációban*, HVG-ORAC, 2018, pp. 496-497; *see also* Fruzsina Gárdos-Orosz, 'Preliminary reference and the Hungarian Constitutional Court: a context of non-reference', *German Law Journal*, Vol. 16, Issue 6, 2015, pp. 1569-1590.

doi: 10.5553/HYIEL/266627012022010001022

4. Conclusions

The above recent changes stand in stark contrast with the earlier careful and responsible approach of the German Constitutional Court and its European counterparts, which were based on the concept of constitutional tolerance[24] and cooperative constitutionalism,[25] as formulated by Weiler and Häberle more than two decades ago.

As Weiler pointed out, constitutional tolerance is *one of Europe's most important constitutional innovation.*[26] Weiler noted, that the concept of constitutional tolerance is not a one-way concept, it applies equally to constitutional actors on EU and national level, to EU institutions, particularly to the CJEU, as well as to national governments and constitutional courts. National constitutional actors are required to be tolerant towards EU constitutional actors, but at the same time, EU institutions must also take into consideration that in an EU with 27 different constitutional traditions, one cannot require Member States' constitutional courts to unconditionally obey EU law. Thus, there is a need for a dialogue, based on mutual respect and shared values.

Häberle underlined, that in the EU, sovereign states decided to cooperate on international level, to confer sovereign competences on international organizations, to provide a higher level of security and welfare. Throughout this cooperation, states did not lose their sovereignty, since they still have an influence over their jointly exercised competences, and they can also withdraw if they wish from this international cooperation. This cooperation however also requires, that (as Weiler pointed out) Member State constitutional actors show more tolerance towards the EU, particularly in the framework of the judicial discourse between national constitutional courts and the CJEU. This approach of self-restraint and tolerance is characterized by di Fabio, as the necessary conditions for the peaceful coexistence.[27]

The concepts of *mutual constitutional tolerance* and *cooperative constitutionalism* are especially relevant, if not an inevitable condition for *peaceful coexistence* in today's EU including 27 different constitutional traditions and identities.

As EU law requires Member States to observe EU law, national constitutional courts duly focus on the protection of the core of their national constitutions, on national constitutional identity, over which Member States cannot accept the supremacy of EU law. This is because such values and core principles of national constitutional law are *taboo* for the constitution-making authority. In this context

24 Joseph H. H. Weiler, 'Federalism and Constitutionalism: Europe's Sonderweg', *Harvard Jean Monnet Paper*, 10/2000.

25 Peter Häberle, 'Der kooperative Verfassungsstaat', *in* Peter Häberle, *Verfassungslehre als Kulturwissenschaft*, 2. Auflage, Duncker & Humblot, 1998.

26 Joseph H. H. Weiler, 'On the power of the Word: Europe's constitutional iconography', *I-CON*, Vol. 3, Issue 2- 3, Special Issue, 2005, pp. 173-190.

27 Udo di Fabio, 'Friedliche Koexistenz', *Frankfurter Allgemeine Zeitung*, 20 October 2010, at www.faz.net/aktuell/politik/staat-und-recht/gastbeitrag-friedliche-koexistenz-11057029.html.

doi: 10.5553/HYIEL/266627012022010001022

of *multilevel constitutionalism,*[28] where a certain constitutionalization of public international law[29] may be observed, core constitutional values are not perceived as competing with the identity and values of the EU, on the contrary, they are *two sides of the same coin*, and shall be equally protected by national courts, as well as the CJEU. Consequently, national constitutional identity and EU identity should *reinforce* each other and sensitivity, *mutual tolerance* and mutual respect[30] should characterize all sides of the judicial dialogue, imposing great *responsibility* on these courts, both on the EU and on national level.

On a practical note, as AG Cruz stated in *Gauweiler,*[31] the CJEU and constitutional courts should be open to cooperation and continue the judicial dialogue as long as it is required, just as it was demonstrated in *Taricco*.[32] Whereas national constitutional courts approach the increased competences of EU institutions and the concept of unconditional supremacy of EU law over the national constitutions with reservations, national constitutional courts also acknowledge their *double identity* under EU law. On the one hand, *national constitutional courts have the duty under EU law to ensure the effective enforcement of EU law* (since their Member State accepted to be bound by the founding treaties and the whole *acquis communautaire* in its entirety). For example, the German Constitutional Court considers it to be unconstitutional, *i.e.* a violation of the fundamental right of *access to justice*, *access to a lawful judge* under the *Grundgesetz*, if a court fails to submit a preliminary reference to the CJEU where there is a question of interpretation or question of validity of EU law in the case before it. On the other hand, national constitutional courts have the duty to *protect the constitution and therewith also the national constitutional identity*. Such a dual identity can only be resolved, if national constitutional courts actively take part in the *judicial dialogue* with the CJEU and their national counterparts.

European and national constitutional law increasingly go hand in hand, while European and national constitutional identity mutually reinforce each other, contributing towards the strengthening of a European constitutional architecture. Protecting national constitutional identity and EU identity at the same time is a joint task of national constitutional courts and the CJEU, where continuous dialogue and *mutual tolerance* ("constitutional tolerance", as Weiler puts it) shall be the cornerstone of *peaceful coexistence*.

28 For more in-depth analysis *see* Ingolf Pernice, 'Multilevel constitutionalism and the crisis of democracy in Europe', *European Constitutional Law Review*, 2015/11, pp. 541-562.

29 Erika de Wet, 'The constitutionalization of public international law', *in* Michel Rosenfeld & András Sajó (eds.), *Oxford Handbook of Comparative Constitutional Law*, Oxford University Press, 2012, pp. 1209-1230; Antje Wiener *et al.*, 'Editorial. Global constitutionalism: human rights, democracy and the rule of law', *Global Constitutionalism*, 2012/1, pp. 1-15; Häberle 1998.

30 András Varga Zs., 'Respect of national identities as european value – European aspects of constitutional identity of Hungary', *Alkotmánybírósági Szemle*, 2020/Különszám.

31 Judgment of 14 January 2015, *Case C-62/14, Gauweiler,* ECLI:EU:C:2015:400, paras. 53-65. In *ultra vires* cases the reviewing criteria would be very similar for the national constitutional court as well as for the CJEU.

32 Judgment of 8 September 2015, *Case C-105/14, Taricco*, ECLI:EU:C:2015:555.

doi: 10.5553/HYIEL/266627012022010001022

Do We Like Majority Decisions?

Aspects of the Majority Principle in Voting on the Different Levels of Political Systems

Péter Smuk[*]

Abstract

This article aims to review the constitutional justifications for majority requirements arising from the democratic principle, and to analyze some current controversial cases. Although the qualified majority requirement is not a new institution in either the national constitutional systems or the functioning of the EU institutions, the democratic legitimacy of majority voting faces several challenges. In order to present aspects that should be re-evaluated in the light of certain new political strategies, this paper analyses the majoritarian requirements in the Treaties, in the rules of procedures of the European Parliament and also case studies pertaining to the constitution-making majority in Hungary and the controversial case of voting on the Sargentini-report. On the basis of this assessment, we may confirm but also reconsider the majority principle.

Keywords: majority principle, qualified majority, voting in parliament, constitution, abstentions.

1. The Majoritarian Principle in Democracy

The simplest justification for the majority principle is that since full consensus in a community is minimal or unattainable, relying on a majority is the simplest and fairest way to resolve disputes. According to Abraham Lincoln's First Inaugural Address,

> "Unanimity is impossible; the rule of a minority, as a permanent arrangement, is wholly inadmissible; so that, rejecting the majority principle, anarchy or despotism in some form is all that is left."[1]

* Péter Smuk: professor of law, Széchenyi István University, Győr.

1 Arend Lijphart, *Thinking about Democracy: Power Sharing and Majority Rule in Theory and Practice*, Routledge, 2008, p. 113.

doi: 10.5553/HYIEL/266627012022010001023

As Sajó noted, it is "truly surprising that such a basic rule of social order like majoritarianism has such poor theoretical foundations."[2] In Lijphard's words,

> "In theory, majority rule tends to be regarded as the crucial decision rule – and hence as the defining criterion – of democracy. In practice, however, strict application of majority rule is extremely rare. Especially with regard to the most important decisions and to issues that cause deep splits in societies, democracies almost uniformly deviate from majoritarian decision-making rules, to adopt mechanisms more likely to rally a broad consensus."[3]

Kis explains that, with certain restrictions, the principle supports political equality through the of one citizen-one vote principle, and meets the requirement of anonymity as well. Everyone can have an equal say in the outcome of a decision and the outcome is not known in advance, so no one can if it is their opinion that will be carried by the majority.[4] At the same time, (permanent) harm to those who remain in a permanent minority requires the elaboration of constitutional guarantees restricting the majority.

According to Sartori, majority voting before the end of the Middle Ages was rare, because officials were usually drawn, and even where the majority decision was tolerated in voting, city-states still preferred consensus. The official recognition of majority decision-making was in the ambit of decisions taken to regulate the internal operation of the monastic communities (*e.g.* the election of abbots).[5] Although one can trace the roots of majority decision-making in Aristotle's references, it nevertheless remained without theoretical foundation in earlier ages, and democracy was also perceived as a distorted form of state. However, the majority principle is not only a feature of democratic systems. For a long time, it functioned as a prerogative of the few, such as democratic life of the county's nobility or guilds; and was also applied in authoritarian and dictatorial political systems of modern times together with the manipulation of the masses. In the language of mathematics, this principle is a necessary, but not a sufficient condition for democracy. Its emergence in the text of the Peace of Westphalia marks the end of earlier (pre-Reformation) universalist thinking, the disintegration of political unity based on mistrust, and the limitations of the majority principle: according to the treaty, majority decisions are not applicable in religious matters.[6]

2 András Sajó, *Limiting Government: An Introduction to Constitutionalism*, CEU Press, Budapest, 1999, p. 57. (in footnotes). For further implications, *see* Stéphanie Novak & Jon Elster, 'Introduction', *in* Stéphanie Novak & Jon Elster (eds.), *Majority Decisions. Principles and Practices*, Cambridge University Press, New York, 2014, pp. 2-8.

3 Lijphart 2008, p. 111.

4 János Kis, *Constitutional Democracy*, Central European University Press, New York-Budapest, 2003, pp. 65-74.

5 Giovanni Sartori, *Demokrácia*, Osiris, Budapest, 1999, p. 80.

6 Martin Morlok, 'The Relationship of Majority and Minority as an Element of Constitutional Culture', *in* Miroslaw Wyrzykowski (ed.), *Constitutional Cultures*, Institute of Public Affairs, Warsaw, 2000, p. 226.

doi: 10.5553/HYIEL/266627012022010001023

In addition to deriving the general will from the majority vote, Rousseau differentiates between majority proportions required to express the general will on certain issues.

> "[...] between unanimity and a tied vote there are various degrees of inequality, each of which can be taken for the proportion in question, according to the condition and needs of the body politic. Two maxims can be used [...] one is that the more important and serious the issue, the closer the deciding vote should be to unanimity; the other, that the greater the urgency of the matter, the smaller the majority required should be."[7]

It is a fairly early lesson of 18th-century US constitution-making that restricting the majority principle in modern democracies is a constitutional requirement. *Jefferson* and *Madison* intended "to impede the operation of majority rule. In few other democratic countries are there so many obstacles in the way of government by electoral and legislative majorities",[8] because the Framers intention was not to establish a pure democracy but rather a balanced republic.[9] In his classic work, Tocqueville examined the tyranny of the majority in the democracies of the US and noted:

> "I regard as impious and detestable the maxim that in matters of government the majority of a people has the right to do everything, and nonetheless I place the origin of all powers in the will of the majority."[10]

Mill has already stated that

> "when society is itself the tyrant – society collectively, over the separate individuals who compose it – its means of tyrannizing are not restricted to the acts which it may do by the hands of its political functionaries. [...] penetrating much more deeply into the details of life, and enslaving the soul itself."[11]

Finally, two theoretical reservations must be considered. *(i)* First, it should be noted that even the concept of majority is not necessarily clear. Lijphart (and Sartori) refer to the varied use of relative, absolute and qualified majorities: so "the term 'majority' is very flexible and ambiguous, consequently, 'majority rule' does not necessarily mean rule by a bare majority (50 percent plus one)."[12] *(ii)* Secondly, while we expect democratic decision-making to lead to the right

7 Jean Jacques Rousseau, *Discourse on Political Economy and The Social Contract*, Oxford University Press, Oxford, 1999, p. 138.

8 Robert A. Dahl, *Dilemmas of Pluralist Democracy,* Yale University Press, 1982, p. 190.

9 Christopher Wolfe, 'Alkotmánybíráskodás és demokrácia', *in* Péter Paczolay (ed.), *Alkotmánybíráskodás, alkotmányértelmezés,* Budapest, 1995, p. 131.

10 Alexis de Tocqueville, *Democracy in America,* University of Chicago Press, 2012, p. 240.

11 John Stuart Mill, *On Liberty,* Yale University Press, New Haven and London, 2003, p. 76.

12 Lijphart 2008, p. 112.

doi: 10.5553/HYIEL/266627012022010001023

results, a quantitative rule in itself can hardly guarantee a high quality outcome. Epistemic considerations justify further corrections to the majoritarian principle.[13]

2. Practical Implications and the Rationale Behind Them

2.1. From Unanimity to Majority – on the International and Supranational Level

In international law,

> "the rule of unanimity has, in fact, been treated by many persons as an inevitable corollary of the theory of sovereignty, which, as it is generally understood, would subject no state to any limitation against its will."[14]

As Hill observed a century ago, "international conferences have been inclined occasionally to allow majority rule on matters of minor importance."[15] In international negotiations, decision-making can be considered a procedural problem, where sovereign states are prone to hurry negotiations in order to arrive at the final issues. At that point however, agreement cannot be reached without consent.

In international organizations, parties establish permanent bodies with their relevant rules of procedures. In the UN Charter[16] (Article 18), the two-thirds majority appears to be the general rule for decision-making, albeit only in 'important questions'. Paragraph 3 also allows for decisions on other questions (including adding new categories of questions to be decided by a two-thirds majority) to be made by a majority of the members present and voting.[17] Decisions of the Security Council on procedural matters shall be made by an affirmative vote of nine members; on all other matters, decisions shall be made by an affirmative vote of nine members including the concurring votes of the permanent members.[18] The five permanent members' right to veto, which is

13 Tamás Győrfi, *Against the New Constitutionalism*, Edward Elgar, Cheltenham, 2016, pp. 37-38. *See also* Bo Rothstein, 'Epistemic Democracy and the Quality of Government', *European Politics and Society*, 2019/1, pp. 16-31. Tocqueville's note is rather disturbing: "The moral empire of the majority is founded in part on the idea that there is more enlightenment and wisdom in many men united than in one alone, in the number of legislators than in their choice." Tocqueville 2012, p. 236.

14 Norman L. Hill, 'Unanimous Consent in International Organization', *The American Journal of International Law*, Vol. 22, Issue 2, 1928, p. 319.

15 Id. pp. 320-321.

16 Other international organizations tend also to opt majority voting, *e.g.* the Constitution of the ILO can be amended by two-thirds majority. *See* Article 36 of the Constitution, at www.ilo.org/dyn/normlex/en/f?p=1000:62:0::NO:62:P62_LIST_ENTRIE_ID:2453907:NO.

17 General Assembly Rules of Procedure Rule 86 [126] provides that "For the purposes of these rules, the phrase 'members present and voting' means members casting an affirmative or negative vote. Members which abstain from voting are considered as not voting." *See* at https://legal.un.org/repertory/art18.shtml.

18 Article 27 UN Charter.

doi: 10.5553/HYIEL/266627012022010001023

based on historical reasons, has introduced some kind of inequality.[19] Between the consensus-requirement as a default on the international level and the majoritarian principle on the national level (especially in legislatures in parliamentary democracies) we find interesting developments on the supranational level. European integration has flourished through the application of qualified majority voting on certain issues, as many have noted.[20] The Masters of the Treaties achieved a milestone with the Nice Treaty, when the differentiated weighting of Member States' votes was matched with a triple majority threshold (74 per cent of Member States' weighted votes, 62 per cent of the population of the EU, and a majority of the Member States) for adopting a legislation. It raised equality and fairness (but also legitimacy) issues, without resulting in a more efficient decision-making process. First, the Convention conceived of new qualified majority rules in the Constitutional Treaty (65 per cent of the EU's population and 55 per cent of Member States, with the caveat that the blocking minority must consist of at least 4 Member States), and these provisions were incorporated into the Lisbon Treaty.[21] Coming into force in 2014, Member States positions changed with the new qualified majority rules, favoring mainly the smaller and the bigger states.[22] Article 16(3) TEU lays down the general rule that the Council is to act by qualified majority, except where the Treaties provide otherwise (*e.g.* where the Council is to act by simple majority or by unanimity).[23]

Among the various majority requirements that apply to the decision-making of the Council, we must mention Article 354 TFEU. This applies for the purposes of Article 7 TEU to the suspension of certain rights, resulting from Union membership; the qualified majority requirements are foreseen under Article 238. (Of course, the Member State in question shall not take part in the vote.) This Article established a special majority requirement, since it prescribes the voting proportion to be achieved in the European Parliament: the EP shall act by a two-thirds majority of the votes cast, representing the majority of its constituent Members. This way, Kochenov argues, the Article provides for the potentially

19 *See* at www.un.org/securitycouncil/content/voting-system.

20 For aspects of the debate on qualified majority voting in the Council, *see* Bálint Ódor, *A kettős többség bevezetésének várható hatásai a Tanács működésére és Magyarország érdekérvényesítési lehetőségeire*, PhD Dissertation, Corvinus University, Budapest, 2013.

21 *See* Article 238 TFEU. Where it is required to act by a simple majority, the Council shall act by a majority of its component members. Where the Council does not act on a proposal from the Commission or from the High Representative of the Union for Foreign Affairs and Security Policy, the qualified majority shall be defined as at least 72 per cent of the members of the Council representing the participating Member States, comprising at least 65 per cent of the population of these States. Abstentions by Members present in person or represented shall not prevent the adoption by the Council of acts which require unanimity.

22 Frank Häge, *The Lisbon Treaty's change to Council voting rules will have important implications for the democratic legitimacy of the EU*, at https://blogs.lse.ac.uk/europpblog/2014/02/03/the-lisbon-treatys-change-to-council-voting-rules-will-have-important-implications-for-the-democratic-legitimacy-of-the-eu/.

23 Paul-John Loewenthal, 'The Council. Articles 237-243', *in* Kellerbauer *et al.* (eds.), *The EU Treaties and the Charter of Fundamental Rights. A Commentary*, Oxford University Press, Oxford, 2019, p. 1730.

doi: 10.5553/HYIEL/266627012022010001023

strictest qualified majority threshold in the Treaties. In addition, it is worth clarifying that while

> "Article 354 TFEU speaks of excluding the MS subjected to the procedure from the procedural thresholds concerning the numbers of MS required to reach Article 7 TEU decisions by the text of that provision, nothing is said in Article 354 TFEU about the population threshold counts, which are part of the QMV."[24]

Notably, the category of *passerelle clauses* is of special importance for the majoritarian principle and the development of integration. These 'bridging provisions' make it possible in specific cases to adopt a decision changing the voting arrangement from unanimity to qualified majority in the Council. The 'general' clause in Article 48(7) TEU foresees that where the Treaty provides for the Council to act by unanimity in a given area or case, the European Council may adopt a decision authorizing the Council to act by a qualified majority in that area or in that case. The Council shall act by unanimity after obtaining the consent of the European Parliament, which shall be given by a majority of its component members. National Parliaments are also notified. The Council can also enact a decision allowing for the adoption of special legislative acts in accordance with the ordinary legislative procedure: these special clauses amount to twenty-seven procedures in the TFEU.[25] Article 48(6) TEU provides that the European Council may even adopt a decision amending all or part of the provisions of Part Three TFEU. The approval of each Member State is necessary, and this paragraph also provides that this decision shall not increase the competences conferred on the Union in the Treaties. Potential future applications of *passerelle clauses* have yet to be explored.[26]

Co-legislation in the European Parliament also implies majority decision-making. Although the government-opposition dualism does not increase the stake of voting, the Treaties or the Rules of Procedure set forth various majority requirements. Given the high number of directly elected members, whose affiliation is not based on their nationality but their political identity, the unanimity principle characteristic of international decision-making regimes does not apply.

The Rules of Procedure of the EP establish several majority thresholds, for example for the election (or rejection) of the Commission by a *majority of the votes cast* (Rule 125.7) or when the EP elects the President of the Commission by a *majority of its component Members* (Rule 124.2). Some instances of qualified majority reflects the relevance of the issue decided upon: *(i)* The Conference of Presidents acting by a majority of three-fifths of the votes cast, representing at

24 Dimitry Kochenov, 'Articles 354-355', *in* Kellerbauer *et al.* (eds.) 2019, p. 2082.

25 Marcus Klamert, 'Article 48', *in* Kellerbauer *et al.* (eds.) 2019, p. 307.

26 Silvia Kotanidis, *Passerelle clauses in the EU Treaties – Opportunities for more flexible supranational decision-making. European Parliamentary Research Service*, 2020, at www.europarl.europa.eu/RegData/etudes/STUD/2020/659420/EPRS_STU(2020)659420_EN.pdf.

doi: 10.5553/HYIEL/266627012022010001023

least three political groups (Rule 21); *(ii)* a two-thirds majority of the votes cast, representing a majority of its component Members. (Rule 89.3, 127.7[27]); *(iii)* a majority representing four-fifths of the Parliament Members (Rule 162); *(iv)* a majority of two-thirds of the members present (Rule 221.2); *(v)* "a large majority of the committee" (Rule 214); and *(vi)* a majority of the commission's component members representing at least three political groups (Rule 235.3).

2.2. Simple and Qualified Majorities in Bodies of Legislation

The majoritarian principle in bodies of legislation,[28] mainly in parliaments and committees, is constitutionally justified by political-democratic equality, expectations surrounding procedural efficiency and responsibility of government. Supporting the majority principle also means supporting the constitutional functions of the legislative body, as this usually exercises its functions and powers through decision-making.

The equal mandate of representatives and the openness of achieving the quorum justify the application of the majority principle. A further procedural threshold is the quorum prescribed: the participation of a certain proportion or number of the members eligible to vote. Those who abstain from voting shall be calculated when considering the quorum, since they participated in the voting with their votes cast.[29]

The Fundamental Law of Hungary [Sections 5(5) and 5(6)] retained the quorum requirement of the former Constitution (Section 24), and the majority requirements was also established in the text shaped in the course of the fourth and fifth amendments:

> "The National Assembly shall have a quorum if more than half of its Members are present at the sitting. Unless otherwise provided in the Fundamental Law, the National Assembly shall make its decisions with the votes of more than half of the Members of the National Assembly present. The provisions of the Rules of Procedure may provide that a qualified majority shall be required for certain decisions to be taken."

It is clear from this provision that, in addition to the simple majority vote of the MPs present (reflecting the parliamentary form of government) there is now a constitutional basis for qualified majority requirements. The constitution or the rules of procedures shall be the legal sources in which a higher rate of democratic support can be prescribed than the simple majority for certain decisions. Based on the previous text of the Constitution, Szente argued that the majority rules of parliamentary decisions are "therefore excluded from the self-regulating powers

27 Two-thirds majority applies when adopting the Motion of censure on the Commission, notably this is a higher majority than in national parliaments at vote of no confidence. *See* Goran Marković, 'European Parliament's Control of the European Commission – Procedural Aspects', *EU and Comparative Law Issues and Challenges Series (ECLIC)*, Vol. 1, 2017, pp. 471-489.

28 We do not examine the majority principle in electoral context.

29 Zoltán Szente, '24. §', *in* András Jakab (ed.), *Az Alkotmány kommentárja*, Századvég, Budapest, 2009, p. 805.

doi: 10.5553/HYIEL/266627012022010001023

of the parliament – therefore the Parliament cannot freely dispose of them"; for this reason, the imposition of special majority requirements is unconstitutional (*e.g.* many of the procedural qualified majorities required by the then House Rules).[30]

Several provisions of both the Fundamental Law and the Act on the National Assembly Chapter V/A. (Section 61/A) cover a fairly large number of qualified majority cases. Reservations made in this respect shall not be discussed here, but the core element of criticisms can be summarized as follows: the regulatory objects, policy issues underlying qualified majority requirements are rather alien to political changes in parliamentary government, the responsibility borne by a government winning a majority in elections; the excessive application of the two-thirds threshold is also likely to undermine confidence in democratic elections.[31]

From the 1990s onwards the qualified majority requirement was elaborated upon in a substantive sense, in a decision of the Constitutional Court which declared that it is "a constitutional guarantee whose essential content is a broad consensus among members of parliament".[32] This is in line with the approach of the Venice Committee to constitutional amendments:

> "The main purpose and effect of a qualified majority requirement is to *(i)* ensure broad political consensus (and thereby strengthen the legitimacy and durability of the amendment), and *(ii)* protect the interests and rights of the political opposition and of minorities."[33]

Based on the electoral system, a direct correlation exists that there is greater social support behind the higher proportion of deputies. However, the function of qualified majority seeking to replace 'ordinary' legislation in certain issues, whether because of their high politics nature or the manifestation of constitutional power, no longer works if the politically disciplined majority of the government has a qualified majority in parliament.[34]

In some constitutional systems qualified majority appears not only in a mathematical form; further lessons can be drawn from these arrangements. Beyond the default majority decision-making, there are cases in which *(i)* affirmative decisions of other entities are required for the decision of the (parliamentary) body to become effective; or *(ii)* a different voting method *(vota ponderantur, non numerantur)* is used within the body.

Another entity upholds a parliamentary decision when it is to be put to an affirmative referendum, or the other House of the bicameral legislature (possibly

30 Id. p. 807.

31 Boldizsár Szentgáli-Tóth, 'Qualified laws as actors of the separation of powers', *Hungarian Journal of Legal Studies*, Vol. 61, Issue 2, 2020, pp. 216-217; *Opinion on the new Constitution of Hungary*, adopted by the Venice Commission, CDL-AD(2011)016-e, para. 24.

32 Decision No. 1/1999. (II. 24.) AB of the Constitutional Court.

33 *Report on Constitutional Amendment*, adopted by the Venice Commission, CDL-AD(2010)001-e, para. 94.

34 *Report on the role of the opposition in a democratic Parliament*, adopted by the Venice Commission, CDL-AD(2010)025, para. 127.

doi: 10.5553/HYIEL/266627012022010001023

composed on the basis of a different principle of representation than the lower house) or in federal states a certain majority of the Member States 'contribute'. This is also the case when a decision requires confirmation by the parliament formed after the next election.[35]

A double qualified majority vote is required when the votes cast by members of the body are not only considered numerically, but also according to additional criteria. An example for this is the qualified majority rule in the capital city of Budapest. The condition for reaching a qualified majority in the General Assembly of the capital is that votes of mayors of the districts of the capital, who together account for more than half of the population of the capital, are necessary to approve a proposal.[36] But the double majority requirement of the EU, investigated above, also combines the criterion of a majority of members with the population requirement of the entities represented by the members.

Some critical comments point to the legitimacy problems raised with this voting calculation. One cannot but agree with Elster who made the following observation:

> "In weighted majority voting, decisions are taken by the majority of votes cast by the units that are present – [...] if the units cast unequal numbers of votes. Although this procedure has also been used at the individual level (plural voting), I consider only its use in voting by aggregate units. Weighted majority voting in two-tiered systems has in common with proportional representation in a one-tiered system the fact that both can be used to translate population differences into voting power. Yet the two are not equivalent. For one thing, the weights used in weighted majority voting may reflect other differences than demographic ones; for another, in weighted majority voting, individual votes are typically used only to determine the vote of an aggregate unit and are not pooled across units."[37]

2.3. *Voting Strategies*

Besides discussing the fundamental questions of the majority rule, one must also consider the decision-making aspects of voting. In community or board decision-making, voting aggregates preferences. In addition to the procedural legitimacy effect of the formal requirements, political science also studies the voting attitudes of MPs and their coordination. Deputies' perceptions of their roles can be extremely diverse regarding the legislative agenda. Not only can Members' resolutions on a given proposal be diverse (supporting or opposing it for different reasons, taking a position for non-rational reasons, *etc.*); but they can also be influenced by the sequence of issues on the voting agenda, and by the fact that decision-making situations that offer more than two alternatives may complicate the situation.

35 With regard of the constitution making procedures, types of these arrangements are listed in CDL-AD(2010)001.

36 Act CLXXXIX of 2011 on Local Governments in Hungary, Section 47(3).

37 Jon Elster, 'Nested majorities', *in* Novak & Elster (eds.) 2011, p. 36.

doi: 10.5553/HYIEL/266627012022010001023

According to the rational choice theory, if individuals are not coordinated, their rational actions often lead to sub-optimal outcomes for them. However, the collective action of legislators, especially the discipline enforced by the parties, can result in a mutually beneficial co-operation on the long run. Parties in larger bodies foster the forging of compromises and long-term agreements to prevent the chaos of choosing between a greater number of alternatives.[38] Compliance with the voting syllabus adopted by political groups can obviously be followed in case the vote is open. The most important difference is clearly the secret and open voting in this respect, but voting methods can also be of additional importance (the rules for casting and counting votes, initiating and ordering roll-call votes are varied). The importance of the voting method is evident, even if a complex statistical correlation can only be shown between the voting methods and the uniform voting discipline/cohesion of the political groups.[39]

In order to meet the required majority requirements, the deputies/parties may prepare the vote in advance. In quite a few cases, the results of a consensual vote are already covered by preliminary agreements, or the likely minority simply refrains from voting against for various reasons.

It has been already noted above, that in EU Council procedures most decisions are made without opposition in the qualified majority area.

> "When the QMV procedure was created, its promoters did not intend that it would be systematically used. Instead, QMV was conceived as a way to avoid that the decision-making process be stuck. QMV was supposed to encourage participants who feared to be outvoted to soften their positions in order to find compromises. QMV is often compared to a 'deterrent weapon' or to the 'sword of Damocles': even if a formal vote is unlikely, each participant is aware that a vote is possible. This general awareness leads participants to have flexible positions."[40]

So, as Novak observes, unanimity – or the right to veto – incentivizes participants to hold out for strong demands; by contrast, when participants know that they can be outvoted, they tend to be more 'constructive'.[41]

38 Gerry Mackie, 'The reception of social choice theory by democratic theory', *in* Novak & Elster (eds.) 2011, pp. 77-102; Zsolt Enyedi & András Körösényi, *Pártok és pártrendszerek*, Osiris, Budapest, 2004, pp. 19-23; Tamás Meszerics, 'Stratégiai viselkedés és bizottsági döntés', *Közgazdasági Szemle*, Vol. 44, Issue 6, 1997, pp. 687-697.

39 Thomas Saalfeld, 'On Dogs and Whips: Recorded Votes', *in* Herbert Döring (ed.), *Parliaments and Majority Rule in Western Europe*, Campus Verlag, Frankfurt, 1995, pp. 528-565. The infamous moment of Hungarian parliamentary practice was the 'secret' vote of the head of state election on the controlled votes in 2005. The votes of each member of the opposition factions were required for the opposition candidate to be the President of the Republic – a relative majority. *See* Péter Smuk, *Magyar közjog és politika 1989-2011*, Osiris, Budapest, 2011, p. 253. *See also* Decision No. 9/2008. (I. 31.) AB of the Constitutional Court.

40 Saalfeld 1995, p. 178

41 Stéphanie Novak, 'Two effects of a high threshold of qualified majority', *in* Novak & Elster 2014, pp. 178-183, and p. 193.

doi: 10.5553/HYIEL/266627012022010001023

3. Majoritarian Voting – Case Studies

3.1. Case Study No. 1 – When Supermajority Is Not Enough or Not Necessary (?)

Generally, the Hungarian Parliament adopts its resolutions with the votes of more than half of the members present, in accordance with the axiom of parliamentarism and the classical majority principle. In the case of the adoption of the Fundamental Law, the main criticism from scholarship was that

> "although the legitimacy of formal adoption is not in question, given that a freely elected Parliament acted in it, but the one-party, rapid constitution-making was not suitable to reflect a consensus or social inclusion in the most important questions."[42]

The constitutional amendments after the 2010 parliamentary elections

> "already reflect the essence of the state philosophy of the later Fundamental Law: the principle of majority, the emphasis on popular sovereignty, the concept of a stronger state, a more capable government compared to the principle of separation of powers."[43]

The essence of the problem in question is that the formal condition for the exercise of constitutional power, qualified majority voting, by no means ensures the achievement of some kind of national, but at least broader consensus beyond the number of pro-government votes.

In the year of writing this article, perhaps the most bizarre topic of the Hungarian constitutional discourse is whether following the elections a simple majority government could abolish the constitutional and political structure established politically unilaterally in the recent decade.[44] The desperation of the opposition can certainly be inferred from this debate, given that during the adoption of the Fundamental Law and other two-thirds decisions, the numerical parliamentary majority rarely sought to achieve additional legitimacy through forging a broader political consensus.

We try to capture this historic, constitutional moment from a legal point of view. First, it is necessary to state that if the Fundamental Law was enacted in the framework of a valid procedure, its amendment and replacement by circumventing the supermajority criterion would in fact constitute revolutionary law. Such 'revolutionary law-making' did not even take place at the time of the regime change in 1989-90.

Nor would a declaration of invalidity of the Fundamental Law be entirely settled in terms of legal proceedings, but the arguments for invalidity itself are

42 István Kukorelli, *Bibó István láthatatlan alkotmánya,* Gondolat, Budapest, 2019, p. 45.

43 István Kukorelli, *Hány éves az Alaptörvény? A régi-új kérdése az Alaptörvényben,* Gondolat, Budapest, 2017, p. 54.

44 The expected win of the opposition just did not arrive in April 2022. For arguments pro and contra the 'simple majority constitution-making', *see* András Jakab, *Hibrid rezsimből jogállamba,* 2022, at https://ssrn.com/abstract=4021427.

doi: 10.5553/HYIEL/266627012022010001023

not solid either: whether we consider the alleged four-fifths criterion of the Constitution [Section 24(5)], the Legislative Act's requirement for preliminary impact assessment, *etc.* or even the presumed 'substantive' unconstitutionality. It is an interesting idea that a conflict with EU law or international law could also provide a legal basis for simple majority constitution-making or, for annulling the Fundamental Law.

The quality of the constitutional political discourse in question is also marred by all these suggestions. Most importantly, our expectations for a consensus on constitutionality are not in the least guaranteed by 'revolutionary' ideas. This evident from the fact that many would call for a referendum to help create a new constitutional foundation.[45]

3.2. Case Study No. 2. – Abstentions (Do Not) Count?

Indirectly, the state of the Hungarian constitutional system is also at stake case. Indeed it can even be referred as an illustration of the practice of parliamentary majority voting – the 'strictest' supermajority threshold in EP, as described above. The controversy surrounding the adoption of the European Parliament's decision to initiate proceedings under Article 7 TEU against Hungary in September 2018 erupted on the question whether the (qualified) majority required for its adoption was reached or whether abstentions should also be taken into account when determining the outcome of the vote. Below, I briefly summarize and evaluate the CJEU's 2021 judgment in *C-650/18, Hungary v European Parliament* concluding the dispute.[46]

The majority criterion stipulated for the voting procedure must be clearly legible from the relevant body's rules of procedure, otherwise the result of the vote may constantly be called into question on a procedural basis by those who remain in the minority. Therefore (following questions on admissibility) the CJEU first reviewed the legal basis for voting, the counting of votes, then the number of abstentions in terms of the result of the vote, and finally the nature of the qualified (double) majority and abstentions were clarified.

Article 7 TFEU provides for the application of Article 354 TFEU to the EP's procedure, according to which the European Parliament "shall act by a two-thirds majority of the votes cast, representing the majority of its component Members." The EP Rules of Procedure Rule 178(3) provided[47] that

> "In calculating whether a text has been adopted or rejected, account shall be taken only of votes cast for and against, except in those cases for which the Treaties lay down a specific majority."

45 Id. p. 40.

46 The so called Sargentini-report [on a proposal calling on the Council to determine, pursuant to Article 7(1) of the Treaty on European Union, the existence of a clear risk of a serious breach by Hungary of the values on which the Union is founded (2017/2131(INL))] has been adopted by the European Parliament by a majority that has been contested by Hungary. Representatives of Hungary alleged that the necessary QMV requirement had not been met. Judgment of 3 June 2021, *Case C-650/18, Hungary v European Parliament*, ECLI:EU:C:2021:426.

47 In EP Rules for the term 2019-2024 this provision can be found in Rule 187(3).

doi: 10.5553/HYIEL/266627012022010001023

In the vote on 12 September 2018, 448 Members supported the proposal, 197 voted against and 48 abstained. The criterion of majority of MEPs was clearly met, but a two-thirds majority of the 'votes cast' were only reached if the abstentions were not taken into account. The Chair of the sitting of the EP announced the result (resolution adopted), which Hungary subsequently challenged before the CJEU. Kochenov remarked on the relevant rules of the TFEU before the judgment was rendered, observing:

> "how to count abstentions is not entirely clear based on the wording of Article 354(4), which posed a problem during the EP vote to activate Article 7 TEU against Hungary in September 2018: following the advice from the Directorate of Legislative Acts, the EP service responsible for the procedures, abstentions were not deemed to be 'votes cast', which affected the majority required. This reading is consistent with the interpretation of 'votes case' in the context of Article 231 TFEU and is supported by Rule 178(3) of the EP Rules of Procedure. By analogy, then, the two-thirds majority of 'votes cast' required in the context of Article 354(4) TFEU is counted disregarding the abstentions."[48]

The CJEU for its part, found that

> "Since the Treaties do not define what is to be understood by 'votes cast', that autonomous concept of EU law must be interpreted in accordance with its usual meaning in everyday language",

taking also into account the context and the purposes of the regulation. In the CJEU's view, the concept of 'votes cast', *in its ordinary meaning*, covers only the positive or negative votes in respect of a given proposal. Abstentions, in the usual sense, should be understood as a refusal to adopt a position on a given proposal, they cannot, therefore, be considered as a 'vote cast'.[49]

The CJEU has held that, by requiring a double majority to be reached for acts adopted by Parliament pursuant to Article 7, the drafters of the Treaty emphasized the importance of such acts, *both politically and constitutionally* – achieving this way 'a specific majority'. Abstentions may be taken into account in order to ascertain (as the fourth paragraph of Article 354 TFEU requires), that the votes in favor represent the majority of the component Members of EP. But concerning the other criteria,

> "account cannot be taken of abstentions for the purpose of determining whether a majority of two thirds of the votes cast has been attained in favor of the adoption of such an act".[50]

48 Kochenov 2019, p. 2082.

49 *Case C-650/18, Hungary v European Parliament,* paras. 83-84.

50 Id. paras. 86-87.

doi: 10.5553/HYIEL/266627012022010001023

Abstentions were taken into account on the basis of the threshold requiring the majority of all Members, and MEPs were informed in advance that abstentions would count for determining the fulfillment the two-thirds condition. (This way, everyone could choose his/her vote with that in mind.[51])

The broader context of the significance of abstentions is also mentioned in the judgment, in response to an argument raised in the Polish intervention. As far as the four-fifths majority required in the Council is concerned, it is not possible to take abstentions into account (Article 354, first paragraph, TFEU), but it does not follow *a contrario* that in the parliamentary procedure (Article 354, fourth paragraph, TFEU) where the Treaty is silent, it is obligatory to take into account the abstentions. According to the CJEU, the purpose of removing any uncertainty in the Council's vote was that abstaining states could not block the adoption of a resolution.[52]

According to the reasoning put forward by Hungary, the value of democracy is also violated in case the abstentions of the deputies are not taken into account. However, according to the CJEU, abstentions were not completely excluded from the vote: they were included in one of the elements of the double majority criterion, namely, the quorum, and MEPs knew the consequences of their possible abstention by prior warning, so the MEPs were not deprived of exercising their prerogatives.[53]

It should be noted that having recourse to an 'ordinary meaning of the words' approach when interpreting the Rules of Procedure is, to say the least, surprising in the context of the internal debates of such a long-established institution. The EP leadership is convinced that this has always been the practice in the past, although the Article 7 procedure has not yet been voted on by the European Parliament.[54] Abstention is an existing option (button) for Members, but the question in a given vote is: when will their position be taken into account? As a means of *preventing* the adoption of the proposal or as a way to *refrain* from such a resolution?

51 In a letter of 10 September 2018, Hungary's Permanent Representative notified the Parliament's Secretary General of the Hungarian Government's position that abstentions should be taken into account in the vote on the Parliament's contested resolution, in accordance with Article 354 TFEU and Rule 178(3) of the Rules of Procedure. On 10 September 2018, the Parliament's Deputy Secretary General informed Members of the European Parliament ('MEPs') via email that, in the context of the calculation of the votes cast, only the votes cast in favor and those cast against the adoption of the resolution would be taken into account, excluding abstentions. *Case C-650/18, Hungary v European Parliament*, paras. 11-12.

52 Id. para. 92.

53 Id. para. 96.

54 As an analogue situation, a voting in the UN General Assembly took place similarly. "The UN General Assembly adopted a resolution [...] calling for Russia to be suspended from the Human Rights Council. The resolution received a two-thirds majority of those voting, in the 193-member Assembly, with 93 nations voting in favor, 24 against", 58 abstained. *See* at https://news.un.org/en/story/2022/04/1115782. As we noted above, General Assembly Rules of Procedure Rule 86 [126] provides that "For the purposes of these rules, the phrase 'members present and voting' means members casting an affirmative or negative vote. Members which abstain from voting are considered as not voting."

doi: 10.5553/HYIEL/266627012022010001023

4. Concluding Remarks

In addition to the theoretical justification and critical literature on the majority principle, I discussed the finding that owing to political responsibility and the effectiveness of parliamentary governance/decision-making, simple and qualified majority is a central element of our form of government. However, in and of itself it cannot contribute to qualitative or democratic legitimacy. This would require an appropriate standard of political culture, which has unfortunately eroded a long time ago.

Board votes are largely organized around strategic considerations. This is particularly the case for multi-divisional bodies, such as multi-party or coalition legislatures, or for states that align themselves on questions of diplomacy in international relations. As far as the latter is concerned, it is seldom possible for the resolution of a body, assembly or parliament to be appealed, therefore, EU procedures represent a particular intermediate level between the national and international dimensions of majority decision-making.

doi: 10.5553/HYIEL/266627012022010001023

CONFERENCE REPORTS

Two Conferences on the European Models of Constitutionalizing Memories and the Hungarian Experience

Report on the 'Conference on the Tradition, Constitution and European Integration' Organized by the Centre for Social Sciences, in Collaboration with the French Embassy in Hungary, 23-24 September 2021, Budapest & the 'Conference on the History, Constitution and Identity in Hungary', Organized by the Centre for Social Sciences, 18 November 2021, Budapest.

*Marina Bán & Boldizsár Szentgáli-Tóth**

Abstract

The two conferences on the European Models of Constitutionalizing Memories and the Hungarian Experience ('Conference on the Tradition, Constitution and European Integration' and 'Conference on the History, Constitution and Identity in Hungary') were organized by the Eötvös Loránd Research Network's Centre for Social Sciences on 23-24 September and 18 November 2021, respectively. The conference report gives an overview of the main topics and findings of these two conferences.

Keywords: conference report, Centre for Social Sciences, European integration, constitutional identity, legal traditions.

The Centre for Social Sciences, Institute for Legal Studies hosted two conferences in the autumn of 2021 on the European models of constitutionalizing legal traditions, with special focus on Hungarian developments. This report gives a cursory overview of the various topics and thoughts explored and debated in these two conferences, focusing on constitutional identity and its different interpretations within the European legal space.

On 23-24 September 2021, in collaboration with the French Embassy in Hungary, the Institute for Legal Studies organized a conference with the title *'Tradition, constitution and European integration'*. Experts from France, Hungary

* Marina Bán: postdoctoral researcher; Center of Excellence for International Courts, University of Copenhagen. Boldizsár Szentgáli-Tóth: senior research fellow, Eötvös Loránd Research Network, Centre for Social Sciences, Budapest.

doi: 10.5553/HYIEL/266627012022010001024

and other jurisdictions provided broad and insightful comparative observations about the different understandings of constitutional identity, with particular focus on the case law of the CJEU. They further examined the interpretation of constitutional identity in Germany, and in Central and Eastern European countries with special regard to Hungary. Fundamental theoretical issues were also raised.

As far as the case law of the CJEU is concerned, presenters called for a substantial cooperation and dialogue with the national constitutional courts. They stressed that instead of mutual recognition and willingness to cooperate, the current judicial dialogue is characterized by hostile rhetoric and attitudes, which leads to the frequent mis-conceptualization of constitutional identity. The participants further underlined the insufficient endeavors of the CJEU to convince the European public about the validity of its judicial reasoning. Furthermore, stakeholders were not satisfied with the efficiency of the dialogue mechanism between national courts and the CJEU. By contrast, the ECtHR was mentioned as a positive example because its jurisprudence provides a broader margin of appreciation for national judges to consider the domestic context and the constitutional identity of the particular country. Furthermore, Protocol 16 ECHR established an opportunity for national judges to request advisory opinions from the ECtHR in case of uncertainty around the interpretation of the ECtHR case law. For these reasons, participants called for a substantive judicial dialogue between the CJEU and national constitutional courts to elaborate on the concept of constitutional identity jointly, based on mutual respect and collegiality.

It has also been argued that national constitutional identity is not considered with sufficient gravity in CJEU case law, as the concept of national identity in its current form could not replace a real reflection on the constitutional characteristics of each Member State. Moreover, the CJEU applies selected interpretative methods in its decisions with the inherent purpose to avoid and eliminate risk factors. This is most probably owed to the Court's fear of potential uncertainties surrounding the interpretation of constitutional identity, and due to the willingness of national constitutional courts to prioritize national constitutional norms and principles over secondary EU law. The long-standing conflict between the national approach vindicating the supremacy of national constitutions over EU law and the European requirement of ensuring priority to European legal instruments over national constitutions should be balanced properly. This cannot be achieved without the strong engagement of both the national constitutional courts and the CJEU. The conference participants further discussed that most fears surrounding the incorporation of constitutional identity into CJEU case law are probably not well-founded, since the CJEU may rely on multiple tools of the founding treaties to avoid an overly broad interpretation of the identity clause stipulated in the TEU.

German and Hungarian constitutional case law on constitutional identity was also analyzed in depth, and several similarities were pointed out between the approaches followed by these constitutional courts. Nevertheless, owing to the decisions' discrepancies, the Hungarian court's concept does not reach the German standard in terms of comprehensibility and cohesion. The Hungarian

doi: 10.5553/HYIEL/266627012022010001024

Constitutional Court has failed to identify an applicable standard behind constitutional identity, declaring that its substance should be determined through a case-by-case assessment. In addition, the Hungarian Constitutional Court stated that constitutional identity is not established, merely acknowledged by the Fundamental Law of Hungary, and the entire text of the Fundamental Law could serve as the basis for identifying the primary elements of constitutional identity. Therefore, the Hungarian interpretation of the concept is closer to the traditional understanding of national identity rather than constitutional identity with a normative and enforceable substance, and should not serve as a normative basis for constitutional identity, such as, for example, the eternity clauses in Germany.

A further problem with the relevant Hungarian constitutional jurisprudence is the lack of differentiation between the internal and external functions of constitutional identity. Constitutional identity should impose a limitation on the primacy of European legal instruments and on the amendments to the constitution. However, according to Hungarian case law, the meaning of constitutional identity may change with the introduction of an amendment to the constitution. In this way, constitutional amendments would not necessarily comply with the principles of the already existing constitutional framework. The conference presenters recommended for the Hungarian Constitutional Court to submit a request for preliminary ruling to the CJEU on the role of constitutional identity in the European legal space, and a substantive review of constitutional amendments based on the concept of constitutional identity.

As far as theoretical issues are concerned, the following questions were raised and elaborated upon in an attempt to answer them in the course of the conference: *(i)* What are the main elements of constitutional identity, and how can one define them? *(ii)* Who is authorized to determine the exact definition of constitutional identity? *(iii)* What are the sources of constitutional identity? *(iv)* Which are the main functions assigned to constitutional identity in the fields of constitutional and legal interpretation? *(v)* Is constitutional identity a static or a dynamic concept?

These were the primary theoretical concerns, but because the answers have far-reaching practical consequences, the gravity of these issues should not be underestimated, and further extensive discussion should be devoted to the clarification of these matters.

The second conference formed part of a postdoctoral research study within the framework of the *Imagine Project*, a research project led by Professor Jan Komárek, at the Center of Excellence for International Courts (iCourts), Faculty of Law, University of Copenhagen, and funded by an ERC Starting Grant. This research consortium delves into the idea of constitutional imaginaries: 'sets of ideas and beliefs that help to motivate and at the same time justify the practice of government and collective self-rule.' These imaginaries are necessary legal fictions in order to support political rule. The baseline of the Imagine Project is the analysis of European constitutional imaginaries, starting from Eric Stein and Joseph Weiler to their present-day successors, contrasting them with case studies on national constitutional imaginaries in Central and Eastern Europe. The

doi: 10.5553/HYIEL/266627012022010001024

conference described below is a part of the Hungarian case study, where distinguished Hungarian experts of the topics discussed the Hungarian model of constitutionalizing historical traditions within the European legal space. The conference took place on 18 November 2021, its title was *'History, constitution and identity in Hungary.'*

The participating experts explained that the historical constitution of Hungary is a theoretical concept originating in the late 18th, early 19th century. In the aftermath of the Hungarian defeat of the 1848 Revolution and War of Independence, the opponents of Germanization, Habsburg imperialism and assimilation relied on a collection of historical documents. They identified them as the country's historical constitution because these documents played a crucial role in the development of the Hungarian state. In the 19th and 20th centuries, the historical constitution was referred to in order to ensure the continuity of the state in times of occupation and oppression. This approach is strongly linked with the Holy Crown of Hungary and its use has been the subject of intense academic and political debate, in particular, the way it is presented in constitutional documents. Although the doctrine of the historical constitution was largely neglected under the communist regime, the debate surrounding it resurfaced amidst the democratic transition. Moreover, in 2011, upon the adoption of the Hungarian Fundamental Law, the country's new constitutional charter, it contributed to the development of a new legal concept, the 'achievements of the historical constitution'. Article R of the Fundamental Law obliges the Constitutional Court to identify and consider these achievements during its decision-making process. Despite lacking basis in case law and possessing a very shaky and heavily debated doctrinal basis, the Constitutional Court at least attempted to integrate the concept. It referred the achievements of the historical constitution to define the constitutional identity of Hungary, and to underline Hungary's sovereignty. In its recent *Decision No. 22/2016. (XII. 5.) AB*, the Constitutional Court strengthened the sovereignty-based discourse and took a stance against the primacy of EU law with the justification that in certain situations the historical constitution of Hungary obliges a departure from EU law. The recurrence of this concept in Hungarian constitutionalism begs the question why the country's historical roots and their presence in constitutional case law remains relevant to this day.

The aim of the conference was twofold. *(i)* First, it sought to examine why historical roots remain present and relevant in Hungarian constitutionalism. *(ii)* Second, it tied to answer the question how history in the country's constitutional development may yield additional, previously unexplored viewpoints and approaches to Hungary's past and current relationship with the EU's constitutional imaginaries.

The conference's framework moved beyond a strictly legal doctrinal setting as regard its methodology, examining the broader implications of the constitutional relevance of the historical past. This involved assessing the intellectual history of how references to the past remained relevant throughout Hungarian constitutionalism, including the concept of the historical constitution, as well as the use of historical narratives in constitutional law and academic

doi: 10.5553/HYIEL/266627012022010001024

debate throughout the years and their impact on the shaping of Hungarian constitutional identity. The conference explored these issues by mapping the historical roots of political and legal thinking about historical narratives. These include the inception of Hungary's historical constitution in the 18th and 19th century, the events of the 20th century and their impact on constitutional debates (such as the Treaty of Trianon, the communist regime and the democratic transition), and how history appears in the Fundamental Law and the case law of the Constitutional Court.

Thus, the conference provided a local constitutional perspective that has remained quite neglected in research on current developments in Hungary. The analysis of how historical references are built into Hungarian constitutional law contributes to the debate surrounding the role of Hungary in the EU constitutional order, and the country's growing opposition of some EU values. In the post-1867 Habsburg Empire, the Hungarian political elite moved from being oppressed to being elevated as equals to the Austrian elite, thus becoming somewhat of an oppressor of other minorities themselves. This imperial role may fuel current ideologies which may be called 'Hungarian exceptionalism' and ambitions to regain the country's role among the leading powers of the EU. This can be rationalized with the historical constitution concept, providing the justification and basis for such continuity and exceptionalism. Opposition to the EU's unifying efforts and the challenges to the primacy of EU law may have their roots in the difference of historical interpretation on the constitutional level. In this way, constitutional doctrines such as the achievements of the historical constitution become tools to define the independence of Hungary and reject ideas perceived as originating from imperial and supranational oppressive powers.

The conference intended to answer the following questions: *(i)* Who shapes and for what reason (or have shaped in the past) the use of history as a constitutional narrative (on the political level)? *(ii)* How do the historical roots of the state appear in Hungarian constitutional law? *(iii)* What role does the reference to history play (or what role has it played) in the Hungarian constitutional vision (at the political, scientific, legal and historical levels)? *(iv)* Why do historical documents and legal concepts remain relevant to this day? *(v)* How can the use of historical narratives in the Hungarian constitutional vision support or reject European constitutional ideas? *(vi)* What unexplored, further perspectives can be gained on the reasons for the current political processes present in Hungary by examining the use of history in Hungarian constitutionalism?

The presentations covered the following main topics: *(i)* History, constitution and identity: The appearance of the historical past in the Hungarian constitution and its influence on Hungarian political identity in different periods from the 19th century to the present day. *(ii)* Hungarian constitutional identity, sovereignty and imperial powers: The use of Hungarian historical narratives to express the country's independence and its relationship with the great powers from the 19th century to the present day. *(iii)* History and the Fundamental Law: The presence of history in the Fundamental Law and 21st century constitutional

Hungarian Yearbook of International Law and European Law 2022 (10) 1
doi: 10.5553/HYIEL/266627012022010001024

law. *(iv)* Historical constitution over the centuries: The evolution of the historical constitution and its definition and changes over the last two hundred years.

In conclusion, both conferences served as valuable platforms for insightful and intense discussion on constitutional identity within the European legal space, and its relationship with national historical traditions. The conferences pointed out that the uncertainties around this concept, especially in the Hungarian model are considerable, therefore, further efforts must be dedicated to tackle these complex issues. For this reason, future conferences and research projects should continue to conceptualize these issues to provide a deeper understanding of the influence of legal traditions on the current constitutional framework of EU Member States, and their role in the strengthening European integration.

doi: 10.5553/HYIEL/266627012022010001024

Csongor István Nagy (ed.), Cross-border Litigation in Central Europe (Book Review)

Kluwer Law International, The Netherlands, 2022, 520 p, ISBN 978-94-035-3705-4

*Gábor Hajdu**

Private international law is a uniquely complex field. Its importance in settling conflict of laws and jurisdictional issues when it comes to cross-border disputes cannot be underestimated. In the past two decades, the field has to a large part come under the aegis of EU law. While national private international law acts continue to exist and exert influence where appropriate, the various EU instruments, such as the Rome I or Brussels I regulations, took the centerstage. The application of these instruments in western EU Member States by courts and other national authorities is fairly well-documented. The same cannot be said however, of the newer, Eastern Member States. In these countries, the application of private international law EU instruments by the courts is still studied in a rather fragmented fashion, often by lone researchers. There is hardly a definite book available on the topic in the reviewer's opinion. This volume, which is essentially a collection of national reports, skillfully edited together by Prof. Csongor István Nagy, aims to correct this issue.

The book is the culmination of years of research conducted by the 'Cross-border litigation in Central-Europe: EU private international law before national courts' (CEPIL) project. This project consisted of a consortium of several universities across the EU. These included the University of Szeged (*Szegedi Tudományegyetem,* Hungary, project coordinator), the *Masarykova univerzita* (Czech Republic), the *Sveučilište u Zagrebu* (Croatia), the *Universitatea Sapientia din municipiul Cluj-Napoca* (Romania), the *Univerzita Mateja Bela v Banskej Bystrici* (Slovakia), and the *Uniwersytet Śląski* (Poland). For the purposes of this review, it would be quite difficult to discuss every single author and researcher involved with the project here. The editor, Prof. Csongor István Nagy, is a renowned expert of private international law himself, chairing the department of private international law at the University of Szeged. The other authors are also recognized experts of private international law in their home countries, as shown by the short biographies of contributors listed in the book's opening pages. In the reviewer's opinion, this level of international cooperation is quite commendable.

* Gábor Hajdu: junior research fellow, Eötvös Loránd Research Network, Centre for Social Sciences, Institute for Legal Studies; junior research fellow, University of Szeged.

Hungarian Yearbook of International Law and European Law 2022 (10) 1
doi: 10.5553/HYIEL/266627012022010001025

An important merit of the volume is that it covered a wide range of newer EU Member States, namely, Croatia, the Czech Republic, Estonia, Hungary, Latvia, Lithuania, Poland, Romania, Slovakia and Slovenia. While this range is impressive, the reader may notice that an EU Member State that otherwise fits into this group is missing: Bulgaria. In the reviewer's opinion, this omission is unfortunate, but perhaps counterbalanced by the otherwise wide scope of countries examined in the book. Nevertheless, the book is capable of ameliorating the lack of consolidated research that was pointed out at the beginning of this review. Its chosen topic is of considerable scientific relevance, if we consider that with each passing decade, the importance of transnational legal relations only increases. From business contracts to mixed marriages, the four fundamental freedoms (goods, services, capital, persons) only enhance the frequency of these legal relations. In this regard, the volume covers all the various legal relations, displaying and interpreting case law related to each in the given national reports.

The reviewer established the relevance of topic and general scope of the work. Thus, it is time to dive into the next aspect of the book, the structure. Each of the countries listed above has a dedicated chapter. These chapters are presented in alphabetic order. In the reviewer's opinion, this is sufficient, but the question arises whether a more thematic grouping would have been possible. For example, the Baltic states are almost together even in the present form but are broken up by the inclusion of Hungary after Estonia. It would have been perhaps possible to group the Member States based on their geographical area, or by finding some common thread of legal traditions that would tie some countries closer together than others. Of course, such an attempt could be hampered by one of the earlier strengths of the volume the reviewer had previously mentioned: the wide range of Member States covered. With so many states included in the book, perhaps it would have been unfeasible to artificially attempt to find common threads to group jurisdictions together. It would be perhaps easy to group the Baltic states together through either method (geographical and legal traditions), but the task may have been much more difficult with the other countries included in the present volume. As such, the alphabetical order of countries was perhaps the most convenient editing solution in the end.

The chapters themselves all follow the same standardized structure. They begin with a descriptive explanation of how the judicial system in their given countries operates, the general legislative framework and how EU private international law instruments are applied before national courts in general. Thereafter, all reports delve into more specific questions. First, civil and commercial disputes (with cross-border elements), from the perspectives of the Rome I, Rome II and Brussels I Regulations. Then they all move on to family law disputes (including Brussels II, Rome III, the Maintenance and Matrimonial Property Regulations), before finishing with succession and insolvency. The reader may typically find a short conclusion at the end of each chapter. Overall, the reviewer cannot find much fault with this chapter structure. The topics have a certain logical flow to them, and it seems wise to put civil and commercial disputes first, since they are undoubtedly the most important and relevant, followed by family law and then succession and insolvency. While it may seem

doi: 10.5553/HYIEL/266627012022010001025

repetitive at first glance, given the nature of the book (an edited collection of individual national reports), a standardized structure and identical thematical templates are very much justified. Still, there is some variation with the exact subheadings, which can be explained by the authors adjusting to the slightly different angles each Member State may present. The reviewer would particularly like to highlight how useful the introductory sections to these chapters are. Few scholars can be considered knowledgeable on the particular court systems and case law databases of all these different EU Member States. The reviewer believes that integrating this information into the chapters not only helps contextualize the analyzed case law, but also provides useful knowledge to the reader that can be potentially applied even outside of the confines of private international law.

It is worth devoting a few words to the somewhat uneven length of the chapters, since this is quite apparent to the readers. Some chapters are of considerable length, while others are comparatively shorter. Of course, this can be owed to the volume of available case law. If a given jurisdiction has fewer cases relating to the application of a particular EU instrument, or if most of those cases involve an 'automatic', unremarkable application of the given instrument by the courts, there is little left for the author to analyze. At least for the reviewer, this unevenness in the chapters' length never seemed to point to a lack of sufficient analysis.

Within the chapters themselves, the attention paid to the different topics is likewise interesting, with most chapters only briefly covering succession matters. This might seem startling at first glance. Given the countries involved, and the high level of emigration taking place towards Western EU Member States (or temporary migration for the sake of work), one would assume that there would be plenty of disputes with cross-border elements that involve matters of succession. However, as Nagy pointed out in the volume's final chapter (discussed below) this does not necessarily imply that there is a dearth of succession disputes with cross-border elements. Rather, in most cases, the dispute simply never reaches the courts. As such, the primary users of the Succession Regulation would be the figures involved in succession proceedings pre-trial, such as public notaries. This is an elegant explanation, but also unfortunately creates a potential gap in the comprehensiveness of the volume. Naturally, accessing succession proceedings that never developed into court disputes is a much more difficult, and a very different task than collating court case law. Furthermore, the book's stated scope and aim was the examination of court cases. Therefore, in the reviewer's opinion, this does not take away from the book's value as a comprehensive overview of EU private international law in the examined Member States.

In the reviewer's opinion, while the various national chapters all present intriguing insights into the application of EU private international law within the Member States, it is the final chapter that ties the book together. Despite the shared subject matter, general structure and standardized methodology, the various chapters each represent partially individual inquiries conducted by the various authors. Thus, the final chapter is an excellent contribution, connecting these individual strands together. Without it, the book would undoubtedly lack a certain focus.

doi: 10.5553/HYIEL/266627012022010001025

There is no space to discuss the full conclusions drawn by the authors regarding EU private international law, but the reviewer will highlight a few that may be considered particularly notable. One of these is the observation that while forum-shopping, parallel proceedings and tendency towards applying the court's own law are popular subjects of private international law scholarship (a statement the reviewer agrees with), the authors' findings were that these particular issues are significantly less common in practice, especially with regards to forum-shopping and parallel proceedings. This is perhaps a surprising result, but the book's findings on the matter seem rather convincing. Another interesting conclusion drawn by the authors was that the application of EU private international law instruments seemingly poses no major conceptual issues to judges of the examined states. According to the authors, this due to the fact that these states are civil-law jurisdictions, finding it easy to follow EU instruments that likewise follow a civil law conceptual framework. However, the authors did highlight that there seems to be one recurring issue: learning the content of foreign law. The authors posit that based on the examined case law, as well as the interviews they conducted, the current systems are rather inadequate. Particularly the 1968 European Convention on Information on Foreign Law and the European Judicial Network were considered to be unsuitable. Furthermore, the authors contended that even if access was feasible (if time-consuming), there are still difficulties surrounding the presentation of sources and the lack of follow-up clarifications. The reviewer believes that this aspect of the research has now provided clear, case law-based evidence of an issue that was already suspected by private international law scholars. This finding thus has a degree of scientific merit in itself. Perhaps most importantly, the book also confirmed the hypothesis that EU private international law rules face special expectations and must meet additional requirements in terms of predictability, clarity and uniformity. In this regard, overall, the authors' research found the instruments to be adequate and sufficient.

In conclusion, *Cross-Border Litigation in Central Europe* is an excellent book. While it presupposes a certain degree of fundamental knowledge on EU private international law from the reader, the reviewer considers this volume highly suitable for both junior and senior scholars, seeking a better understanding on how EU private international law functions in court practice within the examined Member States. Even for those whose own research is unrelated to these countries, there are very likely valuable lessons to learn, with examples for comparison and a solid basis for further developing the existing scholarship.

doi: 10.5553/HYIEL/266627012022010001025

Péter Mezei, Copyright Exhaustion: Law and Policy in the United States and the European Union, 2nd Edition (Book Review)

Cambridge University Press, Cambridge, 2022, 260 p, ISBN 978-1-108-84314-0

Anett Pogácsás & Dávid Ujhelyi[*]

As the author, Péter Mezei notes, "The doctrine of exhaustion, more commonly referred to within the US as the 'first-sale' doctrine, is one of the most fundamental principles of copyright law."[1] The most fundamental principles of any legal discipline are especially challenging to research and write about; this is also the case for copyright law. This is because the principles that provide the foundations of specific fields of law are often regarded or treated as axioms; and axioms by their very nature are difficult, or even impossible to define. Furthermore, it is not uncommon for the origins and initially intended functions of these fundamental legal instruments to fade away or change significantly over the decades.[2] In our view, research on copyright exhaustion faces these very challenges. One of the great achievements of the recently updated book of Mezei is that the author was able to successfully tackle these challenges and peel away the dogmatic, historical, policy and practical layers of copyright exhaustion, to shed light on the very core of this legal instrument.

* Anett Pogácsás: associate professor of law, Pázmány Péter Catholic University, Budapest; member of the Hungarian Council of Copyright Experts. Dávid Ujhelyi: vising lecturer, Pázmány Péter Catholic University, Budapest; member of the Hungarian Council of Copyright Experts; Head of Competition Law and IP Law Department, Ministry of Justice, Budapest.

1 Péter Mezei, *Copyright Exhaustion: Law and Policy in the United States and the European Union*, 2nd edition, Cambridge University Press, Cambridge, 2022, p. 2.

2 The three-step test is also a good example for this, *see* Dávid Ujhelyi, '"That escalated quickly" avagy a háromlépcsős teszt és a paródia kapcsolódási pontjai – I. rész', *Industrial Property and Copyright Review*, 2019/6, pp. 7-41, at www.sztnh.gov.hu/sites/default/files/files/kiadv/szkv/szemle-2019-6/01.pdf.

doi: 10.5553/HYIEL/266627012022010001026

The author's research[3] is structured into four substantive chapters. The first chapter (*The Theory of Copyright Exhaustion*) deals with the dogmatic foundations of the legal instrument in question. The roots of copyright exhaustion – as a limit on the rightholder's exclusive rights – reach down to one of the most basic concepts and goals of the discipline, the balance[4] between the authors and users (or society, in a wider sense). The author builds the four conceptual elements of exhaustion upon this basis, placing them on it just like the walls of a house are erected on the foundation. The 'walls' (or conceptual elements) of exhaustion are identified in the book as follows: *(i)* "the rightholder or another authorized person"; *(ii)* "lawfully distributes and thus transfers the ownership over"; *(iii)* "the original or a copy of a protected subject matter"; and *(iv)* "the lawful owner may resell the copy without the rightholder's permission."[5]

The policy considerations of copyright exhaustion are also discussed in this first chapter, where the Author recounts in great detail the conflict between the superiority of property rights over copyrights, the reward theory, and the restraint of rightholders over market control.[6] As it is stated in the book, the taxonomy of copyright exhaustion is far from settled. In this regard, a number of options emerge, as the legal instrument may be considered a limitation, an exception, an exclusion, a restriction or even an implied license. Choosing one of these options is quite a serious task, and the decision has far reaching legal consequences. It is also worth noting that the Hungarian Copyright Act's codified text[7] on exhaustion is unclear on this matter. Finally, the first chapter concludes with presenting the copyright exhaustion's place in the international legal

3 Some of the Author's recent publications on exhaustion: Péter Mezei, 'Digital Exhaustion: Furthering Social Justice in a Streaming-Dominated Copyright Ecosystem – Critical Remarks After the ECJ's Tom Kabinet Judgment', *in* Stanka Stjepanović *et al.* (eds.), *Zbornik radova: "Izazovi prabnom sistemu"*, Bosnia and Herzegovina, Pravni fakultet univerziteta u Sarajevu, 2021, pp. 190-203; Shubha Ghosh & Péter Mezei, 'The Elusive Quest for Digital Exhaustion in the US and the EU', *Hungarian Yearbook of International Law and European Law*, Vol. 8, 2020, pp. 249-275; Péter Mezei, 'The Doctrine of Exhaustion in Limbo: Critical Remarks on the CJEU's Tom Kabinet Ruling', *Zeszyty Naukowe Uniwersytetu Jagiellońskiego. Prace z Prawa Własności Intelektualnej*, Issue 2, 2020, pp. 130-153; Péter Mezei, 'Meet the unavoidable – the challenges of digital second-hand marketplaces to the doctrine of exhaustion', *in* Pihlajarinne Taina *et al.* (eds.), *Online Distribution of Content in the EU*, Edward Elgar, 2019, pp. 62-78.

4 Christophe Geiger & Elena Izyumenko, 'Copyright on the Human Rights' Trial: Redefining the Boundaries of Exclusivity Through Freedom of Expression', *International Review of Intellectual Property and Competition Law*, Vol. 45, 2014, pp. 326-339; and Anett Pogácsás, *Különbözőség az egységben – A szerzői jogi szabályozás differenciálódásának hatása a jogterület szerepére és hatékonyságára*, Pázmány Press, Budapest, 2017, at http://mek.oszk.hu/18600/18679/18679.pdf.

5 Mezei 2022, pp. 9-10.

6 A similar conflict arises between IP rights and freedom of expression regarding parodies. *See* Dávid Ujhelyi, *A paródiakivétel szükségessége és lehetséges keretrendszere a hazai szerzői jogban*, Ludovika Egyetemi Kiadó, Budapest, 2021.

7 Hungarian Act LXXVI of 1999 on Copyright Law, Section 23(5).

doi: 10.5553/HYIEL/266627012022010001026

framework, with due consideration to the TRIPS agreement,[8] the WIPO internet treaties[9] and the Marrakesh VIP Treaty.[10]

The second chapter ('*The Doctrine of Exhaustion in the Copyright Law of the EU*') logically continues with EU level analysis. The founding Member States' quite different approach was gradually harmonized through the CJEU's practice and judgments, such as *Deutsche Grammophon,*[11] *Membran,*[12] *Coditel I,*[13] *Warner Brothers versus Christiansen,*[14] and *EMI versus Patricia.*[15] These cases paved the way for a uniform EU exhaustion regulation, such as the rule that contractual provisions conflicting with exhaustion cannot be enforced against third parties, the exhaustion of the distribution right is allowed by the first lawful distribution, the free movement of goods and the theory of the common market enjoy priority over copyright law and different royalty rates applied by Member States on the reproduction and distribution of copies are not grounds for preventing the resale of lawfully marketed copies.[16] Following the successful groundwork of the CJEU, the road for adopting vertical and horizontal EU legislation became free: the first Software Directive,[17] the Directive on Rental, Lending and Related Rights,[18] the Database Directive[19] and the InfoSoc Directive[20] all regulate relevant norms on copyright exhaustion. The second chapter also tackles the limitations on copyright exhaustion that arise from the internal logic of EU law, such as parallel importation,[21] regional exhaustion and *droit de suite.*[22]

The picture would not be complete without a separate chapter on the US first sale doctrine. The third chapter ('*The First-Sale Doctrine in the Copyright Law of the*

8 Agreement on Trade-Related Aspects of Intellectual Property Rights, The TRIPS Agreement is Annex 1C of the Marrakesh Agreement Establishing the World Trade Organization, signed in Marrakesh, Morocco on 15 April 1994.

9 WIPO Copyright Treaty, adopted in Geneva on December 20, 1996 and WIPO Performances and Phonograms Treaty, adopted in Geneva on December 20, 1996.

10 Marrakesh Treaty to Facilitate Access to Published Works for Persons Who Are Blind, Visually Impaired or Otherwise Print Disabled, adopted by the Diplomatic Conference to Conclude a Treaty to Facilitate Access to Published Works by Visually Impaired Persons and Persons with Print Disabilities in Marrakesh, on 27 June 2013.

11 Judgment of 8 June 1971, *Case C-78/70, Deutsche Grammophon,* ECLI:EU:C:1971:59.

12 Judgment of 20 January 1981, *Joined Cases C-55/80 and C-57/80, Gema,* ECLI:EU:C:1981:10.

13 Judgment of 6 October 1982, *Case C-262/81, Coditel,* ECLI:EU:C:1982:334.

14 Judgment of 17 May 1988, *Case C-158/86, Warner Brothers and Metronome Video,* ECLI:EU:C: 1988:242.

15 Judgment of 24 January 1989, *Case C-341/87, EMI Electrola,* ECLI:EU:C:1989:30.

16 Mezei 2022, pp. 48-49.

17 Council Directive 91/250/EEC of 14 May 1991 on the legal protection of computer programs.

18 Council Directive 92/100/EEC of 19 November 1992 on rental right and lending right and on certain rights related to copyright in the field of intellectual property.

19 Directive 96/9/EC of the European Parliament and of the Council of 11 March 1996 on the legal protection of databases.

20 Directive 2001/29/EC of the European Parliament and of the Council of 22 May 2001 on the harmonization of certain aspects of copyright and related rights in the information society.

21 Owen H. Dean, 'Parallel Importation – Infringement of Copyright', *South African Law Journal,* Vol. 100, Issue 2, 1983, pp. 258-277.

22 Marilyn J. Krestinger, 'Droit de Suit: The Artist's Right to a Resale Royalty', *Hastings Communications and Entertainment Law Journal,* Vol. 15, Issue 4, 1992, pp. 967-980.

doi: 10.5553/HYIEL/266627012022010001026

US') accordingly provides a comprehensive overview of this legal instrument. This is all the more instructive because it goes back a long way, since US federal courts had been grappling with this issue as early as 1885. "As a direct consequence, the US has experienced far more varied technological and economic challenges regarding the functioning of the limits to the right of distribution."[23] Mezei draws attention to the fact that in the EU the *droit de suite*, as a right for an equitable remuneration, functions as a practical limitation to the doctrine of exhaustion, since free resale is one of the central elements of the doctrine of exhaustion. However, there is no such limitation in US copyright law, in fact, US legislators will be presumably unable to find an internal solution for the resale right in the foreseeable future.[24]

The idea of digital exhaustion is rooted in technological, social and economical changes. Leaving aside a detailed description of the book's most interesting fourth chapter ('*Digital Exhaustion in the EU and the US*'), it is worth pointing out the book's greatest merit and also a key question of the topic. Mezei argues for a more flexible interpretation of international rules to enable copyright law to adapt to the present day, however, the presentation and analysis of the opposing position, the traditional positivist approach, is not neglected either. In the author's view, categorizing the sale of digital contents via the Internet as distribution would implicitly open the door for a digital exhaustion doctrine. "I believe that such an interpretation of the international norms would not contradict WCT Article 1(4) and BC Article 19."[25] As Caterina Sganga also underlines,

> "the advisability of complementing the purely positivistic interpretation of the provision with a deeper consideration of the social, economic and cultural implications of exhaustion, and of its role in facilitating the achievement of copyright goals is at stake."[26]

Adapting copyright to its original purpose would certainly be easier to achieve by amending the relevant international conventions. Not surprisingly, however, the author himself does not see much chance of this happening. But the book's greatest strength is that it does not stop at the seemingly insurmountable, clear obstacles. Despite the fact that no substantial progress can be expected from international conventions, and that the relevant CJEU's judgments further deepened uncertainties in this field,[27] it remains its objective to work on making exhaustion a special limitation, functioning effectively in EU copyright law. To this end, Mezei paves the way for a change of perspective and encourages us to see not only the obstacles, but also the possible solutions, maintaining that "a

23 Mezei 2022, p. 71.
24 Id. p. 105.
25 Id. p. 197.
26 Caterina Sganga, 'A Plea for Digital Exhaustion in EU Copyright Law', *Journal of Intellectual Property, Information Technology, and Electronic Commerce Law*, Vol. 9, Issue 3, 2018, p. 212.
27 Mezei 2020, p. 130.

doi: 10.5553/HYIEL/266627012022010001026

balanced digital exhaustion doctrine can be reached by the combination of technological measures and legal guarantees."[28]

Therefore, the book is highly recommended not only for those who wish to familiarize themselves with all aspects of the doctrine of exhaustion, but those who want a glimmer of hope in the desperate battle of the increasingly complex, inconsistent and unbalanced copyright law itself.

28 Mezei 2022, p. 191.

Hungarian Yearbook of International Law and European Law 2022 (10) 1
doi: 10.5553/HYIEL/266627012022010001026

www.ingramcontent.com/pod-product-compliance
Lightning Source LLC
LaVergne TN
LVHW080745300926
849162LV00008BA/1759
* 9 7 8 9 4 6 2 3 6 6 7 2 5 *